Paragraphs and Essays

A Worktext with Readings

Eighth Edition

Lee Brandon

Mt. San Antonio College

Houghton Mifflin Company   *Boston   New York*

To Sharon

Senior Sponsoring Editor: Mary Jo Southern
Associate Editor: Kellie Cardone
Editorial Associate: Danielle Richardson
Project Editor: Tracy Patruno
Senior Manufacturing Coordinator: Marie Barnes
Senior Marketing Manager: Nancy Lyman

Cover image: © Connie Hayes/SIS

Printed in the U.S.A.

Library of Congress Catalog Card Number: 00-133889

Student Text ISBN: 0-618-04265-2
Instructor's Annotated Edition ISBN: 0-618-04266-0

56789-WEB-04   03   02

Contents

Chapter 7 Narration: Moving Through Time 93

Chapter 16   Literary Analysis: Reacting to Stories   298

Preface

Paragraphs and Essays, Eighth Edition, contains thorough writing coverage, abundant readings, and a handbook designed for use in either developmental or freshman composition writing courses. This new edition continues this book's tradition as a total resource for students and instructors, presenting comprehensive, flexible, relevant, and stimulating instructional material.

Writing Instruction

Writing instruction includes explanations, examples, and exercises at the sentence, paragraph, and essay levels. Instruction for the paragraph and the essay is presented separately in Chapters 4 and 5. Thereafter, it pertains to both through ten chapters of forms of discourse, with occasional separate and specific annotations or instructions. Forms of discourse are exemplified by both paragraph and essay reading selections. This arrangement allows instructors to choose an emphasis of either the paragraph or the essay, or a combined approach, perhaps beginning with paragraphs and culminating with essays. It even permits the instructor teaching students with disparate writing abilities to mix lengths and complexities of assignments within a class, without giving separate reading assignments or using different schedules.

Topic suggestions at the ends of chapters include reading-related, career-related, and general lists so instructors can specify one type or mix types for class assignments.

Chapter 18, The Research Paper, includes forms of documentation as well as a discussion of libraries, online searching, plagiarism, and other research-related topics.

The Handbook presents explanations, examples, and exercises. Half of the exercises have answers in the back, allowing for both class work and independent work.

Reading Selections

Abundant readings from both professional and student writers have been selected as models of exemplary writing on stimulating topics. Readings are culturally diverse and varied in subject material, so they will appeal to students of different backgrounds—generational, ethnic, gender, and regional—while stressing the commonality of experience. Featured readings include mainly paragraphs and essays but also short stories, poems, and even a song. Contemporary cartoons supporting chapter themes and instruction are also included.

Guide questions following the selections direct students to analyze the readings for form and to react to the content. Reading-related writing suggestions cover students' parallel experiences, evaluations, and analyses.

Changes and Enhancements in the Eighth Edition

The eighth edition emphasizes writing the paragraph, essay, and research paper. It includes

- More practical exercises in organization and revision

- Examples of student work that show students how their peers completed assignments by working in stages

- Computer-related writing tips incorporated into the text
- A Writing Process Worksheet suitable for photocopying and designed to provide guidance for students and save time and effort for instructors
- Extended instruction in summary writing combined with other forms of writing
- Updated career-related writing topics added to reading-related topics and general topics
- A chapter on the contemporary research paper, including instruction in documenting online sources and using the electronic library
- More sentence-writing exercises in the Handbook
- New content for some exercises in the Handbook
- A Self-Evaluation Chart to help students track their needs and goals and to promote self-reliance

The eighth edition also stresses the connection between reading and writing. It includes

- More than 40 percent new reading selections
- Readings paired for both pattern and theme in many chapters
- Reading selections that illustrate patterns and stimulate thinking and writing
- Readings that celebrate this country's diverse cultures
- Cartoons that irreverently and hilariously make instructional points

Support Material for Instructors

The Instructor's Annotated Edition contains immediate answers for exercises and activities, along with the following support:

- The Instructor's Guide (all parts included in IAE)
- Reproducible quizzes for the Handbook and many professional essays
- Suggestions for effective and time-saving approaches to instruction
- A sample syllabus

Software Resources

- *English Microlab* for PC and Macintosh. Teaches and reinforces the basics of grammar, punctuation, and mechanics. An accompanying data disk allows instructors to manage and record group results.
- *Expressways*, Second Edition, for PC, Macintosh, and Windows. Interactive software that guides students as they write and revise paragraphs and essays.

Acknowledgments

I am profoundly indebted to the following instructors who have reviewed this textbook: Linda Caywood-Farrell, Piedmont Community College; Sally Hall, Honolulu Community College; Craig Frischkorn, Jamestown Community College; Thomas Beery, Lima Technical College; Jill Lahnstein, Cape Fear Community College; David Throne, Community College of Aurora; Cheryl West, Brewton Parker College; Dorothy Brown, Iowa Western Community College; William

Gilbert, University of Houston—Downtown; Diane Dowdey, Sam Houston State University; Carol S. Hamm, Seminole State College; Herbert Karl Green, Jr., Camden County College; Ida R. Page, Durham Technical Community College; Elisabeth Leyson, Fullerton College; Wayne Rambo, Camden County College; Joseph Szabo, Mercer County Community College; Virginia Burley, Mt. San Antonio College; and Daniel E. M. Landau, Santa Monica College. Thanks also to the faculty members at Mt. San Antonio College, with special recognition to the Basic Courses Review Committee.

I deeply appreciate the work of freelance editors Marilyn Weissman and Margaret Roll, Nancy Benjamin of Books By Design, as well as my colleagues at Houghton Mifflin, Mary Jo Southern, Kellie Cardone, Danielle Richardson, Nancy Lyman, and Tracy Patruno.

I am especially grateful to my family of wife, children and their spouses, and grandchildren for their cheerful, inspiring support: Sharon, Kelly, Erin, Jeanne, Michael, Shane, Lauren, Jarrett, and Matthew.

Student Overview

"Every sentence, paragraph, and essay begins with a single word."

A variation on a familiar saying (Lee Brandon)

THE FAR SIDE   By GARY LARSON

Practice with Principles

Some will tell you that to become a better writer you should practice. Others will say that to become a better writer you should learn the principles of writing.

Each view is a half-truth. If you practice without knowing what to do, you'll get better only within your own limitations; any bad habits are likely to become more ingrained. If you're playing the piano with two fingers and you practice a lot, you may learn to play a great "Chopsticks," but Beethoven's "Moonlight Sonata" will remain beyond your reach.

However, if you learn the principles of writing and do not practice them, they will never become a functioning part of your skills. The solution is in your hands. You are now gazing at a book with a well-rounded approach, one that combines sound techniques and ample writing practice. It is designed for use both in class and on your own.

Each chapter in this book begins with a list of chapter topics.

Chapters 1 through 3 explain the three stages of the writing process.

Chapters 4 through 6 present forms of writing and support: Chapter 4, the paragraph; Chapter 5, the essay; Chapter 6, both the paragraph and the essay with instruction in reading-related writing.

Chapters 7 through 17 focus on forms of discourse, commonly called *patterns of development:* narration, description, exposition (explaining), and argumentation.

Chapter 18 presents a discussion of the research paper.

The Handbook at the end of the book offers instruction in fundamentals and sentence writing. It also includes a brief guide for ESL students.

The three Appendixes include the following: (A) Parts of Speech, (B) Taking Tests, and (C) Writing a Job Application Letter and a Résumé.

A Self-Evaluation Chart appears on the inside front cover of this book (see page 4 for more information about it), and a Correction Chart appears on the inside back cover.

Strategies for Self-Improvement

Here are some strategies you can follow to make the best use of this book and to jump-start the improvement in your writing skills.

1. *Be active and systematic in learning.* Take advantage of your instructor's expertise by being an active class member—one who takes notes, asks questions, and contributes to discussion. Become dedicated to systematic learning: Determine your needs, decide what to do, and do it. Make learning a part of your everyday thinking and behavior.

2. *Read widely.* Samuel Johnson, a great English scholar, once said he didn't want to read anything by people who had written more than they had read. William Faulkner, a Nobel Prize winner in literature, said, "Read, read, read. Read everything—trash, classics, good and bad, and see how writers do it." Read to learn technique, to acquire ideas, and to be stimulated to write. Especially read to satisfy your curiosity and to receive pleasure. If reading is a main component of your course, approach it as systematically as you do writing.

3. *Keep a journal.* Keep a journal even though it may not be required in your particular class. It is a good practice to jot down your observations in a notebook. Here are some topics for daily, or almost daily, journal writing:

- Summarize, evaluate, or react to reading assignments.

- Summarize, evaluate, or react to what you see on television and in movies, and to what you read in newspapers and in magazines.

- Describe and narrate situations or events you experience.

- Write about career-related matters you encounter in other courses or on the job.

Your journal entries may read like an intellectual diary, a record of what you are thinking about at certain times. Keeping a journal will help you to understand reading material better, to develop more language skills, and to think more clearly—as well as to become more confident and to write more easily so that writing becomes a comfortable, everyday activity. Your entries may also provide subject material for longer, more carefully crafted pieces. The most important thing is to get into the habit of writing something each day.

4. *Evaluate your writing skills.* Use the Self-Evaluation Chart inside the front cover of this book to assess your writing skills by listing problem areas you need to work on. You may be adding to these lists throughout the entire term. Drawing on your instructor's comments, make notes on matters such as organization, development, content, spelling, vocabulary, diction, grammar, sentence structure, punctuation, and capitalization. Use this chart for self-motivated study assignments and as a checklist in all stages of writing. As you master each problem area, you can erase it or cross it out.

Most of the elements you record in your Self-Evaluation Chart probably are covered in *Paragraphs and Essays*. The table of contents, the index, and the Correction Chart on the inside back cover of the book will direct you to the additional instruction you decide you need.

- *Organization/Development/Content:* List aspects of your writing, including the techniques of all stages of the writing process, such as freewriting, brainstorming, and clustering; the phrasing of a good topic sentence or thesis; and the design, growth, and refinement of your ideas.

- *Spelling/Vocabulary/Diction:* List common spelling words marked as incorrect on your college assignments. Here, *common* means words that you use often. If you are misspelling these words now, you may have been doing so for years. Look at your list. Is there a pattern to your misspellings? Consult the Spelling section in the Handbook for a set of useful rules. Whatever it takes, master the words on your list. Continue to add troublesome words as you accumulate assignments. If your vocabulary is imprecise or your diction is inappropriate (if you use slang, trite expressions, or words that are too informal), note those problems as well.

- *Grammar/Sentence Structure:* List recurring problems in your grammar or sentence structure. Use the symbols and page references listed on the Correction Chart (inside back cover of this book) or look up the problem in the index.

- *Punctuation/Capitalization:* Treat these problems the same way you treat grammar problems. Note that the Punctuation and Capitalization section in the Handbook numbers some rules; therefore, you can often give exact locations of the remedies for your problems.

Here is an example of how your chart might be used.

Self-Evaluation Chart

Organization/ Development/ Content	Spelling/ Vocabulary/ Diction	Grammar/ Sentence Structure	Punctuation/ Capitalization
needs more specific support such as examples, 136	avoid slang, 33	fragments, 388	difference between semicolons and commas, 452
refine outline, 23	avoid clichés such as "be there for me," 33	subject-verb agreement, 409	comma after long introductory modifier, 448
use clear topic sentence, 17	it's, its, 467	comma splice, 391	
	you're, your, 468	vary sentence patterns, 372	comma in compound sentence, 374, 448
	rec*e*ive, rule on, 464		

5. *Use the Writing Process Worksheet.* Record details about each of your assignments, such as the due date, topic, length, and form. The worksheet will also remind you of the stages of the writing process: explore, organize, and write. A blank Writing Process Worksheet for you to photocopy for assignments appears on page 5. Discussed in Chapter 1, it illustrates student work in almost every chapter. Your instructor may ask you to complete the form and submit it with your assignments.

6. *Take full advantage of technology.* Although using a word processor will not by itself make you a better writer, it will enable you to write and revise more swiftly as you move, alter, and delete material with a few keystrokes. Devices such as the thesaurus, spell checker, grammar checker, and style checker will help you revise and edit. Many colleges have writing labs with good instruction and facilities for networking and researching complicated topics. The Internet, used wisely, can provide resource material for compositions.

7. *Be positive.* To improve your English skills, write with freedom, but revise and edit with rigor. Work with your instructor to set attainable goals, and proceed at a reasonable pace. Soon, seeing what you have mastered and checked off your list will give you a sense of accomplishment.

   While you progress in your English course, notice how you are getting better at content, organization, and mechanics as you read, think, and write.

   Consequently, you can expect writing to become a highly satisfying pleasure. After all, once you learn to write well, writing can be just as enjoyable as talking.

   Finally, don't compare yourself with others. Compare yourself with yourself and, as you improve, consider yourself what you are—a student on the path toward more effective writing, a student on the path toward success.

   It is appropriate to end this overview with the same quotation that introduced it.

   Every sentence, paragraph, and essay begins with a single word.

   Let a word fall.

Writing Process Worksheet

TITLE _____

NAME _____ **DUE DATE** _____

ASSIGNMENT   In the space below, write whatever you need to know about your assignment, including information about the topic, audience, pattern of writing, length, whether to include a rough draft or revised drafts, and whether your paper must be typed.

STAGE ONE   **Explore**   Freewrite, brainstorm (list), cluster, or take notes as directed by your instructor. Use the back of this page or separate paper if you need more space.

STAGE TWO   **Organize**   Write a topic sentence or thesis; label the subject and the treatment parts.

Write an outline or an outline alternative.

STAGE THREE   **Write**   On separate paper, write and then revise your paper as many times as necessary for coherence, language (usage, tone, and diction), unity, emphasis, support, and sentences (CLUESS). Read your paper aloud to hear and correct any grammatical errors or awkward-sounding sentences.

Edit any problems in fundamentals, such as capitalization, omissions, punctuation, and spelling (COPS).

The Writing Process: Stage One

Exploring/Experimenting/ Gathering Information

> "*Writing is easy. All you do is stare at a blank sheet of paper until drops of blood form on your forehead.*"
>
> Gene Fowler
>
> "*My objective is to make the drops of blood smaller.*"
>
> Lee Brandon

THE QUIGMANS   by Buddy Hickerson

B. Hickerson, copyright Los Angeles Times Syndicate.
Reprinted by permission.

The Writing Process Defined

he writing process consists of a set of strategies that will help you proceed from idea or purpose to the final statement of a paragraph or essay. As presented here, the different strategies move from

Stage One: Exploring/Experimenting/Gathering Information

to

Stage Two: Writing the Controlling Idea/Organizing and Developing Support

to

Stage Three: Writing/Revising / Editing.

These stages occupy Chapters 1, 2, and 3, respectively. Collectively they represent what is called the *writing process.*

The process of writing is *recursive,* which means "going back and forth." In this respect writing is like reading. If you do not understand what you have read, you back up and read it again. After you reread the entire passage, you may still go back and reread selectively. The same can be said of your writing. If, for example, you have reached Stage Two and you are working with an outline only to discover that your subject is too broadly considered, you may want to back up and narrow your topic sentence or thesis and then adjust your outline. You may even return to an early cluster of ideas to see how you can use a smaller grouping of them. Revision, in Stage Three, is usually the most recursive part of all. You will go over your material again and again until you are satisfied that you have expressed yourself as well as you possibly can.

The Writing Process Worksheet

The blank Writing Process Worksheet on page 5, with brief directions for the three stages of the writing process, is designed to be duplicated and completed with each major writing assignment. It gives you clear, consistent guidance and provides your instructor with an easy format for finding and checking information. Customarily this worksheet is stapled to the front of your rough and final drafts. Figure 1.1 shows a reduced worksheet.

The Assignment

Particulars of the assignment, frequently the most neglected parts of a writing project, are often the most important. If you do not know, or later cannot recall, specifically what you are supposed to do, you cannot do satisfactory work. An otherwise excellent composition on a misunderstood assignment may get you a failing grade, a sad situation for both you and your instructor.

As an aid to recalling just what you should write about, the Writing Process Worksheet provides space and guidance for you to note these details: information about the topic, audience, pattern of writing, length of the paper, whether to include a rough draft or revised drafts, whether your paper must be typed, and the date the assignment is due.

Figure 1.1
The Writing Process Worksheet: Photocopy the full-size sheet on page 5 to help you with your writing assignments.

Writing Process Worksheet

TITLE _____

NAME _____ DUE DATE _____

ASSIGNMENT In the space below, write whatever you need to know about your assignment, including information about the topic, audience, pattern of writing, length, whether to include a rough draft or revised drafts, and whether your paper must be typed.

STAGE ONE **Explore** Freewrite, brainstorm (list), cluster, or take notes as directed by your instructor. Use the back of this page or a separate sheet of paper if you need more space.

STAGE TWO **Organize** Write a topic sentence or thesis; label the subject and the treatment parts.

Write an outline or an outline alternative.

STAGE THREE **Write** On separate paper, write and then revise your paper as many times as necessary for coherence, language (usage, tone, and diction), unity, emphasis, support, and sentences (CLUESS). Read your paper aloud to hear and correct any grammatical errors or awkward-sounding sentences.
Edit any problems in fundamentals, such as capitalization, omissions, punctuation, and spelling (COPS).

At the time your instructor gives that information, it will probably be clear; a few days later, it may not be. By putting your notes on the assignment portion of the worksheet, you remind yourself of what you should do and also indicate to your instructor what you have done.

Your Audience

More so than most points on the assignment portion of the worksheet, the matter of audience requires special consideration. At the outset of your writing project, you should consider your readers. Their needs, interests, and abilities should determine the focus of your subject, the extent of your explanation, your overall style, and your word choice. We usually make those adjustments automatically when we are speaking; it is easy to forget to do so when we are writing.

Stage One Strategies

Certain strategies commonly grouped under the heading *prewriting* can help you get started and develop your ideas. These strategies—freewriting, brainstorming, clustering, and gathering information—are very much a part of writing. The understandable desire to skip to the finished statement is what causes the most common student-writer grief: that of not filling the blank sheet or of filling it but not significantly improving on the blankness. The prewriting strategies described in this section will help you attack the blank sheet constructively with imaginative thought, analysis, and experimentation. They can lead to clear, effective communication.

Freewriting

One strategy is *freewriting,* an exercise that its originator, Peter Elbow, has called "babbling in print." When you freewrite, you write without stopping, letting your ideas tumble forth. You do not concern yourself unduly with the fundamentals of writing, such as punctuation and spelling. Freewriting is an adventure into your memory and imagination. It is concerned with discovery, invention, and exploration. If you are at a loss for words on your subject, write in a comment such as "I don't know what is coming next" or "blah, blah, blah," and continue when relevant words come. It is important to keep writing. Freewriting immediately eliminates the blank page and thereby helps you break through an emotional barrier, but that is not the only benefit. The words that you sort through in that idea kit will include some you can use. You can then underline or circle those words and even add notes on the side so that the freewriting continues to grow even after its initial spontaneous expression.

The way in which you proceed depends on the type of assignment: working with a topic of your choice, working from a restricted list of topics, or working with a prescribed topic.

The *topic of your choice* affords you the greatest freedom of exploration. You would probably select a subject that interests you and freewrite about it, allowing your mind to wander among its many parts, perhaps mixing fact and fantasy, direct experience, and hearsay. A freewriting about music might uncover areas of special interest and knowledge, such as jazz or folk rock, that you would want to pursue further in freewriting or other prewriting strategies.

Working from a *restricted list* requires a more focused freewriting. With the list, you can, of course, experiment with several topics to discover what is most suitable for you. If, for example, "career choice," "career preparation," "career guidance," and "career prospects" are on the restricted list, you would probably select one and freewrite about it. If it works well for you, you would probably proceed with the next step of your prewriting. If you are not satisfied with what you uncover in freewriting, you would explore another item from the restricted list.

When working with a *prescribed topic,* you focus on a particular topic and try to restrict your freewriting to its boundaries. If your topic specifies a division of a subject area such as "political involvement of your generation," then you would tie those key words to your own information, critical thinking, and imaginative responses. If the topic asks for, let's say, your reactions to a specific poem, then that poem would give you the framework for your free associations with your own experiences, creations, and opinions.

You should learn to use freewriting because it will often serve you well, but you need not use it every time you write. Some very short writing assignments do not call for freewriting. An in-class assignment may not allow time for freewriting.

Nevertheless, freewriting is often a useful strategy in your toolbox of techniques. It can help you get words on paper, break emotional barriers, generate topics, develop new insights, and explore ideas.

Freewriting can lead to other stages of prewriting and writing, and it can also provide content as you develop your topic.

The following example of freewriting, and the writing, revising, and editing examples in Chapters 2 and 3, are from student Betsy Jackson's work on "If I Were a Traffic Cop." She selected her topic, bad drivers, from a restricted list. If she had been working with a prescribed topic, she might have been told to concentrate on only one aspect of bad drivers, such as the need for driver education, the need for better laws, or the cost of bad driving. Then she would have done some research. However, she had no such limitation and, therefore, thought about bad drivers broadly. After her freewriting, she went back over her work looking for an idea that might be limited enough to use as the basis for a paper. Here is what she wrote:

Just driving around on streets and freeways can be a scary experience because of all the bad drivers. Whenever I see them, sometimes I just laugh. Sometimes I get mad. Sometimes I get irritated. Sometimes I get scared. It's not just the young drivers or the old drivers it's <u>all kinds.</u> And all types of people no matter what the nationality or the types of vehicles they drive. Pickup drivers are worse as a group but bad drivers come in all kinds of vehicles. I think someone should do something about them. The worst are the <u>drunk drivers.</u> I don't see them in the morning. But I see them late at night when I'm driving home from work. They should be put away. But a lot of others should be getting serious tickets. Especially the bad ones. <u>Make me a cop</u>—a super-cop—a Rambo cop and I'll go after the bad ones. Some of them cause a lot of accidents and get people all mad. Blah. Blah. Blah. Take <u>tailgaters</u> for example. And what about the drivers that go into the emergency lanes on the free-ways to pass when there's a jam. And then you've got the <u>lane changers</u> that don't even give signals. And those that just <u>keep going</u> and <u>turn left when</u> the <u>light turns red.</u> Then you've got the ones that drive <u>too fast</u> and <u>too slow.</u> And you've got the ones that <u>don't stop</u> for <u>pedestrians.</u> Blah. Blah. Blah. I guess we all have our pet peeves about bad drivers and everyone would like to be a cop sometimes. I guess if you talked to them some would have reasons. Maybe they're <u>late</u> for work or they are <u>mad</u> about something. Or maybe there's an <u>emergency.</u> Whatever it is, I get concerned when they <u>take my life in their hands.</u>

all kinds

drunk drivers

if I were a cop

tailgaters

lane changers
left turners on red
too fast, too slow
don't yield

causes
effect

After her freewriting session, Jackson examined what she had written for possible ideas to develop for a writing assignment. As she recognized those ideas, she underlined key words and phrases and made a few notes in the margins. By reading only the underlined words in her freewriting, you can understand what is important to Jackson; it was not necessary for her to underline whole sentences.

In addition to putting words on that dreaded blank sheet of paper, Jackson discovered that she had quite a lot to say about drivers and that she had selected a favorable topic to develop. The entire process took no more than five minutes. Had she found only a few ideas or no promising ideas at all, she might have freewritten on another topic. Although in going back over her work she saw some errors, especially in wording and sentence structure, she did not correct them because the purpose of freewriting is discovery, not revising or editing. She was confident that she could continue with the process of writing a paper.

Exercise 1	**FREEWRITING**

Try freewriting on a broad topic such as one of the following:

an event that was important to you in your youth

a concert, a movie, or a television program

the ways you use your computer

drugs—causes, effects, a friend with a problem

gangs—causes, effects, an experience

the benefits of using a word processor

ways of disciplining children

why a person is a hero or role model to you

a great or terrible party

a bad or good day at school

why a college education is important

Following the example in Jackson's freewriting, underline and annotate the phrases that may lead to ideas you could explore further.

Brainstorming

This prewriting strategy features key words and phrases that relate in various ways to the subject area or to the specific topic you are concerned with. Brainstorming includes two basic forms: (1) asking and answering questions and (2) listing.

Big Six Questions

One effective way to get started is to ask the "big six questions" about your subject: Who? What? Where? When? Why? How? Then let your mind run free as you jot down answers in single entries or lists. Some of the big six questions may not fit, and some may be more important than others, depending on the purposes of your writing. For example, if you were writing about the causes of a situation, the Why? question could be more important than the others; if you were concerned with how to do something, the How? question would predominate. If you were writing in response to a reading selection, you would confine your thinking to questions appropriately related to the content of that reading selection.

Whatever your focus for the questions is, the result is likely to be numerous ideas that will provide information for continued exploration and development of your topic. Thus your pool of information for writing widens and deepens.

Jackson continued with the topic of bad drivers, and her topic tightened to focus on particular areas.

Who?	bad drivers; me as a cop
What?	driving badly, recklessly, unsafely; a cop's job
Where?	on every roadway
When?	all the time
Why?	hurried, disrespectful, self-centered, sick, addiction, hostile, irresponsible
How?	lane-changing, driving illegally in emergency lane, not signaling, passing on the shoulder, tailgating, turning left on red, rolling stop, speeding, driving while intoxicated

Notice that each question is answered in this example, but with some topics some questions may not fit. As Jackson addressed the Why? and How? questions, her brainstorming produced long lists, suggesting that those areas were strong possibilities for the focus of her paper.

Listing

Another effective way to brainstorm, especially if you have a defined topic and a storehouse of information, is to skip the big-six-questions approach and simply make a list of words and phrases related to your topic. This strategy is favored by many writers.

Knowing from the outset that she was concerned mainly with the behavior of drivers, Jackson might have gone directly to making a list indicating what drivers do or how they drive.

(unsafe lane changers)
driving illegally in the emergency lane
not signaling
passing on the shoulder
(tailgating)
(turning left on red)
turning right on red without stop
rolling stop
speeding
driving too slow in fast lane
(driving while intoxicated)
driving while on cell phone
driving while reading road map
truck in car lanes
drivers dumping trash

From this list, Jackson might have selected perhaps four ideas for her framework and circled them for future reference.

Even if you do not have a focused topic, you may find a somewhat random listing useful, merely writing phrases as they occur to you. This exploratory activity is not unlike freewriting. After you have established such a list, you can sort out and group the phrases as you generate your topic and find its natural divisions. Feel free to accept, reject, or insert phrases.

Exercise 2	**BRAINSTORMING**

Further explore the topic you worked with in Exercise 1 by first answering the big six questions and then making a list.

Big Six Questions

Who? _____

What? _____

Where? _____

When? _____

Why? _____

How? _____

List _____

_____

_____

_____

_____

_____

_____

_____

_____

_____

_____

_____

_____

Clustering

Still another prewriting technique is *clustering*. Start by "double bubbling" your topic; that is, write it down in the middle of the page and draw a double circle around it. Then respond to the question "What comes to mind?" Draw a single bubble around other ideas on spokes radiating out from the hub that contains the topic. Any bubble can lead to another bubble or numerous bubbles in the same way. This strategy is sometimes used instead of or before making an outline to organize and develop ideas.

The more restricted the topic inside the double bubble, the fewer the number of spokes that will radiate with single bubbles. For example, a topic such as "high school dropouts" would have more spokes than "reasons for dropping out of high school."

Here is Jackson's cluster on the subject of bad drivers. She has drawn dotted lines around subclusters that seem to relate to a workable, unified topic.

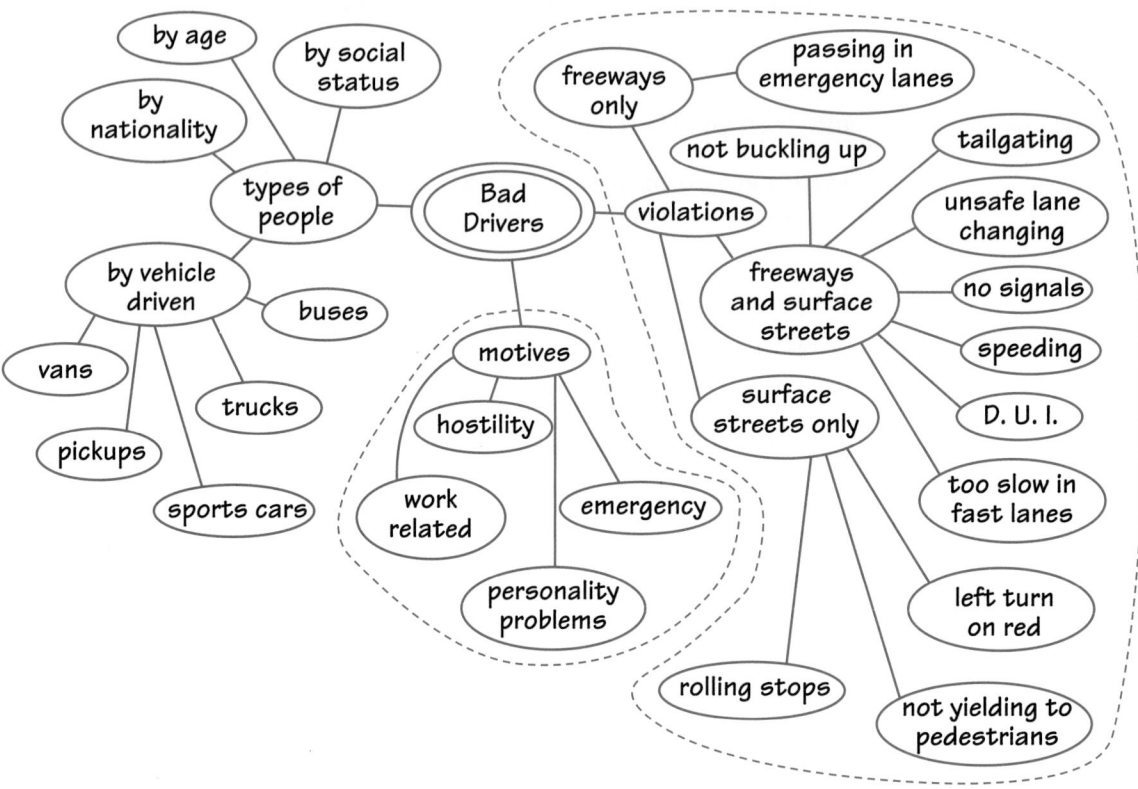

Exercise 3	CLUSTERING

Continuing with your topic, develop a cluster of related ideas. Draw dotted lines around subclusters that have potential for focus and more development.

Gathering Information

For reading-related writing—especially the kind that requires a close examination of the selection—you will read print and/or electronic sources, such as the Internet, make notes, and perhaps outline (see Chapter 2) or summarize (see Chapter 6) the text. Of course, you may also want to make notes for other topics to write about as they occur to you. This kind of note taking can be combined with other strategies such as brainstorming and clustering. It can even take the place of them. It can also be used in conjunction with strategies such as outlining.

Student Betsy Jackson at this point is writing about personal experience. If she wanted to include statistics or an authoritative statement, she might do some library research or interview a police officer. In either case, she would take notes.

Writer's Guidelines: Exploring/Experimenting/Gathering Information

The writing process consists of strategies that will help you proceed from idea or purpose to the final statement of a paragraph or essay. Throughout all stages of the writing process, you should consider your audience. Of the three stages, Stage One offers four approaches:

1. Freewriting consists of writing without stopping, letting ideas tumble forth.

   - Freewriting involves breaking down emotional barriers, generating topics, discovering ideas, and exploring ideas.

   - Your approach to freewriting will depend on whether you work on a topic of your choice (great freedom), a topic from a restricted list (more focused), or an assigned topic (concentration on one idea).

   - You need not use freewriting for all writing experiences. You would probably not use it for very short assignments, in-class assignments with limited time, outline and summary assignments, and assignments on topics you know well.

2. Brainstorming is a technique for quickly developing key words and phrases that relate to your topic. It includes two basic forms: the big six questions or listing.

   - You may ask Who? What? Where? When? Why? and How? questions about your topic, ignoring questions that do not fit.

   - Or you may simply list points on likely divisions of your topic.

3. Clustering is a visual way of showing connections and relationships. It is sometimes used with an outline, and sometimes in place of one.

   - You should start by "double-bubbling" your topic and then, in response to the question What comes to mind? single-bubble other ideas on spokes radiating from the hub.

4. Gathering information can take the form of underlining, annotating, and note taking. These techniques are explored in Chapter 6.

2

The Writing Process: Stage Two

Writing the Controlling Idea/Organizing and Developing Support

"There are no bad writers; there are only writers who have not learned to write."

Linda McCool

© John Callahan, courtesy Levin Represents.

he nine most important words this book can offer you are *State your topic sentence or thesis and support it.* If you have no controlling idea—no topic sentence for a paragraph or thesis for an essay—your writing will be unfocused, and your readers may be confused or bored. But if you organize your material well, so that it supports and develops your controlling idea, you can present your views to your readers with interest, clarity, and persuasion.

Stating the controlling idea and organizing support can be accomplished effectively and systematically. How? This chapter presents several uncomplicated techniques you can use in Stage Two of the writing process.

Defining the Controlling Idea

If you tell a friend you are about to write a paragraph or essay, be prepared to hear the question "What are you writing about?" If you answer, "Public schools," your friend will probably be satisfied with the answer but not very interested. The problem is that the phrase *public schools* offers no sense of limitation or direction. It just indicates your subject, not what you are going to do with it. *An effective controlling statement, called the topic sentence for a paragraph and the thesis for an essay, has both a subject **and** a treatment.* **The subject is what you intend to write about. The treatment is what you intend to do with your subject.**

Example: Glendora High School   offers a well-balanced academic program.
                         subject   treatment

In some instances the subject will follow the treatment:

The time has come for a national law legalizing
                         treatment
physician-assisted suicide for the terminally ill.
                         subject

In other instances the subject will divide the treatment:

Four factors establish Elvis Presley as the greatest
         treatment   subject   treatment
entertainer of the twentieth century: appearance, singing ability, style, and influence.

Writing the Controlling Idea as a Topic Sentence or Thesis

The effective controlling idea presents treatment that can be developed with supporting information. The ineffective one is vague, too broad, or too narrow.

Vague: Public schools   are great.
                       subject   treatment

Better: Public schools   do as well academically as private schools,
                       subject   treatment
according to statistics. (made more specific)

Too broad: <u>Public schools</u>   <u>are too crowded.</u>
              subject   treatment

Better: <u>Bidwell Elementary School</u>   <u>is too crowded.</u> (limiting the subject
              subject   treatment
to a particular school)

Too narrow: <u>American public schools</u>   <u>were first established in Philadelphia</u>
                  subject   treatment
<u>in 1779.</u> (only a fact)

Better: <u>The first public schools in America</u>   <u>were found to meet certain</u>
              subject   treatment
<u>practical needs.</u> (made more specific by indicating aspects)

In writing a sound controlling idea, be sure that you have included both the subject and the treatment and that the whole statement is not vague, too broad, or too narrow. Instead, it should be phrased so that it invites development. Such phrasing can usually be achieved by limiting time, place, or aspect. The limitation may apply to the subject (instead of schools in general, focus on a particular school), or it may apply to the treatment (you might compare the subject to something else, as in "do as well academically"). You might limit both the subject and the treatment.

Exercise 1   **EVALUATING TOPIC SENTENCES**

In the following controlling ideas, underline and label the subjects (S) and treatments (T). Also judge each one as E (effective) or I (ineffective). (See Answer Key for answers.)

Example:

___I___   <u>Basketball</u>   <u>is an interesting sport.</u>
               S   T

_____ 1. Students who cheat in school may be trying to relieve certain emotional pressures.

_____ 2. Shakespeare was an Elizabethan writer.

_____ 3. The quarterback in football and the general of an army are alike in significant ways.

_____ 4. Animals use color chiefly for protection.

_____ 5. Portland is a city in Oregon.

_____ 6. Life in the ocean has distinct realms.

_____ 7. Rome has had a glorious and tragic history.

_____ 8. Boston is the capital of Massachusetts.

_____ 9. The word *macho* has a special meaning to the Hispanic community.

_____ 10. The history of plastics is exciting.

Exercise 2 **EVALUATING TOPIC SENTENCES**

In the following controlling ideas, underline and label the subjects (S) and treatments (T). Also judge each one as E (effective) or I (ineffective).

_E_ 1. An experience in the first grade taught me a valuable lesson about
   S   T

   honesty.

_E_ 2. The Internet has changed the way many people shop.
   S   T

_I_ 3. President Lincoln was assassinated at the Ford Theater.
   S   T

_I_ 4. The dictionary has an interesting history.
   S   T

_I_ 5. The world is a place of many contrasts.
   S   T

_E_ 6. Rap music can be classified on the basis of the intent of its
   S   T

   writers/composers.

_I_ 7. Bombay is one of the most densely populated cities in the world.
   S   T

_T_ 8. What I've seen while working in a fast-food place has made me lose

   my appetite.

_E_ 9. My physical education teacher is called "Coach."
                    S   T

_E_ 10. Count Dracula's reputation is based on his exploits as a nocturnal
                    S   T

   creature.

Exercise 3	WRITING TOPIC SENTENCES

Complete the following entries to make each one a solid topic sentence. Only a subject and part of the treatment are provided. The missing part may be more than a single word.

Example: Car salespeople behave differently, depending on <u>the car they are selling and the kind of customer they are serving.</u>

1. A part-time job can offer *greet financiel supper*

2. My school's athletic program should be *expended*

3. It is almost universally accepted that smoking is _____

4. Students caught cheating should be _____

5. Health care should be _____

6. One of the effects of the rising cost of a college education is _____
_____

7. Offering constructive criticism to a friend who didn't ask can _____
_____

8. People who appear on television talk shows are frequently _____

9. The slang of a particular group reveals _____

10. Gestures and facial expressions usually communicate _____

Exercise 4	WRITING TOPIC SENTENCES

Convert each of the following subjects into a topic sentence.

1. Bumper stickers _____

2. Rudeness _____

3. The true character of my neighbor _____

4. Many homeless people _____

5. Being able to use a computer _____

6. Dieting _____

7. The basic forms of jazz and classical music _____

8. Educated citizens _____

9. The required labeling of rock music albums _____

10. Smoking _____

Your topic sentence or thesis can come from any of several places. You may be able to generate it at Stage One, in your initial freewriting, brainstorming, clustering, or gathering information, or you may be given an assigned topic. In any case, your procedure is the same at this point. You need to work on the statement—just that one sentence—until you have developed an interesting subject and a well-focused treatment. The statement may be a bit more mechanical than the one you actually use in your paragraph or essay, but it can easily be reworded once you reach Stage Three of the writing process: writing, revising, and editing.

The controlling idea will probably not pop into your head full-blown. It is more likely to be the result of repeated revisions. Even when you are revising a paper you have written, you may go back and rephrase your topic sentence or thesis. That is part of the back-and-forth (recursive) nature of the writing process.

In the following example, note how Jackson reworks her controlling idea several times before she settles on a statement that is well focused and capable of being developed.

Subject	Treatment
<u>Bad drivers</u>	<u>can be found everywhere.</u> (too broad)
<u>Someone</u>	<u>should do something about bad drivers.</u> (vague)
<u>Bad driving</u>	<u>has existed in the United States for more than a century.</u> (too broad)
<u>If I were a traffic cop</u>	<u>I'd crack down on certain types of bad drivers.</u> (workable)

She has limited the subject by reducing it to the hypothetical situation of being a traffic cop. She has limited the treatment by dealing with only "certain types of bad drivers," not all bad drivers.

Exercise 5	**WRITING YOUR TOPIC SENTENCE**

Using a topic you worked with in Chapter 1 or one from the list on page 11, write a topic sentence or thesis. Mark the subject and treatment parts.

Organizing Support

You have now studied the first part of the nine-word sentence "State your topic sentence or thesis and support it." In the first stage of the writing process (in Chapter 1), you explored many ideas, experimented with them, and even developed some approaches to writing about them. You may also have gathered information through reading and note taking. The techniques of that first stage have already given you some initial support. The next step is to organize your ideas and information into a paragraph or essay that is interesting, understandable, and compelling.

Three tools can help you organize your supporting material: listing (a form of brainstorming), clustering, and outlining. You will probably use only one of these organizing tools, depending on course requirements, the assignment, or individual preference. In the continuing demonstration of Betsy Jackson's work, each tool is shown.

Listing

Lists are the simplest and most flexible of the organizing tools. Listing need be nothing more than a column of items presenting support material in a useful sequence (time, space, or importance). As you work with your support material, you can cross out words or move them around on the list. By leaving vertical space between items, you can easily insert new examples and details. Jackson took phrases from the list she had made in Stage One and wrote them below her topic sentence.

Subject   Treatment

If I were a traffic cop,   I'd crack down on certain types of bad drivers.

    drunk drivers—most dangerous, top priority, off the road
    tailgaters—hostile, hurried, cause accidents, irritating
    unsafe lane changers—rude, cause accidents
    left-turners on red—reckless, accident prone

Clustering

Chains of circles radiating from a central double-bubbled circle form a cluster that shows the relationship of ideas. In the following example, Jackson has developed part of her Stage One cluster (a section noted by a dotted line on page 14).

Subject   Treatment

If I were a traffic cop,   I'd crack down on certain types of bad drivers.

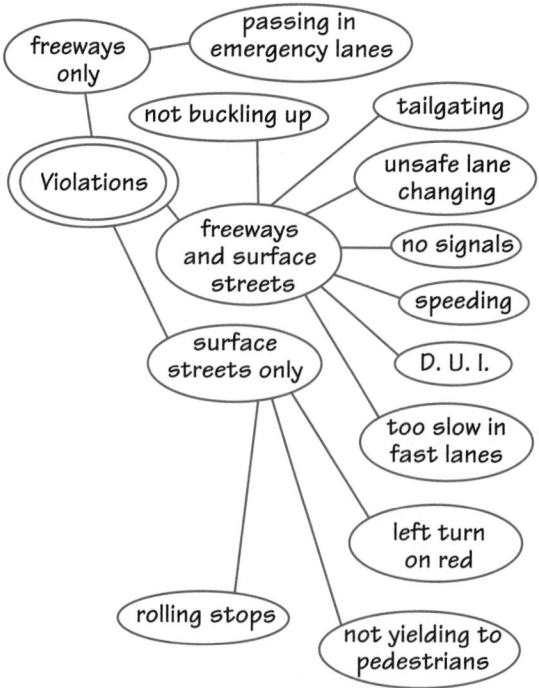

Outlining

Outlining is the tool that most people think of in connection with organizing. Because it is flexible and widely used, it will receive the most emphasis in this stage of the writing process. Outlining does basically the same thing that listing and clustering do. Outlining divides the controlling idea into sections of support material, divides those sections further, and establishes sequence.

An outline is a framework that can be used in two ways. It can indicate the plan for a paragraph or essay you intend to write. It can also show the organization of a passage you are reading. The outline of a reading passage and the outline as a plan for writing are identical in form. If you intend to write a summary of a reading selection, then a single outline might be used for both purposes.

The two main outline forms are the *sentence outline* (each entry is a complete sentence) and the *topic outline* (each entry is a key word or phrase). The topic outline is more common in writing paragraphs and essays.

In the following topic outline, notice first how the parts are arranged on the page: the indentations, the number and letter sequences, the punctuation, and the placement of words. Then read Jackson's outline and see how the ideas in it relate to one another.

Main Idea (will usually be the topic sentence for a paragraph or the thesis for an essay)

   I. Major support
      A. Minor support
         1. Explanation, detail, example
         2. Explanation, detail, example
      B. Minor support
         1. Explanation, detail, example
         2. Explanation, detail, example

  II. Major support
      A. Minor support
         1. Explanation, detail, example
         2. Explanation, detail, example
      B. Minor support
         1. Explanation, detail, example
         2. Explanation, detail, example

Here is Betsy Jackson's outline:

Subject

If I were a traffic cop,

Treatment

I'd crack down on certain types of bad drivers.

   I. Drunks
  II. Unsafe lane changers
      A. Attitude
         1. Rude
         2. Bullying

   B. Results
      1. Accidents
      2. People irritated
III. Left-turners on red
   A. Attitude
      1. Self-centered
      2. Putting self above law
   B. Results
      1. Bad collisions
      2. Mass anger
IV. Tailgaters
   A. Motives
      1. Hostility
      2. Rushed
      3. Impatient
   B. Effects
      1. Accidents
      2. Road fights

The foundation of an effective outline, and, hence, of an effective paragraph or essay, is a strong controlling idea. Always begin by writing a sound topic sentence or thesis, one with a specific subject and well-defined treatment. Then divide the treatment into parts. The nature of the parts will depend on what you are trying to do in the treatment. Just consider the thought process involved. What kinds of material would best support or explain that topic sentence or thesis? How should you organize that material? Should you present a series of examples? A description of a process? A story of human struggle? A combination of methods?

Among the most common forms of dividing and organizing ideas are the following:

- **Narration:** division of time or incident to tell a story
   I. Situation
   II. Conflict
   III. Struggle
   IV. Outcome
   V. Meaning

- **Examples:** division into several examples
   I. First example
   II. Second example
   III. Third example

- **Causes and effects:** division into causes or effects
   I. Cause (or effect) one
   II. Cause (or effect) two
   III. Cause (or effect) three

- **Process analysis:** division of a unit into parts (for example, a pencil has an eraser, a wooden barrel, and a lead)
   I. First part
   II. Second part
   III. Third part

• **Analysis by division:** division into steps telling how something is done

    I. Preparation

    II. Steps

       A. Step 1

       B. Step 2

       C. Step 3

These patterns and others are the subjects of individual chapters in this book.

Exercise 6   **COMPLETING OUTLINES**

Fill in the missing parts of the following outlines. It may be helpful to consider, in each case, whether you are dealing with time, examples, causes, effects, parts, or steps. The answers will vary, depending on your individual experiences and views.

1. <u>Borrowing</u>   <u>is the mother of trouble.</u>
    subject   **treatment**

    I. Received five credit cards in mail

    II. Saw numerous commercials on television

       A. One about _____

       B. Another about _____

    III. Made purchases

    IV. Two months later _____

2. <u>A successful job interview</u>   <u>depends on several factors.</u>
        subject   **treatment**

    I. Good appearance

       A. _____

       B. _____

    II. Behaving properly

    III. Being qualified

       A. Education

       B. _____

    IV. Knowing something about the employer

3. <u>Joe's drug addiction</u>   <u>had significant effects on his life.</u>
    subject   **treatment**

    I. Developed mental health problems

       A. _____

       B. _____

    II. Developed _____

    III. Lost his job

    IV. Lost _____

4. <u>A college education</u> <u>is important for several reasons.</u>
   subject   treatment

  I. Offers personal enrichment

  II. Fulfills curiosity

  III. Provides contacts that may be satisfying later

  IV. _____

5. <u>An ordinary person</u> <u>can be an environmentalist every day.</u>
   subject   treatment

  I. Limit use of internal combustion engines

  II. Avoid using and dumping poisonous chemicals

  III. _____

  IV. _____

    A. Save newspapers

    B. Save _____

    C. _____

6. <u>Cooking spaghetti</u> <u>is not difficult.</u>
   subject   treatment

  I. Get pan, water, and pasta

  II. Boil water in pan

  III. _____

  IV. Cook pasta until _____

  V. Remove pasta from pan and rinse in cold water

7. <u>An excellent doctor</u> <u>must have three qualities.</u>
   subject   treatment

   I. _____

   II. _____

  III. _____

8. <u>Some drivers</u> <u>break traffic laws selectively.</u>
   subject   treatment

  I. Make rolling stops

  II. _____

  III. _____

Exercise 7	WRITING YOUR OUTLINE

Using the subject you converted into a topic sentence or thesis (Exercise 5), compose a topic outline.

Writer's Guidelines: Writing the Controlling Idea/ Organizing and Developing Support

1. The nine most important words this book can offer you are *State your topic sentence or thesis and support it.* If you have no controlling idea—no topic sentence for a paragraph or thesis for an essay—your writing will be unfocused and your readers may be confused or bored. But if you organize your material well, so that it supports and develops your controlling idea, you can present your views to your readers with interest, clarity, and persuasion.

2. An effective controlling statement, called the topic sentence for a paragraph and the thesis for an essay, has both a subject and a treatment. The subject is what you intend to write about. The treatment is what you intend to do with your subject.

   Example: <u>Glendora High School</u>   <u>offers a well-balanced academic program.</u>
                         subject   treatment

3. Three tools can help you organize your supporting material: listing, clustering, and outlining.

   - Listing can be simply a column of items presenting support material in a useful sequence (time, space, or importance).

   - A cluster uses chains of circles radiating from a central double-bubbled circle to show the relationship of ideas.

   - An outline can be used in two ways: to plan the structure and content of something you intend to write and to reveal the structure and content of something you read.

A typical outline looks like this:

Main Idea (will usually be the topic sentence for the paragraph or the thesis for the essay)

  I. Major support

    A. Minor support

      1. Explanation, detail, example

      2. Explanation, detail, example

    B. Minor support

      1. Explanation, detail, example

      2. Explanation, detail, example

 II. Major support

    A. Minor support

      1. Explanation, detail, example

      2. Explanation, detail, example

    B. Minor support

      1. Explanation, detail, example

      2. Explanation, detail, example

The Writing Process: Stage Three

Writing/Revising/Editing

"Writing and rewriting are a constant search for what it is one is saying."

John Updike

THE QUIGMANS   by Buddy Hickerson

Writers' strike

B. Hickerson, copyright 1990, Los Angeles Times Syndicate.
Reprinted by permission.

Writing the First Draft

In Stage Three of the writing process, your work begins to assume its final form. Use your outline or alternative form of organization as a guide in composing your paragraph or essay. For college work, your controlling idea should almost always be clearly stated early in the paper. The Roman numeral parts of the outline will provide the framework for the main ideas of a paragraph assignment or for the topic sentence ideas in an essay. Supporting information—details, examples, quotations—is likely to be used in approximately the same order as it appears in the outline. Keep in mind that you should not be bound absolutely by the outline. Outlines often need to be redone just as your initial writing needs to be redone.

Most writers do best when they go straight through their first draft without stopping to polish sentences or fix small problems. Try that approach. Using the information in your outline and ideas as they occur to you, go ahead and simply write a paragraph or essay. Don't be slowed down by possible misspelled words, flawed punctuation, or ungraceful sentences. You can repair those problems later.

Whether you write in longhand or on a computer depends on what works best for you. Some writers prefer to do a first draft by hand, mark it up, and then go to the computer. Computers save you time in all aspects of your writing, especially revision.

The following paragraph shows how Betsy Jackson wrote her first draft. Notice how it follows the order of topics in her outline; it also includes some new ideas.

Rambo Traffic Cop

I. Drunks
II. Unsafe lane changers
  A. Character
    1. Rude
    2. Bullying
  B. Results
    1. Accidents
    2. People upset
III. Left-turners on red
  A. Attitude
    1. Self-centered
    2. Putting self
      above law
  B. Kinds
    1. Age
    2. Sex
  C. Results
    1. Collisions
    2. Mass irritation
IV. Tailgaters
  A. Motives
    1. Hostility
    2. Rushed
  B. Effects
    1. Accidents
    2. People upset

Make me a traffic cop, and I'll crack down on certain types of drivers. First off are the drunks. I'd zap them off the highways right off, and any cop would. But what I'm really talking about is the jerks of the highway. Near the top are the up-tight lane changers, for example, this morning when I was driving to school, I saw several. I could of carved at least a couple notches in a vilation pad, and I wasn't even cranky. They cut off people and force their way in, and leave behind upset and hurt people. Then there's the left-turn bullies the ones that keep moving out when the yellow turn to red. They come in all ages and sexes, they can be young or old, male or female. Yesterday, I saw this female in a pick-up barrel right out into the teeth of a red light. She had a baby on board. She had lead in her foot. She had evil in her eye. She was hostile and self-centered. Taking advantage of others. She knew that the facing traffic would probably not pull out and risk a head-on crash. The key word there is probably but many times these people with a green light do move out and collide with the left turn bullies. Third, I'd sap the tailgaters. No one goes fast enough for these guys. I'm not alone in this peeve. One bumper sticker reads, "Stay back. I chew tobacky." And James Bond sprayed cars that chased him. Since the first is dirty and the second is against the law, if I had the clout of a Rambo cop I'd just rack up a lot of tailgater tickets. But there's a lot of road demons out there. Maybe it's good I'm not a traffic cop, Rambo or otherwise, cause traffic cops are suppose to inforce hundreds of laws. I don't know if I'd have time cause I have my own pet peeves in mind.

If part of the development of your topic seems out of balance or needs more support, subtract or add material as necessary. Don't be afraid to change the outline. Often going back and forth between the initial draft and the outline will prevent your final work from seeming mechanical. Occasionally, as you discover that you need to expand or diminish a part, it may be useful to review your Stage One for details and opportunities.

Exercise 1	**WRITING YOUR ROUGH DRAFT**

Using the topic you developed in Chapters 1 and 2, write a rough draft of a paragraph or an essay as directed by your instructor.

Revising

The term *first draft* suggests quite accurately that there will be other drafts, or versions, of your writing. Only in the most dire situations, such as an in-class examination when you have time for only one draft, should you be satisfied with a single effort.

What you do beyond the first draft is revision and editing. Revision includes organization, content, and language effectiveness. Editing (discussed later in this chapter) involves a final correcting of simple mistakes and fundamentals such as spelling, punctuation, and capitalization. In practice, editing and revising are not always separate activities, although writers usually wait until the next-to-the-last draft to edit some minor details and attend to other small points that can be easily overlooked.

Successful revision almost always involves intense, systematic rewriting. You should learn to look for certain aspects of skillful writing as you enrich and repair your first draft. To help you recall these aspects so that you can keep them in mind and examine your material in a comprehensive fashion, this textbook offers a memory device—an acronym in which each letter suggests an important feature of good writing and revision. This device enables you to memorize the features of good writing quickly. Soon you will be able to recall and refer to them automatically. These features need not be attended to individually when you revise your writing, although they may be, and they need not be attended to in the order presented here. The acronym is CLUESS (pronounced "clues"), which provides this guide:

Coherence

Language

Unity

Emphasis

Support

Sentences

Each of these features of good writing can be approached with a set of techniques you can apply easily to your first draft. They are presented here with some details, examples, and supporting exercises. The Writer's Guidelines at the end of this chapter provide a concise list of these features and a set of questions you can apply to your own writing and to peer editing.

Coherence

Coherence is the orderly relationship of ideas, each leading smoothly and logically to the next. You must weave your ideas together so skillfully that the reader can easily see how one idea connects to another and to the central thought. This central thought, of course, is expressed in the topic sentence for a paragraph and in the thesis for an essay. You can achieve coherence efficiently by using the following:

Overall pattern

Transitional terms

Repetition of key words and ideas

Pronouns

Consistent point of view

Overall Pattern

Several chapters in this book discuss strategies for an overall pattern of organization or order. Three basic patterns prevail: *time* (chronology), *space* (spatial arrangement), and *emphasis* (stress on ideas). Sometimes you will combine patterns. The coherence of each can be strengthened by using transitional words such as the following:

For a **time** pattern: *first, then, soon, later, following, after, at that point*

For a **space** pattern: *up, down, right, left, beyond, behind, above, below*

For an **emphasis** pattern: *first, second, third, most, more*

Transitional Terms

By using transitional terms, you can help your readers move easily from one idea to another. Each of the following sentences has one of these terms.

> *First,* I realized I had to get a job to stay in school.

> *At the same time,* my track coach wanted the team to spend more hours working out.

> We were, *after all,* the defending champions.

> *Finally,* I dropped one of my courses.

Repetition of Key Words and Ideas

Repeat key words and phrases to keep the main subject in the reader's mind and to maintain the continuity necessary for a smooth flow of logical thought. (See the section on Emphasis later in this chapter.)

Pronouns

Pronouns, such as *he, her, them,* and *it,* provide natural connecting links in your writing. Why? Every pronoun refers to an earlier noun (called the *antecedent* of the pronoun) and thus carries the reader back to that earlier thought. Here are some examples.

> I tried to buy *tickets* for the concert, but *they* were all sold.

> Assertive *people* tend to make decisions quickly. However, *they* may not make the wisest decisions.

> *Roger* painted a picture of *his* father's pickup truck. *It* was so good that *his* professor asked *him* to enter *it* in an art show.

Consistent Point of View

Point of view shows the writer's relationship to the material, the subject, and it usually does not change within a passage.

If you are conveying personal experience, the point of view will be *first person,* or *I,* which can be either involved (a participant) or detached (an observer).

The second person, *you* and *your,* is usually reserved for how-to writing in college assignments.

If you are presenting something from a distance, geographical or historical (for example, telling a story about George Washington), the point of view will be *third person,* and the participants will be referred to as *he, she,* and *they.*

Along with the consistency of perspective, you should avoid shifts in number (*she* to *they*) and verb tense (*is* to *was*).

Being consistent in these matters will promote coherence.

Language

In the revision process, the word *language* takes on a special meaning, referring to usage, tone, and diction. If you are writing with a computer, consider using the thesaurus feature, but keep in mind that no two words share precisely the same meaning.

Usage

Usage is the kind or general style of language we use. All or almost all of us operate on the principle of appropriateness. If I used *ain't* as part of my explanations in this textbook, you would be surprised and probably disappointed; you would think about my word choice rather than what I have to say. Why would you be surprised? Because *ain't* is not appropriate for my audience in this situation. If you write an essay containing slang, you will probably be understood, but if the slang is not appropriate, you will draw unfavorable attention to your message. That does not mean that slang does not have its place—it does. It can be imaginative and colorful. Often, though, it is only a weak substitute for a more precise vocabulary.

Usage is an important part of writing and revising. Judge what is appropriate for your audience and your purpose. What kind of language is expected? What kind of language is best suited for accomplishing your purpose?

Most of the material in the Handbook at the end of this book is grammatical explanation of standard, mainly formal, English. Using standard verb tenses and pronoun cases will help you to write effectively. The Handbook offers clear explanations and examples. It also provides exercises supported by answers in the Answer Key. As you practice the principles of standard English in your writing and revising, you will master them.

Tone

Have you ever heard someone say, "Don't talk to me in that tone of voice" or "I accepted what she was saying, but I didn't like the tone she used when she told me"? *Tone* in these contexts means that the sound of the speaker's voice and maybe the language choices conveyed disrespect to the listener. The tone could have represented any number of feelings about the subject matter and the audience. Tone can have as many variations as you can have feelings: it can, for example, be sarcastic, humorous, serious, cautionary, objective, groveling, angry, bitter, sentimental, enthusiastic, somber, outraged, or loving.

Let's say you are getting a haircut. Looking in those panoramic mirrors bordered with pictures of people with different styles of haircuts, you see that the hair stylist is cutting off too much hair. You could use different tones in giving him or her some timely how-to instructions.

Objective: "If you don't mind, what I meant to say was that I would like a haircut proportioned similar to that one there in the picture of Tom Cruise from *Jerry Maguire.*"

Humorous: "I hesitate to make suggestions to someone who is standing at my back and holding a sharp instrument near my throat, but I'm letting my hair grow out a bit. I don't want you to take off a lot in the back and on the sides."

Angry and sarcastic: "Look man, when I sat down, I said I wanted my hair cut in the design of Tom Cruise in *Jerry Maguire.* The way you're hacking at it, you must've thought I said *Top Gun.*"

Servile: "I really like the way you cut my hair, and I can see that you are proportioning it with great care, but I would like my hair to be a bit longer than the style that I think you're working on. Do you remember how I used to get my hair cut about a year ago, a little longer on the sides and more bushy on top? You came up with a great style that everyone liked. Could you give me one similar to that?"

Overbearing: "Damn it, buddy. Will you watch what you're doing! I asked for a haircut, not a shave. If God had wanted me to have bare skin above my shoulders, he would've put the hair on my feet."

In speech, feelings and attitudes are represented by inflection, loudness, word choice, and language patterns. In writing, tone is conveyed mainly by word choice and order; it is closely related to style—the variations in the way you write, depending on your purpose. Your purpose is simply to present a particular idea in a particular context. The context implies the audience; it is important to use the tone appropriate to your audience.

Usually your tone will be consistent throughout your presentation, although for the informal essay often assigned in college, you may choose to begin in a light-hearted, amusing tone before switching to a more serious, objective mode.

Diction

Diction is word choice. If you use good diction, you are finding the best words for a particular purpose in addressing a certain audience. There is some overlap, therefore, between usage and diction. I may look at an area in the subway and present my reaction in the following way:

Poor Diction

> This part of the subway is really a mess. Everywhere I look I can see things people have thrown away, which have fallen through the grates above. Along with the solid items are liquids. On the walls are a hodgepodge of posters and writing. The whole area is very dirty and very unpleasant.

Note how the scene comes to life with better word choice:

Good Diction

> [Before me I saw] an unspeakable mass of congealed oil, puddles of dubious liquid, and a mishmash of old cigarette packets, mutilated and filthy newspapers, and the debris that filtered down from the street above. [The walls were a display of posters]—here a

Gilbert Highet, "Subway Station"

text from the Bible, there a half-naked girl, here a pair of girl's legs walking up the keys of a cash register—all scribbled over with unknown names and well-known obscenities. . . .

The difference between these two passages is obvious. The first is general. Terms such as "very dirty" and "very unpleasant" carry little meaning. The author has not made us see. The word *very* is an empty modifier. The second passage is specific. You can visualize what the writer is saying through the specific diction, the detail. The first is general and, for content, hardly goes beyond a single phrase—mess in the subway.

Here is a chart showing the difference between general and specific words.

General	*Specific*	*More Specific*
food	fruit	juicy, ripe peach
mess	litter	candy wrappers, empty cans
drink	soda	Pepsi Lite
odor	kitchen smell	aroma of coffee brewing

Another aspect of diction is freshness and originality of expression. To achieve those distinctions, you should avoid clichés, which are trite, familiar phrases. Consider this sentence:

> When the Prince married Cinderella, her sisters went green with envy because she was now on easy street, leaving them out in the cold.

Those words were written by a person who doesn't care about communicating in a clear and interesting manner. It would be far better to say:

> When the Prince married Cinderella, her sisters were envious because they had no suitors.

This list shows some clichés to avoid:

young at heart	quick as a flash
rotten to the core	slow but sure
uphill battle	other side of the coin
more than meets the eye	breathless silence
bitter end	acid test
as luck would have it	better late than never
last but not least	six of one, half dozen of the other

These are ready-made expressions. A cliché master manipulates language as if it were a prefabricated building going up, not bothering to use any imagination and leaving little opportunity for his or her audience to use theirs. Good diction, however, reflects the writer as an individual and is fresh, original, and clear.

Unity

A controlling idea, stated or implied, unifies every piece of good writing. It is the central point around which the supporting material revolves. For a paragraph, the elements are the topic sentence and the supporting sentences. For the essay, the elements are the thesis and the supporting developmental paragraphs. All the supporting material should be related to the topic sentence or thesis, and it should all be subordinate to the topic sentence or thesis. Unity can be strengthened and made more apparent if you restate the topic sentence or thesis at the end of the unit and if you repeat key words and phrases from time to time. A good check on unity is to ask yourself if everything in your paragraph or essay is subordinate to and derived from the controlling idea.

Don't confuse unity and coherence. Whereas coherence involves the clear movement of thought from sentence to sentence or paragraph to paragraph, unity means staying on the topic. A unified and coherent outline would become incoherent if the parts were scrambled, but the outline technically would still be unified. These qualities of writing go together. You should stay on the topic and make clear connections.

Emphasis

Emphasis, a feature of most good writing, helps the reader focus on the main ideas. It can be achieved in several ways but mainly through placement of key ideas and through repetition.

Placement of Ideas

The most emphatic part of any passage, whether a sentence or a book, is the last part, because we usually remember most easily what we read last. The second most emphatic part of a passage is the beginning, because our mind is relatively uncluttered when we read it. For these reasons, among others, the topic sentence or thesis is usually at the beginning of a piece, and it is often restated at the end in an echoing statement.

Repetition of Key Words and Ideas

Repetition is one of the simplest devices in your writer's toolbox. The words repeated may be single words, phrases, slightly altered sentences, or synonyms. Repetition keeps the dominant subject in the reader's mind and maintains the continuity necessary for a smooth flow of logical thought.

You can use this valuable technique easily. If, as is done in the following example, you are discussing the effects of school dropout, then the words *effect(s),* along with synonyms such as *result(s)* or *consequence(s),* and *school dropout(s)* are likely to be repeated several times. Moreover, phrases giving insight into the issue may be repeated, perhaps with slight variation.

The causes of the school <u>dropout</u> problem have received much attention recently, but the <u>effects</u> are just as important. One obvious <u>result</u> is that of unemployment or low-paying employment. The student who <u>drops out</u> of school is likely to be <u>dropping</u> into poverty, perhaps even into a lifelong condition. Another <u>effect</u> is juvenile crime. The young person who has no prospects for a good job and no hope all too frequently turns to illegal activities. A third <u>result</u> concerns the psychological well-being of the <u>dropout</u>. Although <u>withdrawing</u> from school seems to offer a quick, viable solution to perceived problems, it almost immediately has <u>consequences</u> for the <u>dropout</u>'s self-esteem. Of course, these <u>effects</u> may also be tied to causes, such as drugs, poverty, crime, or psychological problems, but devastating <u>repercussions</u> are there at the far end of the causes-and-effects continuum, and youngsters who are contemplating <u>dropping out</u> should consider them with care.

A word of warning: The effective use of word and phrase repetition should not be confused with an irritating misuse of word repetition. We all at times get hung up on certain words, and the result is a negative response from our audience. Consider this awkward use of repetition:

> She looked at him and frowned. He returned the look and then looked away at a stranger looking for his lost keys.

That's too many *look*'s. Consider this version:

> She looked at him [*or, even better,* She frowned at him]. He glared back and then glanced away at a stranger searching for his lost keys.

The second version preserves the idea of people "looking" by using synonyms. It is more precise, and does not grate on the reader's mind as the first does.

Support

How much support does a piece of writing need? A good developmental paragraph fulfills its function by developing the topic sentence. An essay is complete when it fulfills its function of developing a thesis. Obviously, you will have to judge what is complete. With some subjects, you will need little supporting and explanatory material. With others, you will need much more. Incompleteness, not overdevelopment, is more common among beginning writers. Besides having enough support, be sure that the points of support are presented in the best possible sequence.

Consider the following paragraph. Is it complete? Does the writer make the main idea clear and provide adequate support for it? Are the ideas in the right order?

> A cat's tail is a good barometer of its intentions. By various movements of its tail a cat will signal many of its wants. Other movements indicate its attitudes. An excited or aggressively aroused cat will whip its entire tail back and forth.

At first glance, this paragraph seems complete. It begins with a concise topic sentence telling us that a cat's tail is a good barometer of its intentions. It adds information of a general nature in the following two sentences. Then it presents a supporting example about the aggressively aroused cat. But the paragraph is not explicit; there is insufficient supporting material for the opening generalization. The paragraph leaves the reader with too much information to fill in. What are some other ways that cats communicate their intentions with their tails? How do they communicate specific wishes or desires? Is their communication effective? If the passage is to answer these questions that may come into the reader's mind, it must present more material to support the beginning generalization. The original paragraph that follows begins with a concise topic sentence that is then supported with particulars.

> A cat's tail is a good barometer of its intentions. An excited or aggressively aroused cat will whip its entire tail back and forth. When I talk to Sam, he holds up his end of the conversation by occasionally flicking the tip of his tail. Mother cats move their tails back and forth to invite their kittens to play. A kitten raises its tail perpendicularly to beg for attention; older cats may do so to beg for food. When your cat holds its tail aloft while crisscrossing in front of you, it is trying to say, "Follow me"—usually to the kitchen, or more precisely, to the refrigerator. Unfortunately, many cats have lost their tails in refrigerator doors as a consequence.

Michael W. Fox, "What Is Your Pet Trying to Tell You?"

We can strengthen our understanding of good support by analyzing the structure of the model paragraph, putting to use the information we have assimilated to this point in the discussion. The paragraph begins with the highest generalization (the main idea in the topic sentence): "A cat's tail is a good barometer of its intentions." It follows immediately with six supporting statements and ends with a final sentence to add humor to the writing. If we place this material in outline form, we can easily see the recurrent pattern in the flow of thought from general to particular.

Topic sentence (highest generalization)	A cat's tail is a good barometer of its intentions.
Major support	A. An excited or aggressively aroused cat will whip its entire tail back and forth.
Major support	B. When I talk to Sam, he holds up his end of the conversation by occasionally flicking the tip of his tail.
Major support	C. Mother cats move their tails back and forth to invite their kittens to play.
Major support	D. A kitten raises its tail perpendicularly to beg for attention;
Major support	E. older cats may do so to beg for food.
Major support	F. When your cat holds its tail aloft while crisscrossing in front of you, it is trying to say, "Follow me"—usually to the kitchen, or more precisely, to the refrigerator.
Added for humor	Unfortunately, many cats have lost their tails in refrigerator doors as a consequence.

Sentences

In the revision process, the term *sentences* pertains to the variety of sentence patterns and the correctness of sentence structure.

Variety of Sentences

A passage that offers a variety of simple and complicated sentences satisfies the reader, just as a combination of simple and complicated foods go together in a good meal. The writer can introduce variety by including both short and long sentences, by using different sentence patterns, and by beginning sentences in different ways.

Length

In revising, examine your writing to make sure that sentences vary in length. A series of short sentences is likely to make the flow seem choppy and the thoughts disconnected. However, single short sentences often work very well. Because they are uncluttered with supporting points and qualifications, they are often direct and forceful. Consider using short sentences to emphasize points and to introduce ideas. Use longer sentences to provide details or show how ideas are related.

Variety of Sentence Patterns

Good writing includes a variety of sentence patterns. Although there is no limit to the number of sentences you can write, you may be pleased to discover that the conventional English sentence appears in only four basic patterns.

Simple	She did the work well.
Compound	She did the work well, and she was well paid.

Complex	Because she did the work well, she was well paid.
Compound-complex	Because she did the work well, she was well paid, and she was satisfied.

An analysis of these patterns with suggestions and exercises for combining sentences is given in the Handbook.

Each of the four sentence patterns listed has its own purposes and strengths. The simple sentence conveys a single idea. The compound sentence shows, by its structure, that two somewhat equal ideas are connected. The complex sentence shows that one idea is less important than another; that is, it is dependent on, or subordinate to, the idea in the main clause. The compound-complex sentence has the scope of both the compound sentence and the complex sentence.

Variety of Sentence Beginnings

Another way to provide sentence variety is to use different kinds of beginnings. A new beginning may or may not be accompanied by a changed sentence pattern. Among the most common beginnings, other than starting with the subject of the main clause, are those using a prepositional phrase, a dependent clause, or a conjunctive adverb such as *therefore, however,* or *in fact.*

- Prepositional phrase (in italics)

    In your fantasy, you are the star.

    Like casino owners, game show hosts want you to be cheery.

- Dependent clause (in italics)

    When the nighttime "Wheel of Fortune" debuted, the slot was occupied by magazine shows.

    As Pat Sajak noted, viewers often solve the puzzle before the contestants do.

- Conjunctive adverb (in italics)

    Now you know.

    Therefore, you feel happy, excited, and a bit superior.

Problems with Sentences

A complete sentence must generally include an independent clause, which is a group of words that contains a subject and a verb and can stand alone. Some groups of words may sound interesting, but they are not really sentences. Three common problem groupings are the fragment, the comma splice, and the run-on.

- *Fragment:* A word grouping that is structurally incomplete is only a fragment of a sentence.

    Because he left. (This is a dependent clause, not a complete sentence.)

    Went to the library. (This one has no subject.)

    She being the only person there. (This has no verb.)

    Waiting there for help. (This phrase has neither subject nor verb.)

    In the back seat under a book. (Here we have two phrases but no subject or verb.)

- *Comma splice:* The comma splice consists of two independent clauses with only a comma between them.

> The weather was bad, we canceled the picnic. (A comma by itself cannot join two independent clauses.)

- *Run-on:* The run-on differs from the comma splice in only one way: It has no comma between the independent clauses.

> The weather was bad we canceled the picnic.

Fragments, comma splices, and run-ons can easily be fixed (see the Handbook) during the revising and editing stages of your writing. A computerized grammar checker may help you find these problems.

If you frequently have problems with sentence structure and awkwardness of phrasing, be especially suspicious of long sentences. Test each sentence of fifteen or more words for flaws. Try writing shorter, more direct sentences until you gain confidence and competency. Then work with sophisticated patterns.

See the Writer's Guidelines at the end of this chapter for a concise summary of the strategies for effective revision.

Editing

This final stage of the writing process involves a careful examination of your work. Look for problems with capitalization, omissions, punctuation, and spelling (COPS).

Because you can find spelling errors in writing by others more easily than you can in your own, a computerized spell checker is quite useful. However, it will not detect wrong words that are correctly spelled, so you should always proofread. It is often helpful to leave the piece for a few hours or a day, then reread it as if it were someone else's work.

Before you submit your writing to your instructor, do what almost all professional writers do before sending their material along: Read it aloud, to yourself or to a willing audience. Reading material aloud will help you catch any awkwardness of expression, omission and misplacement of words, and other problems that are easily overlooked by an author.

As you can see, writing is a process and is not a matter of just sitting down and banging out a statement. The parts of the process from prewriting to revising to editing are connected, and your movement is ultimately forward, but this process allows you to go back and forth in the recursive manner discussed in Chapters 1 and 2. If your outline is not working, perhaps the flaw is in your topic sentence. You may need to go back and fix it. If one section of your paragraph is skimpy, perhaps you will have to go back and reconsider the pertinent material in your outline or clustering. There you might find more details or alter a statement so that you can move into more fertile areas of thought.

Student Demonstration of All Stages of the Writing Process

Here we see how Betsy Jackson worked through the entire writing process. In Stage One, she freewrote, brainstormed, and developed a cluster of ideas. In Stage Two, she composed a good topic sentence, developed further a part of her cluster from

Stage One, and drew up an outline based on the cluster. Finally, in Stage Three, we see one of her first drafts, her revision and editing of that draft, and finally the finished version.

Note that Jackson has used a Writing Process Worksheet like the one provided at the end of the Student Overview for your major writing assignments. Her worksheet has been lengthened for you to be able to see all parts of her work.

Writing Process Worksheet

TITLE   If I Were a Traffic Cop

NAME   Betsy Jackson   **DUE DATE**   Monday, June 5, 8 a.m.

ASSIGNMENT   In the space below, write whatever you need to know about your assignment, including information about the topic, audience, pattern of writing, length, whether to include a rough draft or revised drafts, and whether your paper must be typed.

Write a paragraph of about 200–300 words on a topic from the list—bad drivers. Discuss types for the pattern. Use some examples. Write for readers who have probably shared your experiences. Include this completed worksheet, one or more rough drafts marked for revision, and a typed final paper.

STAGE ONE   **Explore**   Freewrite, brainstorm (list), cluster, or take notes as directed by your instructor. Use the back of this page or a separate sheet of paper if you need more space.

Freewriting (abbreviated here)

drunks

    Every day when I drive to school I see bad drivers. Sometimes I'm mad. Sometimes I'm irritated. Sometimes I'm scared. I think someone should do something about them. The <u>drunk drivers</u> are the worst. They should be put away. But a lot of the other should be getting tickets too. Some of the drivers are worse than others. Make me a cop, a supercop, a rambo cop, and I'll go after the worst. Maybe I'd just go after the ones that bother me. Some bad drivers cause a lot of accidents and get people all angry. Take the

tailgaters
lane changers
no signals
run lights
too fast/slow
all kinds

<u>tailgaters</u> for example. And what about the <u>drivers that go into the emergency lanes</u> on the freeways to pass when there's a jam. And then you've got the <u>lane changers</u> and the <u>people that don't signal</u> and <u>those that keep going and turning left when</u> the <u>light turns red.</u> Then you've got the people that <u>drive too fast</u> and <u>too slow.</u> And you've got the ones that <u>don't stop</u> for <u>pedestrians.</u> <u>All kinds</u> of bad drivers are out there—young, old, male, female, insane, drunk, angry, and rushed.

Clustering

Brainstorming (Big Six Questions)

Who?   bad drivers; me as a cop

What?   driving badly, recklessly, unsafely; a cop's job

Where?   on every roadway

When?   all the time

Why?   hurried, disrespectful, self-centered, sick, addiction, hostile,
            irresponsible

How?   lane-changing, driving illegally in emergency lane, not sig-
            naling, passing on the shoulder, tailgating, turning left on
            red, rolling stop, speeding, driving while intoxicated

STAGE TWO   **Organize**   Write a topic sentence or thesis; label the subject and the treatment parts.

<u>If I were a traffic cop,</u>   <u>I'd crack down on certain types of drivers.</u>
     subject   treatment

Write an outline or an outline alternative.

   I. Drunks
  II. Unsafe lane changers
     A. Character
        1. Rude
        2. Bullying
     B. Results
        1. Accidents
        2. People upset
 III. Left-turners on red
     A. Attitude
        1. Self-centered
        2. Putting self above law

    B. Kinds
      1. Age
      2. Sex
    C. Results
      1. Collisions
      2. Mass irritation
IV. Tailgaters
    A. Motives
      1. Hostility
      2. Rushed
    B. Effects
      1. Accidents
      2. People upset

STAGE THREE   **Write**   On separate paper, write and then revise your paper as many times as necessary for <u>c</u>oherence, <u>l</u>anguage (usage, tone, and diction), <u>u</u>nity, <u>e</u>mphasis, <u>s</u>upport, and <u>s</u>entences (CLUESS). Read your paper aloud to hear and correct any grammatical errors or awkward-sounding sentences.

Edit any problems in fundamentals, such as <u>c</u>apitalization, <u>o</u>missions, <u>p</u>unctuation, and <u>s</u>pelling (COPS).

Rough Draft: Writing, Revising, Editing

If I were a Traffic Cop
~~Rambo Traffic Cop~~

If I were   *I'd*
~~Make me~~ a traffic cop, and ~~I~~ crack down on certain types of drivers.

My primary target would be drivers arrest   *immediately,*
~~First off are the~~ drunks. I'd ~~zap~~ them ~~off the highways right off,~~ and any cop

concerned   *here.*   *n*
would. But are what I'm really ~~talking~~ about is (the jerks of the highway.) Near

of my hit list   *unsafe*
the top are the ~~up-tight~~ lane changers, ~~for example,~~ This morning when I

have.
was driving to school, ~~I saw several.~~ I could ~~have~~ carved at least a couple
      of

citation   *other drivers*
notches in a ~~vilation~~ pad, and I wasn't even cranky. They cut off ~~people~~ and

ing   *injured*   *are*
force their way in, ~~and~~ leave behind upset and ~~hurt~~ people. Then there's

s
the left-turn bullies the ones who keep moving out when the yellow turn to

red. They come in all ages and sexes, ~~they can be young or old, male or~~

~~female.~~ Yesterday, I saw this female in a pickup barrel right out into the

and
teeth of a red light. She had a baby on board, ~~She had~~ lead in her foot, ~~She~~

t
~~had~~ evil in her eye. She was hostile and self-centered, Taking advantage of

others. She knew that the facing traffic would probably not pull out and

risk a head-on crash. The key word there is "probably" but many times peo-

I   *-*
ple with a green light do move out and colide with the left turn bullies.

Fourth
~~Third~~, I'd zap the tailgaters. No one goes fast enough for ~~these guys. I'm~~ them.

Many of my fellow drivers agree.
~~not alone in this peeve.~~ One bumper sticker reads, "Stay back. I chew

oil on
tobacky." And James Bond sprayed cars that chased him. Since the first is

unsanitary   illegal   authority
~~dirty~~ and the second ~~is against the law~~, if I had the ~~clout~~ of a Rambo-cop I'd

issue   These four types of road demons would feel my
just ~~rack up~~ a lot of tailgater tickets. ~~But there's a lot of road demons out~~

wrath. But   be
~~there.~~ Maybe it's good I'm not a traffic cop, Rambo or otherwise, cause traf-

d   e
fic cops are suppose to inforce hundreds of laws. I don't know if I'd have

be   I'd be concentrating on this private list of obnoxious drivers.
time cause ~~I have my own pet peeves in mind.~~

Final Draft

If I Were A Traffic Cop
Betsy Jackson

Topic sentence   <u>If I were a traffic cop, I'd crack down on certain types of drivers.</u> My pri-

Support   mary target would be <u>drunk drivers.</u> I'd arrest them immediately, and any
cop would. But the jerks on the highway are what I'm really concerned

Support   about here. Near the top of my hit list are the <u>unsafe lane changers.</u> They
cut off other drivers and force their way in, leaving behind upset and
injured people. This morning when I was driving to school, I could have
carved at least a couple of notches in a citation pad, and I wasn't even

Support (example)   cranky. Then there are the <u>left-turn bullies,</u> the ones who keep moving out
when the yellow turns to red. They come in all ages and sexes. Yesterday, I
saw this female in a pickup barrel right out into the teeth of a red light. She
had a baby on board, lead in her foot, and evil in her eye. She was hostile
and self-centered, taking advantage of others. She knew that the facing
traffic would probably not pull out and risk a head-on crash. The key word
there is "probably," but many times people with a green light do move out

Support   and collide with the left-turn bullies. Fourth, I'd zap the <u>tailgaters.</u> No one
goes fast enough for them. Many of my fellow drivers agree. One bumper
sticker reads, "Stay back. I chew tobacky." And James Bond sprayed oil on
cars that chased him. Since the first is unsanitary and the second illegal, if I
had the authority of a traffic cop, I'd just issue a lot of tailgater tickets.

Restated topic sentence   <u>These four types of road demons would feel my wrath.</u> But maybe it's good
I'm not a traffic cop, Rambo or otherwise, because traffic cops are sup-
posed to enforce hundreds of laws. I don't know if I'd have time because I'd
be concentrating on this private list of obnoxious drivers.

| **Exercise 2** | **REVISING AND EDITING A FIRST DRAFT** |

Revise the following student first draft. Then check for <u>c</u>apitalization, <u>o</u>missions (over-sights or grammar problems), <u>p</u>unctuation, and <u>s</u>pelling (COPS). Space is provided for you to add, delete, move, and correct material. (See Answer Key for answers.)

Pain Unforgettable
James Hutchison

One evening in 1968 while I was working the swing shift at the General Tire Recapping Plant. I came up with the greatest pain of my life because of a terible accident. Raw rubber was heated up in a large tank. Pryor to its being fed into an extruder. I was recapping large off-road tires. The lowering platform was in the up position the chain snapped. It sent the heavy platform crashing down into the tank. This caused a huge wave of steaming water to surge out of the tank. Unfortunately, I was in its path the wave hit my back just above my waist. The sudden pain shook me up. I could not move. My clothes were steaming I freaked out. Co-workers ran to my aid and striped the hot clothing from my body, taking skin as they did. I lay face down on the plant floor, naked and shaking for a long time. The paramedics came to pick me up. The painful experience is still scary when I think about it.

| Exercise 3 | **REVISING AND EDITING A FIRST DRAFT** |

Revise the following student first draft. Then check for ͟capitalization, ͟omissions (oversights or grammar problems), ͟punctuation, and ͟spelling (COPS). Space is provided for you to add, delete, move, and correct material.

Quitting School
Doretta McLain

Quitting school was not a big deal for me until I realize all the effects of quitting would bring to my life. At that time I didn't care. I plan to marry a few months later. I was happy then.

Quitting school was a big mistake because when I went out to look for a job I couldn't qualify for any of the good positions because of my lack of education. Instead, I took a job in a fast-food place where I had no future. Then I went to work in a big company just doing simple office work. When it came time for promotions I couldn't pass the tests they gave. That was not all. As a result of quitting school. I couldn't even help my children with their homework or buy the special things for them.

I started my family when I was not even eighteen years. The first year of my marriage was fine, then things started to fall apart. My husband had quit school too, and he didn't make much money, and as I mentioned, I didn't make much either. We argued a lot mainly over money. We couldn't get a big enough house for our family so that we could have the privacy we needed. I quit work to raise my kids and that when I really got in deep. My car was getting old and money was not enough to make big payments I had to buy another old car, which broke down all the time. I started freaking out. The fighting got worse and we had a divorce.

I was lucky that my parents decided to help me, and now I am dedicated to getting a good education. I will work hard to learn so me and my children can have a better life.

Exercise 4	WRITING, REVISING, AND EDITING YOUR PAPER

Using the topic you worked with in Stages One and Two (Chapters 1 and 2), write, revise, and edit a paragraph or essay to complete Stage Three. Alternatively, you may delay this stage until after you have worked with paragraphs and essays in the next two chapters.

Writer's Guidelines: Writing, Revising, Editing

1. **Writing**

   Write your first draft, paying close attention to your outline, list, or cluster. Do not concern yourself with perfect spelling, grammar, or punctuation.

2. **Revising**

   Coherence

   • Are the ideas clearly related, each one to the others and to the central idea?

   • Is there a clear pattern of organization (time, space, or emphasis)?

- Is the pattern supported by words that suggest the basis of that organization (time: *now, then, later;* space: *above, below, up, down;* emphasis: *first, second, last*)?

- Is coherence enhanced by the use of transitional terms, pronouns, repetition, and a consistent point of view?

Language

- Is the general style of language usage appropriate (properly standard and formal or informal) for the purpose of the piece and the intended audience?

- Is the tone (language use showing attitude toward material and audience) appropriate?

- Is the word choice (diction) effective? Are the words precise in conveying meaning? Are they fresh and original?

Unity

- Are the thesis and every topic sentence clear and well stated? Do they indicate both subject and treatment?

- Are all points of support clearly related to and subordinate to the topic sentence of each paragraph and to the thesis of the essay?

Emphasis

- Are ideas properly placed (especially near the beginning and end) for emphasis?

- Are important words and phrases repeated for emphasis?

Support

- Is there adequate material—such as examples, details, quotations, and explanations—to support each topic sentence and thesis?

- Are the points of support placed in the best possible order?

Sentences

- Are the sentences varied in length and beginnings?

- Are the sentences varied in pattern (simple, compound, complex, and compound-complex)?

- Are all problems with sentence structure (fragments, comma splices, run-ons) corrected?

3. **Editing**

- Are all problems in such areas as <u>c</u>apitalization, <u>o</u>missions, <u>p</u>unctuation, and <u>s</u>pelling corrected?

4

Writing the Paragraph

> *"Easy writing makes for hard reading."*
>
> Ernest Hemingway

THE QUIGMANS   by Buddy Hickerson

Scientist in love.

The Paragraph Defined

efining the word *paragraph* is no easy task because there are three different kinds of paragraphs, each one having a different purpose:

Introductory: Usually the first paragraph in an essay, it gives the necessary background and indicates the main idea, called the thesis.

Developmental: A unit of several sentences, it expands on an idea. This book features the writing of developmental paragraphs.

Transitional: A very brief paragraph, it merely directs the reader from one point in the essay to another.

Concluding: Usually the last paragraph in an essay, it makes the final comment on the topic.

The following paragraph is both a definition and an example of the developmental paragraph.

Topic sentence

Support
Support

Support

Concluding sentence

The developmental paragraph contains three parts: the subject, the topic sentence, and the support. The **subject** is what you will write about. It is likely to be broad and must be focused or qualified for specific treatment. The **topic sentence** contains both the subject and the treatment—what you will do with the subject. It carries the central idea to which everything else in the paragraph is subordinated. For example, the first sentence of this paragraph is a topic sentence. Even when not stated, the topic sentence as an underlying idea unifies the paragraph. The **support** is the evidence or reasoning by which a topic sentence is developed. It comes in several basic patterns and serves any of the four forms of expression: narration, description, exposition, and argumentation. These forms, which are usually combined in writing, will be presented with both student and professional examples in the following chapters. *The developmental paragraph, therefore, is a group of sentences, each with the function of supporting a controlling idea called the topic sentence.*

Basic Paragraph Patterns

The most important point about a developmental paragraph is that it should state an idea and support it. The support, or development, can take several forms, all of which you already use. It can

- give an account (tell a story).

- describe people, things, or events.

- explain by analyzing, giving examples, comparing, defining, showing how to do something, or showing causes.

- argue that something should be done or resisted, that something is true or untrue, or that something is good or bad.

(All of these forms of expression are discussed with examples in Chapters 7 through 17.) You will not find it difficult to write solid paragraphs once you understand that good writing requires that main ideas have enough support so that your reader can understand how you have arrived at your main conclusions.

Usually the developmental paragraph will be indented only one time. However, you will note in your reading that some writers, especially journalists, break a paragraph into parts and indent more than once in developing a single idea. That arrangement, called a *paragraph unit,* is fairly common in magazine and newspaper articles (frequently with each sentence indented) but less so in college writing.

Two effective patterns of conventional paragraph structure are shown in Figure 4.1. Pattern A merely states the controlling idea, the topic sentence, and develops it; Pattern B adds a concluding sentence following the development.

Figure 4.1
Paragraph Patterns

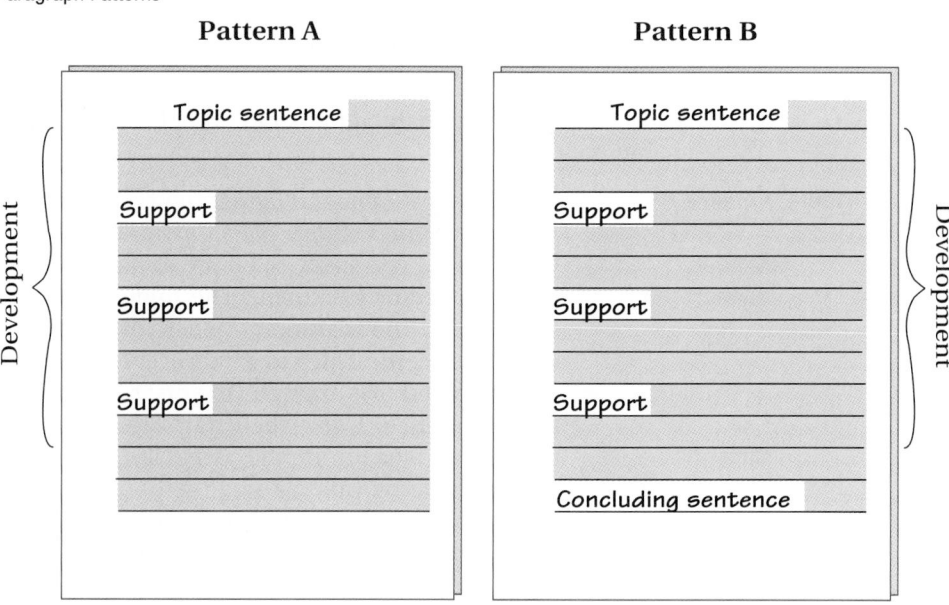

Example of Pattern A:

Pity, Anger, and Achievement Performance

Topic sentence
Support

It is generally thought that pity and sympathy are "good" emotions and that anger is a "bad" emotion. However, attribution theorists have pointed out that the consequences of these emotional expressions are complex. In one investigation, Graham (1984) gave subjects (twelve-year-old children) false failure feedback during an achievement task. For some children, this was accompanied by the remark: "I feel sorry for you" as well as body postures and facial gestures that accompany sympathy (head down, hands folded, etc.). To other students, the experimenter said: "I am angry with you." Students receiving the pity feedback tended to blame the failure on themselves (low ability) and their performance declined. On the other hand, students receiving anger feedback attributed their failure to lack of effort and their performance subsequently
Support
increased. This is not to advocate that sympathy is always detrimental and anger always facilitative. Rather, the consequences of feedback depend on how that feedback is construed and what it

means to the recipient of the communication. Other kinds of feedback, such as praise for success at an easy task and excessive and unsolicited helping, also tend to convey that the student is "unable" and therefore have some negative consequences.

Seymour Feshback and Bernard Weiner, from *Personality*

Seymour Feshback and Bernard Weiner, from *Personality*

Example of Pattern B:

Primitive Methods of Lie Detection

Topic sentence
Support

Throughout history there have been efforts to distinguish the guilty from the innocent and to tell the liars from the truthful. For example, a method of lie detection practiced in Asia involved giving those suspected of a crime a handful of raw rice to chew. After chewing for some time, the persons were instructed to spit out the rice. The innocent person was anticipated to do this easily, whereas the guilty party was expected to have grains of rice sticking to the roof of the mouth and tongue. This technique relied on the increased sympathetic nervous system activity in the presumably fearful and guilty person. This activity would result in the drying up of saliva that, in turn, would cause grains of rice to stick in the mouth.

Support

A similar but more frightening technique involved placing a heated knife blade briefly against the tongue, another method used for criminal detection. An innocent person would not be burned while the guilty party would immediately feel pain, again because of the relative dryness of the mouth.

Concluding sentence

Many of these methods relied (unknowingly) on the basic physiological principles that also guided the creation of the polygraph.

Exercise 1   **ANALYZING A PARAGRAPH**

1. Is the following paragraph developed in Pattern A (topic sentence/development) or Pattern B (topic sentence/development/restated topic sentence)?

2. Identify the parts of the paragraph pattern by underlining and annotating them. Use the two example paragraphs as models.

Types of Nightclubbers
Jerry Lopez

Dancers aren't the only men who go to nightclubs. Having worked in and attended various clubs, I've come to realize they attract about four different types of guys, who can be grouped by the way they act. First there are the dancers. They are out on the floor most of the night. They aren't concerned with their appearance. They usually wear jeans or shorts and a tee shirt. They're there to dance and sweat. Then there are the posers. They go to model and show off their clothes and hair. They won't dance for fear of messing up their appearance, or even worse, sweating! The third group is the scammers. Scammers go to pick up women. They usually stand around and check out the body parts of other people as they pass by. A person close to them can see the lust in their eyes. There are also the boozers or druggies. They can be seen stumbling around, falling down, or lying in some corner where they have passed out. At times I am a member of a fifth group: the observers.

| **Exercise 2** | **ANALYZING A PARAGRAPH** |

1. Is the following paragraph developed in Pattern A (topic sentence/development) or Pattern B (topic sentence/development/restated topic sentence)?

2. Identify the parts of the paragraph pattern by underlining and annotating them. Use the two example paragraphs as models.

The Fighting, Founding Mothers

Maxine Johnson

People argue a lot about the prospects of women in the military fighting in combat, but in the War of Independence, several women distinguished themselves in combat situations. In 1775, Paul Revere got the main credit for riding to warn the Patriots that the British were coming on a military move on Concord and Lexington, Massachusetts. The fact is that, although he did warn some Patriots, he was stopped by the British. Who did get through? Several people, including Sybil Ludington, a teenage woman who fearlessly rode her horse like the wind. Another famous woman was known as Molly Pitcher. Her real name was Mary Hayes. She went with her husband to the battlefield, where she brought the men pitchers of water (hence her nickname) and helped load the cannon her husband fired. When her husband was shot at the Battle of Monmouth in 1778, she took over the cannon and fought bravely. At the end of the battle, won by the Patriots, she carried a wounded man for two miles. More than two hundred years ago, these women proved that their gender can be soldiers in every sense.

The Writing Process and the Paragraph

Learning to write a well-designed developmental paragraph will help you write longer assignments, because the developmental paragraph is often an essay in miniature.

Therefore, you can approach both the developmental paragraph and the essay in the same manner—namely, by working through the three stages of the writing process described in Chapter 1 through 3. In this chapter, we will go through the basic stages and strategies once again. Here is a summary of them:

- Stage One: Exploring, Experimenting, Gathering Information

    Freewrite, brainstorm (answer questions or make lists), cluster, take notes (if doing research or analyzing a reading selection).

- Stage Two: Writing the Controlling Idea, Organizing and Developing Support

    Compose your topic sentence with a subject and treatment.

    Complete an outline or outline alternative.

- Stage Three: Writing, Revising, Editing

    Write a first draft; then revise and edit as many drafts as necessary to reach the final draft.

Student Demonstration of All Stages of the Writing Process

Here is how one student, Vera Harris, moved from an idea to a topic sentence to an outline to a paragraph. Vera Harris returned to college while she still had a full-time job as a hairdresser. When her instructor asked her to write a paragraph about types of people she had encountered, she naturally considered her customers for the subject of her paragraph—what she would write about. But she also had a special interest in dogs, and cleverly she was able to include that interest. Although she knew her topic rather well, she worked with some prewriting techniques that allowed her to get her ideas flowing onto paper.

She used the Writing Process Worksheet for guidance, thus also providing her instructor with a record of the development of her work. Her worksheet has been lengthened for you to be able to see her work in its entirety. You will find a full-size blank worksheet on page 5. It can be photocopied, filled in, and submitted with each assignment if your instructor directs you to do so.

· ·

Writing Process Worksheet

TITLE Customers Are Like Canines

NAME Vera Harris   **DUE DATE** Monday, Nov. 13, 8 a.m.

ASSIGNMENT   In the space below, write whatever you need to know about your assignment, including information about the topic, audience, pattern of writing, length, whether to include a rough draft or revised drafts, and whether your paper must be typed.

Write a paragraph of classification in which you group people according to their behavior. Keep your audience in mind as you select words and as you develop your ideas in an appropriate way. Submit this completed Writing Process Worksheet, a rough draft marked for revision, and a typed final draft of about 250 words.

STAGE ONE   **Explore**   Freewrite, brainstorm (list), cluster, or take notes as directed by your instructor. Use the back of this page or separate paper if you need more space.

Freewriting (partial)

Types of customers

     I have worked in beauty shops for a long time, and I've naturally made a lot of observations about my customers. I could write about what they look like and (how they behave) and how they tip and lots of things. When I first started to work, I guess at first I thought of them as pretty much the same but then I started (to see them as types) mainly as to how they acted and I remember way back then I sometimes thought of how they

Both dogs and customers can be grouped

reminded me of dogs. I don't mean that in any bad way but just that human beings have their personalities and their appearances and all and so do dogs.

Brainstorming: Big Six Questions

Who?   my customers
What?   the way they act
Where?   in the beauty salon
When?   for the years I have worked
Why?   their basic nature
How?   behavior sometimes like dogs—hounds, Dobermans, terriers, bulldogs, cockers, poodles, mixed, retrievers, boxers

Brainstorming: Listing

Kinds of dogs
     hounds
     Dobermans
     terriers
     bulldogs
     cockers
     poodles
     mixed
     retrievers
     pit bulls
     boxers

Clustering

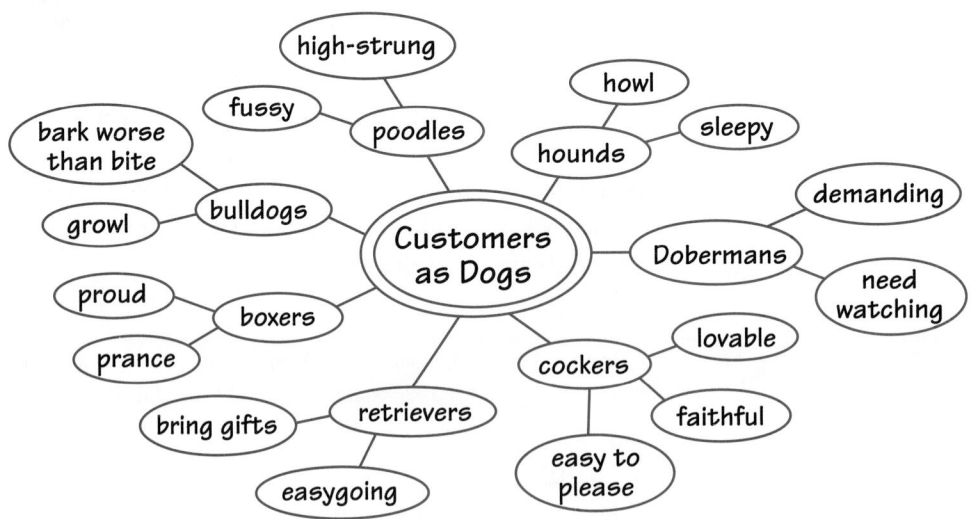

STAGE TWO   **Organize**   Write a topic sentence or thesis; label the subject and the treatment parts.

<u>The customers in the beauty shop where I work</u>   <u>remind me of types</u>
                        subject
<u>of dogs (of which I am fond).</u>
                treatment

Write an outline or an outline alternative.

I. Poodles (major support)
  A. High-strung (minor support)
  B. Need attention (minor support)
II. Doberman pinschers (major support)
  A. Demanding (minor support)
  B. Need watching (minor support)
III. Bulldogs (major support)
  A. Act mean (minor support)
  B. Will back down (minor support)
IV. Cocker spaniels (major support)
  A. Lovable (minor support)
  B. Faithful (minor support)
  C. Easy to please (minor support)

STAGE THREE   **Write**   On separate paper, write and then revise your paper as many times as necessary for coher-ence, language (usage, tone, and diction), unity, emphasis, support, and sentences (CLUESS). Read your paper aloud to hear and correct any grammatical errors or awkward-sounding sentences.

Edit any problems in fundamentals, such as capitalization, omissions, punctuation, and spelling (COPS).

Rough Draft: Revising and Editing

Customers Are Like Canines
Vera Harris

Language
Punctuation
Over the years while working
~~I have worked~~ in a beauty salon ~~for a long time. There,~~ I have come

across almost every kind of salon customer, each with her own unique

Sentences
Because
looks and personality. I am also a dog lover and have observed numerous

Punctuation
Language
relate them to
dogs with care it is easier to classify these people if I ~~compare them with~~

canine types—but in a playful rather than a mean way. The first group is

Language
and high-strung
made up of poodles. Poodles are very prissy, with a constant need for

attention. Their hair is usually over-styled. They think puffballs in soft

Emphasis **Spelling** **Omission** **Language**	colors look great. The ~~next group~~ _last—_ and largest group—is made up of cocker spaniᵉ̶ls. The ¢Cockers are very lovable _and_ the most faithful. They enjoy being groomed and stroked, but they are easy to please ~~pampered~~. Cockers like to see me every week and _to_ visit with others. Some- times I can almost see their tails wagging. Then come the Doberman
Sentences **Sentences** **Language**	pinchers,ˢ T̸his type scares me the most. Dobies are hard to please. If one hair goes the wrong way, I will see their upper lip rise up to ~~show~~ _expose_ eye- teeth, as if they are snarling. I rarely turn my back while working on this
Punctuation **Language**	type—a Dobie might bite. The ~~last~~ _third_ group _members,_ the bulldogs, are not as mean as Dobies. Bulldogs act mean and tough, but if ~~you don't~~ _one doesn't_ show fear when
Punctuation **Language**	they get bossy, they will back down. This type needs to feel in charge, even if ~~it's me~~ _I'm_ leading them around on a leash. No matter what, canines and customers are my best friends.

Final Draft

Customers Are Like Canines
Vera Harris

Topic **sentence**	Over the years while working in a beauty salon, I have come across almost every kind of salon customer, each with her own unique looks and personality. Because I am also a dog lover and have observed numerous dogs with care, it is easier to classify these people if I relate them to
Support	canine types—but in a playful rather than a mean way. The first group is made up of poodles. Poodles are very prissy and high-strung, with a constant need for attention. Their hair is usually over-styled. They think puff-
Support	balls in soft colors look great. Then come the Doberman pinschers. This type scares me the most. Dobies are hard to please. If one hair goes the wrong way, I will see their upper lip rise up to expose eyeteeth. I rarely
Support	turn my back while working on this type—a Dobie might bite. The third group members, the bulldogs, are not as mean as Dobies. Bulldogs act mean and tough, but if one doesn't show fear when they get bossy, they will back down. This type needs to feel in charge, even if I'm leading them
Support	around on a leash. The last—and largest—group is made up of cocker spaniels. The cockers are very lovable and the most faithful. They enjoy being groomed and stroked, but they are easy to please. Cockers like to see me every week and to visit with others. Sometimes I can almost see
Concluding **sentence**	their tails wagging. No matter what, canines and customers are my best friends.

| **Exercise 3** | **WRITING A PARAGRAPH** |

Select one of the topic sentences and write a paragraph based on it.

1. That was an argument I made at that time, but if I had a second chance, I wouldn't repeat it.
2. It was the worst piece of news I ever had to deliver.
3. I confronted authority and learned from the experience.
4. (It) was an act of generosity I will never forget.
5. Sometimes there are good reasons for lying.
6. Alcohol addiction has physical, social, and vocational effects.
7. There are several ways to show affection.
8. The job didn't pay well, but it provided me with a good education in balancing my budget, managing my time, and dealing with the public.
9. Teenagers like music for obvious reasons.
10. Homeless people are in their situation for different reasons.

Writer's Guidelines: Writing the Paragraph

1. The developmental paragraph is a group of sentences, each with the function of stating or supporting a controlling idea called the topic sentence.
2. The developmental paragraph contains three parts: the subject, the topic sentence, and the support.
3. The two main patterns of the developmental paragraph are these:

Pattern A

Topic sentence

Support

Support

Support

Development

Pattern B

Topic sentence

Support

Support

Support

Concluding sentence

Development

4. The topic sentence includes what you are writing about—the *subject*—and what you intend to do with that subject—the *treatment*.

<u>Being a good parent</u> <u>is more than providing financial support.</u>
        subject   treatment

5. The outline is a pattern for showing the relationship of ideas. It can be used to reveal the structure and content of something you read or to plan the structure and content of something you intend to write. The following topic outline shows how the parts are arranged on the page as well as how the ideas in it relate to one another.

Main Idea (will usually be the topic sentence for the paragraph or the thesis for the essay)

  I. Major support
     A. Minor support
        1. Details (specific information of various kinds)
        2. Details
     B. Minor support
        1. Details
        2. Details
 II. Major support
     A. Minor support
     B. Minor support
        1. Details
        2. Details
        3. Details

Writing the Essay

"I wouldn't show my first draft to even my most merciful friend."

Roger Summers

THE QUIGMANS   by Buddy Hickerson

*Repressive Celibate and the Seven Politically Correct Height-Challenged.

B. Hickerson, copyright Los Angeles Times Syndicate. Reprinted by permission.

The Essay Defined in Relation to the Developmental Paragraph

he essay is as difficult to define as the paragraph, but the paragraph definition gives us a framework. Consider the definition from Chapter 4:

> The *developmental paragraph* . . . is a group of sentences, each with the function of supporting a controlling idea called the topic sentence.

The main parts of the developmental paragraph are the topic sentence (subject and treatment), support (evidence and reasoning), and, often, a concluding sentence. Now let's use that framework to define the essay:

> The *essay* is a group of paragraphs, each with the function of supporting a controlling idea called the thesis.

These are the main parts of the essay:

Introduction: presents the thesis, which states the controlling idea—much like the topic sentence for a paragraph but on a larger scale.

Development: introduces evidence and reasoning—the support.

Transition: points out divisions of the essay (seldom used in the short essay).

Conclusion: provides an appropriate ending—often a restatement of or reflection on the thesis.

Thus, considered structurally, the developmental paragraph is often an essay in miniature. That does not mean that all paragraphs can grow to be essays or that all essays can shrink to become paragraphs. For college writing, however, a good understanding of the parallel between well-organized paragraphs and well-organized essays is useful. As you learn how to write effective paragraphs—with strong topic sentences and strong support—you also learn how to organize an essay. You just magnify the process, as shown in Figure 5.1.

Figure 5.1
Paragraph and Essay Compared

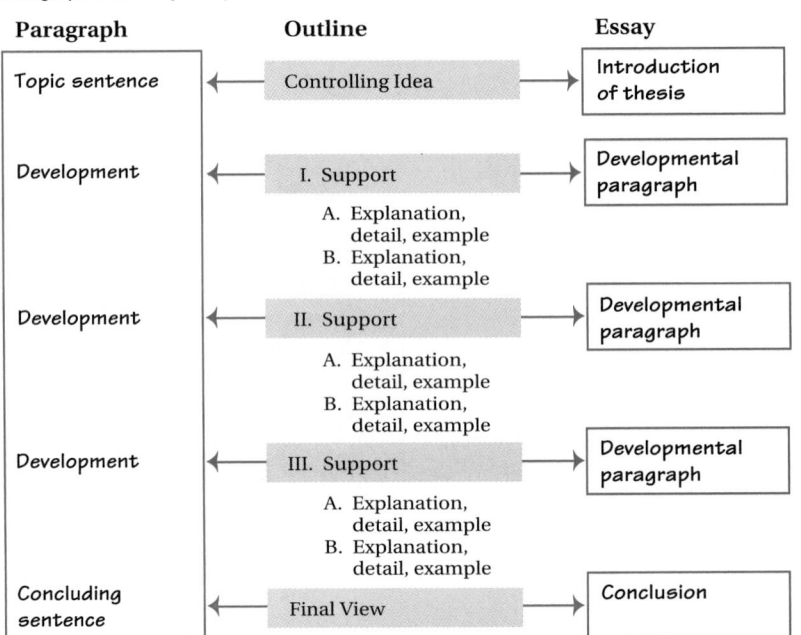

Paragraph:

Short Essay:

Good King Elvis

A messiah, a jester, a reckless jerk—or a soulful singer from the Deep South—Elvis at different times to different people was all these things. <u>His fans mirror every facet of their idol.</u>

Topic sentence

Support

Support

Support

Concluding sentence

A messiah, a jester, a reckless jerk—or a soulful singer from the Deep South—Elvis at different times to different people was all these things. <u>His fans mirror every facet of their idol.</u> "I liked him because of his looks," says Sue Scarborough, forty-nine, of Lexington, Kentucky, as she waits with her husband to tour Graceland. "He didn't put on airs," says Jeff Graff, twenty, of Cleveland, Ohio. "He went out of his way to help people." "I met him in 1960 when I was twelve years old," says Billie Le Jeune of Memphis, who visits Graceland once or twice a month: "He asked me what my favorite subject was." On the pink field-stone wall outside Graceland, which for years has functioned as an unauthorized bulletin board, the graffiti runs like this: ELVIS IS LOVE; I DID DRUGS WITH ELVIS; and most cryptic of all—ELVIS DIDN'T DESERVE TO BE WHITE.

I. Appearance

II. Helped people

III. Basic goodness

Jim Miller, "Forever Elvis"

Good King Elvis

A messiah, a jester, a reckless jerk—or a soulful singer from the Deep South—Elvis at different times to different people was all these things. <u>His fans mirror every facet of their idol.</u>

For some fans the attraction is appearance. "I liked him because of his looks," says Sue Scarborough, forty-nine of Lexington, Kentucky, as she waits for her husband to tour Graceland. (She grins good-naturedly at her husband and gives him an affectionate nudge in the ribs when he says, "My wife really likes Elvis, but I'm not jealous because he is dead—I think." Her response tells all: "My husband's a good man at drivin' a truck and fishin' for bass, but no one'll ever paint his picture on velvet.")

(For others, Elvis was a king with a common touch and humanitarian instincts.) "He didn't put on airs," says Jeff Graff, twenty, of Cleveland, Ohio. "He went out of his way to help people." (His friend nods his head in agreement. "Elvis must've given away a hundred Cadillacs in his day." Others in line break in to tell stories about the generosity of this good man who once walked among them.)

(The speakers at Graceland who get the most attention are those who actually met Elvis and have information about his basic goodness.) "I met him in 1960 when I was twelve years old," says Billie Le Jeune of Memphis, who visits Graceland once or twice a month: "He asked me what my favorite subject was." (A few others have stories equally compelling. The crowd listens in awe.)

(Along with these talkers at Graceland are the writers, who sum up the range of Elvis's qualities.) On the pink fieldstone wall outside Graceland, which for years has functioned as an unauthorized bulletin board, the graffiti runs like this: ELVIS IS LOVE; I DID DRUGS WITH ELVIS; and most cryptic of all—ELVIS DIDN'T DESERVE TO BE WHITE.

Introduction

Thesis

Topic sentence

Support

Topic sentence

Support

Topic sentence

Support

Conclusion

Like the paragraph, the essay may also assume different patterns. It may be principally one form of discourse: narration, description, exposition, or argumentation. It may also be a combination, varying from paragraph to paragraph and even within paragraphs. Regardless of its pattern, the essay will be unified around a central idea, or thesis. The *thesis* is the assertion or controlling purpose. All the other parts of the essay will be subordinate to the thesis and will support it. As with the paragraph, the main point, here the thesis, will almost certainly be stated, usually in the first paragraph, and again, more frequently than not, at the end of the essay. The essay on Elvis illustrates this pattern.

The only difference in concept between the topic sentence and the thesis is one of scope: The topic sentence unifies and controls the content of the paragraph, and the thesis does the same for the essay. Because the essay is longer and more complex than the typical paragraph, the thesis may suggest a broader scope and may more explicitly indicate the parts.

Special Paragraphs Within the Essay

Developmental paragraphs were discussed in Chapter 4, and paragraphs of transition (usually short and having a simple structure) are almost never needed in short essays. Let's focus our attention, therefore, on paragraphs of introduction and conclusion.

Introductions

A good introductory paragraph does many things. It attracts the reader's interest, states or points toward the thesis, and moves the reader smoothly into the body paragraphs, the developmental paragraphs. Here are some introductory methods:

- a direct statement of the thesis

- background

- definition of term(s)

- quotation(s)

- a shocking statement

- question(s)

- a combination of two or more methods on this list

You should not decide that some of the methods are good and some are bad. Indeed, all are valid, and the most common one is the last, the combination. Use the approach that best fits each essay. Resist the temptation to use the same kind of introduction in every essay you write.

Each of the following statements is an introductory paragraph. The thesis is the same in all of them, yet each uses a different introductory method. Notice the great variety here.

Direct Statement of Thesis:

**Subject
Treatment**

Anyone on the road in any city near midnight on Friday and Saturday is among dangerous people. They're not the product of the witching hour; they're the product of the "happy hour." They're called drunk drivers. These threats to our lives and limbs need to be controlled by federal laws with strong provisions.

Background:

**Subject
Treatment**

In one four-year period in California (1995–1998), 15,363 people were injured and 5,954 were killed by drunk drivers. Each year, the same kinds of figures come in from all our states. The state laws vary. The federal government does virtually nothing. Drunk driving has reached the point of being a national problem of huge proportions. This slaughter of innocent citizens should be stopped by following the lead of many other nations and passing federal legislation with strong provisions.

Definition:

Here's a recipe. Take two thousand pounds of plastic, rubber, and steel, pour in ten gallons of gas, and start the engine. Then take one human being of two hundred pounds of flesh, blood, and bones, pour in two glasses of beer in one hour, and put him or her

Subject
Treatment

behind the wheel. Mix the two together, and the result may be a drunken driver ready to cause death and destruction. <u>This problem of drunk driving can and should be controlled by federal legislation with strong provisions.</u>

Quotation:

Subject
Treatment

The National Highway Traffic Safety Administration has stated that 50 percent of all fatal accidents involve intoxicated drivers and that "75 percent of those drivers have a Blood Alcohol Content of .10 percent or greater." That kind of information is widely known, yet the carnage on the highways continues. <u>This problem of drunk driving should be addressed by a federal law with strict provisions.</u>

Shocking Statement and Questions:

Subject
Treatment

Almost 60,000 Americans were killed in the Vietnam War. What other war kills more than that number every four years? Give up? It's the war with drunk drivers. The war in Vietnam ended about three decades ago, but our DUI war goes on, and the drunks are winning. <u>This deadly conflict should be controlled by a federal law with strong provisions.</u>

Questions and a Definition:

Subject
Treatment

What is a drunk driver? In California it's a person with a blood alcohol content of .08 percent or more who is operating a motor vehicle. What do those drivers do? Some of them kill. Every year more than 16,000 people nationwide die. Those are easy questions. The difficult one is, What can be done? One answer is clear: <u>Drunk drivers should be controlled by federal laws with strong provisions.</u>

All these introductory methods are effective. Some others, however, are ineffective because they are too vague to carry the thesis or because they carry the thesis in a mechanical way. The mechanical approach may be direct and explicit, but it usually numbs the reader's imagination and interest.

Avoid: The purpose of this essay is to write about the need for strong national laws against drunk driving.

Avoid: I will now write a paper about the need for strong national laws against drunk driving.

The length of an introduction can vary, but the typical length for the introductory paragraph of a student essay is three to five sentences. If your introduction is shorter than three, be certain that it conveys all that you want to say. If it is longer than five, be certain that it only introduces and does not try to expand on ideas. That function is reserved for the developmental paragraphs; a long and complicated introduction may make your essay top-heavy.

Exercise 1　　**WRITING AN INTRODUCTION**

Pick one of the following theses (altering it a bit to suit your own ideas, if you like) and write at least three introductions for it, using a different method for each one. Underline the thesis in each paragraph, and label the subject and treatment parts.

1. Marriages come in different shapes and sizes.

2. Career choices are greatly influenced by a person's background.

3. *Friendship* is just one word, but friends are of different kinds.

4. The spirit of sports has been corrupted by money.

5. Sexual harassment at work often goes unreported for practical reasons.

Conclusions

Your concluding paragraph should give the reader the feeling that you have said all you want to say about your subject. Like introductory paragraphs, concluding paragraphs are of various types. Here are some effective ways of concluding a paper:

- Conclude with a final paragraph or sentence that is a logical part of the body of the paper; that is, it functions as part of the support. In the following example, there is no formal conclusion. This form is more common in the published essay than in the student essay.

> One day he hit me. He said he was sorry and even cried, but I could not forgive him. We got a divorce. It took me a while before I could look back and see what the causes really were, but by then it was too late to make any changes.

Maria Campos, "A Divorce with Reasons"

- Conclude with a restatement of the thesis in slightly different words, perhaps pointing out its significance or making applications.

> Don't blame it on the referee. Don't even blame it on the fight managers. Put the blame where it belongs—on the prevailing mores that regard prize fighting as a perfectly proper enterprise and vehicle of entertainment. No one doubts that many people enjoy prize fighting and will miss it if it should be thrown out. And that is precisely the point.

Norman Cousins, "Who Killed Benny Paret?"

- Conclude with a review of the main points of the discussion—a kind of summary. This is appropriate only if the complexity of the essay makes a summary necessary.

> As we have been made all too aware lately in this country, the more energy we conserve now, the more we'll have for the future. The same holds true for skiing. So take the Soft Path of energy conservation as you ski. You'll not only be able to make longer nonstop runs, but you'll have more energy to burn on the dance floor.

Carl Wingus, "Conserving Energy as You Ski"

- Conclude with an anecdote related to the thesis.

> Over the harsh traffic sounds of motors and horns and blaring radios came the faint whang-whang of a would-be musician with a beat-up guitar and a money-drop hat turned up at his feet. It all reminded me of when I had first experienced the conglomeration of things that now assailed my senses. This jumbled mixture of things both human and nonhuman was, in fact, the reason I had come to live here. Then it was different and exciting. Now it was the reason I was leaving.

Brian Maxwell, "Leaving Los Angeles"

- Conclude with a quotation related to the thesis.

> Fifty percent of all fatal traffic accidents involve intoxicated drivers, according to the National Highway Traffic Safety Administration. Cavenaugh and Associates, research specialists, say that

drunk drivers killed 83,824 people in the five-year period from 1993 through 1999. They go on to say that intoxicated drivers cost us somewhere between $11 and $24 billion each year. It is time to give drunk drivers a message: "Stay off the road. You are costing us pain, injury, and death, and no one has the right to do that."

There are also many ineffective ways of concluding a paper. Do not conclude with the following:

- a summary when a summary is unnecessary

- a complaint about the assignment or an apology about the quality of the work

- an afterthought—that is, something you forgot to discuss in the body of the paper

- a tagged conclusion—that is, a sentence beginning with such phrases as *In conclusion, To conclude,* or *I would like to conclude this discussion*

- a conclusion that raises additional problems that should have been settled during the discussion

The conclusion is an integral part of the essay and is often a reflection of the introduction. If you have trouble with the conclusion, reread your introduction. Then work for a roundness or completeness in the whole paper.

Student Demonstration of All Stages of the Writing Process

Let's see now how one student wrote an essay by working her way through all the stages of the writing process.

Our student writer, Leah, is an inmate at a California prison where, for several years, she was enrolled in a small, low-cost college program. In her English class, her assignment was to write a personal essay of 500 to 800 words. Her instructor suggested she concentrate on a recent development or event at the prison that had changed her life, for better or worse.

Several topics interested her. There was the problem of overcrowding: She lived in an institution built for 900 inmates, and the population was now 2,200. She also considered education. After spending some time in routine prison work and aimless activities, she discovered school and found it highly satisfying. Then there were the accomplishments of her Native-American friends at the prison. After years of arguing their case, they had finally obtained permission from the institution to build a sweat lodge for religious purposes, and it was now in operation. That was a subject she knew well, and it was one for which she held the most enthusiasm. She was ready to proceed, knowing that the writing process would provide her with strategies and give her direction.

Leah used the Writing Process Worksheet for guidance, thus also providing her instructor with a record of the development of her work. Her worksheet has been lengthened for you to be able to see parts of her work in their entirety. You will find a full-size blank worksheet on page 5. It can be photocopied, filled in, and submitted with each assignment if your instructor directs you to do so.

Writing Process Worksheet

TITLE   Prison Sweat Lodge

NAME   Leah   **DUE DATE**   Tuesday, April 11, at 1 p.m.

ASSIGNMENT   In the space below, write whatever you need to know about your assignment, including information about the topic, audience, pattern of writing, length, whether to include a rough draft or revised drafts, and whether your paper must be typed.

Write a personal essay of 500 to 800 words about some aspect of your prison life that has changed recently. This will be mainly process analysis; therefore, you will probably organize your discussion by time. Write for a general cross section of the population, one that will probably not have shared the experience you write about. Submit this completed worksheet, a rough draft marked for revision, and a typed final draft.

STAGE ONE   **Explore**   Freewrite, brainstorm (list), cluster, or take notes as directed by your instructor. Use the back of this page or separate paper if you need more space.

Freewriting

• First Leah started freewriting, which enabled her to probe her memory and see which aspects of the subject most interested her. She wrote without stopping, letting her ideas tumble forth in a rich free association on the subject of "sweat lodge." •

For several years I have wanted to worship in the way that I did when I was on the reservation. These people here at prison were discriminating against me, I thought. I knew that the other people here could go to the chaplain and to the chapel and they could do so without people complaining or going to any bother. I didn't know why they did not allow me to follow my own religious preference. Then I talked to the other Indian sisters here at prison and they told me that they had been working for many years to get a sweat lodge. I started working with them. It took years of work, *have sweat* but it is worth it for now <u>we have a sweat lodge</u> where we can go for our *lodge now* ceremonies. It makes me feel good. I look forward to it. I <u>have used it once a week for most</u> of the <u>last year.</u> When I am nervous and when things are tense on the prison grounds, I think about the sweat lodge and just thinking about it gives me some peace. Then <u>when I go there and sweat</u> for a period of time I seem to feel that I am leaving the prison grounds and I am *ceremony* <u>at peace</u> with the universe. It is <u>a ceremony</u> that is <u>important</u> to me and *important* also to the prison. We even have women who are not Indians who are interested and we teach them about Indian ways and we all learn from what we do. What else is there to say. I could go on and on. That is what I have to say. I love the sweat lodge which we call the sweats. I think it is the most important thing in my life now. I used to be bitter toward the prison for denying me my rights, but now I am even <u>at peace</u> with them—most of the *at peace* time. I remember when we were trying to get approval and . . . [partial]

Brainstorming: Big Six Questions

• Leah continued with the subject of prison sweat lodge, and her topic tightened to focus on particular areas. Although she could have listed the annotations and the words she underlined in her freewriting, she began with the Big Six Questions for her framework. •

Who?	American Indian inmates and others
What?	sweat lodge—how it was started—the politics—the ceremonies
Where?	California Institution for Women—off the yard
When?	1989, before, after, long time in planning and building
Why?	spiritual, physical, self-esteem, educational
How?	preparation, steps

Brainstorming: Listing

• Leah then proceeded to write three useful lists based on her answers to the questions. •

Sweat lodge	Ceremony	Result
Problems in building it	Preparation	Relaxed
Reasons	Blankets	Spiritually clean
Fairness	Rocks	Peaceful
Who helped	Fire	
Time to build	Water	
	Tobacco and sweet grass	
	Sweating	
	Passing pipe	
	Tearing down	

Clustering

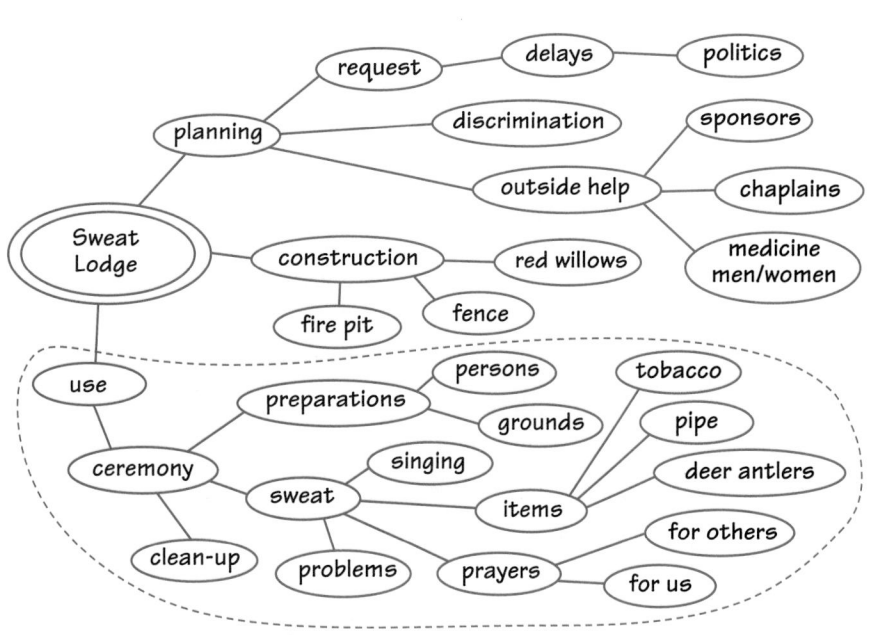

• Notice that after completing her basic cluster, Leah went back and drew a broken boundary around subclusters that offered encouraging areas for focus. Some sub-clusters, usually with further clustering to provide details, can work as well as an outline for providing structure and content for the development of an essay. •

STAGE TWO   **Organize**   Write a topic sentence or thesis; label the subject and the treatment parts.

Composing the Thesis

• After freewriting, brainstorming, and clustering, Leah was ready to focus. She was ready to concentrate on one aspect of her larger topic that could reasonably be developed in an essay of 500 to 800 words. She also wanted to establish a direction for the essay that would target her audience, who knew little about her topic. It would be necessary to explain her topic in detail so that uninformed readers could easily understand. Moreover, she would avoid any Native-American words that her audience might not know. Although the sweat lodge was developed in an atmosphere of controversy in which she and others often had to be persuasive, she anticipated that readers of this essay would be open-minded and interested. She would simply inform them about her experience with the sweat lodge, giving a personal perspective. She would also have to avoid using prison slang, because this essay was for an assignment in a college writing class.

Leah made three attempts to write a sentence with both a subject (what she would write about) and a treatment (what she would do with her subject). She wanted the treatment to be just right, not vague or too broad or too narrow. •

I want to explain how we use sweats and why.

Using the prison sweat lodge involves specific practices that contribute to my well-being.

Subject   I want to discuss the <u>prison sweat lodge,</u> <u>what we do in the preparation</u>
Treatment   <u>period, what we do when we're inside for the ceremony, and what we do</u>
<u>afterwards.</u>

• Her third attempt satisfied her, and the statement became her thesis. Later she would reword it. •

Write an outline or an outline alternative.

• Leah's next task was to organize her material. Although she might have used the part of her cluster marked by the dotted lines, she chose the outline form.

The outline shows the relationship of ideas, suggests ways to divide the essay according to Leah's thesis, and indicates support. The divisions are Preparation, Ceremony, and Ceremony completion and site restoration. Those items are Leah's Roman numeral headings. •

I. Preparation
   A. Fasting
      1. Duration
      2. Only water
   B. Heat rocks
      1. Thirty to fifty
      2. Build fire

C. Set up lodge
   1. Permission from sponsor
   2. Cover framework
II. Ceremony
   A. Movement
      1. Going and coming
      2. Passing sacred objects
   B. Establishing attitude
   C. Sweating
   D. Praying and singing
   E. Purification rites
      1. Tobacco ties
      2. Sage
      3. Sweet grass
III. Ceremony completion and site restoration
   A. Personal
      1. Water down
      2. Eat and drink
      3. Change
   B. Site
      1. Remove and store blankets
      2. Move rocks

STAGE THREE   **Write**   On separate paper, write and then revise your paper as many times as necessary for coherence, language (usage, tone, and diction), unity, emphasis, support, and sentences (CLUESS). Read your paper aloud to hear and correct any grammatical errors or awkward-sounding sentences.

Edit any problems in fundamentals, such as capitalization, omissions, punctuation, and spelling (COPS).

• The following is an early draft that shows Leah's revision process. The draft also includes some editing (COPS). •

Razor Wire Sweat Lodge

My tribe is   twenty-one represented   always
I am a Pomo ~~Indian~~, one ~~tribe~~ of ~~many here~~ on the prison grounds. I have
                         ancestors   in
had tremendous interest in my ~~Ancestry~~ and their customs, and the cultures   ] Rewrite
of all Indian tribes. The sacred sweat ceremonies, I've found to be one of the   ]
                     cultural practices   other
most interesting. Many women of ~~all~~ races here in the facility have also taken   ] Rewrite
                    other benefits
interest and found ~~peace~~ within themselves from participating in the sweats.   ]

I want to discuss the prison sweat lodge, what we do in the preparation

period, what we do when we're inside for the ceremony, and what we do

afterwards.

Rewrite for stronger topic sentence [

The first step to sweating is the preparation period. Before anyone can [*in our prison facility*] sweat there are many requirements ~~in~~ [*concerning*] what we wear/ ~~how we are instructed (depending on how many times we've gone),~~ and how we act. ~~T~~[*For*]wenty-four hours before the sweat we fast. ~~We can only drink~~ [*Participants should drink only*] water or juices, but if someone has health problems we will excuse them. The lava [*coherence*] rocks have to [*heat*] in the fire approximately three hours before we start sweat-

Organize. Be more concise [

ing. The fire has to be built just right in a little house shape. ~~Putting~~ [*We put*] all the rocks in the middle with the wood standing like a teepee around them; then the paper [*is*] stuffed between and around the wood. Once there's a good fire going then we ~~start~~ tend to the sweat lodge itself. Because we have no tarp to put on the sweat lodge, the state has provided us with plenty of blankets. The blankets have to cover the s[w]eat lodge fully. We put at least three layers of blankets on the sweat lodge. We make sure we leave about eight inches of blanket around the bottom of the sweat lodge. ~~Around~~ [*By*] this

coherence |

time, some women have started making their tobacco ties. These ties are used for ~~putting your~~ [*sending*] prayer on. We'~~ve got to~~ [*must*] make sure the sponsor is somewhere by the sweat lodge at all times. ~~Also about~~ [*As for*] the rock[s] we use thirty to fifty of them[;] it depends on their size and how many women are sweating that day. Then the women are told to change into only muu muu[s]; the state provides them also. Then we're read[y] to go inside. The preparation period is very important[,] ~~and~~ [*but*] everyone looks forward to it being over.

Once everyone is inside the sweat lodge, there are certain things ~~you~~ [*we*] must do. ~~The way we enter is~~ first we enter counterclockwise[,] and [*once*] inside we ~~maintain everything we do~~ [*conduct all parts of the ceremony*] counterclockwise. There are four rounds in the sweat which last about twenty to thirty minutes ~~each.~~ [*each of*] We stress that no one [*should*] break our circle inside the sweat lodge, but it ~~is possible.~~ [*sometimes happens.*] Some

coherence |

women can't handle the heat inside[,] [*so*] we never make them stay. The praying

Rephrase |

and singing is in the Sioux language because our outside sponsor is Sioux. Not

the individual.

everyone has to sing or pray. It's up to ~~them.~~ As someone finishes a prayer

she mentions all her relatives

~~they say for all their relations/~~ then the next person prays. Before ~~anyone~~

we

~~even~~ enters the sweat, ~~they~~ have to make sure they have peace and good   Agr

feelings with all other members. The tobacco ties hang over our heads in

the sweat or around our necks. (Also) we take in sage with us and smudge

for purification

ourselves with it. After each round, new hot rocks are brought in. As these

verb tense | rocks are place*d* in the fire, sweet grass is put on them. ~~All~~ *What* we do inside the   Be more concise

through

sweat lodge is not only for ourselves, but ~~for~~ our prayers for others. We

maintain ourselves with humility during the whole sweat.

When the sweat is over, we enter the final phase. We come out and

to   n

throw our tobacco ties in the fire pit. The ~~first thing~~ we ~~do is~~ hose ourselves

down with plenty of cold water. The refreshments are opened and someone

goes after food. Once we've eaten and changed our clothes, we start taking

down the sweat. The blankets have to be taken off the same way they

carefully

were put on and folded up ~~good.~~ The leftover wood has to be put away

must be covered

and ~~on both~~ the blankets and the wood ~~we put their covers.~~ Any garbage

to

that's been left around is thrown in the dumpster. Then we lock the gate   move to end

f   we

and bid our farewells until the next weekend. After it's all over ~~you really~~   to end

physically   ed

feel ~~a sense of~~ refresh~~ness~~ clean and peaceful.

Using

The sweat lodge is a custom of most~~ly all~~ Indian tribes. Certain Indian

from

tribes go about it differently ~~than~~ others but once they're all inside everyone   Rewrite

feels of one whole being. All three steps I've gone through are helpful for

Each week we

a successful sweat ceremony. ~~Many of us members~~ look forward to these

ceremonies ~~every week.~~ They help us cope better with the prison system.

Final Draft

Razor Wire Sweat Lodge

Leah

My Indian tribe is Pomo, one of twenty-one represented at this prison. I
have always had tremendous interest in my ancestors and their customs,
and in the cultures of all Indian tribes. The sacred sweat ceremony itself is

at the center of my life. Here at prison it has taken on a special meaning. In fact, many women of other races here have also found peace within themselves as a result of participating with me and other Native Americans in the sweats. **Thesis** <u>Each Saturday we have a routine: We make preparations, we sweat, and we conclude with a post-sweat activity.</u>

Topic sentence <u>Before we sweat, we must prepare ourselves and the facility.</u> For twenty-four hours before the sweat, we fast. We do not eat anything and drink only water or juices, but if someone has a health problem, we will excuse her. As for clothing, we wear simple, loose dresses such as the prison-issued muu muus. We bring tobacco ties, sage leaves, sweet grass, and sometimes a pipe. Preparing the facility is more complicated than preparing ourselves. About thirty-five lava rocks must be heated in a fire approximately three hours before we start sweating. The wood for the fire has to be placed in a tepee shape around the pile of rocks and ignited. Once the fire is hot, we tend to the sweat lodge itself. Because we have no tarp to put on the sweat lodge frame, the state provides us with blankets. We use these to cover the lodge fully, draping it with about three layers and leaving an opening to the east. Finally we are ready to go inside. The preparation period is very important, but everyone looks forward to its being over.

Topic sentence <u>From this point on through the ceremony, everything must be done according to rules.</u> First we enter counterclockwise, and once inside we conduct all parts of the ceremony counterclockwise. There are four rounds in the sweat, each of which lasts about twenty to thirty minutes. We stress that no one should break our circle inside the sweat lodge, but it sometimes happens. Some women can't handle the steam and the heat, so we never make them stay. Those who do stay are free to participate in the singing and praying or not. The four rounds are similar. For each, six hot rocks are brought in, and six dippers of water are poured onto the rocks. The number six indicates the four directions and the sky and the ground. As someone finishes a prayer (usually in Sioux because our sponsor is a Sioux), she mentions her relatives, for this ceremony is also for others. Then another person follows. As sweet grass burns outside on the fire, we sit in the hot steam and rub sage leaves on our bodies for purification. We maintain ourselves with humility during the whole event.

Topic sentence <u>When the sweat is over, we enter the final phase.</u> We come out and throw our tobacco ties into the fire pit, and the smoke takes our prayers to the sky. Then we hose ourselves down with plenty of cold water and open the refreshments we brought. Once we've eaten and changed our clothes, we start dismantling the sweat. The blankets have to be taken off the same way they were put up and then folded carefully. The leftover wood has to be put away, and the blankets and wood must be covered. Any garbage that's been left around is thrown into the dumpster. Then we lock the gate to our facility and bid farewell.

Using a sweat lodge is a custom of most Indian tribes. Certain Indian tribes go about it differently from others, but in here when we are together in the lodge, we feel like one whole being. Each week we look forward to this ceremony. It helps us cope better with the prison system. After it's over, we feel physically refreshed, clean, and peaceful.

Exercise 2   **COMPLETING A WRITING PROCESS WORKSHEET**

Select one of the following theses and complete a Writing Process Worksheet at least through Stage Two. (Photocopy the blank form on page 5 at the end of the Student Overview.) Alter the topic if you like, even by taking the opposite position.

1. The date (marriage, class, game, job) was a disaster (success).

2. I will never forget my first encounter with racial prejudice (cruelty to animals, inhumanity).

3. The kind of music I listen to reflects the kind of person I would like to be.

4. A preoccupation with a single activity or concern throws life out of balance.

5. The importance of student government is often overlooked.

6. A death in the family can teach a person a great deal about life.

7. The way a person drives reveals his or her personality.

8. The way I drive depends on my mood.

9. The way I keep my room (car, house, yard, desk) is a reflection of the way I think (regard life).

10. One of my most embarrassing moments has become, in retrospect, only a humorous recollection.

Writer's Guidelines: Writing the Essay

1. The essay is a group of paragraphs, each with the function of stating or supporting a controlling idea called the thesis.

   • The main parts of an essay are the introduction, development, and conclusion.

   • The essay can be considered an amplification of a developmental paragraph.

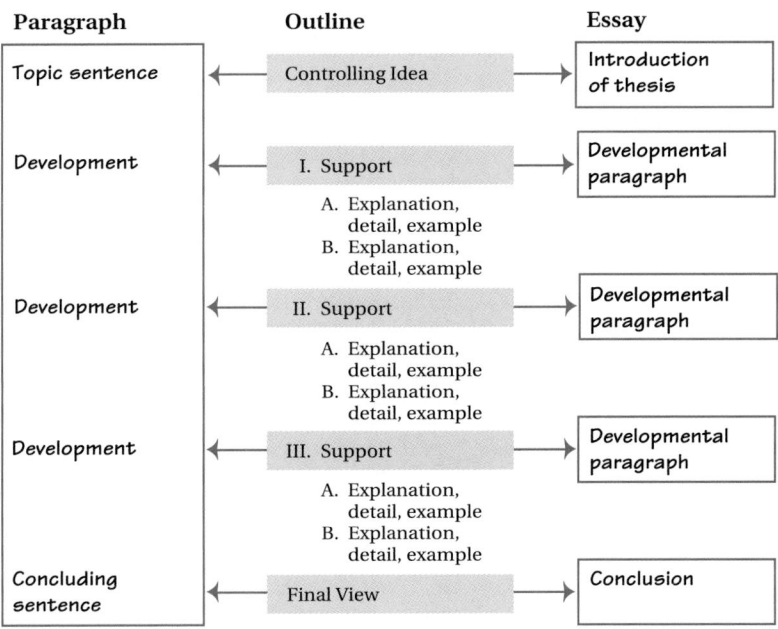

2. The introduction contains the thesis within a context of comments that give an adequate perspective on the topic. There are many good introductory methods, which include presenting a direct statement of the thesis, background, definition of term(s), quotation(s), a shocking statement, question(s), and a combination of two or more of these methods.

3. The conclusion makes a final comment on the development of your thesis. If you do not know how to conclude, reread your introduction for ideas.

4. You can depend on the three stages of the writing process to help you write paragraphs and essays. In the first stage, you are encouraged to explore relevant ideas and perhaps generate a topic sentence or thesis. In the second stage, you move naturally to a precise statement of your topic sentence or thesis and to an organized plan for your support material. Finally, you do the actual writing, revising, and editing of your paragraph or essay. This process also allows for recursive movement: You can go back and forth as you rework your material.

Reading-Related Writing

> "*Read, read, read. Read everything—trash, classics, good and bad, and see how they do it. Just like a carpenter who works as an apprentice and studies the Master.*"
>
> William Faulkner

THE QUIGMANS   by Buddy Hickerson

"So . . . where's the 'on' switch?"

B. Hickerson, copyright Los Angeles Times Syndicate. Reprinted by permission.

Reading for Writing

ecause most college writing assignments are connected with reading, it is worthwhile to consider how to focus thoughtful attention on the written word. Of course, if you know about writing assignments or tests beforehand, your reading can be more concentrated. You should always begin a reading assignment by asking yourself why you are reading that particular material and how it relates to your course work and interests. For example, most selections in this book are presented as ideas to stimulate thought and invite reflective comparisons, to provide material for analysis and evaluation, and to show how a pattern or process of writing can be done effectively. The discussion and critical-thinking questions and activities that follow the selections arise from these purposes. Other questions raised by your instructor or on your own can also direct you in purposeful reading. Consider such questions and activities at the outset. Then, as you read, use strategies that are appropriate for the kind of assignment you are working on. Among the most common strategies are underlining, annotating, and outlining. Used correctly, they will help you attain a critical, receptive, and focused state of mind as you prepare for writing assignments.

Underlining

Imagine you are reading a chapter of several pages, and you decide to underline and write in the margins. Immediately, the underlining takes you out of the passive, television-watching frame of mind. You are involved. You are participating. It is now necessary for you to discriminate, to distinguish more important from less important ideas. Perhaps you have thought of underlining as a method designed only to help you with reviewing. That is, when you study the material the next time, you won't have to reread all of it; instead, you can deal only with the most important, underlined parts. While you are underlining, you are benefiting from an imposed concentration, because this procedure forces you to think, to focus. Consider the following suggestions for underlining:

1. Underline the main ideas in paragraphs. The most important statement, the topic sentence, is likely to be at the beginning of the paragraph.

2. Underline the support for those main ideas.

3. Underline answers to questions that you bring to the reading assignment. These questions may have come from the end of the chapter, from subheadings that you turn into questions, or from your independent concerns about the topic.

4. Underline only the key words. You would seldom underline all the words in a sentence and almost never a whole paragraph.

Does that fit your approach to underlining? Possibly not. Most students, in their enthusiasm to do a good job, overdo underlining.

The trick is to figure out what to underline. You would seldom underline more than about 30 percent of a passage, although the amount would depend on your purpose and the nature of the material. Following the preceding four suggestions will be useful. Learning more about the principles of sentence, paragraph, and essay organization will also be helpful.

Annotating

Annotating, writing notes in the margins, is a practice related to underlining. You can do it independently, although it usually appears in conjunction with underlining to signal your understanding and to extend your involvement in your reading.

Writing in the margins represents intense involvement because it turns a reader into a writer. If you read material and write something in the margin as a reaction to it, then in a way you have had a conversation with the author. The author has made a statement and you have responded. In fact, you may have added something to the text; therefore, for your purposes you have become a co-author or collaborator. The comments you make in the margin are of your own choosing according to your interests and the purpose you bring to the reading assignment. Your response in the margin may merely echo the author's ideas, it may question them critically, it may relate them to something else, or it may add to them.

The comments and marks on the following essay will help you understand the connection between writing and reading. Both techniques—underlining to indicate main and supporting ideas and annotating to indicate their importance and relevance to the task at hand—will enhance thinking, reading, and writing.

Total Institutions
Seymour Feshback and Bernard Weiner

Total institution encompasses individual (thesis)

1   A total institution completely encompasses the individual, forming a barrier to the types of social intercourse that occur outside such a setting. Monasteries, jails, homes for the aged, boarding schools, and military academies are a few examples of total institutions.

1. Individual activities in same setting

2. All life within group

3. Activities tightly scheduled

2   Total institutions have certain common characteristics. First, the individuals in such environments must sleep, play, and work within the same setting. These are generally segmented spheres of activity in the lives of most individuals, but within a total institution one sphere of activity overlaps with others. Second, each phase of life takes place in the company of a large group of others. Frequently, sleeping is done in a barracks, food is served in a cafeteria, and so on. In such activities everyone is treated alike and must perform certain essential tasks. Third, activities in an institution are tightly scheduled according to a master plan, with set times to rise, to eat, to exercise, and to sleep. These institutional characteristics result in a bureaucratic society, which requires the hiring of other people for surveillance. What often results is a split in the groups within an institution into a large, managed group (inmates) and a small supervisory staff. There tends to be great social distance between the groups, who perceive each other according to stereotypes and have severely restricted communications.

Managed groups and staff at distance

Two worlds—inside and outside

Personality altered

3   The world of the inmate differs greatly from the outside world. When one enters a total institution, all previous roles, such as father or husband, are disrupted. The individual is further depersonalized by the issuance of a uniform, confiscation of belongings, and gathering of personal information, as well as by more subtle touches like doorless toilets, record keeping, and bedchecks. The effects of an institutional setting are so all-encompassing that one can meaningfully speak of an "institutional personality": a persistent manner of behaving compliantly and without emotional involvement.

Becomes psychotic, childlike, or depressive

4   Of course, there are <u>individual differences in adaptation</u> to the situation. They can be as extreme as <u>psychosis</u>, <u>childlike regression</u>, and <u>depression</u> or as mild as resigned compliance. <u>Most individuals do adjust</u> and build up a system of satisfactions, such as close friendships and cliques.

Individuals adjust but have trouble later on street

5   But because of these bonds and the fact that the habits needed to function in the outside world have been lost, <u>inmates face</u> great <u>problems</u> upon <u>leaving an institution</u>. A <u>shift from</u> the <u>top of</u> a <u>small society</u> to the <u>bottom of</u> a <u>larger one</u> may be <u>further demoralizing</u>.

Outlining Reading Material

After reading, underlining, and annotating the piece, the next step could be to outline it. If the piece is well organized, you should be able to reduce it to a simple outline so that you can, at a glance, see the relationship of ideas (sequence, relative importance, and interdependence).

The essay on total institutions can be outlined very easily:

Total Institutions

  I. Common characteristics

    A. All activities in the same setting

    B. All phases of life within larger group

    C. Activities scheduled according to a master plan

      1. Bureaucratic society

      2. Social distance between inmates and staff

 II. Adjusting to the world inside

    A. Individual depersonalized

      1. Wears uniform

      2. No personal belongings

      3. No privacy

    B. Adaptation

      1. Negative

        a. Psychosis

        b. Regression

        c. Depression

      2. Positive

III. Problems upon release outside

    A. Adjusting to a different system

    B. Encountering shock of going to the bottom of a new order

Exercise 1	**UNDERLINING, ANNOTATING, AND OUTLINING**

Underline and annotate this passage. Then complete the outline that follows.

Effective E-Mail Practices

1   Use short lines and short paragraphs. A short line length (perhaps 50 to 60 characters) is much easier to read than the 80-character line of most text editors. Similarly, short paragraphs (especially the

first and last paragraph) are more inviting to read. Avoid formatting a long message as one solid paragraph.

2   Don't shout. Use all-capital letters only for emphasis or to substitute for italicized text (such as book titles). Do NOT type your entire message in all capitals: It is a text-based form of *shouting* at your reader and is considered rude (not to mention being more difficult to read).

3   Proofread your message before sending it. Don't let the speed and convenience of e-mail lull you into being careless. While an occasional typo or other surface error will probably be overlooked by the reader, excessive errors or sloppy language creates an unprofessional image of the sender.

4   Append previous messages appropriately. Most e-mail systems allow you to append the original message to your reply. Use this feature judiciously. Occasionally, it may be helpful for the reader to see his or her entire message replayed. More often, however, you can save the reader time by establishing the context of the original message in your reply. If necessary, quote pertinent parts of the original message. If the entire original message is needed, treat it as an appendix and insert it at the *end* of your reply—not at the beginning.

5   Use a direct style of writing and think twice; write once. Put your major idea in the first sentence or two. If the message is so sensitive or emotionally laden that a more indirect organization would be appropriate, you should reconsider whether e-mail is the most effective medium for the message. Because it is so easy to respond immediately to a message, you might be tempted to let your emotions take over. Such behavior is called "flaming" and should be avoided. Always assume the message you send will never be destroyed but will be saved permanently in somebody's computer file.

6   Don't neglect your greeting and closing. Downplay the seeming impersonality of computerized mail by starting your message with a friendly salutation, such as "Hi, Amos" or "Dear Mr. Fisher."

7   An effective closing is equally important. Some e-mail programs identify only the e-mail address (for example, "70511.753 @compuserve.com") in the message header they transmit. Don't take a chance that your reader won't recognize you. Include your name, e-mail address, and any other appropriate identifying information at the end of your message.

Adapted from Scot Ober, *Contemporary Business Communication*

I. Short lines; short paragraphs

   A. _____

   B. _____

II. No shouting

   A. No entire message in capital letters

   B. Causes problems

      1. _____

      2. _____

III. Proofread message before sending

   A. Resist temptation to send without checking

   B. Errors create unprofessional image

IV. Append messages appropriately

    A. _____

    B. Often better to establish context in your message

    C. _____

V. Direct style with deliberation

    A. _____

    B. _____

VI. Greetings and closings

    A. _____

    B. Provide necessary information in closing

        1. _____

        2. _____

        3. _____

Types of Reading-Related Writing

So far the writing you have considered, in both the student examples and your assignments, has been of a personal nature. The content derives from direct and indirect experience (reading and listening), and often involves opinion. Mastering this kind of writing is important, because you do have something to say. Many college writing tasks, however, will require you to evaluate and reflect on what you read, rather than write only about personal experience. You will be expected to read, think, and write. Your reading-related writing assignment may call for

- a *summary* (main ideas in your own words).

- a *reaction* (usually ideas on how the reading relates specifically to you, your experiences, and your attitudes but also often a critique of the worth and logic of the reading).

- a *two-part response* (includes both a summary and a reaction but separates them).

These kinds of writing have certain points in common. They all

- originate as a response to something you have read.

- indicate, to some degree, the content of the piece.

Writing a Summary

A **summary** is a rewritten, shortened version of a piece of writing in which you use your own wording to express the main ideas. Learning to summarize effectively will help you in many ways. Summary writing reinforces comprehension skills in reading. It requires you to discriminate among the ideas in the target reading passage. Summaries are usually written in the form of a well-designed paragraph or paragraph unit. Frequently, they are used in collecting material for research papers and in writing conclusions to essays.

The following rules will guide you in writing effective summaries. A summary

1. cites the author and title of the text.

2. is usually shorter than the original by about two-thirds, although the exact reduction will vary depending on the content of the original.

3. concentrates on the main ideas and includes details only infrequently.

4. changes the original wording without changing the idea.

5. does not evaluate the content or give an opinion in any way (even if you see an error in logic or fact).

6. does not add ideas (even if you have an abundance of related information).

7. does not include any personal comments by the author of the summary (therefore, no use of *I* referring to self).

8. seldom contains quotations (but if you do use quotations, do so only with quotation marks).

9. uses some author tags ("says York," "according to York," or "the author explains") to remind the reader(s) that you are summarizing the material of another author.

Exercise 2   **EVALUATING A SUMMARY**

Apply the rules of summary writing to the following summary of "Total Institutions," p. 77. Mark the instances of poor summary writing by using rule numbers from the preceding list.

Total Institutions

A total institution completely encompasses the individual. Total institu-

tions have certain common characteristics. Institutions provide the setting for

all rest, recreation, and labor. Residents function only within the group. And

residents are directed by a highly organized schedule, which, I think, is what

they need or they wouldn't be there. There residents are depersonalized by

being required to wear a uniform, abandon personal items, and give up pri-

vacy. Some adapt in a negative way by developing psychological problems,

but most adapt in a positive way by forming relationships with other resi-

dents. Several popular movies, such as *The Shawshank Redemption,* show

how prison society works, to use one example. Once outside the total institu-

tion, individuals must deal with the problem of relearning old coping habits.

They must also withstand the shock of going from the top of a small society to the bottom of a larger one. Society needs these total institutions, especially the jails.

The following is an example of an effective summary.

A Summary of "Total Institutions"
Michael Balleau

In "Total Institutions" Seymour Feshback and Bernard Weiner explain that a total institution encompasses the lives of its residents, who share three common traits: The residents must do everything in the same place, must do things together, and must do things according to the institution's schedule. The institution takes away the residents' roles they had in society, takes away their appearance by issuing uniforms, takes away their personal property by confiscation, and takes away their privacy by making life communal. The authors say that some residents adapt negatively by having psychological problems, but most form relationships and new roles within the institution. Upon release, these residents must learn to function in the free world all over again as they start at the bottom of society. This shift "may be further demoralizing."

Writing a Reaction

The reaction statement is another kind of reading-related writing. Some reactions require evaluation with a critical-thinking emphasis. Some focus on simple discussion of the content presented in the reading and include summary material. Others concentrate on the writer's experiences as related to the content of the passage.

The following paragraph is a student's reaction statement to "Total Institutions."

Institutions Always Win
Tanya Morris

The short essay "Total Institutions," by Seymour Feshback and Bernard Weiner, is a study of conflicts in different settings. The common characteristics of such an institution are in personal combat with the individual, in which the resident is stripped of his or her choices and left to participate in all activities in the same setting, with no opportunity for a sanctuary. Further, the resident who tries to assert his or her uniqueness is controlled by a master plan. That plan is enforced by police personnel, who become the masters, set up social barriers, and maintain control over their underlings. Cut off from the free world, the resident is in conflict with significant matters of newness—clothes, facilities, regulations, and roles. The authors explain that inexorably the institution wins, converting the resident into a disturbed person or an amiable robot among others who are similarly institutionalized. But at that moment of conversion, the now-depersonalized individual may be thrust back into society to try to reclaim old roles and behaviors in another cycle of conflicts. The authors of this essay are very clear in showing just how comprehensive these institutions are in waging their war, for good or bad, against individuality. After all, they are "total."

Writing a Two-Part Response

As you have seen, the reaction response includes a partial summary or is written with the assumption that readers have read the original piece. However, your instructor may prefer that you separate each form—for example, by presenting a clear, concise summary followed by a reaction response. This format is especially useful for critical examination of a text or for problem-solving assignments, because it requires you to understand and repeat another's views or experiences before responding. The two-part approach also helps you avoid the common problem of writing only a summary of the text when your instructor wants you to both summarize and evaluate or otherwise react. In writing a summary and a reaction it is a good idea to ask your instructor if you should separate your summary from your response.

Part I: Summary

Total Institutions: A Summary and a Reaction

Michael Balleau

In "Total Institutions" Seymour Feshback and Bernard Weiner explain that a total institution encompasses the lives of its residents, who share three common traits: The residents must do everything in the same place, must do things together, and must do things according to the institution's schedule. The institution takes away the residents' roles they had in society, takes away their appearance by issuing uniforms, takes away their personal property by confiscation, and takes away their privacy by making life communal. The authors say that some residents adapt negatively by having psychological problems, but most form relationships and new roles within the institution. Upon release, these residents must learn to function in the free world all over again as they start at the bottom of society. This shift "may be further demoralizing."

Part 2: Reaction

The basic ideas in "Total Institutions" gave me an insight into the behavior of my cousin. Let's call him George. He spent almost five years in prison for white collar crime at the bank where he worked. When George was incarcerated, he was an individual, almost to the extreme of being a rebel. When he got out, he was clearly an institutionalized person. Cut off from the consumer society, George was reluctant to enter stores and go through checkout lines. He was fearful of being left alone. Because his prison setting was very noisy, silence made him uncomfortable, and he wanted a radio or television on all the time. Accustomed to being around people in the institution, George couldn't stand being alone, and he depended on others to suggest times for meals and chores. Of course, his new reputation and behavior now set him apart from his former roles. It took him almost three years to readjust.

Journal Writing

Your journal entries are likely to be concerned primarily with the relationship between the reading material and you—your life experiences, your views, your imagination. The reading material will give you something of substance to write about, but you will be writing especially for yourself, developing confidence and ease in writing, so that writing becomes a comfortable part of your everyday activities, as speaking already is.

These journal entries will be part of your intellectual diary, recording what you are thinking about a certain issue. They will be of use in helping you understand the reading material, in helping you develop your writing skills, in uncovering ideas that can be used on other assignments, and in helping you think more clearly and imaginatively. Because these entries are of a more spontaneous nature than the more structured writing assignments, organization and editing are likely to be of less concern.

Each journal entry should be clearly dated and, if reading related, should specify the title and author of the original piece.

Even if your instructor wants you to concentrate on what you read for your journal writing, he or she might not want you to be restricted to the material in this text. Fortunately, you are surrounded by reading material in newspapers, magazines, and, of course, textbooks from other courses. These topics can serve you well, especially if you want to begin your journal writing now.

Career-Related Writing

This textbook includes career-related writing topics at the end of Chapters 7 through 17. They are a special feature designed to offer options for students who would like to write about jobs they currently hold, major areas of study, and intended careers. Because students are often studying materials in other classes and have access to other published sources, career-related writing may include ideas from reading material. Those ideas can be documented with a listing of the source, which usually includes the name of the author, title of the work, place of publication, publisher, date, and page numbers. The citations for quotations or specific references can be made in the same fashion as the ones for textbook sources (see the following three sections in this chapter).

Supporting Ideas with Quotations and References

In your reading-related writing assignments, you are likely to use three methods in developing your ideas: explanation, direct reference to the reading selection, and quotation from the reading. The explanations can take different forms, such as causes or effects, comparison, definition, or exemplification. These forms are explored later in this book. The references point the reader directly toward the reading selection. The more specific the reference—including even the page number—the more helpful it is to your readers. As for quotations, remember that the words are borrowed. They can be very effective as support, but you must give credit to the original writer.

These concepts are quite important in all reading-related writing, but especially in the writing that you will be doing in Chapters 7 through 17 of this textbook. Your references should be very clear and direct. Your quotations should be exact and should always appear within quotation marks to indicate that you have borrowed words. The form for quotations is presented on pages 455–456 in the Handbook at the end of this book.

In addition to these few requirements for reading-related writing based on material in this text, your instructor may also expect you to document your ideas. This means that you must indicate the sources of all the original ideas you have borrowed, even when you have changed the words.

Basic Documentation

Borrowing words or ideas without giving credit to the originators is called plagiarism, a kind of intellectual theft. Therefore, your instructor may ask you to document your reading-related writing.

Documenting sources for papers based on written material is usually quite simple. One documentation method is MLA (Modern Language Association) style. See Chapter 18, "The Research Paper," for more explanation. Here are its most common principles that can be used for textbook or other restricted sources, with some examples.

- If you use material from a source you have read, identify that source so the reader will recognize it or be able to find it.

- Document any original idea borrowed, whether it is quoted, paraphrased (written in your words but not shorter), or summarized (written in your words and shorter). Basic situations include the following:

  > Normally, you need give only the author's name and a page number: (Rivera 45).

  > If you state the author's name in introducing the quotation or idea, then usually give only the page number: (45).

  > If the author has written more than one piece in the book, then a title or shortened form of the title is also required: (Rivera, *The Land* 45).

Here is an example of documenting a quotation by an author represented only once in a textbook.

- Using the author's name to introduce:

  > Suzanne Britt says that "neat people are bums and clods at heart" (255).

Following is an example of documenting an idea borrowed from an author but not quoted.

- Using the author's name to introduce:

  > Suzanne Britt believes that neat people are weak in character (255).

- Not using the author's name to introduce:

  > Music often helps Alzheimer's patients think more clearly (Weiss 112).

Documentation in Action

Your paragraph or essay may include ideas from newspapers, magazines, or books. To make life simpler for you, most of the reading-related assignments in this book are based on selections included in this book. When you are writing about something you have read, just write as you usually would, but bring in ideas and quotations from that source. You may also want to refer to more than one source. You may even use ideas from other sources to contrast with your own. For example, you may say, "Unlike Fred M. Hechlinger in 'The First Step in Improving Sex Education: Remove the Hellfire' (351), I believe that public schools should not offer sex education." Do not feel that each point you make must be directly related to sources.

Here is a paragraph illustrating how to incorporate ideas and document them:

Jackie Malone, "Sexist Men as Victims"

> Sexist men are victims of their own bias against females. Because they cannot accept women as full human beings, they themselves are smaller in dimension. In Irwin Shaw's "The Girls in Their Summer Dresses," Michael looks at his wife, but he doesn't see a full human being; he just sees a sexual object: "what a pretty girl, what nice legs" (314). Because he sees her and other women that way, he cannot ever have the relationship with her that she deserves and that he would find fulfilling. Of course, thinking of women as just soft and cuddly has its effects on men in other ways. The man as father who thinks that way may very well regard his own daughter as one limited in her ranges of activities and limited in her potential. He may be one of those fathers who immediately stereotype their daughters as headed for a "life of the affections," not like a son's, "earning a living" (Lurie 249). Unfortunately, these men cannot accept females as their equals in any important respect, and, in doing so, they deprive themselves, as well as others.

Essays and Applications

The following essays demonstrate many of the elements of good writing that we have been exploring. To help you evaluate and write in response to those selections, each essay is accompanied first by a set of discussion and critical thinking questions and then by several reading-related writing suggestions. As you read, underline and annotate the material.

The Struggle to Be an All-American Girl

Elizabeth Wong

The title of the reading may suggest that Elizabeth Wong would experience success if she became an "all-American girl." But then the question is, Would she enjoy as an adult what she had wanted as a child? Another question comes to mind: Must one relinquish one's own cultural identity to assume another cultural identity?

1   It's still there, the Chinese school on Yale Street where my brother and I used to go. Despite the new coat of paint and the high wire fence, the school I knew ten years ago remains remarkably, stoically the same.

2   Every day at 5 P.M., instead of playing with our fourth- and fifth-grade friends or sneaking out to the empty lot to hunt ghosts and animal bones, my brother and I had to go to Chinese school. No amount of kicking, screaming, or pleading could dissuade my mother, who was solidly determined to have us learn the language of our heritage.

3   Forcibly, she walked us the seven long, hilly blocks from our home to school, depositing our defiant tearful faces before the stern principal. My only memory of him is that he swayed on his heels like a palm tree, and he always clasped his impatient twitching hands behind his back. I recognized him as a repressed maniacal child killer, and knew that if we ever saw his hands we'd be in big trouble.

4   We all sat in little chairs in an empty auditorium. The room smelled like Chinese medicine, and imported faraway mustiness. Like ancient mothballs or dirty closets. I hated that smell. I favored crisp new scents. Like the soft French perfume that my American teacher wore in public school.

5   Although the emphasis at the school was mainly language—speaking, reading, writing—the lessons always began with an exercise in politeness. With the entrance of the teacher, the best student would tap a bell and everyone would get up, kowtow, and chant, *"sing san ho,"* the phonetic for "How are you, teacher?"

6   Being ten years old, I had better things to learn than ideographs copied painstakingly in lines that ran right to left from the tip of a *moc but,* a real ink pen that had to be held in an awkward way if blotches were to be avoided. After all, I could do the multiplication tables, name the satellites of Mars, and write reports on "Little Women" and "Black Beauty." Nancy Drew, my favorite book heroine, never spoke Chinese.

7   The language was a source of embarrassment. More times than not, I had tried to disassociate myself from the nagging loud voice that followed me wherever I wandered in the nearby American supermarket outside Chinatown. The voice belonged to my grandmother, a fragile woman in her seventies who could outshout the best of the street vendors. Her humor was raunchy, her Chinese rhythmless, patternless. It was quick, it was loud, it was unbeautiful. It was not like the quiet, lilting romance of French or the gentle refinement of the American South. Chinese sounded pedestrian. Public.

8   In Chinatown, the comings and goings of hundreds of Chinese on their daily tasks sounded chaotic and frenzied. I did not want to be thought of as mad, as talking gibberish. When I spoke English, people nodded at me, smiled sweetly, said encouraging words. Even the people in my culture would cluck and say that I'd do well in life. "My, doesn't she move her lips fast," they would say, meaning that I'd be able to keep up with the world outside Chinatown.

9   My brother was even more fanatical than I about speaking English. He was especially hard on my mother, criticizing her, often cruelly, for her pidgin speech—smatterings of Chinese scattered like chop suey in her conversation. "It's not 'What it is' Mom," he'd say in exasperation. "It's 'What *is* it; what *is* it, what *is* it!'" Sometimes Mom might leave out an occasional "the" or "a," or perhaps a verb of being. He would stop her in mid-sentences: "Say

it again, Mom. Say it right." When he tripped over his own tongue, he'd blame it on her: "See, Mom, it's all your fault. You set a bad example."

10   After two years of writing with a *moc but* and reciting words with multiples of meanings, I finally was granted a cultural divorce. I was permitted to stop Chinese school.

11   I thought of myself as multicultural. I preferred tacos to egg rolls; I enjoyed Cinco de Mayo more than Chinese New Year.

12   At last, I was one of you; I wasn't one of them.

13   Sadly, I still am.

Exercise 3   **DISCUSSION AND CRITICAL THINKING**

1. By what steps is Wong transformed into an "all-American girl"?

2. Who or what influenced her the most?

3. How does she feel about her transformation?

4. Why can't she do anything about her transformation?

5. What advice would you give to her?

6. What advice do you think the author would give to her daughter?

Exercise 4   SUGGESTIONS FOR READING-RELATED WRITING

Complete one of the following reading-related responses.

1. Write a summary.

2. Write a two-part piece composed of labeled summary and reaction parts.

3. Analyze the essay as a transformation that Wong experienced. Concentrate on stages of her change, using time as the principle for order. As you emphasize stages, resist any temptation to write only a summary.

4. Discuss how different parts of society—school, neighborhood, and family—influenced Wong. Use references to her essay and quotations from it.

Native American Core Values and Cooperative Learning

Lee Little Soldier

As a professor of education at Texas Tech University, Lee Little Soldier has made a specific study of ways of learning in relation to cultural needs and values. For Native Americans, she matches core values with learning styles and concludes that cooperative learning is especially effective. This excerpt is from "Cooperative Learning and the Native American Student," first published in *Phi Delta Kappan*.

1   It is a truism that education must have personal meaning for students. Thus educators must begin where the students are, with material that is relevant to their culture. Yet if education is to provide students with an array of life choices, then mastery of basic skills is also essential. Bridging the gap between the Indian and non-Indian worlds is crucial to the success of schooling for Native Americans.

2   Despite vast differences among Native American tribes, certain core values characterize these diverse cultures. For example, Native Americans respect and value the dignity of the individual, and children are afforded the same respect as adults. Although outsiders may view Native American parents as too permissive, nonetheless they teach their children to seek the wisdom and counsel of their elders. At the same time, traditional Indian families encourage children to develop independence, to make wise decisions, and to abide by them. Thus the locus of control of Indian children is internal, rather than external, and they are not accustomed to viewing adults as authorities who impose their will on others. Native American students entering school for the first time may respond with confusion and passivity to an authoritarian teacher who places many external controls on them.

3   Other core values of Native Americans include cooperation and sharing. The idea of personal property may be foreign. Because traditionally they come from extended families, Native American children tend to be group-centered rather than self-centered. They are accustomed to sharing what-

ever they have with many family members, a habit that can unnerve non-Indian teachers who emphasize labeling possessions and taking care of one's *own* belongings. If such teachers do not understand the notion of common ownership, they can easily mislabel certain behaviors as "stealing."

4   Moreover, Native American students may enter school far more advanced than their non-Indian counterparts in such social behaviors as getting along with others, working in groups, taking turns, and sharing. Too often these strengths are not recognized or rewarded in school.

5   Harmony is another core value of Native Americans—harmony with self, with others, and with nature. Paleo-Indians could not have survived had they not used their environment productively. Even today, Native Americans generally take no more than they can use and live in balance with their surroundings.

6   The problem facing educators is to build a warm, supportive learning environment for Native American students without compromising educational goals and without investing a lot of money—which most school districts don't have. The answer to this problem may lie at least partly in an old concept that is receiving renewed emphasis: cooperative learning.

7   To make cooperative learning work, we must rid ourselves of the notion that students who help other students are somehow "cheating." We in American education are so programmed to view learning as an individual—indeed, a competitive—activity that we tend to overlook the value of group methods for reaching individual goals. Certainly, individual effort has its value, and group effort is not always appropriate, but opportunities abound for cooperation that enhanced individual achievement.

8   Cooperative learning is based on principles of team sports, and Indian students have a heritage of playing team sports and are avid team competitors. When teachers label Native American students as noncompetitive, they often base their conclusion on pitting one student against another in an academic setting. Such individual competition creates a dilemma for the Native American student whose culture traditionally teaches helping rather than competing with others.

9   The potential benefits of cooperative learning for Native American students are clear. Cooperative learning appears to improve student achievement, and it also matches such traditional Indian values and behaviors as respect for the individual, development of an internal locus of control, cooperation, sharing, and harmony. Cooperative learning can improve the attitudes of students toward themselves, toward others, and toward school, as well as increasing cross-racial sharing, understanding and acceptance.

Exercise 5	**DISCUSSION AND CRITICAL THINKING**

1. What is Little Soldier's thesis (par. 1)?

2. What is the difference between being inner-willed (internal locus of control) and outer-willed (par. 2)?

3. Do you feel your reason for behavior comes mainly from inside or outside forces? Or are the reasons complex? Do they vary depending on the situation?

4. In what way are Native American students advanced (par. 4)?

5. According to Little Soldier, is cooperative learning always best?

6. On what principles is cooperative learning based?

7. In what ways are Native American students both competitive and not competitive?

8. In your opinion which three Native American values and behaviors relate most directly to the intentions of cooperative learning (par. 9)?

9. What is your opinion of cooperative, or shared, learning? How does your opinion relate to your own set of values?

Exercise 6	**SUGGESTIONS FOR READING-RELATED WRITING**

Complete one of the following reading-related responses.

1. Write a summary.

2. Write a two-part piece composed of labeled summary and reaction parts.

3. In a reaction response explain how three Native American core values or behaviors such as cooperation, sharing, and harmony relate to cooperative learning.

4. Explain how some of Little Soldier's ideas relate to your experiences with group work, placing you either in agreement or disagreement with her.

5. Explain how your values and behaviors relate to your preferred way(s) of learning.

6. Referring to Little Soldier's essay and to your own experiences, discuss the proper blending of individual and group effort in learning.

Writer's Guidelines: Reading-Related Writing

1. Underlining helps you to read with discrimination.

   - Underline the main ideas in paragraphs.

   - Underline the support for those ideas.

   - Underline answers to questions that you bring to the reading assignment.

   - Underline only the key words.

2. Annotating enables you to actively engage the reading material.

   - Number parts if appropriate.

   - Make comments according to your interests and needs.

3. Outlining the passages you read sheds light on the relationship of ideas, including the major divisions of the passage and their relative importance.

4. Summarizing helps you concentrate on main ideas. A summary

   - cites the author and title of the text.

   - is usually shorter than the original by about two-thirds, although the exact reduction will vary depending on the content of the original.

   - concentrates on the main ideas and includes details only infrequently.

   - changes the original wording without changing the idea.

   - does not evaluate the content or give an opinion in any way (even if you see an error in logic or fact).

   - does not add ideas (even if you have an abundance of related information).

   - does not include any personal comments by the author of the summary (therefore, no use of *I* referring to self).

   - seldom uses quotations (but if you do, only with quotation marks).

   - uses some author tags ("says York," "according to York," or "the author explains") to remind the reader(s) that you are summarizing the material of another writer.

5. Two other types of reading-related writing are

   - the reaction—how the reading relates to you, your experiences, and your attitudes; also, often your critique of the worth and logic of the piece.

   - the two-part response—separates a summary from a reaction.

6. Most ideas in reading-related papers are developed in one or more of these three ways:

   - explanation

   - direct references

   - quotations

7. Documenting is giving credit to borrowed ideas and words.

Narration: Moving Through Time

"The art of writing is the art of applying the seat of the pants to the seat of the chair."

M. H. Vorse

THE QUIGMANS　　　　by Buddy Hickerson

WHADAYA *MEAN* I DO NOTHING? WHY, TODAY ALONE, I PROPPED UP MY FEET, DODGED RESPONSIBILITY, PUSHED MY LUCK AND SAWED IMAGINARY LOGS!

B. Hickerson, copyright Los Angeles Times Syndicate. Reprinted by permission.

Writing Narratives

*I*n our everyday lives, we tell stories and invite other people to do so by asking questions such as "What happened at work today?" and "What did you do last weekend?" We are disappointed when the answer is "Nothing much." We may be equally disappointed when a person doesn't give us enough details or gives us too many and spoils the effect. After all, we are interested in people's stories and in the people who tell them. We like narratives.

What is a narrative? A **narrative** is an account of an incident or a series of incidents that make up a complete and significant action. A narrative can be as short as a joke, as long as a novel, or anything between, including a single paragraph. Each narrative has five properties: situation, conflict, struggle, outcome, and meaning.

Situation

Situation is the background for the action. The situation may be described only briefly, or it may even be implied. ("To celebrate my seventeenth birthday, I went to the Department of Motor Vehicles to take my practical test for my driver's license.")

Conflict

Conflict is friction, such as a problem in the surroundings, with another person, or within the individual. The conflict, which is at the heart of each story, produces struggle. ("It was raining and my appointment was the last one of the day. The examiner was a serious, weary-looking man who reminded me of a bad boss I once had, and I was nervous.")

Struggle

Struggle, which need not be physical, is the manner of dealing with conflict. The struggle adds action or engagement and generates the plot. ("After grinding on the ignition because the engine was already on, I had trouble finding the windshield wiper control. Next I forgot to signal until after I had pulled away from the curb. As we crept slowly down the rain-glazed street, the examiner told me to take the emergency brake off. All the while I listened to his pen scratching on his clipboard. 'Pull over and park,' he said solemnly.")

Outcome

Outcome is the result of the struggle. ("After I parked the car, the examiner told me to relax, and then he talked to me about school. When we continued, somehow I didn't make any errors, and I got my license.")

Meaning

Meaning is the significance of the story, which may be deeply philosophical or simple, stated or implied ("Calmness promotes calmness").

Verb Tense

Because most narratives relate experience in time order, the verb tense is likely to be the past ("She *walked* into the room") rather than the present ("She *walks* into the room"), although you may use either. An unnecessary change in tense tends to distract or confuse readers.

Two generalizations may be useful as you work with verb tense.

- Most narratives (often summaries) based on literature are written in *present tense*.

  > Tom Sawyer *pretends* that painting the fence *is* a special pleasure. His friends *watch* him eagerly. He *talks* and *displays* his joy. They *pay* him to do his work.

- Most historical events and personal experiences are written in the *past tense*.

  > The Battle of Gettysburg *was* the decisive encounter in the Civil War. Although General Lee, the Confederate general in charge of the overall strategy, *was* a wise and experienced man, he *made* some tactical blunders that *led* to a devastating victory by the Union forces.

  > We *walked* down the path to the well-house, attracted by the fragrance of the honeysuckle with which it *was covered*. Someone *was* drawing water and my teacher *placed* my hand under the spout. As the cool stream *gushed* over one hand she *spelled* into the other the word *water*, first slowly, then rapidly.

Helen Keller, *The Story of My Life*

Although Helen Keller chose the conventional past tense for verbs in the past passage, she might have chosen the present tense for a sense of immediacy.

The two main points about tense are the following:

- The generalizations about verb tense selection (using past for the historical and the personal and using present for fiction) are useful.

- The verb tense in a passage should change only when the shift is needed for clarity and emphasis.

Point of View

Point of view shows the writer's relationship to the material, the subject, and it usually does not change within a passage.

If you are conveying personal experience, the point of view will be *first person,* which can be either involved (as a participant) or detached (as an observer). The involved perspective uses *I* more prominently than the detached does.

If you are presenting something from a distance—geographical or historical (for example, telling a story about George Washington)—the point of view will usually be *third person,* and the participants will be referred to as "he," "she," and "they."

Description

A good descriptive writer presents material so that the perceptive reader can read and re-experience the writer's ideas. One device important to that writer is imagery. Images can be perceived through the senses (sight, sound, taste, smell, and touch). A good descriptive writer also gives specific details and presents concrete particulars (actual things) in a convincing way. We read, we visualize, we identify, and—*zap*—we connect with a narrative account.

In the following paragraphs, the images are italicized to emphasize how the author has made us hear, smell, touch, and see. Also note the other specific details.

> Before she had quite arisen, she *called* our names and *issued* orders, and *pushed* her large feet into homemade slippers and *across* the *bare lye-washed wooden floor* to *light* the coal-oil lamp.

> The *lamplight* in the Store gave a *soft* make-believe feeling to our world which made me want to *whisper* and walk about on tip-toe. The *odors* of onions and oranges and kerosene had been *mixing* all night and wouldn't be disturbed until the wooded slat was removed from the door and the early morning air forced its way in with the bodies of people who had walked miles to reach the pickup place.

Maya Angelou, "Cotton-Picking Time"

Note the use of specific information in the next paragraph.

> On one recent Saturday afternoon a Latino fifth-grader, wearing the same type of hightop tennis shoes I wore as a ten-year-old on that same street corner, strode up to Señor Farrillas' snow-cone pushcart. The kid pulled out a pocketful of dimes and bought two *raspadas*. One for himself, and one for his school chum—a Vietnamese kid. He was wearing hightops, too. They both ordered strawberry, as I recall.

Luis Torres, "Los Chinos Discover el Barrio"

Torres presents the material so you can visualize it. Try to picture this, instead: "The other day I saw a youngster buy a refreshment for himself and his friend." Of course, that is what happened, but very little narrative/descriptive communication takes place in this abbreviated version. In Torres's account, you know when and where the action took place. You know what the kids were wearing, and you know that the author (point of view as technique) identifies with the kids. They buy strawberry *raspadas* from Señor Farrillas. The Latino kid pays for the *raspadas* with "a pocketful of dimes." Did you ever, as a kid, put your hand in the pocket of some tight jeans and try to pull out those dimes with a balled fist? We identify, and the imagery registers. We may not have visited that street corner in reality, but vicariously we take a trip with Torres.

Dialogue

Dialogue is used purposefully in narration to characterize, particularize, and support ideas. It shows us how people talk and think, as individuals or as representatives of society. Not every narrative requires dialogue.

Note in the following paragraph that the snatches of dialogue are brief. The language will ring true to Asian immigrants and those who have been around Asian immigrants. It is starkly realistic yet sympathetically engaging in context so that we are convinced of its authenticity and drawn into the story. This passage is from "The Struggle to Be an All-American Girl." As narrator, the author was present when the utterances in this paragraph were made.

> My brother was even more fanatical than I about speaking English. He was especially hard on my mother, criticizing her, often cruelly, for her pidgin speech—smatterings of Chinese scattered like chop suey in her conversation. "It's not 'What it is,' Mom," he'd say in exasperation. "It's 'What *is* it, what *is* it!'" Sometimes Mom might leave out an occasional "the" or "a," or perhaps a verb of being. He would stop her in mid-sentence: "Say it again, Mom. Say it right." When he tripped over his own tongue, he'd blame it on her: "See, Mom, it's all your fault. You set a bad example."

Elizabeth Wong, "The Struggle to Be an All-American Girl"

Before turning to your own writing of narratives, let's look at a range of them, some composed by professional writers and some by students. These examples will show you different forms and different techniques, and they will furnish you with subject material for your own composition in paragraphs, essays, and journals.

Connecting Reading and Writing

W-A-T-E-R
Helen Keller

Helen Keller was a remarkable person. With the help of her teacher and companion, Anne Sullivan, she conquered the handicaps of blindness and deafness and became one of the most famous and admired persons of her time. In this paragraph unit, she wrote about what was perhaps the most important, constructive event in her life.

1   One day, while I was playing with my new doll, Miss Sullivan put my big rag doll into my lap also, spelled "d-o-l-l" and tried to make me understand that "d-o-l-l" applied to both. Earlier in the day we had had a tussle over the words "m-u-g" and "w-a-t-e-r." Miss Sullivan had tried to impress it upon me that "m-u-g" is *mug* and that "w-a-t-e-r" is *water,* but I persisted in confounding the two. In despair she had dropped the subject for the time, only to renew it at the first opportunity. I became impatient at her repeated attempts and, seizing the new doll, I dashed it upon the floor. I was keenly delighted when I felt the fragments of the broken doll at my feet. Neither sorrow nor regret followed my passionate outburst. I had not loved the doll. In the still, dark world in which I lived there was no strong sentiment of tenderness. I felt my teacher sweep the fragments to one side of the hearth, and I had a sense of satisfaction that the cause of my discomfort was removed. She brought me my hat, and I knew I was going out into the warm sunshine. This thought, if a wordless sensation may be called a thought, made me hop and skip with pleasure.

2   We walked down the path to the well-house, attracted by the fragrance of the honeysuckle with which it was covered. Someone was drawing water and my teacher placed my hand under the spout. As the cool stream gushed over one hand she spelled into the other the word *water,* first slowly, then rapidly. I stood still, my whole attention fixed upon the motions of her fingers. Suddenly I felt a misty consciousness as of something forgotten—a thrill of returning thought; and somehow the mystery of language was revealed to me. I knew then that "w-a-t-e-r" meant the wonderful cool something that was flowing over my hand. That living word awakened my soul, gave it light, hope, joy, set it free! There were barriers still, it is true, but barriers that could in time be swept away.

Exercise 1   **DISCUSSION AND CRITICAL THINKING**

1. What is the situation?

2. What is the conflict?

3. What struggle occurs?

4. What is the outcome of the struggle?

5. What is the meaning of this narrative?

B. B. King Live!
Andrea Lee

As narrated in The Blues Abroad, *the situation here is potentially dramatic. The audience in the concert hall is Russian; the performer is African American. The audience loves music but is not familiar with B. B. King's style. King wants involvement from audience members, but they don't know what to do.*

A slick-haired Russian M.C. announced B. B. King ("A great Negritanski musician"), and then King was on stage with his well-known guitar—Lucille—and a ten-man ensemble. As King and the ensemble swung into "Why I Sing the Blues," one could sense the puzzlement of the Russian audience. "Negro" music to them meant jazz or spirituals, but this was something else. Also, there was the question of response. B. B. King is a great, warm presence when he performs, and he asks his audiences to pour themselves out to him in return. King teases his audiences, urging them to clap along, to whistle, to hoot their appreciation, like the congregations in the Southern churches in which he grew up. But to Russians, such behavior suggests a lack of culture and an almost frightening disorder. Though obviously impressed, the audience at first kept a respectful silence during the numbers, as it might at the symphony. (Only the foreigners shouted and stomped out the beat; we found the Russians around us staring at us openmouthed.) Then King played an irresistible riff, stopped, and leaned toward the audience with his hand cupped to his ear. The audience caught on and began to clap. King changed the beat, and waited for the audience to catch up. Then he changed it again. Soon the whole place was clapping along to "Get Off My Back, Woman," and there were even a few timid shouts and whistles. King, who has carried the blues to Europe, Africa, and the Far East, had broken the ice one more time.

Exercise 2   **DISCUSSION AND CRITICAL THINKING**

1. What is the situation?

2. What is the conflict?

3. What struggle occurs?

4. What is the outcome?

5. What is the meaning?

The Pie
Gary Soto

Author and teacher Gary Soto here discusses the time when he gave in to temptation, swapping immediate gratification for ensuing guilt. After committing his act, he returned to his home, where he "knew" that others knew. It is the classic story of crime and self-punishment, filtered through childhood perceptions, which, of course, magnify and distort. This is taken from his collection of essays *A Summer Life* (1990).

1   I knew enough about hell to stop me from stealing. I was holy in almost every bone. Some days I recognized the shadows of angels flopping on the backyard grass, and other days I heard faraway messages in the plumbing that howled underneath the house when I crawled there looking for something to do.

2   But boredom made me sin. Once, at the German Market, I stood before a rack of pies, my sweet tooth gleaming and the juice of guilt wetting my underarms. I gazed at the nine kinds of pie, pecan and apple being my favorites, although cherry looked good, and my dear, fat-faced chocolate was always a good bet. I nearly wept trying to decide which to steal and, forgetting the flowery dust priests give off, the shadow of angels and the proximity of God howling in the plumbing underneath the house, sneaked a pie behind my coffee-lid frisbee and walked to the door, grinning to the bald grocer whose forehead shone with a window of light.

3   "No one saw," I muttered to myself, the pie like a discus in my hand, and hurried across the street, where I sat on someone's lawn. The sun wavered between the branches of a yellowish sycamore. A squirrel nailed itself high on the trunk, where it forked into two large bark-scabbed limbs. Just as I was going to work my cleanest finger into the pie, a neighbor came out to the porch for his mail. He looked at me, and I got up and headed for home. I raced on skinny legs to my block, but slowed to a quick walk when I couldn't wait any longer. I held the pie to my nose and breathed in its sweetness. I licked some of the crust and closed my eyes as I took a small bite.

4   In my front yard, I leaned against a car fender and panicked about stealing the apple pie. I knew an apple got Eve in deep trouble with snakes because Sister Marie had shown us a film about Adam and Eve being cast into the desert, and what scared me more than falling from grace was being thirsty for the rest of my life. But even that didn't stop me from clawing a chunk from the pie tin and pushing it into the cavern of my mouth. The slop was sweet and gold-colored in the afternoon sun. I laid more pieces on my tongue, wet finger-dipping pieces, until I was finished and felt like crying because it was about the best thing I had ever tasted. I realized right there and then, in my sixth year, in my tiny body of two hundred bones and three or four sins, that the best things in life came stolen. I wiped my sticky

fingers on the grass and rolled my tongue over the corners of my mouth. A burp perfumed the air.

5   I felt bad not sharing with Cross-Eyed Johnny, a neighbor kid. He stood over my shoulder and asked, "Can I have some?" Crust fell from my mouth, and my teeth were bathed with the jam-like filling. Tears blurred my eyes as I remembered the grocer's forehead. I remembered the other pies on the rack, the warm air of the fan above the door and the car that honked as I crossed the street without looking.

6   "Get away," I had answered Cross-Eyed Johnny. He watched my fingers greedily push big chunks of pie down my throat. He swallowed and said in a whisper, "Your hands are dirty," then returned home to climb his roof and sit watching me eat the pie by myself. After a while, he jumped off and hobbled away because the fall had hurt him.

7   I sat on the curb. The pie tin glared at me and rolled away when the wind picked up. My face was sticky with guilt. A car honked, and the driver knew. Mrs. Hancock stood on her lawn, hands on hip, and she knew. My mom, peeling a mountain of potatoes at the Redi-Spud factory, knew. I got to my feet, stomach taut, mouth tired of chewing, and flung my frisbee across the street, its shadow like the shadow of an angel fleeing bad deeds. I retrieved it, jogging slowly. I flung it again until I was bored and thirsty.

8   I returned home to drink water and help my sister glue bottle caps onto cardboard, a project for summer school. But the bottle caps bored me, and the water soon filled me up more than the pie. With the kitchen stifling with heat and lunatic flies, I decided to crawl underneath our house and lie in the cool shadows listening to the howling sound of plumbing. Was it God? Was it Father, speaking from death, or Uncle with his last shiny dime? I listened, ear pressed to a cold pipe, and heard a howl like the sea. I lay until I was cold and then crawled back to the light, rising from one knee, then another, to dust off my pants and squint in the harsh light. I looked and saw the glare of a pie tin on a hot day. I knew sin was what you take and didn't give back.

Exercise 3   **DISCUSSION AND CRITICAL THINKING**

1. What is Soto's motive—the real motive—in taking the pie?

2. What occurs between temptation and conscience?

3. What forms does guilt take?

4. How realistic is this story of youthful crime and self-punishment?

5. If you were Soto's parent (or the shop owner) and you knew what he had done and what he had felt, what would you do?

Closets and Keepsakes
Willi Coleman

Certain moments of growing up are indelible, and recalling them can be a comfort, especially when we have problems. Those were the times when someone listened and made us feel special. Willi Coleman had such moments with her mother. Coming across mementos from her childhood brings back with poignant clarity just what her mother did for her. This is about closets, and keepsakes, and pivotal moments.

1   Closets are the city dweller's storeroom, attic, and basement. Although I've been known to keep boxes under my bed or stuffed behind the sofa, it is the shelves and back recesses of a closet which seem to hold a rare assortment of items. There are some very special memories contained in cardboard boxes and brown paper bags of varying sizes. Such things I make no pretense of wanting to throw away or share with others during sophisticated wine and cheese romps down memory lane. Some things are too precious for either category. Occasionally it is up to scraps of paper and old photographs to link you with yourself through the passing of time and shifts in lifestyles. And so, we move battered boxes and newspaper-protected, oddly shaped bundles into cramped studio or tenth-floor "garden" apartments. Inside these packages are parts of ourselves that we sometimes refuse to share with curious lovers and newfound friends. Decor and lifestyles change, but the stuff in the back of the closet remains a constant beacon calling us back.

2   Sitting on the floor with the contents of two boxes spread out before me, I feel the weight of a wrinkled brown paper bag. It is heavy and crumpled to fit the shape of its contents. The straightening comb inside has slightly bent teeth, contoured by years of being dropped from less than skillful hands and blackened by just as much use. A few remaining glints of bright metal transport me instantly to a time when I was very small, very southern . . . and quite happy. There was a time . . . there really was a time when hot combs were for holidays and permanents did not exist. Political correctness be damned, we loved the ritual as well as the end results. Both were powerful lines of love held in the hands of women and shaping the lives of girls. The route taken was as old as fire and remains equally as irreplaceable.

3   I remember being eight years old and sitting on the floor, my head even with my mother's knees. She above me, seated on a chair, shifted her weight from side to side organizing wide tooth comb, brush, pins, straightening comb and serious hair grease. Her hands pulled, darted, twisted and patted as if she were directing the Sunday morning choir for "Light of the World" Baptist Church. Two smart taps on the left side of my head was the signal for me to turn my head to the right and vice versa. When I allowed my head to wander out of her reach or without her direction my reward was three sharp raps on the top of my head. It never hurt, and the ritual never gave way to verbal directions. It was always three slaps on the head with a wide tooth comb . . . never two or four.

4   Mama was a creature of habit and our sessions together could halt time, still waters, and predict the future. Any soul-wrenching childhood catastrophe could be borne until it was again my turn on the floor between my

mother's knees. On some occasions the first flap of the comb brought not my usual obedient response but a sniffle. On the second flap I escalated to a whimper and the third was almost anticipated by a full-scale yell. Always an overly dramatic child, I played the sniffle, whimper, yell routine for a full three minutes to my one-woman audience. In due time I would quiet down just enough to hear the head tapper inquire in words that never changed . . . "Lil old negro . . . what in the world is wrong with you?" The sentence had a rhythm all its own. Negro came out "knee-grow" and "world" was drawn out as if to give the sound a chance to circle the entire universe. Mama had her way of pampering each of her children. She did not like "nobody's rotten kids" and had no intentions of raising any in her house. Behavior which would not have been tolerated otherwise received lesser penalties on hair day. The invitation of her words immediately prompted me to unburden myself. It never crossed my mind to hold back the hurt, fear, or anger. Long before I was four I knew that with me on the floor and Mama waving her comb I could get more mileage out of a mere whimper than a loud wail at any other time.

5   Except for special occasions Mama came home from work early on Saturdays. She spent six days a week mopping, waxing, and dusting other women's houses and keeping out of reach of other women's husbands. Saturday nights were reserved for "taking care of them girls' hair" and the telling of stories. Some of which included a recitation of what she had endured and how she had triumphed over "folks that were lower than dirt" and "no-good snakes in the grass." She combed, patted, twisted, and talked, saying things which would have embarrassed or shamed her at other times. There were days when I was sure that she had ceased to be the mother we all knew. The smell of warm oils, clean hair, and a Black working woman's anger had transformed her into somebody else. She talked with ease and listened with undivided attention. Sometimes the magic lasted for hours. By the time my sister had taken her place on the floor I had covered the two blocks to the store. With whatever change could be squeezed out of Mama's "four dollars a day plus carfare," I would carefully choose day-old pastry and get back home before my sister's last plait was in place. There never was a time when I did not wonder just what tales and secrets I had missed. The eleven months which separated my sister and me were, I suspected, most evident in what was said during my absence.

6   But even this small slight has carved out a warm place to hide in my memories. For, at my mother's signal, I had moved away from those Saturday hair sessions, as if from a safe harbor, carrying with me: "Child, go look at yourself in the mirror." It was always said as if whatever I saw surpassed good and bordered on the truly wonderful. And I, searching for my own reflection, walked away oblivious to the love and life-sustaining messages which had seeped into my pores as I sat on the floor of my mother's kitchen.

| **Exercise 4** | **VOCABULARY HIGHLIGHTS** |

Write a short definition of each word as it is used in the essay. (Paragraph numbers are given in parentheses.) Be prepared to use the words in your own sentences.

sophisticated (1)   escalated (4)

decor (1)   sustaining (6)

contoured (2)

Exercise 5	DISCUSSION AND CRITICAL THINKING

1. At what point in Coleman's life did the sessions with her mother become important to her?

2. Were the sessions deliberately planned by her mother?

3. Were the sessions mutually satisfying? Explain.

4. Precisely why were the sessions pivotal experiences for Coleman?

Student Writers: Demonstrations and Readings

Brittany Markovic is by nature an adventurer. As a student pilot, she soars the skies and shoots touch-and-go landings at her local airport as if she has no fear. But the thought of allowing someone to stick a needle through her tongue was another matter. Like most dramatic events in life, this one, with all its details, became fixed vividly in her mind and was a natural topic for her narrative.

Markovic's Writing Process Worksheet, which follows, shows you how her writing evolved from idea to final draft. To conserve space here, the freewriting and the rough draft marked for revision have been omitted. The balance of her worksheet has been lengthened for you to be able to see parts of her work in their entirety.

You will find a full-size blank worksheet on page 5. It can be photocopied, filled in, and submitted with each assignment if your instructor directs you to do so.

Writing Process Worksheet

TITLE I Get a Pierce

NAME Britanny Markovic   **DUE DATE** Friday, April 28, at 9 a.m.

ASSIGNMENT	In the space below, write whatever you need to know about your assignment, including information about the topic, audience, pattern of writing, length, whether to include a rough draft or revised drafts, and whether your paper must be typed.

Write a narrative paragraph of about three hundred words on something you did that was daring, perhaps surprising even yourself. Because only you have experienced this in your fashion, explain to your audience in this class how you felt about what was happening. Submit this completed form, a rough draft marked for revision, and a typed final draft.

STAGE ONE   **Explore**   Freewrite, brainstorm (list), cluster, or take notes as directed by your instructor. Use the back of this page or separate paper if you need more space.

Listing

plan
talk to friends
get reference
situation | trip to Hollywood
friend with me
slow to go inside
_____ go in
talk to piercer
look at jewelry
go through prep
conflict | go to room
stick out tongue
_____ close my eyes
tongue marked
struggle | tongue stabbed
_____ pain
all over
outcome | relieved
pleased
_____
meaning | look back to event
look ahead to tattoo

STAGE TWO   **Organize**   Write a topic sentence or thesis; label the subject and the treatment parts.

<u>I</u> <u>am a person with a special mission as I enter the the tattoo and</u>
subject   treatment
<u>piercing shop.</u>

Write an outline or an outline alternative.

I. Situation
   A. Mission
   B. Enter shop
II. Conflict
   A. Fear
     1. Sweaty palms
     2. Butterflies
   B. Meet my piercer

   III. Struggle
      A. Select jewelry
      B. Present tongue
      C. Feel pain
      D. Tongue returns with pierce
   IV. Outcome
      A. Deed done
      B. Tongue pierced
    V. Meaning
      A. Relieved
      B. Pleased

STAGE THREE   **Write**   On separate paper, write and then revise your paper as many times as necessary for <u>c</u>oherence, <u>l</u>anguage (usage, tone, and diction), <u>u</u>nity, <u>e</u>mphasis, <u>s</u>upport, and <u>s</u>entences (CLUESS). Read your paper aloud to hear and correct any grammatical errors or awkward-sounding sentences.

Edit any problems in fundamentals, such as <u>c</u>apitalization, <u>o</u>missions, <u>p</u>unctuation, and <u>s</u>pelling (COPS).

Final Draft

I Get a Pierce
Brittany Markovic

Topic sentence <u>I am a person with a special mission as I enter The Gauntlet tattoo and piercing shop with sweaty palms and butterflies in my stomach.</u> I walk up **Situation** to the heavily tattooed and pierced girl standing behind a glass display case and tell her I have an appointment for a tongue piercing. She is sur- **Conflict** prisingly friendly (in comparison to her tough appearance) and tells me that she will be my piercer. After I select the length and thickness of the barbell-shaped jewelry, I follow her up a narrow staircase to a small room **Struggle** that looks like a doctor's office. She instructs me to rinse with mouthwash and sit up on the padded table. She then gives me a detailed description of what is going to happen. Most people feel no pain, she says. I answer quickly "yes" when she asks if I am ready. I stick out my tongue, and she holds onto it with a pair of forceps. She marks the spot with a blue ink dot. She picks up the needle with the jewelry inside and poises it over my tongue. She tells me she will count to three and then pierce me. My mind is racing with thoughts about the anticipated pain and the unexplainable reason I am doing this. She counts to three and WHOOSH my whole body is hit with a wave of pain. The suddenness and severity of it is a rush. She continues to narrate as she assembles the jewelry, and when she releases the tongue, it falls back into my mouth with a heavy KERPLUNK that makes me smile. The deed is done and I am happy both that it is over and that I was **Outcome** able to do something I had wanted to do for a long time. After two years, I still don't know exactly why I did it except that I just wanted to see what it **Meaning** was like. It felt good to crawl out of my plain Jane jeans and T-shirt image and do something totally out of character. Next mission—tattoo!

Exercise 6	DISCUSSION AND CRITICAL THINKING

1. Is there any point at which Markovic is close to deciding not to get the pierce?

2. Does she have a good understanding of her motive? Discuss.

3. Does she omit any information you wished you knew?

4. If you were Markovic's parent and you read this account, how would you react?

5. Now Markovic is considering a tattoo. It is two years later. What would you advise? Why?

6. Is it acceptable to have a meaning that is actually not completely clear to the writer?

A Bee in My Bonnet
Elizabeth Brock

This story from student Elizabeth Brock's childhood is much more amusing to her now than it once was, and at a deeper level it reminds her of a love that transcends all the embarrassment of a little girl. The setting of the narrative is one that Brock expects to revisit, for she intends to become an elementary school teacher.

My grandmother, who came from the hill country of Oklahoma, had a wonderful vocabulary of folk expressions and country words. She also had a collection of stories that I got to know by heart. In short, she was my favorite person—the owner of all wisdom and goodness—and whatever she said was, as she would phrase it, "the gospel truth." Of course, as a child before I started to school, I wanted to talk like her. Then in the first grade, I discovered that Grandma's language could get me laughed at.

At the beginning of that school year, we were reading little books about many countries, places that I had never heard of. One book was about Greece. It was full of all kinds of difficult words such as "Socrates" and "olympics," and it had pictures of buildings that were on top of hills and looked different from any I'd seen. All of us in the Blue group had copies of the book on Greece, but our teacher had a special book. It was large with colorful paintings and drawings.

One day she brought it to our table and began to read. Then she got to the word *pillar*. "Does anyone know what the word *pillar* means?" she asked. I was shy and didn't want to answer, but when no one else knew, my hand rose slowly as if I thought someone might slap it at any time. When she called me by name, I said, "A pillar is something you put your head on when you're going to sleep." For a brief moment there was silence, and I felt proud. I even thought of my grandmother saying, "Take your pillar and go in there and get your nap."

Then the teacher began laughing. "No, Elizabeth," she said. "You're talking about a pillow. A pillow is what you put under your head." With that explanation, the students began to laugh, and I tried to laugh too, but my face was both frozen and red. The teacher held up her book and pointed to some large round supports on a Greek temple. "These are pillars," she said.

That one incident would set me back for the whole year in volunteering to answer questions. I could never seem to forget it. But I didn't tell anyone in my family about it. After school, I just went home and stomped around a little, and Grandma said, "You got a bee in your bonnet today, honey?" and I said I did. I still liked the way she talked, but right then I started sorting out the Grandma language from my school language.

Though Grandma has died, I look back and remember her words with great fondness. They didn't help me in school, but they are my family words— my country grandma words that bring back poignant memories—and those words are some of the best I've ever heard.

| **Exercise 7** | **DISCUSSION AND CRITICAL THINKING** |

1. Annotate the essay for situation, conflict, struggle, outcome, and meaning.

2. As Brock looks at this experience in retrospect, what are her feelings about it?

3. Why is dialogue especially useful and relevant in Brock's essay?

4. Does she wish her grandmother had spoken any other way?

5. The introduction to this essay points out that Brock intends to be a teacher. How might she use this experience in her profession, especially in dealing with students who are just learning the language or are learning standard English?

Practicing Narrative Patterns

Some narratives seem more structured than others, but all have the same basic patterns. The parts, especially conflict and struggle, will vary in extent, depending on the circumstances.

| **Exercise 8** | **COMPLETING NARRATIVE PATTERNS** |

Fill in the blanks to complete the following pattern of this narrative based on the short story "The Gift of the Magi," by O. Henry.

I. Situation

    A. A poor man and woman much in love

        1. Man with a watch but no watch chain

        2. Woman with a fine head of hair but no comb

    B. Holiday time

II. Conflict

    A. Mutual desire to give holiday presents

    B. No money to _____

III. Struggle

    A. Man sells watch to buy woman _____

    B. Woman cuts off hair and sells it to buy man _____

IV. Outcome

    A. Man gives hairless woman _____

    B. Woman gives watchless man _____

V. Meaning

    A. Love in _____

    B. Ends with _____

✎ Topics for Writing Narratives

**Reading-Related
Topics**

"W-A-T-E-R"

1. This passage is an epiphany—a moment that reveals an important truth (through setup, incident, and understanding). After Helen Keller went through that one experience, her life was transformed. Using the "w-a-t-e-r" passage as a model, write your own epiphany about the first time you knew or understood something about a concept such as love, caring, or family. Or write about the first time you realized you could read or learn another language.

"B. B. King Live!"

2. Using the paragraph on B. B. King as a model for organization, write a narrative account of the first few minutes of a concert you attended, showing how the audience became involved in the event. Or, present the factors that negatively influenced the audience so that it did *not* become involved.

3. Pretend you are a Russian music lover at the B. B. King concert in Moscow. Write a narrative about how you became involved in the audience response.

"The Pie"

4. Write about the incident from the pie's point of view.

5. Write about one of your own childhood experiences in which you did something wrong or perceived that you did.

"Closets and Keepsakes"

6. Create and describe a comfort session. Include specific information that would be believable for both mother and daughter, or father and son, to relate.

7. Write about occasions (work, play, walks, eating out) when you had comfort conversations with grown-ups such as parents or grandparents.

"I Get a Pierce"

8. Write about a time when you or someone you know did something that was daring or out of character.

9. Write about a time when you were tempted and almost did something that was out of character.

"A Bee in My Bonnet"

10. Write about a language- or culture-based incident that caused you momentary embarrassment.

11. Write about a time when you helped a person avoid or get over an incident that was embarrassing because of a language or cultural matter.

Career-Related Topics

12. Write a narrative account of a work-related encounter between a manager and a worker and briefly explain the significance of the event.

13. Write a narrative account of an encounter between a customer and a salesperson. Explain what went right and what went wrong.

14. Write a narrative account of how a person solved a work-related problem perhaps by using technology.

15. Write a narrative account of a salesperson handling a customer's complaint. Critique the procedure.

General Topics *Each of the following topics concerns the writing of a narrative with meaning beyond the story itself. The narrative will be used to inform or persuade in relation to a clearly stated idea.*

16. Write a narrative based on a topic sentence such as this: "One experience showed me what _____ [pain, fear, anger, love, sacrifice, dedication, joy, sorrow, shame, pride] was really like."

17. Write a simple narrative about a fire, a riot, an automobile accident, a rescue, shoplifting, or some other unusual happening you witnessed.

18. Write a narrative that supports (or opposes) the idea of a familiar saying such as one of the following:

You never know who a friend is 'til you need one.

It isn't what you know, it's who you know.

A bird in the hand is worth two in the bush.

Fools and their money are soon parted.

A person who is absent is soon forgotten.

Better to be alone than to be in bad company.

A person in a passion rides a mad horse.

Borrowing is the mother of trouble.

A person who marries for money earns it.

The person who lies down with dogs gets up with fleas.

Never give advice to a friend.

If it isn't broken, don't fix it.

Nice people finish last.

Every person has a price.

You get what you pay for.

Haste makes waste.

The greatest remedy for anger is delay.

A person full of him- or herself is empty.

To forget a wrong is the best revenge.

Money is honey, my little sonny,
And a rich man's joke is always funny.

Writer's Guidelines: Narration

1. Include these points so you will be sure you have a complete narrative:

   - situation

   - conflict

   - struggle

   - outcome

   - meaning

2. Use these techniques or devices as appropriate:

   - images that appeal to the senses (sight, smell, taste, hearing, touch) and other details to advance action

   - dialogue

   - transitional devices (such as *next, soon, after, later, then, finally, when, following*) to indicate chronological order

3. Give details concerning action.

4. Be consistent with point of view and verb tense.

5. Keep in mind that most narratives written as college assignments will have an expository purpose; that is, they explain a specific idea.

6. Consider working with a short time frame for short writing assignments. The scope would usually be no more than one incident of brief duration for one paragraph. For example, writing about an entire graduation ceremony might be too complicated, but concentrating on the moment when you walked forward to receive the diploma or the moment when the relatives and friends come down on the field could work very well.

8

Description: Moving Through Space

"My task . . . is, by the power of the written word, to make you hear, to make you feel—it is, before all, to make you see. That—and no more—is everything."

Joseph Conrad

THE QUIGMANS   by Buddy Hickerson

B. Hickerson, copyright Los Angeles Times Syndicate. Reprinted by permission.

Writing Description

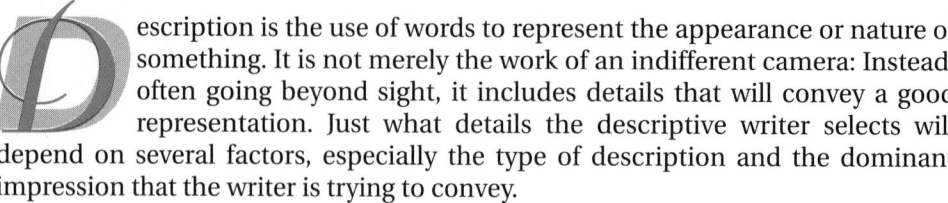

escription is the use of words to represent the appearance or nature of something. It is not merely the work of an indifferent camera: Instead, often going beyond sight, it includes details that will convey a good representation. Just what details the descriptive writer selects will depend on several factors, especially the type of description and the dominant impression that the writer is trying to convey.

Types of Description

Depending on how you wish to treat your subject material, your description is likely to be either objective or subjective.

Effective *objective description* presents the subject clearly and directly as it exists outside the realm of emotions. If you are explaining the function of the heart, the characteristics of a computer chip, or the renovation of a manufacturing facility, your description will probably feature specific, impersonal details. Most technical and scientific writing is objective in this sense. It is likely to be practical and utilitarian, making little use of speculation or poetic technique and featuring mainly what can be seen.

Effective *subjective description* is also concerned with clarity and it may be direct, but it conveys a feeling about the subject and sets a mood while making a point. Because most expression involves personal views, even when it explains by analysis, subjective description (often called *emotional description*) has a broader range of uses than objective description.

Descriptive passages can be a combination of objective and subjective description; only the larger context of the passage will reveal the main intent. The following description of a baseball begins with objective treatment and then moves to subjective.

Objective treatment moving to subjective treatment

> It weighs just over five ounces and measures between 2.86 and 2.94 inches in diameter. It is made of a composition-cork nucleus encased in two thin layers of rubber, one black and one red, surrounded by 121 yards of tightly wrapped blue-gray wool yarn, 45 yards of white wool yarn, 53 more yards of blue-gray wool yarn, 150 yards of fine cotton yarn, a coat of rubber cement, and a cowhide (formerly horsehide) exterior, which is held together with 216 slightly raised red cotton stitches. Printed certifications, endorsements, and outdoor advertising spherically attest to its authenticity. . . . Feel the ball, turn it over in your hand; hold it across the seam or the other way, with the seam just to the side of your middle finger. Speculation stirs. You want to get outdoors and throw this spare and sensual object to somebody or, at the very least, watch somebody else throw it. The game has begun.

Roger Angell, "On the Ball"

The following subjective description, also on the subject of baseball, is designed to move the emotions while informing.

The following details relate to the paradoxes.

Note the emotional appeals, the subjective approach.

> The Babe was a bundle of paradoxes. Somehow one of the most appealing things about him was that he was neither built, nor did he look like, an athlete. He did not even look like a ballplayer. Although he stood six feet two inches and weighed 220 pounds, his body was pear-shaped and even when in tip-top condition he had a bit of a belly. His barrel always seemed too much for his legs, which tapered into a pair of ankles as slender almost as those of a girl. The great head perched upon a pair of round and unathletic shoulders, presented a moon of a face, the feature of which was the

flaring nostrils of a nose that was rather like a snout. His voice was deep and hoarse, his speech crude and earthy, his ever-ready laughter a great, rumbling gurgle that arose from the caverns of his middle. He had an eye that was abnormally quick, nerves and muscular reactions to match, a supple wrist, a murderous swing, and a gorgeously truculent, competitive spirit.

Paul Gallico, "Babe Ruth"

Techniques of Descriptive Writing

As a writer of description, you will need to focus your work to accomplish three specific tasks:

- Emphasize a single point (dominant impression).
- Establish a perspective from which to describe your subject (point of view).
- Position the details for coherence (order).

Dominant Impression

See if you can find the dominant impression in this description:

> Please help me find my dog. He is a mongrel with the head of a poodle and the body of a wolfhound, and his fur is patchy and dingy-gray. He has only three legs, but despite his arthritis, he uses them pretty well to hobble around and scratch his fleas and mange. His one seeing eye is cloudy, so he runs with his head sideways. His ragged, twisted ears enable him to hear loud sounds, which startle his troubled nervous system and cause him to howl pitifully. If you give him a scrap of food, he will gum it up rapidly and try to wag his broken tail. He answers to the name of Lucky.

Of course, the dominant impression, what is being emphasized, is "misery," or "unlucky," not "lucky." The dominant impression emerges from a pattern of details, often involving repetition of one idea with different particulars. Word choice, which is of paramount importance, depends on your purpose in writing and on your audience.

If you are eating hamburgers in a restaurant, and you say to your companion, "This food is good," your companion may understand all he or she needs to understand on the subject. After all, your companion can see you sitting there chewing the food, smacking your lips, and wiping the sauce off your chin. But if you write that sentence and send it to someone, your reader may be puzzled. Although the reader may know you fairly well, he or she may not know the meaning of "good" (to eat? to purchase for others? to sell?) or of "this food" (What kind? Where is it? How is it special? How is it prepared? What qualities does it have?).

To convey your main concern effectively to readers, you will want to give some sensory impressions. These sensory impressions, collectively called *imagery*, refer to that which can be experienced by the senses—what we can see, smell, taste, hear, and touch. You may use *figures of speech* to convey these sensory impressions; figures of speech involve comparisons of unlike things that, nevertheless, have something in common.

The imagery in this passage is italicized.

Topic sentence
Dominant impression

Image (touch)
Images (sight)
Image (sound)

Sitting here in Harold's Hefty Burgers at midnight, I am convinced that I am eating the <u>ultimate form of food</u>. The *buns* are *feathery soft* to the touch but *heavy* in the hand and *soggy* inside. As I take a full-mouth, no-nonsense bite, the *melted cheese* and *juices cascade* over my fingers and make little *oil slicks* on the *vinyl table* below. I *chew noisily* and happily like a puppy at a food bowl, stopping occasionally to flush down the *rich, thick taste* of *spicy animal fat* with a *swig* from a *chilled mug of fizzing root beer* that *prickles* my *nose.* Over at the grill, *the smell of frying onions creeps away* stealthily on *invisible feet* to conquer the neighborhood, turning hundreds of ordinary *citizens* like me into drooling, stomach growling, fast-food addicts, who *trudge* in from the night like the walking dead and *call out* the same order, time after time. "Hefty Burger." "Hefty Burger." "Hefty Burger."

Image (taste)
Image (smell)
Figure of speech

Image (sight)
Image (sound)

Note movement through time and space

Dale Scott, "Hefty Burger"

In reading Scott's enthusiastic endorsement of the Hefty Burger, the reader will have no trouble understanding the idea that he liked the food. Through imagery, Scott has involved the reader in what he has seen, smelled, heard, tasted, and touched. He has also used figures of speech, including these examples:

Simile: a comparison using *like* or *as* — "chew noisily and happily like a puppy"

Metaphor: a comparison using word replacement — "feathery [instead of 'delicately'] soft"

Personification: an expression giving human characteristics to something not human — "smell of frying onions creeps away stealthily on invisible feet to conquer" [instead of "spreads to entice"]

Subjective description is likely to make more use of imagery, figurative language, and words rich in associations than is objective description. But just as a fine line cannot always be drawn between the objective and the subjective, a fine line cannot always be drawn between word choice in one and in the other. However, we can say with certainty that whatever the type of description, careful word choice will always be important. Consider the following points about word choice (diction), point of view, and order.

Word Choice: General and Specific, Abstract and Concrete

To move from the general to the specific is to move from the whole class or group of items to individual ones; for example,

General	*Specific*	*More Specific*
food	hamburger	Hefty Burger
mess	grease	oil slicks on the table
drink	soda	mug of root beer
odor	smell from grill	smell of frying onions

Words are classified as abstract or concrete, depending on what they refer to. *Abstract words* refer to qualities or ideas: *good, ordinary, ultimate, truth, beauty, maturity, love. Concrete words* refer to things or a substance; they have reality: *onions, grease, buns, tables, food.* Specific concrete words, sometimes called *concrete particulars,* often support generalizations effectively and convince the reader of the accuracy of the description.

Never try to give all the details in a description. Instead, be selective. Pick only those details that you need to project a dominant impression, always taking into account the knowledge and attitudes of your readers. To reintroduce an idea from the beginning of this chapter, description is not photographic. If you wish to describe a person, select the traits that will project your intended dominant impression. If you wish to describe a landscape, do not give all the details that you might find in a picture; on the contrary, pick the details that support your intended dominant impression. That extremely important dominant impression is directly linked to your purpose. It is created by the judicious choice and arrangement of images, figurative language, and revealing details.

Point of View

Point of view shows the writer's relationship to the subject, thereby establishing the perspective from which the subject is described. It rarely changes within a passage. Two terms usually associated with fiction writing, *first person* and *third person,* also pertain to descriptive writing.

If you want to convey personal experience, your point of view will be *first person,* which can be either involved (point of view of a participant) or uninvolved (point of view of an observer). The involved perspective uses *I* more prominently than the uninvolved. Student Dale Scott's paragraph "Hefty Burgers" uses first person, involved.

If you want to present something from a detached position, especially from a geographical or historical distance (see "Babe Ruth" and "On the Ball"), your point of view will be *third person,* and you will refer to your subjects by name or by third-person pronouns such as *he, she, him, her, it, they,* and *them,* without imposing yourself as an *I* person.

Order

The point of view you select may indicate or even dictate the order in which you present descriptive details. If you are describing your immediate surroundings while taking a walk (first person, involved), the descriptive account would naturally develop spatially as well as chronologically—in other words, in both space and time.

- To indicate space, use terms such as *next to, below, under, above, behind, in front of, beyond, in the foreground, in the background, to the left,* and *to the right.*

- To indicate time, use words such as *first, second, then, soon, finally, while, after, next, later, now,* and *before.*

Some descriptive pieces, for example, the one on Babe Ruth, may follow an idea progression for emphasis and not move primarily through space or time. Whatever appropriate techniques you use will guide your reader and thereby aid coherence.

All three elements—dominant impression, point of view, and order—work together in a well-written description.

The dominant impression of the paragraph "On the Ball" is of an object remarkably well designed for its purpose. The point of view is third person, and the order of the description moves from the core of the baseball outward.

The paragraph "Babe Ruth" emphasizes the idea of paradox (something that appears to be a contradiction). The details are presented from a detached point of view (third person) and appear in order from physique to overall appearance to behavior. The details show a person who wasn't built like an athlete and didn't look like an athlete yet was one of the most famous athletes of all time. Collectively those details convey the dominant impression of "Ruth, the paradox."

Scott's "Hefty Burger" can also be evaluated for all three elements:

- *Dominant impression:* good food (images, figurative language, other diction). The reader experiences the incident as the writer did because of the diction.

The general and abstract have been made clear by use of the specific and the concrete. Of course, not all abstract words need to be tied to the concrete, nor do all general words need to be transformed to the specific. As you describe, use your judgment to decide which words fit your purposes—those needed to enable your audience to understand your ideas and to be persuaded or informed.

- *Point of view:* first person, involved

- *Order:* spatial, from restaurant table to grill, to outside, and back to restaurant

Useful Procedure for Writing Description

What is your subject? (school campus during summer vacation)

What is the dominant impression? (deserted)

What is the situation? (You are walking across the campus in early August.)

What is the order of details? (time and place)

What details support the dominant impression?

1. (smell of flowers and cut grass rather than food and smoke and perfume)

2. (dust accumulated on white porcelain drinking fountain)

3. (sound of the wind, wildlife, and silence rather than people)

4. (crunch of dead leaves underfoot)

5. (echo of footsteps)

This form may be useful. (See the Writing Process Worksheet on page 5.)

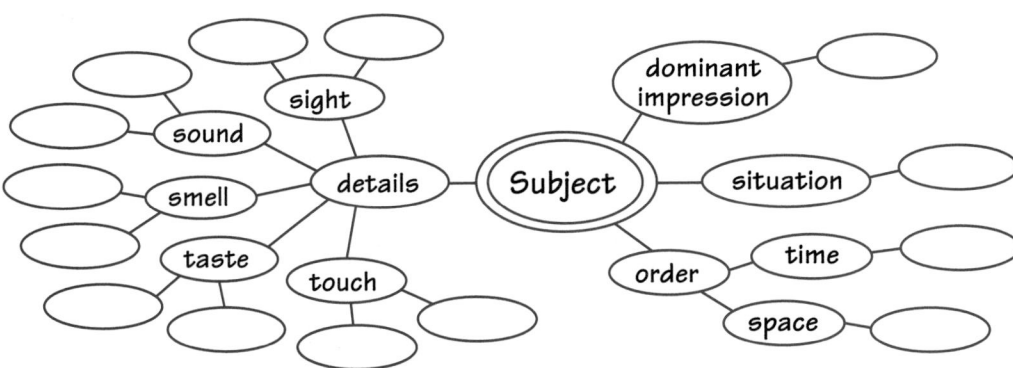

Consider giving your description a narrative framework. Include some action if it fits your purpose.

Exercise 1	**DISCUSSION AND CRITICAL THINKING**

Improve the following sentences by supplying specific and concrete words. Use images when they serve your purposes.

Example: The animal was restless and hungry.

The gaunt lion paced about the cage and chewed hungrily on an old shoe.

1. The fans were happy.

2. She was in love.

3. Confusion surrounded him.

4. The traffic was congested.

5. The dessert impressed the diner.

6. The woman liked her date.

7. The salesman was obnoxious.

8. The room was cluttered.

9. His hair was unkempt.

10. The room smelled bad.

Connecting Reading and Writing

The Mousetrap
Craig Finley

Freelance writer Craig Finley begins this paragraph with a stark description of the mousetrap and then dispassionately explains its function. In his clear and concise presentation, the paragraph is as practical, effective, and impersonal as the object it depicts.

The mousetrap is a remarkably simple and efficient instrument. The platform is a rectangular piece of soft pine wood, two and a half inches wide, six inches long, and a quarter-inch thick. The plane surface of the piece of wood is evenly divided by a square strike bar, which is attached to the middle by three staples. The staples are evenly spaced, with one in the middle. Between the middle and end staples on each side is a strong metal spring coiled around the bar. Each spring is taut and kept that way by the use of a straight piece of metal thrust out from the coil and tucked up under the kill bar on one side and placed against the board on the other. Also attached to the center kill bar is a bait pad, a little rectangular piece of flat metal with a grooved edge extending up from one side to hold the trigger rod. At the open end of the board, from an eye-screw, dangles the trigger rod, a long piece of metal that can move freely in a half circle from a point behind the screw to the grooved bait pad. To set the trap, place the bait, preferably cheese, on the bait pad, then cock the kill bar by pulling the free end over in a half circle to the other side and tucking it under the trigger rod. Then secure the kill bar by moving the trigger rod into the groove on the side of the bait pad. When the rodent nibbles on the cheese, it will move the bait pad, which will loosen the trigger rod and, in turn, release the kill bar in its fatal arc to pin the rodent against the board.

| Exercise 2 | DISCUSSION AND CRITICAL THINKING |

1. Underline the topic sentence.

2. Is the description objective or subjective?

3. Write an X to mark the spot where description becomes an explanation of how the mousetrap works.

4. Use phrases from the description to label the ten parts of the drawing. If you are artistically inclined, add a rodent.

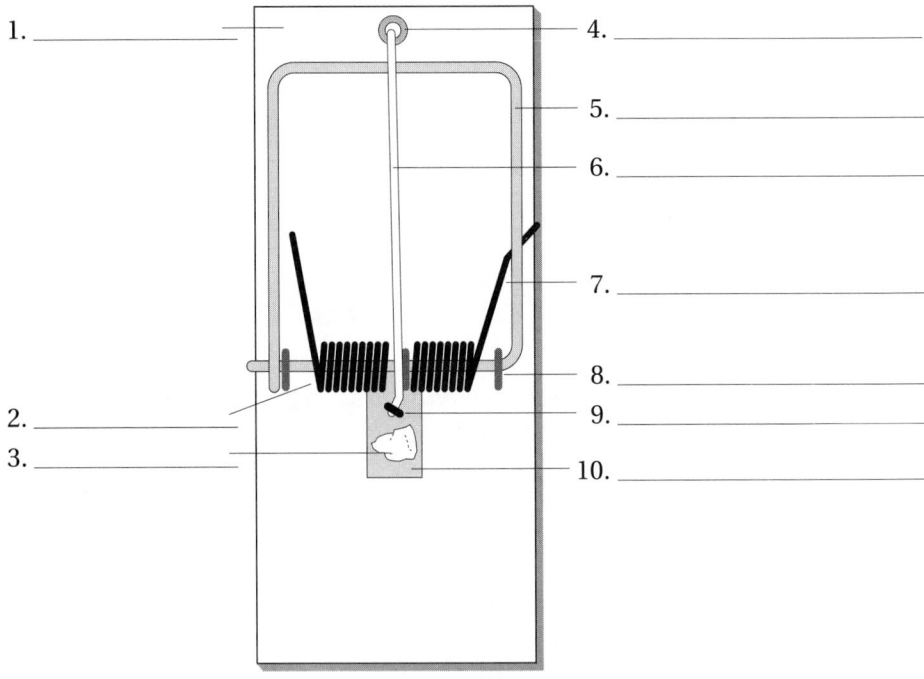

1. _____   4. _____

                                     5. _____

                                     6. _____

                                     7. _____

                                     8. _____
2. _____   9. _____
3. _____   10. _____

Phoenix Jackson
Eudora Welty

Taken from the celebrated short story "A Worn Path," this description allows you to see a person in action. Of course, you learn more about her than a few descriptive characteristics. You discover an important part of her character.

It was December—a bright frozen day in the early morning. Far out in the country there was an old Negro woman with her head tied in a red rag, coming along a path through the pinewoods. Her name was Phoenix Jackson. She was very old and small and she walked slowly in the dark pine shadows, moving a little from side to side in her steps, with the balanced heaviness and lightness of a pendulum in a grandfather clock. She carried a thin, small cane made from an umbrella, and with this she kept tapping the frozen earth in front of her. This made a grave and persistent noise in the still air, that seemed meditative, like the chirping of a solitary little bird. She wore a dark striped dress reaching down to her shoetops, and an equally long apron of bleached sugar sacks, with a full pocket; all neat and tidy, but every time she took a step she might have fallen over her shoelaces, which dragged from her unlaced shoes. She looked straight ahead. Her eyes were blue with age. Her skin had a pattern all its own of numberless branching wrinkles and as though a whole little tree stood in the middle of her forehead, but a golden color ran underneath, and the two knobs of her cheeks were illuminated by a yellow burning under the dark. Under the red rag her hair came down on her neck in the frailest of ringlets, still black, and with an odor like copper.

Exercise 3   **DISCUSSION AND CRITICAL THINKING**

1. Briefly state the dominant impression.

2. Underline the key words that support the dominant impression.

3. Give examples of images of sight, sound, smell, and touch.

4. Give two examples of figures of speech.

The Alley
Amy Tan

These paragraphs are taken from The Joy Luck Club, a novel composed of sixteen tales that reflect author Amy Tan's childhood in San Francisco. Here, in brief narrative and rich descriptive treatment, she reveals her childhood neighborhood as it lives in her memory.

1   We lived on Waverly Place, in a warm, clean, two-bedroom flat that sat above a small Chinese bakery specializing in steamed pastries and dim sum. In the early morning, when the alley was still quiet, I could smell fragrant red beans as they were cooked down to a pasty sweetness. By daybreak, our flat was heavy with the odor of fried sesame balls and sweet curried chicken

crescents. From my bed, I would listen as my father got ready for work, then locked the door behind him, one-two-three clicks.

2   At the end of our two-block alley was a small sandlot playground with swings and slides well-shined down the middle with use. The play area was bordered by wood-slat benches where old-country people sat cracking roasted watermelon seeds with their golden teeth and scattering the husks to an impatient gathering of gurgling pigeons. The best playground, however, was the dark alley itself. It was crammed with daily mysteries and adventures. My brothers and I would peer into the medicinal herb shop, watching old Li dole out onto a stiff sheet of white paper the right amount of insect shells, saffron-colored seeds, and pungent leaves for his ailing customers. It was said that he once cured a woman dying of an ancestral curse that had eluded the best of American doctors. Next to the pharmacy was a printer who specialized in gold-embossed wedding invitations and festive red banners.

Exercise 4	DISCUSSION AND CRITICAL THINKING

1. Is the dominant impression concerned with a static or a dynamic environment?

2. Which paragraph is based on time, and which is based on space?

3. Give examples of images of touch, smell, sound, sight, and taste.

4. In the second paragraph, what words guide the reader through space?

5. Why do the children prefer the alley to the playground?

In the Land of "Coke-Cola"
William Least Heat-Moon

William Trogdon, of English-Irish-Osage ancestry, writes under the pen name William Least Heat-Moon. Traveling around the country in the old van he called Ghost Dancing, he sought out locales on secondary highways marked in blue on road maps. A collection of his descriptions of these adventures subsequently became the best-selling book *Blue Highways*. Here he visits a folksy all-you-can-eat restaurant in rural Georgia.

1   In the land of "Coke-Cola" it was hot and dry. The artesian water was finished. Along route 72, an hour west of Ninety-Six, I tried not to look for a spring; I knew I wouldn't find one, but I kept looking. The Savannah River, dammed to an unnatural wideness, lay below, wet and cool. I'd come into

Georgia. The sun seemed to press on the roadway, and inside the truck, hot light bounced off chrome, flickering like a torch. Then I saw what I was trying not to look for: in a coppice, a long-handled pump.

2   I stopped and took my bottles to the well. A small sign: WATER UNSAFE FOR DRINKING. I drooped like warm tallow. What fungicide, herbicide, nematicide, fumigant, or growth regulant—potions that rebuilt Southern agriculture—had seeped into the ground water? In the old movie Westerns there is commonly a scene where a dehydrated man, crossing the barren waste, at last comes to a water hole; he lies flat to drink the tepid stuff. Just as lips touch water, he sees on the other side a steer skull. I drove off thirsty but feeling a part of mythic history.

3   The thirst subsided when hunger took over. I hadn't eaten since morning. Sunset arrived west of Oglesby, and the air cooled. Then a roadsign:

SWAMP GUINEA'S FISH LODGE
ALL YOU CAN EAT!

An arrow pointed down a county highway. I would gorge myself. A record would be set. They'd ask me to leave. An embarrassment to all.

4   The road through the orange earth of north Georgia passed an old, three-story house with a thin black child hanging out of every window like an illustration for "The Old Woman Who Lived in a Shoe"; on into hills and finally to Swamp Guinea's, a conglomerate of plywood and two-by-fours laid over with the smell of damp pine woods.

5   Inside, wherever an oddity of natural phenomenon could hang, one hung: stuffed rump of a deer, snowshoe, flintlock, hornet's nest. The place looked as if a Boy Scout troop had decorated it. Thirty or so people, black and white, sat around tables almost foundering under piled platters of food. I took a seat by the reproduction of a seventeenth-century woodcut depicting some Rabelaisian banquet at the groaning board.

6   The diners were mostly Oglethorpe County red-dirt farmers. In Georgia tones they talked about their husbandry in terms of rain and nitrogen and hope. An immense woman with a glossy picture of a hooked bass leaping the front of her shirt said, "I'm gonna be sick from how much I've ate."

7   I was watching everyone else and didn't see the waitress standing quietly by. Her voice was deep and soft like water moving in a cavern. I ordered the $4.50 special. In a few minutes she wheeled up a cart and began offloading dinner: ham and eggs, fried catfish, fried perch fingerlings, fried shrimp, chunks of barbecued beef, fried chicken, French fries, hush puppies, a broad bowl of cole slaw, another of lemon, a quart of ice tea, a quart of ice, and an entire loaf of factory-wrapped white bread. The table was covered.

8   "Call me if y'all want any more." She wasn't joking. I quenched the thirst and then—slowly—went to the eating. I had to stand to reach plates across the table, but I intended to do the supper in. It was all Southern fried and good, except the Southern-style sweetened ice tea; still I took care of a quart of it. As I ate, making up for meals lost, the Old-Woman-in-the-Shoe house flashed before me, lightning in darkness. I had no moral right to eat so much. But I did. Headline: STOMACH PUMP FAILS TO REVIVE TRAVELER.

9   The loaf of bread lay unopened when I finally abandoned the meal. At the register, I paid a man who looked as if he'd been chipped out of Georgia chert. The Swamp Guinea. I asked about the name. He spoke of himself in the third person like the Wizard of Oz. "The Swamp Guinea only tells regulars."

10   "I'd be one, Mr. Guinea, if I didn't live in Missouri."

11   "Y'all from the North? Here, I got somethin' for you." He went to the office and returned with a 45 rpm record. "It's my daughter singin'. A little promotion we did. Take it along." Later, I heard a husky north Georgia voice let go a down-home lyric rendering of Swamp Guinea's menu:

> *That's all you can eat*
> *For a dollar fifty,*
> *Hey! The barbecue's nifty!*

And so on through the fried chicken and potatoes.

12   As I left, the Swamp Guinea, a former antique dealer whose name was Rudell Burroughs, said, "The nickname don't mean anything. Just made it up. Tried to figure a good one so we can franchise someday."

13   The frogs, high and low, shrilled and bellowed from the trees and ponds. It was cool going into Athens, a city suffering from a nasty case of the sprawls. On the University of Georgia campus, I tried to walk down Swamp Guinea's supper. Everywhere couples entwined like moonflower vines, each waiting for the blossom that opens only once.

Exercise 5   **VOCABULARY HIGHLIGHTS**

Write a short definition of each word as it is used in the essay. (Paragraph numbers are given in parentheses.) Be prepared to use the words in your own sentences.

artesian (1)   fumigant (2)

coppice (1)   dehydrated (2)

fungicide (2)   conglomerate (4)

herbicide (2)   chert (9)

nematicide (2)   entwined (13)

Exercise 6   **DISCUSSION AND CRITICAL THINKING**

1. How many of the five senses are represented in the imagery? Give an example of each one you find.

2. Give examples of these different figures of speech: simile, personification, metaphor.

3. What ideas dominate each section as the writer moves from one phase of his experience to another?

4. You learn a great deal about the location and the residents in this passage. What do you learn about William Least Heat-Moon by the way he describes his experience?

5. What kind of audience does the author anticipate? Why?

Ode to an Orange
Larry Woiwode

Winner of the fiction award from the American Academy and National Institute of Arts and Letters and poet laureate of North Dakota, Larry Woiwode has been greatly influenced by the harsh and austere northern prairies of his youth. It is from the winters in those bleak days that he conjures up the image of the simple orange. Read this and you will never again see an orange in the same way, never again take this fruit for granted.

1 Oh, those oranges arriving in the midst of the North Dakota winters of the forties—the mere color of them, carried through the door in a net bag or a crate from out of the white winter landscape. Their appearance was enough to set my brother and me to thinking that it might be about time to develop an illness, which was the surest way of receiving a steady supply of them.

2 "Mom, we think we're getting a cold."

3 "*We?* You mean, you two want an orange?"

4 This was difficult for us to answer or dispute; the matter seemed moved beyond our mere wanting.

5 "If you want an orange," she would say, "why don't you ask for one?"

6 "We want an orange."

7 "'We' again, '*We want an orange.*'"

8 "May we have an orange, please."

9 "That's the way you know I like you to ask for one. Now, why don't each of you ask for one in that same way, but separately?"

10 "Mom . . ." And so on. There was no depth of degradation that we wouldn't descend to in order to get one. If the oranges hadn't wended their way northward by Thanksgiving, they were sure to arrive before the Christmas season, stacked first in crates at the depot, filling the musty place, where pews sat back to back, with a springtime acidity, as if the building had been rinsed with a renewing elixir that set it right for yet another year. Then the crates would appear at the local grocery store, often with the top slats pried back on a few of them, so that we were aware of the resinous smell of fresh wood in addition to the already orangy atmosphere that foretold the season more explicitly than any calendar.

11 And in the broken-open crates (as if burst by the power of the oranges themselves), one or two of the lovely spheres would lie free of the tissue they came wrapped in—always purple tissue, as if that were the only color that could contain the populations of them in their nestled positions. The crates bore paper labels at one end—of an orange against a blue background, or of a blue goose against an orange background—signifying the colorful otherworld (unlike our wintry one) that these phenomena had arisen from. Each orange, stripped of its protective wrapping, as vivid in your vision as a pebbled sun, encouraged you to picture a whole pyramid of them in a bowl on your dining room table, glowing in the light, as if giving off the warmth that came through the windows from the real winter sun. And all of them came stamped with a blue-purple name as foreign as the otherworld that you might imagine as their place of origin, so that on Christmas day you

would find yourself digging past everything else in your Christmas stocking, as if tunneling down to the country of China, in order to reach the rounded bulge at the tip of the toe which meant that you had received a personal reminder of another state of existence, wholly separate from your own.

12 The packed heft and texture, finally, of an orange in your hand—this is it!—and the eruption of smell and the watery fireworks as a knife, in the hand of someone skilled, like our mother, goes slicing through the skin so perfect for slicing. This gaseous spray can form a mist like smoke, which can then be lit with a match to create actual fireworks if there is a chance to hide alone with a match (matches being forbidden) and the peel from one. Sputtery ignitions can also be produced by squeezing a peel near a candle (at least one candle is generally always going at Christmastime), and the leftover peels are set on the stove top to scent the house.

13 And the ingenious way in which oranges come packed into their globes! The green nib at the top, like a detonator, can be bitten off, as if disarming the orange, in order to clear a place for you to sink a tooth under the peel. This is the best way to start. If you bite at the peel too much, your front teeth will feel scraped, like dry bone, and your lips will begin to burn from the bitter oil. Better to sink a tooth into this greenish or creamy depression, and then pick at that point with the nail of your thumb, removing a little piece of the peel at a time. Later, you might want to practice to see how large a piece you can remove intact. The peel can also be undone in one continuous ribbon, a feat which maybe your father is able to perform, so that after the orange is freed, looking yellowish, the peel, rewound, will stand in its original shape, although empty.

14 The yellowish whole of the orange can now be divided into sections, usually about a dozen, by beginning with a division down the middle; after this, each section, enclosed in its papery skin, will be able to be lifted and torn loose more easily. There is a stem up the center of the section like a mushroom stalk, but tougher; this can be eaten. A special variety of orange, without any pits, has an extra growth, or nubbin, like half of a tiny orange, tucked into its bottom. This nubbin is nearly as bitter as the peel, but it can be eaten, too; don't worry. Some of the sections will have miniature sections embedded in them and clinging as if for life, giving the impression that babies are being hatched, and should you happen to find some of these you've found the sweetest morsels of any.

15 If you prefer to have your orange sliced in half, as some people do, the edges of the peel will abrade the corners of your mouth, making them feel raw, as you eat down into the white of the rind (which is the only way to do it) until you can see daylight through the orangy bubbles composing its outside. Your eyes might burn; there is no proper way to eat an orange. If there are pits, they can get in the way, and the slower you eat an orange, the more you'll find your fingers sticking together. And no matter how carefully you eat one, or bite into a quarter, juice can always fly or slip from a corner of your mouth; this happens to everyone. Close your eyes to be on the safe side, and for the eruption in your mouth of the slivers of watery meat, which should be broken and rolled fine over your tongue for the essence of orange. And if indeed you have sensed yourself coming down with a cold, there is a chance that you will feel it driven from your head—your nose and sinuses suddenly opening—in the midst of the scent of a peel and eating an orange.

16 And oranges can also be eaten whole—rolled into a spongy mass and punctured with a pencil (if you don't find this offensive) or a knife, and then sucked upon. Then, once the juice is gone, you can disembowel the orange as you wish and eat away its pulpy remains, and eat once more into the whitish interior of the peel, which scours the coating from your teeth and makes your numbing lips and tip of your tongue start to tingle and swell up from behind, until, in the light from the windows (shining through an empty glass bowl), you see orange again from the inside. Oh, oranges, solid *o*'s, light from afar in the midst of the freeze, and not unlike the unspherical fruit which first went from Eve to Adam and from there (to abbreviate matters) to my brother and me.

17 "Mom, we think we're getting a cold."

18 "You mean, you want an orange?"

19 This is difficult to answer or dispute or even to acknowledge, finally, with the fullness that the subject deserves, and that each orange bears, within its own makeup, into this hard-edged yet insubstantial, incomplete, cold, wintry world.

Exercise 7 **VOCABULARY HIGHLIGHTS**

Write a short definition of each word as it is used in the essay. (Paragraph numbers are given in parentheses.) Be prepared to use the words in your own sentences.

ode (title)	heft (12)
degradation (10)	detonator (13)
wended (10)	feat (13)
elixir (10)	abrade (15)
resinous (10)	disembowel (16)

Exercise 8 **DISCUSSION AND CRITICAL THINKING**

1. Is this description objective, subjective, or a combination of the two?

2. In paragraph 14 write an *X* at the point where the description goes from objective to subjective.

3. Instead of just giving description, what does Woiwode do to give form to his discussion in paragraphs 13 through 16?

4. How does Woiwode's conclusion reflect back on the introduction?

5. Use short quotations to give an example of the images of sight, sound, smell, touch, and taste, as found in paragraphs 12 and 13:

6. How does Woiwode use narration to give a framework for his essay?

Student Writers: Demonstrations and Readings

When student Mike Kavanagh looked at the assignment to write a descriptive paragraph about something he knew well, he had no trouble in selecting a subject. As a drag racer for sport and prize money, he had built up his car, a 1968 Camaro, to thunder down the track at more than two hundred miles per hour, with all his senses raw to the wind.

His Writing Process Worksheet shows you how his writing evolved from idea to final draft. To conserve space here, the freewriting and the rough draft marked for revision have been omitted. The balance of his worksheet has been lengthened for you to be able to see parts of his work in their entirety.

You will find a full-size blank worksheet on page 5. It can be photocopied, filled in, and submitted with each assignment if your instructor directs you to do so.

Writing Process Worksheet

TITLE The Drag

NAME Mike Kavanagh   **DUE DATE** Monday, March 27, 9 a.m.

ASSIGNMENT   In the space below, write whatever you need to know about your assignment, including information about the topic, audience, pattern of writing, length, whether to include a rough draft or revised drafts, and whether your paper must be typed.

Write a paragraph of description with a narrative framework about something you have experienced, an event that occurred in a short period of time, maybe a minute or less. Write so that an uninformed audience can understand what you did, how you did it, and how you felt. About 250 to 300 words. Submit this completed worksheet, a rough draft marked for revision, and a typed final draft.

STAGE ONE   **Explore**   Freewrite, brainstorm (list), cluster, or take notes as directed by your instructor. Use the back of this page or separate paper if you need more space.

Cluster

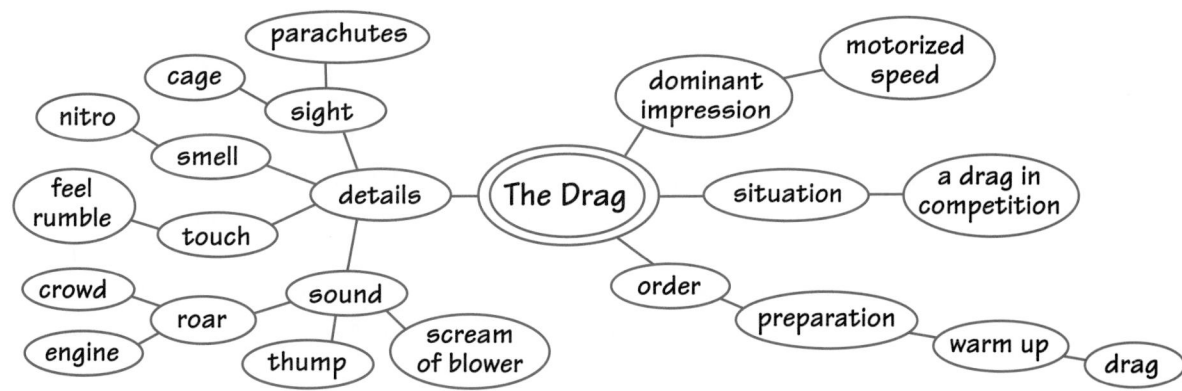

STAGE TWO   **Organize**   Write a topic sentence or thesis; label the subject and the treatment parts.

I <u>climb into the cockpit for my drag.</u>
subject   treatment

Write an outline or an outline alternative.

I. Preparation
   A. Take position
   B. Strap in
      1. Straps merge
      2. Buckle
II. Warm up
   A. Fire motor
      1. Feel rumble
      2. Hear blower
      3. Smell nitro
   B. Dry hop tires
III. Drag
   A. Green light
   B. Thrust
   C. Braking
      1. Regular brakes
      2. Parachutes
   D. Success
      1. Scoreboard
      2. Feeling

STAGE THREE   **Write**   On separate paper, write and then revise your paper as many times as necessary for <u>c</u>oherence, <u>l</u>anguage (usage, tone, and diction), <u>u</u>nity, <u>e</u>mphasis, <u>s</u>upport, and <u>s</u>entences (CLUESS). Read your paper aloud to hear and correct any grammatical errors or awkward-sounding sentences.

Edit any problems in fundamentals, such as <u>c</u>apitalization, <u>o</u>missions, <u>p</u>unctuation, and <u>s</u>pelling (COPS).

Final Draft

The Drag

Mike Kavanagh

Topic sentence — As I climb into the cockpit for my drag, I hear the roar of the crowd and the thundering blasts in the background. Engulfed in an iron cage, I strap myself down. First over the shoulders, then from the waist, and finally from between my legs the straps merge and then buckle at my belly button. This is to ensure my stability in the ironclad, two-hundred-and-thirty-miles-per-hour street rocket. My crew then signals me to fire up the three thousand horsepower motor mounted at my back. With the push of a button, I feel the rumble of the motor, hear the scream of the blower, and smell the distinctive odor of nitro in the air. I then move up to the starting line to

Description and narrative frame — dry hop my rear tires for better traction. I quickly thrust the accelerator pedal to the floor. I am shot forward about two hundred feet. Letting off the accelerator pedal and pulling the brake handle allows me to come to a slow stop. A low continuous thump from the motor echoes through my head as I reverse back to the starting line. As I creep forward, I stage the beast and wait for the lights to change to green. This feels like an eternity. The lights flicker yellow, yellow, yellow, GREEN! I stab the pedal to the floor. I am flung thirteen hundred and twenty feet faster than I can say my name. When I pull the brake and parachute handles simultaneously, I lunge back from the force of the billowing chutes. I climb out of the jungle gym and

Concluding sentence — look up at the scoreboard, which reads 5.26 seconds at 230.57. There's nothing else like rocketing down the track at 230 m.p.h.

Exercise 9   **DISCUSSION AND CRITICAL THINKING**

1. Is this paragraph mainly descriptive, mainly narrative, or equally balanced?

2. Annotate in the margin and underline at least one image of sound, sight, touch, and smell.

3. Although you probably have not drag raced competitively, you can get a good sense of what it is like to do so by reading this paragraph. What details and what phrasing convince you that the author is writing from experience?

4. What is the dominant impression?

The Incense Bowl
Nguyet Anh Nguyen

In this beautifully evocative essay, student Nguyet Anh Nguyen writes of a family heirloom. She says it is not valuable in a monetary sense, but to her family it is beyond price. It is an incense bowl, an object of beauty that ties her to her family and her revered ancestors. This highly effective essay is exceptionally moving and revealing of culture.

I don't know exactly when the incense bowl came to my house. It was there when I was born. This incense bowl, together with a set of two candlesticks, is a family heirloom, so it has been kept and maintained carefully by all the descendants in my family, even though most people would see it as a simple, common object. As a child, I was told that my father was the unexpected heir to the bowl and had a right to keep it because his oldest brother had died early without having children. Of course, my only brother will be the next heir following my father. According to Vietnamese custom, daughters are seldom allowed to become heiresses, so my sister and I will never have a chance to own the bowl.

Made of copper and used to burn incense, the incense bowl is round, golden in color, heavy, and compact, with a diameter of about fifteen inches. It

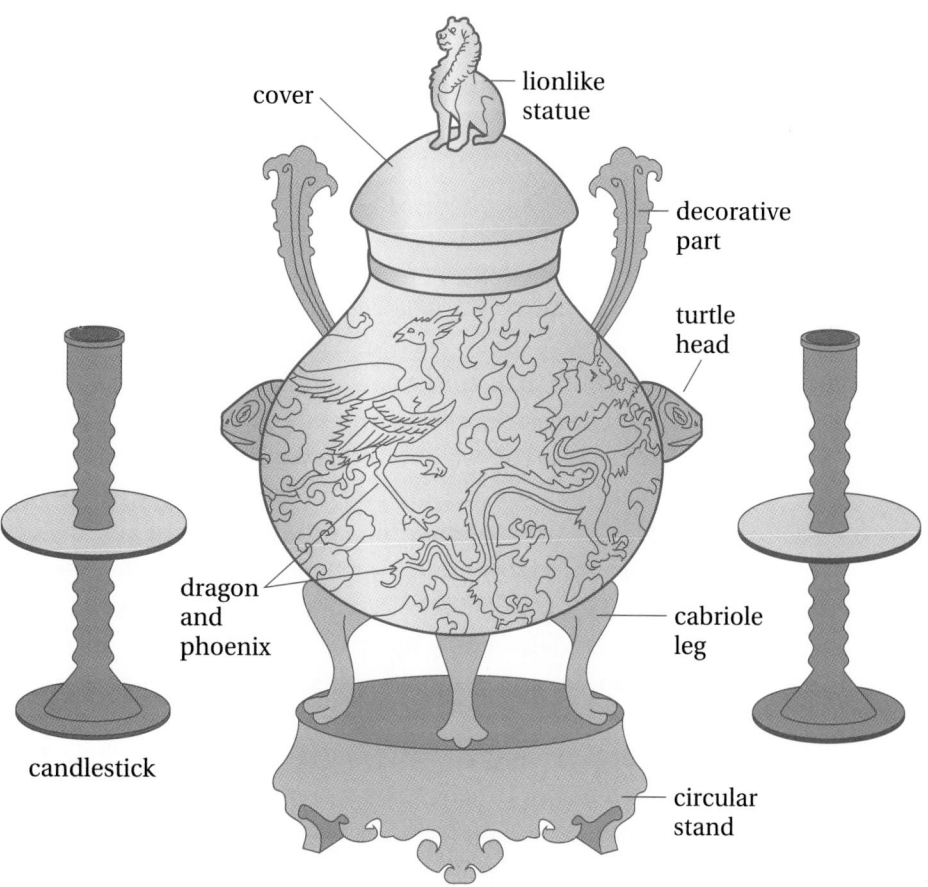

cover — lionlike statue

decorative part

turtle head

dragon and phoenix

cabriole leg

candlestick

circular stand

sits on a prayer table, which is wide and strong enough to hold it. Before every ceremony, my father cleans and polishes the incense bowl and candlesticks by hand at home rather than bringing them to a cleaning service store. This task takes him several hours to finish. First, he uses lemon liquid to clean the outside of the bowl before rubbing the polish on it. This method is very effective. The copper surface of the bowl becomes dull after being exposed to the air for a long time. The acid in lemon liquid can wash away the outer layer of copper oxide. Then, after rinsing the bowl with water, he rubs it again with a soft towel and polish. The harder he rubs, the brighter it becomes. By watching my father's work, I can understand how much he esteems his ancestors and deceased parents. And his manner is unintentionally transferred directly to my soul without using language.

The cleaning process takes much time because the outer surface of the incense bowl is not smooth. Each side of the bowl is decorated with the relief figures of a flying dragon and a dancing phoenix-like creature blending well with carved cloud and flower images. The incense bowl is supported by three S-shaped cabriole legs, which fit into a circular stand made of copper as well. On top of the incense bowl's cover, there is a separate part, a copper statue of a sitting lionlike creature, which is attached to serve as the handle. We occasionally use this cover when the bowl contains only burning sandalwood, and put it aside when using stick incense. Also, two turtle head figures are carved on opposite sides of the bowl to use as its handles. These creatures—the dragon, the phoenix-like bird, the turtle heads, and the lionlike animal—are the four Chinese mythical animals that have the magical power to bring peace and good fortune to people according to ancient belief. Besides those creatures, the incense bowl is decorated with features of Chinese classical architecture.

In our family, the incense bowl is also a witness of all notable events such as birthdays, weddings, new years, funerals, anniversaries of the deaths of deceased ancestors, and even simple prayers of my family. On the important ceremonial days, we usually place on the prayer table some fresh flowers and tropical fruits, varied according to the season, such as durian, longans, mangoes, pineapple, watermelon, green oranges, bananas, custard apples, coconuts, persimmons, mangosteens, mulberries, grapes, grapefruits, plums, papayas, Jacknut tangerines, and so on, together with a tray of plentiful food, and some hot tea or wine as an offering to our ancestors. One candlestick is placed on the left and one on the right side of the incense bowl, which is located at the center of the prayer table. Then the candles are lighted. In the solemn atmosphere, the whole family stands in line and bows formally in front of the table while the aromatic white smoke of burning incense and smoldering sandalwood fly up to the air (from the incense bowl). In this worship, we believe that the smoke transmits our prayers to our ancestors.

This incense bowl has shared intimately with my family in difficult times. Once, my father was very poor. He had to toil hard to maintain his family's well being. However, he never thought about selling this copper bowl for money. Such behavior, which is common among most Vietnamese people, can be compared with the Asian Indians' love for cows. Even those who are starving in India refuse to eat their sacred cows. In much the same spirit, the incense bowl has been handed down from generation to generation, no matter what the family's situation.

As one can see, the copper incense bowl has a special position in my family, even though it is not very valuable. Definitely, it carries much cultural meaning and is a symbol of the sentiment or bond shared through the generations. And more importantly, the incense bowl's history embraces both the prosperity and poverty of our lives.

Exercise 10	DISCUSSION AND CRITICAL THINKING

1. Does Nguyen seem disappointed that she will never own the bowl? Why?

2. How are the description and narration blended in this essay?

3. Why is the bowl so valuable?

4. Which paragraph emphasizes visual description?

5. Underline the thesis of this essay.

Practicing Descriptive Patterns

Description, which is almost always used with other patterns, is very important and often neglected. This exercise features descriptive writing that supports a dominant impression of colorful action.

Exercise 11	COMPLETING DESCRIPTIVE PATTERNS

Inside the Movie Theater

I. Getting refreshments

  A. See

    1. _____

    2. _____

  B. Smell

    1. _____

    2. _____

  C. Touch

    1. _____

    2. _____

II. Watching the movie

   A. Sights

      1. On the screen

         a. _____

         b. _____

      2. In the audience

         a. _____

         b. _____

   B. Sounds

      1. On the screen

         a. _____

         b. _____

      2. In the audience

         a. _____

         b. _____

   C. Enjoyment

      1. Group experience

      2. Refreshments

         a. _____

         b. _____

✎ Topics for Writing Description

Reading-Related Topics

"The Mousetrap"

1. Describe a simple item and explain how it functions. Consider items such as a yo-yo, a Slinky, a flashlight, a pair of scissors, nail clippers, a cigarette lighter, a pocket knife, a baby bottle, a diaper, a music box, a windup toy, a broom, a special wrench, or a can opener.

"Phoenix Jackson"

2. Using this paragraph as a model, describe someone you know. Involve your subject in some purposeful activity, and use a dominant trait to unify your writing.

"The Alley"

3. Describe your neighborhood as it was when you were growing up. Populate it with one or more of the people (not necessarily family members) who influenced you. Limit your description in time and place, and unify it around a dominant impression.

4. Describe an exciting area you visited as a child, perhaps a forbidden place, one that alternately attracted and frightened you.

"In the Land of 'Coke-Cola'"

5. Describe a colorful restaurant, concentrating on food, service, and ambiance. Integrate the parts of your description by presenting a scene involving someone ordering or eating food or someone serving food to a customer.

"Ode to an Orange"

6. Describe one item of food such as a fruit or vegetable that you liked during your childhood. Put this description into a cultural framework, explaining why the item was preferred (season, area where you lived, customs of your family) and how you prepared (if applicable) and consumed it.

"The Drag"

7. Describe an exciting moment that you experienced; it need not be a sporting event, but it can be. It could be an accident, a rescue, an unexpected pleasure, or any personal triumph. Pick an event that you can describe colorfully.

"The Incense Bowl"

8. Describe a family heirloom (ring, watch, wedding dress, religious item, silverware, dishes, tools) or another relic that is being passed down from generation to generation in your family and explain why it is prized by you (or explain your apprehension about being responsible for it).

9. Describe another object such as a photo album that depicts relatives from different generations and represents the roots of your family. Include descriptions of some of your favorite photos. Include copies of photos if you like.

Career-Related Topics

10. Describe a well-furnished, well-functioning office or other work area. Be specific.

11. Describe a computer-related product; give special attention to the dominant trait that gives the product its reputation.

12. Describe a person groomed and attired for a particular job or interview. Be specific in giving details pertaining to the person and in naming the place or situation. Describe yourself from a detached point of view if you like.

General Topics

Objective Description

Give your topic some kind of framework or purpose beyond simply writing a description. As you develop your purpose, consider the knowledge and attitudes of your readers. You might be describing a lung for a biology instructor, a geode for a geology instructor, a painting for an art instructor, or a comet for an astronomy instructor. Or maybe you could pose as the seller of an object, such as a desk, a table, or a bicycle. Describe one of the following topics:

13. A simple object, such as a pencil, cup, sock, dollar bill, coin, ring, or notebook.

14. A human organ, such as a heart, liver, lung, or kidney.

15. A visible part of your body, such as a toe, finger, ear, nose, or eye.

16. A construction, such as a room, desk, chair, commode, or table.

17. A mechanism, such as a bicycle, tricycle, wagon, car, motorcycle, can opener, or stapler.

Subjective Description

The following topics also should be developed with a purpose other than merely writing a description. Your intent can be as simple as giving a subjective reaction to your topic. However, unless you are dealing with a topic you can present reflectively or a topic as interesting in itself as the one in "On the Ball" (p. 112), you will usually need some kind of situation. The narrative framework (something happening) is especially useful in providing order and vitality to writing. Here are three possibilities for you to consider:

18. Personalize a trip to a supermarket, a stadium, an airport, an unusual house, a mall, the beach, a court, a church, a club, a business, the library, or the police station. Describe a simple conflict in one of those places while emphasizing descriptive details.

19. Pick a high point in any event and describe the most important few seconds. Think how a scene can be captured by a video camera and then give focus by applying the dominant impression principle, using relevant images of sight, sound, taste, touch, and smell. The event might be a ball game, a graduation ceremony, a wedding ceremony, a funeral, a dance, a concert, a family gathering, a class meeting, a rally, a riot, a robbery, a fight, a proposal, or a meal. Focus on subject material that you can cover effectively in the passage you write.

20. Pick a moment when you were angry, sad, happy, confused, lost, rattled, afraid, courageous, meek, depressed, or elated. Describe how the total context of the situation contributed to your feeling.

Writer's Guidelines: Description

1. In objective description, use direct, practical language appealing mainly to the sense of sight.

2. In subjective description, appeal to the reader's feelings, especially through the use of figurative language and through images of sight, sound, smell, taste, and touch.

3. Use concrete, specific words if appropriate.

4. Apply these questions to your writing:

   • What is the dominant impression I am trying to convey?

   • What details support the dominant impression?

   • What is the order of the details?

   • What is the point of view? Is it first or third person? Involved or objective?

5. Consider giving the description a narrative framework. Include some action.

Exemplification: Writing with Examples

"Like a picture, a specific vivid example may be worth a thousand words of explanation."

Karen Glen

THE QUIGMANS   by Buddy Hickerson

After his human mating technique fails, Bob tries the traditional, love-snaring neck bloat of the common toad.

Surveying Exposition

ith this chapter on exemplification, we turn to *exposition,* a form of writing whose main purpose is to explain. This and the following six chapters will explore these questions:

Examples	Can you give me an example or examples of what you mean?
Analysis by Division	How do the parts work together?
Process Analysis	How do I do it? How is it done?
Cause and Effect	What is the reason for this? What is the outcome?
Classification	What types of things are these?
Comparison and Contrast	How are these similar and dissimilar?
Definition	What does this term mean?

In most informative writing, these various methods of organizing and developing thought are used in combination, with one method dominating according to the writer's purpose for explaining. The other forms of discourse can be used in combination with these. You have already learned that narration and description are frequently used for expository purposes. In Chapter 17 you will see how persuasive and expository writing are often blended, becoming interdependent.

Writing Paragraphs and Essays of Exemplification

Exemplification means using examples to explain, convince, or amuse. Lending interest and information to writing, exemplification is one of the most common and effective ways of developing ideas. Examples may be developed in a sentence or more, or they may be only phrases or even single words, as in the following sentence: "Children like packaged breakfast foods, such as *Wheaties, Cheerios,* and *Rice Krispies.*"

Characteristics of Good Examples

As supporting information, the best examples are specific, vivid, and representative. These three qualities are closely linked; collectively, they must support the topic sentence of a paragraph and the thesis of an essay.

You use examples to inform or convince your reader. Of course, an example by itself does not necessarily prove anything. We know that examples can be found on either side of an argument, even at the extreme edges. Therefore, in addition to providing specific examples so that your reader can follow you precisely and vivid ones so that your reader will be interested, you should choose examples that are representative. Representative examples are examples that your reader can consider, accept as appropriate, and even match with examples of his or her own. If you are writing about cheating and you give one specific, vivid, and representative example, your reader should be able to say, "That's exactly what happens. I can imagine just how the incident occurred, and I could give some examples that are similar."

Techniques for Finding Examples: Listing and Clustering

Writing a good paragraph or essay of exemplification begins, as always, with prewriting. The techniques you use will depend on what you are writing about. If you were writing about cheating at school, you might work effectively with a list, perhaps including a few insights into your topic if you have not already formulated your controlling statement. The following is one such list compiled by student Lara Olivas as she developed her essay in the demonstration on p. 148; she has circled items she thinks she can use.

Student Cheating
When I copied homework
Looking at a friend's test answers
A student with hand signals
Jake and his electronic system
Time for planned cheating
Those who got caught
(A person who bought a research paper)
Jess, who copied from me
The Internet "Cheaters" source
The two students who exchanged identities
(More work than it's worth)
(More stress than it's worth)
The teacher's assistant and his friends
(The girl from the biology class)

If you are pretty well settled on your subject and you expect to use several different kinds of examples, clustering may work very well for you. Student Garabed Yegavian, whose paragraph begins on p. 145, first used clustering to explore and then transferred much of his information to an outline. Yegavian's cluster is shown here.

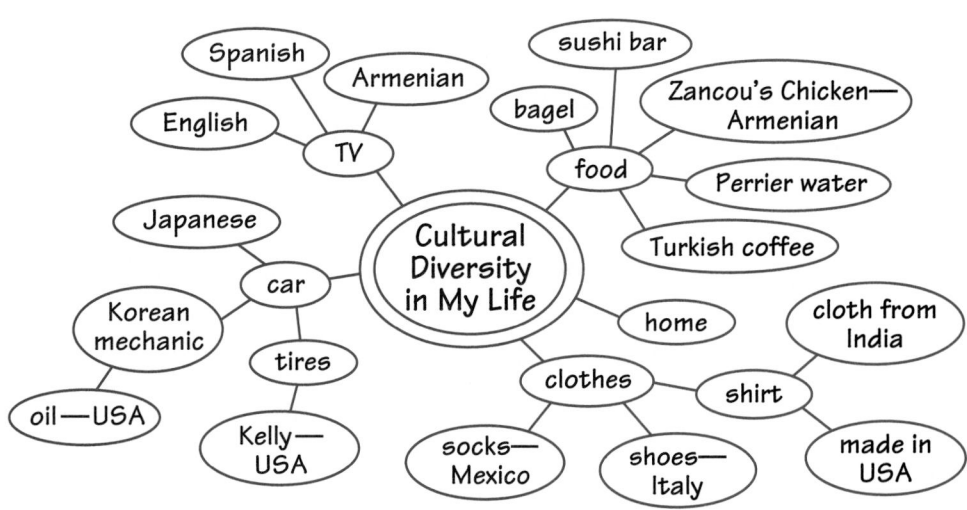

Number and Order of Examples

After you have explored your topic and collected information, you must decide whether to use only one example with a detailed explanation, a few examples with a bit less information, or a cluster of examples. A well-stated topic sentence or thesis will guide you in making this decision. When you are writing about a personal topic, you will probably have far more examples than you can use.

If your example is an incident or a series of incidents, you will probably use time order, reinforcing that arrangement with terms such as *next, then, soon, later, last,* and *finally.* If your examples exist in space (maybe in different parts of a room), then you would use space references (*up, down, left, right, east, west, north,* and *south*). Arranging examples by emphasis means going from the most important example to the least important or from the least to the most important.

Connecting Reading and Writing

Who Are Our Heroes?
Ponchitta Pierce

In this passage taken from Ponchitta Pierce's essay by the same name, we have a definition of a "hero/shero" by the author Maya Angelou. Notice how Angelou's examples clarify her definition.

The poet Maya Angelou, whose works include the autobiography *I Know Why the Caged Bird Sings,* doesn't use the word *hero.* She prefers the term *hero/shero,* because *hero* too often is thought of as male. "Young women and young men need to know that there are women who give encouragement and succor, nourishment and insight," explained Angelou. "A hero/shero encourages people to see the good inside themselves and to expand it." Angelou lists Eleanor Roosevelt, the author Pearl S. Buck, and the abolitionist Frederick Douglass among her heroes. "They confronted societies that did not believe in their ideas and faced hostile adversaries," she said. "At times they were angry. Anger is very good—but I have not seen any case where any of them became bitter." We can develop the heroic in ourselves, Angelou continued, by seeking to do right by others. "Are you concerned about the poor, the lonely, and the ill?" she asked. "Do you follow your concern with action? I try to act as I would want my hero/shero to act. I want to display courtesy, courage, patience, and strength all the time. Now, I blow it 84 times a day. But I'm trying."

Exercise 1	DISCUSSION AND CRITICAL THINKING

1. Underline the topic sentence of the paragraph.

2. Circle Angelou's examples.

3. Why does Angelou use the term *hero/shero?*

4. What are the four qualities of being a hero/shero that Angelou applies to herself?

5. Are her examples effective?

6. What is the difference between anger and bitterness? Can you think of examples of people living today who illustrate both terms?

I'm Outta Here

David Levine

Every day, three thousand students give up on high school—for good. They push open the doors and walk out. They turn their backs on school. Drop out. Now what? Here we have one of numerous examples of dropout experiences discussed by David Levine in an essay first published in *Seventeen* magazine.

Think about it. In some ways it seems perfect. Quit school. Just say No—no more pressure, no more stupid rules, no more deadlines, no more uncaring teachers, no more snobby, clique-conscious peers. Nearly every high school student has imagined what it would be like. Beth Kierny did more than imagine. A few months into her senior year at Columbia High School, in East Greenbush, New York, she dropped out of school. Beth is a shy eighteen-year-old with dark, curly hair who hated getting up early for classes. She thought it would be great. She'd just get a job, sleep in later, work at some cool place instead of sitting in boring classes, and lead an easier, more interesting life. But without a diploma, Beth found it difficult to get a job. She had to finally settle for one at the Hessmart gas station a few miles down Route 20. Being the youngest and newest employee, she got stuck working the worst shifts. Often she had to get up even earlier than she had to for school—sometimes she had to be *at work* by 7:00 A.M. Or she'd have to work the midnight shift, which was scary because one never knew if the place might get held up. Or she'd have to work weekends, when her friends were all out partying. The money was terrible—at minimum wage she cleared maybe $90 a week—and she couldn't afford a car, so she had to take cabs to and from work, which cost almost ten bucks a day. That didn't leave much for her share of the $425 a month in rent on their small apartment behind the Burger King.

Exercise 2   **DISCUSSION AND CRITICAL THINKING**

1. What topic is illustrated?

2. Does Levine use one example or many examples? Why?

3. What are the main narrative points in the example?

4. Does this example correspond to what you know about dropping out of school? Therefore, does the example work well?

In Defense of Talk Shows

Barbara Ehrenreich

Author of nine books and columnist for *Time* magazine, Barbara Ehrenreich has addressed a broad range of subjects, but her specialty is social and political commentary. Here she comments on the crass motives of those who operate the most exploitative talk shows and ridicules the blindness of certain politicians who, she says, are more offended by the subject material than the plight of the guests.

1   Up until now, the targets of Bill (*The Book of Virtues*) Bennett's[1] crusades have at least been plausible sources of evil. But the latest victim of his wrath—TV talk shows of the *Sally Jessy Raphael* variety—are in a whole different category from drugs and gangsta rap. As anyone who actually watches them knows, the talk shows are one of the most excruciatingly moralistic forums the culture has to offer. Disturbing and sometimes disgusting, yes, but their very business is to preach the middle-class virtues of responsibility, reason, and self-control.

2   Take the case of Susan, recently featured on *Montel Williams* as an example of a woman being stalked by her ex-boyfriend. Turns out Susan is also stalking the boyfriend and—here's the sexual frisson—has slept with him only days ago. In fact, Susan is neck deep in trouble without any help from the boyfriend: She's serving a yearlong stretch of home incarceration for assaulting another woman, and home is the tiny trailer she shares with her nine-year-old daughter.

3   But no one is applauding this life spun out of control. Montel scolds Susan roundly for neglecting her daughter and failing to confront her role in the mutual stalking. A therapist lectures her about this unhealthy "obsessive kind of love." The studio audience jeers at her every evasion. By the end Susan has lost her cocky charm and dissolved into tears of shame.

4   The plot is always the same. People with problems—"husband says she looks like a cow," "pressured to lose her virginity or else," "mate wants more sex than I do"—are introduced to rational methods of problem solving. People with moral failings—"boy crazy," "dresses like a tramp," "a hundred sex partners"—are introduced to external standards of morality. The preaching—delivered alternately by the studio audience, the host, and the

1. An activist in Republican politics, William Bennett is the editor of *The Book of Virtues,* a book extolling traditional morals and culture.—Au.

ever present guest therapist—is relentless. "This is wrong to do this," Sally Jessy tells a cheating husband. "Feel bad?" Geraldo asks the girl who stole her best friend's boyfriend. "Any sense of remorse?" The expectation is that the sinner, so hectored, will see her way to reform. And indeed, a Sally Jessy update found "boy crazy," who'd been a guest only weeks ago, now dressed in schoolgirlish plaid and claiming her "attitude [had] changed"—thanks to the rough-and-ready therapy dispensed on the show.

5   All right, the subjects are often lurid and even bizarre. But there's no part of the entertainment spectacle, from *Hard Copy* to *Jade*, that doesn't trade in the lurid and bizarre. At least in the talk shows, the moral is always loud and clear: Respect yourself, listen to others, stop beating on your wife. In fact, it's hard to see how *The Bill Bennett Show*, if there were to be such a thing, could deliver a more pointed sermon. Or would he prefer to see the feckless Susan, for example, tarred and feathered by the studio audience instead of being merely booed and shamed?

6   There *is* something morally repulsive about the talks, but it's not anything Bennett or his co-crusader Senator Joseph Lieberman has seen fit to mention. Watch for a few hours, and you get the claustrophobic sense of lives that have never seen the light of some external judgment, or people who have never before been listened to, and certainly never been taken seriously if they were. "What kind of people would let themselves be humiliated like this?" is often asked, sniffily, by the show's detractors. And the answer, for the most part, is people who are so needy—of social support, of education, of material resources and self-esteem—that they mistake being the center of attention for being actually loved and respected.

7   What the talks are about, in large part, is poverty and the distortions it visits on the human spirit. You'll never find investment bankers bickering on *Rolonda*, or the host of *Gabrielle* recommending therapy to sobbing professors. With few exceptions the guests are drawn from trailer parks and tenements, from bleak streets and narrow, crowded rooms. Listen long enough, and you hear references to unpaid bills, to welfare, to twelve-hour workdays and double shifts. And this is the real shame of the talks: that they take lives bent out of shape by poverty and hold them up as entertaining exhibits. An announcement appearing between segments of *Montel* says it all: The show is looking for "pregnant women who sell their bodies to make ends meet."

8   This is class exploitation, pure and simple. What next—"homeless people so hungry they eat their own scabs"? Or would the next step be to pay people outright to submit to public humiliation? For $50 would you confess to adultery in your wife's presence? For $500 would you reveal your thirteen-year-old's girlish secrets on *Rikki Lake*? If you were poor enough, you might.

9   It is easy enough for those who can afford spacious homes and private therapy to sneer at their financial inferiors and label their pathetic moments of stardom vulgar. But if I had a talk show, it would feature a whole different cast of characters and category of crimes than you'll ever find on the talks: "CEOs who rake in millions while their employees get downsized" would be an obvious theme, along with "Senators who voted for welfare and Medicaid cuts"—and, if he'll agree to appear, "well-fed Republicans who dithered about talk shows while trailer-park residents slipped into madness and despair."

Exercise 3	**VOCABULARY HIGHLIGHTS**

Write a short definition of each word as it is used in the essay. (Paragraph numbers are given in parentheses.) Be prepared to use the words in your own sentences.

plausible (1)   hectored (4)

excruciatingly (1)   feckless (5)

forums (1)   claustrophobic (6)

frisson (2)   detractors (6)

incarceration (2)   dithered (9)

Exercise 4	**DISCUSSION AND CRITICAL THINKING**

1. What role do each of the following play in the talk show: the host, the guests, the audience, the guest therapist, the plot?

2. Ehrenreich mentions that the shows are plotted to occur within both a chronological and a moral framework (with guests often repenting near the end of the show). To what extent do other television programs do that? What about wrestling? What about prime-time action programs? Can you think of others?

3. What do you say to those who maintain that most troubled talk-show guests are more typical of troubled normal people than we would like to admit?

4. Some talk shows are worse than others. Discuss three and give examples of the kinds of guests each host is likely to invite. Include common techniques the hosts use to encourage guests to talk and to act out.

5. According to Ehrenreich, how do Bill Bennett and Senator Lieberman miss the point?

6. Consider the title of Ehrenreich's essay: "In Defense of Talk Shows." In what way is the essay a defense? In what way is it not?

Raised on Rock-and-Roll

Anna Quindlen

A highly respected columnist, Anna Quindlen looks back on the media that influenced her as a youth. There she finds the early rock of *American Bandstand.* She and rock music grew up together. Others may analyze the music; Quindlen feels.

1   *Mister Ed* is back on television, indicating that, as most middle-of-the-road antique shops suggest, Americans cannot discriminate between things worth saving and things that simply exist. *The Donna Reed Show* is on, too, and *My Three Sons*, and those dopey folks from *Gilligan's Island.* There's *Leave It to Beaver* and *The Beverly Hillbillies* and even *Lassie,* whose plaintive theme song leaves my husband all mushy around the edges.

2   Social historians say these images, and those of Howdy Doody and Pinky Lee and Lamb Chop and Annette have forever shaped my consciousness. But I have memories far stronger than that. I remember sitting cross-legged in front of the tube, one of the console sets with the ersatz lamé netting over the speakers, but I was not watching puppets or pratfalls. I was born in Philadelphia, a city where if you can't dance you might as well stay home, and I was raised on rock-and-roll. My earliest television memory is of *American Bandstand*, and the central question of my childhood was: Can you dance to it?

3   When I was fifteen and a wild devotee of Mitch Ryder and the Detroit Wheels, it sometimes crossed my mind that when I was thirty-four years old, decrepit, wrinkled as a prune and near death, I would have moved on to some nameless kind of dreadful show music, something akin to Muzak. I did not think about the fact that my parents were still listening to the music that had been popular when they were kids; I only thought that they played "Pennsylvania 6-5000" to torment me and keep my friends away from the house.

4   But I know now that I'm never going to stop loving rock-and-roll, all kinds of rock-and-roll; the Beatles, the Rolling Stones, Hall and Oates, Talking Heads, the Doors, the Supremes, Tina Turner, Elvis Costello, Elvis Presley. I even like really bad rock-and-roll, although I guess that's where my age shows; I don't have the tolerance for Bon Jovi that I once had for the Raspberries.

5   We have friends who, when their son was a baby, used to put a record on and say, "Drop your butt, Phillip." And Phillip did. That's what I love: drop-your-butt music. It's one of the few things left in my life that makes me feel good without even thinking about it. I can walk into any bookstore and find dozens of books about motherhood and love and human relations and so many other things that we once did through a combination of intuition and emotion. I even heard recently that some school is giving a course on kissing, which makes me wonder if I'm missing something. But rock-and-roll flows through my veins, not my brain. There's nothing else that feels the same to me as, say, the faint sound of the opening dum-doo-doo-doo-doo-doo of "My Girl" coming from a radio on a summer day. I feel the way I felt when I first heard it. I feel good, as James Brown says.

6   There are lots of people who don't feel this way about rock-and-roll. Some of them don't understand it, like the Senate wives who said that records should have rating stickers on them so that you would know

whether the lyrics were dirty. The kids who hang out at Mr. Big's sub shop in my neighborhood thought this would make record shopping a lot easier, because you could choose albums by how bad the rating was. Most of the people who love rock-and-roll just thought the labeling idea was dumb. Lyrics, after all, are not the point of rock-and-roll, despite how beautifully people like Bruce Springsteen and Joni Mitchell write. Lyrics are the point only in the case of "Louie, Louie"; the words have never been deciphered, but it is widely understood that they are about sex. That's understandable, because rock-and-roll is a lot like sex: If you talk seriously about it, it takes a lot of the feeling away—and feeling is the point.

7   Some people over-analyze rock-and-roll, just as they over-analyze everything else. They say things like "Bruce Springsteen is the poet laureate of the American dream gone sour," when all I need to know about Bruce Springsteen is that the saxophone bridge on "Jungleland" makes the back of my neck feel exactly the same way I felt the first time a boy kissed me, only over and over and over again. People write about Prince's "psychedelic masturbatory fantasies," but when I think about Prince, I don't really think, I just feel—feel the moment when, driving to the beach, I first heard "Kiss" on the radio and started bopping up and down in my seat like a seventeen-year-old on a day trip.

8   I've got precious few things in my life anymore that just make me feel, that make me jump and dance, that make me forget the schedule and the job and the mortgage payments and just let me thrash around inside my skin. I've got precious few things I haven't studied and considered and reconsidered and studied some more. I don't know a chord change from a snare drum, but I know what I like, and I like feeling this way sometimes. I love rock-and-roll because in a time of talk, talk, talk, it's about action.

9   Here's a test: Get hold of a two-year-old, a person who has never read a single word about how heavy-metal musicians should be put in jail or about Tina Turner's "throaty alto range." Put "I Heard It Through the Grapevine" on the stereo. Stand the two-year-old in front of the stereo. The two-year-old will begin to dance. The two-year-old will drop his butt. Enough said.

| **Exercise 5** | **VOCABULARY HIGHLIGHTS** |

Write a short definition of each word as it is used in the essay. (Paragraph numbers are given in parentheses.) Be prepared to use the words in your own sentences.

discriminate (1)	intuition (5)
plaintive (1)	deciphered (6)
ersatz (2)	laureate (7)
lamé (2)	psychedelic (7)
decrepit (3)	fantasies (7)

| **Exercise 6** | **DISCUSSION AND CRITICAL THINKING** |

1. Why is it understandable that Quindlen does not give many examples of rock lyrics?

2. According to Quindlen, what examples would be used by social historians to show how she has been influenced?

3. What examples does she provide of strong memories from her childhood?

4. Why does she use the sample of "Louie, Louie"?

5. What does the example of Bruce Springsteen represent?

6. What does the two-year-old represent as an example?

Student Writers: Demonstrations and Readings

Lara Olivas was asked to write an essay on unproductive student behavior, developing her ideas mainly with examples. Of numerous topics that came to mind, one stood out: cheating. It was a practice she had observed for years and one that she had very briefly experimented with and rejected. Wanting to do something a bit different, she considered all the reasons that cheating is not a good idea and came up with a practical one: Cheating is hard work, and cheaters sometimes work harder at cheating than others do at their work.

Olivas's Writing Process Worksheet shows how her writing evolved from idea to final draft. To conserve space here, the free writing and the rough drafts marked for revision have been omitted. The balance of her worksheet has been lengthened for you to be able to see her other work in its entirety.

You will find a full-size blank worksheet on page 5. It can be photocopied, filled in, and submitted with each assignment if your instructor directs you to do so.

• •

Writing Process Worksheet

TITLE Cheating Is Not Worth the Bother

NAME Lara Olivas　　　　　　　　　　　　　　　　**DUE DATE** Wednesday, May 17, 9:00 a.m.

ASSIGNMENT　In the space below, write whatever you need to know about your assignment, including information about the topic, audience, pattern of writing, length, whether to include a rough draft or revised drafts, and whether your paper must be typed.

Write a 500- to 750-word essay of exemplification on the topic of unproductive student behavior. Fellow students and the instructor will probably be familiar with your subject but not your examples and your view. Submit this completed worksheet, one or more rough drafts marked for revision, and a typed final draft.

STAGE ONE **Explore** Freewrite, brainstorm (list), cluster, or take notes as directed by your instructor. Use the back of this page or separate paper if you need more space.

Listing

Student Cheating

When I copied homework
Looking at a friend's test answers
A student with hand signals
Jake and his electronic system
Time for planned cheating
Those who got caught
(A person who bought a research paper)
Jess, who copied from me
The Internet "Cheaters" source
The two students who exchanged identities
(More work than it's worth)
(More stress than it's worth)
The teacher's assistant and his friends
(The girl from the biology class)

STAGE TWO **Organize** Write a topic sentence or thesis; label the subject and the treatment parts.

<u>Cheating students</u> <u>often put themselves under more stress than honest</u>
       subject   treatment
<u>students.</u>

Write an outline or an outline alternative.

  I. Student who bought paper
     A. Had trouble with form
        1. Prewriting
        2. Drafts
     B. Had trouble with quality
     C. Drops class
 II. Student with cheat cards
     A. Had a system
     B. Sometimes under suspicion
     C. Experienced stress

STAGE THREE

Write On separate paper, write and then revise your paper as many times as necessary for coherence, language (usage, tone, and diction), unity, emphasis, support, and sentences (CLUESS). Read your paper aloud to hear and correct any grammatical errors or awkward-sounding sentences.

Edit any problems in fundamentals, such as capitalization, omissions, punctuation, and spelling (COPS).

Final Draft

Cheating Is Not Worth the Bother
Lara Olivas

I knew many students who took college prep classes all the way through high school and never read a book in an English class. They read Cliff's Notes or Monarch Notes, or they copied work from other people who did. But they weren't cheating just in English classes. They had systems of cheating in every class. Cheating became a way of life. They were always conniving and scheming. I'm not that pure. I've tried cheating, but I soon rejected it. I didn't learn that way, and I lost my self-esteem. I also feared getting caught; and I discovered that most of the time cheating was hard, stressful work. So I never became, like some of my friends, a master cheater, but I did become a master observer of cheaters because students almost always see more than teachers do. **Thesis** What I learned was that cheaters often put themselves under more stress than honest students.

Topic sentence Even the student who pays for school work can become a victim of **Specific example** stress. I remember a student in my junior composition class who needed a research paper, so he found a source and bought one for seventy-five dollars. **Order by time** The first trouble was that he had to submit the work in stages: the topic, the working bibliography, the note cards, the outline, the rough draft, and the final. Therefore, he went to the library and started working backwards. Of course, he couldn't turn in only the bib cards actually used in the paper, and next he had to make out note cards for the material he "would be" documenting, and even make out more. After having all kinds of trouble, he realized that the bought paper was of "A" quality, whereas he had been a "C" student. He went back to his source and was told he should change the sentence structure and so on to make the paper weaker. Finally he dropped the class after spending more time on his paper than I did on mine.

Topic sentence Then during my senior year, a female student in Biology 4 became another subject for my study in cheating. She was sitting next to me, so I **Specific example** could see everything she did. She kept her cheat cards in her bra. This is **Order by time** the way she did it. On the day of the test, she would wear a loose-fitting blouse or dress. Then when the instructor wasn't watching, she would hunch her shoulders like a buzzard sleeping and slump so she could look down the front of her own dress. Sometimes she'd have to fiddle around down there to get the cheat card to pop into place. Her writing was tiny. I know about the writing because one day the teacher left the room, and she just took a card out and used it openly. If the instructor stared at her when she was looking down, she would blow inside her dress as if she were trying to cool off her bosom or something. Then she would smile at the instructor and shake her head and pucker her lips to show how hot it was. Her strategy worked because she did perspire due to the stress. The tests were mainly on muscles and bones and weren't that difficult. She probably worked harder in rigging the cheat cards on her underwear than I did in memorizing information.

Cluster of examples   There were dozens of other examples—the writing on seats, hands, arms, legs, and cuffs; the hand signs, blinks, and coughs; and the plagiarism of all kinds. There were even the classes where cheating would never be caught because some teachers didn't watch carefully during the tests, and others didn't read carefully later. But for the most part, the cheaters were the ones who had the most anxiety and often the ones who did the most work—work that was never directed toward learning.

Exercise 7	**DISCUSSION AND CRITICAL THINKING**

1. Why did Olivas give up cheating?

2. What evidence is there that the two students she discusses experienced stress?

3. Does Olivas use a large number of specific examples to support her points or does she develop her examples in detail?

4. As she develops her examples in paragraphs, what other pattern of writing emerges?

Traveling the World at Home
Garabed Yegavian

An Armenian-American student, Garabed Yegavian has traveled to many countries and encountered many cultures. Living in Southern California, he is constantly reminded that he lives in a global community, but this assignment focused his attention on specific, persuasive examples.

Living in California can be like traveling the world. It is morning! Responding to my alarm clock made in China, I get out of my bed, which was constructed in the United States, and step onto a Persian rug. I'm ready to start my Saturday. I walk to my closet to find my clothes: pants from Indonesia, shirt of fabric from India but made in North Carolina, socks from Mexico, shoes from Italy. For late breakfast I have a bagel and cream cheese. I sit in front of my television to see what's happening in the world today. I flip through the channels—English, Spanish, Chinese—until I get to the local Armenian station for an update. After an hour I'm ready to go. I drive to my Korean friend's garage, where he fills my car with oil refined in a plant down by Long Beach. I pay him with my American dollars, and I'm off for tires. On the way to the tire shop, I stop for some lunch. Zancou's Chicken is the place for me today. I order Armenian-style chicken and a bottle of Perrier water and enjoy my feast. Done with lunch, I motor to the tire shop where an immigrant worker from El Salvador fits American Kelly tires on my car. I drink a small cup of Turkish coffee with the manager and talk about business here in America. After a while, my car is ready, and I leave for a mid-afternoon snack. Where to go? There are just too many choices. I decide to go to a Japanese restaurant near my home. There I eat sushi made with fish caught from the waters off Peru, drink Japanese saki, and reflect on my day's experiences. In miles I hadn't gone far, but who needs to travel the world when one lives in Southern California?

Exercise 8	DISCUSSION AND CRITICAL THINKING

1. Underline the topic sentence of the paragraph.

2. Circle each specific example.

3. As Yegavian's community becomes more global, does it become less American, more American, or just a different kind of American?

4. Do you welcome this kind of change and find it rather exciting, as Yegavian apparently does? Why or why not?

5. To what extent is your environment similar to the one presented in this paragraph?

Practicing Patterns of Exemplification

The simple patterns in this exercise will help you see the relationship between purpose and example(s). In an actual writing assignment, you would include more divisions for details.

Exercise 9	COMPLETING PATTERNS OF EXEMPLIFICATION

Fill in the blanks to add (more) examples that support the controlling idea.

1. Controlling idea: Some people let television watching interfere with their social lives.

    I. Watching football games at a family gathering on holidays

    II. Watching television in a _____

    III. _____

2. Controlling idea: Most successful movies are more concerned with action than with character, and the action is violent.

   I. (Name of movie) _____

  II. (Name of movie) _____

 III. (Name of movie) _____

✎ Topics for Writing Exemplification

Reading-Related Topics

"Who Are Our Heroes?"

1. Using the traits of a hero offered by Angelou (courtesy, courage, patience, and strength) or similar traits, define your hero/shero through an extended example.

2. Use an ordinary person as an extended example to define what you mean by a term such as *role model, good doctor, neighbor, parent, teacher, friend, sibling, co-worker, coach,* or *police officer.*

"I'm Outta Here"

3. Write about the reasons for dropping out of school, using someone you know as an example.

4. Write about the effect(s) of dropping out of school, using someone you know as an example.

"In Defense of Talk Shows"

5. Select one of the following statements from the essay and develop or explain it by using examples from your own experience of watching television.

> The preaching—delivered alternatively by the studio audience, the host, and the ever present guest therapist—is relentless

> At least in the talk shows, the moral is always loud and clear: Respect yourself, listen to others, stop beating on your wife.

> And this is the real shame of the talks: that they take lives bent out of shape by poverty and hold them up as entertaining exhibits.

6. If you believe that talk shows give voice to troubled ordinary people and instruction to some viewers, as some talk-show hosts maintain, use an example or several examples to support your view.

"Raised on Rock-and-Roll"

7. Write about the experiences you had with rock music while you were growing up, supporting the idea that you were not corrupted.

8. Support the opposing view that some rock lyrics have a bad effect on youth because they promote violence or convey racist, sexist, and homophobic views.

9. Use, paraphrase, or modify this statement, and support it with your own examples: "That's what I love: drop-your-butt music. It's one of the few things left in my life that makes me feel good without even thinking about it."

"Cheating Is Not Worth the Bother"

10. Use the main idea of this essay as your topic sentence or thesis and develop it with your own example(s) for a paragraph or essay.

11. Use this essay as a model to write about employee theft or shoplifting.

"Traveling the World at Home"

12. Write about a typical day or moment in your community, using examples of products, services, and ideas that make you part of a global village.

13. Write about someone you know who has chosen a simplified life and is only marginally dependent on resources from around the world. Give examples.

Career-Related Topics

14. Use specific examples to support one of the following statements as applied to business or work.

    It's not what you know, it's who you know.

    Don't burn your bridges.

    Like Legos, business is a matter of connections.

    Tact is the lubricant that oils the wheels of industry.

    The customer is always right.

    If you take care of the pennies, the dollars will take care of themselves.

    A kind word turns away wrath.

15. Use another common saying or invent one of your own and illustrate it with an example or examples.

16. Discuss how a specific service or product can benefit its users. Use an example or examples.

General Topics

Choose one of the following statements as a topic sentence for a paragraph or a thesis for an essay. Support the statement with specific examples.

17. Television commercials are often amusing [misleading, irritating, sexist, racist, useless, fascinating].

18. Rap music often carries important messages [makes me sick, brings out the best in people, brings out the worst in people, degrades women, promotes violence, presents reality, appeals to our better instincts, tells funny stories].

19. Rock groups don't have to be sensational in presentation and appearance to be popular.

20. A person can be an environmentalist in everyday life.

21. Many people who consider themselves law-abiding citizens break laws on a selective basis.

22. Television news is full of stories of violence, but we can also find acts of kindness in everyday life.

23. Car salespeople behave differently depending on the kind of car they are selling and the kind of customer they have.

24. The kinds of toys people buy for their children tell us much about their social values.

25. People who do not have a satisfying family life will find a family substitute.

26. One painful experience reminded me of the importance of human rights [student rights, worker rights, gender rights].

27. Drug abuse, including alcohol abuse, may be a problem even with people who seem to be functioning well.

28. Country music appeals to some of our most basic concerns.

Writer's Guidelines: Exemplification

1. Use examples to explain, convince, or amuse.

2. Use examples that are vivid, specific, and representative.

   • Vivid examples attract attention.

   • Specific examples are identifiable.

   • Representative examples are typical and therefore the basis for generalization.

3. Tie your examples clearly to your thesis.

4. Draw your examples from what you have read, heard, and experienced.

5. Brainstorm a list or cluster of possible examples before you write.

6. The order and number of your examples will depend on the purpose stated in your topic sentence or thesis.

10

Analysis by Division: Examining the Parts

"Writing is the art of putting black words on white paper in succession until the impression is created that something has been said."

Alexander Woollcott

THE QUIGMANS   by Buddy Hickerson

"WOO! Check out the third and seventh
segments on THAT babe. YEAH!"

B. Hickerson, copyright Los Angeles Times Syndicate. Reprinted by permission.

Writing Analysis by Division

If you need to explain how something works or exists as a unit, you will write an analysis by division. You will break down a unit (your subject) into its parts and explain how each part functions in relation to the operation or existence of the whole. The most important word here is *unit.* You begin with something that can stand alone or can be regarded separately: a poem, a heart, a painting, a car, a bike, a person, a school, a committee. The following procedure will guide you in writing an analysis by division. Move from subject to principle, to division, to relationship.

Step 1: Select something that is a unit.

Step 2: State one principle by which the unit can function.

Step 3: Divide the unit into parts according to that principle (the perceived purpose or role).

Step 4: Discuss each of the parts in relation to the unit.

Here's how a writer might apply this general procedure to a real object (unit).

Step 1: For the unit, I choose a pencil.

Step 2: For our principle, I see the pencil as a writing instrument.

Step 3: For dividing the unit into parts based on the principle of a pencil as a writing instrument, I divide the pencil into an eraser, an eraser holder, a wooden barrel, and a thin graphite core with a sharpened point.

Step 4: For our discussion of the parts in relation to the unit, I will say something like this: "At the top of the wooden barrel is a strip of metal encircling an eraser and clamping it to the barrel. In the center of the barrel is a core of graphite that can be sharpened to a point at the end and used for writing. The eraser is used to remove marks made by the graphite point. Thus I have a complete writing tool, one that marks and erases marks."

Like many things, a pencil can be regarded in different ways. For example, an artist might *not* consider a pencil mainly as a writing tool. Instead, an artist might look at a pencil and see it as an object of simple functional beauty that could be used as a subject in a still-life painting. Here is how an artist might follow the procedure.

Step 1: For the unit, I choose a pencil.

Step 2: For the principle or way of regarding the unit, I see the pencil as an object of simple functional beauty.

Step 3: For the division into parts based on my principle, I divide the pencil into texture, shape, and color.

Step 4: For the discussion of parts in relation to the unit, I will explain how the textures of the metal, graphite, and wood, along with their shapes and colors, produce a beautiful object.

Either treatment of the same unit, the pencil, is valid, but mixing the treatments by applying more than one principle at a time causes problems. For example, if we were to say that a pencil has an eraser, an eraser holder, a wooden barrel, a graphite core, and a beautiful coat of yellow paint, we would have an illogical analysis by division, because all parts but the "beautiful coat of yellow paint" relate to the pencil as a writing instrument.

Organization

In a paragraph or an essay of analysis by division, the main parts are likely to be the main points of your outline or main extensions of your cluster. If they are anything else, reconsider your organization. For the pencil, your outline might look like this:

I. Eraser

II. Eraser holder

III. Wooden barrel

IV. Graphite core with point at one end

Sequence of Parts

The order in which you discuss the parts will vary according to the nature of the unit and the way in which you view it. Here are some possible sequences for organizing the parts of a unit.

Time: The sequence of the parts in your composition can be mainly chronological, or time-based (if you are writing about something that functions on its own, such as a heart, with the parts presented in relation to stages of the function).

Space: If your unit is a visual object and if, like the pencil, it does nothing by itself, you may discuss the parts in relation to space. In the example about the pencil, the parts of the pencil begin at the top with the eraser and end at the bottom with the graphite point.

Emphasis: Because the most emphatic part of any piece of writing is the end (the second most emphatic point is the beginning), consider placing the most significant part of the unit at the end. In the example, both space and emphasis govern the placement of the pencil point at the end of the order.

Connecting Reading and Writing

The Family and Its Parts

Ian Robertson

Author and college professor Ian Robertson gives his definition of family with its necessary components.

What characteristics, then, are common to all family forms? First, the family consists of a group of people who are in some way related to one another. Second, its members live together for long periods. Third, the adults in the group assume responsibility for any offspring. And, fourth, the members of the family form an economic unit—often for producing goods and services (as when all members share agricultural tasks) and always for consuming goods and services (such as food or housing). We may say, then, that the "family" is a relatively permanent group of people related by ancestry, marriage, or adoption, who live together, form an economic unit, and take care of their young. If this definition seems a little cumbersome, it is only because it has to include such a great variety of family forms.

| Exercise 1 | DISCUSSION AND CRITICAL THINKING |

1. According to Robertson, what are the four characteristics of the family?

2. Must this family include children?

3. Does this definition rule out groups of people headed by nonmarried couples or homosexual couples? If not, explain. If so, explain how the definition might be modified to include the two other groups.

4. Do you prefer a broad or narrow definition of *family?* Why?

The Zones of the Sea

Leonard Engel

In this paragraph reprinted from *The Sea*, published by Time-Life Books, the author shows that the sea can be divided into four zones.

The life of the ocean is divided into distinct realms, each with its own group of creatures that feed upon each other and depend on each other in different ways. There is, first of all, the tidal zone, where land and sea meet. Then comes the realm of the shallow seas around the continents, which goes down to about 500 feet. It is in these two zones that the vast majority of marine life occurs. The deep ocean adds two regions, the zone of light and the zone of perpetual darkness. In the clear waters of the western Pacific, light could still be seen at a depth of 1,000 feet through the portholes of the *Trieste* on its seven-mile dive. But for practical purposes the zone of light ends at about 600 feet. Below that level there is too little light to support the growth of the "grass" of the sea—the tiny, single-celled green plants whose ability to form sugar and starch with the aid of sunlight makes them the base of the great food pyramid of the ocean.

| Exercise 2 | DISCUSSION AND CRITICAL THINKING |

1. What are the four zones of the sea?

2. Is the paragraph organized by space or by time?

3. What characterizes each zone?

4. Draw a cross section of the sea to show the four zones. Make it as elaborate as you like.

Paired Essays on What We Are—Heritage as Hyphenation

We are all individuals, unique and separate, but we are also very much connected to those who went before us and to those who surround us. Therefore, we are all pluralistic because we have been shaped by many individuals of different cultures. Increasingly, American society is multicultural, a condition that can be traced especially to intermarriage and immigration. In response to the question "What are you?" some would answer merely, "American," but others would mention the parts of their heritage. The length of the hyphenated phrase will depend on the number of contributing factors an individual wishes to include. The term may be as long as Chinese-Irish-German-American-Woman-Buddhist-Protestant-Catholic.

In this pair of essays, two authors address the issue of multiple parts of self. Kesaya Noda says in "Growing Up Asian in America" that she is a Japanese, a Japanese-American, and a Japanese-American woman, although her humanity transcends all designations. In "Intermarried . . . with Children," Jill Smolowe concentrates on a broader study of the blending of cultures in America through mixed marriages and the offspring of mixed marriages, focusing on historical developments and recent trends.

THE QUIGMANS by Buddy Hickerson

"Lemme guess . . . . You were a test-tube baby, right?

Growing Up Asian in America

Kesaya E. Noda

Who are you? Can you classify yourself with a single word? Kesaya E. Noda has grown up Asian in America but she needs several words to characterize herself because her identity has many facets.

1   Sometimes when I was growing up, my identity seemed to hurtle toward me and paste itself right to my face. I felt that way, encountering the stereotypes of my race perpetuated by non-Japanese people (primarily white) who may or may not have had contact with other Japanese in America. "You don't like cheese, do you?" someone would ask. "I know your people don't like cheese." Sometimes questions came making allusions to history. That was another aspect of the identity. Events that had happened quite apart from the me who stood silent in that moment connected my face with an incomprehensible past. "Your parents were in California? Were they in those camps during the war?" And sometimes there were phrases or nicknames: "Lotus Blossom." I was sometimes addressed or referred to as racially Japanese, sometimes as Japanese-American, and sometimes as an Asian woman. Confusions and distortions abounded.

2   How is one to know and define oneself? From the inside—within a context that is self-defined from a grounding in community and a connection with culture and history that are comfortably accepted? Or from the outside—in terms of messages received from the media and people who are

often ignorant? Even as an adult I can still see two sides of my face and past. I can see from the inside out, in freedom. And I can see from the outside in, driven by the old voices of childhood and lost in anger and fear.

I Am Racially Japanese

3   A voice from my childhood says: "You are other. You are less than. You are unalterably alien." This voice has its own history. We have indeed been seen as other and alien since the early years of our arrival in the United States. The very first immigrants were welcomed and sought as laborers to replace the dwindling numbers of Chinese, whose influx had been cut off by the Chinese Exclusion Act of 1882. The Japanese fell natural heir to the same anti-Asian prejudice that had arisen against the Chinese. As soon as they began striking for better wages, they were no longer welcomed.

4   I can see myself today as a person historically defined by law and custom as being forever alien. Being neither "free white," nor "African," our people in California were deemed "aliens, ineligible for citizenship," no matter how long they intended to stay here. Aliens ineligible for citizenship were prohibited from owning, buying, or leasing land. They did not and could not belong here. The voice in me remembers that I am always a *Japanese*-American in the eyes of many. A third-generation German-American is an American. A third-generation Japanese-American is a Japanese-American. Being Japanese means being a danger to the country during the war and knowing how to use chopsticks. I wear this history on my face.

5   I move to the other side. I see a different light and claim a different context. My race is a line that stretches across ocean and time to link me to the shrine where my grandmother was raised. Two high, white banners lift in the wind at the top of the stone steps leading to the shrine. It is time for the summer festival. Black characters are written against the sky as boldly as the clouds, as lightly as kites, as sharply as the big black crows I used to see above the fields in New Hampshire. At festival time there is liquor and food, ritual, discipline, and abandonment. There is music and drunkenness and invocation. There is hope. Another season has come. Another season has gone.

6   I am racially Japanese. I have a certain claim to this crazy place where the prayers intoned by a neighboring Shinto priest (standing in for my grandmother's nephew who is sick) are drowned out by the rehearsals for the pop singing contest in which most of the villagers will compete later that night. The village elders, the priest, and I stand respectfully upon the immaculate, shining wooden floor of the outer shrine, bowing our heads before the hidden powers. During the patchy intervals when I can hear him, I notice the priest has a stutter. His voice flutters up to my ears only occasionally because two men and a woman are singing gustily into a microphone in the compound, testing the sound system. A prerecorded tape of guitars, samisens, and drums accompanies them. Rock music and Shinto prayers. That night, to loud applause and cheers, a young man is given the award for the most *net-suretsu*—passionate, burning—rendition of a song. We roar our approval of the reward. Never mind that his voice had wandered and slid, now slightly above, now slightly below the given line of the melody. Netsuretsu. Netsuretsu.

7   In the morning, my grandmother's sister kneels at the foot of the stone stairs to offer her morning prayers. She is too crippled to climb the stairs, so each morning she kneels here upon the path. She shuts her eyes for a few seconds, her motions as matter of fact as when she washes rice. I linger

longer than she does, so reluctant to leave, savoring the connection I feel with my grandmother in America, the past, and the power that lives and shines in the morning sun.

8   Our family has served this shrine for generations. The family's need to protect this claim to identity and place outweighs any individual claim to any individual hope. I am Japanese.

I Am a Japanese-American

9   "Weak." I hear the voice from my childhood years. "Passive," I hear. Our parents and grandparents were the ones who were put into those camps. They went without resistance, they offered cooperation as proof of loyalty to America. "Victim," I hear. And, "Silent."

10   Our parents are painted as hard workers who were socially uncomfortable and had difficulty expressing even the smallest opinion. Clean, quiet, motivated, and determined to match the American way; that is us, and that is the story of our time here.

11   "Why did you go into those camps?" I raged at my parents, frightened by my own inner silence and timidity. "Why didn't you do anything to resist? Why didn't you name it the injustice it was?" Couldn't our parents even think? Couldn't they? Why were we so passive?

12   I shift my vision and my stance. I am in California. My uncle is in the midst of the sweet potato harvest. He is pressed, trying to get the harvesting crews onto the field as quickly as possible, worried about the flow of equipment and people. His big pickup is pulled off to the side, motor running, door ajar. I see two tractors in the yard in front of an old shed; the flatbed harvesting platform on which the workers will stand has already been brought over from the other field. It's early morning. The workers stand loosely grouped and at ease, but my uncle looks as harried and tense as a police officer trying to unsnarl a New York City traffic jam. Driving toward the shed, I pull my car off the road to make way for an approaching tractor. The front wheels of the car sink luxuriously into the soft, white sand by the roadside and the car slides to a dreamy halt, tail still on the road. I try to move forward. I try to move back. The front bites contentedly into the sand, the back lifts itself at a jaunty angle. My uncle sees me and storms down the road, running. He is shouting before he is even near me.

13   "What's the matter with you?" he screams. "What the hell are you doing?" In his frenzy, he grabs his hat off his head and slashes it through the air across his knee. He is beside himself. "Don't you know how to drive in sand? What's the matter with you? You've blocked the whole roadway. How am I supposed to get my tractors out of here? Can't you use your head? You've cut off the whole roadway, and we've got to get out of here."

14   I stand on the road before him helplessly thinking, "No, I don't know how to drive in sand. I've never driven in sand."

15   "I'm sorry, uncle," I say, burying a smile beneath a look of sincere apology. I notice my deep amusement and my affection for him with great curiosity. I am usually devastated by anger. Not this time.

16   During the several years that follow I learn about the people and the place, and much more about what has happened in this California village where my parents grew up. The issei, or grandparents, made this settlement in the desert. Their first crops were eaten by rabbits and ravaged by insects. The land was so barren that men walking from house to house sometimes

got lost. Women came here too. They bore children in 114-degree heat, then carried the babies with them into the fields to nurse when they reached the end of each row of grapes or other truck-farm crops.

17   I had no idea what it meant to buy this kind of land and make it grow green. Or how, when the war came, there was no space at all for the subtlety of being who we were—Japanese-Americans. Either/or was the way. I hadn't understood that people were literally afraid for their lives then, that their money had been frozen in banks; that there was a five-mile travel limit; that when the early evening curfew came and they were inside their houses, some of them watched helplessly as people they knew went into their barns to steal their belongings. The police were patrolling the road, interested only in violators of curfew. There was no help for them in the face of thievery. I had not been able to imagine before what it must have felt like to be an American—to know absolutely that one is an American—and yet to have almost everyone else deny it. Not only deny it, but challenge that identity with machine guns and troops of white American soldiers. In those circumstances it was difficult to say, "I'm Japanese-American." "American" had to do.

18   But now I can say that I am a Japanese-American. It means I have a place here in this country, too. I have a place here on the East Coast, where our neighbor is so much a part of our family that my mother never passes her house at night without glancing at the lights to see if she is home and safe; where my parents have hauled hundreds of pounds of rocks from fields and arduously planted Christmas trees and blueberries, lilacs, asparagus, and crab apples, where my father still dreams of angling a stream to a new bed so that he can dig a pond in the field and fill it with water and fish. "The neighbors already came for their Christmas tree?" he asks in December. "Did they like it? Did they like it?"

19   I have a place on the West Coast where my relatives still farm, where I heard the stories of feuds and backbiting, and where I saw that people survived and flourished because fundamentally they trusted and relied upon one another. A death in the family is not just a death in a family; it is a death in the community. I saw people help each other with money, materials, labor, attention, and time. I saw men gather once a year, without fail, to clean the grounds of a ninety-year-old woman who had helped the community before, during, and after the war. I saw her remembering them with birthday cards sent to each of their children.

20   I come from a people with a long memory and a distinctive grace. We live our thanks. And we are Americans. Japanese-Americans.

I Am a Japanese-American Woman

21   Woman. The last piece of my identity. It has been easier by far for me to know myself in Japan and to see my place in America than it has been to accept my line of connection with my own mother. She was my dark self, a figure in whom I thought I saw all that I feared most in myself. Growing into womanhood and looking for some model of strength, I turned away from her. Of course, I could not find what I sought. I was looking for a black feminist or a white feminist. My mother is neither white nor black.

22   My mother is a woman who speaks with her life as much as with her tongue. I think of her with her own mother. Grandmother had Parkinson's disease and it had frozen her gait and set her fingers, tongue, and feet jerking and trembling in a terrible dance. My aunts and uncles wanted her to be

able to live in her own home. They fed her, bathed her, dressed her, awoke at midnight to take her for one last trip to the bathroom. My aunts (her daughters-in-law) did most of the care, but my mother went from New Hampshire to California each summer to spend a month living with Grandmother, because she wanted to and because she wanted to give my aunts at least a small rest. During those hot summer days, mother lay on the couch watching the television or reading, cooking foods that Grandmother liked, and speaking little. Grandmother thrived under her care.

23   The time finally came when it was too dangerous for Grandmother to live alone. My relatives kept finding her on the floor beside her bed when they went to wake her in the mornings. My mother flew to California to help clean the house and make arrangements for Grandmother to enter a local nursing home. On her last day at home, while Grandmother was sitting in her big, overstuffed armchair, hair combed and wearing a green summer dress, my mother went to her and knelt at her feet. "Here, Mamma," she said. "I've polished your shoes." She lifted Grandmother's legs and helped her into the shiny black shoes. My Grandmother looked down and smiled slightly. She left her house walking, supported by her children, carrying her pocketbook, and wearing her polished black shoes. "Look, Mamma," my mom had said, kneeling. "I've polished your shoes."

24   Just the other day, my mother came to Boston to visit. She had recently lost a lot of weight and was pleased with her new shape and her feeling of good health. "Look at me, Kes," she exclaimed, turning toward me, front and back, as naked as the day she was born. I saw her small breasts and the wide, brown scar, belly button to pubic hair, that marked her because my brother and I were both born by Caesarean section. Her hips were small. I was not a large baby, but there was so little room for me in her that when she was carrying me she could not even begin to bend over toward the floor. She hated it, she said.

25   "Don't I look good? Don't you think I look good?"

26   I looked at my mother, smiling and as happy as she, thinking of all the times I have seen her naked. I have seen both my parents naked throughout my life, as they have seen me. From childhood through adulthood we've had our naked moments, sharing baths, idle conversations picked up as we moved between showers and closets, hurried moments at the beginning of days, quiet moments at the end of days.

27   I know this to be Japanese, this ease with the physical, and it makes me think of an old Japanese folk song. A young nursemaid, a fifteen-year-old girl, is singing a lullaby to a baby who is strapped to her back. The nursemaid has been sent as a servant to a place far from her own home. "We're the beggars," she says, "and they are the nice people. Nice people wear fine sashes. Nice clothes."

> If I should drop dead,
> bury me by the roadside!
> I'll give a flower
> to everyone who passes.
>
> What kind of flower?
> The cam-cam-camellia [tsun-tsun-tsubaki]
> watered by Heaven:
> alms water.

28   The nursemaid is the intersection of heaven and earth, the intersection of the human, the natural world, the body, and the soul. In this song, with clear eyes, she looks steadily at life, which is sometimes so very terrible and sad. I think of her while looking at my mother, who is standing on the red and purple carpet before me, laughing, without any clothes.

29   I am my mother's daughter. And I am myself.

30   I am a Japanese-American woman.

Epilogue

31   I recently heard a man from West Africa share some memories of his child-hood. He was raised Muslim, but when he was a young man, he found himself deeply drawn to Christianity. He struggled against his inner impulse for years, trying to avoid the church yet feeling pushed to return to it again and again. "I would have done *anything* to avoid the change," he said. At last, he became Christian. Afterwards he was afraid to go home, fearing that he would not be accepted. The fear was groundless, he discovered, when at last he returned—he had separated himself, but his family and friends (all Muslim) had not separated themselves from him.

32   The man, who is now a professor of religion, said that in the Africa he knew as a child and a young man, pluralism was embraced rather than feared. There was "a kind of tolerance that did not deny your particularity," he said. He alluded to zestful, spontaneous debates that would sometimes loudly erupt between Muslims and Christians in the village's public spaces. His memories of an atheist who harangued the villagers when he came to visit them once a week moved me deeply. Perhaps the man was an agricultural advisor or inspector. He harassed the women. He would say: "Don't go to the fields! Don't even bother to go to the fields. Let God take care of you. He'll send you the food. If you believe in God, why do you need to work? You don't need to work! Let God put the seeds in the ground. Stay home."

33   The professor said, "The women laughed, you know? They just laughed. Their attitude was, 'Here is a child of God. When will he come home?'"

34   The storyteller, the professor of religion, smiled a most fantastic tender smile as he told this story. "In my country, there is a deep affirmation of the oneness of God," he said. "The atheist and the women were having quite different experiences in their encounter, though the atheist did not know this. He saw himself as quite separate from the women. But the women did not see themselves as being separate from him. 'Here is a child of God,' they said. 'When will he come home?'"

| **Exercise 3** | **VOCABULARY HIGHLIGHTS** |

Write a short definition of each word as it is used in the essay. (Paragraph numbers are given in parentheses.) Be prepared to use the words in your own sentences.

perpetuated (1)	spontaneous (32)
devastated (15)	harangued (32)
arduously (18)	harassed (32)
gait (22)	affirmation (34)
pluralism (32)	encounter (34)

1. What is the unit?

2. What is the principle by which the unit is divided?

3. What are the parts of the unit?

4. What does Noda say about the people who stereotyped her?

5. What are some of the characteristics of the stereotyping she encountered?

6. Simply, what does it meant to the author to say she is Japanese-American (paragraph 18)?

7. As a Japanese-American woman, what is her legacy, what values are passed down in her family?

8. What is the significance of Noda's story about the nursemaid (paragraphs 27 and 28)?

9. Why does the author end her essay with an epilogue about the African professor of religion?

Intermarried . . . with Children

Jill Smolowe

In a special issue of *Time* magazine, the cover image is what appears to be a photograph of an attractive young woman. The caption says, "Take a good look at this woman. She was created by a computer from a mix of several races. What you see is a remarkable preview of . . . The New Face of America: How Immigrants Are Shaping the World's First Multicultural Society." Inside, among numerous articles on cultural diversity in the United States, is this essay by Jill Smolowe. Using supporting material from reporters from Chicago, New York, and Los Angeles, she writes of the significance of the mixing of race, culture, and faith in marriage and child rearing.

1   Hostile stares and epithets were the least of their problems when Edgar and Jean Cahn first dated. Twice the couple—he a white Jew, she a black Baptist—were arrested simply for walking the streets of Baltimore arm in arm. When they wed in 1957, Maryland law barred interracial marriages, so the ceremony was held in New York City. Although Jean had converted by then, the only rabbi who would agree to officiate denied them a huppah and the traditional breaking of glass. As law students at Yale in the 1960s, the couple lived in a basement because no landlord would rent them a flat.

2   In 1963 the Cahns moved to Washington, D.C., where they raised two sons, Reuben and Jonathan. By 1971, as co-deans of the Antioch School of Law, the high profile couple had received so many death threats that they needed bodyguards. The boys' mixed ancestry caused near riots at their public school. One principal said they "brought a dark force to the school" and called for their expulsion.

3   Now the generational wheel has turned. In 1990 young Reuben married Marna, a white Lutheran from rural Pine Grove, Pennsylvania. Although both a rabbi and a minister officiated, none of Marna's relatives, except her mother, attended the wedding. Her father fumed, "I can't believe you expect me to accept a black person, and a Jewish one at that!" But with the birth last year of towheaded Aaron, Marna's family softened considerably.

4   Intermarriage, of course, is as old as the Bible. But during the past two decades, America has produced the greatest variety of hybrid households in the history of the world. As ever increasing numbers of couples crash through racial, ethnic and religious barriers to invent a life together, Americans are being forced to rethink and redefine themselves. For all the divisive talk of cultural separatism and resurgent ethnic pride, never before has a society struggled so hard to fuse such a jumble of traditions, beliefs and values.

5   The huddled masses have already given way to the muddled masses. "Marriage is the main assimilator," says Karen Stephenson, an anthropologist at UCLA. "If you really want to affect change, it's through marriage and child rearing." This is not assimilation in the Eurocentric sense of the word: one nation, under white, Anglo-Saxon Protestant rule, divided, with liberty and justice for some. Rather it is an extended hyphenation. If, say, the daughter of Japanese and Filipino parents marries the son of German and Irish immigrants, together they may beget a Japanese-Filipino-German-Irish-Buddhist-Catholic-American child. "Assimilation never really happens," says Stephenson. "Over time you get a bunch of little assimilations."

6   The profusion of couples breaching once impregnable barriers of color, ethnicity and faith is startling. Over a period of roughly two decades, the number of interracial marriages in the U.S. has escalated from 310,000 to more than 1.1 million; 72% of those polled by *Time* know married couples who are of different races. The incidence of births of mixed-race babies has multiplied 26 times as fast as that of any other group. Among Jews the number marrying out of their faith has shot up from 10% to 52% since 1960. Among Japanese Americans, 65% marry people who have no Japanese heritage; Native Americans have nudged that number to 70%. In both groups the incidence of children sired by mixed couples exceeds the number born into uni-ethnic homes.

7   Some critics fret that all this criss-crossing will damage society's essential "American" core. By this they usually mean a confluence of attitudes, values and assumptions that drive Americans' centuries-old quest for a better life. What they fail to acknowledge is that legal, educational and economic changes continuously alter the priorities within that same set of social variables. A few generations back, religion, race and custom superseded all other considerations. When Kathleen Hobson and Atul Gawande, both 27, married last year, however, they based their vision of a shared future on a different set of common values: an upper-middle-class upbringing in tightknit families, a Stanford education and a love of intellectual pursuits.

8   Unlike many other mixed couples, Gawande, an Indian American, and Hobson, a white Episcopalian of old Southern stock, have always enjoyed a warm reception from both sets of parents. Still, when Hobson first visited the Gawandes in Ohio, not every one of their friends was ready to celebrate. "One Indian family didn't want to come because they were concerned about their children being influenced," Hobson says. Their wedding in Virginia was a harmonious blend of two cultures: although Kathleen wore a white gown and her minister officiated, the ceremony included readings from both Hindu and Christian texts.

9   Tortured solutions to mixed-marriage ceremonies are common. Weddings, like funerals, are a time when family resentments, disappointments and expectations bubble to the surface. The tugging and tussling over matters that may seem frivolous set the stage for a couple's lifelong quest to create an environment that will be welcoming to both families, yet uniquely their own.

10   Accommodation and compromise only begin at the altar. The qualities that attracted Dan Kalmanson, an Anglo of European extraction, to Yilva Martinez in a Miami reggae club—her Spanish accent, exotic style of dance, and playfulness—had a more challenging echo in their married life. After they wed in 1988, Ignacio, Yilva's then eight-year-old son by a previous marriage, moved from Venezuela to join the couple. Dan, 33, spoke no Spanish, the boy no English. The couple decided to compel Ignacio to speak English. He caught on so fast that his Spanish soon degenerated. Says Yilva: "We have literally forced him to learn Spanish again."

11   For Yilva, 35, the struggle is not just to preserve her native tongue; she also wants to suffuse her home, which has grown with the addition of Kristen, 3, with the Latin ethnic that values family above all else. "Here, you live to work. There, we work to live," she says. "In Venezuela we take a two-hour lunch break; we don't cram in a hamburger at McDonald's."

12   Children also force mixed couples to confront hard decisions about religion. Blanche Speiser, 43, was certain that Mark, 40, would yield if she wanted to raise their two kids Christian, but she also knew that her Jewish husband would never attend church with the family or participate in holiday celebrations. After much soul searching, she opted for a Jewish upbringing. "I knew it would be O.K. as long as the children had some belief," she says. "I didn't want a mishmash." Although Blanche remains comfortable with that decision and has grown accustomed to attending synagogue with her family, she admits that it pricks when Brad, 7, says, "Mommy, I wish you were Jewish." Other couples expose their families to both religions, then leave the choice to the kids.

13   When it comes to racial identity, many couples feel that a child should never have to "choose" between parents. The 1990 U.S. census form, with its "Black," "White" and "Other" boxes, particularly grated. "'Other' is not acceptable, pure and simple," says Nancy Brown, 40. "It is psychologically damaging to force somebody to choose one identity when physiologically and biologically they are more than one." Nancy, who is white, thinks the census form should include a "Multiracial" box for her two daughters; her black husband Roosevelt, 44, argues that there should be no race box at all. Both agree that people should be able to celebrate all parts of their heritage without conflict. "It's like an equation," says Nancy, who is president of an interracial family support group. "Interracial marriage that works equals multiracial children at ease with their mixed identity, which equals more people in the world who can deal with this diversity."

14   The world still has much to learn about living with diversity. "What people say, what people do and what they say they do are three entirely different things," says anthropologist Stephenson. "We are walking contradictions." Kyoung-Hi Song, 27, was born in Korea but lived much of her youth abroad as her father was posted from one United Nations assignment to the next. Despite that cosmopolitan upbringing, her parents balked when Kyoung-Hi married Robert Dickson, a WASP from Connecticut. They boycotted the 1990 wedding, and have not contacted their daughter since. The Dicksons hope that the birth of their first child, expected in April, will change that.

15   Intolerance need not be that blatant to inflict wounds. If Tony Jeffreys, 34, and Alice Sakuda Flores, 28, have a child, that hypothetical Japanese-Filipino-German-Irish-Buddhist-Catholic-American will become flesh and blood. In their one year of marriage, Tony says, "I've heard friends say stupid stuff about Asians right in front of Alice. It is really hypocritical because a lot of them have Mexican or black girlfriends or wives." Sometimes the more subtle the rejection, the sharper the sting. Says Candy Mills, 29, the daughter of black and Native American parents, who is married to Gabe Grosz, a white European immigrant: "I know that people are tolerating me, not accepting me."

16   Such pain is evidence that America has yet to harvest the full rewards of its founding principles. The land of immigrants may be giving way to a land of hyphenations, but the hyphen still divides even as it compounds. Those who intermarry have perhaps the strongest sense of what it will take to return America to an unhyphenated whole. "It's American culture that we all share," says Mills. "We should capitalize on that." Perhaps her two Native American-black-white-Hungarian-French-Catholic-Jewish-American children will lead the way.

Exercise 5	**VOCABULARY HIGHLIGHTS**

Write a short definition of each word as it is used in the essay. (Paragraph numbers are given in parentheses.) Be prepared to use the words in your own sentences.

epithets (1)   resurgent (4)

towheaded (3)   profusion (6)

confluence (7)   degenerated (10)

frivolous (9)   suffuse (11)

exotic (10)   boycotted (14)

Exercise 6	DISCUSSION AND CRITICAL THINKING

1. In what way is the hyphenation discussed in this essay another way of saying "analysis by division"?

2. How does the marriage of Marna and Reuben illustrate both the change and lack of change in interracial marriages?

3. What is anthropologist Karen Stephenson's view of assimilation?

4. What is a mixed marriage?

5. What role do common values have in mate selection (paragraph 7)?

6. What are two common solutions to the issue of mixed-faith marriages and child rearing? Which do you think is better? Why?

7. Explain this statement: "The land of immigrants may be giving way to a land of hyphenations, but the hyphen still divides even as it compounds."

Exercise 7	CONNECTING THE PAIRED ESSAYS

1. Both Noda and Smolowe are concerned with hyphenation. Why is Noda's system less complicated?

2. Is Noda at odds with Smolowe or are her views essentially consistent with Smolowe's?

3. Noda is concerned with gender in saying that she is a Japanese-American woman. Why doesn't Smolowe bring up that issue?

4. What does each author say about prejudice and stereotyping?

5. What solution does each author have for relieving the hostility among different groups?

6. Which author has made a deeper impression on your thinking? Why?

Student Writers: Demonstrations and Readings

When Selin Simon received her assignment to write a paper of analysis by division on something that was a physical unit, she naturally turned to another class she was taking: biology. From that broad subject she chose *skin* as an organ of the human body.

Her Writing Process Worksheet shows how her writing evolved from idea to final draft. Notice that her clustering as part of Stage One was truly an exploration. She was able to use that information as she slightly reorganized her thoughts in her topic sentence and her well-structured outline. To conserve space here, the free writing and the rough draft marked for revision have been omitted. The balance of her worksheet has been lengthened for you to be able to see her other work in its entirety.

You will find a full-size blank worksheet on page 5. It can be photocopied, filled in, and submitted with each assignment if your instructor directs you to do so.

. . . .

Writing Process Worksheet

TITLE Skin

NAME Selin Simon   **DUE DATE** Friday, June 2, 8 a.m.

ASSIGNMENT In the space below, write whatever you need to know about your assignment, including information about the topic, audience, pattern of writing, length, whether to include a rough draft or revised drafts, and whether your paper must be typed.

Write a paragraph of analysis by division about a physical object. Discuss the parts and explain how the object functions. It might be a machine or an organ of the human body. You should assume that your audience knows very little about your subject. Submit this completed worksheet, a rough draft, marked for revision, and a typed final draft of about 200 to 250 words.

STAGE ONE **Explore** Freewrite, brainstorm (list), cluster, or take notes as directed by your instructor. Use the back of this page or separate paper if you need more space.

Clustering

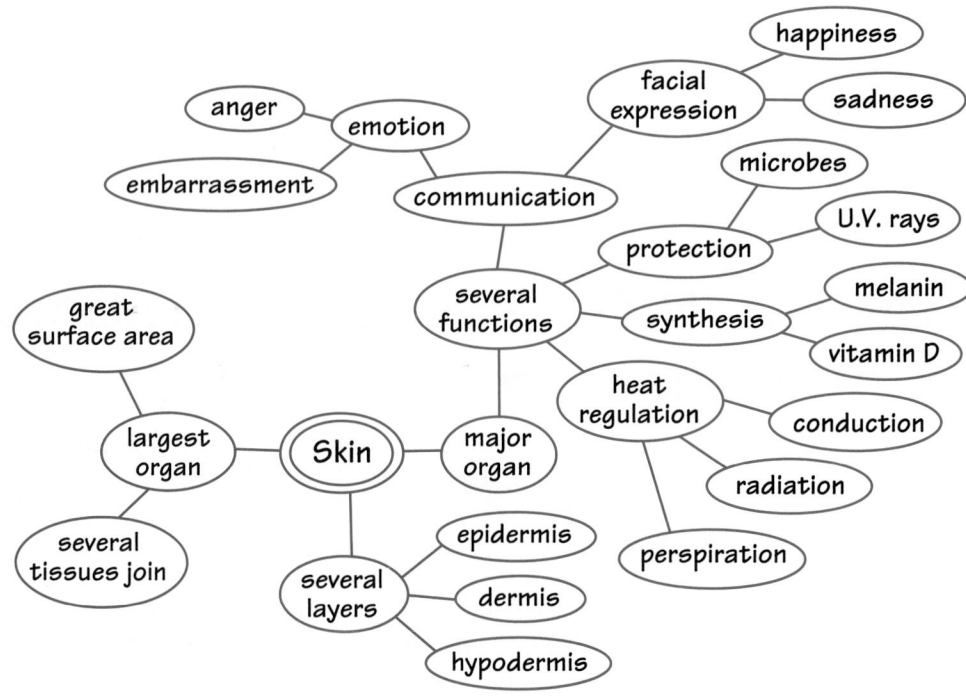

STAGE TWO **Organize** Write a topic sentence or thesis; label the subject and the treatment parts.

<u>The skin</u> <u>is composed of three different layers: epidermis, dermis, and</u>
    subject   treatment
<u>hypodermis.</u>

Write an outline or an outline alternative.

I. Epidermis
   A. Superficial layer
   B. Protective role
      1. Against organisms
      2. Against water
      3. Against ultraviolet rays
   C. Synthesizes melanin for skin color
   D. Synthesizes keratin
      1. For bone growth
      2. For bone maintenance
II. Dermis
   A. Deeper and thicker than epidermis
   B. Nourishes tissue
   C. Provides for elasticity
   D. Cools body with its sweat glands

III. Hypodermis
    A. Innermost layer
    B. Binds dermis to underlying organs
    C. Has fat
       1. For insulation
       2. For shock absorption
       3. For energy

STAGE THREE   **Write**   On separate paper, write and then revise your paper as many times as necessary for coherence, language (usage, tone, and diction), unity, emphasis, support, and sentences (CLUESS). Read your paper aloud to hear and correct any grammatical errors or awkward-sounding sentences.
Edit any problems in fundamentals, such as capitalization, omissions, punctuation, and spelling (COPS).

Final Draft

Skin

Selin Simon

Skin is technically an organ because it is composed of several kinds of tissues that are structurally arranged to function together. In fact, it is the largest organ of the body, occupying approximately 19,344 sq. cm. of surface area. It is composed of three different layers: epidermis, dermis, and hypodermis. Epidermis is the superficial layer of the skin. It plays an important protective role as a physical barrier to organisms, water, and ultraviolet rays. It also helps in the synthesis of melanin, which gives color to the skin, and of keratin, which, as a skin protein with vitamin D, helps in the metabolism of calcium and phosphate in bones. Dermis, deeper and thicker than epidermis, contains blood vessels and nerves to nourish the tissue and elastic fibers that provide skin flexibility. Moreover, it contains glands that produce sweat, thereby helping to regulate the body temperature. Hypodermis, the innermost layer, binds the dermis to the underlying organs. Composed of adipose tissues storing fat, it serves as an insulator, a shock absorber, and a source of energy. These layers work together to perform the major functions of the skin.

Topic sentence, Part 1, Part 2, Part 3, Concluding sentence

Exercise 8   **DISCUSSION AND CRITICAL THINKING**

1. What adjustment did Simon make as she moved from her cluster in Stage One to her outline in Stage Two?

2. Circle the words that support the idea of function. You will be looking for words such as *function* and *help.*

More Than Book 'Em

Jerry Price

A veteran police officer of fifteen years, Jerry Price knows well that every call has its unique characteristics, so he must be much more than simply a cop. Here he discusses the different roles he might assume when he answers a call concerning a family dispute.

1   As a police officer, when I am on patrol I have a wide variety of duties. I respond to several different types of calls. One of the most common calls involves a family dispute between a husband and wife. When I respond to that kind of problem, I have to play one or more quite different roles. The main roles for family disputes are counselor, referee, and law enforcer.

2   The most common family dispute involves a husband and wife arguing. Usually the argument is almost over when I arrive. I need to talk to both sides. Depending on how intense they are, I either separate them or talk to them together. Both the husband and wife will tell me they are right and the other spouse is wrong. I then become a counselor. In this role I must be a good listener to both parties, and when they are done talking, it's my turn to talk. In the worst situation I may tell them it looks as if they are headed for a separation or divorce. However, most of the time I tell them to act like adults and talk to their spouse as they talked to me. I may suggest that they seek professional counseling. With the husband and wife now having everything off their chests, and after their having received my small lecture, they may be able to go back to living relatively peaceful lives together.

3   In a different scenario, if the yelling and screaming is still gong on when I arrive, I may want to just stand back and be a referee. I usually allow the wife to talk first. She typically tells her husband off. Not forgetting my role as referee, I step in only if the argument gets extremely ugly. When this happens, I send the wife to a neutral corner to cool off. Then I allow her to continue her verbal assault. When I feel the husband has had enough, I stop the wife and give the husband a turn. All the time I am watching and listening. My main task is to keep the fight clean. If I think progress is being made with the couple, I let it continue. If the argument is going in circles, I may stop the flight. At this time I may send one of the fighters out for a drive or to a friend's house to cool off. This diversion is, however, only a temporary solution to the problem, for when the couple gets back together I will probably be needed for round two.

4   When the family dispute turns into a fist fight, it's usually the husband hitting his wife. Wives do hit their husbands, but the male ego usually won't let the men call the police. When the husband has hit his wife, and she has only a very minor injury, it will be up to her to have her husband arrested. If the wife is bleeding or has several bruises, then I make the decision. In these cases I become the enforcer of the law. I always place the husband under arrest even if the wife doesn't want it. As the enforcer I then take the husband to jail. The severity of the wife's injuries will determine how long the husband will stay in jail. He may be released in a couple of hours with a ticket and a court date, or

he may be in jail until he can be seen by a judge. Prior convictions and restraining orders are considerations.

5   As a typical police officer on patrol, I make many decisions and play many roles in domestic disturbance cases. The circumstances of these cases dictate the way each is handled. As an experienced officer, I should be able to make the right decision, and I should know when to be a counselor, a referee, or a law enforcer.

Exercise 9	DISCUSSION AND CRITICAL THINKING

1. The subject of this piece is "police officer," which is the larger unit for analysis. How did Price apply a principle to limit his subject for analysis by division? In other words, with which aspect of being a police officer is he concerned?

2. What are the different roles he may assume (as indicated in the last sentence of the introductory paragraph)? These roles become the parts for the functional analysis.

3. Of the three roles, which one requires the least judgment?

4. Of these roles, which are seldom thought of in connection with police work?

Practicing Patterns of Analysis by Division

In analysis by division, Roman numeral headings are almost always parts of the unit you are discussing as your subject. Learning to divide the unit into parts will help you move through your assignment quickly and efficiently.

Exercise 10	COMPLETING PATTERNS OF ANALYSIS BY DIVISION

Fill in the blanks to complete each analysis by division.

1. Unit: Doctor

   Principle: effective as a general practitioner

   Parts based on the principle

   I. Ability to _____

   II. Knowledge of _____

   III. Knowledge of _____

2. Unit: Newspaper

   Principle: Sections for readers

   Parts based on the principle

   I. News

   II. _____

III. _____

IV. _____

V. _____

✎ Topics for Writing Analysis by Division

Reading-Related Topics

"The Family and Its Parts"

1. Use this definition of a family, with its parts, as a pattern for writing about a family you are familiar with.

2. Use this definition of a family as a model for discussing why a particular family is dysfunctional.

3. Evaluate this definition and discuss how it might be broadened to include parents who are not married or other people with uncommon living arrangements.

"The Zones of the Sea"

4. Using this paragraph as a model, write about something else that has layers, such as a bone, a tree, the atmosphere, the earth, or a snowfield. Consult an encyclopedia or textbook for specific information on your topic.

5. Use the information and framework of this paragraph to expand on the zones of life, plants, and animals found in different locations.

"Growing Up Asian in America"

6. Write an analysis by division in which you discuss your own or someone else's origin. *Origin* here may mean ethnic group, class, or region (part of the country such as South, Midwest, East).

7. Using this essay as a model, write about who you are and why by referring to your parents and grandparents. How are they different from each other and from yourself? More important, what have you learned or inherited from them?

"Intermarried . . . with Children"

8. Write an analysis by division about the mixing of different factors in a family (for example, race, culture, faith, values, gender, generation) that have worked together but are still separate.

9. If you are a first-generation American, analyze what values or behaviors you have adopted from your contacts with American schooling and society.

10. Analyze a mixed marriage in which at least three other factors (such as education, values, interests) were more important than race, culture, or religion.

11. Considering your parents, grandparents, and any others who have significantly influenced you, give yourself a hyphenated designation and write an analysis by division about what each has contributed to you as a person. You may even include regional differences (North, South, West, East, Midwest) or different societies (country, city, inner city, suburbia).

Paired Essays on What We Are—Heritage as Hyphenation

12. Write about your own cultural makeup by discussing your hyphenated status and referring to one or both of the essays for insights or support. The hyphenation need not be exotic. It could be as simple as "Hill Country Texas-Chicago-Irish-Native American-Protestant-Free Thinker."

"Skin"

13. Using this paragraph as a model, write about how a particular unit functions. Consider another organ of the human body such as the heart, liver, or lungs. Other subjects include a piece of technology such as a computer, a printer, or a scanner.

"More Than Book 'Em"

14. Using Price's basic idea that he must be flexible and respond to the needs of the people he deals with, write about how you, in some function, must also fulfill several roles. Consider such roles as parent, family member, friend, employee, referee, guide, spouse, and student.

15. Write about someone else's multiple roles, such as those mentioned in the previous suggestion.

Career-Related Topics

16. Explain how the parts of a product function together as a unit.

17. Explain how each of several qualities of a specific person—such as his or her intelligence, sincerity, knowledgeability, ability to communicate, manner, attitude, and appearance—makes that individual an effective salesperson, manager, or employee.

18. Explain how the demands or requirements for a particular job represent a comprehensive picture of that job.

19. Explain how the aspects of a particular service (such as friendly, competent, punctual, confidential) work together in a satisfactory manner.

General Topics

Some of the following topics are too broad for a short writing assignment and should be narrowed. For example, the general "a wedding ceremony" could be narrowed to the particular: "José and María's wedding ceremony." Your focused topic should then be divided into parts and analyzed.

20. A machine such as an automobile, a computer, a camera

21. A city administration, a governmental agency, a school board, a student council

22. A ceremony—wedding, graduation

23. A holiday celebration, a pep rally, a sales convention, a religious revival

24. An offensive team in football (any team in any game)

25. A family, a relationship, a gang, a club, a sorority, a fraternity

26. An album, a performance, a song, a singer, an actor, a musical group, a musical instrument

27. A movie, a television program, a video game

28. Any well-known person—athlete, politician, criminal, writer

Writer's Guidelines: Analysis by Division

Almost anything can be analyzed by division—for example, how the parts of the ear work in hearing, how the parts of the eye work in seeing, or how the parts of the heart work in pumping blood throughout the body. Subjects such as these are all approached with the same systematic procedure.

1. This is the procedure.

   - *Step 1.*   Begin with something that is a unit.
   - *Step 2.*   State the principle by which that unit functions.
   - *Step 3.*   Divide the unit into parts according to the principle.
   - *Step 4.*   Discuss each of the parts in relation to the unit.

2. This is the way you might apply that procedure to a good boss.

   - Unit.   Manager
   - Principle of function.   Effective as a leader
   - Parts based on the principle: Fair, intelligent, stable, competent in field
   - Discussion: Consider each part in relation to the person's effectiveness as a manager.

3. This is how a basic outline of analysis by division might look.

   Thesis: To be effective as a leader, a manager needs specific qualities.
   - I. Fair
   - II. Intelligent
   - III. Stable
   - IV. Competent in field

Process Analysis: Writing about Doing

"Writing is not hard. Just sit down and write as it occurs to you. The writing is easy—it's the occurring that's hard."

Stephen Leacock

THE QUIGMANS   by Buddy Hickerson

Bad hints from Heloise.

B. Hickerson, copyright Los Angeles Times Syndicate. Reprinted by permission.

Writing Process Analysis

*I*f you have any doubt about how frequently we use process analysis, just think about how many times you have heard people say, "How do you do it?" or "How is [was] it done?" Even when you are not hearing those questions, you are posing them yourself when you need to make something, cook a meal, assemble an item, take some medicine, repair something, or figure out what happened. In your college classes, you may have to discover how osmosis occurs, how a rock changes form, how a mountain was formed, how a battle was won, or how a bill goes through the legislature.

If you need to explain how to do something or how something was (is) done, you will engage in *process analysis.* You will break down your topic into stages, explaining each so that your reader can duplicate or understand the process.

Two Types of Process Analysis: Directive and Informative

The questions How do I do it? and How is (was) it done? will lead you into two different types of process analysis—directive and informative.

Directive process analysis explains how to do something. As the name suggests, it gives directions for the reader to follow. It says, for example, "Read me, and you can bake a pie (tune up your car, read a book critically, write an essay, take some medicine)." Because it is presented directly to the reader, it usually addresses the reader as "you," or it implies the "you" by saying something such as "First [you] purchase a large pumpkin, and then [you]...." In the same way, this textbook addresses you or implies "you" because it is a long how-to-do-it (directive process analysis) statement.

Informative process analysis explains how something was (is) done by giving data (information). Whereas the directive process analysis tells you what to do in the future, the informative process analysis tells you what has occurred or what is occurring. If it is something in nature, such as the formation of a mountain, you can read and understand the process by which it emerged. In this type of process analysis, you do not tell the reader what to do; therefore, you will seldom use the words *you* or *your.*

Working with Stages

Preparation or Background

In the first stage of the directive type of process analysis, list the materials or equipment needed for the process and discuss the necessary setup arrangements. For some topics, this stage will also provide technical terms and definitions. The degree to which this stage is detailed will depend on both the subject itself and the expected knowledge and experience of the projected audience.

The informative type of process analysis may begin with background or context rather than with preparation. For example, a statement explaining how mountains form might begin with a description of a flat portion of the earth made up of plates that are arranged like a jigsaw puzzle.

Steps or Sequence

The actual process will be presented here. Each step or sequence must be explained clearly and directly, and phrased to accommodate the audience. The language, especially in directive process analysis, is likely to be simple and concise; however, avoid dropping words such as *and, a, an, the,* and *of,* and thereby lapsing into "recipe language." The steps may be accompanied by explanations about why certain procedures are necessary and how not following directions carefully can lead to trouble.

Order

The order will usually be chronological (time based) in some sense. Certain transitional words are commonly used to promote coherence: *first, second, third, then, soon, now, next, finally, at last, therefore, consequently,* and—especially for informative process analysis—words used to show the passage of time such as hours, days of the week, and so on.

Basic Forms

Consider using this form for the directive process (with topics such as how to cook something or how to fix something).

How to Prepare Spring Rolls

    I. Preparation
      A. Suitable cooking area
      B. Utensils, equipment
      C. Spring roll wrappers
      D. Vegetables, sauce
    II. Steps
      A. Season vegetables
      B. Wrap vegetables
      C. Fold wrappers
      D. Deep fry rolls
      E. Serve rolls with sauce

Consider using this form for the informative process (with topics such as how a volcano functions or how a battle was won).

How Coal Is Formed

    I. Background or context
      A. Accumulation of land plants
      B. Bacterial action
      C. Muck formation
    II. Sequence
      A. Lignite from pressure
      B. Bituminous from deep burial and heat
      C. Anthracite from metamorphic conditions

Combined Forms

Combination process analysis occurs when directive process analysis and informative process analysis are blended, usually when the writer personalizes the account. For example, if I tell you from a detached view how to write a research paper, my writing is directive process analysis, but if I tell you how I once wrote a research paper and give you the details in an informative account, then you may very well learn enough so that you can duplicate what I did. Thus, you would be both informed and instructed. Often the personalized account is more interesting to the general reader, but if you need to assemble a toy the night before your child's birthday, for example, you just want information.

Many assignments are done as a personalized account. A paper about planting radish seeds may be informative—but uninspiring. However, a paper about the time you helped your grandpa plant his spring garden (giving all the details) may be informative, directive, and entertaining. It is often the cultural framework provided by personal experience that transforms a pedestrian directive account into something memorable. That's why some instructors ask their students to explain how to do something within the context of experience.

Useful Prewriting Procedure

All the strategies of freewriting, brainstorming, and clustering can be useful in writing a process analysis. However, if you already know your subject well, you can simply make two lists, one headed *Preparation* or *Background* and the other *Steps* or *Sequence*. Then jot down ideas for each. After you have finished with your listing, you can delete parts, combine parts, and rearrange parts for better order. That editing of your lists will lead directly to a formal outline you can use in Stage Two of the writing process. Following is an example of listing for the topic of how to prepare spring rolls.

Preparation	*Steps*
stainless steel bowl	slice and mix vegetables
deep-fry pan	add sauce to vegetables
spoon	beat eggs
damp cloth	place wrappers on damp cloth
spring roll wrappers	add 2 to 3 tablespoons of vegetables per wrapper
eggs	fold and seal wrapper with egg
sauce	freeze for later or deep fry immediately
cabbage	serve with sweet and sour sauce
celery	
carrots	
bean sprouts	

Connecting Reading and Writing

Popping the Cork

A. Del Turco

The author of this passage begins with a scenario. Your mission, should you choose to accept it, is to open a bottle of champagne while a host of friends watch. Are you fearful that you might not perform with grace? If the answer is yes or if you are just a bit hesitant, A. Del Turco provides the directions you need.

1   All of the guests have arrived. Everyone has been seated at the dinner table. Light conversation abounds. Amid all of the explanations of what

everyone "does," your wife leans over to you and speaks the words of doom: "Why don't you open the champagne?" All conversation ceases. Suddenly you are aware of seven pairs of eyes, all looking at you. Each guest in turn mentally sizes you up. "Is he man enough?" "Will he embarrass himself again this year?" "Did they really have to re-carpet?" There it sits, ten feet away, smugly chilling in an ice bucket. The enemy. Relax. Opening a good bottle of champagne is not an ordeal once you know how. The necessary materials are few. All that is needed is an ice bucket, a table napkin, a little bravery, and some patience. To start, do yourself a favor by choosing a good champagne. Well-chilled good champagnes won't explode, while bad champagnes are potentially embarrassing. The wine should be chilled in the ice bucket for at least twenty minutes. This is done to reduce pressure in the bottle and allow for an uneventful opening.

2   First, remove the bottle from the bucket and quickly dry it. Wrap the table napkin around the neck of the bottle. This affords you a better grip. Next remove the neck wrapping to expose the wire basket. Removing the wire basket is the first tricky bit. The basket can be removed by twisting the wire braid counterclockwise six turns. This is an international standard among champagne vintners. Then pull the table napkin over the cork. This is done, once again, to allow for a better grip. Now comes the fun part. At the bottom of the champagne bottle is a deep indentation. This is not a manufacturing defect; it is called the "punt." Hold the bottle in your left hand by the punt. With your right, grip the cork between thumb and forefinger. Gently begin rocking the cork back and forth, slowly pulling at the cork. Soon the cork will begin to loosen and move more quickly. This is a critical point in the opening. Slow it down! Hold the cork back and slowly work it out of the neck. If the cork is removed properly, only the slightest sigh should be heard. From the champagne—not you.

Exercise 1   **DISCUSSION AND CRITICAL THINKING**

1. What type of process analysis (informative or directive) is used in "Popping the Cork"?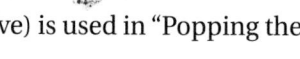

2. To what type of audience (well informed, moderately informed, or poorly informed on the topic) does Del Turco direct this selection? On what do you base your answer?

3. What is the prevailing tone of this material (objective, humorous, reverent, argumentative, cautionary, playful, ironic, ridiculing)?

4. Where does the preparation stage end?

5. How many steps does the writer use? Number them in the margin of the text.

6. Underline the transitional words in the pages that indicate time or other progression.

The Birth of an Island
Rachel Carson

We usually think of birth in a biological sense, but Rachel Carson describes a different kind—a geological birth. It requires no coach, no midwife, no obstetrician. But unless you can live for thousands or even millions of years, you cannot witness the whole process. Nevertheless, it is a process, and it can be described in steps.

The birth of a volcanic island is an event marked by prolonged and violent travail: the forces of the earth striving to create, and all the forces of the sea opposing. The sea floor, where an island begins, is probably nowhere more than about fifty miles thick—a thin covering over the vast bulk of the earth. In it are deep cracks and fissures, the results of unequal cooling and shrinkage in past ages. Along such lines of weakness the molten lava from the earth's interior presses up and finally bursts forth into the sea. But a submarine volcano is different from a terrestrial eruption, where lava, molten rocks, gases, and other ejecta are hurled into the air through an open crater. Here on the bottom of the ocean the volcano has resisting it all the weight of the ocean water above it. Despite the immense pressure of, it may be, two or three miles of sea water, the new volcanic cone builds upward toward the surface in flow after flow of lava. Once within reach of the waves, its soft ash and tuff are violently attacked, and for a long period the potential island may remain a shoal, unable to emerge. But, eventually, in new eruptions, the cone is pushed up into the air and a rampart against the attacks of the waves is built of hardened lava.

Exercise 2   **DISCUSSION AND CRITICAL THINKING**

1. What type of process analysis (informative or directive) is used here?

2. To what type of audience (well informed, moderately informed, or poorly informed on the topic) does Carson direct this selection?

3. What is the prevailing tone of this material (objective, humorous, reverent, argumentative, cautionary, playful, ironic, ridiculing)?

4. At what point does the setup material end and the informative process begin? Underline that pivotal sentence.

5. How many stages are there? Number them in the margin of the text.

6. What five transitional terms are used? Underline them.

Fast, Sleek, and Shiny: Using the Internet to Help Buy New Cars

Preston Gralla

In this essay adapted from *The Complete Idiot's Guide to Online Shopping,* **Preston Gralla presents down-to-earth advice on how to shop for a car on the Internet and how to avoid getting taken. Cars are only one of the many products featured in this book. This essay includes a discussion on how to buy a car and finance it, all through using your computer.**

1   Whether or not you plan to buy your new car over the Internet, make sure to do your prepurchase research online. Use the Internet to help decide which car to buy and to get the best deal possible from the dealer— or even to buy online. You'll get pleasure not only out of saving money, but also out of seeing car dealers gnash their teeth over the thought of how you were able to bargain them down to very little profit. There goes their trip to Cancun this year!

Step 1: Go Online to Research and Find Your Dream Machine

2   Your clunker has finally spit the last bit of black exhaust out of its tail pipe, and it's time to get a new dream machine. But what should you get? Should it be a supermacho, ego-enhancing sports utility vehicle? A trusty family station wagon? A hell-bent-for-leather sports car? Or just a plain old sedan? And which is the best model for your needs and pocketbook?

3   You'll find many sites to help you narrow down what you should buy. If you're not quite sure what you want, immediately head to the GTE Super-pages Consumer Guide at www.consumerguide.com. Use the Interactive Car Finder—think of it as the "Complete Idiot's Guide to Choosing a Car." You select the kind of car (compact, sports utility vehicle, and so on) the price range, fuel economy, and features such as air-conditioning, and voilà—you'll get a list of cars that match your pocketbook and the features you want.

4   Car aficionados who want to know what the insiders think about cars should head to the online site of *Car and Driver* magazine at www.carand driver.com. As you might guess, many, many more car sites online can help you decide which car to buy, and many also offer car reviews. I'd suggest that after you use the Consumer Guide and the *Car and Driver* site to narrow down your choices, you check in with as many sites as possible to get their takes on the cars of your dreams. One excellent site is Edmund's at www.edmunds.com.

Step 2: Get Ready to Bargain—Find Out the True Dealer Invoice Price

5   Sure, the last time you bought a car, you probably thought you got a pretty good deal. The dealer may even have said something like, "You got the best of me that time, Buddy." Guess what? The dealer was lying. (What a shock!)

You got taken for a ride. The dealer got the best of you. And it's not because you're not smart enough to drive a good bargain. It's because the dealer knows exactly how much the car cost, and you don't have a clue. Sticker price, retail price, rebates, MSRP (what in the world does that stand for, anyway?—oh, yeah, Manufacturer's Suggested Retail Price), the costs of all the "extras" (such as doors and an engine, it seems)—trying to put it all together makes your head start to spin. The whole pricing scheme for new cars is designed to confuse you. So what's a poor car buyer to do?

6   It's simple. Head to the Internet and find out exactly how much the dealer paid for the car (the dealer cost) to the dollar—including all the extras. When you're armed with that information, you can force the dealer to meet your price—or you can walk out the door and find a dealer who *will* meet it.

7   You can find the dealer invoice price at a number of sites on the Internet. But head to www.edmunds.com to get the best lowdown. It not only provides the most comprehensive information but also explains the ins and outs of car pricing, which is arcane enough to have confused a medieval philosopher. This site offers excellent how-to-buy articles as well.

8   The MSRP is the car's base price that the dealer will quote to you. Never, ever, ever pay that price for a car. If you do, the dealer and salesperson will be breaking out the champagne after you leave.

9   Find the invoice price. That's the most important number on the page. It's the price that the dealer pays the manufacturer for the base model of the car, without any extras. That's the number you're going to use when you start to bargain. Do you notice something interesting about the MSRP price and the invoice price? I thought you did; you have sharp eyes. The MSRP (sticker) price is several thousand dollars higher than the invoice price. So if a dealer knocks off $1,000 from the sticker price, you might think you're getting a good deal, but you're not—the dealer is still making out like a bandit.

10   Next, check out the invoice prices of the options you want—things like automatic transmission, a luggage rack, and a stereo. As you can see, each item has an MSRP as well as an invoice price, which means that the dealer is making money by marking up all your extras as well. The dealer also has to pay a destination charge, which can be $500 or more. Edmund's reports that charge as well.

11   To figure out the true cost to the dealer of the car you're interested in buying, do this math:

Invoice Price + Invoice Price of Extras + Destination Charge = Dealer's Costs

Now here's a strange fact: Even if you pay only the dealer's invoice costs for a car, in most instances the dealer *still* makes a profit. That's because of a little-known program called the "Dealer Hold Back." The dealer hold back is a percentage of the MSRP of the vehicle, including all extras. When a dealer sells a vehicle, the manufacturer sends the dealer a check based on the hold back percentage and the MSRP of the vehicle. Domestic carmakers typically pay a 3 percent dealer hold back, and foreign makers often pay 2 percent. But the amount varies from manufacturer to manufacturer. Edmund's tells you the dealer hold back for the car you're buying.

12   Let's take an example. Say the MSRP of the car and extras you've bought is $25,000, and the dealer hold back is 3 percent. According to this formula, after you buy the car, the manufacturer sends the dealer a check for $750.

Therefore, even if the dealer sells the car at invoice price, he or she is still making money. Note, though, that the money doesn't go to your salesperson—it goes straight to the dealer. So, no salesperson is going to agree to give you a car at invoice price.

13　　Another way to save hundreds or even thousands of dollars when buying your next car is to find out what kinds of rebates and dealer incentives are available; on the www.edmunds.com site, just click on Incentives and Rebates.

Step 3: Psyching Out Your Dealer with Information You Got Online

14　　So now you know the invoice cost of the car you want to buy, the destination charge, the dealer hold back, and any kinds of rebates and incentives available on the car you're interested in buying. What next? Let's say you want to buy a car from a dealer, not through the Web.

15　　First, print everything out directly from the Web so that you have a sheaf of papers you can refer to. When you walk in with the printouts, the dealer will realize you know your business and won't try to pull a fast one on you. (Well, the dealer may *try* to pull a fast one, but won't be able to succeed.)

16　　Also, figure out on a sheet of paper how much you're willing to pay for the car. Base it on the invoice price of the car. You should hold the line at 3 percent over invoice cost if you can—and if the car isn't very popular or new models are about to come out, try to get it at 2 percent or less over invoice cost. If you're looking to buy a hot-selling car, you might not be able to drive such a hard bargain, but it's worth a try. For cars that aren't moving fast, you should be able to bargain down to your 2 percent or 3 percent figure. Also, when figuring the price you should pay for a car, be sure to consider any rebates or incentives.

| **Exercise 3** | **DISCUSSION AND CRITICAL THINKING** |

1. Is this essay informative or directive?

2. Sometimes the preparation stage is implied or assumed. To shop on the Internet, of course, a person needs a computer with Internet access. Does Gralla specify the preparation stage, or does he simply make an assumption about the computer and Internet access?

3. Gralla gives much information, but he also is writing with a particular audience in mind. Just what does he expect the reader to know about computers?

4. How many steps does Gralla use?

5. In tone (the way the author regards the subject and the reader), what distinguishes this essay from many directive process analysis statements?

A Successful Interview

C. Edward Good and William Fitzpatrick

Freelance authors C. Edward Good and William Fitzpatrick describe the interview as systematic. To be successful in an interview, a person being interviewed must understand the system. In this way, the interviewee will not only follow what is going on and anticipate questions but also, in some instances, be able to control the flow of the interview.

1   Facing the interview might make you apprehensive, but there is no reason to fear it. It is your real opportunity to get face to face with your product's potential buyer and bring to bear all of your personal selling skills. If you go into the situation with confidence based on preparation and not on ego, you will come out a winner. Take the time to prepare properly. The interview has been your goal thus far in the job search, so it is your stepping stone to future success. Be positive, be enthusiastic, and rely on your experience in communicating with people.

The Interview

2   The interviewer will most likely take the following steps with you:

Establish Rapport.   The interviewer's responsibility is to put you at ease, both physically and emotionally. The more relaxed you are, the more you will trust the interviewer and open up to him or her. Skilled interviewers will not put you in front of a desk. They will put the chair beside the desk so there are no barriers between you or will not use a desk at all. Initial conversation will be about trivial matters such as the weather, parking, or any subject to get you talking.

3   *Determine Your Qualifications.*   The interviewer has to find out as early as possible if you are technically qualified (on the surface) for the job. Time is valuable, and an interviewer can't waste it on unqualified candidates. The determination is made by a review of the application and your resume. This can turn into a simple yes and no session as the interviewer matches your qualifications against the requirements for the position. During this phase, information is gathered to develop questions later on in the conversation. This technique is called blueprinting.

4   *Explain the Company and the Job.*   At this point in the interview, the interviewer will try to get you excited about wanting to work for the company. He or she generally will cover job responsibilities and company benefits to interest you even further.

5   *Determine Your Suitability.*   The interviewer now has to determine if you are the best candidate. In many cases this is a subjective judgment based upon impressions of your conduct and your ability to handle the questions posed to you. In this part of the interview you will be asked situational questions, which may or may not be directly related to your future duties. The interviewer may even ask some startling questions to get your

response. The technique used is to ask open-ended questions (those that require more than a one-word answer) during this phase, rather than close-ended questions (those that only require a simple yes or no).

6   *Conclusion.*   Now it is the interviewer's responsibility to review the major points you covered during the interview and get you out of the office in a timely manner. The interviewer should ensure all of your questions have been answered and will generally let you know what the next step is and when a decision will be made.

7   As you can see, an interview is a planned and controlled process. As stated, a trained and skilled interviewer will guide you through the steps and will know exactly how to keep you on track. The managers in the second and subsequent interviews may not follow a planned agenda and may even have trouble staying on track themselves. If you understand what is happening, you can take control. The rules for the interview are based on one theory only. If you were called, you probably are qualified for the job. Your task is to show the company you are the best qualified of the candidates who are competing. Here are some suggestions for doing that.

8   *Always Be Positive.*   Losers dwell on past losses, winners dwell on future successes. Don't worry about where you have been, worry about where you're going. Make sure your accomplishments are related to your capabilities.

9   *Listen, Listen, Listen.*   Throughout the interview, concentrate to be sure you're really listening to what the interviewer has to say. It looks very bad when you ask a question the interviewer just answered.

10   *State Your Qualifications, Not Your Drawbacks.*   Tell them what you can do; let them wonder about what you can't do.

11   *Ask Questions.*   Be sure to ask intelligent, well-thought-out questions that indicate you are trying to find out what you can do for the company. Base any statements on proven experience, not dreams and hopes.

12   *Watch Out for Close-Ended Questions.*   Be wary of interviewers who ask close-ended questions. They probably don't know what they are doing. If you begin to hear a series of questions that require only a yes or no, the other candidates are probably hearing the same questions. If the interviewer asks three candidates the same question and all he gets are three no answers, he won't be able to distinguish among the three. If all the answers are the same, he can't make an intelligent choice. Your strategy, then, is to turn these close-ended questions into open-ended ones so you can put a few intelligent sentences together. In this way, you will distinguish yourself from the other yes and no candidates.

13   *Stay Focused.*   Concentrate on the conversation at hand. Don't get off on extraneous matters that have nothing to do with the job or your qualifications.

14   *Don't Get Personal.*   Keep personal issues out of the interview. Never confide in an interviewer no matter how relaxed and comfortable you feel. If you feel the urge to bare your soul, your feelings should tell you the interviewer is very skilled and followed the first step of the interview extremely well.

15 *Rehearse.* Plan some answers to obvious questions. Why did you leave your previous position? Why did you choose your academic major? What are your training and experience going to do for the company?

16 *Maintain Eye Contact.* If you can't look interviewers in the eye, they won't believe your answer. Further, there are no answers written on the ceiling, so if you get in a bind, don't look up for divine guidance. The answer is not on the ceiling. It's in your head.

17 *Pause a Moment.* Take a moment before each answer to consider what you will say. Don't answer the question in a rush, but reflect a moment to get it straight.

18 *Take Notes.* If you plan on taking notes, ask first. Some people are uncomfortable when their words are written down. Do not attempt to record the conversation.

19 *Multiple Interviewers.* If you are interviewed by more than one person, answer all of them equally. Begin with the questioner, let your eyes go to each of the others as you continue your answer, and finally come back to the original questioner. Each of them will then feel you are speaking to him or her alone.

20 *Don't Drink, Don't Smoke.* In fact, don't ingest anything at all. Although it is polite to accept a proffered cup of coffee or a soft drink, it is not polite to spill it in your lap. You will be nervous, so don't take the chance. Remember, they are merely trying to establish rapport. Besides, you can't maintain eye contact while drinking or eating.

21 *Likely Open-Ended Questions.* What follows are some properly formulated open-ended questions you may hear later. Get used to the format and prepare answers. Keep them down to a couple of sentences, not paragraphs.

1. In your relationship with your previous supervisor, would you mind giving an example of how you were alike or not alike?

2. How would you define success?

3. Would you demonstrate some methods you would use to cause a marginal employee to rise to his or her full potential?

4. How can a team atmosphere improve your personal effectiveness?

5. If you were a problem, how would you solve yourself?

After the Interview

22 When the interview concludes, don't linger, but don't run out the door, either. If the interviewers haven't indicated when a decision will be reached, ask them. This will give them the impression that you might have other offers you are considering. When you get back to your car, take out a professional-looking note card (purchased in advance for just this purpose) and write (in longhand with roller pen or a fountain pen) a brief thank-you note to all the people in the company who interviewed you.

23 Take the note to the post office and mail it the same day. It is important that the note reach the interviewers the next day. You hope it will hit their desk at the same time they are comparing your resume with those of other

candidates. You now have the advantage of having at least two documents on their desk. It might not help, but it certainly won't hurt.

| Exercise 4 | DISCUSSION AND CRITICAL THINKING |

1. Is this essay informative or directive?

2. What are the major steps that an interviewer is likely to follow?

3. Are the suggestions presented in any sequence that need be followed?

4. Is the interview process discussed here formal or informal or a combination?

5. How does this "planned and controlled process" compare with interviews you have participated in?

Student Writers: Demonstrations and Readings

Many of us reclaim our ethnic origin at our New Year as we celebrate by eating a meal that is intended to bring us happiness, peace, and prosperity for the next twelve months. For Maysim Mondegaran, the meal is Sabzi Polo Mahi, and each phase of the preparation and cooking is done with care and feeling. Reading her paragraph will make you hungry. Notice how she includes both directive and informative elements.

Mondegaran's Writing Process Worksheet shows you how her writing evolved from idea to final draft. To conserve space here, the free writing and the rough draft marked for revision have been omitted. The balance of her worksheet has been lengthened for you to be able to see her other work in its entirety.

You will find a full-size blank worksheet on page 5. It can be photocopied, filled in, and submitted with each assignment if your instructor directs you to do so.

. . . .

Writing Process Worksheet:

TITLE Sabzi Polo Mahi

NAME Maysim Mondegaran   **DUE DATE** Thursday, March 9, 11 a.m.

| **ASSIGNMENT** | In the space below, write whatever you need to know about your assignment, including information about the topic, audience, pattern of writing, length, whether to include a rough draft or revised drafts, and whether your paper must be typed. |

Write a long paragraph (about 300 words) about a holiday meal, dish, or ritual. Explain how something is done, and place your subject within a cultural framework. Submit your completed Writing Process Worksheet, a rough draft marked for revision, and a typed final draft.

STAGE ONE **Explore**   Freewrite, brainstorm (list), cluster, or take notes as directed by your instructor. Use the back of this page or separate paper if you need more space.

Clustering

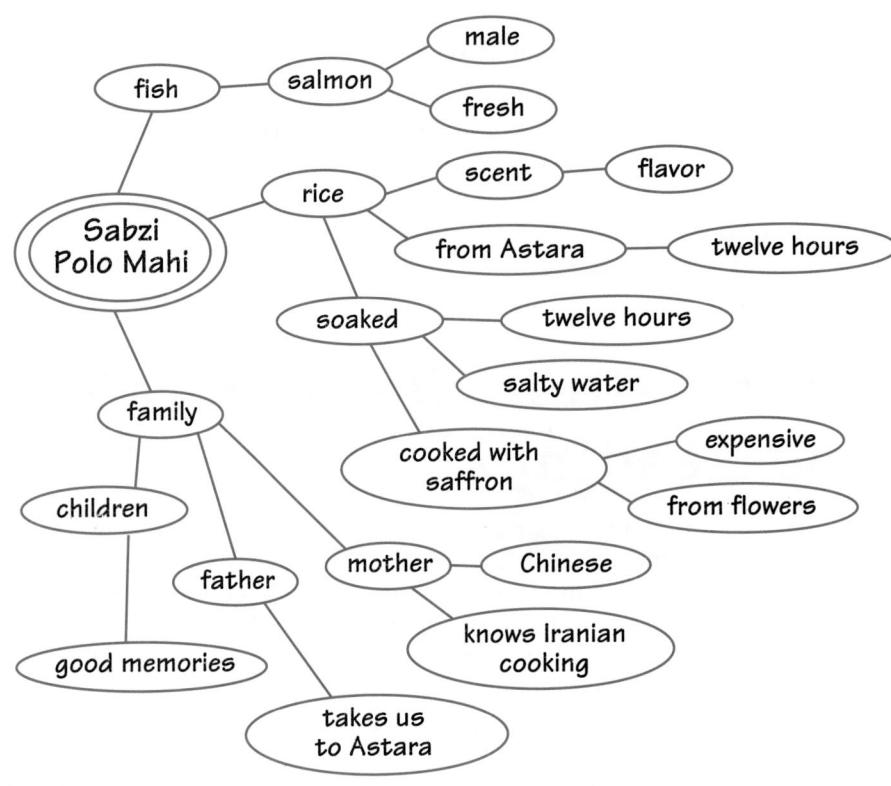

Listing

— Preparation	— Steps
Get fish	Cook fish
Find good rice	Cook rice
Get vegetables	Cook vegetables
Butter	Season
Saffron	

STAGE TWO **Organize**   Write a topic sentence or thesis; label the subject and the treatment parts.

In order to make Sabzi Polo Mahi properly, you need to know how to pick
        subject   **treatment**
the right ingredients and how to cook them.

Write an outline or an outline alternative.

I. Preparation
   A. Picking the fish
      1. Fresh
      2. Salmon
      3. Male
   B. Picking the rice
      1. Appearance
      2. Scent
      3. Where found
   C. Vegetables
      1. Leafy
      2. Garlic
   D. Picking the seasoning
      1. Butter
      2. Saffron
II. Cooking
   A. Fish
      1. Baked
      2. Flaky, white, juicy
   B. Rice
      1. Soaked for twelve hours
      2. Boiled
      3. Drained
   C. Vegetables
      1. Stir-fried
      2. Steamed with rice
   D. Seasoning
      1. Butter
      2. Saffron

STAGE THREE   **Write**   On separate paper, write and then revise your paper as many times as necessary for c̲oherence, l̲anguage (usage, tone, and diction), u̲nity, e̲mphasis, s̲upport, and s̲entences (CLUESS). Read your paper aloud to hear and correct any grammatical errors or awkward-sounding sentences.

Edit any problems in fundamentals, such as c̲apitalization, o̲missions, p̲unctuation, and s̲pelling (COPS).

Final Draft

Sabzi Polo Mahi

Maysim Mondegaran

    In Iran, families like to celebrate the beginning of the New Year each spring with a meal called Sabzi Polo Mahi, which means fish with vegetables and rice. The preparation is as important as the cooking. In order to

Transitional words are circled   make this special dish, one must (first) know how to pick the right fish, rice, vegetables, and seasoning. A fresh fish is required for the main part of the meal. It should have shiny bright eyes, nonsticky light grey skin, and pale pink meat. Salmon is recommended. In my family we usually buy one that weighs about eight kilograms. It is best to pick a male fish because the meat is more tender and tastier than that of the female. The males always have several black round dots that look like moles on top of their heads. (Second,) the rice must be excellent, and the best is grown in Astara, in

Preparation

Northern Iran. Although my mother is Chinese, she likes to follow the Iranian custom, so every now and then we drive six hours to Astara and buy several big bags of Astarian rice with long grains and a good scent. To get the

Steps 1 best results, the rice must be soaked in salty water for twelve hours before it is cooked. When the rice is almost through soaking, the fish is placed in

2 the oven preheated to about 350 degrees and baked. (From time to time) it should be basted. The baking time will vary, depending on the size of the fish. It is done when the flesh is white and flaky but still moist. (While) the

3 fish is cooking, the rice should be boiled and drained. (While) the rice is draining, the vegetables should be prepared. The vegetables (in my family,

4 mainly leafy green ones like spinach or parsley) are chopped fine and stir-

5 fried with garlic. (After) the vegetables are done, they should be combined

6 with the rice and steamed so that the flavors mix. (After) they are steamed, melted butter and ground saffron mixed with a few drops of water are poured over them. Saffron has a bright yellow color and a rich flavor. My mother buys it raw and grinds it specially for this meal. (At last) the Sabzi Polo Mahi is ready—the succulent baked fish and the mixture of spicy green vegetables and rice, (now) made vibrant yellow and flavorful by the saffron and butter. This is one of my favorite dishes, and I look forward to the next time when I can have it with my family.

Exercise 5 **DISCUSSION AND CRITICAL THINKING**

1. What type of process analysis (informative, directive, or both) is used?

2. To what kind of audience (well informed, moderately informed, or poorly informed on the topic) does the writer direct this selection?

3. What is the prevailing tone (objective, humorous, reverent, argumentative, cautionary, playful, ironic, ridiculing) of this material?

Making a Perfect Paper Airplane

John L. Tillman

John Tillman has a special interest in engineering, and here his expertise shows as he explains how to use simple materials to do something we have all dreamed about: building a perfect paper airplane. Follow the directions, and you'll get a lot of admiring glances. This approach is guaranteed.

Most people know how to make a paper airplane. Generally, these paper airplanes end up looking like a sleek delta-winged fighter, but there are other types. What you are about to read is a set of directions for making an unusual paper airplane that most people would claim, some adamantly, to be unflyable.

At the outset, you must gather the necessary materials. A standard piece of notebook paper, preferably one with squared corners and no holes for binder rings, is the most essential item. If you are a novice paper airplane maker, use a pen or pencil and a ruler at least as long as the diagonal corner-to-corner length of the paper.

Now the construction can begin. First set the piece of paper flat on a desk or table in front of you with the long dimension of the paper's rectangular shape facing side to side. Using a pencil and ruler, draw a line diagonally across the paper from the lower left-hand corner to the upper right-hand corner, as you face it. Grab the upper left-hand corner and pull it up and toward your lower right, creating a fold along the line you have drawn.

After you have made the fold, take the paper and slightly rotate the paper clockwise so that the long flat edge is on top and the sawtooth edge is facing you. Next, using the ruler and pencil, draw a line parallel to the top long flat edge, about one-third to one-half inch below the top edge. Fold the paper along this line, bringing the top edge up, over and toward you. Where this now former top edge is now located is your next fold line; fold again as described in the preceding sentence. Once again, repeat this fold sequence for a third and last time. What you now have should look like a sawtooth pattern facing you with a laterally extended flat leading edge at the top. Take the left and right ends of this leading edge and bend them up toward the ceiling. Continue bending these ends until they start coming together, forming a circle. Push these two ends together into one another, connecting them and creating an object that looks like a crown. If necessary, work with this crownlike object so that the leading edge is as perfectly round as you can get it.

What you now have is an aerodynamically viable object. With the leading edge facing forward and away from you, and the leading edge connection facing up toward the ceiling, place your index and middle fingers in the middle and on top of the sawtooth trailing edge. Your thumb should naturally fall into place on the bottom of the trailing edge. Lifting your hand so that the forward circular part of this paper airplane is facing well above the horizon, flick your wrist from up to forward, letting it go with a firm shove. A forceful throw is not necessary. If it does not fly straight (a gentle curve is permissible), check to see if either the circular leading edge or the trailing sawtooth shaped wing is warped. If they aren't circular when looking at it in a fore-aft direction, bend it or play around with it until it is. Happy flying.

| **Exercise 6** | **DISCUSSION AND CRITICAL THINKING** |

1. What type of process analysis (informative, directive, or both) is used?

2. To what type of audience (well informed, moderately informed, or poorly informed on the topic) does the writer direct this selection?

3. What is the prevailing tone (objective, humorous, reverent, argumentative, cautionary, playful, ironic, ridiculing) of this material?

4. Draw a line at the point at which the preparation (materials, setup, explaining words, and so on) ends and the steps begin.

5. Write numbers in the margin to indicate the steps or stages in the process.

6. Circle any transitional words indicating time or other progression (*first, second, then, soon, now, next, after, before, when, finally, at last, therefore, consequently,* and—especially for the informative process analysis—words used to show the passage of time, such as hours, days of the week, and so on).

Practicing Patterns of Process Analysis

A definite pattern underlies a process analysis. In some presentations, such as directions with merchandise to be assembled, the content reads as mechanically as an outline, and no reader objects. The same can be said of most recipes. In other presentations, such as your typical college assignments, the pattern is submerged in flowing discussion. The directions or information must be included, but the writing should be well-developed and interesting. Regardless of the form you use or the audience you anticipate, keep in mind that in process analysis the pattern will provide a foundation for the content.

Exercise 7   **COMPLETING PATTERNS OF PROCESS ANALYSIS**

Reread "Popping the Cork," which begins on p. 180, and convert it into an outline of directive process analysis.

I. Preparation

    A. Basic materials

        1. _____

        2. _____

        3. _____

        4. _____

    B. Champagne

        1. _____

        2. _____

II. Steps

    A. _____

    B. _____

    C. _____

D. _____

E. _____

F. _____

✎ Topics for Writing Process Analysis

Reading-Related Topics

"Popping the Cork"

1. Discuss how to perform a specialty such as barbecuing a steak, carving a turkey, making a toast, or flambéing cherries jubilee. Don't just relate a mechanical procedure. Explain how to do the task with style and confidence.

"The Birth of an Island"

2. Use this reading selection as a guide to writing about the formation of some other geological feature: an alluvial plain, a beach, a mountain lake, a mountain, a desert, or a delta. Consult a science textbook or an encyclopedia for basic information.

"Fast, Sleek, and Shiny: Using the Internet to Help Buy New Cars"

3. Using this essay as a model, explain how to purchase another item on the Internet.

4. Using the steps of the model in this essay, write an informative process analysis in which you explain how you shopped for a car or a similar product on the Internet.

"A Successful Interview"

5. Using the interview process discussed in this essay, describe an interview you experienced as either an interviewer or an interviewee.

6. As a group, prepare for a practice interview, conduct it, and write about the results of this activity.
   a. Create and define an imaginary company or decide on a company you are all familiar with, such as Wal*Mart, JCPenney, or Sears.
   b. Divide the class into three groups: those who are interviewing; those who are being interviewed (looking for a job); and those who are watching, taking notes, and advising other groups.
   c. All groups prepare for mock interviews: deciding on job specifications (duties, pay, benefits, etc.), phrasing questions, and anticipating questions.
   d. Rehearse.
   e. Conduct interviews.
   f. Take notes.
   g. Write an informative process analysis based on a particular interview and related to the procedure described in the essay. You will discuss the background and sequence parts and evaluate the performance of the interviewers and the person being interviewed. For a more focused piece of writing, you could concentrate only on the person being interviewed.

"Sabzi Polo Mahi"

7. Write about a special holiday dish prepared in your home. Follow Monde-garan's lead in discussing the source and quality of the foods, and try to capture her warmth of tone. Try to blend the directive and informative approaches.

"Making a Perfect Paper Airplane"

8. Write a directive process analysis in which you explain how to make a paper airplane (or some other simple object approved by your instructor) of a different design. After you finish your first draft, give it to someone else in the class and ask him or her to follow your directions, make the paper airplane, and deliver both the draft and the airplane to you. See if you can figure out what went wrong (if anything does) and write a final draft.

Career-Related Topics

9. Explain how to display, package, sell, or demonstrate a product.

10. Explain how to perform a service or to repair or install a product.

11. Explain the procedure for operating a machine, computer, piece of equipment, or other device.

12. Explain how to manufacture, construct, or cook something.

General Topics

Most of the following topics are directive as they are phrased. However, each can be transformed into a how-it-was-done informative topic by personalizing it and explaining stage by stage how you, someone else, or a group did something. For example, you could write either a directive process analysis about how to deal with an obnoxious person or an informative process analysis about how you or someone else dealt with an obnoxious person. Keep in mind that the two types of process analysis are often blended, especially in the personal approach. Many of these topics will be more interesting to you and your readers if they are personalized.

Most of the topics require some narrowing to be treated in a paragraph. For example, writing about playing baseball is too broad; writing about how to throw a curve ball may be manageable.

13. How to end a relationship without hurting someone's feelings

14. How to pass a test for a driver's license

15. How to get a job at _____

16. How to eat _____

17. How to perform a magic trick

18. How to repair _____

19. How to assemble _____

20. How to learn about another culture

21. How to approach someone you would like to know better

Writer's Guidelines: Process Analysis

1. Decide whether your process analysis is mainly directive or informative, and be appropriately consistent in using pronouns and other designations.

- For the directive analysis, use the second person, addressing the reader as *you*. The *you* may be understood, even if it is not written.

- For the informative analysis, use the first person, speaking as *I* or *we*, or the third person, speaking about the subject as *he, she, it*, or *they*, or by name.

2. Consider using these basic forms.

Directive	**Informative**
I. Preparation	I. Background
A.	A.
B.	B.
II. Steps	II. Sequence
A.	A.
B.	B.
C.	C.

3. Listing is a useful prewriting activity for this form. Begin with the Roman numeral headings indicated in number 2.

4. The order of a process analysis will usually be chronological (time based) in some sense. Certain transitional words are commonly used to promote coherence: *first, second, third, then, soon, now, next, finally, at last, therefore,* and *consequently.*

Cause and Effect: Determining Reasons and Outcomes

"Originality doesn't mean saying what no one has ever said before; it means saying exactly what you think yourself."

James Stephen

THE QUIGMANS   by Buddy Hickerson

The desert wedding is a greatly feared event, mostly because
of the tossing of the bridal cactus.

Writing Cause and Effect

Causes and effects deal with reasons and results; they are sometimes discussed together and sometimes separately. Like other forms of writing to explain, writing about causes and effects is based on natural thought processes. The shortest, and arguably the most provocative, poem in the English language—"I/Why?"—is posed by an anonymous author about cause. Children are preoccupied with delightful and often exasperating "why" questions. Daily we encounter all kinds of causes and effects. The same subject may raise questions of both kinds.

> The car won't start. Why? *(cause)*
> The car won't start. What now? *(effect)*

At school, from the biology lab to the political science classroom, and at work, from maintaining relationships to changing procedures, causes and effects are found everywhere.

Exploring and Organizing

One useful approach to developing a cause-or-effect analysis is listing. Write down the event, situation, or trend you are concerned about. Then on the left side, list the cause, and on the right side, list the effects. From them you will select the main causes or effects for your paragraph or essay. Here is an example.

Causes	Event, Situation, or Trend	Effects
Low self-esteem	Joining a gang	Life of crime
Drugs		Drug addiction
Tradition		Surrogate family relationship
Fear		Protection
Surrogate family		Ostracism
Protection		Restricted vocational opportunities
Neighborhood status		

As you use prewriting techniques to explore your ideas, you need to decide whether your topic should mainly inform or mainly persuade. If you intend to inform, your tone should be coolly objective. If you intend to persuade, your tone should be subjective. In either case, you should take into account the views of your audience as you phrase your ideas. You should also take into account how much your audience understands about your topic and develop your ideas accordingly.

Composing a Topic Sentence or a Thesis

Now that you have listed your ideas under causes and effects, you are ready to focus on the causes, on the effects, or, occasionally, on both.

Your controlling idea, the topic sentence or the thesis, might be one of the causes: "It is not just chance; people have reasons for joining gangs." Later, as you use the idea, you would rephrase it to make it less mechanical, allowing it to become part of the flow of your discussion. If you wanted to personalize the work—thereby probably making it more interesting—you could write about someone you know who joined a gang. You could use the same basic framework, the main causes, to indicate why this particular person joined a gang.

Writing an Outline

Your selection of a controlling idea takes you to the next writing phase: completing an outline or outline alternative. There you need to

- consider kinds of causes and effects.

- evaluate the importance of sequence.

- introduce ideas and work with patterns.

In its most basic form, your outline, derived mainly from points in your listing, might look like one of the following:

Paragraph of causes

Topic sentence: It is not just chance; people have reasons for joining gangs.

  I. Low self-esteem (cause 1)

  II. Surrogate family (cause 2)

  III. Protection (cause 3)

Essay of effects

Thesis: One is not a gang member without consequences.

  I. Restricted vocational opportunities (effect 1)

  II. Life of crime (effect 2)

  III. Drug addiction (effect 3)

  IV. Ostracism from mainstream society (effect 4)

Considering Kinds of Causes and Effects

Causes and effects can be primary or secondary, immediate or remote.

Primary or Secondary

Primary means "major," and *secondary* means "minor." A primary cause may be sufficient to bring about the situation (subject). For example, infidelity may be a primary (and possibly sufficient by itself) cause of divorce for some people but not for others, who regard it as secondary. Or if country X is attacked by country Y, the attack itself, as a primary cause, may be sufficient to bring on a declaration of war. But a diplomatic blunder regarding visas for workers may be of secondary importance, and though significant, it is certainly not enough to start a war over.

Immediate or Remote

Causes and effects often occur at a distance in time or place from the situation. The immediate effect of sulfur in the atmosphere may be atmospheric pollution, but the long-range, or remote, effect may be acid rain and the loss of species. The immediate cause of the greenhouse effect may be the depletion of the ozone layer, whereas the long-range, or remote, cause is the use of CFCs (commonly called Freons, which are found in such items as Styrofoam cups). Even more remote, the ultimate cause may be the people who use the products containing Freons. Your purpose will determine the causes and effects appropriate for your essay.

Evaluating the Importance of Sequence

The sequence in which events occur(red) may or may not be significant. When you are dealing with several sequential events, determine whether the sequence of events has causal connections; that is, does one event bring about another?

Consider this sequence of events: Joe's parents get divorced, and Joe joins a gang. We know that one reason for joining a gang is to gain family companionship. Therefore, we may conclude that Joe joined the gang in order to satisfy his needs for family companionship, which he lost when his parents were divorced. But if we do so, we may have reached a wrong conclusion, because Joe's joining the gang after the family breakup does not necessarily mean that the two events are related. Maybe Joe joined the gang because of drug dependency, low self-esteem, or a need for protection.

In each case, examine the connections. To assume that one event is *caused* by another just because it *follows* the other is a logical error called a *post hoc* ("after this") fallacy. An economic depression may occur after a president takes office, but that does not necessarily mean the depression was caused by the new administration. It might have occurred anyway, perhaps in an even more severe form.

Order

The order of the causes and effects you discuss in your paper may be based on time, space, emphasis, or a combination.

- *Time:* If one stage leads to another, as in a discussion of the causes and effects of upper atmospheric pollution, your paper would be organized best by time.

- *Space:* In some instances, causes and effects are best organized by their relation in space. For example, the causes of an economic recession could be discussed in terms of local factors, regional factors, national factors, and international factors.

- *Emphasis:* Some causes and effects may be more important than others. For instance, if some causes of divorce are primary (perhaps infidelity and physical abuse) and others are secondary (such as annoying habits and laziness), a paper about divorce could present the secondary causes first, and then move on to primary causes to emphasize the latter as more important.

In some situations, two or more factors (such as time and emphasis) may be linked; in that case, select the order that best fits what you are trying to say, or combine orders.

Introducing Ideas and Working with Patterns

In presenting your controlling idea—probably near the beginning for a paragraph or in an introductory paragraph for an essay—you will almost certainly want to perform two functions:

1. *Discuss your subject.* For example, if you are writing about the causes or effects of divorce, begin with a statement about divorce as a subject.

2. *Indicate whether you will concentrate on causes or effects or combine them.* That indication should be made clear early in the paper. Concentrating on one—causes or effects—does not mean you will not mention the other; it only means you will emphasize one of them. You can bring attention to your main concern(s)—causes, or effects, or a combination—by repeating key words such as *cause, reason, effect, result, consequence,* and *outcome.*

The most likely pattern for your work is one of those shown in Figure 12.1. These patterns may look familiar to you. We discussed similar patterns in Chapters 4 and 5.

Figure 12.1
Patterns for Paragraph and Essay

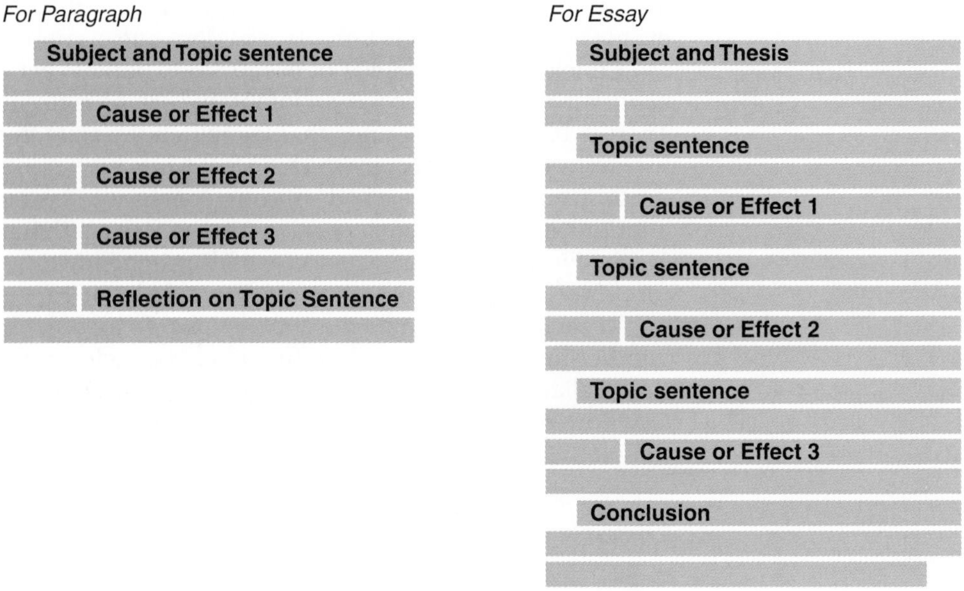

For Paragraph

Subject and Topic sentence
Cause or Effect 1
Cause or Effect 2
Cause or Effect 3
Reflection on Topic Sentence

For Essay

Subject and Thesis
Topic sentence
Cause or Effect 1
Topic sentence
Cause or Effect 2
Topic sentence
Cause or Effect 3
Conclusion

Exercise 1	**COMPLETING PATTERNS OF CAUSE AND EFFECT**

Complete the following cluster on teenage parenthood. Then select three primary causes or three primary effects that could be used in writing a paragraph or essay on this topic.

Causes   **Effects**

Teenage
Parenthood

Primary causes   Primary effects

1. _____   1. _____

2. _____   2. _____

3. _____   3. _____

Connecting Reading and Writing

What Happens to Steroid Studs?

Anastasia Toufexis

Young men take steroids because they want the Rambo look. But they get much more than muscles in their steroids effects package—and what they get, no one wants.

But the drug-enhanced physiques are a hazardous bargain. Steroids can cause temporary acne and balding, upset hormonal production, and damage the heart and kidneys. Doctors suspect they may contribute to liver cancer and atherosclerosis. Teens, who are already undergoing physical and psychological stresses, may run some enhanced risks. The drugs can stunt growth by accelerating bone maturation. Physicians also speculate that the chemicals may compromise youngsters' still developing reproductive systems. Steroid users have experienced a shrinking of the testicles and impotence. Dr. Richard Dominguez, a sports specialist in suburban Chicago, starts his lectures to youths with a surefire attention grabber: "You want to shrink your balls? Take steroids." Just as worrisome is the threat to mental health. Drug users are prone to moodiness, depression, irritability and what are known as "roid rages." Ex-user Darren Allen Chamberlain, 26, of Pasadena, California, describes himself as an "easy-going guy" before picking up steroids at age 16. Then he turned into a teen Terminator.

Exercise 2	DISCUSSION AND CRITICAL THINKING

1. What is the subject (a situation, circumstances, or trend) at the center of this discussion?

2. Which sentence most clearly indicates the author's intention of writing about cause or effect, or a combination?

3. Is this passage concerned most with causes, effects, or a combination of both?

4. Underline the sentences that indicate the specific effects.

5. In what order (time, space, emphasis, or a combination) are the parts presented?

6. Is the author's purpose mainly to inform or to persuade?

Family Heroes and Role Models

Marian Wright Edelman

We are not born with values. We do not survive and prosper by ourselves. Any person who has succeeded should be able to look back and recognize those who provided a heritage through example and instruction. Marian Wright Edelman pays homage to her family and community for what her generation of black children received. This paragraph comes from her book *The Measure of Our Success: A Letter to My Children and Yours* (1992).

The legacies that parents and church and teachers left to my generation of Black children were priceless but not material: a living faith reflected in daily service, the discipline of hard work and stick-to-it-ness, and a capacity to struggle in the face of adversity. Giving up and "burnout" were not part of the language of my elders—you got up every morning and you did what you had to do and you got up every time you fell down and tried as many times as you had to to get it done right. They had grit. They valued family life, family rituals, and tried to be and to expose us to good role models. Role models were of two kinds: those who achieved in the outside world (like Marian Anderson, my namesake) and those who didn't have a whole lot of education or fancy clothes but who taught us by the special grace of their lives the message of Christ and Tolstoy and Gandhi and Heschel and Dorothy Day and Romero and King that the Kingdom of God was within—in what you are, not what you have. I still hope I can be half as good as Black church and community elders like Miz Lucy McQueen, Miz Tee Kelly, and Miz Kate Winston, extraordinary women who were kind and patient and loving with children and others and who, when I went to Spelman College, sent me shoeboxes with chicken and biscuits and greasy dollar bills.

Exercise 3	**DISCUSSION AND CRITICAL THINKING**

1. What is the subject at the center of this discussion?

2. Which sentence most clearly indicates why black children of Edelman's generation developed a good set of values?

3. What were the three main legacies, or causes, of the value system of Edelman's generation?

4. What kinds of role models were causal factors?

5. Give two examples of role models (one of each kind) offered by Edelman.

The Purposes of Shopping

Phyllis Rose

Author of scholarly books, university professor, book reviewer, and freelance writer—Phyllis Rose is also a student of shopping. To her, shopping is not just something we do to acquire the necessities or a few frills. This brief paragraph comes from her essay "Shopping and Other Spiritual Adventures."

It is a misunderstanding of the American retail store to think we go there necessarily to buy. Some of us shop. There's a difference. Shopping has many purposes, the least interesting of which is to acquire new articles. We shop to cheer ourselves up. We shop to practice decision-making. We shop to be useful and productive members of our class and society. We shop to remind ourselves how much is available to us. We shop to remind ourselves how much is to be striven for. We shop to assert our superiority to the material objects that spread themselves before us.

Exercise 4	DISCUSSION AND CRITICAL THINKING

1. Is the emphasis mainly causes or effects?

2. Underline the topic sentence.

3. Place numbers in the text to indicate the reasons (causes) for shopping.

4. According to Phyllis Rose, what is the difference between buying and shopping?

5. Which of these reasons for shopping apply to you? What place does shopping occupy in your life? What are the items you buy and what are the items you shop for?

6. Does the paragraph convey an implied philosophy or value system?

A Hole in the Head?

U.S. News and World Report

Subtitled "A Parent's Guide to Tattoos, Piercings, and Worse," this essay is especially concerned with cause—why are so many young people altering their bodies?—and effects—what are the results of a practice called art by some and mutilation by others?

1   "Doesn't that hurt?" asks Jessica Brown, age 10½, as she rivets her gaze on the ivory spike through graduate student Shawn Arthur's nose. She stares at the needles skewering the skin on either side of his chest. "That's got to be painful."

2   Her parents, Mark and JoEllen Brown from Nanticoke, Pennsylvania, listen approvingly. After an afternoon of gaping at living canvases at the "Inkin' the Valley" body-art convention in Wilkes-Barre, Pennsylvania, Jessica no longer craves a tattoo. She says they "make people uglier." She'll settle for just a navel ring.

3   Jessica's parents might consider that a victory, given that teenagers today seem to comb the *National Geographic* for fashion tips. (Don't laugh. Branding, scarification, and stretched earlobe holes are showing up among kids in California and New York.) Tattoos and piercing are far more mainstream than most parents realize. In a forthcoming study of more than 2,100 adolescents from schools in eight states, Texas Tech University School of Nursing Professor Myrna Armstrong found that 1 in 10 had a tattoo and that over half were interested in getting one. The young body-art enthusiasts came from all income levels and ethnic groups. A majority earned A's and B's.

4   What's a parent to do? Many child-raising experts would have you believe that resistance is futile. It isn't. But the social and commercial currents are powerful. Tattoos and piercings have become widely acceptable, if not respectable. They turn up on celebrities, in toy stores (the Tattoodles doll), and as games on the Internet (Piercing Mildred [http://www.mildred.com]). Young Jessica can tick off every pierced part of her favorite pop singers, the Spice Girls. "I've got people bringing in pictures from *Glamour* magazine and wanting me to reproduce some star's tattoo," says Scranton, Pennsylvania, tattooer Marc Fairchild, who—like most professionals—refuses to work on minors. "Pamela Anderson [of TV's *Baywatch*] has made me thousands with that barbed wire around her arm." One Miss America contestant even bared a bellybutton ring in this year's pageant.

5   That's why tattooing emerged as the country's sixth-fastest-growing retail business last year—after Internet and paging services and bagel, computer, and cellular phone shops. Since then, the industry has been expanding by more than one studio a day, to 2,926—a 13.9 percent jump in nine months. These brightly lighted establishments are springing up near suburban malls and colleges.

6   What the heck. While it may alarm parents, the body-art fad is "nothing pathological," says University of Missouri psychiatrist Armando Favazza, an authority on self-mutilation and author of *Bodies Under Siege*. Indeed, studies show that young people indulge in body art for many of the same reasons adults do: to differentiate themselves, commemorate an event in their lives, or simply for the heck of it. "I like expressing myself that way—it expresses me," explains senior Tiffanie Gillis, a former varsity volleyball and soccer player at Piedmont Hills High School in San Jose, California. She sports a dozen perforations in her ears, a pierced bellybutton, tongue, and nipple, and five discreet tattoos, including a cartoon character she now regrets inking on her ankle two years ago, at age 15. Though her father has begged her to stop, Gillis intends to get more markings when she turns 18 and no longer needs to fake parental consent. "To tell you the truth, it's addictive," she says.

7   "Frankly, I like being shocking," says alternative music fan Amy Elizabeth Eisenberg, 20, a former scholarship student in marine biology at the University of Maryland who got the first of her eight facial piercings at age 16. "Why not?"

8   How about the pain? Though tattoo and piercing initiates often ask about it, most experience only a modicum of discomfort. Biting your tongue hurts more than getting it pierced. Tattooing feels like hair electrolysis.

9   Parents would do better to emphasize the potential medical complications. Naval piercings can take 12 months to heal, for instance, and can hurt for much of that time, since they are prone to infection and easily irritated by waistbands. Tongues, though quick to mend, swell tremendously when first pierced and can remain tender. "I had to live on Slurpees for a week," recalls Bridget McNicholas, a 14-year-old sophomore from Bowie High School in Maryland who had her tongue pierced this summer. The health risks include hepatitis B and tetanus, as well as skin reactions that can occur with red and yellow dyes. An improperly placed piercing can damage nerves. Dentists have seen tongue studs cause problems from chipped teeth to speech impairment.

10   If a kid shows any concern about the pain, that could be an opening for parents to suggest faux piercings with magnetic studs or temporary tattoos such as mehndi skin paintings.

11   Though many states ban the tattooing or piercing of minors, parents can't count on that to protect their kids. Wily teens will find ways to thwart ID checks and permission forms. Tiffanie Gillis got a friend's father to accompany her to the tattoo parlor at 15; she then returned alone, using that first tattoo as "proof" she was of age. When Philip Wheeler, an 18-year-old senior from Gaithersburg, Maryland, and his girlfriend drove three hours to Ocean City, Maryland, for her to get her tongue pierced two years ago, they grabbed a stranger off the boardwalk to sign the parental consent form. And those were legitimate establishments. Amateurs known as "scratchers," operating out of flea markets and fruit stands, rarely demand ID—or pay attention to hygiene. Kits that include needles and ink sell for a few hundred dollars through skin-art magazines.

12   Many teens resort to do-it-yourself jobs. Elizabeth Fisher, 15, an honors student in Manchester, Maryland, and her friend inked ladybugs on their ankles last summer. Her mother let her cover the mess with a professionally done blue bear rather than remove it.

13   For the parent of the persistent teen, there is the risky strategy of a field trip. "Luckily, we ran into people who said what we wanted to hear," says JoEllen Brown, mother of preteen Jessica.

14   Parents who feel they have exhausted all other avenues can still stress to their children the wise words of heavily tattooed rock star W. Axl Rose: Think before you ink.

15   "Start out small, and put it in an inconspicuous place," recommends Steven Snyder, an Owings Mills, Maryland, dermatologist and laser surgeon who has removed over 10,000 tattoos. The bulk of his business is older people who have spent years regretting their youthful exuberance and keeping the evidence covered in long sleeves or folks who broke up with the partners whose names are emblazoned on their bodies. Depending on the size and color—black ink is easier to remove than green—most tattoos take several painful laser sessions and cost between $800 and $1,600 to remove.

Homemade jobs often prove more difficult than a professional piece because the ink may get etched deeper into the epidermis, or leave scars.

16   If all else fails, parents can still try to protect their kids from major damage. Visit several tattoo and piercing parlors. First impressions count for a lot: If a place isn't clean, walk away. "Ask to see the autoclave," recommends Las Vegas tattooer Mari DeVine, who says no one has ever asked to see hers in the three years since she opened Tattoos-R-Us. These sterilizers work like pressure cookers and can kill hepatitis B. Needles should come in sealed packages and be opened in front of you. Each pot of ink or petroleum jelly should be fresh for you. Tattooers and piercers should wear latex gloves. Guns used for punching holes in earlobes are inappropriate for other body parts. "Most piercing shops are dangerous and have no concept of what they're doing. You have to be really careful," says Jhan Dean Egg, a San Francisco piercer.

17   It may come as sweet consolation to learn that even the experts—tattooers, piercers, body-art enthusiasts—also grapple with dissuading their kids. "Ear piercing, that's where I draw the line," declares Jim McNulty, a heavily tattooed database administrator from Dickson City, Pennsylvania, whose 14-year-old, Ashley, wants to get a tongue stud and thinks navel rings are "the coolest-looking things in the world." For a tattoo, it's age 18 or no go. Reasons McNulty, "The larger tattoo is a decision on a lifestyle, not just what you want to wear on your body." Unless, of course, the whole point is to needle your parents.

Exercise 5	**DISCUSSION AND CRITICAL THINKING**

1. How is this essay slanted toward a particular audience?

2. Is the essay a fair appraisal of today's body alteration practices?

3. In addition to cause and effect, what other patterns are used extensively?

4. What cause is emphasized in paragraph 4?

5. What three causes of body art are given in paragraph 6?

6. What are the potential medical complications?

7. Jim McNulty says, "The larger tattoo is a decision on a lifestyle, not just what you want to wear on your body." What does he mean? Do you agree?

8. What are your feelings about body alteration and about the writers of this article?

Road Warriors

Lynn Bulmahn

Staff writer for the *Waco Tribune-Herald* newspaper, Lynn Bulmahn interviewed officers from the Texas Department of Public Safety, professional counselors, and driving school instructors to confirm what she had found in her statistical research. Road rage is widespread and dangerous, and it is increasing in both degree and extent.

1　　You see him in your rearview mirror, a terrifying sight. Red-faced and angry, he gets on your bumper and tries to intimidate you into revving up to his idea of the correct speed—95 miles an hour, no doubt. When you don't cooperate, he'll make an obscene gesture, then zoom around your car, turning his head to shout curses to you instead of looking at the road ahead. Screeeech! This temper-tantrum on four wheels narrowly misses some other cars. Horns blare and tempers flare as this automotive ogre weaves in and out of traffic lanes in a manner that would put an NFL running back to shame. Reckless—if not wreck-less—drivers are one of the scariest hazards on the road today. And incidents of road rage—accidents and violence caused by angry, stressed-out drivers—are increasing nationwide.

2　　A study by the American Automobile Association for Traffic Safety shows a 51 percent jump in road violence, or incidents dubbed "road rage," from 1990 to 1995. Nationwide, AAA reported 10,037 violent clashes, which led to 218 deaths and 12,610 injuries over the five-year period studied. In Southern California, where freeways are a way of life, those taking the wheel face a daily barrage of hostility. Freeway violence is so common that it has become acceptable parody in such movies as *LA Story.* As society is becoming less polite, people may be more prone to express their negative feelings in public—and behind the wheel.

3　　Alice Wilson, a licensed professional counselor who deals in anger management cases, said chronically angry people may see the road as a battlefield. Such drivers are dangerous, she warns. "People like this refuse to slow down, even if they're going through a school zone," she said. "They feel it's an imposition on them when they're going somewhere."

4　　Although there is no one typical aggressive driver, patterns do emerge from the AAA study. The majority are males age 18 to 26. Most are "poorly educated with criminal records, histories of violence and drug or alcohol problems, and many have recently suffered an emotional or professional setback," the report said. Only about 4 percent of aggressive driving incidents involve women. But when women are on the attack, they'll often use their vehicle as a weapon. This occurs about 70 percent of the time, the study determined.

5　　Wilson said angry drivers aren't always young people. But, she said, such drivers may have one, two or more identifying characteristics. They're typically from a home environment where coping skills and a solid value system were never observed or learned. Many angry drivers come from dysfunctional families where there was a lot of fighting and arguing. This gives such people a predisposition to become angry, and yet they lack coping skills to properly deal with their quarrelsome emotions. Often, Wilson explained, the misuse of alcohol or drugs or physical and sexual abuse may have come into the picture.

6   Angry drivers may be under extreme stress or anxiety, she said. "They may have identity problems, such as low self-esteem," Wilson said. "If they suffer from self-hatred, they will have no respect for themselves or others. If they feel they're not as successful as other people, they may resent seeing other drivers who appear to be confident. Their minds may play games on them, so that they feel others are always out to get them," she said.

7   Like violent, win-at-any-cost athletes, angry drivers are often competitive to the point of aggression. They may see driving as a game or the road as a battlefield, Wilson said. She said some hostile drivers are territorial to the point that they feel the lane they drive in is their personal property. Should other drivers cut in, the hostile drivers may resent their "trespassing" on "their" area. Hostile drivers may see anger as a way to be important and powerful. Throwing a fit may give them a way to feel important because they've noticed people who scream and act out a temper tantrum can instill fear in others.

Exercise 6	DISCUSSION AND CRITICAL THINKING

1. Is this essay mainly one of causes or effects?

2. What pattern of causes is given in paragraph 4?

3. What identifying characteristics are discussed in paragraph 5 as causes of road rage?

4. What causes some angry drivers to feel the way they do about other drivers?

5. For what reasons does driving become an angry game for some?

Student Writers: Demonstrations and Readings

Responding to an assignment on cause and effect, Emmett Davis quite naturally turned to his special interest, the early days of rock and roll, and discussed the qualities that gave Elvis Presley his legendary status.

Davis's Writing Process Worksheet shows you how his writing evolved from idea to final draft. To conserve space here, the freewriting has been omitted. The balance of his worksheet has been lengthened for you to be able to see his other work in its entirety.

You will find a full-size blank worksheet on page 5. It can be photocopied, filled in, and submitted with each assignment if your instructor directs you to do so.

Writing Process Worksheet

TITLE Elvis Presley: Twentieth-Century Legend

NAME Emmett Davis   **DUE DATE** Tuesday, January 8, noon

ASSIGNMENT

In the space below, write whatever you need to know about your assignment, including information about the topic, audience, pattern of writing, length, whether to include a rough draft or revised drafts, and whether your paper must be typed.

Discuss why a well-known person achieved his or her stature, or discuss the results of a well-known person's achieving stature. You can assume that your audience will be familiar with your subject but probably will not know some of the particulars you include. Your writing of mainly causes or effects should be about 200 to 300 words. Submit this completed worksheet, a rough draft marked for revision and editing, and a typed final draft.

STAGE ONE

Explore Freewrite, brainstorm (list), cluster, or take notes as directed by your instructor. Use the back of this page or separate paper if you need more space.

Clustering

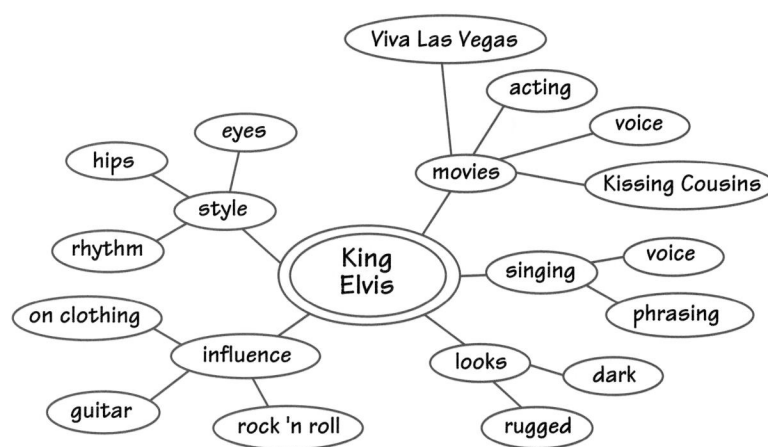

Listing

Causes	Event, Situation, or Trend	Effects
singing	Elvis becomes King.	isolation
style		drugs
influence		wealth
looks		loss of privacy
personality		attention
success		fame
movies		idolization
reputation		well-connected
promotion		

| **STAGE TWO** | **Organize**   Write a topic sentence or thesis; label the subject and the treatment parts. |

Four factors establish Elvis Presley as the greatest entertainer of the
      treatment   subject
twentieth century: appearance, singing ability, style, and influence.

Write an outline or an outline alternative.

   I. Appearance
      A. Rugged good looks
      B. Dress
      C. Grooming
  II. Singing ability
      A. Range
      B. Quality
 III. Style
      A. Personal
      B. Animal magnetism
  IV. Influence
      A. Innovated
      B. Inspired others

| **STAGE THREE** | **Write**   On separate paper, write and then revise your paper as many times as necessary for coherence, language (usage, tone, and diction), unity, emphasis, support, and sentences (CLUESS). Read your paper aloud to hear and correct any grammatical errors or awkward-sounding sentences. |
| | Edit any problems in fundamentals, such as capitalization, omissions, punctuation, and spelling (COPS). |

Rough Draft with Revision and Editing

Elvis Presley: Twentieth-Century Legend

                Now   it is only natural to   a
     At the end of the twentieth century, ~~we~~ look back and make lists of
                                              One person on the list would certainly be
the greatest people of that time. ~~The one I am most interested in is~~ the
                                              Although
Greatest Performer in Popular Music. I would have trouble choosing the top
        for some areas   F
person, in this case, I don't. Of course, it's Elvis Presley, ~~and~~ four factors

make my choice easy: he was good looking, he could sing, he had style, and
                                                           , which
he influenced the whole world of popular music. Most young people just call
                                                           ly
~~popular music~~ "rock 'n' roll." As for his looks, he was dark, ~~and~~ handsome,
                       even   unruly
~~to the point of being~~ beautiful, with thick, ~~floppy~~ hair and a sneering smile
                       rebellious
that appealed to the ~~fighting~~ side of young people. He looked good in

everything from a leather jacket to a spanggled outfit, though at the end he

did put on a little too much w̲ḙi̲ght. As for singing, he had a powerful deep

voice/ ~~He had~~ *with* a wide range similar to the big voices in rhythm and blues

and black gospel music/∅n stage, his style was personal/Ⱨe shook his hips *he had listened to and loved. When he was   , as*

and belted out songs like "Heartbreak Hotel" and "You Ain't Nothin' But a

Hound Dog." Because he was so different and so good, he influenced and

inspired others who would become famous artists of rock 'n' roll. While

making the guitar respectable, he popularized the driving rhythm of rock.

He made music more personal and more ag̲gressive. Groups like the Beatles

and the Rolling Stones gave him credit for his innovations. Some believe

that he's in the witness protection program, ~~I think~~ he's alive in a more *but, to me*

important way/he's a legend/the Greatest Performer in Popular Music for

the Twentieth Century.

Final Draft

Elvis Presley: Twentieth-Century Legend
Emmett Davis

Now, at the end of the twentieth century, it is only natural we look back and make a list of the greatest people of that time. One position on the list would certainly be the Greatest Performer in Popular Music. Although I would have trouble choosing the top person for some areas, in this case, I have no problem. Of course, it's Elvis Presley. <u>Four factors make my choice easy: he was good looking, he could sing, he had style, and he influenced the whole world of popular music, which most young people just call "rock 'n' roll."</u> As for his <u>looks</u>, he was darkly handsome, even beautiful, with thick, unruly hair and a sneering smile that appealed to the rebellious side of young people. He looked good in everything from a leather jacket to a spangled outfit, though at the end he did put on a little too much weight. As for <u>singing</u>, he had a powerful, deep voice with a wide range similar to the big voices in rhythm and blues and black gospel music he had listened to and loved. When he was on stage, his <u>style</u> was personal, as he shook his hips and belted out songs like "Heartbreak Hotel" and "You Ain't Nothin' But a Hound Dog." While making the guitar respectable, he popularized the driving rhythm of rock. He made music more personal and more aggressive. Because he was so different and so good, he <u>influenced</u> and inspired others who would become famous artists

Topic sentence

Cause 1

Cause 2

Cause 3

Cause 4

of rock 'n' roll. Groups like the Beatles and the Rolling Stones gave him credit for his innovations. Some believe that he's in the witness protection program, but, to me, he's alive in a more important way: he's a legend— he's the Greatest Performer in Popular Music for the Twentieth Century.

| Exercise 7 | **DISCUSSION AND CRITICAL THINKING** |

1. What patterns of writing besides cause and effect does Emmett Davis use in his paragraph?

2. What are some examples Davis uses for support?

3. What descriptive details does Davis use?

A Child with a Child

Ana Reyes

Student Ana Reyes, writing about a friend, explains that having a baby at fifteen may produce effects that will not be recognized for several years or more.

Roxanne was only a fifteen-year-old sophomore in high school when she became pregnant. Her boyfriend was the same age, but his emotional maturity was even lower. While she was dealing with being pregnant, he was going out with his friends and getting into trouble, even having serious fights with other youngsters. The causes of her getting pregnant would be much simpler than the results.

Roxanne and her boyfriend had been dating since the eighth grade, and her boyfriend had always been the type to hang out with the guys. She told me that she often felt insecure and was afraid of losing him. Therefore, she began sleeping with him, thinking that he would love her more and want to spend more time with her. But her plan didn't work. He roamed and she became pregnant. After her pregnancy, she dropped out of regular school and enrolled in home studies. Soon she was living with a daughter named Jessica and working for the school district, making $4.25 an hour. While Roxanne left her daughter every day at home with her mother, the father of the child did nothing but get into trouble with the law and even his family. Roxanne was not emotionally ready for her role as a mother, so Roxanne's mother took on the duty of raising Jessica.

Roxanne is not alone in becoming a young teenage mother. Many young girls are getting pregnant because they don't know any better. They have parents who don't emphasize enough that raising a child is difficult. However, many teenagers are careless and think of nothing but having fun. They believe that by sleeping with their boyfriend and getting pregnant, they will establish a bond, but love and affection require a stronger foundation. Others like the attention they get for being pregnant while so young, or they feel lonely and want somebody to love them. They may feel that there is no hope ahead and that having a baby is one way of making a statement. But in most cases, if the teenager gave any thought whatsoever to motive, the baby does not fulfill the need the teenager had when she became pregnant.

A lot of times, when the teenage mother becomes an adult who was never really around for her baby while the baby was growing up, their relationship becomes distant. As for my friend Roxanne, she never concentrated enough on raising her daughter alone. And now that she is twenty years old and her daughter is five, she wants her daughter to listen to her and do what she says. But Jessica has been raised by her grandmother, whom she considers her mother. She calls her grandmother "Mom" and Roxanne "Roxanne." When Roxanne tries to make Jessica refer to her as mother, Jessica just laughs as if Roxanne were joking, or she starts to cry when Roxanne becomes angry.

Teenage pregnancy has always been a big issue, especially in the past several years. During the time Roxanne and I have talked about raising a child at such an early age, she has said that she often regrets having a child. She says if she could go back and do it again, she would completely change her life. Far too often, that is what happens. The person regrets having a baby, and it is really sad because the baby is not at fault, and will often have a difficult time growing up.

| **Exercise 8** | **DISCUSSION AND CRITICAL THINKING** |

1. Is this an essay of mainly causes or effects, or is it balanced?

2. What was the main cause of her pregnancy, according to Roxanne?

3. What were the immediate effects of the teenage pregnancy and what were the long-range effects?

4. Who suffered more in this, the child or the mother? Explain.

5. In what way is Jessica fortunate?

Practicing Patterns of Cause and Effect

A detailed outline and your subsequent writing may include a combination of causes and effects, but you almost always will emphasize one concern—either causes or effects—over the other. The emphasis will provide the main structure, reflecting your topic sentence. Whether you are writing a basic outline for an assignment outside class without a significant time constraint or you are writing in class under the pressure of time, you will always have time to jot down prewriting lists and create cause and effect outlines.

| **Exercise 9** | **COMPLETING PATTERNS OF CAUSE AND EFFECT** |

Fill in the blanks to complete first the causes outline and then the effects outline.

1. Causes for dropping out of high school

   I. Family tradition

   II. _____

   III. _____

   IV. _____

2. Effects of getting a college education

   I. Better informed

   II. _____

   III. _____

   IV. _____

✎ Topics for Writing Cause and Effect

Reading-Related Topics

"What Happens to Steroid Studs?"

1. Write about the causes or effects of steroid use on someone you know.

2. Write about the effects of other drugs such as tobacco, heroin, cocaine, marijuana, LSD, or alcohol on someone you know. Consider doing a detailed study based on information from the counseling office, health office, library, American Heart Association, American Lung Association, or a police station. Pamphlets are readily available.

"Family Heroes and Role Models"

3. Write about people who have influenced you in important ways. How have they caused you to be who you are? Consider family members, friends, and people you know at church, at school, or in the community. Or write about the ways a public figure has influenced you.

4. Write about one role model who has influenced you in three or more important ways, or about three or more role models, each of whom has influenced you in an important way.

"The Purposes of Shopping"

5. Discuss buying and shopping in terms of the causes and effects of each activity.

6. Use Rose's ideas to discuss online shopping. Explain whether the causes and effects are the same.

7. As a buyer, explain why you go to a particular store.

8. As a shopper, explain why you go to a particular store.

9. Rose does not discuss big sales days. Explain how the whole sales atmosphere in a store contributes to the shopping experience and suggests the reasons for and the results of the activity.

"A Hole in the Head?"

10. Discuss the reasons why someone you know got a tattoo or body pierce or why someone you know did not get a tattoo or body pierce.

11. Discuss the effects for someone you know who got a tattoo or body pierce. Consider the relevant physical, psychological, social, family, and vocational effects.

"Road Warriors"

12. Discuss someone you know who is an overaggressive driver in terms of the causes of that aggression, or write about the effects of the aggression.

13. Write about a specific experience you had in observing or being involved in a road-rage incident. Stress causes or effects.

14. Use this essay as a model to write mainly about the causes or effects of rage related to shopping (especially at sales), work (high-pressure jobs), or sports (Little League, in stadiums, or at sports bars).

"Elvis Presley: Twentieth-Century Legend"

15. Write about the reasons why another well-known person achieved great fame. You might choose another performer or a thinker, artist, writer, scientist, or political or social leader.

16. Write about an ordinary person who has achieved excellence within a family, neighborhood, or community. Write about causes or effects or both.

"A Child with a Child"

17. Use this essay as a model for writing about someone you know who has gone through a similar experience.

18. Write about a problem in a larger sense, generalizing about mainly the causes or mainly the effects of teen pregnancy or parenthood.

Career-Related Topics

19. Discuss the effects (benefits) of a particular product or service on the business community, family life, society generally, a specific group (age, income, interest), or an individual.

20. Discuss the needs (thus the cause of development) by individuals, families, or institutions for a particular product or type of product.

21. Discuss the effects of using a certain approach or philosophy in sales, human resources management, or customer service.

General Topics

Select one of these topics as a subject (situation, circumstance, or trend) for your paragraph or essay and then determine whether you will concentrate on causes, effects, or a combination. You can probably write a more interesting, well-developed, and therefore successful paragraph or essay on a topic you can personalize. For example, a discussion about a specific young person who contemplated, attempted, or committed suicide is probably a better topic idea than a general discussion of suicide. If you do not personalize the topic, you will probably have to do some basic research to supply details for development.

22. Attending or completing college

23. Having or getting a job

24. Change in policy or administration

25. Change in coaches, teachers, officeholder(s)

26. Alcoholism

27. Gambling

28. Moving to another country, state, or home

29. Exercise

30. Passing or failing a test or course

31. Popularity of a certain TV program or song

32. Early marriage

Writer's Guidelines: Cause and Effect

1. Determine whether your topic should mainly inform or mainly persuade, and use the right tone for your purpose and audience.

2. Use listing to brainstorm cause-and-effect ideas. This is a useful form:

Causes	Event, Situation or Trend	Effects
1.		1.
2.		2.
3.		3.
4.		4.

3. Decide whether to concentrate on causes, effects, or a combination of causes and effects. Most paragraphs will focus only on causes or only on effects. Many short essays will discuss causes and effects but will use one as the framework for the piece. A typical basic outline might look like this:

    Topic sentence of paragraph or thesis of essay
    I. Cause or Effect 1
    II. Cause or Effect 2
    III. Cause or Effect 3

4. Do not conclude that something is an effect merely because it follows something else.

5. Lend emphasis to your main concern(s)—causes, effects, or a combination—by repeating key words such as *cause, reason, effect, result, consequence,* and *outcome.*

6. Causes and effects can be primary or secondary, immediate or remote.

7. The order of causes and effects in your paper may be based on time, space, emphasis, or a combination.

13

Classification: Establishing Groups

"You don't write because you want to say something; you write because you've something to say."

F. Scott Fitzgerald

THE QUIGMANS   by Buddy Hickerson

B. Hickerson, copyright 1997. Los Angeles Times Syndicate. Reprinted by permission.

Writing Classification

To explain by classification, you put persons, places, things, or ideas into groups or classes based on their characteristics. Whereas analysis by division deals with the characteristics of just one unit, classification deals with more than one unit, so the subject is plural.

To classify efficiently, try following this procedure:

1. Select a plural subject.

2. Decide on a principle for grouping the units of your subject.

3. Establish the groups, or classes.

4. Write about the classes.

Selecting a Subject

When you say you have different kinds of neighbors, friends, teachers, bosses, or interests, you are classifying; that is, you are forming groups.

In naming the different kinds of people in your neighborhood, you might think of different groupings of your neighbors, the units. For example, some neighbors are friendly, some are meddlesome, and some are private. Some neighbors have yards like Japanese gardens, some have yards like neat-but-cozy parks, and some have yards like abandoned lots. Some neighbors are affluent, some are comfortable, and some are struggling. Each of these sets is a classification system and could be the focus of one paragraph in your essay.

Using a Principle to Avoid Overlapping

All the sets in the preceding section are sound because each group is based on a single concern: neighborly involvement, appearance of the yard, or wealth. This one concern, or controlling idea, is called the *principle*. For example, the principle of neighborly involvement controls the grouping of neighbors into three classes: friendly, meddlesome, and private.

All the classes in any one group must adhere to the controlling principle for that group. You would not say, for example, that your neighbors can be classified as friendly, meddlesome, private, and affluent, because the first three classes relate to neighborly involvement, but the fourth, relating to wealth, refers to another principle. Any one of the first three—the friendly, meddlesome, and private—might also be affluent. The classes should not overlap in this way. Also, every member should fit into one of the available classes.

Establishing Classes

As you name your classes, rule out easy, unimaginative phrasing such as *fast/medium/slow, good/average/bad,* and *beautiful/ordinary/ugly.* Look for creative, original phrases and unusual perspectives.

Subject: neighbors

Principle: neighborhood involvement

Classes: friendly, meddlesome, private

Subject: neighbors

Principle: yard upkeep

Classes: immaculate, neat, messy

Subject: neighbors

Principle: wealth

Classes: affluent, comfortable, struggling

Using Simple and Complex Forms

Classification can take two forms: simple and complex. The simple form does not go beyond main divisions in its groupings.

Subject: Neighbors

Principle: Involvement

Classes: I. Friendly

  II. Meddlesome

  III. Private

Complex classifications are based on one principle and then subgrouped by another related principle. The following example classifies neighbors by their neighborly involvement. It then subgroups the classes on the basis of motive.

  I. Friendly
  A. Civic-minded
  B. Want to be accepted
  C. Gregarious

  II. Meddlesome
  A. Controlling
  B. Emotionally needy
  C. Suspicious of others

  III. Private
  A. Shy
  B. Snobbish
  C. Secretive

Here are two examples by professional writers on other topics, one organized as a simple form and the other organized as a complex form.

Subject
Development of classes
I. Some do not listen.
II. Some only half-listen.
III. Some listen with
passive acceptance.
IV. Some listen with
discrimination.

Glenn R. Capp, *Listen Up!*

Subject main class
Main class I
Principle

Simple

　　Listeners can be classified into four groups: (1) Some do not listen; they "tune the speaker out" and think of matters foreign to the speaker's subject. They get little from a speech. (2) Some only half-listen; their spasmodic listening fluctuates all the way from careful attention to no attention. They understand fragments of the speech, but they do not see the idea as a whole. (3) Some listen with passive acceptance; they accept all the speaker says without question. Because of their lack of discrimination, they add little to what the speaker says from their own experiences. (4) Some listen with discrimination; this critical type of listener gets the most from a speech.

Complex

　　There are two principal types of <u>glaciers:</u> the <u>continental</u> and the <u>valley.</u> The <u>continental glaciers</u> are great sheets of ice, called ice caps, that cover parts of continents. The earth has two continental glaciers at present: one spreads over most of Greenland and one over all of Antarctica save for a small window of rock and the peaks of several ranges. The Greenland ice sheet is over 10,000 ft. thick in the central part and covers an area of about 650,000 sq. miles. The Antarctic sheet has been sounded, in one place at least, to a depth of 14,000 ft., and it spreads over an area of 5,500,000 sq. miles. This is larger than conterminous United States in the proportion of 5½:3. It is calculated to store 7 million cu. miles of ice, which if melted would raise the ocean level 250 ft.

Main class II

Subclass A (conventional)

Subclass B

Subclass C

Valley glaciers are ice streams that originate in the high snow fields of mountain ranges and flow down valleys to warmer climates, where they melt. Some break up into icebergs and eventually melt in the ocean. In certain places the valley glaciers flow down the mountain valleys to adjacent plains and there spread out as lobate feet. These are called expanded-foot glaciers. Generally the sprawling feet of several valley glaciers coalesce to form one major sheet, and this is called a piedmont glacier.

Notice that the valley glacier is subdivided:

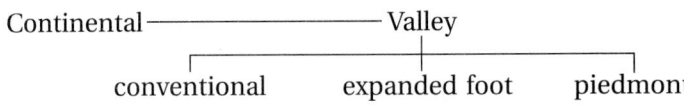

A. J. Eardley, "Glaciers: Types and Subtypes"

As you can see, glaciers are of two types based on their location (with implications for size:): (1) the continental glacier, such as the huge one in the Antarctic, and (2) the valley glacier. The valley glacier can be subdivided into the conventional valley glacier, flowing straight; the expanded-foot glacier, which spreads out; and the piedmont glacier, which is made up of several expanded-foot glaciers. This information could be organized in a simple outline as follows:

I. Continental glacier

II. Valley glacier

   A. Conventional

   B. Expanded-foot

   C. Piedmont

This outline on glaciers could be cut down to just the "valley glacier" part and developed into a paragraph or an essay. Moving in the other direction, we can say that almost all classifications can be part of a higher level of classification. For example, glaciers are one type of earth-altering process. (Others include earthquakes, volcanoes, and wind erosion.)

Most papers of classification will be simple (based on one principle) in concept, informative in purpose, and organized class by class.

Exercise 1	AVOIDING OVERLAPPED CLASSES

Mark each set of classes as OK or OL (overlapping); circle the classes that overlap.

	Subject	Principle	Classes
Example:			
OL	community college students	intentions	vocational academic transfer specialty needs hardworking

_____	1. airline flights	passenger seating	first class business coach
_____	2. country singers	clothing trademark	hat overalls decorative costume expensive
_____	3. schools	ownership	private religious public
_____	4. faces	shape	round square oval beautiful broad long
_____	5. dates	behavior resembling aquatic animals	sharks clams jellyfish cute octopuses

Connecting Reading and Writing

Musical Instruments: Beating, Blowing, and Bowing

Louise Dudley and Austin Faricy

We know that certain kinds of instruments are grouped in orchestras, but what is the basis for the arrangement? Louise Dudley and Austin Faricy point out that a simple principle provides for the classification and that the same principle gives us insight into the sequence in which these instruments were probably developed.

Musical instruments may be classified roughly according to the way the vibrator is set in motion, by bowing, blowing, or beating. Those in which the sound is made by beating are called the *instruments of percussion:* drum, xylophone, cymbals. Those in which the sound is made by blowing are *wind instruments:* horn, trumpet, flute. Those in which the sound is made by bowing are string instruments: violin, cello. The last name is the least satisfactory because certain of the stringed instruments, the harp, for example, are not bowed. Therefore, they are called stringed instruments, not *bowed instruments.* This is the usual classification of instruments: percussion, wind, strings. It is supposed that instruments of percussion came first, then wind instruments, and last, strings. A child follows this order in his natural development; at first he likes rattles and other toys that make noise by beating. Later he learns to whistle, and he likes the wind instruments, pipes of all kinds. Still later he begins to play on the strings, violin or cello.

| Exercise 2 | DISCUSSION AND CRITICAL THINKING |

1. Which sentence is the topic sentence?

2. What principle do Dudley and Faricy use for classifying the instruments? Where is that principle stated?

3. Into what classes do the writers break down the subject?

4. Do the authors admit any weakness in their terms?

5. What makes the order of these classes appropriate: percussion, then wind, then stringed instruments?

Nobles, Peasants, and Clergy

T. Walter Wallbank

In this passage taken from *The Story of Civilization,* historian T. Walter Wallbank classifies medieval society (456–1453 c.e.) into three groups.

Though at times there was considerable social mobility, medieval society conventionally consisted of three classes: the nobles, the peasants, and the clergy. Each of these groups had its own task to perform. Since the vassals [land owners] usually gave military service to their lord in return for their fiefs [estates], the nobles were primarily fighters, belonging to an honored society distinct from the peasant people—freemen, villeins, and serfs. In an age of physical violence, society obviously would accord first place to the man with the sword rather than to the man with the hoe. The peasants were the workers; attached to the manors, they produced the crops and did all the menial labor. The Church drew on both the noble and the peasant classes for the clergy. Although the higher churchmen held land as vassals under the feudal system, the clergy formed a class which was considered separate from the nobility and peasantry.

| Exercise 3 | DISCUSSION AND CRITICAL THINKING |

1. What sentence carries the topic idea?

2. Into what classes does Wallbank break down his subject?

3. What principle does Wallbank use as a basis for classifying members of society?

4. Why was it necessary to discuss the clergy class more fully than the other two classes?

5. Were the classes set inflexibly?

Paired Essays on Ways of Controlling

Some would argue that the greatest motivator in society, even stronger than the desire to produce offspring or make money, is the drive to control. We all know that the person with the TV remote control is the one with power, and we would all like to be the one holding that little zapper. Unfortunately, after the television set is cold and the remote is at rest, the urge to control persists.

The paired essays in this chapter deal with those who control, or at least seek control—the bosses and the naggers. In "Why We Carp and Harp," Mary Ann Hogan examines the struggle for control carried on by naggers—whether friendly, social, professional, or domestic. Naturally, naggers say all they want to do is make people better. At work, controllers are called *bosses,* and our awareness is sharpened when bosses are "bad bosses." According to some psychologists, the bad news is that all bosses are bad in certain ways. In "How to Deal with a Difficult Boss," Donna Brown Hogarty concentrates on five kinds of bad bosses: the bully, the workaholic, the jellyfish, the perfectionist, and the aloof boss—all exerting control but having trouble with it.

THE QUIGMANS   by Buddy Hickerson

"Quigman, you've been an employee of mine for some time.
I'd like to bounce something off you."

B. Hickerson, copyright Los Angeles Times Syndicate. Reprinted by permission.

Why We Carp and Harp

Mary Ann Hogan

Nag. Nag. Nag. Stop! Stop! Stop! We know nagging, don't we? After all, we've heard so much of it that we're experts, right? Maybe not. Listen to what this expert says about types of naggers. She points out that in this sophisticated world, some people specialize in certain kinds of nagging. This article was first published in the *Los Angeles Times*

1 Bring those dishes down from your room! Put those scissors away. . . . I told you not to smoke in the kitchen and you shouldn't be smoking anyway! Take your feet off the table! Why do I have to tell you again and again! . . . ? The hills are alive with the sound of nagging—the gnawing, crescendoing timbre of people getting in each other's face. Parents nag children, wives nag husbands, husbands nag wives, friends nag friends . . . "*Use* your fork . . . *Stop* spending money like water . . . *Can't* you be ready on time? . . . *Act* like an adult. . . ." Nagging, of course, has been around since the first cave husband refused to take out the cave garbage. But linguists, psychologists, and other scholars are just now piecing together what nagging really is, why we do it, and how to stop it before we nag each other to death.

2 Common perception holds that a nag is an unreasonably demanding wife who carps at a long-suffering husband. But in truth, nagging is universal. It happens in romances, in families, in businesses, in society—wherever people gather and one person wants another to do something he or she doesn't want to do. "It's a virus. You pick it up through kissing, shaking hands and standing in crowded rooms with people who have perfect children, wonderful husbands and sterilized homes," says humor columnist Erma Bombeck, whose family members nag her as artfully as she nags them. "It makes you feel good—like you're getting something done. Most of us want perfection in this world," she adds.

3 Thus, doctors can nag patients to lose their potbellies; accountants can nag timid clients to buy low; bosses can nag workers to get things done on time; special interest groups can nag the public to save the planet and send money, and the government can nag everyone to pay their taxes on time, to abstain from drink if they're pregnant, and, while they're at it, to Buy American. And when the going gets desperate, the desperate get nagging: Our recession-plagued nation, experts say, could be headed for a giant nag jag.

4 "When people are generally dissatisfied, they tend to harp at other people more," says Bernard Zilbergeld, a Bay Area psychologist. Naggers tend to fall into four categories—friendly, professional, social, and domestic—that range from the socially acceptable to the toxic.

5 The Friendly Ones are proud of their art. "My sisters call me a nag, but that's not necessarily a bad thing," says Bari Brenner, a 44-year-old Castro Valley resident who describes herself as "a third-generation nag" with a low tolerance for procrastinators. "I get things done. The truth is I'm organized, they're not. I can see the big *picture.* They can't. We're going on a trip to England. 'Did you call the travel agent?' 'No.' 'Well, *call* the travel agent . . . book the hotel . . . call *now!*' It's the same thing at work. Nagging can be a means to an end."

6 Professional Nags—people who do it for a living—have to disguise what they do to get what they want. "I have to nag all the time—but you have to

be careful about using the word *nag*," says Ruth Holton, a lobbyist for Common Cause, the good-government advocacy group. "I have to ask [legislators] for the same thing over and over again, year in, year out. But if they perceive what you're doing as nagging, they'll say, 'I've heard this 100 times before,' and they'll shut down. There's a fine line between artful persistence and being perceived as a nag."

7   Social nags don't see themselves as naggers. The U.S. Surgeon General's office peppers us with health warnings and calls it education. Environmentalists harp on people to recycle and save the rain forest, all in the name of the Greater Good. "One person's nagger is another person trying to save the world," says Arthur Asa Berger, a popular culture critic at San Francisco State University.

8   Then, somewhere beyond the limits of social convention, lies the dangerous world of the good old-fashioned Domestic Nag. Observers of the human condition, from the Roman poets to the purveyors of prime-time TV, have mined domestic nagging's quirkiness for laughs. But behavioral experts say that's where nagging can run amok. At best, domestic nagging is irritating. In Neil Simon's *The Odd Couple,* Felix wanted Oscar to clean up his act. Oscar liked being a slob, Felix nagged, nothing changed, and Felix finally moved out. At its worst, domestic nagging is murderous. In England last May, a 44-year-old businessman strangled his wife after 15 years of her nagging finally made him snap. In January, a judge ruled that the wife's verbal abuse justifiably provoked him and gave the husband an 18-month suspended sentence.

9   What causes this dynamic of domestic demolition? At the root of nagging, behavioralists say, lies a battle for control. It begins with a legitimate request: "I need you to hear me . . . to be with me . . . to be around, to do things like take out the garbage." But the person being asked doesn't want to change and sees the request as a threat to his or her control of the status quo. So the request is ignored.

10 "From the nagger's point of view, the naggee isn't listening," says Andrew Christensen, a UCLA psychology professor who has studied nagging for four years. "From there, it escalates. The further you withdraw, the more I nag. The naggee's point of view is, 'If I don't respond, maybe you'll shut up.'" The original request gets lost in the power struggle. The nagging takes on a life of its own. The desperate refrain of "Take out the garbage" can stand for a whole universe of complaints, from "You never do anything around here" to "I hate your stupid brown shoes!" "Sometimes I go through the house saying, 'Dammit, close the cupboards! Don't leave the towels on the floor! What's so hard about moving a vacuum cleaner across the hall. . . .' Bang! Bang! Bang! The list goes on," says a 40-year-old Mill Valley mother of two schoolchildren. "It's like the tape is stuck on replay and nobody's listening."

11 UCLA's Christensen calls it the "demand-withdraw pattern." In 60 percent of the couples he's studied, women were in the demanding, or nagging, role. In 30 percent of the cases, men were the demanders. In 10 percent, the roles were equal. "It may be that, traditionally, women have been more interested in closeness and sharing feelings, and men have been more interested in privacy," he says.

12 The scenario of the man coming home from work and the woman spending the day with the kids feeds the gender stereotype of the female nag. "He wants to sit in front of the TV, she's primed to have an empathetic

listener," Christensen says. "The reverse is true with sex. There, men tend to be in the nagging role. Either way, one feels abandoned, neglected, and deprived, the other feels intruded upon. It's a stalemate."

13   Communications experts say there is a way to end the nagging. Both people have the power to stop. What it takes is earnest willingness to step out of the ritual. The naggee could say: "You keep bringing up the issue of the garbage. I'd like to sit down and talk about it." But the gesture would have to be heartfelt, not an exercise in lip service. The nagger could write a note instead of carping. "People tend to react differently to written communication," says Zilbergeld. In either case, the effect is paradoxical: When the nagger stops, it leaves room for the naggee to act. When the naggee listens, there's nothing to nag about.

14   And if it doesn't stop? "It gets more and more robotic," says Gahan Wilson, the *New Yorker* magazine artist who explored the fate of the Nag Eternal in a recent cartoon. "We spend much of our lives on automatic pilot."

Exercise 4   VOCABULARY HIGHLIGHTS

Write a short definition of each word as it is used in the essay. (Paragraph numbers are given in parentheses.) Be prepared to use the words in your own sentences.

crescendoing (1)   status quo (9)

timbre (1)   escalates (10)

advocacy (adj.) (6)   scenario (12)

purveyors (8)   stalemate (12)

demolition (9)   paradoxical (13)

Exercise 5   DISCUSSION AND CRITICAL THINKING

1. What is being classified?

2. What is the classification based on?

3. Where is the thesis stated?

4. Translate the basic parts of the classification into a simple topic outline.

    I. _____   III. _____

        A. _____   A. _____

        B. _____   B. _____

    II. _____   IV. _____

        A. _____   A. _____

        B. _____   B. _____

5. What do the behavioralists say is at the root of nagging?

6. How does the idea of control relate to each of the four groups of naggers?

7. How do you react to nagging from family and close friends?

8. Do some people like to be nagged and even depend on naggers for direction?

How to Deal with a Difficult Boss

Donna Brown Hogarty

Journalist Donna Brown Hogarty makes it clear that if you've ever had a boss, you've had a bad boss in certain respects. Bosses who are particularly bad, she says, can be grouped in five categories, and being able to recognize the kind of bad boss you have is the first step in dealing with discomfort and frustration at work. This article was published in *Reader's Digest* in 1993.

1   Harvey Gittler knew his new boss was high-strung—the two had worked together on the factory floor. But Gittler was not prepared for his co-worker's personality change when the man was promoted to plant manager.

2   Just two days later, the boss angrily ordered a standing desk removed because he'd seen a worker leaning on it to look up an order. He routinely dressed down employees at the top of his lungs. At one time or another he threatened to fire almost everyone in the plant. And after employees went home, he searched through trash cans for evidence of treason.

3   For many workers, Gittler's experience is frighteningly familiar. Millions of Americans have temperamental bosses. In a 1984 Center for Creative Leadership study of corporate executives, nearly 75 percent of the subjects reported having had at least one intolerable boss.

4   "Virtually all bosses are problem bosses, in one way or another," says psychologist Mardy Grothe, co-author with Peter Wylie of *Problem Bosses: Who They Are and How to Deal with Them.* The reason, he said, lies in lack of training. Most bosses were promoted to management because they excelled at earlier jobs—not because they have experience motivating others.

5   Uncertain economic times worsen the bad-boss syndrome. "There is an acceptance of getting results at any price," says Stanley Bing, a business executive and author of *Crazy Bosses.* "As a result, the people corporations select to be bosses are the most rigid and demanding, and the least able to roll with the punches."

6   Bad bosses often have a recognizable *modus operandi.* Harry Levinson, a management psychologist in Waltham, Massachusetts, has catalogued problem bosses, from the bully to the jellyfish to the disapproving perfec-

tionist. If you're suffering from a bad boss, chances are he or she combines several of these traits and can be dealt with effectively if you use the right strategy.

The Bully

7   During his first week on the job, a new account manager at a small Pennsylvania advertising agency agreed to return some materials to a client. When he mentioned this at a staff meeting, the boss turned beet red, his lips began to quiver and he shouted that the new employee should call his client and confess he didn't know anything about the advertising business, and would *not* be returning the materials.

8   Over the next few months, as the account manager watched co-workers cower under the boss's browbeating, he realized that the tyrant fed on fear. Employees who tried hardest to avoid his ire were most likely to catch it. "He was like a schoolyard bully," the manager recalls, "and I've known since childhood that, when confronted, most bullies back down."

9   Armed with new-found confidence and growing knowledge of the ad business, he matched his boss's behavior. "If he raised his voice, I'd raise mine," the manager recalls. True to type, the boss started to treat him with grudging respect. Eventually, the young man moved up the ranks and was rarely subjected to his boss's outbursts.

10 Although standing up to the bully often works, it *could* make matters worse. Mardy Grothe recommends a different strategy: reasoning with him after he's calmed down. "Some bosses have had a problem with temper control all their lives, and are not pleased with this aspect of their personality," he explains. Want a litmus test? If the boss attempts to compensate for his outburst by overreacting and trying to "make nice" the next day, says Grothe, he or she feels guilty about yesterday's bad behavior.

11 Grothe suggests explaining to your boss how his temper affects you. For instance, you might say, "I know you're trying to improve my performance, but yelling makes me less productive because it upsets me."

12 Whatever strategy you choose, deal with the bully as soon as possible, because "once a dominant/subservient relationship is established, it becomes difficult to loosen," warns industrial psychologist James Fisher. Fisher also suggests confronting your boss behind closed doors whenever possible, to avoid being disrespectful. If your boss continues to be overbearing, try these strategies from psychologist Leonard Felder, author of *Does Someone at Work Treat You Badly?*

13 • To keep your composure while the boss is screaming, repeat a calming phrase to yourself, such as "Ignore the anger. It isn't yours."

14 • Focus on a humorous aspect of your boss's appearance. If she's got a double chin, watch her flesh shake while she's yammering. "By realizing that even the most intimidating people are vulnerable, you can more easily relax," explains Felder.

15 • Wait for your boss to take a breath, then try this comeback line: "I want to hear what you're saying. You've got to slow down."

16 Finally, never relax with an abusive boss, no matter how charming he or she can be, says Stanley Bing. "The bully will worm his or her way into your heart as a way of positioning your face under his foot."

The Workaholic

17 "Some bosses don't know the difference between work and play," says Nancy Ahlrichs, vice president of client services at the Indianapolis office of Right Associates, an international outplacement firm. "If you want to reach them at night or on a Saturday, just call the office." Worse, such a boss invades your every waking hour, making it all but impossible to separate your own home life from the office.

18 Ahlrichs advises setting limits on your availability. Make sure the boss knows you can be reached in crisis, but as a matter of practice go home at a set time. If he responds angrily, reassure him that you will tackle any project first thing in the morning. Get him to set the priorities, so you can decide which tasks can wait.

19 If you have good rapport with the boss, says Mardy Grothe, consider discussing the problem openly. Your goal is to convince him that just as he needs to meet deadlines, you have personal responsibilities that are equally important.

The Jellyfish

20 "My boss hires people with the assumption that we all know our jobs," says a woman who works for a small firm in New England. "Unfortunately, he hates conflict. If someone makes a mistake, we have to tiptoe around instead of moving to correct it, so we don't hurt anyone's feelings."

21 Her boss is a jellyfish. He has refused to establish even a basic pecking order in his office. As a result, a secretary sat on important correspondence for over a month, risking a client's tax write-offs. Because no one supervises the firm's support staff, the secretary never received a reprimand, and nobody was able to prevent such mishaps from recurring. The jellyfish simply can't take charge because he's afraid of creating conflicts.

22 So "*you* must take charge," suggests Lee Colby, a Minneapolis-based management consultant. "Tell the jellyfish: 'This is what I think I ought to be doing. What do you think?' You are taking the first step, without stepping on your boss's toes."

23 Building an indecisive supervisor's confidence is another good strategy. For example, if you can supply hard facts and figures, you can then use them to justify any course you recommend—and gently ease the jellyfish into taking a firmer position.

The Perfectionist

24 When Nancy Ahlrichs was fresh out of college, she landed her first full-time job, supervising the advertising design and layout of a small-town newspaper. On deadline day, the paper's irritable general manager would suddenly appear over her shoulder, inspecting her work for errors. Then he'd ask a barrage of questions, ending with the one Ahlrichs dreaded most: "Are you sure you'll make deadline?"

25 "I never missed a single deadline," Ahlrichs says, "yet every week he'd ask that same question. I felt belittled by his lack of confidence in me."

26 Ironically, the general manager was lowering the staff's productivity. To paraphrase Voltaire, the perfect is the enemy of the good. According to psychiatrist Allan Mallinger, co-author with Jeannette DeWyze of *Too Perfect:*

When Being in Control Gets Out of Control, "The perfectionist's overconcern for thoroughness slows down everyone's work. When everything has to be done perfectly, tasks loom larger." The nit-picking boss who is behind schedule becomes even more difficult, making subordinates ever more miserable.

27   "Remember," says Leonard Felder, "the perfectionist *needs* to find something to worry about." To improve your lot with a perfectionist boss, get her to focus on the big picture. If she demands that you redo a task you've just completed, mention your other assignments, and ask her to prioritize. Often, a boss will let the work you've completed stand—especially when she realizes another project may be put on hold. If your boss is nervous about a particular project, offer regular reports. By keeping the perfectionist posted, you might circumvent constant supervision.

28   Finally, protect yourself emotionally. "You can't depend on the perfectionist for encouragement," says Mallinger. "You owe it to yourself to get a second opinion of your work by asking others."

The Aloof Boss

29   When Gene Bergoffen, now CEO of the National Private Truck Council, worked for another trade association and asked to be included in the decision-making process, his boss was brusque and inattentive. The boss made decisions alone, and very quickly. "We used to call him 'Ready, Fire, Aim,'" says Bergoffen.

30   Many workers feel frozen out by their boss in subtle ways. Perhaps he doesn't invite them to key meetings or he might never be available to discuss projects. "At the core of every good boss is the ability to communicate expectations clearly," says Gerard Roche, chairman of Heidrick & Struggles, an executive search firm. "Employees should never have to wonder what's on a boss's mind."

31   If your boss fails to give you direction, Roche says, "the worst thing you can do is nothing. Determine the best course of action, then say to your boss: 'Unless I hear otherwise, here's what I'm going to do.'"

32   Other strategies: When your boss does not invite you to meetings or include you in decision making, speak up. "Tell her you have information that might prove to be valuable," suggests Lee Colby. If that approach doesn't work, find an intermediary who respects your work and can persuade the boss to listen to your views.

33   To understand your boss's inability to communicate, it's vital to examine his work style. "Some like hard data, logically arranged in writing," says Colby. "Others prefer face-to-face meetings. Find out what makes your boss tick—and speak in his or her language."

34   Understanding your boss can make your job more bearable in a number of ways. For instance, try offering the boss two solutions to a problem—one that will make him happy, and one that will help you to reach your goals. Even the most difficult boss will usually allow you to solve problems in your own way—as long as he's convinced of your loyalty to him.

35   No matter which type of bad boss you have, think twice before going over his head. Try forming a committee with your colleagues and approaching the boss all together. The difficult boss is usually unaware of the problem and often is eager to make amends.

36 Before embarking on any course of action, engage in some self-analysis. Chances are, no matter how difficult your job is, you are also contributing to the conflict. "Talk to people who know you both, and get some honest feedback," suggests Mardy Grothe. "If you can fix the ways in which you're contributing to the problem, you'll be more likely to get your boss to change."

37 Even if you can't, there's a silver lining: the worst bosses often have the most to teach you. Bullies, for example, are frequently masters at reaching difficult goals. Perfectionists can often prod you into exceeding your own expectations.

38 As a young resident psychologist at the Menninger psychiatric hospital in Topeka, Kansas, Harry Levinson was initially overwhelmed by the high standards of founder Karl Menninger. "I felt I was never going to be able to diagnose patients as well as he did or perform to such high academic requirements," Levinson recalls. He even considered quitting. But in the end, he rose to the challenge, and today he believes he owes much of his success to what he learned during that critical period.

39 Dealing with a difficult boss forces you to set priorities, to overcome fears, to stay calm under the gun, and to negotiate for better working conditions. And the skills you sharpen to ease a tense relationship will stand you in good stead throughout your career. "Employees who are able to survive a trying boss often earn the respect of higher-ups for their ability to manage a situation," says Levinson. "And because a difficult boss can cause rapid turnover, those who stick it out often advance quickly."

40 Your bad boss can also teach you what *not* to do with subordinates as you move up—and one day enable you to be a better boss yourself.

Exercise 6	**VOCABULARY HIGHLIGHTS**

Write a short definition of each word as it is used in the essay. (Paragraph numbers are given in parentheses.) Be prepared to use the words in your own sentences.

modus operandi (6)	invades (17)
cower (8)	rapport (19)
browbeating (8)	recurring (21)
litmus test (10)	paraphrase (26)
subservient (12)	prioritize (27)
vulnerable (14)	brusque (29)

Exercise 7	**DISCUSSION AND CRITICAL THINKING**

1. What is being classified?

2. What is the purpose of the classification?

3. What are the five classes of bad bosses?

4. Of the five classes, which is the most difficult for most people to deal with? for you to deal with? Can you give any examples?

5. Hogarty suggests that sometimes the boss's behavior is caused to some extent by the behavior of the workers. How would you explain that? Provide examples, if possible.

6. Which of the five types of behavior are sometimes found in combination?

| Exercise 8 | CONNECTING THE PAIRED ESSAYS |

For quick reference, these are the classes discussed in the essays:

Naggers (Hogan): friendly, professional, social, domestic

Bad bosses (Hogarty): bully, workaholic, perfectionist, jellyfish, aloof boss

1. Assuming that domestic nags can be like bosses and can vary in the same way, to what classes of bad bosses might the domestic nags be similar?

2. Would you deal with the extremely aggressive domestic nagger and the bully bad boss in the same way? Note that in Hogarty's essay, one person suggested confrontation, even yelling back, and another advised against that tactic. What factors are different in the two situations?

3. Of the five groups in the Hogarty essay, which ones are most inclined to be naggers?

4. Which of Hogarty's groups are likely to be especially concerned with control? Rank them from most concerned to least concerned.

5. In regard to control, is the main difference between naggers and bad bosses one of causes or one of effects?

Student Writers: Demonstrations and Readings

For all the years he could remember, Boris Belinsky has observed doctors from up close and at a distance. It was only natural, therefore, that when asked to classify a group of people according to their behavior, he chose doctors.

His Writing Process Worksheet shows you how this writing evolved from idea to final draft. To conserve space here, the freewriting and two rough drafts have been omitted. The balance of his worksheet has been lengthened for you to be able to see his other work in its entirety.

You will find a full-size blank worksheet on page 5. It can be photocopied, filled in, and submitted with each assignment if your instructor directs you to do so.

Writing Process Worksheet

TITLE Doctors Have Their Symptoms, Too

NAME Boris Belinsky   **DUE DATE** Friday, March 20, 8 a.m.

ASSIGNMENT In the space below, write whatever you need to know about your assignment, including information about the topic, audience, pattern of writing, length, whether to include a rough draft or revised drafts, and whether your paper must be typed.

Write a paragraph of classification in which you group people according to their behavior in a particular vocation area. Your audience, your instructor and your peers, will be somewhat aware of the career field you select but will lack your insights. Submit a completed worksheet, a rough draft marked for revision, and a typed final draft of about 250 words.

STAGE ONE **Explore** Freewrite, brainstorm (list), cluster, or take notes as directed by your instructor. Use the back of this page or separate paper if you need more space.

Clustering

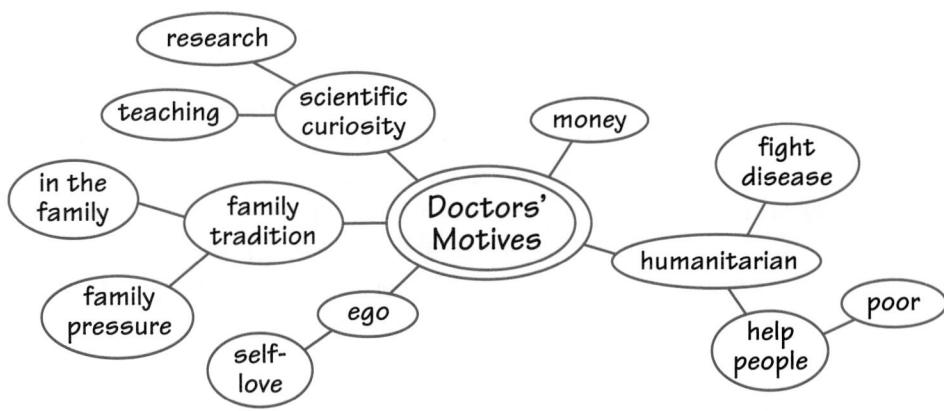

STAGE TWO **Organize** Write a topic sentence or thesis; label the subject and the treatment parts.

<u>Doctors</u> can be classified according to <u>their motives for choosing their field</u>

    subject   treatment

<u>of work.</u>

Write an outline or an outline alternative.

   I. Motive: to make money

      A. Slow with patients

      B. Fast with bills

  II. Motive: to pursue scientific interests

      A. Work in labs

      B. Teach in medical schools

 III. Motive: to help people

      A. Spend much time with patients

      B. Have good standards

         1. May locate in poor areas

         2. Advocate preventative methods

         3. Do volunteer work

STAGE THREE   **Write**   On separate paper, write and then revise your paper as many times as necessary for coherence, language (usage, tone, and diction), unity, emphasis, support, and sentences (CLUESS). Read your paper aloud to hear and correct any grammatical errors or awkward-sounding sentences.

Edit any problems in fundamentals, such as capitalization, omissions, punctuation, and spelling (COPS).

Final Draft

Doctors Have Their Symptoms, Too

Boris Belinsky

Because I come from a large family that unfortunately has had a lot of illnesses, I have learned to classify doctors according to why they became doctors. **Topic sentence** <u>As doctors can diagnose illnesses by the symptoms they identify, I can figure out doctors' motives by their symptoms, by which I mean behavior.</u> Some doctors have chosen the field of medicine because they want to **Support (class)** make <u>money.</u> They hurry their patients (customers) through their multiple office spaces, answering few questions and never sitting down. Although slow to answer the desperate phone calls, they're fast with the bills. The **Support (class)** second class is the group with <u>scientific</u> interests. Not as much concerned about money, they're often found in university hospitals, where they teach and work on special medical problems. They may be a bit remote and explain symptoms in technical terms. The third group is my favorite: those **Support (class)** who became doctors to <u>help people.</u> They spend much time with patients, often practice in areas that are not affluent, advocate preventative meth-**Concluding sentence** ods, and do volunteer work. <u>Not all doctors easily fall into these three groups, but virtually every one has a tendency to do so.</u>

Exercise 9   **DISCUSSION AND CRITICAL THINKING**

1. What is the principle on which Belinsky's classification is based?

2. How does Belinsky protect himself against a charge that some doctors are not easily classified?

3. Why has Belinsky had occasion to make the observations on which this paragraph is based?

Types of Hepatitis

Annie Chen

While volunteering to donate blood, Annie Chen discovered that she had hepatitis. After going to the doctor, she went to the library in search of medical information. Propelling her was one of the strongest motives she had ever had for doing research: concern about her health. She soon became a lay expert and was able to write about the different kinds of hepatitis.

Two years ago when I stopped at a hospital to donate blood, a simple screening procedure determined that I had hepatitis, a disease that involves the inflammation of the liver. After going to my doctor, who gave me information, instructions, and a shot of gamma globulin, I immediately went to the library. Nothing could stop me from learning what I could about this disease I thought only other people had. What I found there confirmed in more detail what the doctor had told me. Hepatitis has distinct symptoms: jaundice, vomiting, nausea, poor appetite, and general weakness. Nevertheless, hepatitis is not a single disease coming from the same source; instead, it mainly takes three different forms, which are known as type A, type B, and type C.

Hepatitis A is the seventh most commonly reported infectious disease in the United States (behind gonorrhea, chicken pox, syphilis, AIDS, salmonellosis, and shigellosis). Type A hepatitis, the kind I had, is highly contagious and is commonly transmitted by human waste. It is also acquired by the ingestion of contaminated food, milk, or water; therefore, this type is said to be toxic. Outbreaks of this type are often traced to eating seafood from polluted water. The highest incidence of hepatitis A is in children, about thirty percent of them younger than fifteen. Fortunately, when treated with medicines such as gamma globulin, symptoms are gone in less than six weeks.

Unlike hepatitis A, hepatitis B is caused by a virus. Though it can also be transmitted by contact with human secretions and feces, it is most frequently spread during intimate sexual contact and the sharing of needles by drug abusers. Nurses, doctors, laboratory technicians, and dentists are often exposed to type B hepatitis. A common infectious disease in Southeast Asian countries, hepatitis B is much more serious than A. Although most patients recover completely, some with weak immune systems may carry the virus for more than a year and may become chronic carriers.

In 1990, the hepatitis C virus was identified. It is spread by blood-to-blood contact. Therefore, any way that one person's blood may be in contact with an infected person's blood will spread the hepatitis C virus. Some of the most common means of transmission are blood transfusions, intravenous drug use,

(margin notes: Subject Principle, Thesis, Topic sentence Class 1, Topic sentence Class 2, Topic sentence Class 3)

tattooing, body piercing, and sharing needles. Type C now accounts for about twenty percent of all viral hepatitis cases.

In most hepatitis patients, the liver cells will eventually regenerate with little or no residual damage. I feel perfectly fine, and there are no worries for other patients like me. Although hepatitis is an extremely troublesome disease, blood screening for transfusions, effective medicines, and good health practices have minimized the effects, at least for the informed and careful public.

Exercise 10	**DISCUSSION AND CRITICAL THINKING**

1. Double underline the thesis.

2. What is the principle on which the classification is based?

3. Underline the topic sentences (which also indicate the classes by name) of paragraphs 2, 3, and 4.

Practicing Patterns of Classification

Because the basic pattern of classification consists of classes, the initial outline is predictable: It uses Roman numeral headings for the classes, although some classes may be longer and more complex than others.

Exercise 11	**COMPLETING PATTERNS OF CLASSIFICATION**

Fill in the blanks to identify classes that could be discussed for each subject.

1. Subject: Professional athletes
   Principle: Why they participate in sports
   Classes:

   I. Glory

   II. _____

   III. _____

2. Subject: Pet owners
   Principle: Why they own (need) pets
   Classes:

   I. Companionship

   II. _____

   III. _____

3. Subject: Dates or prospective spouses
   Principle: The way they can be compared to vehicles

I. Economy (Taurus, Chevelle, Corolla, Civic)

   A. Low cost

   B. Low maintenance

   C. _____

II. SUVs or minivans (Caravan, Quest, Suburban)

   A. Practical

   B. _____

   C. _____

III. Luxury (Porsche, BMW, Mercedes, Lexus)

   A. High cost

      1. Initial

      2. _____

   B. _____

   C. Impressive features

      1. _____

      2. Unnecessary

✎ Topics for Writing Classification

Reading-Related Topics

"Musical Instruments: Beating, Blowing, and Bowing"

1. Write a piece in which you classify instruments according to how difficult they are to play.

2. Write a piece in which you discuss the subdivisions of one of the three groups, for example, kinds of instruments that are blown.

3. Write a paper in which you classify instruments in terms of the principal mood you associate them with: warlike, romantic, nostalgic, excited, anxious, peaceful.

4. Write a paper in which you classify guitars.

"Nobles, Peasants, and Clergy"

5. In a paragraph or essay, discuss contemporary social classes in a particular community, region, or country.

6. Using the Wallbank paragraph as a model, write about the divisions within a particular company (such as management, sales, manufacturing, distribution) or within a particular school (such as administration, faculty, certified support staff). Name the company or school.

"Why We Carp and Harp"

7. Pick one of the classes of naggers (such as domestic) and show in a paragraph or essay how the category can be divided into subclasses.

8. Write a paper in which you classify people who are frequently nagged (the naggees), such as those in a family, at work, and at school.

9. Using Hogan's set of classes as a framework, discuss each kind of nagger with examples from your experience and your reading.

10. In a paragraph or essay, discuss how control can be related to each of Hogan's four classes.

"How to Deal with a Difficult Boss"

11. Write about each of the five types of bad bosses, giving examples from your own experience.

12. Discuss a subdivision of the bully bosses (such as those who use words, threats of job loss, and physical threats) and explain how each functions.

13. Discuss how the idea of control relates to the five classes of bad bosses. For example, does the perfectionist seek perfection or merely control?

14. Using this article as a framework, write a classification of good bosses.

15. Hogarty mentions that bad bosses are often made worse by bad employees. Write a classification of bad employees, perhaps from a good boss's perspective.

Paired Essays on Ways of Controlling

16. Discuss the extent to which the four types of naggers are like bosses (either good or bad).

17. Discuss whether the idea of control is good or bad, necessary or unnecessary in nagging and bossing. Is the desire to control always bad? Use the authors' patterns of classification as a framework.

18. Use the same idea as in question 17, but use only one essay as a framework.

"Doctors Have Their Symptoms, Too"

19. Classify another vocational group (clergy, teachers, lawyers, police officers, shop owners) according to their reasons for selecting their field.

"Types of Hepatitis"

20. Write an essay in which you discuss the various types of another disease, such as diabetes, skin cancer, arthritis, herpes, pneumonia, leukemia, or lupus. Some of these diseases not only have classes but also have subclasses. Medical books and encyclopedias can provide you with basic information.

Career-Related Topics

21. Discuss different types of managers you have encountered (democratic, authoritative, autocratic, buddy, aloof).

22. Discuss different types of customers with whom you have dealt (perhaps according to their purpose for seeking your services or products).

23. Discuss different types of employees you have observed.

24. Discuss different qualities of products or services in a particular field.

25. Discuss different kinds of chat rooms on the Internet.

General Topics *Write a paragraph or an essay using one of the topics listed here. Divide your topic into groups according to a single principle.*

26. Intelligence	36. Dopers	45. Mothers or fathers
27. Waitresses	37. Sports fans	46. Rock music
28. Dates	38. Churchgoers	47. Talkers on the telephone
29. Smokers	39. Laughs	
30. Smiles	40. Bus drivers	48. Pick-up lines (as in a bar)
31. Liars	41. Riders on buses or airplanes	49. Chicken eaters
32. Gossips		50. Surfers (Internet or ocean)
33. TV watchers	42. Junk food	
34. Styles in clothing	43. Graffiti	51. Beards
35. Sports	44. Home computers	52. Pet owners

Writer's Guidelines: Classification

1. Follow this procedure for writing paragraphs and essays of classification:
   - Select a plural subject.
   - Decide on a principle for grouping the units of your subject.
   - Establish the groups, or classes.
   - Write about the classes.

2. Avoid uninteresting phrases for your classes, such as *good/average/bad*, *fast/medium/slow*, and *beautiful/ordinary/ugly.*

3. Avoid overlapping classes.

4. The Roman numeral parts of your outline will probably indicate your classes.
   - I. Class one
   - II. Class two
   - III. Class three

5. If you use subclasses, clearly indicate the different levels.

6. Following your outline alternative, give somewhat equal (however much is appropriate) space to each class.

Comparison and Contrast: Showing Similarities and Differences

"My first draft usually has only a few elements worth keeping. I have to find what they are and build from them and throw out what doesn't work."

Susan Sontag

THE QUIGMANS   by Buddy Hickerson

B. Hickerson, copyright Los Angeles Times Syndicate. Reprinted by permission.

Comparison and Contrast Defined

Comparison and contrast is a method of showing similarities and differences between subjects. *Comparison* is concerned with organizing and developing points of similarity; *contrast* serves the same function for differences. In some instances, a writing assignment may require that you cover only similarities or only differences. Occasionally, an instructor may ask you to separate one from the other. Usually, you will combine them within the larger design of your paragraph or essay. For convenience, the term *comparison* is often used for both comparison and contrast, because both use the same techniques and are regularly combined into one operation.

This chapter will help you deal with topics and choose strategies for developing comparison and contrast.

Generating Topics and Working with the 4 *P*'s

Comparison and contrast are basic to your thinking. In your daily activities, you consider similarities and differences between persons, things, concepts, political leaders, doctors, friends, instructors, schools, nations, classes, movies, and so on. You naturally turn to comparison and contrast to solve problems and make decisions in your life and in your writing. Because you have had so much experience with comparing, finding a topic to write about is likely to be easy and interesting. Freewriting, brainstorming, and listing will help you generate topics that are especially workable and appropriate for particular assignments.

Many college writing assignments will specify a topic or direct you to choose one from a list. Regardless of the source of your topic, the procedure for developing your ideas by comparison and contrast is the same. That procedure can appropriately be called the *4 P's:* purpose, points, patterns, and presentation.

Purpose

In most of your writing, the main purpose will be either to inform or to persuade.

Informative Writing

If you want to explain something about a topic by showing each subject in relationship with others, then your purpose is informative. For example, you might be comparing two composers, Beethoven and Mozart. Both were musical geniuses, so you might decide that it would be senseless to argue that one is superior to the other. Instead, you choose to reveal interesting information about both by showing them in relation to each other. The emphasis of your writing would be on insights into their characteristics, the insights heightened because the characteristics are placed alongside each other.

Persuasive Writing

If you want to show that one actor, one movie, one writer, one president, one product, or one idea is better than another, your purpose will be persuasive. Your argument will take shape as you write, beginning with emphasis in the topic sentence or thesis and reinforcement by repetition throughout your paper, in each case indicating that one side is superior.

Let's say, as an extended illustration, that you are taking a course in twentieth-century European history and you are asked to write about two leaders. You choose to write about Mussolini and Hitler as dictators. In freewriting, you discover that you know quite a bit about the two leaders. By brainstorming, you come up with some specific information.

Who?	Mussolini and Hitler
What?	fascist leaders, racists—with Hitler being more extreme
Where?	in Italy and Germany, respectively
When?	the decade before and during World War II
Why?	greed, morals, possible psychological problems, with Hitler being more extreme
How?	setting up totalitarian states

You tentatively decide that your purpose will be to persuade readers that, although both men were fascists, Hitler was more extreme in all important respects. If you need more information, you will have to consult your textbooks, your lecture notes, or sources in the library or on the Internet.

Points

The points are the ideas that will be applied somewhat equally to both sides of your comparison and contrast. They begin to emerge in freewriting, take on more precision in brainstorming, acquire a main position in listing, and assume the major part of the framework in the outline.

When writing on an assigned topic based on lectures and reading, you will probably be able to decide these points quickly. The subject material itself may dictate the points. For example, if you were comparing the governments of the United States and Great Britain, you would probably use these three points: executive, legislative, and judicial.

Using listing as a technique for finding points is simple. Follow this procedure:

1. Select one side of your two-part subject (the side you know better) and compose a list in relation to a basic treatment you expect to extend to your comparative study.

   <u>Hitler</u> <u>was a fascist dictator with racist views</u>.
     subject   **treatment**

2. Make a list of points (about Hitler as a fascist dictator).

   commitment

   racial views

   beliefs

   fascism

   flexibility

   militaristic designs

3. Decide which points can also be applied in a useful way to the other subject, in this case, Mussolini. (You can also reverse the approach.) In this instance, all of the points can be applied in a useful way.

4. Select the points for your topic sentence or thesis.

   racial views

   commitment

   militaristic designs

5. Incorporate these points into a topic sentence or thesis. (Your final topic sentence or thesis need not specify the points.)

   <u>Although Mussolini and Hitler were both fascist dictators, they</u> <u>were significantly</u>
   subject
   <u>different in their racial views, commitment, and militaristic designs.</u>
   treatment (with points)

   You now have a purpose and points. An outline or outline alternative will help you select and develop a pattern for your comparison.

Patterns

Now you will choose between two basic patterns of organization: (1) subject by subject (opposing) or (2) point by point (alternating). In long papers you may mix the two patterns, but in most college assignments, you will probably select just one and make it your basic organizational plan.

In comparison and contrast, the outline works especially well in indicting relationships and sequence. As with most other writing forms we have worked with, the sequence of a comparison-and-contrast paragraph or essay can be based on time, space, or emphasis. Emphasis is the most likely order.

Figures 14.1 and 14.2 show you the two patterns as they are applied to both the paragraph (on the left) and the essay (on the right).

In the subject-by-subject approach, organize your material around the subjects—the sides of the comparative study, as shown in Figure 14.1. In the point-by-point approach, organize your paper mainly around the points that you apply to the two subjects, as shown in Figure 14.2.

Figure 14.1
Subject-by-Subject Organization

For Paragraph

> **Topic sentence**
> **I. Mussolini**
> > **A. Racial views**
> >
> > **B. Commitment**
> >
> > **C. Militaristic designs**
>
> **II. Hitler**
> > **A. Racial views**
> >
> > **B. Commitment**
> >
> > **C. Militaristic designs**

For Essay

> **Introduction with thesis**
>
> **I. Mussolini**
> > **A. Racial views**
> >
> > **B. Commitment**
> >
> > **C. Militaristic designs**
>
> **II. Hitler**
> > **A. Racial views**
> >
> > **B. Commitment**
> >
> > **C. Militaristic designs**
>
> **Conclusion**

Figure 14.2
Point-by-Point Organization

For Paragraph

Topic sentence
I. Racial views
   A. Mussolini

   B. Hitler

II. Commitment
   A. Mussolini

   B. Hitler

III. Militaristic designs
   A. Mussolini

   B. Hitler

For Essay

Introduction with thesis

I. Racial views
   A. Mussolini

   B. Hitler

II. Commitment
   A. Mussolini

   B. Hitler

III. Militaristic designs
   A. Mussolini

   B. Hitler

Conclusion

Presentation

The two patterns of organization—subject by subject and point by point—are equally valid, and each has its strengths for presentation of ideas.

As shown in Figure 14.1, the subject-by-subject pattern presents materials in large blocks, which means the reader can see a body of material that is complete. However, if the material is also complex, the reader has the burden of remembering ideas in going from one part to the next. Parallel development of ideas and cross-references in the second portion of the paragraph or essay can often offset that problem. Transitional words and phrases also help to establish coherence.

The point-by-point pattern shown in Figure 14.2 provides an immediate and direct relationship of points to subject. Therefore, it is especially useful in arguing that one side is superior to the other, in dealing with complex topics, and in working with longer compositions. But because of its systematic nature, if development is not sufficient, it can appear mechanical and monotonous. You can avoid that appearance by developing each idea thoroughly.

Some writers believe that the subject-by-subject form works best for short (paragraph-length) assignments, and the point-by-point form works best for longer pieces (essays).

In the following examples, the topic of Mussolini and Hitler is presented first in the final draft stage of the paragraph form and then in the essay form. Note that the paragraph (often, as here, an essay in miniature) is expanded into an essay by developing the topic sentence, the supporting points, and the restated topic sentence into separate paragraphs: introduction, middle paragraph, middle paragraph, middle paragraph, and conclusion. Although both the paragraph and the essay make good observations and illustrate the use of pattern, for this topic the full essay would probably be more suitable in fulfilling the writer's purpose. Both the paragraph and the essay use a point-by-point arrangement.

Here is the paragraph:

Topic sentence

Point 1: Racism

Hitler and Mussolini often have been thought of as twin dictators, but there was considerable difference between the two men and their regimes, and Hitler was more extreme. Racism is justly associated with all fascism at that time; therefore, Mussolini is impli-

Transition

Point 2: Commitment

Transition

Point 3: Militaristic designs

Transition

Restated topic sentence

cated. It should be pointed out, however, that the Italians' blatant racism occurred after Mussolini's deep association with Hitler. *But* Hitler had held racist views from the beginning of his political movement, and it was a main motive in the Nazi movement. Their degree of commitment to act also varied. Mussolini merely talked and strutted for the most part. He had few fixed doctrines and increasingly accommodated himself to circumstances. *But* Hitler meant every bit of his bellicosity, and he was willing to wage the most frightful war of all time. A study of their involvement in that war, however, reveals striking differences. Italian fascism was comparatively restrained and conservative until the Nazi example spurred it to new activity. *In contrast,* Hitler's radical and dynamic pace hardly flagged from January 1933 to April 1945. In the process, anti-Semitism, concentration camps, and total war produced a febrile and sadistic nightmare without any parallel in the Italian experience. Though both Hitler and Mussolini were fascist, history shows them to be different in all of these respects, and in each one Hitler was more radical.

Here is the essay:

Introduction with thesis

Hitler and Mussolini have often been thought of as twin dictators, but there were considerable differences between the two men and their regimes, and Hitler was more extreme. These differences become apparent when one considers their racial views, their commitment, and their militaristic designs.

Topic sentence

(Middle paragraph)

Racism is justly associated with all fascism at that time; therefore, Mussolini, along with Hitler, is implicated. It should be pointed out, however, that the Italians' blatant racism occurred after Mussolini's deep association with Hitler. Prior to that, for many years there had been no racial doctrine in Italian fascist ideology. But Hitler held racist views from the beginning of his political movement, and it was a main motive in the Nazi movement. To resolve the "Jewish problem," he eventually slaughtered at least six million people.

Topic sentence

(Middle paragraph)

Their degree of commitment to act also varied. From a distance toward the end of the war, they may have seemed quite similar, but over the span of their reigns, they were different. Mussolini merely talked and strutted for the most part. He had few fixed doctrines and increasingly accommodated himself to circumstances. But Hitler meant every bit of his bellicosity and was willing to wage the most frightful war of all time.

Topic sentence

(Middle paragraph)

A study of their involvement in that war, however, reveals striking differences. Italian fascism was comparatively restrained and conservative until the Nazi example spurred it to new activity. Mussolini talked of a militaristic policy, but he followed a more temperate course in practice and kept the peace for thirteen years, knowing that Italy could not gain from a major war. In contrast, Hitler's radical and dynamic pace hardly flagged from January 1933 to April 1945. In the process, anti-Semitism, concentration camps, and total war produced a febrile and sadistic nightmare without any parallel in the Italian experience.

Conclusion

Thus, though both were fascist, history shows the two men to be different in both ideas and actions. Only at the end of their relationship, when Mussolini succumbed to Hitler's domination, do the two leaders appear as twin dictators, but beneath appearances it is Hitler who was the true believer, the fascist dictator.

Analogy

Analogy is a method of organizing and developing ideas by comparison. In an analogy, a writer explains or clarifies an unfamiliar subject by likening it to a familiar but strikingly different subject. Writers use analogy to make the new, the different, the complex, or the difficult more understandable for the reader. Analogy, therefore, explains, clarifies, illustrates, and simplifies; it does not prove anything.

In the following model analogy, Emerson compares society to a wave. Most analogies, like this model, are part of a larger piece of writing.

> Society is a wave. The wave moves onward, but the water of which it is composed does not. The same particle does not rise from the valley to the ridge. Its unity is only phenomenal. The persons who make up a nation today, next year die, and their experience dies with them.

Ralph Waldo Emerson, "Self-Reliance"

Writers usually announce the analogy and then develop it. In addition, analogies, as a rule, rise spontaneously from the material as the writer's thoughts flow. Study the following model. Notice that the writer announces the comparison in the first sentence. To make the meaning clear, he compares the atmosphere of the earth to a window.

> The atmosphere of Earth acts like any window in serving two very important functions. It lets light in and it permits us to look out. It also serves as a shield to keep out dangerous or uncomfortable things. A normal glazed window lets us keep our house warm by keeping out cold air, and it prevents rain, dirt, and unwelcome insects and animals from coming in. As we have already seen, Earth's atmospheric window also helps to keep our planet to a comfortable temperature by holding back radiated heat and protecting us from dangerous levels of ultraviolet light.
>
> Lately, we have discovered that space is full of a great many very dangerous things against which our atmosphere guards us. It is not a perfect shield, and sometimes one of these dangerous objects does get through. There is even some evidence that a few of these messengers from space contain life, though this has by no means been proven yet.

Lester Del Ray, *The Mysterious Sky*

The steps for writing the analogy are identical to those of writing comparison and contrast.

Connecting Reading and Writing

Heavenly Father, Divine Goalie

Charles Prebish

Not many thinkers would connect sports with religion. Beginning with a basic idea from fellow writer Richard Lipsky about the religious overtones of games, Charles Prebish extended the comparison and produced an intriguing analogy.

In *How We Play the Game*, Richard Lipsky tells us (of baseball), "The game takes place in an atmosphere of piety. In many ways the ballplayers themselves can be seen as priests who represent us in a liturgy (game) that is part of a sacred tradition." Lipsky's comment reveals that far too little has been said about the role of the player in sport religion. In other words, we need to reflect on the actors in sport religion. It would be incorrect, though, to suggest that it is only the actual players who fulfill the role of religious participants in sport. We must include the coaches and officials as well, in their role as functionaries in the religious process. They are not untrained, either. Sport, no doubt, has its own seminaries and divinity schools in the various minor leagues and training camps that school the participants in all aspects of the tradition, from theology to ritual. The spectators, as video viewers, radio listeners, or game-going die-hards, form the congregation of sport religion. Their attendance is not required for all religious observances, but they do attend at specified times to share in religious rites. And they bear the religious symbols of their faith: the pennants, emblems, hats, coats, gloves, and whatever other objects the media geniuses can promote to signify the glory of sport in general and the home team in particular. The sport symbol may not be the cross, rosary, mezuzah, but it is no less valuable to the owner, and is likely considered to be just as powerful as its traditional counterpart, or more so.

Exercise 1	DISCUSSION AND CRITICAL THINKING

1. What is the basis of the analogy?

2. What are the points of comparison?

Pink Kittens and Blue Spaceships

Alison Lurie

What are the sources of gender identity? In this passage from her book *The Language of Clothes*, Alison Lurie shows that people condition children from birth.

1 Sex-typing in dress begins at birth with the assignment of pale-pink layettes, toys, bedding and furniture to girl babies, and pale-blue ones to boy babies. Pink, in this culture, is associated with sentiment; blue with service. The implication is that the little girl's future concern will be the life of the affections; the boy's, earning a living. As they grow older, light blue becomes a popular color for girls' clothes—after all, women must work as well as weep—but pink is rare on boys'; the emotional life is never quite manly.

2 In early childhood girls' and boys' clothes are often identical in cut and fabric, as if in recognition of the fact that their bodies are much alike. But the T-shirts, pull-on slacks and zip jackets intended for boys are usually

made in darker colors (especially forest green, navy, red and brown) and printed with designs involving sports, transportation and cute wild animals. Girls' clothes are made in paler colors (especially pink, yellow and green) and decorated with flowers and cute domestic animals. The suggestion is that the boy will play vigorously and travel over long distances; the girl will stay home and nurture plants and small mammals. Alternatively, these designs may symbolize their wearers: the boy is a cuddly bear or a smiling tiger, the girl a flower or a kitten. There is also a tendency for boys' clothes to be fullest at the shoulders and girls' at the hips, anticipating their adult figures. Boys' and men's garments also emphasize the shoulders with horizontal stripes, epaulets or yokes of contrasting color. Girls' and women's garments emphasize the hips and rear through the strategic placement of gathers and trimmings.

| **Exercise 2** | **DISCUSSION AND CRITICAL THINKING** |

1. Does this selection stress comparison or contrast?

2. Is the purpose mainly to inform, to persuade, or to do both?

3. What are the two main points used for comparing and contrasting girls' and boys' clothes?

4. Is the pattern of the piece point by point or subject by subject?

5. Fill in the parts of this outline of the piece.

    I. Color   II. Design

       A. _____   A. _____

       B. _____   1. _____

                                2. _____

                           B. _____

                                  1. _____

                                  2. _____

6. Now that most mothers work outside the home, do you think the preferred colors and designs will change?

The Small Town and the Big City

Craig Calhoun

Presentations of comparison and contrast are used frequently in college textbooks. In this paragraph from *Sociology,* sixth edition, Craig Calhoun discusses human behavior and the reasons for that behavior in a small community and in a large one.

In almost every way, Diagonal [Iowa] and the Upper West Side of Manhattan appear to be opposites. In Diagonal, everyone knows everyone else personally; people are involved in a continual round of community-centered activities (the few who do not participate are thought aloof and antisocial); and everyone's activities are subject to close scrutiny. Gossip keeps most Diagonal residents from stepping very far out of line. Of course, sexual transgressions, public drunkenness, and teenage vandalism occasionally take place, but serious crime is rare. On the Upper West Side most people know only a few of the people who live in their apartment building; everyone has his or her own circle of friends; and community-based activities are rare (such as the occasional block party). Neighborliness is often considered nosiness. Anonymity is the norm, and widely different lifestyles are tolerated or simply ignored. At the same time, crime is common: most Upper West Side residents either have been the victim of a mugging or robbery or know someone who has been.

Exercise 3	DISCUSSION AND CRITICAL THINKING

1. Underline the topic sentence of the paragraph.

2. Is the paragraph pattern subject by subject or point by point?

3. Fill in the parts of this basic outline:

   I. Diagonal

      A. People involved

      B. _____

      C. Serious crime rare

  II. _____

      A. _____

      B. Mostly anonymous

      C. _____

4. Could the paragraph be improved by using some transitional words such as *on the other hand, unlike,* or *to the contrary?* If so, where would you put them?

Los Chinos Discover el Barrio

Luis Torres

Blending nostalgic recollections and astute insights, Luis Torres chronicles the cultural changes of a Northeast Los Angeles neighborhood. Note how the concluding scene parallels the introductory scene. If, after you have finished reading the piece, you are not certain whether it is optimistic or pessimistic, reread the first and last paragraphs.

1   There's a colorful mural on the asphalt playground of Hillside Elementary School, in the neighborhood called Lincoln Heights. Painted on the beige handball wall, the mural is of life-sized youngsters holding hands. Depicted are Asian and Latino kids with bright faces and ear-to-ear smiles.

2   The mural is a mirror of the makeup of the neighborhood today: Latinos living side-by-side with Asians. But it's not all smiles and happy faces in the Northeast Los Angeles community, located just a couple of miles up Broadway from City Hall. On the surface there's harmony between Latinos and Asians. But there are indications of simmering ethnic-based tensions.

3   That became clear to me recently when I took a walk through the old neighborhood—the one where I grew up. As I walked along North Broadway, I thought of a joke that comic Paul Rodriguez often tells on the stage. He paints the picture of a young Chicano walking down a street on L.A.'s Eastside. He comes upon two Asians having an animated conversation in what sounds like babble. "Hey, you guys, knock off that foreign talk. This is America—speak Spanish!"

4   When I was growing up in Lincoln Heights 30 years ago most of us spoke Spanish—and English. There was a sometimes uneasy coexistence in the neighborhood between brown and white. Back then we Latinos were moving in and essentially displacing the working-class Italians (to us, they were just *los gringos*) who had moved there and thrived after World War II.

5   Because I was an extremely fair-skinned Latino kid I would often overhear remarks by gringos in Lincoln Heights that were not intended for Latino ears, disparaging comments about "smelly wetbacks," and worse. The transition was, for the most part, a gradual process. And as I recall—except for the slurs that sometimes stung me directly—a process marked only occasionally by outright hostility.

6   A trend that began about ten years ago in Lincoln Heights seems to have hit a critical point now. It's similar to the ethnic tug-of-war of yesteryear, but different colors, different words are involved. Today Chinese and Vietnamese are displacing the Latinos who, by choice or circumstance, had Lincoln Heights virtually to themselves for two solid generations.

7   Evidence of the transition is clear.

8   The bank where I opened my first meager savings account in the late 1950s has changed hands. It's now the East-West Federal Bank, an Asian-owned enterprise.

9   The public library on Workman Street, where I checked out *Charlotte's Web* with my first library card, abounds with signs of the new times: It's called "La Biblioteca del Pueblo de Lincoln Heights," and on the door there's a notice advising that the building is closed because of the Oct. 1 earthquake; it's written in Chinese.

10   The white, wood-frame house on Griffin Avenue that I once lived in is now owned by a Chinese family.

11   What used to be a Latino-run mortuary at the corner of Sichel Street and North Broadway is now the Chung Wah Funeral Home.

12   A block down the street from the funeral home is a *panaderia*, a bakery. As I would listen to radio reports of the U.S. war in faraway Indochina while walking from class at Lincoln High School, I often used to drop in the *panaderia* for a snack.

13   The word *panaderia*, now faded and chipped, is still painted on the shop window that fronts North Broadway. But another sign, a gleaming plastic one, hangs above the window. The sign proclaims that it is a Vietnamese-Chinese bakery. The proprietor, Sam Lee, bought the business less than a year ago. With a wave of his arm, he indicates that *La Opinion,* the Spanish-language daily newspaper, is still for sale on the counter. Two signs hang side by side behind the counter announcing in Spanish and in Chinese that cakes are made to order for all occasions.

14   Out on North Broadway, Fidel Farrillas sells *raspadas* (snow-cones) from his pushcart. He has lived and worked in Lincoln Heights "for 30 years and a pinch more," he says, his voice nearly whistling through two gold-framed teeth. He has seen the neighborhood change. Twice.

15   Like many older Latinos he remembers the tension felt between *los gringos y la raza* years ago—even though most people went about their business ostensibly coexisting politely. And others who have been around as long will tell an inquiring reporter scratching away in his notebook, "We're going out of our way to treat the *chinos* nice—better than the *gringos* sometimes treated us back then." But when the notebook is closed, they're likely to whisper, "But you know, the thing is, they smell funny, and they talk behind your back, and they are so arrogant—the way they're buying up everything in our neighborhood."

16   Neighborhood transitions can be tough to reconcile.

17   It isn't easy for the blue-collar Latinos of Lincoln Heights. They haven't possessed much. But they had the barrio, "a little chunk of the world where we belonged," as one described it. There may be some hard times and hard feelings ahead as *los chinos* continue to make inroads into what had been an exclusively Latino enclave. But there are hopeful signs as well.

18   On one recent Saturday afternoon a Latino fifth-grader, wearing the same type of hightop tennis shoes I wore as a 10-year-old on that same street corner, strode up to Señor Farrillas' snow-cone pushcart. The kid pulled out a pocketful of dimes and bought two *raspadas*. One for himself, and one for his school chum—a Vietnamese kid. He was wearing hightops, too. They both ordered strawberry, as I recall.

Exercise 4   **VOCABULARY HIGHLIGHTS**

Write a short definition of each word as it is used in the essay. (Paragraph numbers are given in parentheses.) Be prepared to use the words in your own sentences.

depicted (1)	*los gringos y la raza* (15)
simmering (2)	ostensibly (15)
Chicano (3)	*chinos* (15)
animated (3)	barrio (17)
disparaging (5)	enclave (17)

| Exercise 5 | DISCUSSION AND CRITICAL THINKING |

1. Although this essay is not a highly structured comparative study, Torres is mainly concerned with Lincoln Heights then and Lincoln Heights now, thirty years later. What are the main points he uses to show the similarities?

2. What are some of the similarities?

3. What are some of the differences?

4. What is the implied comparison between the first and the last paragraphs?

5. What is Torres's main message? Specifically, is he mostly optimistic or pessimistic? What evidence do you find? Do you agree with him?

Paired Essays on Orderly and Disorderly People

Are you fundamentally orderly or disorderly? We all have tendencies toward one or the other extreme. Some of us are hardcore, to our shame or pride. If we lean toward the disorderly, we may scoff at the opposite, referring to them as "uptight" or "anal retentive." If we are in the orderly camp, we may pity the disorderly for failures in work ethic, analytical power, self-discipline, even personal hygiene.

As we read Suzanne Britt's essay, we are probably first surprised and then charmed by her wit and satirical jibes. She insists that the neat (orderly) people are the bad guys and that the sloppy (disorderly) people are the good guys. Moreover, to her, the distinction is not even close. She says, "Neat people are lazier and meaner than sloppy people." She doesn't use the slang term "neat freaks," but she makes it clear that the neat are twisted, self-centered individuals who "cut a clean swath through the organic as well as the inorganic world."

Joyce Gallagher, author of "The Messy Are in Denial," is one of those people whom she characterizes as the organized. Her group has a preordained mission—to save and sustain the less fortunate, the disorganized, the sloppy. A bemused and grudgingly forgiving participant (after all, the disorganized can't help themselves), she traces the history of the organized and disorganized from a recent yard sale back to cave dwellers, saying that human nature hasn't changed much. The disorganized flounder, often in endearing ways, and the organized come to their rescue because of a genetic imperative.

THE QUIGMANS   by Buddy Hickerson

"AAUGH! It'll take me weeks to clean this place up! *Dirt everywhere!!* And as for you, my friend, I have two words: public restroom!"

B. Hickerson, copyright Los Angeles Times. Reprinted by permission.

Neat People vs. Sloppy People

Suzanne Britt

In this essay from her book *Show and Tell*, Suzanne Britt discusses two kinds of people, the neat and the sloppy. Wouldn't the world be a better place if we were all a bit neater? If you think so, prepare to argue with Suzanne Britt.

1   I've finally figured out the difference between neat people and sloppy people. The distinction is, as always, moral. Neat people are lazier and meaner than sloppy people.

2   Sloppy people, you see, are not really sloppy. Their sloppiness is merely the unfortunate consequence of their extreme moral rectitude. Sloppy people carry in their mind's eye a heavenly vision, a precise plan, that is so stupendous, so perfect, it can't be achieved in this world or the next.

3   Sloppy people live in Never-Never Land. Someday is their métier. Someday they are planning to alphabetize all their books and set up home catalogs. Someday they will go through their wardrobes and mark certain items for tentative mending and certain items for passing on to relatives of similar shape and size. Someday sloppy people will make family scrapbooks into which they will put newspaper clippings, postcards, locks of hair, and the dried corsage from their senior prom. Someday they will file everything on the surface of their desk, including the cash receipts from coffee purchases

at the snack shop. Someday they will sit down and read all the back issues of *The New Yorker.*

4　　For all these noble reasons and more, sloppy people never get neat. They aim too high and wide. They save everything, planning someday to file, order, and straighten out the world. But while these ambitious plans take clearer and clearer shape in their heads, the books spill from the shelves onto the floor, the clothes pile up in the hamper and closet, the family mementos accumulate in every drawer, the surface of the desk is buried under mounds of paper and the unread magazines threaten to reach the ceiling.

5　　Sloppy people can't bear to part with anything. They give loving attention to every detail. When sloppy people say they're going to tackle the surface of the desk, they really mean it. Not a paper will go unturned; not a rubber band will go unboxed. Four hours or two weeks into their excavation, the desk looks exactly the same, primarily because the sloppy person is meticulously creating new piles of papers with new headings and scrupulously stopping to read all the old book catalogs before he throws them away. A neat person would just bulldoze the desk.

6　　Neat people are bums and clods at heart. They have cavalier attitudes toward possessions, including family heirlooms. Everything is just another dust-catcher to them. If anything collects dust, it's got to go and that's that. Neat people will toy with the idea of throwing the children out of the house just to cut down on the clutter.

7　　Neat people don't care about process. They like results. What they want to do is get the whole thing over with so they can sit down and watch the rasslin' on TV. Neat people operate on two unvarying principles: Never handle any item twice, and throw everything away.

8　　The only thing messy in a neat person's house is the trash can. The minute something comes to a neat person's hand, he will look at it, try to decide if it has immediate use and, finding none, throw it in the trash.

9　　Neat people are especially vicious with mail. They never go through their mail unless they are standing directly over a trash can. If the trash can is beside the mailbox, even better. All ads, catalogs, pleas for charitable contributions, church bulletins and money-saving coupons go straight into the trash can without being opened. All letters from home, postcards from Europe, bills and paychecks are opened, immediately responded to, then dropped in the trash can. Neat people keep their receipts only for tax purposes. That's it. No sentimental salvaging of birthday cards or the last letter a dying relative ever wrote. Into the trash it goes.

10　　Neat people place neatness above everything, even economics. They are incredibly wasteful. Neat people throw away several toys every time they walk through the den. I knew a neat person once who threw away a perfectly good dish drainer because it had mold on it. The drainer was too much trouble to wash. And neat people sell their furniture when they move. They will sell a La-Z-Boy recliner while you are reclining in it.

11　　Neat people are no good to borrow from. Neat people buy everything in expensive little single portions. They get their flour and sugar in two-pound bags. They wouldn't consider clipping a coupon, saving a leftover, reusing plastic nondairy whipped cream containers or rinsing off tin foil and draping it over the unmoldy dish drainer. You can never borrow a neat person's newspaper to see what's playing at the movies. Neat people have the paper all wadded up and in the trash by 7:05 A.M.

12   Neat people cut a clean swath through the organic as well as the inorganic world. People, animals, and things are all one to them. They are so insensitive. After they've finished with the pantry, the medicine cabinet, and the attic, they will throw out the red geranium (too many leaves), sell the dog (too many fleas), and send the children off to boarding school (too many scuff marks on the hardwood floors).

Exercise 6 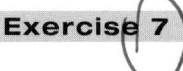   **VOCABULARY HIGHLIGHTS**

Write a short definition of each word as it is used in the essay. (Paragraph numbers are given in parentheses.) Be prepared to use the words in your own sentences.

rectitude (2)   meticulously (5)

stupendous (2)   scrupulously (5)

métier (3)   cavalier (6)

tentative (3)   heirlooms (6)

excavation (5)   swath (12)

Exercise 7   **DISCUSSION AND CRITICAL THINKING**

1. Is this essay mainly comparison or contrast?

2. Is Britt trying mainly to inform or persuade?

3. What are the main points for this study?

4. Is the pattern mainly point by point or subject by subject?

5. What is the moral distinction between the neat and the sloppy?

6. Britt says that sloppy people are morally superior to neat people. How does that idea differ from common assumptions?

7. To what extent is Britt serious, and to what extent is she just being humorous?

8. Britt presents two extremes. What qualities would a person in the middle have?

The Messy Are in Denial

Joyce Gallagher

Freelance journalist Joyce Gallagher gives us some insights into why the disorganized often marry the organized. She says it's all part of a design in Nature. Reasoning and her personal experience tell her so.

1   Others may see the disorganized as carefree people wallowing happily in the cluttered chaos of their own making. I see their conduct for what it so obviously is—a crying out for help. If they are so contented, then why are so many of them latching onto and becoming entirely dependent on those of us who are organized? Complaining all the while about being controlled, they, nevertheless, behave like mistletoe nailing itself to oaks, fleas colonizing St. Bernards, and funguses invading feet.

2   That tendency is easy to document and understand. Anyone can see why the disorganized (the messy, the sloppy, the disorderly, the Pisces, the idealist, the daydreamer) need the organized (the orderly, the systematic, the tidy, the Virgo, the neat, the realistic, the practical). But that leaves the more complicated question: Why would the organized even tolerate the disorganized? Or to use our figures of speech, why would oaks, St. Bernards, and feet be so submissive? I say the answer to all such connections can be found in the phrase "balance in nature." Every creature-type occupies a niche or plunges into extinction. One role of those who are neat (while they are enjoying their own practical and artistic triumphs) is to provide a secure directive system so the sloppy can experience their measure of fulfillment. Like a stoical whale with a barnacle, the organized hang in there while the disorganized hang on.

3   Of course, hanging on, or even hanging around, doesn't mean the disorganized are always complete parasites. Far from it. In fact, the disorganized are often writers, artists, musicians, pop philosophers, and lovable flakes. They may even be fun to be around, even get married to—even stay married to, if you can get past their messiness.

4   If you will just listen, the disorganized will explain *ad nauseam* their lives as works in progress. And in a sense their lives are works in progress, not in advanced stages of progress such as revision or editing, but in freewriting, brainstorming, clustering. Without a thesis, they freewrite through the material world, not yet knowing what to keep or discard. They brainstorm through life, jumping from one acquisition to another, clustering their "treasures" in attics, work rooms, garages, and other handy, unprotected spaces. Finally, if not directed by an organized person, they run the risk of inundating themselves with their own junk.

5   Fortunately, when Nature has its way, an organizer comes to the rescue—as a friend, a relative, or, perhaps, an official. In my situation, I'm the organized spouse, sometimes succumbing to my disorganized companion's pathetic romanticism, but more often, saving him from himself.

6   I do what I can. As he busily accumulates, I busily distribute. It's not easy. Toil as I might, I look around and see him effortlessly acquiring, like a tornado sucking in stuff faster than I can throw it away. I especially donate to thrift stores. Hapless children, the disabled of all kinds, and veterans of all wars depend mightily on us organized people to provide merchandise to their benefactors. Unfortunately for the organized, the thrift industry also depends on the disorganized as customers to cart home items such as scratchy records, manual typewriters, vintage clothing, and myriad unspeakable artifacts called "collectibles."

7   And if it's not a thrift store providing a game preserve for the disorganized, it's a yard sale. Organized people conduct yard sales. The disorganized attend them. As slack-jawed, hollow-eyed hulks, they drive compulsively from one location to another, not knowing what they are looking for. I sup-

pose it's an ancient yearning for the hunt, even when the belly, larder, and garage are full. I've known my significant disorganized other to stake out a promising sale site a full hour before opening time, peering through the windshield of his motorized blind, stalking the forlorn, unwanted inanimate prey. Way back in the distance, I shovel out junk, knowing it is the burden of the neat to offset every shopping binge of the sloppy.

8 Despite my taking credit for rescuing and sustaining my disorganized mate, pride didn't prompt me to write this. In fact, I don't particularly relish my lot as an organized person with a directive mission. My behavior is quite beyond my control. As mentioned previously, it's probably instinctive, genetic. Tens of thousands of evolutionary years have made my opposite and me what we are.

9 My spouse's counterpart was perhaps an ancient daydreaming troglodyte, who decorated sandstone cave walls with drawings of hunts, imagining the glories of bringing down that mammoth with one club whomp. If so, there was a well-groomed organizer in the background, arranging his clubs all in a row and his life generally. If she hadn't done so, he couldn't have contributed to the diverse gene pool into which we now dip.

10 Reason tells me that's what happened to the Neanderthals—there was too much inbreeding among the disorganized. Consider the artists' uniform depictions of these creatures: messy to the max, with grubby fingers and tousled hair, their privates barely concealed by scrappy animal-hide clothing. It's no wonder science has failed to establish kinship between them and the surviving relatively neat- and tidy-looking *homo sapiens*.

| Exercise 8 | VOCABULARY HIGHLIGHTS |

Write a short definition of each word as it is used in the essay. (Paragraph numbers are given in parentheses.) Be prepared to use the words in your own sentences.

stoical (2)	inanimate (7)
parasites (3)	sustaining (8)
ad nauseam (4)	troglodyte (9)
inundating (4)	Neanderthals (10)
artifacts (6)	*homo sapiens* (10)

| Exercise 9 | DISCUSSION AND CRITICAL THINKING |

1. Is this essay mainly comparison or contrast?

2. Is Gallagher trying mainly to inform or persuade?

3. What points of contrast are applied to the two types?

4. How much truth do you find amid the humor?

5. Do you agree that disorganized people need organized people?

6. Can one also make the point that organized people need disorganized people?

7. Can the high rate of divorce be partly traced to how organized people and disorganized people do or do not pair up?

| **Exercise 10** | **CONNECTING THE PAIRED ESSAYS** |

1. In comparing the two essays, what subjects are equivalent?

2. Britt says that neat people are lazy and mean. Does Gallagher say anything similar about the disorganized? If Gallagher doesn't go that far, then how far does she go in characterizing the disorganized?

3. Are the differences mainly in the types (neat and messy) being discussed or the interpretation of the two types?

4. Both authors use humor to exaggerate traits. Which author distorts reality more?

5. Which author seems more flexible? Explain.

6. With which side of which comparison do you identify, if at all?

Student Writers: Demonstrations and Readings

Jennifer Jeffries considered several topics before she selected different kinds of love. Just a bit of freewriting convinced her that she had the information and interest to do a good job. In a psychology course she had recently taken, she had read about and discussed ideas about love. At first, she planned to use the subject-by-subject approach; then, as her paragraph grew longer and more complicated, she switched to the point-by-point form.

Jeffries's Writing Process Worksheet shows you how her writing evolved from idea to final draft. To conserve space here, her three rough drafts marked for revision have been omitted. The balance of the worksheet has been lengthened for you to be able to see her other work in its entirety.

You will find a full-size blank worksheet on page 5. It can be photocopied, filled in, and submitted with each assignment if your instructor directs you to do so.

Writing Process Worksheet

TITLE Two Loves: Puppy and True

NAME Jennifer Jeffries   **DUE DATE** Monday, May 16, 8 a.m.

ASSIGNMENT

In the space below, write whatever you need to know about your assignment, including information about the topic, audience, pattern of writing, length, whether to include a rough draft or revised drafts, and whether your paper must be typed.

Compare and contrast two abstract terms in a paragraph with the appropriate pattern. Write for a general audience. If your term is extremely technical, use explanations that can be understood by those outside the field you are discussing. Submit this completed worksheet, a rough draft marked for revision, and a typed final draft of about 250 to 300 words.

STAGE ONE

Explore Freewrite, brainstorm (list), cluster, or take notes as directed by your instructor. Use the back of this page or separate paper if you need more space.

Freewriting

Love as common word

Puppy love and true love

Time will tell

Love is one of the most common words in the English language. It is one of the first words a person hears when coming into this world and it is one of the last a person hears when leaving the world. There are many kinds of love, the two that we are likely to remember the best are the first love and the last love. Those two are puppy love and true love. That is true if everything works out all right. I guess it's difficult to tell what kind of love one is in when one is in it, but later one can look at the love and figure out what kind it was, or in the case of true love that may last for a long time and even to the end of life you can figure out what it is while you are still experiencing it. These are two good ideas to compare and contrast because they are similar but mostly dissimilar.

Brainstorming

Who?	people in love
What?	puppy love and true love
Where?	everywhere where people are free to fall in love
When?	throughout life
Why?	because all human beings of sound mind want to love and be loved
How?	by using their own qualities and responding to the situation

Listing

True love is special. [These circled points can also be applied to puppy love.]
    -duration
    -commitment

(-intimacy)
(-passion)
-age
-circumstances
-common beliefs
-sincerity

STAGE TWO **Organize** Write a topic sentence or thesis; label the subject and the treatment parts.

<u>True love and puppy love</u> <u>are mainly different when compared and</u>
          subject   treatment
<u>contrasted in terms of passion, intimacy, and commitment.</u>

Write an outline or an outline alternative.

  I. Passion
      A. Puppy love
          1. Consuming
          2. Intense
      B. True love
          1. Present
          2. Proportional
 II. Intimacy
      A. Puppy love
          1. Lots of talking
          2. Superficial
      B. True love
          1. Good communication
             a. Feelings
             b. Ideas
          2. Deep
III. Commitment
      A. Puppy love
          1. Not tested
          2. Weak, if at all
      B. True love
          1. Proven
          2. Profound

STAGE THREE **Write** On separate paper, write and then revise your paper as many times as necessary for <u>c</u>oherence, <u>l</u>anguage (usage, tone, and diction), <u>u</u>nity, <u>e</u>mphasis, <u>s</u>upport, and <u>s</u>entences (CLUESS). Read your paper aloud to hear and correct any grammatical errors or awkward-sounding sentences.

Edit any problems in fundamentals, such as <u>c</u>apitalization, <u>o</u>missions, <u>p</u>unctuation, and <u>s</u>pelling (COPS).

Final Draft

Two Loves: Puppy and True
Jennifer Jeffries

Topic sentence   Of the many forms of love, the two opposite extremes are puppy love and true love. <u>If love in its fullest form has three parts—passion, intimacy, and commitment—then puppy love and true love could be called *incomplete* and *complete*, respectively.</u> <u>Passion</u> is common to both. Puppy love

Point couldn't exist without *passion*, hence the word puppy—an immature animal that jumps around excitedly licking somebody's face. A person in

Subject A <u>puppy love</u> is attracted physically to someone and is constantly aroused. A

Subject B person in <u>true love</u> is also passionate, but the passion is proportional to other parts of love—and life. True love passion is based on more than physical attraction, though that should not be discounted. It is with the

Point <u>intimacy</u> factor that puppy love really begins to differ from true love. <u>Puppy</u>

Subject A <u>love</u> may promote a lot of talk, but most of it can be attributed to the arousal factor. There's no closeness and depth of shared experience. But

Subject B with <u>true love</u> there is a genuine closeness and shared concern for each other that is supportive and reassuring. That closeness usually comes from years of shared experience, which also proves commitment. And it is just

Point that factor, the <u>commitment</u>, that is probably the main difference between

Subject A puppy love and true love. The people in <u>puppy love</u> may talk about eternity, but their love hasn't really gotten outside the physical realm. Their love has not been tested, whereas those in true love have a proven commit-

Subject B ment. <u>True love</u> has survived troubles in this imperfect world and become stronger. And it has survived because it has more than the one dimension. These considerations show that these two loves are very different, though puppy love may, with time, become true love. That possibility doesn't mean that age necessarily corresponds with one form of love. A person of any age can, by knowing passion, intimacy, and commitment, experience true love, but true love is more likely to develop over a period of time.

Exercise 11   **DISCUSSION AND CRITICAL THINKING**

1. Do you agree with Jeffries's decision to use the point-by-point pattern rather than the subject-by-subject one? Why or why not?

2. The author says that puppy love can become true love. Can true love ever become puppy love?

3. Jeffries implies that one is much more likely to fall out of puppy love than true love. Do you agree? Why or why not?

4. How much time is required for true love to develop?

The Piper Cherokee and the Cessna 172

Brittany Markovic

As a student pilot and a student in a community college, Brittany Markovic leads a life rich in variety and excitement. She rides to school in an automobile, but her mind is in the skies where she flies training aircraft. This comparison-and-contrast assignment provided her with an opportunity to compare and contrast two aircraft often used in training student pilots.

When most people think of an airplane, the picture that comes to mind is likely that of a large aircraft such as a Boeing 747. Commercial airlines are what the public is most familiar with, for that is what travelers ordinarily use for long-distance transportation. However, most business handled by airplanes—in fact about 80 percent of all flights—is done by small planes in what is called general aviation. When a student pilot thinks of an airplane, it is probably a small training plane, the Cessna 172. Later, the student's attention may turn to another small aircraft, the Piper Cherokee. Although either can be used for training, I believe that certain features make the Cessna 172 the better aircraft for the student.

For the student at the controls, two key characteristics probably come to mind, all related to movement, namely the power for thrust and the landing speed. In all those respects, the two aircraft are similar. The Piper Cherokee must have enough thrust to lift a maximum of 2,350 pounds at takeoff, for which it has 150 horsepower. Then in landing, the Cherokee should come in at 63 knots. The Cessna 172 has quite similar ratings: it can lift 2,400 pounds, has 160 horsepower, and lands at a speed between 60 and 70 knots. All of those factors should be considered in relation to the particular flight. The maximum weight matters little in training flights because they are made without extra passengers and baggage. The landing speeds for the two are also about the same and nonconsequential. The only significant matter is found in the power plant, which favors the Cessna 172 by 10 horsepower, small but in some situations crucial.

That power and speed, of course, must be seen in relation to the design of the aircraft, especially the wing placement. For the Piper Cherokee, the wing is mounted below the cockpit. That design allows for great visibility above the aircraft, which, in turn, is better for observing other aircraft and certain weather conditions. The big problem for the student pilot is that the wing-under arrangement partially blocks the pilot's view of the runway. On the contrary, the Cessna 172 features a wing over the fuselage, providing the new pilot with a much appreciated better view of the runway. That design allows the student pilot to more easily master the two most difficult maneuvers: taking off and landing.

Another point to consider seriously is the fuel system, for the new pilot has enough things to take care of without having to worry about getting gas to the carburetor. In the wing-under Piper Cherokee, the tanks are in the wing, but because the wings are lower than the engine, the fuel must be pushed to the engine by a fuel pump, and a fuel pump may not work. But that possible problem does not exist in the high-wing Cessna 172. It also has its gas tank in the wing; however, because the wing is above the engine, gravity delivers fuel to the carburetor without need of a pump. When it comes to airplanes, less may be more. We all know that gravity is more reliable than a fuel pump.

The first features, the power for thrust and the landing speed, give the Cessna 172 only a slight edge over the Piper Cherokee. But the other two factors are decisive. Better visibility for takeoffs and landings afforded by the high wing and gas delivered by gravity make the Cessna 172 the better aircraft for student pilots.

Exercise 12	**DISCUSSION AND CRITICAL THINKING**

1. Is Markovic's purpose to inform or persuade?

2. Markovic is writing for an audience that knows little about aerodynamics. How does her writing reflect her understanding of her audience?

3. Double underline the thesis of the essay and underline the topic sentence of paragraphs 2, 3, and 4.

4. Does Markovic use the subject-by-subject or point-by-point pattern?

5. Circle the words that provide a smooth transition between paragraphs 2 and 3 and between paragraphs 3 and 4.

Practicing Patterns of Comparison and Contrast

Understanding the two basic patterns of comparison and contrast and knowing which one to use for a particular assignment will serve you well in writing for all occasions.

Exercise 13	**COMPLETING PATTERNS OF COMPARISON AND CONTRAST**

Fill in the blanks to complete the comparisons and contrasts in the following outlines.

Point-by-Point Outline

John: Before and after marriage

   I. Way of talking (content and manner)

      A. _____

      B. John: After

II. _____

    A. John: Before

    B. John: After

III. _____

    A. John: Before

    B. _____

Subject-by-Subject Outline

Two vans: Nissan Quest and Dodge Caravan (would be more specific if for a particular year)

  I. Quest

    A. Horsepower and gears

    B. _____

    C. Cargo area

  II. Caravan

    A. _____

    B. Safety

    C. _____

✐ Topics for Writing Comparison and Contrast

The following topics lend themselves to unique and creative analogies. Choose a topic that strikes your fancy and write a paragraph or essay on that topic using analogy.

1. Riding the merry-go-round and dating

2. Juggling and paying bills

3. Driving on the freeway and pursuing a career

4. Going fishing and looking for a job

5. Shopping in a supermarket and getting an education

6. Caring for a child and for a dog

7. Driving in traffic and fighting on a battlefield

8. Sleeping and watching television

9. Learning a new culture from an immigrant's viewpoint and learning an environment from an infant's viewpoint

10. Looking for Elvis and looking for truth (or for the Holy Grail, an honest person, a unicorn, the Loch Ness monster, Big Foot, or the Abominable Snowman)

Reading-Related Topics

"Pink Kittens and Blue Spaceships"

11. Compare and contrast the toys traditionally given to boys and to girls.

12. Compare and contrast the games or recreation generally made available to girls and to boys.

"The Small Town and the Big City"

13. Compare and contrast two communities (for example, urban and suburban, city and country) that you have lived in, showing that one is more safe, friendly, or charitable than the other.

14. Compare and contrast two schools (small and large, city and rural) to show that one is different from the other in some respect, such as school spirit, seriousness about education, safety, and so on.

"Los Chinos Discover el Barrio"

15. Compare and contrast a neighborhood, a community, or a school as it once was and now is. Consider such points as change, lack of change, behavior, appearance, attitudes, and convictions. Use specific examples.

"Neat People vs. Sloppy People"

16. Using ideas and points from this essay, discuss two people you know or have read about to argue that Britt's conclusions are valid.

17. Using ideas and points from this essay, discuss two people you know or have read about to argue that her ideas are not valid.

18. Write a comparative study on people with good table manners and those with bad table manners. Explain the causes and effects of their behavior.

19. Using Britt's essay as a model of exaggerated humor, write a comparative study of one of the following:

    • People who exercise a lot and those who hardly exercise

    • People who diet and those who do not

    • Men with beards and those without

    • Women with extremely long fingernails and those with short fingernails

    • People who dye their hair and those who do not

    • People who take care of their yards and those who do not

    • People who take care of their children (or pets) and those who do not

"The Messy Are in Denial"

20. Using Gallagher's points and insights, discuss two people you know or have read about to argue that her conclusions are valid.

21. Using Gallagher's points and insights, discuss two people you know or have read about to argue that her ideas are not valid.

Paired Essays on Orderly and Disorderly People

22. Compare and contrast Britt's sloppy person with Gallagher's disorganized person.

23. Compare and contrast Britt's neat person with Gallagher's organized person.

"Two Loves: Puppy and True"

24. Using the terms and the patterns shown in this paragraph, write a comparison-and-contrast piece on two couples you know who are in love.

25. Write a comparative study of two other kinds of love, such as those based mostly on companionship and those based mostly on romance. You could use the same points that Jeffries does: passion, intimacy, and commitment.

"The Piper Cherokee and the Cessna 172"

26. Compare and contrast two pickup trucks to show that one is better than the other for particular needs or purposes (everyday driving, certain kinds of work or recreation, making a good impression on peers). If you have a computer, use the Internet to collect specific information. Give credit to your source(s).

27. Compare any other two products to show that one is better or more useful for a particular need or purpose.

Career-Related Topics

28. Compare and contrast two pieces of office equipment or two services with the purpose of showing that one is better.

29. Compare and contrast two management styles or two working styles.

30. Compare and contrast two career fields to argue that one is better for you.

31. Compare and contrast a public school with a business.

32. Compare and contrast two computers or two software programs.

General Topics

Compare and contrast one or more of the following topics. After you limit your topic, personalize it or do some research so that you will have specific support.

33. Two generations of college students

34. Two automobiles, bicycles, motorcycles, snowmobiles

35. Two types of (or specific) police officers, doctors, teachers, preachers, students, athletes

36. Two famous persons—authors, generals, actors, athletes

37. Two philosophies, religions, ideologies

38. Cross-country skiing and downhill skiing

39. Living at college and living at home

40. A small college and a large college or a four-year college and a community college

41. Two gangs or two kinds of gangs

42. Two roommates, neighbors, friends, dates

43. Two movies, television shows, commercials, songs, singers

44. Dating and going steady, living together and being married, a person before and after marriage

45. Shopping malls and neighborhood stores

46. Two political candidates or office holders

Writer's Guidelines: Comparison and Contrast

1. Purpose: During the exploration of your topic, define your purpose clearly.

   - Decide whether you are writing a work that is primarily comparison, primarily contrast, or balanced.

   - Determine whether your main purpose is to inform or to persuade.

2. Points

   - Indicate your points of comparison or contrast, perhaps by listing.

   - Eliminate irrelevant points.

3. Pattern

   - Select the subject-by-subject or the point-by-point pattern after considering your topic and planned treatment. The point-by-point pattern is usually preferred in essays. Only in long papers is there likely to be a mixture of patterns.

   - Compose an outline reflecting the pattern you select.

   - Use this basic subject-by-subject pattern:

     I. Subject X
       A. Point 1
       B. Point 2
     II. Subject Y
       A. Point 1
       B. Point 2

   - Use this basic point-by-point pattern:

     I. Point 1
       A. Subject X
       B. Subject Y
     II. Point 2
       A. Subject X
       B. Subject Y

4. Presentation

   - Be sure to give each point more or less equal treatment. Attention to each part of the outline will usually ensure balanced development.

   - Use transitional words and phrases to indicate comparison and contrast and to establish coherence.

   - Use a carefully stated topic sentence for a paragraph and a clear thesis for an essay. Each developmental paragraph should have a topic sentence broad enough to embrace its content.

Definition: Clarifying Terms

"$\mathcal{A}$ definition is the enclosing of a wilderness of ideas within a wall of words."

Samuel Butler

THE QUIGMANS   by Buddy Hickerson

Jane Goodall in the wilds of Milwaukee.

B. Hickerson, copyright 1998. Los Angeles Times Syndicate. Reprinted by permission.

Writing Definition

M̲ost definitions are short; they consist of a *synonym* (a word or phrase that has about the same meaning as the term to be defined), a phrase, or a sentence. For example, we might say that a hypocrite is a person "professing beliefs or virtues he or she does not possess." Terms can also be defined by *etymology,* or word history. *Hypocrite* once meant "actor" *(hypocrites)* in Greek because an actor was pretending to be someone else. We may find this information interesting and revealing, but the history of a word may be of no use because the meaning has changed drastically over the years. Sometimes definitions occupy a paragraph or an entire essay. The short definition is called a *simple definition;* the longer one is known as an *extended definition.*

Techniques for Writing Simple Definitions

If you want to define a term without being abrupt and mechanical, you have several alternatives. All of the following techniques allow you to blend the definition into your developing thought.

- *Basic dictionary meaning.* You can quote the dictionary's definition, but if you do, you are obliged to indicate your source, which you should do directly and explicitly. Always give the complete title of the dictionary, such as "*The American Heritage Dictionary* says," not simply "Webster says." Dozens of dictionaries use the "Webster" designation.

- *Synomyms.* Although no two words have exactly the same meaning, synonyms often follow as if in parentheses.

Example: He was guilty of the ancient sin of *hubris,* of excessive pride.

- *Direct explanation.* You can state the definition.

James Harvey Robinson, "On Various Kinds of Thinking"

Example: This spontaneous and loyal support of our preconception—this process of finding "good" reasons to justify our routine beliefs—is known to modern psychologists as *rationalizing*—clearly a new name for a very ancient thing.

- *Indirect explanation.* You can imply the definition.

Ruth Benedict, *Patterns of Culture*

Example: Trance is a similar abnormality in our society. Even a mild mystic is *aberrant* in Western civilization.

- *Analytical or formal definition.* In using this method, you define by placing the term (the subject) in a class (genus) and then identifying it with characteristics that show how it differs from other members of the same class, as the following examples show:

Subject	Class	Characteristics
A democracy	is a form of government	in which voters elect representatives to manage society.
A wolf	is a dog-like mammal	that is large and carnivorous, with coarse fur, erect, pointed ears, and a bushy tail.
Jazz	is a style of music	that features improvisation and performance.

Exercise 1	WRITING SIMPLE DEFINITIONS

Complete the following formal definitions.

	Subject	Class	Characteristics
1.	Rock	is a style of music	
2.	Rap	is a style of music	
3.	Psychology	is a field of study	
4.	Recreation	is a sport, exercise, or pastime	
5.	Capitalism	is an economic system	
6.	Racism		
7.	Family		
8.	An elephant		
9.	A bicycle		
10.	Happiness		

Dictionary Entries—Which One to Use

Suppose that you do not know the meaning of the term in italics in the following sentence:

> That kind of cactus is *indigenous* to the Mojave Desert.

As you consider the term in context, you look at the dictionary definitions.

> **in•dig•e•nous** \ in-'di-jə-nəs \ *adj* [LL *indigenus,* fr. L *indigena,*
> n., native, fr. OL *indu, endo* in, within + L *gignere* to beget—more
> at END-, KIN] (1646) **1:** having originated in and being produced,
> growing, living, or occurring naturally in a particular region or
> environment **2:** INNATE, INBORN ***syn*** see NATIVE—**in•dig•e-nous•ly**
> *adv*—**in•dig•e•nous•ness** *n*

The first definition seems to offer an insight. *Produced* doesn't work, but *grow-ing* and *living naturally in a particular region or environment* seem to fit. Yet *grow-ing* and *living* are not precisely the same. Then you look at the second set of defini-tions: INBORN, INNATE ***syn*** *see* NATIVE. The words are synonyms. You can see that of the three words, only *native* fits. To provide more information for the reader, the dictio-nary also presents *native* with a special treatment of synonyms (hence the *syn*) in its own place. Looking under the word *native,* you find this definition:

> ¹**na•tive** \ 'nāt-iv \ *adj* [ME *natif,* fr. MF, fr. L *nativus,* fr. *natus,* pp. of
> *nasci* to be born—more at NATION] (14c) **1:** INBORN, INNATE <~ talents>

2: belonging to a particular place by birth <~ to Wisconsin> 3: *archaic:* closely related 4: belonging to or associated with one by birth 5: NATURAL, NORMAL 6a: grown, produced, or originating in a particular place or in the vicinity: LOCAL b: living or growing naturally in a particular region: INDIGENOUS 7: SIMPLE, UNAFFECTED 8a: constituting the original substance or source b: found in nature esp. in an unadulterated form <mining ~ silver> 9: *chiefly Austral:* having a usu. superficial resemblance to a specified English plant or animal—**na•tive•ly** *adv*—**na•tive•ness** *n*

syn NATIVE, INDIGENOUS, ENDEMIC, ABORIGINAL mean belonging to a locality. NATIVE implies birth or origin in a place or region and may suggest compatibility with it <*native* tribal customs>. INDIGENOUS applies to species or races and adds to NATIVE the implication of not having been introduced from elsewhere <maize is *indigenous* to America>. ENDEMIC implies being peculiar to a region <edelweiss is *endemic* in the Alps>. ABORIGINAL implies having no known race preceding in occupancy of the region <the *aboriginal* peoples of Australia>.

Merriam-Webster's Collegiate Dictionary, Tenth Edition

In the synonyms at the close of the entry, did you observe the various shades of meaning, especially the meaning of *indigenous* and *native?* A dictionary is an invaluable aid to definition, but it must be used with care if you want to express yourself clearly and precisely. No two words have exactly the same meaning, and a word may have many meanings, some that extend to very different concepts.

Avoiding Common Problems

- Do not use the expression *is where* or *is when* in beginning the main part of the definition. The verb *is* (a linking verb) should be followed by a noun, a pronoun, or an adjective.

  Weak: A stadium is where they hold sports spectaculars.

  Better: A stadium is a structure in which sports spectaculars are held.

  Weak: Socialism is when the ownership and operation of the means of production and distribution are vested in the community as a whole.

  Better: Socialism is a theory or system of community organization that advocates that the ownership and control of the means of production, capital, land, and so forth, be vested in the community as a whole.

- Do not use the *circular definition,* a practice of defining a term with the term itself.

  Circular: An aristocracy is a form of government based on rule by the aristocrats.

  Direct: An aristocracy is a form of government in which the power resides in the hands of the best individuals or a small privileged class.

- Do not define the subject in more complicated language than the original.

  Murky: *Surreptitious* means "clandestine."

  Clear: *Surreptitious* means "secret."

- Do not substitute the example for the definition; the example may be excellent for clarification, but it does not completely define.

Weak: Political conservatives are people like William F. Buckley, Jr., and Pat Robertson.

Better: Political conservatives are people who are dedicated to preserving existing conditions. Examples of conservatives are William F. Buckley, Jr., and Pat Robertson.

Techniques for Writing Extended Definitions

Essays of definitions can take many forms. Among the more common techniques for writing a paragraph or short essay of definition are the patterns we have worked with in previous chapters. Consider each of those patterns when you need to write an extended definition. For a particular term, some forms will be more useful than others; use the pattern or patterns that best fulfill your purpose.

Each of the following questions takes a pattern of writing and directs it toward definition.

- *Narration:* Can I tell an anecdote or story to define this subject (such as *jerk, humanitarian,* or *citizen*)? This form may overlap with description and exemplification.

- *Description:* Can I describe this subject (such as *a whale* or *the moon*)?

- *Exemplification:* Can I give examples of this subject (such as naming individuals, to provide examples of *actors, diplomats,* or *satirists*)?

- *Analysis by Division:* Can I divide this subject into parts (for example, the parts of a *heart, cell,* or *carburetor*)?

- *Process Analysis:* Can I define this subject (such as *lasagna, tornado, hurricane, blood pressure,* or any number of scientific processes) by describing how to make it or how it occurs? (Common to the methodology of communicating in science, this approach is sometimes called the "operational definition.")

- *Cause and Effect:* Can I define this subject (such as *a flood, a drought, a riot,* or *a cancer*) by its causes and effects?

- *Classification:* Can I group this subject (such as kinds of *families, cultures, religions,* or *governments*) into classes?

Subject	*Class*	*Characteristics*
A republic	is a form of government	in which power resides in the people (the electorate).

- *Comparison and Contrast:* Can I define this subject (such as *extremist* or *patriot*) by explaining what it is similar to and different from? If you are defining *orangutan* to a person who has never heard of one but is familiar with the gorilla, then you could make comparison-and-contrast statements. If you want to define *patriot,* then you might want to stress what it is not (the contrast) before you explain what it is: a patriot is not a one-dimensional flag waver, not someone who hates "foreigners" because America is always right and always best.

When you use prewriting strategies to develop ideas for a definition, you can effectively consider all the patterns you have learned by using a modified clustering form (Figure 15.1). Put a double bubble around the subject to be defined. Then put a single bubble around each pattern and add appropriate words. If a pattern is not

Figure 15.1
Bubble cluster showing how a term could be defined using different essay patterns.

relevant to what you are defining, leave it blank. If you want to expand your range of information, you could add a bubble for a simple dictionary definition and another for an etymological definition.

Order

The organization of your extended definition is likely to be one of emphasis, but it may be space or time, depending on the subject material. You may use just one pattern of development for the overall sequence. If so, you would use the principles of organization discussed in previous chapters.

Introduction and Development

Consider these ways of introducing a definition: with a question, with a statement of what it is not, with a statement of what it originally meant, or with a discussion of why a clear definition is important. You may use a combination of these ways or all of them before you continue with your definition.

Development, whether in the form of sentences for the paragraph or of paragraphs for the essay, is likely to represent one or more of the patterns of narration, description, exposition (with its own subdivisions), and argumentation.

Whether you personalize a definition depends on your purpose and your audience. Your instructor may ask you to write about a word within the context of your experience or to write about it from a detached, clinical viewpoint.

Connecting Reading and Writing

The Amusement Park
Russell B. Nye

A freelance writer, Russell B. Nye is especially interested in popular culture and was drawn to the idea of the amusement park as an American institution. Places such as Disneyland, Disney World, Magic Mountain, Coney Island, Cedar Point, and Six (more or fewer) Flags engage our emotions as much as they entertain us. Nye gives us a definition that measures the depth and breadth of our experiences at places like those.

The amusement park, separated by fences and guards from the outside world, is itself a kind of play field, through whose gates visitors come expecting to be both spectators and participants. It is a place of action, noise, color, and confusion, which people enter only to play, filled with nothing but devices and situations to help them do so. There are games of competition—all sorts of shooting and throwing games, weight-guessing, strength-testing devices, and whole buildings devoted to pinball and other competitive machines. Games of chance abound—lotteries, spinning fortune wheels, and the ubiquitous bingo hall. Mimicry, of course, is the entire purpose of the theme park. Many parks also hire clowns, actors of book characters and animals and other masked or costumed players to wander the grounds. Vertigo-inducing rides such as whips, Ferris wheels, swings and slides form the backbone of the park's traditional attractions. Roller coasters, in particular, combine real speed, simulated danger and sensory disorder, and relief—in two- to three-minute intervals—to produce the most powerful vertiginous effect of all. Nowhere else in modern life may one put together in the space of a few hours and with such minor expenditure of money and energy so complete a play experience.

| Exercise 2 | DISCUSSION AND CRITICAL THINKING |

1. Underline the topic sentence of the paragraph.

2. Circle the closing sentence if there is one.

3. According to the author, "Mimicry . . . is the entire purpose of the theme park." What does he mean by that?

4. Name some of the patterns of writing that Nye uses.

5. Is *amusement park* the kind of term that could easily be explained by a phrase or is an extended definition such as Nye's necessary?

Georgia on My Mind

Ray Jenkins

What was it like to be a poor white Southerner in the Old South? Ray Jenkins knows. As you read this selection, anticipate a reading-related writing topic asking you to indicate what it is like to live in your neighborhood or in the neighborhood where your parents grew up.

Unless a man has picked cotton all day in August; has sat in an outhouse in 20 degrees in January and passed this time of necessity by reading last year's Sears Roebuck catalogue; has eaten a possum and liked it; has castrated a live pig with a dull pocket knife and has wrung a chicken's neck with his own hands; has learned at least a few chords on a fiddle and guitar; has tried to lure a sharecropper's daughter into the woods for mischievous purposes; has watched a man who had succeeded in doing just that have his sins washed away in the Blood of the Lamb in a baptism in a muddy creek; has been kicked by a mean milch cow and kicked her back; has drunk busthead likker knowing full well it might kill him; has wished the next day it had killed him; has watched a neighbor's house burn down; has drawn a knife on an adversary in fear and anger; has half-soled his one pair of shoes with a tire repair kit; has gone into a deep dark well to get out a dead chicken that had fallen in; has waited beside a dusty road in the midday heat, hoping the R.F.D. postman would bring some long-coveted item ordered from the catalogue; has been in close quarters with a snake; has, in thirsty desperation, drunk water that worked alive with mosquito larvae called wiggletails; has eaten sardines out of a can with a stick; has killed a cat just for the hell of it; . . . has stepped in the droppings of a chicken and not really cared; has been cheated by someone he worked hard for; has gone to bed at sundown because he could no longer endure the crushing isolation; has ridden a bareback mule three miles to visit a pretty girl who waited in a clean, flimsy cotton dress—unless he has done these things, then he cannot understand what it was like in my South.

Exercise 3   **DISCUSSION AND CRITICAL THINKING**

1. This unconventional definition has no stated topic sentence. What is the unstated topic sentence?

2. What is the effect of using one exceedingly long sentence to develop the definition?

3. What pattern of development is featured in this definition?

4. Is there any overall pattern to Jenkins's use of examples?

Tortillas

José Antonio Burciaga

A distinguished publisher and writer, José Antonio Burciaga died in 1996, leaving a rich legacy of poems, short stories, and essays. His essay here defines one of the most basic Hispanic foods, *tortillas.* Much more than a mere recipe, this definition is colorfully layered with historical, regional, and personal context.

1   My earliest memory of *tortillas* is my *Mamá* telling me not to play with them. I had bitten eyeholes in one and was wearing it as a mask at the dinner table.

2   As a child, I also used *tortillas* as hand warmers on cold days, and my family claims that I owe my career as an artist to my early experiments with *tortillas.* According to them, my clowning around helped me develop a strong artistic foundation. I'm not so sure, though. Sometimes I wore a *tortilla* on my head, like a *yarmulke,* and yet I never had any great urge to convert from Catholicism to Judaism. But who knows? They may be right.

3   For Mexicans over the centuries, the *tortilla* has served as the spoon and the fork, the plate and the napkin. *Tortillas* originated before the Mayan civilizations, perhaps predating Europe's wheat bread. According to Mayan mythology, the great god Quetzalcoatl, realizing that the red ants knew the secret of using maize as food, transformed himself into a black ant, infiltrated the colony of red ants, and absconded with a grain of corn. (Is it any wonder that to this day, black ants and red ants do not get along?) Quetzalcoatl then put maize on the lips of the first man and woman, Oxomoco and Cipactonal, so that they would become strong. Maize festivals are still celebrated by many Indian cultures of the Americas.

4   When I was growing up in El Paso, *tortillas* were part of my daily life. I used to visit a tortilla factory in an ancient adobe building near the open *mercado* in Ciudad Juárez. As I approached, I could hear the rhythmic slapping of the *masa* as the skilled vendors outside the factory formed it into balls and patted them into perfectly round corn cakes between the palms of their hands. The wonderful aroma and the speed with which the women counted so many dozens of *tortillas* out of warm wicker baskets still linger in my mind. Watching them at work convinced me that the most handsome and *deliciosas tortillas* are handmade. Although machines are faster, they

can never adequately replace generation-to-generation experience. There's no place in the factory assembly line for the tender slaps that give each *tortilla* character. The best thing that can be said about mass-producing *tortillas* is that it makes it possible for many people to enjoy them.

5　In the *mercado* where my mother shopped, we frequently bought *taquitos de nopalitos,* small tacos filled with diced cactus, onions, tomatoes, and *jalapeños.* Our friend Don Toribio showed us how to make delicious, crunchy *taquitos* with dried, salted pumpkin seeds. When you had no money for the filling, a poor man's *taco* could be made by placing a warm *tortilla* on the left palm, applying a sprinkle of salt, then rolling the *tortilla* up quickly with the fingertips of the right hand. My own kids put peanut butter and jelly on *tortillas,* which I think is truly bicultural. And speaking of fast food for kids, nothing beats a *quesadilla,* a *tortilla* grilled-cheese sandwich.

6　Depending on what you intend to use them for, *tortillas* may be made in various ways. Even a run-of-the-mill *tortilla* is more than a flat corn cake. A skillfully cooked homemade *tortilla* has a bottom and a top; the top skin forms a pocket in which you put the filling that folds your *tortilla* into a taco. Paper-thin *tortillas* are used specifically for *flautas,* a type of taco that is filled, rolled, and then fried until crisp. The name *flauta* means *flute,* which probably refers to the Mayan bamboo flute; however, the only sound that comes from an edible *flauta* is a delicious crunch that is music to the palate. In México *flautas* are sometimes made as long as two feet and then cut into manageable segments. The opposite of *flautas* is *gorditas,* meaning *little fat ones.* These are very thick small *tortillas.*

7　The versatility of *tortillas* and corn does not end here. Besides being tasty and nourishing, they have spiritual and artistic qualities as well. The Tarahumara Indians of Chihuahua, for example, concocted a corn-based beer called *tesgüino,* which their descendants still make today. And everyone has read about the woman in New Mexico who was cooking her husband a *tortilla* one morning when the image of Jesus Christ miraculously appeared on it. Before they knew what was happening, the man's breakfast had become a local shrine.

8　Then there is *tortilla* art. Various Chicano artists throughout the Southwest have, when short of materials or just in a whimsical mood, used a dry *tortilla* as a small, round canvas. And a few years back, at the height of the Chicano movement, a priest in Arizona got into trouble with the Church after he was discovered celebrating mass using a *tortilla* as the host. All of which only goes to show that while the *tortilla* may be a lowly corn cake, when the necessity arises, it can reach unexpected distinction.

Exercise 4	**DISCUSSION AND CRITICAL THINKING**

1. Does the author assume his audience already knows what a *tortilla* is?

2. Where is the simplest, most direct definition?

3. Which of these patterns of development—description, narration, process analysis, classification, and exemplification—does Burciaga use?

4. What does Burciaga's use of personal experience add to his extended definition?

5. What different aspects of life does he bring into his definition?

Paired Essays on Sexual Harassment and Sex Bias

What comes to mind when you see these two terms: *sexual harassment* and *sex bias?* Probably unwanted sexual attention and on-the-job gender discrimination, respectively. Moreover, the common denominator for those two phrases is likely to be the word *female,* though both phrases can also relate to the male by definition and by law.

The first of the paired essays ("Is It Sexual Harassment?") in this chapter will introduce you to the myths of sexual harassment while giving you the opportunity to consider some scenarios and draw your own line between acceptable and unacceptable, legal and illegal behavior. The second essay is "What Does Sex/Gender Have to Do with Your Job?" The answer to that question is, of course, that if sex/gender limits career advancement or pay, it is probably illegal.

Bringing the two social and economic problems into focus, you may conclude that they are sometimes one, and that ultimately both sexual harassment and sex bias spring from a single view. But those issues are for you to decide.

Francine's newly-installed Security Dweeb Alarm
begins to pay for itself.

B. Hickerson, copyright 1997. Los Angeles Times Syndicate. Reprinted by permission.

Is It Sexual Harassment?

Ellen Bravo and Ellen Cassedy

From the mailroom to Senate chambers, the debate goes on. It's still not always clear how to define harassment or how to stop it. Here, the authors attempt to show the difference between what's merely annoying and what's illegal. First published in *Redbook*, July 1992, the article is excerpted from Bravo and Cassedy's *The 1995 Guide to Combating Sexual Harassment: Candid Advice from the National Association of Working Women*. The authors credit the consulting firm Jane C. Edmonds and Associates for additional information.

1   Who decides what constitutes offensive behavior in the workplace? You—the recipient. Try testing your instincts about whether the following scenarios are examples of sexual harassment. Then read the authors' expert analyses.

Is This Abuse?

2   *Scenario 1:* Justine works in a predominantly male department at Company XYZ. She has tried to fit in, and occasionally even laughs at the frequent, off-color sex jokes. But she gets more irritated every day. It's well-known in the department that Justine has an out-of-town boyfriend she sees most weekends. It's also known that one of her coworkers, Scott, has the hots for her. Boyfriend or not, he's willing to do almost anything to get a date with Justine. Recently, one of Justine's coworkers overheard their boss talking to Scott in the hallway. "If you get her into bed," the boss said, "I owe you a dinner. Good luck!" They chuckled and went their separate ways.

3   *Analysis:* The boss is out of line. He probably didn't intend anyone to overhear him—but he shouldn't have been having such a conversation at all. The boss is responsible for keeping the workplace free of harassment and telling employees the consequences of violating the law. Instead, he gave Scott an incentive to make sexual advances toward a coworker. Some may argue that whether Scott and Justine get together socially is a personal matter—but public workplace boasting or dares clearly is not. The law doesn't require Justine to be tough enough to speak up on her own; it says her company must provide an atmosphere free of offensive or hostile behavior. Instead of making Scott think the way to win favor with a supervisor is to pressure a coworker into bed, the boss might arrange for a department-wide seminar on sexual harassment.

4   *Scenario 2:* Freda has been working for Bruce for three years. She has never complained about anything and appears to be happy in her job. Bruce regularly compliments Freda on her outfits; in his opinion, she has a good figure and excellent taste in clothes. Typically, he'll remark, "You sure look good today." Last week, Freda was having a bad day and told Bruce she was "sick and tired of being treated like a sex object." Bruce was stunned at the angry comment. He had always thought they had a good working relationship.

5   *Analysis:* Context and delivery are everything in examining a case like this. When Bruce says, "You sure look good today," does Freda usually answer, "So do you"? Or does Bruce murmur suggestively, "Mmm, you sure

look g-o-o-o-o-d," and stare at her chest while she crosses her arms? Does Bruce ever compliment other women? Men? Does he praise Freda's work performance as well?

6   Freda might have been upset earlier about Bruce's comments but failed to speak up because he is her boss. It's not uncommon for someone in her situation to keep quiet for fear of looking foolish or appearing to be a "bad sport." Even if she were just having a bad day, Freda probably wouldn't say she was tired of being treated like a sex object unless she'd felt that way before.

7   Since Bruce was "stunned" that Freda blew up at him, he needs to consider whether she may have sent him signals he ignored. He may be guilty only of not being tuned in. Or perhaps Freda doesn't really mind the personal praise, but wants more attention paid to her work.

8   Bruce and Freda should sit down and talk. He should listen to what she has to say, then let her know that he values her work *and* her feelings. He should also encourage her to speak up promptly in the future about issues that concern her rather than let them fester.

9   *Scenario 3:* Barbara is a receptionist for a printing company. Surrounding her desk are five ads printed by the company for a beer distributor. The posters feature provocatively posed women holding cans of beer and the slogan, What'll you have? Many times male customers have walked in, looked at the posters, and commented, "I'll have *you,* honey." When Barbara tells her boss she wants the posters removed, he replies that they represent the company's work, and he's proud to display them. He claims no one but Barbara is bothered by the posters, so what's her problem?

10   *Analysis:* The standard here is not how the boss feels but whether a "reasonable woman" might object to being surrounded by such posters, especially since the company has other products it could display. Because women are disproportionately victims of rape and sexual assault, women have a stronger incentive to be concerned with sexual behavior.

11   Barbara did not insist that the company refuse the account or exclude the posters from its portfolio. She merely said she didn't want them displayed around *her* desk. Barbara's view certainly is substantiated by how she's been treated; the posters seem to prompt customers to make suggestive remarks to her.

12   *Scenario 4:* Therese tells Andrew, her subordinate, that she needs him to escort her to a party. She says she's selecting him because he's the most handsome guy on her staff. Andrew says he's busy. Therese responds that she expects people on her staff to be team players.

13   *Analysis:* Therese may have wanted Andrew merely to accompany her to the party, not to have a sexual relationship with her. And Andrew might have been willing to go along if he hadn't been busy. Nevertheless, a reasonable employee may worry about what the boss means by such a request, particularly when it's coupled with remarks about personal appearance.

14   Andrew might not mind that Therese finds him handsome. But most people would object to having their job tied to their willingness to make a social appearance with the boss outside of work. The implicit threat also makes Therese's request unacceptable. The company should prohibit managers from requiring subordinates to escort them to social engagements.

15   *Scenario 5:* Darlene asks her coworker Dan out on a date. Their romance lasts several months before Darlene ends it. Dan is crushed and wants to keep seeing her. During the workday he frequently buzzes her on the intercom and stops by her desk to chat. Darlene tries to brush him off, with no success. She asks her manager to intervene. The manager says he doesn't get involved in personal matters.

[Analysis omitted. See Question 9 under "Discussion and Critical Thinking."]

16   *Scenario 6:* Someone has posted an explicit magazine centerfold in the men's rest room. No women, obviously, ever go in there.

[Analysis omitted. See Question 10 under "Discussion and Critical Thinking."]

Exploding the Myths

17   MYTH: Sexual harassment doesn't deserve all this attention. It happens rarely, and it's done by a few dumb—or sick—men.

18   FACT: Studies suggest that at least 50 percent of women experience harassment at some point in their work or academic careers. And though only a small percentage of men are considered "chronic harassers," most who engage in the abuse are not psychopaths. Many other men, intentionally or not, end up condoning or encouraging the harassers even if only by remaining silent.

19   MYTH: Boys will be boys. Sexual harassment is so widespread it's pointless to try to stamp it out.

20   FACT: Yes, sexual harassment is widespread. So is littering. So is stealing. The answer is to stop it, not accept it. To suggest that men aren't capable of controlling their behavior insults men's intelligence. Besides, like other forms of sexual abuse, harassment is usually a means of exerting power, not expressing passion.

21   MYTH: Most men accused of harassment are just kidding around or trying to flatter.

22   FACT: Chronic harassers *know* their behavior makes women uncomfortable; that's why they do it. Even if women tell them no again and again, this resistance is simply ignored. Other men are genuinely surprised to find that what they intend as innocent teasing isn't perceived that way. In the workplace, a man should assume a female coworker *won't* like sexual comments or gestures until he learns otherwise. And if he is told that he has offended someone, he should apologize at once.

23   MYTH: If women want to be treated as equals on the job, they can't expect special treatment.

24   FACT: A harassment-free workplace doesn't "coddle" women—it simply provides them with the same respectful treatment that men want. Rather than demanding that women adjust to a workplace that's comfortable only for men, management ought to provide an environment that reflects the sensitivities of *all* workers.

25 MYTH: All this talk about harassment will make women hypersensitive, causing them to imagine problems where there are none.

26 FACT: In the short run, defining sexual harassment and providing women with ways to speak up probably *will* lead to an increase in the number of reports filed—most of them regarding real, not imagined, offenses. In the long run, however, public discussion will cut down on unwelcome sexual attention on the job, resulting in fewer harassment complaints and a more productive workplace for everybody.

27 MYTH: You can't blame a guy for looking. Women invite attention by the way they dress.

28 FACT: If a woman's clothes are truly inappropriate for the job, management should tell her so. But a woman's dress *doesn't* give a male employee license to say or do whatever he likes. Once a woman tells him she doesn't like his comments about her clothing, he should back off—or be made to do so.

Harassment by Any Other Name . . .

29 Most cases of illegal sexual harassment fall into three categories:

30 1. *Quid pro quo*   This is Latin for "something in return for something." In other words, put out or else. A supervisor makes unwelcome sexual advances and either states or implies that the victim *must* submit if she wants to keep her job or receive a raise, promotion, or job assignment. These cases are the most clear-cut. The courts generally hold the employer liable for any such harassment whether he knew about it or not. That's because anyone who holds a supervisory position, with power over terms of employment, is considered to be an "agent" of the employer.

31 2. *Hostile environment*   An employee doesn't have to be fired, demoted, or denied a raise or promotion to be sexually harassed and to file a charge. Sexually explicit jokes, pinups, graffiti, vulgar statements, and abusive language and innuendos can poison the victim's work environment. The incidents generally must be shown to be repeated, pervasive, and harmful to the victim's emotional well-being. The employer is considered liable if he knew or should have known of the harassment and did nothing to stop it.

32 3. *Sexual favoritism*   In these situations, a supervisor rewards only those employees who submit to his sexual demands. The *other* employees—those who are denied raises or promotions—can claim that they're being penalized by the sexual attention directed at the favored coworkers.

| Exercise 5 | VOCABULARY HIGHLIGHTS |

Write a short definition of each word as it is used in the essay. (Paragraph numbers are given in parentheses.) Be prepared to use the words in your own sentences.

constitutes (1)	disproportionately (10)
incentive (3)	portfolio (11)
murmur (5)	substantiated (11)
fester (8)	intervene (12)
unique (10)	quid pro quo (30)

Exercise 6 **DISCUSSION AND CRITICAL THINKING**

1. Which three paragraphs give a dictionary-like definition of sexual harassment?

2. The definition, divided into three parts, is a good example of the use of what other pattern of development?

3. Besides the three-part definition, what pattern of development is used most extensively in this article?

4. How are the causes and effects (as a pattern of development) relevant in this essay?

5. Do the authors go too far in defining sexual harassment?

6. Is having two female authors writing on this subject especially appropriate because the authors can reflect on personal experience? Or does it raise doubts about the objectivity of their observations? Does the gender of the authors matter at this time on this topic?

7. What kind of audience do the authors apparently expect?

8. In what way can men benefit from an enforcement of sexual harassment policies?

9. Analyze scenario 5 (paragraph 15).

10. Analyze scenario 6 (paragraph 16).

What Does Sex/Gender Have to Do with Your Job?

Jeffrey Bernbach

If the federal legislation called Title VII worked perfectly, freelance writer Jeffrey Bernbach would not need to pose the question that serves as the title for this essay. Focusing on the on-the-job aspects of sex bias, he gives abundant examples of the more troubling behavior of those who would separate society into "man's world" and "woman's world," with unfairness to some men and to many women. This piece is an excerpt from *Job Discrimination: How to Fight, How to Win*, 1996.

1   Although there have been laws against employment discrimination for more than a hundred years in the United States, they varied from state to state. Not until some thirty years ago did Title VII (in addition to prohibiting discrimination based on race, color, religion, and national origin) establish federal uniformity, making it unlawful to discriminate against females—or, for that matter, males—on the basis of their sex. On-the-job gender discrimination occurs when an employee is treated differently from a person of the opposite sex under similar circumstances for reasons based solely on the employee's sex.

More Are Less Equal Than Others—Wage Bias

2   Historically, the most obvious example of sex bias has been paying women less than men for doing the same work. Although unlawful, the practice is pervasive, and even now, after years of strong feminist (and other) efforts to correct this inequity, women still earn only seventy cents for every dollar earned by men. This is *wage inequality,* not to be confused with the *glass ceiling,* which denies women the opportunity to *advance* up the corporate ladder (which also, of course, impinges on wage increases). Let's say you're a woman working as a publicity director for a large corporation, and you earn $35,000; your male counterpart, publicity director for another division of the same corporation, is earning $50,000. You and he have almost identical curriculum vitae—in fact, you went to the same college, worked together at another company, and then each of you got your "dream job."

3   Although you are worth as much as your male colleague in terms of employee value (or conversely, maybe he is worth only as much as *you*), nothing will be done to correct this unfair (read that *unlawful*) situation for two reasons, both very related:

1. Understandably, you don't want to quit your job—you love it, and protesting could lead to dismissal or, at the very least, rocking the corporate boat to your detriment,

and

2. Your company knows it can get away with such inequities.

So there you are: making seventy cents for every dollar your colleague makes. This goes on at every level of employment, from factory workers to upper-echelon managers. It's a sad, unlawful truth of life in the workplace. And, until recently, most women didn't challenge it because they wanted to keep their jobs.

4 Among the women who do take on such challenges, the litigant most feared by any employer is a minority female over forty years old. This is enough to make executives at even the grandest corporations quake in their boots because such plaintiffs fall into *three* categories protected by federal and state laws: age, sex, and race.

5 While women are victims of sex discrimination far more often than men, remember that if a male worker is treated less favorably than his female colleagues because of his sex, he has just as much a right to challenge this inequity. Here's a hypothetical example: A man is hired as an editor at a fashion magazine where all the other editors are women. Although he has similar editorial experience and a similar position, on the organizational chart, the female editors are making more than he is simply *because he's a man.* So workplace discrimination based on gender (sex) can work both ways.

6 Those who do fight for on-the-job equality may find themselves in double trouble: victims first of sexual discrimination and later of sexual harassment.

7 Ironically, some of the most frequently cited sources of gender bias occur in professions where women not only do the same jobs but also wear the same or similar uniforms as men: the military, police and fire departments. And often, female protests have less to do with wage inequities and more to do with the way they are perceived, or treated by their peers.

8 One New Jersey policewoman, for example, reported that in over five years with a local police force, officers on the midnight tour watched pornographic movies at the station house while she patrolled the town—alone. Another policewoman reported that although she outscored two men on physical tests, and tied with another man on written tests, the men were hired promptly, while it took her five years (and a lawsuit) to gain her rightful place on the force.

9 Similar news reports show that women in the military are struggling for acceptance in what still seems to be a man's world. Two hundred officers in the air force, along with their supporters, have formed a group called WANDAS Watch (Women Active in our Nation's Defense, their Advocates and their Supporters). One target of their protests was the recently retired air force chief of staff, who had vocalized his opposition to women assuming increased roles in the air force. A few years ago he reportedly told a Senate panel he would "rather fly with a less-qualified male pilot than with a top-notch woman aviator."

10 Last year, when the first female astronaut to pilot a space shuttle successfully linked up with a Russian space flight, a group of former female pilots, thirteen women who called themselves FLATS (Fellow Lady Astronaut Trainees), recalled that when they had trained with NASA thirty years earlier, they were never called up as pilots. One FLAT, now sixty-five and a retired pilot, told the *New York Times,* "We could have done it, but the guys didn't want us." She remembered that one NASA official said at the time

that he would "just as soon orbit with a bunch of monkeys than with a bunch of women."

11 In these "uniformed" cases, the problem is not one of wage or promotion, but of limited opportunities to perform the task for which these women were hired or were qualified to perform. The time-worn excuse of denying certain jobs to females in order to "protect" them from damage to their reproductive systems or possible harm to an unborn fetus has been held by the courts to constitute sex discrimination. Similarly, restricting the weight that females can be required to lift on a job or the number of hours they may work, in order to "protect" them (which obviously limits employment opportunities), also constitutes sex discrimination. In the same way, height and weight standards adversely affect job possibilities for women and are illegal unless it can be demonstrated that they are a *bona fide occupational requirement of the job,* that is, necessary for performance.

12 Speaker of the House of Representatives Newt Gingrich committed "verbal discrimination" while infuriating millions of men and women in 1995 when he said, "If combat means living in a ditch, females have biological problems staying in a ditch for thirty days because they get infections, and they don't have upper-body strength. I mean some do, but they're relatively rare. On the other hand, men are basically little piglets—you drop them in the ditch, they roll around in it, doesn't matter, you know."

13 Aside from Speaker Gingrich's skewed view, some common sense considerations should and do apply. For example, if a job at a trucking company requires lifting two-hundred-pound boxes for eight hours a day, an employer might justifiably refuse to give that job to a five-foot-two 110-pound woman (or man, for that matter). However, if the applicant could demonstrate that he or she could do the job, the employer would have no basis to deny it to him or her. As another instance, if a man is applying for a job as an attendant for the women's rest room in a restaurant or hotel, and is denied the job, that's not sexual discrimination; nor would a vice versa situation of a woman looking for a job as an attendant in a men's room be the case. In either of these examples, sex would be a bona fide occupational qualification.

14 If a woman has a license—and a desire—to drive an eighteen-wheeler, there's no *lawful reason* why she shouldn't have the job. If a man is licensed as a nursery school educator, there's no *lawful reason* why he shouldn't have the job. But stereotypical perceptions persist.

| **Exercise 7** | **VOCABULARY HIGHLIGHTS** |

Write a short definition of each word as it is used in the essay. (Paragraph numbers are given in parentheses.) Be prepared to use the words in your own sentences.

pervasive (2)	litigant (4)
curriculum vitae (2)	plaintiffs (4)
conversely (3)	hypothetical (5)
detriment (3)	bona fide (11)
echelon (3)	stereotypical (14)

| Exercise 8 | **DISCUSSION AND CRITICAL THINKING** |

1. How does Bernbach define "on-the-job discrimination"?

2. What is the difference between "wage inequality" and the "glass ceiling"?

3. According to Bernbach, why have not women who were discriminated against, until recently, filed charges?

4. Explain Bernbach's statement (paragraph 7), "Often, female protests have less to do with wage inequities and more to do with the way they are perceived, or treated by their peers."

5. Speculate what the retired air force chief of staff meant when he said he would "rather fly with a less-qualified male pilot than a top-notch woman aviator."

6. What is your response to Newt Gingrich's statement (paragraph 12) about women's unsuitability for combat duty?

7. How do you feel about women serving in combat?

8. What are some vocations that are often thought of as being almost exclusively female? male? Does the pay in those vocations reflect a sex bias? Explain.

9. Some people believe that women should stay out of jobs that are part of a "man's world" and that men demean themselves by taking jobs in a "woman's world." How do you react to such thinking?

10. Bernbach uses several forms of writing to define sex discrimination. Indicate at least one use of each of the following forms by using paragraph numbers.

| Exercise 9 | **CONNECTING THE PAIRED ESSAYS** |

1. Paragraph 25 in "Is It Sexual Harassment?" presents this myth: "All this talk about harassment will make women hypersensitive, causing them to imagine problems where there are none." Paragraph 26 offers commentary. Give your

own view of how these ideas relate to both sexual harassment and sex bias as defined in the two essays.

2. Why do sexual harassment and sex bias apply mainly, though not exclusively, to females? Discuss how prevailing stereotypical views influence public opinion.

Student Writers: Demonstrations and Readings

Linda Wong looked at a list of abstract terms for her assignment to write an extended definition and almost immediately found one that intrigued her. She had often heard people say things such as "I just can't love him [or her] enough," and "It was too much of a good thing," and she connected those ideas with one of the terms: *extremist.*

Wong's Writing Process Worksheet shows you how her writing evolved from idea to final draft. To conserve space here, the freewriting and the rough drafts marked for revision have been omitted. The balance of the worksheet has been lengthened for you to be able to see her other work in its entirety.

You will find a full-size blank worksheet on page 5. It can be photocopied, filled in, and submitted with each assignment if your instructor directs you to do so.

Writing Process Worksheet

TITLE Going Too Far

NAME Linda Wong   **DUE DATE** Monday, December 3, 8 a.m.

ASSIGNMENT In the space below, write whatever you need to know about your assignment, including information about the topic, audience, pattern of writing, length, whether to include a rough draft or revised drafts, and whether your paper must be typed.

Write a paragraph that defines an abstract word. Use at least three patterns of writing in your extended definition. Keep in mind that members of your audience may use your term in different ways, so using examples and clear explanations will be helpful for clarification. Submit your completed worksheet, one or more rough drafts marked for revision, and a typed final draft of about three hundred words.

STAGE ONE **Explore** Freewrite, brainstorm (list), cluster, or take notes as directed by your instructor. Use the back of this page or separate paper if you need more space.

Clustering

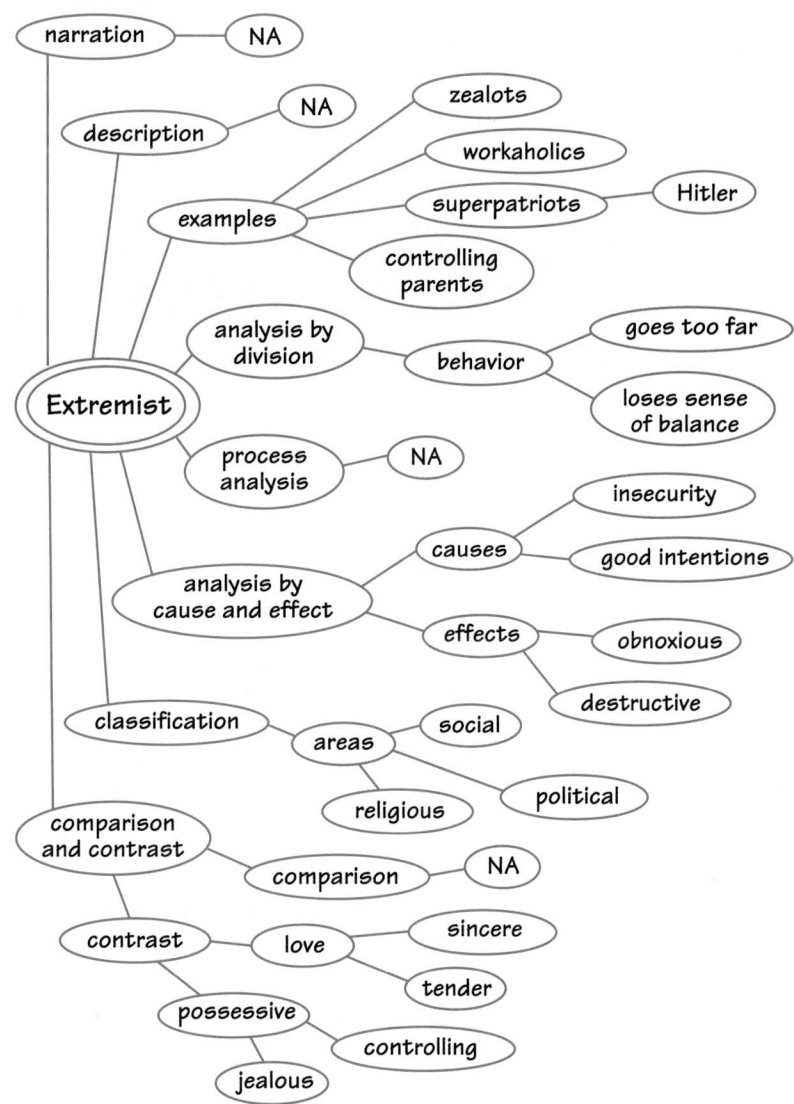

STAGE TWO   **Organize**   Write a topic sentence or thesis; label the subject and the treatment parts.

<u>Extremists</u> <u>are involved people who lose their sense of balance and go too</u>
  subject   treatment
<u>far in concentrating on one thing.</u>

Write an outline or an outline alternative.

  I. Going too far
    A. Become preoccupied with one thing
    B. Lose sense of balance
  II. Produce bad effect
    A. Are unpleasant to be around
    B. Are often destructive

III. Become incomplete
   A. Are often thought of as one kind of person
      1. Workaholics
      2. Zealots
      3. Superpatriots
   B. Diminished by loss of perspective

STAGE THREE **Write** On separate paper, write and then revise your paper as many times as necessary for coherence, language (usage, tone, and diction), unity, emphasis, support, and sentences (CLUESS). Read your paper aloud to hear and correct any grammatical errors or awkward-sounding sentences. Edit any problems in fundamentals, such as capitalization, omissions, punctuation, and spelling (COPS).

Final Draft

Going Too Far

Linda Wong

What the term does not mean

Some people believe that it is good to be an extremist in some areas, but those people are actually changing the meaning of the word. According to the Random House Dictionary of the English Language, the word extremism itself means "excessively biased ideas, intemperate conduct." The extremist goes too far; that means going too far in whatever the person is doing. I once heard someone say that it is good for people to be extremists in love. But that is not true. It is good to be enthusiastically and sincerely in love, but extremists in love love excessively and intemperately. People who love well may be tender and sensitive and attentive, but extremists are possessive or smothering. The same can be said of parents. We all want good parents, but parental extremists involve themselves too much in the lives of their children, who, in turn, may find it difficult to develop as individuals and become independent. Even in patriotism, good patriots are to be distinguished from extreme patriots. Good patriots love their country, but extreme patriots love their country so much that they think citizens from other countries are inferior and suspect. Extreme patriots may have Hitlerlike tendencies. Just what is wrong with extremists then? It is the loss of perspective. The extremists are so preoccupied with one concern that they lose their sense of balance. They are the workaholics, the zealots, the superpatriots of the world. They may begin with a good objective, but they focus on it so much that they can become destructive, obnoxious, and often pitiful. The worst effect is that these extremists lose their completeness as human beings.

Simple definition
Topic sentence

Example/contrast

Example/contrast

Example/contrast

Examples

Effect and concluding sentence

Exercise 10   **DISCUSSION AND CRITICAL THINKING**

1. Wong says that extremists "can become destructive, obnoxious, and often pitiful." Can you think of any good effects from people who were extremists? For example, what about a scientist who works fifteen hours a day to find a cure for a horrible disease? Is it possible that the scientist may succeed in his or her profession and fail in his or her personal life? But what if the scientist does not want a personal life? Discuss.

2. Why does Wong use contrast so much?

3. According to Wong, is it bad for a person to be an extremist in religion? Discuss.

Prison Slang
Louise Rubec

Almost every subculture has certain words that are understandable only to people who live in that culture. American prison slang has been around for more than a hundred years. It is richly and colorfully complex, yet simple and direct. Prison student Louise Rubec presents a brief language lesson.

1   Prison slang is like other slang in that it is language used in a special way for special reasons. As with conventional slang, some words have unusual, nonstandard meanings, and some words are invented.

2   Most slang is used by people who want to conform to group language customs. In prison it is used both by people who don't want others to know what they are talking about and by those who are seeking group identity. As a variety of language, it is technically a dialect because it is an integral part of the culture of that group. Prison slang covers many areas, but it especially reflects prisoners' concerns such as violence, talking, and reputation.

3   The very idea of violence is strangely muted by the terms used to discuss brutal acts. If a person is attacked by a group of people who throw a blanket over her head before they beat her, she is said to be the recipient of a "blanket party" given by a "rat pack." If she "caught a cold" or they "took her wind," she died. They may have killed her with a sharp instrument called a "shank" or a "shiv." Perhaps she didn't know there was a "raven" (contract) out on her; she thought they were only "putting on a floor show" (pretending) or "selling wolf tickets" (bluffing).

4   She should have listened with more care to what both her enemies and her friend were saying. Her foes claimed she had "snitched them off" (informed), but she didn't take the charge seriously enough. Then as a brave act of kindness, her friend "pulled her coat" (told her something she should know). Unfortunately a cop came by and she whispered to her friend, "Radio it," "Dog-face it," "Dummy up" (all meaning "shut up"). She actually thought about the danger and considered sending a "kite" (note) to a "homey" (close friend, perhaps someone from her neighborhood) asking for protection. But then she got distracted and "put the grapes on hold" (filed the bit of gossip away for future use).

5   That was her mistake because the woman out to get her was a "diehard" (will not conform to prison rules of conduct), "hard core" (career criminal), or "cold piece" (psychopath or sociopath) who was a "hog" (enforcer), "dancer" (fighter), and sometimes a "jive bitch" (agitator).

6   These are only a few of the hundreds of slang words used by women behind bars. They are part of prison life. All female convicts learn them—or else.

| Exercise 11 | **DISCUSSION AND CRITICAL THINKING** |

1. The essay begins with both a thesis and a definition. Which following sentence repeats that idea?

2. How are examples and causes used as patterns of development?

3. How is classification (meaning types of something) used?

4. How are comparison and contrast used as a pattern of development?

Practicing Patterns of Definition

Doing the following exercise will help you remember the patterns of writing used in extended definitions.

| Exercise 12 | **COMPLETING PATTERNS OF DEFINITION** |

Fill in the double bubble with a term to be defined. You might want to define cultur-ally diverse society, educated person, leader, role model, friend, infatuation, true love, success, *or* intelligence. *Then complete a bubble on the right for each para-graph or essay pattern. If the pattern does not apply (that is, if it would not provide useful information for your definition), mark it NA ("not applicable").*

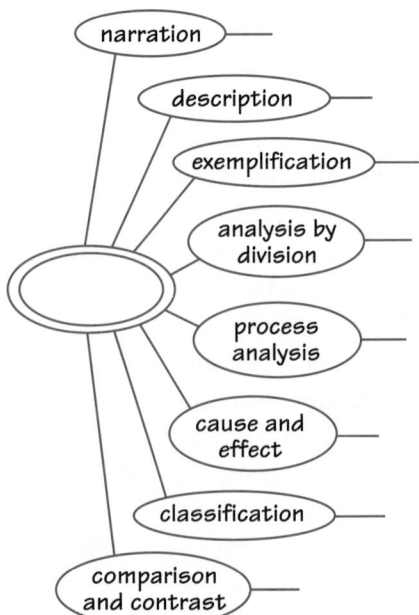

✎ **Topics for Writing Definition**

Reading-Related Topics

"The Amusement Park"

1. Define one of these other places for amusement: state or county fair, sports bar, championship game in a particular sport, Oktoberfest (or any other festival), spring break at a particular location, a religious revival, or a political rally.

"Georgia on My Mind"

2. Ray Jenkins defines *traditional rural white southerner* by listing the unique and colorful experiences of such a person. Define a person by listing his or her associations with a housing project, barrio, working-class neighborhood, streets, prison, affluent suburb, migrant worker camp, small town, reservation, or refugee camp. You may use the same form as Jenkins, but keep in mind that the extremely long sentence form he uses so well here is unconventional and should be used sparingly.

3. Using Jenkins's paragraph as a model, define a daycare worker, security guard, police officer, preacher, nurse, firefighter, parent, coach, or attendant in an extended-care facility.

"Tortillas"

4. Write a definition of one of the basic foods of your culture or your family. Consider dumplings, corn bread, biscuits, rice, potatoes, *pupusas*, beans, fry bread, bagels, muffins, spaghetti, and crumpets. Develop your paragraph or essay by relating the food to its cultural context and history and to your own experiences. Also consider classifying the main varieties of your basic food.

"Is It Sexual Harassment?"

5. Write a paragraph or essay in response to scenario 4 or 5. Use the three categories of illegal sexual harassment in paragraphs 30 through 32 as guiding principles. Be sure your response has a clear definition.

6. Apply one of the three categories of illegal sexual harassment in paragraphs 30 through 32 to a situation with which you are familiar.

7. Discuss one of the myths in terms of its truth or accuracy. Use your own reasoning and experience as support for your views.

"What Does Sex/Gender Have to Do with Your Job?"

8. Write a two-part response (summary and reaction, separated) to the views of an individual mentioned by Bernbach—the retired air force chief of staff, the NASA official, former Speaker of the House Newt Gingrich, or a police or fire department worker who holds gender bias. Your summary should be brief. Your reaction should relate your ideas to those in the summary. As an option, you could combine the summary and reaction in a single response. Either form should include a clear definition of sex bias.

9. Write about a sex bias situation with which you are familiar. It could involve employment or restricted pay or advancement that occurred because of gender discrimination. Include a definition of sex bias.

Paired Essays on Sexual Harassment and Sex Bias

10. Discuss how gender stereotyping is the underlying cause of both sexual harassment and sex bias. Express your own views and include ideas from the two essays.

11. Use hypothetical or real examples, along with observations from the essays, to explain how the definitions of sexual harassment and sex bias can relate to men as well as women.

"Going Too Far"

12. Apply the definition of *extremist* from this paragraph to a situation with which you are familiar: an overprotective parent, a controlling companion, an over-controlling boss, a too-strict police officer or teacher, a too-virtuous friend or preacher, a too-clean housekeeper (companion, parent), a zealous patriot, a person fanatical about a diet, or a person concerned too much with good health or exercise. You might begin your paragraph or essay with the statement: "It is good to be _____, but when _____ is carried to the extreme, the result is _____."

"Prison Slang"

13. Define another term for language usage such as *jargon* ("shop talk" by a group of people in a restricted activity, especially vocational or recreational), regional slang, age-group slang, or sign-language slang.

14. Using Rubec's essay as a model, develop a definition of *body language.*

Career-Related Topics

15. Define one of the following terms by using other patterns of development (such as exemplification, cause and effect, narration, comparison and contrast): *total quality management, quality control, business ethics, customer satisfaction, cost effectiveness, Internet, temporary worker, union, outsource,* or *downsize.*

16. Define a good boss, good employee, good workplace, good employer, or good job. Be specific.

17. Define a term from computer technology such as *Internet, World Wide Web, search engine,* or *chat room.*

General Topics

The following topics are appropriate for extended development of definitions; most of them will also serve well for writing simple definitions.

18. Conservative	28. Clotheshorse	38. School spirit
19. Asian American	29. Educated	39. Feminist
20. Bonding	30. Gang	40. Chicano
21. Sexist	31. Freedom	41. Jock
22. Cult	32. Body language	42. Hispanic American
23. Biker	33. Hero	43. African American
24. Liberal	34. Druggie	44. Macho
25. Workaholic	35. Convict	45. Cool
26. Surfer	36. Teen slang	46. Native American
27. Personal space	37. Psychopath	47. Jerk

Writer's Guidelines: Definition

Simple Definition

1. No two words have exactly the same meaning.

2. Several forms of simple definitions can be blended into your discussion: basic dictionary definitions, synonyms, direct explanations, indirect explanations, and analytical definitions.

3. For a formal or analytical definition, specify the term, class, and characteristic(s).

   Example: <u>Capitalism</u> <u>is an economic system</u> <u>characterized by investment</u>
                 term   class
   <u>of money, private ownership, and free enterprise.</u>
                  characteristics

4. Avoid "is where" and "is when" definitions, circular definitions, and the use of words in the definition that are more difficult than the word being defined.

Extended Definition

1. Use clustering to consider other patterns of development that may be used to define your term.

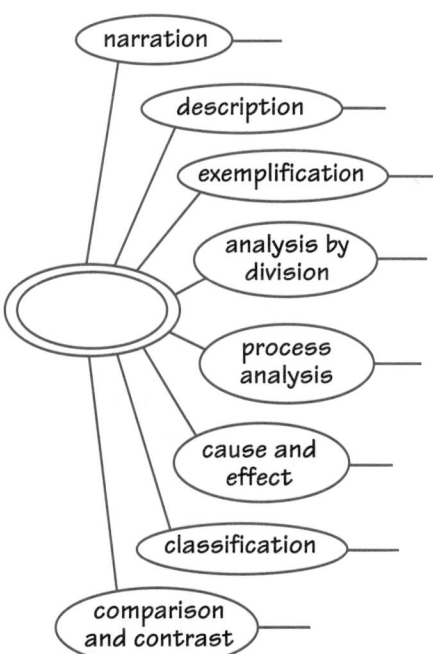

2. The organization of your extended definition is likely to be one of emphasis, but it may be space or time, depending on the subject material. You may use just one pattern of development for the overall organization.

3. Consider these ways of introducing a definition: with a question, with a statement of what it is not, with a statement of what it originally meant, or with a discussion of why a clear definition is important. You may use a combination of these ways before you continue with your definition.

4. Whether you personalize a definition depends on your purpose and your audience. Your instructor may ask you to write about a word within the context of your own experience or to write about it from a detached, clinical viewpoint.

Literary Analysis:
Reacting to Stories

"A professional writer is an amateur who didn't quit."

Richard Bach

THE QUIGMANS   by Buddy Hickerson

Date with a movie critic.

B. Hickerson, copyright Los Angeles Times Syndicate. Reprinted by permission.

Why We Read Stories

N arrative literature tells stories. Why do we read stories? Among the possible answers is one particularly intriguing theory by Robert Penn Warren. He said that we often find life disjointed and our own behavior beyond clear, reasonable explanation, but if we read stories we discover understandable patterns of human life. If the writers are good, we can see parallels with what we have experienced and causes and effects that make sense. Stories, including story poems, give us little reflective universes to ponder, to discuss with others, to marvel at, and to question.

Interpreting Narrative Literature

Because narrative literature is a representation of life, it may be discussed from many perspectives. A single short story or poem may be a study in philosophy, psychology, history, or some other field. Prepare to engage your full intellect and complete knowledge in considering the stories you read. Keep in mind that no two people will interpret them in precisely the same way, because all of us are different in our experiences, ways of thinking, and values. However, we also have much in common, and we will usually be able to agree on one or more reasonable interpretations based on the evidence we find within the narrative framework.

Writing about Literature

In previous chapters, we have discussed how to write paragraphs and essays. In this chapter, we turn our attention to the short story and the narrative poem for subject material. The change is not significant. Stories and poems contain many of the forms emphasized in this book: narrative, description, examples, analysis by division, causal analysis, classification, definition, comparison and contrast, and argumentation. Stories and poems also have raw materials that can be transformed into these patterns of writing. Therefore, learning to write about literature extends what you are learning about writing while providing a new dimension of experience. This new dimension lays the groundwork for writing in more advanced composition classes, literature classes, and other humanities classes.

The forms of narrative we work with in this chapter are not complicated. Because short stories and narrative poems both tell stories, we can use the same principles to discuss them in a broad fashion. The following discussion of setting, conflict, characters, plot, theme, point of view, and analysis will provide you with a good framework for basic reading for understanding, as well as for annotating your text, interpreting stories and poems, and even generating topics for writing.

Setting

In its simplest form, the *setting* is the environment in which the literary work takes place. It may be merely appropriate, without calling attention to itself. It may also be supportive, reinforcing the theme. For example, a story about death may occur in the winter, whereas a story about birth or rediscovery of life may occur in springtime or early summer. Edgar Allan Poe uses this reinforcing technique in "The Fall of the House of Usher," a story about a disintegrating family living in a decrepit limestone house located in the midst of a swamp stewing with decaying plants. In this instance, the setting is more than its descriptive details; certain aspects such as the house are *symbolic* (representing something in addition to itself). The house, poised precipitously above the water, is about to descend into its "grave." But in "The Lottery," an almost equally well-known story, the author, Shirley Jackson, sets her story of the barbaric execution of an innocent citizen in a bucolic village on a beautiful early summer day. The brutal act is all the more shocking because of the contrast between setting and event.

Conflict

Conflict is at the heart of every fictional work, whether it be a feature film or a prose story. In a short story, the conflict is likely to relate mostly to the main character. That main character may be at odds with forces such as another character, something in the environment, or even something within him- or herself.

Characters

The main character, the one who deals most directly and most intimately with the conflict, is often called the *protagonist*. The opposition to the protagonist in dealing with his or her problem is often called the *antagonist*. In certain stories these terms may not fit well, but the principle of the main character dealing consciously or unconsciously with conflict is basic to fiction.

In dealing with conflict, the central character or characters are likely to change, resist change, or make some self-discovery. This character or these characters will not necessarily be aware of the significance of what is occurring or even that something *is* occurring.

Plot

As the character or characters deal with conflict, a sequence of events will ensue. That sequence is called the *plot*. It begins with an *exposition*—an introduction to the situation and the basic conflict. Then it continues through an event or series of events to the *climax,* or highest point in the struggle. Finally, it ends with the *resolution* or a final comment on the situation.

Theme

If the plot is basically "what happens," the *theme* is the significance of what happens. The theme is what the story means in terms of human nature, the human condition, one individual, or particular institutions. The theme is sometimes called the *fictional point*. In some contemporary stories that represent a fragmented, illogical reality, the theme may not be easily stated because the depicted reality itself often defies clear comprehension.

Point of View

Each work is told from a certain perspective, or in rare instances from more than one. That perspective is called *point of view,* which in most stories is either *first person* or *third person*.

In the first person story, the reader hears the story from the narrator. That narrator may be the central character in the work; for example, Holden Caulfield in *The Catcher in the Rye* is both narrator and central character. The narrator can also be a minor character or merely an observer. Regardless of the role of the narrator, we get the freshness and directness of someone who is there; the "I" person speaks.

The other common point of view is third person. With this perspective we have a narrator who reports from a detached view, never using "I" to refer to him- or herself but instead using third person pronouns such as "he" and "she." The author may choose to restrict him- or herself further by writing in *third person objective.* This point of view presents characters and situations as we would ordinarily perceive them. We get to know people mainly by considering (1) how they look, (2) what they say, (3) how they act, (4) how others react to them, and (5) what others say about them.

The author may claim one other prerogative and reveal what a character or characters are thinking. Thus the author seems all-knowing. This enhanced point of view can be broadly called *third person omniscient* (a term that may be qualified, depending on the author's self-imposed limitations or focus). The third person omniscient point of view (with whatever limitation) is the most common in contemporary fiction. Most thrillers, for example, are told in the third person omniscient point of view with a shifting or multiple approach to allow for a close scrutiny of several characters and their situations.

Analysis

The elements of narrative literature can be considered for emphasis in the analysis of a work, either separately or in combination. You can write a composition mainly about the use of setting in a particular work, or you can write an analysis that is equally concerned with character and theme. But regardless of the emphasis, because you are writing about a work that is made up of interdependent parts, you cannot easily write about one part and completely exclude the others. The theme of the work, the meaning of it, could scarcely be omitted when you consider the various parts, because each part is directed toward the fictional point.

Finding Topics for Literary Analysis

Analytical Writing

Any one of the aspects of a narrative can serve as a good topic for a paragraph or essay. Here are some to stimulate your thinking:

- *Setting:* Write about the appropriateness of the setting (with or without symbols) in supporting or even in representing the theme. You might use your knowledge of the techniques of good descriptive writing by analyzing what the author has done with diction, images, and figurative language.

- *Conflict:* Discuss the extent to which the main character perceives and deals with the conflict.

- *Character:* Write about the character's changing, not changing, or gaining self-knowledge. Or write an analysis by division based on a few of the central character's traits (such as honesty, dedication, insecurity, immaturity, cleverness, or low self-esteem); use clustering or brainstorming to find these traits. You can also discuss characters in studies of comparison and contrast, definition (perhaps combined with analysis by division as in "Character X is a sexist"), or analysis of causes or effects (the whys or the results of a situation).

- *Plot:* Unless you are going to write about some idea such as irony or reversal, avoid writing about this aspect of narrative literature. The reason is that it's always a temptation to fall into the "plot summary" trap, merely telling what happens in the story rather than analyzing and interpreting.

- *Point of view:* An author selects a point of view that is advantageous to the story he or she wants to tell. Explain why a particular point of view is advantageous; for example, the first-person perspective may characterize, and the third-person objective may provide a sense of detachment or distance.

- *Theme:* Discuss how other aspects of the story (especially setting, conflict, character, and plot) support or establish the theme, the meaning of the story.

Speculative Writing

There are also more imaginative ways of writing about literature. You can personalize aspects of plot, theme, or characterization by applying them to your own life. Or you can creatively alter stories by inventing new scenes for a character, projecting a character into the future to speculate about development, moving a character from one story to another, or fabricating flashbacks that would explain behavior found in a story. You can explore these and other imaginative ways of writing about fiction by trying some of the Topics for Writing about Literature at the end of this chapter. Regardless of the type of assignment you do, you will need to support your ideas in a clear and logical manner.

Student Writers: Demonstrations and Readings

Consider these key points in the following models of student writing:

- *Development:* Study these examples, especially for their clear statements of purpose. Observe also how the examples develop the analysis through the use of references to, summaries and paraphrases of, and quotations and explanations from the story itself.

- *Verb tense:* As is customary in writing about literature, each student essay is written in the present tense. For example, the writers relate events in the story as "He *goes* to the farm house," "She *eyes* him with suspicion."

- *Quotations:* Quotations can effectively give the flavor of the original story while supporting the point the student writer is making. Use short quotations and blend them into your summary writing and commentary rather than quoting long passages.

Examine the following three examples for correct punctuation, and remember these main points about punctuating quotations:

- With an indirect quotation, you usually do not need commas:

  > The girl looked at him "with cold steady eyes."
  > He mounts the "final unreasoning assault."

- If you introduce a quotation with a statement that is grammatically complete (an independent clause), you must use a colon:

The doctor knows why the parents are not volunteering information: "That's why they were spending three dollars on me."

- With a conversational tag such as "he said," you have a choice between a comma and a colon, but a comma is more typical:

He said, "It is a social necessity."

The following student paragraph and essay are based on "The Use of Force," a short story by William Carlos Williams. Told from the first person point of view, it is a fictional account of a doctor making a house call to attend to a young girl. When she refuses to allow the doctor to examine her throat (there have been cases of diphtheria, and he feels the procedure is necessary), the doctor decides to force her mouth open. During the struggle, he becomes emotionally involved until he is aware of a "fury," although only he knows he has lost sight of his original objective. However necessary, using force has made her hostile and him furious. He doesn't like what he sees of himself.

In writing about the short story "The Use of Force," Ajax Mylonas was intrigued by the way the central character struggled with two conflicts: one on the surface and one inside the mind.

Mylonas's Writing Process Worksheet shows how his writing evolved from idea to final draft. Notice how he attached short quotations to his outline and then used them in his drafts. To conserve space here, the freewriting has been omitted. The balance of his worksheet has been lengthened for you to be able to see his other work in its entirety.

You will find a full-size blank worksheet on page 5. It can be photocopied, filled in, and submitted with each assignment if your instructor directs you to do so.

··

Writing Process Worksheet

TITLE More Than Just a House Call

NAME Ajax Mylonas   **DUE DATE** Tuesday, May 4, 9 a.m.

ASSIGNMENT	In the space below, write whatever you need to know about your assignment, including information about the topic, audience, pattern of writing, length, whether to include a rough draft or revised drafts, and whether your paper must be typed.

Write a paragraph in which you discuss how the central character deals with his or her conflict(s). Assume that your readers are at least familiar with the story "The Use of Force." Include some short quotations from the story, submit the completed worksheet, a rough draft marked for revision, and a typed final draft of about 200 to 300 words.

STAGE ONE	**Explore** Freewrite, brainstorm (list), cluster, or take notes as directed by your instructor. Use the back of this page or separate paper if you need more space.

Clustering

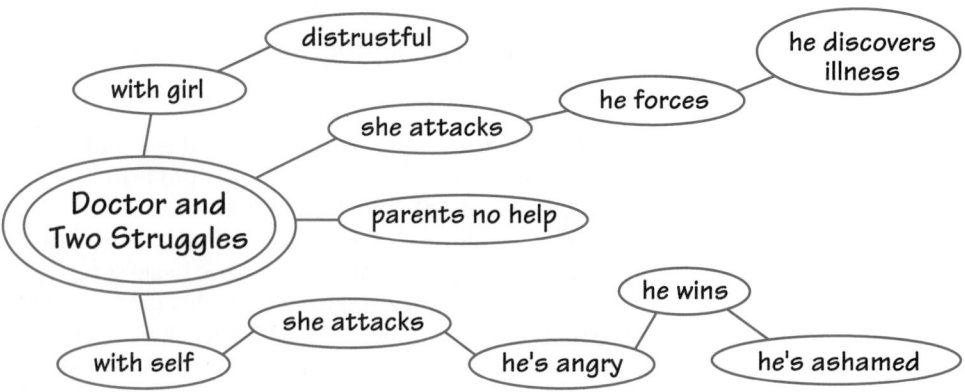

STAGE TWO   **Organize**   Write a topic sentence or thesis; label the subject and the treatment parts.

<u>The story</u> <u>has two story lines based on two related conflicts.</u>
    subject   treatment

Write an outline or an outline alternative.

(For literary analysis add short quotations)

I. The surface conflict
   A. Doctor-patient relationship
   B. Physical struggle
      1. Girl won't cooperate
      2. Doctor uses force
      3. Doctor examines her throat
   C. Job done

II. The inner conflict
   A. Doctor versus himself
      1. Tries to be professional
      2. Loses self-control ("attractive little thing," "damned little brat," "furious")
      3. Loses sight of objective ("got beyond reason")
   B. Emotional (brutal) side wins ("It was a pleasure to attack her," "blind fury")

STAGE THREE   **Write**   On separate paper, write and then revise your paper as many times as necessary for <u>c</u>oherence, <u>l</u>anguage (usage, tone, and diction), <u>u</u>nity, <u>e</u>mphasis, <u>s</u>upport, and <u>s</u>entences (CLUESS). Read your paper aloud to hear and correct any grammatical errors or awkward-sounding sentences.
Edit any problems in fundamentals, such as <u>c</u>apitalization, <u>o</u>missions, <u>p</u>unctuation, and <u>s</u>pelling (COPS).

Rough Draft with Revision and Editing

More Than Just a House Call

"The Use of Force," by William Carlos Williams, has two story lines. One appears on the surface and moves the plot along. If the author had only written about it, the ~~story~~ *account* would be no more than ~~journalism~~ *a news story*. The doctor makes a house call because a little girl is sick. Her parents are self-conscious, and the doctor is out of his comfortable environment. The girl won't open ~~up~~ *her mouth* for an examination. The doctor insists, ~~and~~ *A*after a scuffle ~~and some use of~~ *he uses* force, ~~he~~ *and* discovers that she has an infected throat. She will be treated. The story has a happy ending. But weave it *in* with the other part of the story, and the ending is not happy. The surface story is all between the girl and the doctor, ~~T~~*but t*he ~~subterranean~~ *deep* story is between the doctor and himself, ~~and it~~*I*'s all about the use of force from the forcer's perspective. He's ~~mixed up~~ *ambivalent* about the experience at first. The girl is an "attractive little thing," ~~but is obviously spoiled.~~ *who will soon become a "damned little brat."* She struggles with such vigor that he is jolted out of his easy professional manner. He struggles with her, *and* she is a worthwhile opponent. He ~~gets caught up in the combat.~~ He doesn't like what is happening, but he has "got beyond reason." ~~He~~ *Although he* struggles with himself, ~~and the~~ *his* bad side wins. He gets what he wants, and no one else knows that he has his own ~~meanness~~ *aggression* inside, just below the surface. ~~He has~~ *His new role of forcing turns that aggression to even more savage feelings. He remembers that "it was a pleasure to attack her."* ~~tasted the feeling of combat to win.~~ *which* The struggle had nothing to do with medicine, and everything to do with passion for triumph, *took the form of a "blind fury."* He won the battle ~~for~~ *in* the first story, but he lost the battle ~~for~~ *in* the second. *We may forgive him for being an imperfect human being, but he won't let himself off that easily.*

Final Draft

More Than Just a House Call
Ajax Mylonas

Topic sentence   "The Use of Force," by William Carlos Williams, has two story lines. One appears on the surface and moves the plot along. If the author had written only about it, the account would be no more than a news story. The doctor

Surface conflict

Struggle

Outcome

makes a house call because a little girl is sick. Her parents are self-conscious, and the doctor is out of his comfortable environment. The girl won't open her mouth for an examination. The doctor insists. After a scuffle he uses force and discovers that she has an infected throat. She will be treated. The story has a happy ending. But weave it in with the other part of the story, and the ending is not happy. The surface story is all between

Inner conflict

the girl and the doctor, but the deep story is between the doctor and himself. It's all about the use of force from the forcer's perspective. He's ambivalent about the experience at first. The girl is an "attractive little

Struggle

thing," who will soon become a "damned little brat." She struggles with such vigor that he is jolted out of his easy professional manner. He struggles with her, and she is a worthwhile opponent. He becomes "furious." He doesn't like what is happening, but he has "got beyond reason." Although

Outcome

he struggles with himself, his bad side wins. He gets what he wants, and no one else knows that he has his own aggression inside, just below the surface. His new role of forcing turns that aggression to even more savage instincts. He remembers that "it was a pleasure to attack her." The strug-

Meaning

gle, which had nothing to do with medicine, and everything to do with passion for triumph, took the form of a "blind fury." He won the battle in the first story, but he lost the battle in the second. We may forgive him for being an imperfect human being, but he won't let himself off that easily.

The Use of Self-Analysis

Gloria Mendez

This essay explains that the first-person point of view places the central character in "The Use of Force" in close focus, with all his strengths and weaknesses there on the surface for our analysis—and for his own. The underlinings and margin notes have been added to show how Mendez organized her final draft.

Thesis

One of the main thrusts in "The Use of Force" is point of view. <u>The narrator, a doctor, tells his own story, a story about his encounter with an uncooperative patient but also—and mainly—a story about the narrator's transformation from a mature, rational person to someone of a lower order who has lost</u>

Parts of support

<u>considerable self-respect.</u> This transformation happens in stages of attitudinal change that occur during his arrival, his early attempt at obtaining cooperation, his loss of self-control, and his reflection on his behavior.

Topic sentence

<u>When the doctor arrives at the small farmhouse, he feels like an outsider</u>. The family is self-conscious and not sure about how to act around a doctor. They are poor, and out of concern for the daughter, are spending some of their meager funds to get a diagnosis and possible treatment. The doctor observes that they are "all very nervous, eyeing me up and down distrustfully." They tell him very little, wanting to get their money's worth.

Topic sentence <u>The doctor initially follows standard procedure</u>. He sees that she is feverish and panting. With concern about a local diphtheria epidemic, he asks the mother if she had looked at the girl's throat. In a foreshadowing that the doctor does not catch, the mother says, "I tried to . . . , but I couldn't see." Moving to the hands-on stage, he asks the girl to open her mouth. "Nothing doing." He tries a gentle approach, shows her he has no concealed weapons by opening his hands. But her mother mentions the word "hurt," and the doctor grinds his "teeth in disgust." He maintains his composure as he approaches her. She loses hers, as she tries to scratch his eyes out and succeeds in knocking his glasses to the floor.

Topic sentence <u>Both his tact and his attitude change</u>. The parents are embarrassed; they apologize, threaten the daughter, and awkwardly try to help the doctor. He's disgusted with them, however; they've done all the wrong things. But he admires the girl, even saying he had "already fallen in love with the savage brat." He knows that her anger is caused by her fear of him. He decides to use force—for her own good. The possibility that she has diphtheria is there. The girl's resistance builds: she screams and struggles. He uses a "wooden tongue depressor," and she chews it "into splinters."

Topic sentence <u>It is during this phase of the incident that the doctor joins the struggle at her level</u>. As he admits, "But now I also had grown furious—at a child. I tried to hold myself down but I couldn't." He goes for heavier equipment—a metal spoon. He convinces himself that he must get the "diagnosis now or never." Whether his rationality or truth prevailed in that decision, he does know that he "had got beyond reason. I could have torn the child apart in my fury. It was a pleasure to attack her. My face was burning with it." He has truth and reason on his side, but his emotions as "a blind fury" are in control. He mounts the "final unreasoning assault" and wins. She has an infected throat, and he has exposed it, but she still tries to attack "while tears of defeat blinded her eyes."

Topic sentence <u>The final stage, the recognition, is there throughout the last part of the story</u>. If the doctor had dismissed the incident, we would have thought him insensitive. If the doctor had savored the experience, we would have called him sadistic. But the doctor, with obvious regret, has admitted that he had "grown furious," lost restraint, "got beyond reason," felt a "longing for muscular release," and gone on "to the end."

Conclusion The "use of force" has two effects in this story. The girl resents the force and becomes alternately defensive and offensive. The doctor uses force and becomes so caught up in the physical and emotional conflicts that he is responding to the wrong motive for acting. It is the point of view that highlights the doctor's feelings of guilt in retrospect. This feeling comes across much more poignantly because this story is, after all, a confessional.

Reading Selections on the Theme of Love

In place of the usual brief introduction for thematically grouped reading selections, here is a well-known essay classifying eight different types of love. It will serve as a good set of criteria for evaluating the theme of love as developed in the two prose and two verse stories that follow.

The stories offer a wide spectrum of expressions of love: a man with a wandering eye in "The Girls in Their Summer Dresses"; a woman who finds brief happiness in hearing of her husband's death in "The Story of an Hour"; a loving woman and a two-timing man in "Frankie and Johnny"; and an iron-willed, autocratic, possessive husband in "My Last Duchess."

"Your wedding announcement's in the paper, Bob. But the bride's name has been withheld, pending notification of next of kin."

B. Hickerson, copyright Los Angeles Times Syndicate. Reprinted by permission.

How Do I Love Thee?

Robert J. Trotter

How one loves depends on many things, including who is loving and who is being loved, but each love has certain components. Robert Trotter, using the system developed by R. J. Sternberg, details the different types of love by giving explanations and providing examples.

1   Intimacy, passion, and commitment are the warm, hot, and cold vertices of Sternberg's love triangle. Alone and in combination they give rise to

eight possible kinds of love relationships. The first is nonlove—the absence of all three components. This describes the large majority of our personal relationships, which are simply casual interactions.

2   The second kind of love is liking. "If you just have intimacy," Sternberg explains, "that's liking. You can talk to the person, tell about your life. And if that's all there is to it, that's what we mean by liking." It is more than nonlove. It refers to the feelings experienced in true friendships. Liking includes such things as closeness and warmth but not the intense feelings of passion or commitment.

3   If you just have passion, it's called infatuated love—the "love at first sight" that can rise almost instantaneously and dissipate just as quickly. It involves a high degree of physiological arousal but no intimacy or commitment. It's the tenth-grader who falls madly in love with the beautiful girl in his biology class but never gets up the courage to talk to her or gets to know her, Sternberg says, describing his past.

4   Empty love is commitment without intimacy or passion, the kind of love sometimes seen in a 30-year-old marriage that has become stagnant. The couple used to be intimate, but they don't talk to each other any more. They used to be passionate, but that's died out. All that remains is the commitment to stay with the other person. In societies in which marriages are arranged, Sternberg points out, empty love may precede the other kinds of love.

5   Romantic love, the Romeo and Juliet type of love, is a combination of intimacy and passion. More than infatuation, it's liking with the added excitement of physical attraction and arousal but without commitment. A summer affair can be very romantic, Sternberg explains, but you know it will end when she goes back to Hawaii and you go back to Florida, or wherever.

6   Passion plus commitment is what Sternberg calls fatuous love. It's Hollywood love: Boy meets girl, a week later they're engaged, a month later they're married. They are committed on the basis of their passion, but because intimacy takes time to develop, they don't have the emotional core necessary to sustain the commitment. This kind of love, Sternberg warns, usually doesn't work out.

7   Companionate love is intimacy with commitment but no passion. It's a long-term friendship, the kind of committed love and intimacy frequently seen in marriages in which the physical attraction has died down.

8   When all three elements of Sternberg's love triangle come together in a relationship, you get what he calls consummate love, or complete love. It's the kind of love toward which many people strive, especially in romantic relationships. Achieving consummate love, says Sternberg, is like trying to lose weight, difficult but not impossible. The really hard thing is keeping the weight off after you have lost it, or keeping the consummate love alive after you have achieved it. Consummate love is possible only in very special relationships.

(a) Nonlove (b) Friendship (c) Infatuation (d) Empty love

(e) Romantic love (f) Fatuous love (g) Companionate love (h) Consummate love

.... indicates absence   _____ indicates presence

---

Exercise 1   **DISCUSSION AND CRITICAL THINKING**

1. What are the eight different types of love described by Trotter?

2. What examples does Trotter use? Which ones are general and which are specific? What additional examples can you think of, taken from what you have read and what you have seen in movies and on television?

3. What are some specific examples of the types of love for which Trotter does not provide his own examples?

The Girls in Their Summer Dresses

Irwin Shaw

Michael looks at the girls, and his wife, Frances, becomes annoyed. Is Irwin Shaw writing only about two individuals in this short story, or do the characters represent a general, and long-standing, division between the sexes?

1   Fifth Avenue was shining in the sun when they left the Brevoort. The sun was warm, even though it was February, and everything looked like Sunday

morning—the buses and the well-dressed people walking slowly in couples and the quiet buildings with the windows closed.

2 Michael held Frances' arm tightly as they walked toward Washington Square in the sunlight. They walked lightly, almost smiling, because they had slept late and had a good breakfast and it was Sunday. Michael unbuttoned his coat and let it flap around him in the mild wind.

3 "Look out," Frances said as they crossed Eighth Street. "You'll break your neck."

4 Michael laughed and Frances laughed with him.

5 "She's not so pretty," Frances said. "Anyway, not pretty enough to take a chance of breaking your neck."

6 Michael laughed again. "How did you know I was looking at her?"

7 Frances cocked her head to one side and smiled at her husband under the brim of her hat. "Mike, darling," she said.

8 "O.K.," he said. "Excuse me."

9 Frances patted his arm lightly and pulled him along a little faster toward Washington Square. "Let's not see anybody all day," she said. "Let's just hang around with each other. You and me. We're always up to our neck in people, drinking their Scotch or drinking our Scotch; we only see each other in bed. I want to go out with my husband all day long. I want him to talk only to me and listen only to me."

10 "What's to stop us?" Michael asked.

11 "The Stevensons. They want us to drop by around one o'clock and they'll drive us into the country."

12 "The cunning Stevensons," Mike said. "Transparent. They can whistle. They can go driving in the country by themselves."

13 "Is it a date?"

14 "It's a date."

15 Frances leaned over and kissed him on the tip of the ear.

16 "Darling," Michael said, "this is Fifth Avenue."

17 "Let me arrange a program," Frances said. "A planned Sunday in New York for a young couple with money to throw away."

18 "Go easy."

19 "First let's go to the Metropolitan Museum of Art," Frances suggested, because Michael had said during the week he wanted to go. "I haven't been there in three years and there're at least ten pictures I want to see again. Then we can take the bus down to Radio City and watch them skate. And later we'll go down to Cavanaugh's and get a steak as big as a blacksmith's apron, with a bottle of wine, and after that there's a French picture at the Filmarte that everybody says—say, are you listening to me?"

20 "Sure," he said. He took his eyes off the hatless girl with the dark hair, cut dancer-style like a helmet, who was walking past him.

21 "That's the program for the day," Frances said flatly. "Or maybe you'd just rather walk up and down Fifth Avenue."

22 "No," Michael said. "Not at all."

23 "You always look at other women," Frances said. "Everywhere. Every damned place we go."

24 "No, darling," Michael said, "I look at everything. God gave me eyes and I look at women and men and subway excavations and moving pictures and the little flowers of the field. I casually inspect the universe."

25   "You ought to see the look in your eye," Frances said, "as you casually inspect the universe on Fifth Avenue."

26   "I'm a happily married man." Michael pressed her elbow tenderly. "Example for the whole twentieth century—Mr. and Mrs. Mike Loomis. Hey, let's have a drink," he said, stopping.

27   "We just had breakfast."

28   "Now listen, darling," Mike said, choosing his words with care, "it's a nice day and we both felt good and there's no reason why we have to break it up. Let's have a nice Sunday."

29   "All right. I don't know why I started this. Let's drop it. Let's have a good time."

30   They joined hands consciously and walked without talking among the baby carriages and the old Italian men in their Sunday clothes and the young women with Scotties in Washington Square Park.

31   "At least once a year everyone should go to the Metropolitan Museum of Art," Frances said after a while, her tone a good imitation of the tone she had used at breakfast and at the beginning of their walk. "And it's nice on Sunday. There're a lot of people looking at the pictures and you get the feeling maybe Art isn't on the decline in New York City, after all—"

32   "I want to tell you something," Michael said very seriously. "I have not touched another woman. Not once. In all the five years."

33   "All right," Frances said.

34   "You believe that, don't you?"

35   "All right."

36   They walked between the crowded benches, under the scrubby city-park trees.

37   "I try not to notice it," Frances said, "but I feel rotten inside, in my stomach, when we pass a woman and you look at her and I see that look in your eye and that's the way you looked at me the first time. In Alice Maxwell's house. Standing there in the living room, next to the radio, with a green hat on and all those people."

38   "I remember the hat," Michael said.

39   "The same look," Frances said. "And it makes me feel bad. It makes me feel terrible."

40   "Sh-h-h, please, darling, sh-h-h."

41   "I think I would like a drink now," Frances said.

42   They walked over to a bar on Eighth Street, not saying anything, Michael automatically helping her over curbstones and guiding her past automobiles. They sat near a window in the bar and the sun streamed in and there was a small, cheerful fire in the fireplace. A little Japanese waiter came over and put down some pretzels and smiled happily at them.

43   "What do you order after breakfast?" Michael asked.

44   "Brandy, I suppose," Frances said.

45   "Courvoisier," Michael told the waiter. "Two Courvoisiers."

46   The waiter came with the glasses and they sat drinking the brandy in the sunlight. Michael finished half his and drank a little water.

47   "I look at women," he said. "Correct. I don't say it's wrong or right. I look at them. If I pass them on the street and I don't look at them, I'm fooling you, I'm fooling myself."

48   "You look at them as though you want them," Frances said, playing with her brandy glass. "Every one of them."

49   "In a way," Michael said, speaking softly and not to his wife, "in a way that's true. I don't do anything about it, but it's true."

50   "I know it. That's why I feel bad."

51   "Another brandy," Michael called. "Waiter, two more brandies."

52   He sighed and closed his eyes and rubbed them gently with his fingertips. "I love the way women look. One of the things I like best about New York is the battalions of women. When I first came to New York from Ohio that was the first thing I noticed, the million wonderful women, all over the city. I walked around with my heart in my throat."

53   "A kid," Frances said. "That's a kid's feeling."

54   "Guess again," Michael said. "Guess again. I'm older now. I'm a man getting near middle age, putting on a little fat and I still love to walk along Fifth Avenue at three o'clock on the east side of the street between Fiftieth and Fifty-seventh Streets. They're all out then, shopping, in their furs and their crazy hats, everything all concentrated from all over the world into seven blocks—the best furs, the best clothes, the handsomest women, out to spend money and feeling good about it."

55   The Japanese waiter put the two drinks down, smiling with great happiness.

56   "Everything is all right?" he asked.

57   "Everything is wonderful," Michael said.

58   "If it's just a couple of fur coats," Frances said, "and forty-five-dollar hats—"

59   "It's not the fur coats. Or the hats. That's just the scenery for that particular kind of woman. Understand," he said, "you don't have to listen to this."

60   "I want to listen."

61   "I like the girls in the offices. Neat, with their eyeglasses, smart, chipper, knowing what everything is about. I like the girls on Forty-fourth Street at lunchtime, the actresses, all dressed up on nothing a week. I like the salesgirls in the stores, paying attention to you first because you're a man, leaving lady customers waiting. I got all this stuff accumulated in me because I've been thinking about it for ten years and now you've asked for it and here it is."

62   "Go ahead," Frances said.

63   "When I think of New York City, I think of all the girls on parade in the city. I don't know whether it's something special with me or whether every man in the city walks around with the same feeling inside him, but I feel as though I'm at a picnic in this city. I like to sit near the women in the theatres, the famous beauties who've taken six hours to get ready and look it. And the young girls at the football games, with the red cheeks, and when the warm weather comes, the girls in their summer dresses." He finished his drink. "That's the story."

64   Frances finished her drink and swallowed two or three times extra. "You say you love me?"

65   "I love you."

66   "I'm pretty, too," Frances said. "As pretty as any of them."

67   "You're beautiful," Michael said.

68   "I'm good for you," Frances said, pleading. "I've made a good wife, a good housekeeper, a good friend. I'd do any damn thing for you."

69   "I know," Michael said. He put his hand out and grasped hers.

70   "You'd like to be free to—" Frances said.

71   "Sh-h-h."

72   "Tell the truth." She took her hand away from under his.

73   Michael flicked the edge of his glass with his finger. "O.K," he said gently. "Sometimes I feel I would like to be free."

74   "Well," Frances said, "any time you say."

75   "Don't be foolish." Michael swung his chair around to her side of the table and patted her thigh.

76   She began to cry silently into her handkerchief, bent over just enough so nobody else in the bar would notice. "Someday," she said, crying, "you're going to make a move."

77   Michael didn't say anything. He sat watching the bartender slowly peel a lemon.

78   "Aren't you?" Frances asked harshly. "Come on, tell me. Talk. Aren't you?"

79   "Maybe," Michael said. He moved his chair back again. "How the hell do I know?"

80   "You know," Frances persisted. "Don't you know?"

81   "Yes," Michael said after a while, "I know."

82   Frances stopped crying then. Two or three snuffles into the handkerchief and she put it away and her face didn't tell anything to anybody. "At least do me a favor," she said.

83   "Sure."

84   "Stop talking about how pretty this woman is or that one. Nice eyes, nice breasts, a pretty figure, good voice." She mimicked his voice. "Keep it to yourself. I'm not interested."

85   Michael waved to the waiter. "I'll keep it to myself," he said.

86   Frances flicked the corners of her eyes. "Another brandy," she told the waiter.

87   "Two," Michael said.

88   "Yes, Ma'am; yes, Sir," said the waiter, backing away.

89   Frances regarded Michael coolly cross the table. "Do you want me to call the Stevensons?" she asked. "It'll be nice in the country."

90   "Sure," Michael said. "Call them."

91   She got up from the table and walked across the room toward the telephone. Michael watched her walk, thinking what a pretty girl, what nice legs.

| **Exercise 2** | **DISCUSSION AND CRITICAL THINKING** |

1. Point out the significance of the setting, either stated or implied.

2. Indicate the main conflict (and any secondary conflict).

3. Name the central character(s) and his or her (their) traits.

4. State the point of view (first or third person).

5. How does the behavior of both characters change after Michael starts looking at other women?

6. Would you say one is more at fault in this argument? Explain.

7. What is the significance of Michael's last observation of Frances?

8. What do you think will happen to their marriage? Why?

9. What would be your "Dear Abby" advice to them?

10. Briefly discuss the theme (what the story means, what it says about an individual specifically or human nature generally).

The Story of an Hour

Kate Chopin

The author of this famous story on love and marriage, Kate Chopin, was left a widow with six children at age thirty-two. Turning to writing seriously, she wrote stories set mainly in the Creole bayou country around New Orleans. Her independent thinking, especially about women's emotions, attracted a firestorm of critical attention to her novel *The Awakening,* and two collections of short stories, *Bayou Folk* and *A Night in Acadie,* and established her reputation as a feminist.

1   Knowing that Mrs. Mallard was afflicted with a heart trouble, great care was taken to break to her as gently as possible the news of her husband's death.

2   It was her sister Josephine who told her, in broken sentences, veiled hints that revealed in half concealing. Her husband's friend Richards was

there, too, near her. It was he who had been in the newspaper office when intelligence of the railroad disaster was received, with Brently Mallard's name leading the list of "killed." He had only taken the time to assure himself of its truth by a second telegram, and had hastened to forestall any less careful, less tender friend in bearing the sad message.

3   She did not hear the story as many women have heard the same, with a paralyzed inability to accept its significance. She wept at once, with sudden, wild abandonment, in her sister's arms. When the storm of grief had spent itself she went to her room alone. She would have no one follow her.

4   There stood, facing the open window, a comfortable, roomy armchair. Into this she sank, pressed down by a physical exhaustion that haunted her body and seemed to reach into her soul.

5   She could see in the open square before her house the tops of trees that were all aquiver with the new spring life. The delicious breath of rain was in the air. In the street below a peddler was crying his wares. The notes of a distant song which some one was singing reached her faintly, and countless sparrows were twittering in the eaves.

6   There were patches of blue sky showing here and there through the clouds that had met and piled above the other in the west facing her window.

7   She sat with her head thrown back upon the cushion of the chair quite motionless, except when a sob came up into her throat and shook her, as a child who has cried itself to sleep continues to sob in its dreams.

8   She was young, with a fair, calm face, whose lines bespoke repression and even a certain strength. But now there was a dull stare in her eyes, whose gaze was fixed away off yonder on one of those patches of blue sky. It was not a glance of reflection, but rather indicated a suspension of intelligent thought.

9   There was something coming to her and she was waiting for it, fearfully. What was it? She did not know; it was too subtle and elusive to name. But she felt it, creeping out of the sky, reaching toward her through the sounds, the scents, the color that filled the air.

10   Now her bosom rose and fell tumultuously. She was beginning to recognize this thing that was approaching to possess her, and she was striving to beat it back with her will—as powerless as her two white slender hands would have been.

11   When she abandoned herself a little whispered word escaped her slightly parted lips. She said it over and over under her breath: "Free, free, free!" The vacant stare and the look of terror that had followed it went from her eyes. They stayed keen and bright. Her pulses beat fast, and the coursing blood warmed and relaxed every inch of her body.

12   She did not stop to ask if it were not a monstrous joy that held her. A clear and exalted perception enabled her to dismiss the suggestion as trivial.

13   She knew that she would weep again when she saw the kind, tender hands folded in death; the face that had never looked save with love upon her, fixed and gray and dead. But she saw beyond that bitter moment a long procession of years to come that would belong to her absolutely. And she opened and spread her arms out to them in welcome.

14   There would be no one to live for during those coming years; she would live for herself. There would be no powerful will bending her in that blind persistence with which men and women believe they have a right to impose a private will upon a fellow-creature. A kind intention or a cruel intention

made the act seem no less a crime as she looked upon it in that brief moment of illumination.

15   And yet she had loved him—sometimes. Often she had not. What did it matter! What could love, the unsolved mystery, count for in face of this possession of self-assertion which she suddenly recognized as the strongest impulse of her being!

16   "Free! Body and soul free!" she kept whispering.

17   Josephine was kneeling before the closed door with her lips to the keyhole, imploring for admission. "Louise, open the door! I beg; open the door—you will make yourself ill. What are you doing, Louise? For heaven's sake open the door."

18   "Go away. I am not making myself ill." No; she was drinking in a very elixir of life through that open window.

19   Her fancy was running riot along those days ahead of her. Spring days, and summer days, and all sorts of days that would be her own. She breathed a quick prayer that life might be long. It was only yesterday she had thought with a shudder that life might be long.

20   She arose at length and opened the door to her sister's importunities. There was a feverish triumph in her eyes, and she carried herself unwittingly like a goddess of Victory. She clasped her sister's waist, and together they descended the stairs. Richards stood waiting for them at the bottom.

21   Some one was opening the door with a latchkey. It was Brently Mallard who entered, a little travel-stained, composedly carrying his grip-sack and umbrella. He had been far from the scene of accident, and did not even know there had been one. He stood amazed at Josephine's piercing cry; at Richards's quick motion to screen him from the view of his wife.

22   But Richards was too late.

23   When the doctors came they said she had died of heart disease—of joy that kills.

Exercise 3   **DISCUSSION AND CRITICAL THINKING**

1. What is Mrs. Mallard's first reaction in hearing of her husband's death?

2. What is her second reaction?

3. Why hasn't she considered freedom before?

4. Did her husband love her? Did she love him?

5. Did he abuse her?

6. Is this story mainly about women's rights, freedom, or some other subject?

7. Why does Mrs. Mallard die?

Frankie and Johnny

Anonymous

Frankie really loved this guy, but he "was doing her wrong," and, well, she took action. This song narrates one of the best-known crimes of passion in folk literature.

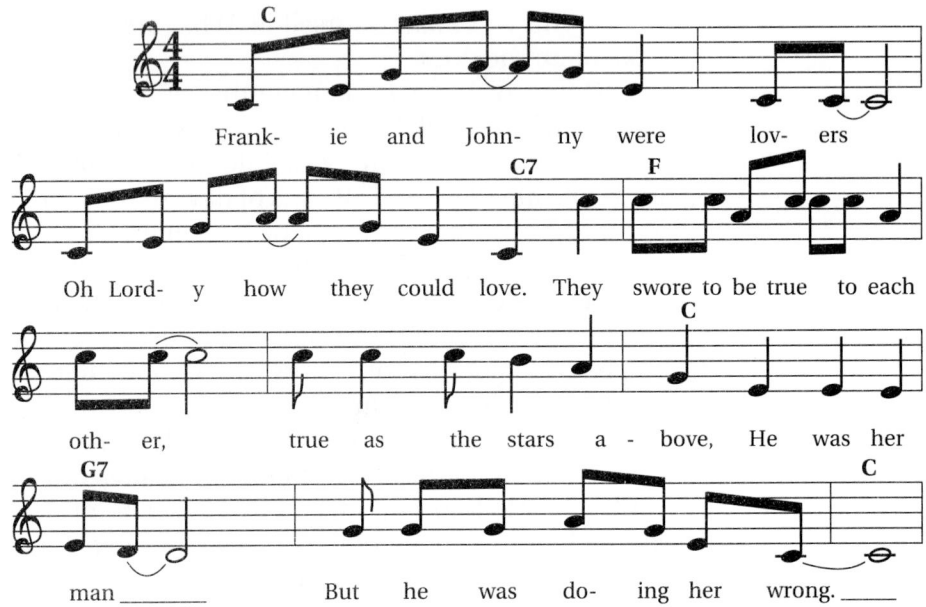

Frankie she was a good woman
As everybody knows,
Spent a hundred dollars
Just to buy her man some clothes.
5   He was her man, but he was doing her wrong.

Frankie went down to the corner
Just for a bucket of beer,
She said, "Mr. Bartender,
Has my loving Johnny been here?
10   He was my man, but he's a-doing me wrong."

"Now I don't want to tell you no stories
And I don't want to tell you no lies
I saw your man about an hour ago
With a gal named Nellie Bligh
15   He was your man, but he's a-doing you wrong."

Frankie went down to the hotel
Didn't go there for fun,
Underneath her kimona
She carried a forty-four gun.
20   He was her man, but he was doing her wrong.

Frankie looked over the transom
To see what she could spy,
There sat Johnny on the sofa
Just loving up Nellie Bligh.
25 He was her man, but he was doing her wrong.

Frankie got off that ladder
She didn't want to see no more;
Rooty-toot-toot three times she did shoot
Right through that hardwood door.
30 He was her man, but he was doing her wrong.

Now the first time Frankie shot Johnny
He let out an awful yell,
The second time she shot him
There was a new man's face in hell.
35 He was her man, but he was doing her wrong.

"Oh, roll me over easy
Roll me over slow
Roll me over on the right side
For the left side hurts me so."
40 He was her man, but he was doing her wrong.

Sixteen rubber-tired carriages
Sixteen rubber-tired hacks
They take poor Johnny to the graveyard
They ain't gonna bring him back.
45 He was her man, but he was doing her wrong.

Frankie looked out of the jailhouse
To see what she could see,
All she could hear was a two-string bow
Crying, "Nearer my God to thee."
50 He was her man, but he was doing her wrong.

Frankie she said to the sheriff,
"What do you reckon they'll do?"
The sheriff he said to Frankie,
"It's the electric chair for you."
55 He was her man, but he was doing her wrong.

This story has no moral
This story has no end
This story only goes to show
That there ain't no good in men!
60 He was her man, but he was doing her wrong.

Exercise 4   **DISCUSSION AND CRITICAL THINKING**

1. Point out the significance of the setting, either stated or implied.

2. Indicate the main conflict (and any secondary conflicts).

3. Name the central character(s), and give his or her (their) traits.

4. State the point of view (first or third person).

5. Briefly discuss the theme (what the story means, what it says about an individual specifically or human nature generally).

My Last Duchess
Ferrara, Italy
Robert Browning

Poet Robert Browning creates a chilling character who tells about his "last duchess." Approach this poem with care. It's not easy to understand at first reading, but once you know what to look for, a person within a story will emerge, one you will not forget.

The duke lived centuries ago in Italy. He was a proud man, powerful and self-centered. Like a king, he more or less owned the city-state of Ferrara and everything in it, even the duchess, his wife. The duchess was *his* duchess. He had given her *his* nine-hundred-year-old name. That should have been enough for her, he assumed. Naturally, he wanted her to be happy and smile—but only for him. Unfortunately, she didn't understand. Instead, she smiled frequently at things such as a bough of cherries, a local mule, a casual comment by somebody else. The duke was offended by her democratic spirit, but he didn't feel like explaining his pique. Instead he "gave commands; / Then all smiles stopped together." He did keep her portrait, where her image is "as if alive."

In the painting, she smiles in a very fetching pose. The duke has installed a curtain in front of the picture. When he wants to see *his* last duchess smile, he pulls the curtain. Now she smiles only for him. He is very pleased.

But time has passed, and at the time of this poem he is entertaining a representative of a wealthy neighbor who has a daughter eligible for marriage. She could be the next duchess. The duke pulls the curtain and tells the representative about *his* "last duchess," the one who had a heart "too soon made glad." It would not be good for *his* next duchess to be so indiscriminate. The poet does not judge the duke. He lets the duke talk. And talk he does. The duke is a gracious host. He has rare objects to point out. They are all *his*. If only his last duchess could have understood that! Of course, he couldn't "stoop to blame." Perhaps the next duchess will be prepared if the representative will be so kind as to carry the message. But the duke will not come right out and say that *his* duchess should derive pleasure only from him. It would be ill-bred and undignified for him to do so.

That's my last Duchess painted on the wall,
Looking as if she were alive. I call
That piece a wonder, now: Frà Pandolf's hands
Worked busily a day, and there she stands

5   Will't please you sit and look at her? I said
"Frà Pandolf" by design, for never read
Strangers like you that pictured countenance,
The depth and passion of its earnest glance,
But to myself they tuned (since none puts by

10   The curtain I have drawn for you, but I)
And seemed as they would ask me, if they durst,
How such a glance came there; so, not the first
Are you to turn and ask thus. Sir, 'twas not
Her husband's presence only, called that spot

15   Of joy into the Duchess' cheek: perhaps
Frà Pandolf chanced to say "Her mantle laps
Over my lady's wrist too much," or "Paint
Must never hope to reproduce the faint
Half-flush that dies along her throat": such stuff

20   Was courtesy, she thought, and cause enough
For calling up that spot of joy. She had
A heart—how shall I say?—too soon made glad,
Too easily impressed; she liked whate'er
She looked on, and her looks went everywhere.

25   Sir, 'twas all one! My favor at her breast,
The dropping of the daylight in the West,
The bough of cherries some officious fool
Broke in the orchard for her, the white mule
She rode with round the terrace—all and each

30   Would draw from her alike the approving speech,
Or blush, at least. She thanked men,—good! but thanked
Somehow—I know not how—as if she ranked
My gift of a nine-hundred-years-old name
With anybody's gift. Who'd stoop to blame

35   This sort of trifling? Even had you skill
In speech—which I have not—to make your will
Quite clear to such an one, and say, "Just this
Or that in you disgusts me; here you miss,
Or there exceed the mark"—and if she let

40   Herself be lessoned so, nor plainly set
Her wits to yours, forsooth, and made excuse,
—E'en then would be some stooping; and I choose
Never to stoop. Oh sir, she smiled, no doubt,
Whene'er I passed her; but who passed without

45   Much the same smile? This grew; I gave commands;
Then all smiles stopped together. There she stands
As if alive. Will't please you rise? We'll meet
The company below, then. I repeat,
The Count your master's known munificence

50   Is ample warrant that no just pretense
Of mine for dowry will be disallowed;

> Though his fair daughter's self, as I avowed
> At starting, is my object. Nay, we'll go
> Together down, sir. Notice Neptune, though,
> 55 Taming a sea-horse, thought a rarity,
> Which Claus of Innsbruck cast in bronze for me!

Exercise 5	DISCUSSION AND CRITICAL THINKING

1. Point out the significance of the setting, either stated or implied.

2. Indicate the main conflict (and any secondary conflicts).

3. Name the central character(s) and give his or her (their) traits.

4. State the point of view (first or third person).

5. What happened to the duchess? On what evidence or reasoning do you base your answer?

6. How does the portrait covered by a curtain represent the kind of control the duke wants?

7. Briefly discuss the theme (what the story means, what it says about an individual specifically or human nature generally).

Exercise 6	COMPARING THE SELECTIONS

1. How might each of the four couples from the four selections be classified according to the eight categories in "How Do I Love Thee?" Point out the differences between the companions. For example, Michael and Frances have different views on what a loving relationship means.

2. How is the couple in "The Girls in Their Summer Dresses" different from the couple in "Frankie and Johnny"?

3. In these four selections, which depiction of love is the most realistic? Why? Are any of them realistic?

✎ Topics for Writing about Literature

Reading-Related Topics

"The Girls in Their Summer Dresses"

1. Write a comparison and contrast piece about Michael and Frances. Use particular moments in their conversation (such as at the beginning, then when she becomes annoyed, when they decide to have a drink, and when they decide to visit with friends) or character traits (such as honesty, loyalty, love, affection, lust, forgiveness) for points in your organization.

2. Write an analysis by division of Francis or Michael, using character traits such as those indicated in question 1.

3. Write about the significance of setting.

4. State the theme that you think the author implies, and then agree or disagree with it.

5. Write a piece in which you show how the characters' behavior becomes more self-conscious, mechanical, and detached as the story progresses.

6. Develop a persuasive piece in which you argue that either Michael or Frances is primarily at fault.

7. Argue that neither Michael nor Frances is at fault because men and women simply have different views toward male-female relationships.

8. Imagine the couple a year or so in the future, and write about them at that time.

"The Story of an Hour"

9. Write a diary account of some of the experiences Mrs. Mallard went through in her marriage—experiences that made her long for freedom.

10. Pose as the husband and write a eulogy that he would deliver at his wife's funeral. Include examples of the love they shared. Through his words, have him reveal what type of husband he was. For instance, he may reveal himself as a well-intentioned yet controlling person, but he will not recognize himself as such.

11. Write a piece in which you argue that Mrs. Mallard's reaction is far more likely to be experienced by a woman than by a man; or argue against that view.

12. Discuss the issue of whether, if the roles were reversed, Mr. Mallard could die of the same shock that killed Mrs. Mallard.

13. Assume that Mrs. Mallard has empty love and Mr. Mallard has companionate love, and compare and contrast these two characters in relation to the story's theme.

"Frankie and Johnny"

14. Write a paper on both the causes and effects of Frankie's shooting Johnny.

15. Write a paper in which you discuss the songwriter's techniques in using language and in developing a narrative account. You may want to refer to the instructions in this book on narration (Chapter 7) and description (Chapter 8).

"My Last Duchess"

16. Write a character study (using functional analysis) of the duke, drawing supporting information from the poem. His traits, such as intelligence, arrogance, and pride (try brainstorming and clustering for more), could provide a framework for your statement.

17. Write a character study of the duchess, drawing supporting information from the poem. If you speculate to round out your study, label your speculation as such.

18. Write a piece that explains what happened to the duchess. Use evidence from the poem.

19. Assume that you are the duchess just before the duke took whatever steps he took, and write a diary entry about your life on his estate.

20. The person listening to the duke is an envoy from the leader of another city-state. The leader's daughter is the duke's prospective bride. Write out a statement about the duke that the envoy might deliver to the young woman. His report can either state the situation outright or be subtle and suggestive.

Reading Selections on the Theme of Love

21. Write a piece in which you classify and analyze the love in one of the four selections according to the eight types of love in "How Do I Love Thee?"

22. Compare and contrast Michael from "The Girls in Their Summer Dresses" with Johnny from "Frankie and Johnny."

23. Compare and contrast Frances from "The Girls in Their Summer Dresses" with Frankie from "Frankie and Johnny."

24. Write an essay on love in which you show that these four selections illustrate the main types of love. (References to "How Do I Love Thee?" are optional.)

25. Using the same stanzaic patterns as in "Frankie and Johnny," write a ballad about Frances and Michael from "The Girls in Their Summer Dresses."

26. Pose as the duke from "My Last Duchess" and write a statement in which he asks Frankie of "Frankie and Johnny" to be his new bride. Then write her answer to him.

27. Write a paragraph or essay in which you argue that one of these four pieces is the most realistic view of the true nature of love. You may refer to more than one. Include insights from "How Do I Love Thee?" if you like.

28. Compare the duke from "My Last Duchess" with Brently Mallard from "The Story of an Hour."

Career-Related Topics

29. Discuss the idea of dating among employees. Is it usually a good or a bad idea? Does dating generally improve or damage workplace morale in the long run? Should there be any company guidelines? Use whatever ideas you have

acquired from considering the five reading selections on the theme of love as supporting information.

30. Discuss the benefits and problems associated with finding and getting to know potential dates online.

General Topic   31. Write about another story from a source other than this book according to the guidelines for writing about literature presented in this chapter.

Writer's Guidelines: Literary Analysis

1. In analyzing a piece of literature, consider its setting, conflict, characters, plot, point of view, and especially its theme. You would usually emphasize one of those aspects.

2. Writing about literature may be analytical (as in point 1), or it may be more speculative, personal, or comparative.

3. Develop your ideas by referring directly to the story; by explaining; and by using summaries, paraphrases, and quotations.

4. Use the present tense in relating events in the story.

5. Use quotation marks correctly around the words you borrow.

6. For organization, consider patterns of development such as analysis by division, comparison and contrast, and cause and effect.

17

Argument: Writing to Persuade

"People are never so likely to settle a question rightly as when they discuss it freely."

Robert Southey

THE QUIGMANS   by Buddy Hickerson

"Oh, please, Cedric. Must you turn every argument we have into a psychodrama?"

B. Hickerson, copyright Los Angeles Times Syndicate. Reprinted by permission.

Writing Paragraphs and Essays of Argument

*P*ersuasion is a broad term. When we persuade, we try to influence people to think in a certain way or to do something.

Argument is persuasion on a topic about which reasonable people disagree. Argument involves controversy. Whereas exercising appropriately is probably not controversial because reasonable people do not dispute the idea, an issue such as gun control is. In this chapter, we will be concerned mainly with the kind of persuasion that involves argument.

Techniques for Developing Argument

Statements of argument are informal or formal. An opinion column in a newspaper is likely to have little set structure, whereas an argument in college writing is likely to be tightly organized. Nevertheless, the opinion column and the college paper have much in common. Both provide a proposition, which is the main point of the argument, and both provide support, which is the evidence or the reasons that back up the proposition.

For a well-structured college paragraph or essay, an organization plan is desirable. Consider these elements when you write an argument, and ask yourself the following questions as you develop your ideas:

Background: What is the historical or social context for this controversial issue?

Proposition (the thesis of the essay): What do I want my audience to believe or do?

Qualification of proposition: Can I limit my propositions so that those who disagree cannot easily challenge me with exceptions? If, for example, I am in favor of using animals for scientific experimentation, am I concerned only with medical experiments or with any use, including experiments for the cosmetic industry?

Refutation (taking the opposing view into account, mainly to point out its fundamental weakness): What is the view on the other side, and why is it flawed in reasoning or evidence?

Support: In addition to sound reasoning, can I use appropriate facts, examples, statistics, and opinions of authorities?

This is the most commonly used pattern for an essay, which is abbreviated for a paragraph.

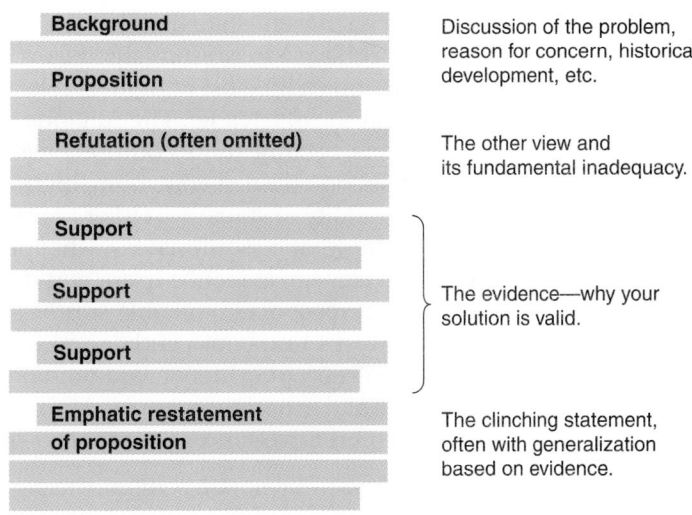

Background	Discussion of the problem, reason for concern, historical development, etc.
Proposition	
Refutation (often omitted)	The other view and its fundamental inadequacy.
Support	The evidence—why your solution is valid.
Support	
Support	
Emphatic restatement of proposition	The clinching statement, often with generalization based on evidence.

There are, of course, other variants, and there are also several methods of developing the material within each pattern. You may organize the supporting facts by comparison, one side at a time or one issue at a time (present an issue favoring your position, then refute one of your opponent's claims). You may develop the argument (or persuasive writing, in a broader sense) by a method such as cause and effect, comparison and contrast, or a combination of methods.

Your Audience

Your audience may be uninformed, informed, biased, hostile, receptive, apathetic, sympathetic, empathetic—any one, a combination, or something else. The point is that you should be intensely concerned about who will read your composition. If your readers are likely to be uninformed about the social and historical background of the issue, then you need to set the issue in context. The discussion of the background should lead to the problem for which you have a proposition or solution. If your readers are likely to be biased or even hostile to your view, take special care to refute the opposing side in a thoughtful, incisive way that does not further antagonize them. If your readers are already receptive and perhaps even sympathetic, and you wish to move them to action, then you might appeal to their conscience and the need for their commitment.

Kinds of Evidence

In addition to sound reasoning generally, you can use these kinds of evidence: facts, examples, statistics, and authorities.

First, you can offer facts. Martin Luther King, Jr., was killed in Memphis, Tennessee, on April 4, 1968. Because an event that has happened is true and can be verified, this statement about King is a fact. But that James Earl Ray acted alone in killing King is to some questionable. That King was the greatest of all civil rights leaders is also opinion because it cannot be verified.

Some facts are readily accepted because they are general knowledge—you and your reader know them to be true, because they can be or have been verified. Other "facts" are based on personal observation and are reported in various publications but may be false or questionable. You should always be concerned about the reliability of the source for both the information you use and the information used by those with other viewpoints. Still other so-called facts are genuinely debatable because of their complexity or the incompleteness of the knowledge available.

Second, you can cite examples. Keep in mind that you must present a sufficient number of examples and that the examples must be relevant.

Third, you can present statistics. Statistics are numerical facts and data that are classified and tabulated to present significant information about a given subject.

Avoid presenting a long list of figures; select statistics carefully and relate them to things familiar to your reader. The millions of dollars spent on a war in a single week, for example, become more comprehensible when expressed in terms of what the money would purchase in education, highways, or urban renewal.

To test the validity of statistics, either yours or your opponent's, ask: Who gathered them? Under what conditions? For what purpose? How are they used?

Fourth, you can cite evidence from, and opinions of, authorities. Most readers accept facts from recognized, reliable sources—governmental publications, standard reference works, and books and periodicals published by established firms. In addition, they will accept evidence and opinions from individuals who, because of their knowledge and experience, are recognized as experts.

In using authoritative sources as proof, keep these points in mind:

- Select authorities who are generally recognized as experts in their field.

- Use authorities who qualify in the field pertinent to your argument.

- Select authorities whose views are not biased.

- Try to use several authorities.

- Identify the authority's credentials clearly in your essay.

Logical Fallacies

Certain thought patterns are inherently flawed. Commonly called *logical fallacies*, these thought patterns are of primary concern in argumentation. You should be able to identify them in the arguments of those on the other side of an issue, and you should be sure to avoid them in your own writing.

Eight kinds of logical fallacies are very common.

1. *Post hoc, ergo propter hoc* ("after this, therefore because of this"): When one event precedes another in time, the first is assumed to cause the other. "If *A* comes before *B*, then *A* must be causing *B*."

   Examples: "I knew I'd have a day like this when I saw that black cat run across my driveway this morning."

   What did I tell you? We elected him president, and now we have high inflation."

2. *False analogy:* False analogies ignore differences and stress similarities, often in an attempt to prove something.

   Examples: "People have to get a driver's license because unqualified drivers could have bad effects on society. Therefore, couples should also have to get a license to bear children because unqualified parents can produce delinquent children."

   "The leader of that country is a mad dog dictator, and you know what you do with a mad dog. You get a club and kill it."

3. *Hasty generalization:* This is a conclusion based on too few reliable instances.

   Example: "Everyone I met this morning is going to vote for Johnson, so I know Johnson is going to win."

   "How many people did you meet?"

   "Three."

4. *False dilemma:* This fallacy presents the reader with only two alternatives from which to choose. The solution may lie elsewhere.

   Examples: "Now, only two things can be done with the savings and loan places. You either shut them down or let them go bankrupt."

   "The way I see it, you either bomb them back into the Stone Age or let them keep on pushing us around."

5. *Argumentation ad hominem* (argument against the person): This is the practice of abusing and discrediting your opponent rather than keeping to the main issues of the argument.

   Examples: "Who cares what he has to say? After all, he's a wild-eyed liberal who has been divorced twice."

   "Let's put aside the legislative issue for a moment and talk about the person who proposed it. For one thing he's a Southerner. For another he's Catholic. Enough said."

6. *Begging the question:* This fallacy assumes something is true without proof. It occurs when a thinker assumes a position is right before offering proof.

   Examples: "Those savages can never be civilized."

   "I have one simple question. When is he going to stop ripping off his customers? Case closed."

7. *Circular reasoning:* This thought pattern asserts proof that is no more than a repetition of the initial assertion.

   Example: "You can judge good art by reading what good critics say about it."

   "But who are good critics?"

   "The people who spend their time judging good art."

8. *Non sequitur:* This fallacy draws a conclusion that does not follow.

   Examples: "He's my first cousin, so of course you can trust him."

   "You can count on Gizmo computers; they were designed by native Californians."

Exercise 1	**IDENTIFYING LOGICAL FALLACIES**

Identify the logical fallacy in the following sentences.

1. "If politicians can hire ghostwriters, why can't a little student like me be allowed to buy a research paper?"

2. "Stamp out dirty books, I say. Just look at all the crime we have since they started allowing this stuff."

3. "I was starting to have my doubts about the accuracy of newspapers until I read a newspaper editorial last week saying how reliable newspapers actually are."

4. "I can tell from listening to my family that the school bond issue will never pass."

5. "Blaming a company for making big profits is like blaming a cow for giving too much milk."

6. "Okay, so my spouse left me. Who cares? They're like buses; you miss one, and another one'll come along in a minute or two."

7. "I used to think Hemingway was a great writer until I read about his life. The guy was a self-centered, pompous jerk, and I'll never read any of his stuff again."

8. "I was really shocked until she told me it happened in New York, and then I just said, 'What's new?'"

9. "Like I say, you either fish or you cut bait. Will you marry me or won't you? Take your choice." (Two fallacies here)

10. "Mark my words. If they start controllin' hand guns, it's just a matter of time 'til we're back to defendin' ourselves with clubs and rocks against criminals with bazookas."

| **Exercise 2** | **WRITING EXAMPLES OF LOGICAL FALLACIES** |

Provide examples of the following logical fallacies. Work in a group or individually as directed by your instructor.

1. *Post hoc:* _____

    _____

    _____

2. False analogy: _____

    _____

    _____

3. Hasty generalization: _____

    _____

    _____

4. False dilemma: _____

    _____

    _____

5. *Argumentum ad hominem:* _____

    _____

    _____

6. Begging the question: _____

    _____

    _____

7. Circular reasoning: _____

    _____

    _____

8. *Non sequitur:* _____

    _____

    _____

Connecting Reading and Writing

The New Prohibitionism

Charles Krauthammer

Psychiatrist, former science advisor to President Carter, and Pulitzer Prize–winning journalist, Charles Krauthammer brings passion and intellect to the issues he covers in his weekly columns for the *Washington Post* and his monthly columns in *Time* magazine. In this essay he takes on alcohol, not only discussing its effect on society but comparing it with another product, tobacco. Both have devastating effects, but one, he argues, is treated differently.

1.   The oddest thing about the current national crusade against tobacco is not its frenzy—our culture lives from one frenzy to the next—but its selectivity. Of course tobacco is a great national killer. It deserves all the pummeling it gets. But alcohol is a great national killer too, and it has enjoyed an amazingly free ride amid the fury of the New Prohibitionism.

2.   Joe Camel has been banished forever, but those beloved Budweiser frogs—succeeded by even cuter Budweiser lizards—keep marching along, right into the consciousness of every TV-watching kid in the country.

3.   For 26 years television has been free of cigarette ads. Why? Because TV persuades as nothing else, and we don't want young people—inveterate TV watchers—persuaded. Yet television is bursting with exhortations to drink. TV sports in particular, a staple of adolescents, is one long hymn to the glories of beer.

4.   And the sports-worshipping years are precisely the time that kids learn to drink. The median age at which they start drinking is just over 13. A 1990 survey found that 56 percent of students in Grades 5 through 12 say alcohol advertising encourages them to drink. Surprise!

5.   Am I for Prohibition? No. But I am for a little perspective. We tend to think of the turn-of-the-century temperance movement as little blue-haired ladies trying to prevent people from having a good time on Saturday night. In fact, the temperance movement was part of a much larger progressive movement seeking to improve the appalling conditions of the urban working class. These were greatly exacerbated by rampant alcoholism that contributed to extraordinary levels of spousal and child abuse, abandonment, and destitution.

6.   Alcohol is still a cause of staggering devastation. It kills 100,000 Americans a year—not only from disease but also from accidents. In 1996, 41 percent of all U.S. traffic fatalities were alcohol related. It causes huge economic losses and untold suffering. Why, then, do the Bud frogs get to play the Super Bowl while Joe Camel goes the way of the Marlboro Man?

7.   The most plausible answer is that tobacco is worse because it kills more people. Indeed it does. But 100,000 people a year is still a fair carnage. Moreover, the really compelling comparison is this: alcohol is far more deadly than tobacco *to innocent bystanders*. In a free society, should we not

consider behavior that injures others more worthy of regulation than behavior that merely injures oneself? The primary motive for gun control, after all, is concern about homicide, not suicide.

8   The antitobacco folk, aware of this bedrock belief, try to play up the harm smokers cause others. Thus the attorneys general seeking billions of dollars in damages from the tobacco companies are claiming that taxpayers have been unfairly made to pay for the treatment of smoking-related illnesses.

9   A clever ploy. But the hardheaded truth is that premature death from smoking, which generally affects people in their late-middle and early retirement years, is an economic boon to society. The money saved on pensions and on the truly expensive health care that comes with old age—something these smokers never achieve—surely balances, if it does not exceed, the cost of treating tobacco-related diseases.

10   The alternative and more dramatic antitobacco tactic is to portray smoking as an assault on nonsmokers via secondhand smoke. Now, secondhand smoke is certainly a nuisance. But the claim that it is a killer is highly dubious. "The statistical evidence," reported the nonpartisan Congressional Research Service in 1994, "does not appear to support a conclusion that there are substantive health effects of passive smoking."

11   Unlike secondhand smoke, secondhand booze is a world-class killer. Drunk driving alone kills 17,000 people a year. And alcohol's influence extends far beyond driving: it contributes to everything from bar fights to domestic violence. One study found that 44 percent of assailants in cases of marital abuse had been drinking. Another study found that 60 percent of wife batterers had been under the influence. Whatever claims you make against tobacco, you'd have quite a time looking for cases of the nicotine-crazed turning on their wives with a butcher knife.

12   Moreover, look at the *kinds* of people alcohol kills. Drunk drivers kill toddlers. They kill teens. They kill whole families. Tobacco does not kill toddlers and teens. Tobacco strikes late. It kills, but at a very long remove in time. Its victims generally have already had their chance at life. Tobacco merely shortens life; alcohol can deprive people of it.

13   Still undecided which of the two poisons is more deserving of social disapprobation? Here's the ultimate test. Ask yourself this: If you knew your child was going to become addicted to either alcohol or tobacco, which would you choose?

| **Exercise 3** | **VOCABULARY HIGHLIGHTS** |

Write a short definition of each word as it is used in the essay. (Paragraph numbers are given in parentheses.) Be prepared to use the words in your own sentences.

pummeling (1)	destitution (5)
inveterate (3)	plausible (7)
exhortations (3)	carnage (7)
exacerbated (5)	ploy (9)
rampant (5)	disapprobation (13)

| Exercise 4 | DISCUSSION AND CRITICAL THINKING |

1. What is the implied proposition in paragraph 1?

2. What kind of evidence does Krauthammer use in paragraph 4? What else might have been included to make the evidence stronger?

3. Why is alcohol worse than tobacco according to the author?

4. What other issue does Krauthammer use for comparison in paragraph 7?

5. What kind of evidence does he use in paragraph 10?

6. How many effects of "secondhand booze" does he give? What are they?

7. Does society in general treat alcohol less negatively than tobacco? If so, why?

8. What legislation should a person who agrees with Krauthammer propose?

9. How would you respond to Krauthammer's question at the end of this essay? Explain.

The First Step in Improving Sex Education: Remove the Hellfire

Fred M. Hechinger

To journalist Fred M. Hechinger the first step in improving sex education is a matter of attitude. He believes that the problems of unwanted teen pregnancies and sexually transmitted diseases can be addressed only if we first set aside the "hellfire reaction." This article initially appeared in the *New York Times*.

1   "Analysis of sex education in Sweden, Holland, France, Great Britain, and Canada shows us lagging far behind," Zella Luria, a psychology professor at Tufts University, wrote in *Independent School* magazine.

2   "In America, hellfire is still close to sexuality and thus shapes our education and services. Who pays the price? Our children do," Professor Luria wrote in his article, "The Adolescent Years and Sexuality."

3   Lately, America has been trying to catch up. Sex education in public schools has grown dramatically in the last five years, in part driven by the

fear of AIDS. More than 40 states require or encourage some sex education, and at least 6 out of 10 American teenagers now receive it before high school graduation.

4   But the issue is still plagued by poorly informed teachers, lack of effective teaching materials, and many teachers' fear of opposition from parents, school administrators, and some religious leaders when "safe sex," abortion, and homosexuality are discussed. Hellfire reaction persists.

5   The state education authorities are more interested in providing information about AIDS and other sexually transmitted diseases than about prevention of unwanted pregnancies, concluded a report by the Alan Guttmacher Institute, a nonprofit research and education organization.

6   The report, "Risk and Responsibility: Teaching Sex Education in America's Schools Today," says that many teachers consider even the stepped-up attention to sex education "too little and too late." They call for such instruction to begin not later than the seventh grade, and preferably even sooner. They estimate that at least a quarter of tenth graders are already sexually active.

7   Opposition to sex education is felt or perceived by many teachers, even though national polls show that more than 85 percent of American adults favor such instruction, up from 69 percent in 1965.

8   Continuing reluctance to let schools deal with the issue of unwanted pregnancies appears to stem from the controversial nature of birth control and abortion. Yet, more than a million teenagers become pregnant each year, most unintentionally. About 416,000 have abortions, 472,000 give birth, and the rest miscarry.

9   Contrary to the assertion of some opponents of sex education that it encourages intercourse and promiscuity, most sex education instructors stress the moral and pregnancy-preventing appeal of abstinence.

10   They also discuss the consequences of sexual activity; the responsibility of males in helping to prevent unintended pregnancies; the practical and psychological problems created by teenage pregnancy; the demands of parenthood; and the false message sent by the media, particularly television, in showing "sex without consequences." Most teachers also urge students to resist peer pressure to have sexual intercourse.

11   Still, to ignore reality by skirting birth control and abortion cripples sex education, advocates say.

12   Pregnancy is not the only matter of concern. Each year, a quarter of the sexually active women between 15 and 19 years old seek treatment for a sexually transmitted disease.

13   Even where sex education is offered, the time spent on it may be insufficient. The Guttmacher report found that typically fewer than 12 hours of instruction are devoted to it in the seventh grade, and not much more in the twelfth grade.

14   Other obstacles remain. "Changing students' attitudes is the hardest part," a health teacher in New York told researchers. "They believe, 'It can't happen to me.'"

15   A teacher in North Carolina added, "Students have a lot of personal knowledge about sex—most of which is inaccurate."

16   Teachers' knowledge is often inaccurate, too. While the birth control pill is the most widely used contraceptive among teenagers, the Guttmacher report found that three-quarters of the teachers believed that the pill

should be given occasional "rests," which, the institute says, "medical evidence shows are not needed and may expose the user to an unnecessary risk to become pregnant."

17 Fortunately for American teenagers and the nation's health, more parents and communities are beginning to learn how to shed old taboos and deal rationally with new realities.

Exercise 5   **DISCUSSION AND CRITICAL THINKING**

1. Which sentence best expresses Hechinger's proposition?

2. What reasons for sex education does Hechinger cite?

3. What rebuttal does Hechinger offer?

4. What are the obstacles to good sex education besides opposition by some of the public?

5. Give an example of each kind of support: fact, opinion, statistics, authoritative statement (one example may cover more than one kind of support).

Of Headless Mice . . . and Men

Charles Krauthammer

In this essay for *Time* magazine, Charles Krauthammer says if we peer into the future we may see our cloned selves slouching there just over the horizon, loaded with body parts for us to harvest. Since his statement of moral outrage was first published, several biotechnical breakthroughs have occurred, including the cloning of clones and the transplanting of two human arms. Another essay by Krauthammer appears on pages 332–333.

1 Last year Dolly the cloned sheep was received with wonder, titters and some vague apprehension. Last week the announcement by a Chicago physicist that he is assembling a team to produce the first human clone

occasioned yet another wave of Brave New World anxiety. But the scariest news of all—and largely overlooked—comes from two obscure labs, at the University of Texas and at the University of Bath. During the past four years, one group created headless mice; the other, headless tadpoles.

2   For sheer Frankenstein wattage, the purposeful creation of these animal monsters has no equal. Take the mice. Researchers found the gene that tells the embryo to produce the head. They deleted it. They did this in a thousand mice embryos, four of which were born. I use the term loosely. Having no way to breathe, the mice died instantly.

3   Why then create them? The Texas researchers want to learn how genes determine embryo development. But you don't have to be a genius to see the true utility of manufacturing headless creatures: for their organs—fully formed, perfectly useful, ripe for plundering.

4   Why should you be panicked? Because humans are next. "It would almost certainly be possible to produce human bodies without a forebrain," Princeton biologist Lee Silver told the London *Sunday Times.* "These human bodies without any semblance of consciousness would not be considered persons, and thus it would be perfectly legal to keep them 'alive' as a future source of organs."

5   "Alive." Never have a pair of quotation marks loomed so ominously. Take the mouse-frog technology, apply it to humans, combine it with cloning, and you become a god: with a single cell taken from, say, your finger, you produce a headless replica of yourself, a mutant twin, arguably lifeless, that becomes your own personal, precisely tissue-matched organ farm.

6   There are, of course, technical hurdles along the way. Suppressing the equivalent "head" gene in man. Incubating tiny infant organs to grow into larger ones that adults could use. And creating artificial wombs (as per Aldous Huxley),[1] given that it might be difficult to recruit sane women to carry headless fetuses to their birth/death.

7   It won't be long, however, before these technical barriers are breached. The ethical barriers are already cracking. Lewis Wolpert, professor of biology at University College, London, finds producing headless humans "personally distasteful" but, given the storage of organs, does not think distaste is sufficient reason not to go ahead with something that would save lives. And Professor Silver not only sees "nothing wrong, philosophically or rationally," with producing headless humans for organ harvesting, he wants to convince a skeptical public that it is perfectly O.K.

8   When prominent scientists are prepared to acquiesce in—or indeed encourage—the deliberate creation of deformed and dying quasi-human life, you know we are facing a bioethical abyss. Human beings are ends, not means. There is no grosser corruption of biotechnology than creating a human mutant and disemboweling it at our pleasure for spare parts.

9   The prospect of headless human clones should put the whole debate about "normal" cloning in a new light. Normal cloning is less a treatment for infertility than a treatment for vanity. It is a way to produce an exact genetic replica of yourself that will walk the earth years after you're gone.

[1] Aldous Huxley (1894–1963) is the author of *Brave New World,* a satirical novel about a technological society that self-medicates and develops embryos in bottles.

10   But there is a problem with a clone. It is not really you. It is but a twin, a perfect John Doe Jr., but still a junior. With its own independent consciousness, it is, alas, just a facsimile of you.

11   The headless clone solves the facsimile problem. It is a gateway to the ultimate vanity: immortality. If you create a real clone, you cannot transfer your consciousness into it to truly live on. But if you create a headless clone of just your body, you have created a ready source of replacement parts to keep you—your consciousness—going indefinitely.

12   Which is why one form of cloning will inevitably lead to the other. Cloning is the technology of narcissism, and nothing satisfies narcissism like immortality. Headlessness will be cloning's crowning achievement.

13   The time to put a stop to this is now. Dolly moved President Clinton to create a commission that recommended a temporary ban on human cloning. But with physicist Richard Seed threatening to clone humans, and with headless animals already here, we are past the time for toothless commissions and meaningless bans.

14   Clinton banned federal funding of human-cloning research, of which there is none anyway. He then proposed a five-year ban on cloning. This is not enough. Congress should ban human cloning now. Totally. And regarding one particular form, it should be draconian: the deliberate creation of headless humans must be a crime, indeed a capital crime. If we flinch in the face of this high-tech barbarity, we'll deserve to live in the hell it heralds.

Exercise 6	**VOCABULARY HIGHLIGHTS**

Write a short definition of each word as it is used in the essay. (Paragraph numbers are given in parentheses.) Be prepared to use the words in your own sentences.

wattage (2)	abyss (8)
semblance (4)	mutant (8)
ominously (5)	disemboweling (8)
acquiesce (8)	narcissism (12)
quasi- (8)	draconian (14)

Exercise 7	**DISCUSSION AND CRITICAL THINKING**

1. What sentence most clearly states Krauthammer's proposition?

2. To whom does Krauthammer address as the main audience—scientists, legislators, or general readers?

3. Which paragraph serves as the main refutation?

4. What tone is suggested by words such as "scariest" (par. 1), "monsters" (par. 2), and "plundering" (par. 3)? What words might be used by someone with a different view to alter the tone?

5. In paragraphs 9–12, Krauthammer discusses normal cloning and headless cloning. According to him, what weakness (as reflected in human vanity and self-centeredness) in normal cloning makes the advance to headless cloning inevitable?

6. Do you approve of the idea of human cloning for the replacement of body parts?

7. How is your view on human cloning related to your religious or philosophical views?

8. Do you agree with Krauthammer's suggestion for a congressional ban on human cloning, which includes making the cloning of headless human beings a capital crime?

Student Writers: Demonstrations and Readings

After Angela DeSarro received a list of topics from which to select, she went to the library to obtain some information about the ones that interested her. One such topic was euthanasia. Her electronic data bank offered her an essay in the *Journal of the American Medical Association* about a doctor who illegally assisted a suffering, terminally ill patient. DeSarro's mind and emotions came together on the issue and she had her topic.

Her Writing Process Worksheet shows you how her writing evolved from idea to final draft. Notice how she turns her listing into an outline, which becomes the structure for her paragraph. To conserve space here, her freewriting and two rough drafts marked for revision and editing have been omitted. The balance of the worksheet has been lengthened for you to be able to see her other work in its entirety.

You will find a full-size blank worksheet on page 5. It can be photocopied, filled in, and submitted with each assignment if your instructor directs you to do so.

· ·

Writing Process Worksheet

TITLE My Life to Live—or Not

NAME Angela DeSarro **DUE DATE** Tuesday, October 14, 10 a.m.

ASSIGNMENT In the space below, write whatever you need to know about your assignment, including information about the topic, audience, pattern of writing, length, whether to include a rough draft or revised drafts, and whether your paper must be typed.

Write a paragraph of 200 to 300 words in which you argue for a particular action or restraint. Include at least three supporting points. Keep in mind that some thoughtful readers will disagree with your proposition. Submit this completed worksheet, a rough draft marked for revision and editing, and a typed final draft

STAGE ONE **Explore** Freewrite, brainstorm (list), cluster, or take notes as directed by your instructor. Use the back of this page or separate paper if you need more space.

Listing

Debbie's struggle
   (from *JAMA*)
—terminally ill with cancer
—nauseous, emaciated, suffering
—wants to die with a bit of
   dignity intact
—physician helps her
—an illegal act
—shouldn't be illegal

Proposal
—physician-assisted suicide
—patient terminally ill,
   little time left
—must be suffering
—must want suicide
—physician can assist
—must be regulated
—should be national law
—similar to the one in Oregon

STAGE TWO **Organize** Write a topic sentence or thesis; label the subject and the treatment parts.

The time has come for a national law legalizing physician-assisted suicide
                       treatment   subject
for the terminally ill.

Write an outline or an outline alternative.

  I. Person dying
    A. Pain
    B. Extreme discomfort
    C. Example: Debbie
 II. Person desiring death with dignity
    A. Not wanting to wither away
    B. Not wanting to be alive on tubes and machines
    C. Example: Debbie

III. Person demanding choice in dying
   A. Of time
   B. Of method
   C. Example: Debbie
IV. A law that works
   A. Chosen by voters in Oregon
   B. Is not abused
V. Plea for a national law

STAGE THREE | **Write** On separate paper, write and then revise your paper as many times as necessary for coherence, language (usage, tone, and diction), unity, emphasis, support, and sentences (CLUESS). Read your paper aloud to hear and correct any grammatical errors or awkward-sounding sentences.

Edit any problems in fundamentals, such as capitalization, omissions, punctuation, and spelling (COPS).

Final Draft

My Life to Live—or Not

Angela DeSarro

Debbie, 20, was dying of ovarian cancer. Racked with pain, nauseous, emaciated, she sought the ultimate relief and found it in euthanasia. A doctor administered a drug and she died. It was a hidden, secret act. It was also illegal in Debbie's state, but this case was written up in the *Journal of the American Medical Association.* Surely the time has come for a nationwide law legalizing this practice under specific provisions and regulations.

Proposition

Support Debbie had reached the point of not only enduring terrible pain but of vomiting constantly and not being able to sleep. Pain-killing medication no longer worked. She wanted to die with what she regarded as a degree of dignity. She had already become a withered, suffering human being with tubes coming out of her nose, throat, and urinary tract, and she was losing all self-control. She also believed that it should be up to her, under these conditions, to decide when and how she should die. Laws in most places prohibit terminally ill patients from choosing death and physicians from assisting them. One state, Oregon, has a law favoring physician-assisted suicide, at least in the limited cases of terminally ill people expected to live less than six months. In 1998, fifteen people benefited from that law; it was not abused. It, or a similar form, should be enacted nationwide.

Support

Concluding sentence as a restated proposition

Exercise 8 | **DISCUSSION AND CRITICAL THINKING**

1. What kinds of evidence does DeSarro use to support her argument?

2. What might be the objections to her reasoned argument?

3. Do you agree or disagree with DeSarro's argument? Why?

Teaching Our Kids to Shoot 'Em Up

Tina Sergio

Tina Sergio's instructor had directed her to write an essay that included ideas from at least three newspaper, magazine, or journal sources. She was to document the ideas she incorporated into the content of her essay and submit photocopies of the works she cited. (See Chapter 18 for MLA style.) A suggested writing topic about the negative effects of media on youth intrigued her. The issue was something that most people of her generation could relate to as they reflected on their childhood: the confusing blur of fact and fantasy in all media but especially in video games and in television cartoons, sitcoms, dramas, and news.

Why is it that if video games or television shows contain any type of nudity, many parents become outraged and forbid their children from involvement; however, when video games and television shows feature shooting and killing, these parents don't bat an eye? What does absorbing all this violence teach children? A Surgeon General's special report has told us that viewing violence on the media can teach aggressive attitudes and behaviors, and can desensitize feelings ("Media Violence" 78). It is now a matter of responsibility for all parties involved. Parents need to monitor their children's consumption of media, and video-game manufacturers and television networks need to reduce the amount of violence they display.

Media have become a central force in children's lives. Educator Donald J. Graff points out that children now average 35 hours per week watching television and playing video games (21). A majority of that time is spent watching cartoons, and cartoons can sometimes be more violent than cop shows on prime-time television. Studies have shown that prime-time action shows stage three to five violent acts per hour, whereas violence in Saturday morning children's programming ranges between 20 and 25 violent acts per hour (Graff 22). According to psychologist Richard Lieberman of Cornell University, we're seeing an especially high-risk population for lethal violence in the 10- to 14-year age group because developmentally their concept of death is still magical. Children think of death as temporary ("Death Doesn't Count" 33). For instance, in the cartoon *South Park,* there's a character named Kenny who gets killed in every episode but always reappears in the next episode. Although *South Park* is an adult cartoon, some parents allow their children to watch it, mainly because it is a cartoon.

Video games are another major contributor to media violence, and kids are spending more and more time playing them. Over the years, video-game action has become much more graphic and grizzly. For example, in the game called *Doom,* the players wander through corridors blasting the guts out of their enemies. What effects do these games have on children when day after day they sit in front of the screens pretending to shoot and kill? Arguably some may lose touch with reality, maybe even lose respect for life. Because video games are not yet rated by the Federal Communications Commission, parents don't realize that video games such as *Doom* are not meant for children.

Unfortunately, violent entertainment survives on television because the audience has been conditioned to expect the harsher realities. The kind of show that contains both of these components—entertainment and violence—is the news. The ratings soar with live coverage of such events as a car chase down a freeway and a man shooting his brains out. It is scary the way the media cover tragedies like the massacre at Columbine High School, where two kids kill their classmates and themselves. Surely the nonstop pictures and commentary sometimes give desperate and troubled kids ideas about ways to get attention on network news. It is time for the news media to take some responsibility for what to show and to whom.

Violence in the media has become a public-health issue that affects us all. Parents should stop using video games and cartoons as babysitters, and Americans should be a little less hung up on nudity in the media and a little more worried about the violence their children are absorbing. The media and video producers need to exercise concern and restraint. If all parties were to show responsibility, legislation would be unnecessary.

Works Cited
"Media Violence." *Pediatrics* 1 June 1995: 78–79.
"Death Doesn't Count." *Newsweek* 21 Feb. 1999: 33.
Graff, Donald J. "Violence in the Media." *Business First* 28 Apr. 1997: 22.

Exercise 9	**DISCUSSION AND CRITICAL THINKING**

1. Draw a line around Sergio's proposition.

2. Underline the topic sentences, which are also the support for Sergio's contention that violence in the media represents a threat to society.

3. On what does the success of Sergio's proposition depend?

4. What kinds of evidence does Sergio present to support her argument?

5. How would you argue against her view?

6. Professional wrestling and certain talk shows also present aggression and staged violence. Would you include those as other examples of media violence? Suggest additional examples.

Practicing Patterns of Argument

The formal pattern of argument is not always followed in a set sequence, but the main components—the proposition and the support—are always included. You should also consider whether to qualify your proposition and whether to include a refutation.

| Exercise 10 | **COMPLETING PATTERNS OF ARGUMENT** |

Fill in the blanks with supporting statements for each proposition. Each outline uses this pattern:

Proposition
  I. Support
  II. Support
  III. Support

1. Proposition: School uniforms should be required at Kennedy Elementary School.

   I. Buying only uniforms would save parents money.

   II. _____

   III. _____

   IV. _____

2. Proposition: School uniforms should not be required at Kennedy Elementary School.

   I. No conclusive evidence supports the benefits of requiring uniforms.

   II. _____

   III. _____

✎ Topics for Writing Argument

"The New Prohibitionism"

1. Write a two-part response in which you first summarize Krauthammer's article and then react to his ideas by agreeing or disagreeing with him point by point. Label the two parts as summary and reaction. (See page 8 for form.)

2. If the use of alcohol or tobacco has troubled your life, write an argument in which you agree or disagree with Krauthammer and relate your views to your knowledge and experience.

3. The tobacco industry has been restricted in its advertising, required to pay compensation for smoking-related illnesses and deaths, and heavily taxed. It has also been subjected to an antismoking public-relations campaign designed to influence young people not to smoke. Some of the legislation has been national. What measures should be taken against the alcohol industry? Write your views as argument.

4. If you disagree with Krauthammer about the effects of secondhand smoke, research the issue on the World Wide Web and in the library, and write an argument.

5. If you somehow had the power to remove either alcohol or tobacco from the world, which one would you remove? Use three or more points in your argument.

"The First Step in Improving Sex Education: Remove the Hellfire"

6. In a paragraph or an essay, argue that Hechinger's ideas are sound or unsound.

7. Choose one of his points, such as the "hellfire" (morality) issue, and argue that it is significant or not significant.

8. In relation to Hechinger's proposal, write about the sex education program in the high school you attended and argue that it was adequate or inadequate.

9. Consider the statement by the North Carolina teacher, "Students have a lot of personal knowledge about sex—most of which is inaccurate," and argue that it is true or not true by relating it to whatever information you have or can acquire.

10. Argue that significant progress in sex education cannot be made because of obstacles Hechinger mentions: poorly informed teachers, not enough time, and student attitudes. You may want to take another view.

"Of Headless Mice . . . and Men"

11. Write a two-part response in which you first summarize Krauthammer's article and then react to his ideas by agreeing or disagreeing with him point by point. Label the two parts as summary and reaction. (See page 83 for form.)

12. Krauthammer is morally outraged about the possible cloning of headless human beings for replacement of body parts. Yet some others believe that since these beings would not, and could not, have their own consciousness, the issue should not be moral. Write an argument in which you explain your position on the topic in relation to your value system.

13. Krauthammer also questions the motives of those who would practice the "normal" cloning of human beings (with heads). He says it "is less a treatment of infertility than a treatment for vanity." In a short argument, agree or disagree with that view.

14. Search library periodicals or the World Wide Web for other articles on human cloning. Incorporate ideas you find in those sources to show that human cloning can have several purposes—such as dealing with infertility, satisfying vanity through transplants, saving lives through transplants, creating genetically superior human beings—and argue that the whole issue should be approached with caution but not dismissed as the creation of Frankenstein monsters.

"My Life to Live—or Not"

15. Write an argument in which you agree or disagree with DeSarro. Incorporate your own value system, religious or secular, into your discussion.

16. Use the World Wide Web or the library to research a state law that permits doctors to assist in suicides under certain conditions (Oregon's is one good example). Discuss how well the law has worked and whether it should be enacted as a national law or a law in other states.

"Teaching Our Kids to Shoot 'Em Up"

17. Use your own examples of the behavior of children and television programming to either support or attack Sergio's views. Include your own experiences if they are relevant.

18. Research this issue on the World Wide Web or in the library and use the evidence you find to either support or disagree with Sergio.

19. If you were to take one step beyond Sergio and suggest legislation to control the effects of media violence, what would the provisions be?

20. Argue that professional wrestling and talk shows do much to promote the idea of using violent means to solve human problems. Use specific examples.

Career-Related Topics

21. Write an essay of argument to convince people that workers at a particular company should or should not be laid off.

22. Write an essay of argument to convince people that workers in a particular service industry should or should not go on strike.

General Topics

The following are broad subject areas; you will have to limit your focus for an essay of argument. You may modify the topics to fit specific situations.

23. Sexual harassment

24. Juvenile justice

25. Endangered species legislation

26. Advertising tobacco

27. Homelessness

28. State-run lotteries

29. Jury reform

30. Legalizing prostitution

31. Censoring rap or rock music

32. Cost of illegal immigration

33. Installation of local traffic signs

34. Foot patrols by local police

35. Change in (your) college registration procedure

36. Local rapid transit

37. Surveillance by video (on campus, in neighborhoods, or in shopping areas)

38. Zone changes for stores selling liquor

39. Curfew for teenagers

40. Laws keeping known gang members out of parks

Writer's Guidelines: Argument

1. Ask yourself the following questions. Then consider which parts of the formal argument you should include in your paragraph or essay.

   - *Background:* What is the historical or social context for this controversial issue?

   - *Proposition* (the thesis of the essay): What do I want my audience to believe or do?

- *Qualification of proposition:* Can I limit my proposition so that those who disagree cannot easily challenge me with exceptions?

- *Refutation* (taking the opposing view into account, mainly to point out its fundamental weakness): What is the view on the other side, and why is it flawed in reasoning or evidence?

- *Support:* In addition to sound reasoning, can I use appropriate facts, examples, statistics, and opinions of authorities?

2. The basic pattern of a paragraph or an essay of argument is likely to be in this form:

Proposition (the thesis of the essay)

 I. Support 1
 II. Support 2
 III. Support 3

18

The Research Paper

"Think of your next piece of writing as a lifeless but strangely viable monster sprawled on a lab table—and you're Dr. Frankenstein."

J. N. Williamson

THE QUIGMANS   by Buddy Hickerson

"So I take it you haven't seen much action around here since the whole Internet thing?"

B. Hickerson, copyright 1997. Los Angeles Times Syndicate. Reprinted by permission.

The Library

The main parts of the library pertaining to the research paper are the book collection and the periodical collection. Books are arranged on shelves by subject according to the Library of Congress system or the Dewey Decimal system. Periodicals, including newspapers, are stored in a variety of ways: in unbound form (very recent editions), in bound form, on microfilm, or in online computer systems.

Books

Today most academic and municipal libraries provide information about books on online computer terminals, with data banks accessible by author, title, subject, or other key words. Usually a printout of sources is available. Selecting key words and their synonyms is crucial to effective use of these online terminals. A combination of words will help you focus your search. In the following sample printout on the topic *animal?* and *conservation,* the user has keyed in the topic and then clicked to the title to check for location and availability:

```
BOOK - Record 1 of 20 Entries Found                        Brief View
-----------------------------------------------------------------------
Title:        The atlas of endangered species
Published:    New York : Macmillan : Toronto : Maxwell Macmillan
                 Canada, 1991.
Subjects:     Endangered species.
              Endangered plants.
              Nature conservation.
              Rare animals.
              Rare plants.
              Wildlife conservation.
              Enviromental protection.
--------------------------------------------- + Page 1 of 2 -----------
Search Request: K-ANIMAL? AND CONSERVATION    MS<ENTER>-Book catalog
BOOK - Record 1 of 20 Entries Found                        Brief View
-----------------------------------------------------------------------
Title:        The atlas of endangered species
-----------------------------------------------------------------------
LOCATION:              CALL NUMBER:           STATUS:
REFERENCE SHELVES      333.9516 At65          Not checked out
(Non-Circulating)
```

Printed Material Other Than Books

For the typical college research paper, the main printed nonbook sources are periodicals, such as newspapers, magazines, and journals. Various indexes will provide you with information for finding the source material you need. Depending on the library and the publication, periodicals are listed in indexes printed on paper or in electronic form. The most common index in bound volumes is the *Readers' Guide to Periodical Literature* (now also computerized). It indexes more than 200 popular magazines such as *Time* and *Newsweek,* which means that it is useful for basic research but not for more scholarly studies. The *New York Times* and numerous other metropolitan newspapers are also covered by indexes. For more academic searches, check with a reference librarian for indexes in specific fields such as anthropology or art. Indexes are usually kept in one area of the reference section. The following figure shows three sample entries from the *Readers' Guide.*

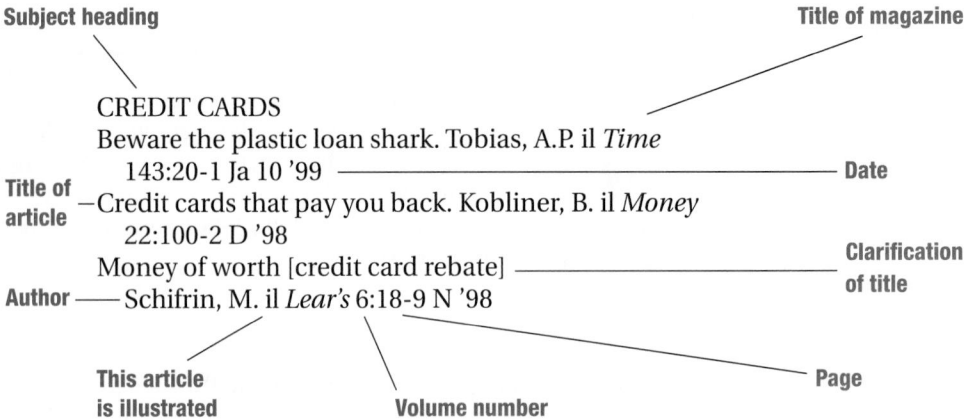

Subject heading

Title of magazine

CREDIT CARDS
Beware the plastic loan shark. Tobias, A.P. il *Time*
143:20-1 Ja 10 '99 —————————————————— Date

Title of article — Credit cards that pay you back. Kobliner, B. il *Money*
22:100-2 D '98

Money of worth [credit card rebate] ——————————— Clarification of title
Author —— Schifrin, M. il *Lear's* 6:18-9 N '98

This article is illustrated

Volume number

Page

Computerized Indexes and Other Online Services

Computerized indexes, such as *InfoTrac, Periodical Abstracts,* and *Newspaper Abstracts Ondisc,* can be accessed in basically the same way as the online book catalogs, using key words and word combinations. They provide source information, perhaps with printouts. Some indexes include short abstracts (brief summaries) of the individual entries. Some indexes even provide the full text of material. One such index is *NEXIS,* an online service that can help you find sources and then provide the text of the original source material, all of which can be printed out.

An online essay originally published in, say, *Time* magazine, usually will be published without illustrations and in a different format. Therefore, it is important that you give full bibliographical information about your particular source (source citation instructions appear later in this chapter).

Government publications, pamphlets, and other materials are cataloged in several ways. Procedures for searching all electronic indexes and sources routinely are posted alongside terminals, and librarians are available for further explanations and demonstrations. Many libraries also have pamphlets listing the periodicals they carry, their arrangements with other libraries for sharing or borrowing materials, access to the Internet, databases stored on CD-ROMs, and various online services.

Steps to Writing a Research Paper

The *research paper* is a long documented essay based on a thorough examination of your topic and supported by your explanations and by both references to and quotations from your sources. The traditional research paper in the style of the Modern Language Association, typically called MLA style, includes a title page (often omitted), a thesis and outline, a documented essay (text), and a list of sources (called "Works Cited," referring to the works used specifically in the essay).

This section will introduce you to eight steps for writing a research paper. Don't be apprehensive; if you can write an effective essay, you can write an effective research paper. Just pick a feasible topic and don't get behind schedule (the two main problems for students working on research papers). The form for documentation follows in the next section of this chapter.

Although specific aims and methods may vary from one research activity to another, most nonexperimental, objective research tasks depend on eight basic steps. See the following explanation and then review the same student work for illustration. Excerpts from a student final draft follow this discussion.

1. Select your topic, and make a scratch outline.

As soon as possible construct a thesis as you did for writing essays by choosing what you intend to write about (subject) and then by deciding how you will limit or focus your subject (treatment).

- Your topic should interest you and be appropriate in subject and scope for your assignment.

- Your topic should be researchable and covered in library and other relevant sources, such as the Internet. Avoid topics that are too subjective or are so new that good source material is not available.

To write a treatment for your subject, you may need to scan a general discussion of your topic area so you can consider it in perspective and begin to see the parts or aspects on which you will want to concentrate. Relevant sections of encyclopedias and comprehensive books, such as textbooks, are often useful in establishing the initial overview. At this point, the closer you can come to a well-defined topic with a functional scratch outline of its divisions, the more likely you are to make a smooth, rapid, effective journey through the process.

Student Examples

Tentative thesis: Despite some valid criticism, <u>the zoo as an institution</u>
subject

<u>will probably survive because of its roles in entertainment, education, and</u>
treatment

<u>conservation.</u>

- I. Entertainment
  - A. Money
  - B. Problems
- II. Conservation
  - A. Science
  - B. Breeding
- III. Education
  - A. General public
  - B. Students
- IV. Criticism
  - A. Pro
  - B. Con
- V. Zoos of future
  - A. Education
  - B. Conservation

2. Find sources for your investigation.

With your topic and its divisions in mind, use the resources and the electronic databases available in your college library to identify books, articles, and other materials pertaining to your topic. The list of these items, called the *bibliography*, should be prepared on cards in the form appropriate for your assignment (MLA in this text). Seek different kinds of materials (books, periodicals, newspapers, electronic databases), different types of source information (primary, meaning coming from direct study, participation, observation, involvement; and secondary, meaning coming from indirect means—usually reporting on what others have done, observed, or been involved in), and credible writers (authorities and relatively unbiased, reliable reporters on your topic).

Student Examples

Periodical

Diamond, Fared. "Playing God at the Zoo." <u>Discover</u> Mar. 1995: 79–85.

Book

Douglas-Hamilton, Ian. <u>Battle for the Elephants</u>. New York: Viking, 1992.

3. Take notes.

Resist the temptation to write down everything that interests you. Instead, take notes that pertain to divisions of your topic as stated in your thesis or scratch outline. Locate, read, and take notes on the sources listed in the preliminary bibliography. Some of these sources need to be printed out from electronic databases, some photocopied, and some checked out. Your notes will usually be on cards, with each card indicating key pieces of information:

A. Division of topic (usually the Roman numeral part of your scratch outline or divisions of your thesis)

B. Identification of topic (by author's last name or title of piece)

C. Location of material (usually by page number)

D. Text of statement as originally worded (with quotation marks; editorial comments in brackets), summarized or paraphrased (in student's own words, without quotation marks), and statement of relevance of material, if possible

Student Example

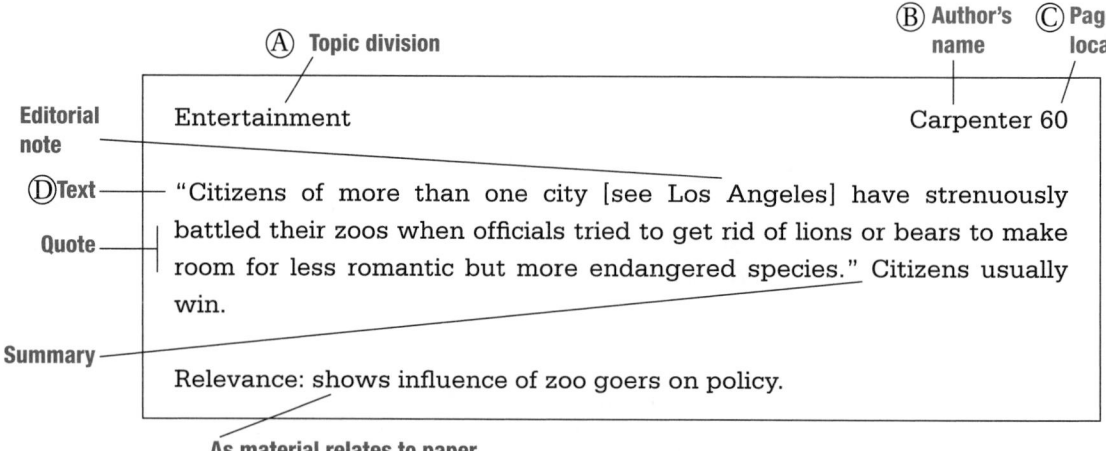

4. Refine your thesis statement and outline to reflect more precisely what you intend to write.

Student Example

Thesis: Throughout the world, despite determined opposition, the modern zoo with a new image and compound purpose is taking shape.

I. Zoos as entertainment

    A. Attendance

    B. Income

    C. Customer preferences

II. Captive breeding success

    A. National

        1. Bison

        2. California condor

    B. International

        1. Arabian oryx

        2. White rhino

        3. Komodo dragon

III. Scientific success

    A. Embryo transfers

    B. Artificial insemination

    C. Test-tube fertilization

    D. Storage of eggs, sperm, and tissue

    E. Computer projects

        1. Lab studies

        2. Animal tracking

IV. Education

    A. Purpose—change attitude

    B. Basic idea—show animals in ecosystem

    C. School applications

V. Different models of zoos

    A. Zoo/park

    B. Safari zoo

    C. Regional zoo

5. Referring to your thesis, outline, and note cards keyed to your outline, write the first draft of your research paper.

6. Evaluate your first draft, and amend it as needed (perhaps researching an area not well-covered for additional support material and adding or deleting sections of your outline to reflect the way your paper has grown).

Use the writing process guidelines as you would in writing any other essay:

- Write and then revise your assignment as many times as necessary for coherence, language (usage, tone, and diction), unity, emphasis, support, and sentences (CLUESS).

- Correct problems in fundamentals such as capitalization, omissions, punctuation, and spelling (COPS). Before writing the final draft, read your paper aloud to discover any errors or awkwardnesses of expression.

Use the guidelines in the next section of this chapter (pp. 355–362) to include proper research paper form in documentation.

7. Using the same form as on the preliminary bibliography, prepare a "Works Cited" section (a list of works you have referred to or quoted and identified by parenthetical markers in the text).

8. Write your final research paper (and submit it with any preliminary material required by your instructor).

The final draft will probably include these parts:

A. Title page (often omitted)

B. Thesis and outline (topical or sentence, as directed)

C. Documented text

D. List of sources used

Student Example

• Title page

Zoos—An Endangered Species?
Michael Chung
Professor Lee Brandon
English 1A
9 January 2000

• Thesis and outline (previously given)

• Excerpt from the documented text (from pages 7–8)

In a spectacular captive breeding success in 1992, the National Zoo in Washington, D.C., may have saved the endangered Komodo dragon from extinction by successfully incubating thirty eggs. This ten-foot dangerous, ugly creature that resembles a dinosaur numbers only somewhere around 5,000–8,000 in the wild but soon will be represented in numerous zoos (Browne C1). Now that the incubation process is established, the entire program offers opportunity to restock the Komodo's habitat in Indonesia.

Not all captive breeding projects can end with a reintroduction of the species to the wild. For those species, the zoos have turned to science, which has been used in a variety of ways. In "Preserving the Genetic Legacies," Karen F. Schmidt says:

> Zoos are increasingly adapting the latest in human and agricultural reproductive technologies to aid beleaguered species by boosting their numbers, increasing gene variety in small populations and controlling inbreeding. . . . Although still in the early stages, embryo transfers, artificial insemination and even test-tube fertilization are seen by zoologists as having real or potential application in conserving endangered wildlife. (60)

These scientific endeavors began in the 1970s and now some of them are commonplace. Female apes are on the pill and surrogate mother tigers are receiving embryos. Schmidt reports that the Cincinnati Zoo Center for Reproduction of Endangered Wildlife has frozen "eggs from a rare female Sumatran rhino that died, hoping one day to obtain some sperm and learn how to make test-tube rhino embryos" (60). In many zoos, eggs, sperm, and skin for DNA storage have been frozen in zoo labs, awaiting scientific development by future generations.

Margin annotations:

(Statistics)
Paraphrased material
Citation

Quotation introduced with title and author's name
Block-indented quotation, no quotation marks

Words omitted (ellipses)

Citation after period for long quotation

Reference introduced with author's name
Blended paraphrase and quotation
Citation after quotation marks for short quotation

• List of sources used

Works Cited [partial]

Newspaper Browne, Malcolm W. "They're Back! Komodos Avoid Extinction." <u>New York Times</u> 1 Mar. 1994: C1, C4.

Book Douglas-Hamilton, Ian. <u>Battle for the Elephants</u>. New York: Viking, 1992.

Magazine "Not Endangered." <u>The Economist</u> 13 Apr. 1991: 55–56.

Web site "Project Technology." <u>The Malaysian Elephant Satellite Tracking Project</u>. 27 Apr. 1997 <http://www.si.edu/elephant/eleintro.htm>.

Internet Rainey, James. "Dogfight at the Zoo." <u>Los Angeles Times</u> 30 Jan. 1994. 29 Apr. 1997 <http://www.latimes.com/cgi-bin 1994>.

Magazine Schmidt, Karen F. "Preserving the Genetic Legacies." <u>U.S. News & World Report</u> 24 Aug. 1992: 60.

Magazine Tarpy, Cliff. "New Zoos." <u>National Geographic</u> July 1993: 6–37.

Magazine Tudge, Colin. "Captive Audiences for Future Conservation." <u>New Scientist</u> 28 Jan. 1995: 51.

Second piece by same author—book ——<u>Last Animals at the Zoo: How Mass Extinction Can Be Stopped</u>. London: Hutchinson Radius, 1999.

Bibliography and Works Cited, MLA Style

You will list source material in two phases of your research paper project: the preliminary bibliography and the works cited.

When you begin your research, make a list of works that may provide useful information on your topic. At this time, do not stop to make a careful examination and evaluation of each entry, although you should keep in mind that your material usually should come from a variety of sources and that they ideally should be objective, authoritative, and current. For various reasons, some items may not find their way into your research paper at all. As you read them, you may discover that some are superficial, poorly researched, overly technical, off the topic, or unavailable. The preliminary bibliography is nothing more than a list of sources to consider and select from.

The sources that are actually used in the paper—meaning those referred to by name or quoted—become part of the Works Cited list at the end of the final draft.

The MLA research paper form is commonly used for both the preliminary bibliography and the list of works cited. This format is unlike the formats used in catalogs and indexes. The following examples show the difference between printout forms from library files and the MLA research paper forms.

In using Internet material, consider that some of the material is a copy of well-edited, carefully selected text and that some is published by those who happen to have a server, a bit of computer expertise, and a desire to publish. Some of those writers and others may be biased, illogical, and foolish. As you research and develop your topic, you should evaluate all content, with special concern for anonymous Internet material. Note the difference between printout forms from library files and the MLA research paper forms.

Books

Printout Form

```
Author:      DiSilvestro, Roger L.
Title:       The African elephant: twilight in Eden
Published:   New York: Wiley, ©1991.
```

MLA Research Paper Form

Titles of longer works are either underlined or italicized; be consistent.

> DiSilvestro, Roger L. <u>The African Elephant: Twilight in Eden</u>.
> New York: Wiley, 1991.

Periodicals

Printout Form

Author:	Ormrod, Stefan A.
Title:	Boo for zoos.
Source:	New Scientist v. 145 (Mar. 18 '95) p. 48

MLA Research Paper Form

> Ormrod, Stefan A. "Boo for Zoos." <u>New Scientist</u> 18 Mar. 1995: 48.

Form for Printed Sources

Books

A Book by One Author
> Adeler, Thomas L. <u>In a New York Minute</u>. New York: Harper, 1990.

An Anthology
List the name of the editor, followed by a comma, a space, and "ed."
> Grumet, Robert S., ed. <u>Northeastern Indian Lives</u>. Amherst: U
> of Massachusetts P, 1996.

Two or More Books by the Same Author
> Walker, Alice. <u>The Color Purple: A Novel</u>. New York: Harcourt,
> 1982.
> ———. <u>Meridian</u>. New York: Harcourt, 1976.

A Book by Two or More Authors
> Current, Richard Nelson, Marcia Ewing Current, and Louis
> Fuller. <u>Goddess of Light</u>. Boston: Northeastern UP, 1997.

Use *et al.* for four or more authors.
> Danziger, James N., et al. <u>Computers and Politics: High
> Technology in American Local Governments</u>. New York:
> Columbia UP, 1982.

A Book with a Corporate Author
> Detroit Commission on the Renaissance. <u>Toward the Future</u>.
> Detroit: Wolverine, 1989.

Articles

Article in a Journal
> Butterick, George. "Charles Olson's 'The Kingfishers' and the
> Poetics of Change." <u>American Poetry</u> 6.2 (1989): 28–59.

Article in a Weekly or Biweekly Magazine, Author Unknown
> "How the Missiles Help California." <u>Time</u> 1 Apr. 1996: 45.

Article in a Monthly or Bimonthly Magazine
```
Fallows, James. "Why Americans Hate the Media." Atlantic
     Monthly Feb. 1996: 45-64.
```

Newspaper Article
```
Gregory, Tina. "When All Else Fails." Philadelphia Inquirer 2
     Apr. 1990: C12.
```

Editorial
```
Lewis, Anthony. "Black and White." Editorial. New York Times
     18 June 1992, natl. ed.: A19.
```

A Work in an Anthology

```
Booth, Wayne C. "The Scholar in Society." Introduction to
     Scholarship in Modern Languages and Literatures. Ed.
     Joseph Gibaldi. New York: MLA, 1981. 116-143.
```

An Article in an Encyclopedia

```
Cheney, Ralph Holt. "Coffee." Collier's Encyclopedia. 1993 ed.
```

Government Publications

```
United States. Dept. of Transportation. National Highway
     Traffic Safety Admin. Driver Licensing Laws Annotated
     1980. Washington: GPO, 1980.
```

Citations from the *Congressional Record* require only a date and page number.
```
Cong. Rec. 11 Sept. 1992: 12019-24.
```

Published Proceedings of a Conference

```
Proceedings of the 34th Annual International Technical
     Communication Conference. Denver, 10-13 May 1987. San
     Diego: Univelt, 1987.
```

Treat particular presentations in the proceedings as you would pieces in a collection.
```
Wise, Mary R. "The Main Event Is Desktop Publishing."
     Proceedings of the 34th International Technical
     Communication Conference. Denver, 10-13 May 1987. San
     Diego: Univelt, 1987.
```

A Lecture, Speech, or Address

```
Kern, David. "Recent Trends in Occupational Medicine."
     Memorial Hospital, Pawtucket, RI. 2 Oct. 1997.
```

A Personal Interview

```
Thomas, Carolyn. Personal interview. 5 Jan. 2000.
```

Form for Electronic Sources

Formats vary widely in electronic media because of rapidly changing systems and terms. The information you provide in your bibliography and works cited will inform your reader about such matters as the subject of each source, who has worked on it, where it came from originally, when it was first written and last changed, when you found it, where you found it, and how you found it. Be sure that you give enough information. If you cannot find directions for citing a source, you should identify a form used for similar content as a model, improvise if necessary, and be as consistent as possible.

Do not be intimidated by the length and seeming complexity of the citations. Every part is reasonable and every part is necessary. If you are not certain whether to include some information, you probably should. As you present your orderly sequence of parts in your entries, you must take great care in attending to detail, for a single keystroke can leave your source concealed in cyberspace with no electronic map for your reader.

The examples in this section are based on guidelines authorized by MLA. More details can be found at <www.mla.org>. Because the nature of electronic sources and references to them are constantly evolving, check that Web site for changes and updates.

This is the basic form for Internet and World Wide Web sources for your bibliography and works-cited entries:

- Author's last name, first name, middle initial (or editor, compiler, or translator)
- "Title of article or other short work" or *Title of Book*
- Publication date or date of last revision for any printed version
- Subject of forum or discussion group
- Indication of online posting or Web page
- Title of electronic journal
- Editor's name (if available)
- Page numbers or the numbers of paragraphs or sections
- Name of institution or organization sponsoring or affiliated with Web site
- Date of access to the source
- <electronic address or URL>

Online Services—Library and Personal

Library Subscription Services (Database with full texts)
Online library subscription services provide databases mainly of articles in journals, magazines, and newspapers. They are accessed either at a library terminal or by the student's computer. They often include hundreds of publications and enable students to find and print out entire texts rapidly. Although most have complete printed versions, the illustrations are usually omitted, page numbers are changed or not given, and some material may be reformatted. For brief documented papers, instructors sometimes ask their students to include copies of the printouts with the final submission. Content ranges from works intended for the general reader to those written for scholarly purposes. Some are listed as "juried," which means that the selections have been evaluated for credible content by a group of experts in the field. Library online services include ProQuest Direct, Lexis-Nexis, and EBSCOhost.

The basic form is author, title, publication information, service company, library, and date of access. Include the URL of the service in angle brackets if it is available.

Fox, Justin. "What in the World Happened to Economics?" <u>Fortune</u>
15 Mar. 1999: 90–102. <u>ABI/INFORM Global</u>. ProQuest
Direct. Regional Community Coll. Lib., Little Rock. 2
Mar. 1999 <http://www.umi.com/proquest/>.

Rivenburg, Roy. "The Mean Season." <u>Los Angeles Times</u> 14 July
1995: E-1. NewsBank InfoWeb. Mt. San Antonio Coll. Lib.,
Walnut, CA. 8 Sept. 1999.

*Personal Subscription Services (databases with full texts supplied by companies such
as AOL)*

Typically indicate author, title, publication information (if any), name of service,
date of access, and the *Keyword* you used or the *Path* (sequence of topics) you followed in locating the source.

"Cloning." <u>BioTech's Life and Science Dictionary</u>. 30 June 1998.
Indiana U. America Online. 4 July 1998. Path: Research
and Learning; Science; Biology; Biotechnology
Dictionary.

"Tecumseh." <u>Compton's Encyclopedia Online</u>. Vers. 3.0. 1998.
America Online. 8 April 2000. Keyword: Compton's

Professional Site

<u>MLA on the Web</u>. 25 November 1997. Modern Language Association of
America. 25 Mar. 1998 <http://www.mla.org>.

Personal Site

Hawisher, Gail. Home page. University of Illinois Urbana-
Champaign/The Women, Information Technology, and
Scholarship Colloquium. 18 Mar. 1998
<http://www.art.uiuc.edu/wits/members/hawisher.html>.

Book

Conrad, Joseph. <u>Lord Jim</u>. London: Blackwoods, 1900. <u>Oxford Text
Archive</u>. 12 July 1993. Oxford University Computing
Services. 20 Feb. 1998 <ftp://ota.ox.ac.uk/pub/
ota/public/english/conrad/lordjim.1924>.

Dickens, Charles. <u>A Christmas Carol</u>. London 1843. <u>The Electronic
Text Center</u>. Ed. David Seaman. Dec. 1997. U of Virginia
Library. 4 Feb. 1998 (http://etext.lib.virginia.edu/
cgibin/browse-mixed?id=DicChri&tag=public&images=
images/modeng&data=/lvl/Archive/eng-parsed).

Poem

Hampl, Patricia. "Who We Will Love." <u>Woman Before an Aquarium</u>.
Pittsburgh: U of Pittsburgh P, 1978: 27–28. A Poem a
Week. Rice University. 13 Mar. 1998
<http://www.ruf.rice.edu/~alisa/Jun24html>.

Article in a Journal

Bieder, Robert A. "The Representation of Indian Bodies in
Nineteenth-Century American Anthropology." <u>The American
Indian Quarterly</u> 20.2 (1996). 28 Mar. 1998
<http://www/uoknor.edu/aiq/aiq202.html#beider>.

Killiam, Rosemary. "Cognitive Dissonance: Should Twentieth-Century Women Composers Be Grouped with Focault's Mad Criminals?" <u>Music Theory Online</u> 3.2 (1997): 30 pars. 10 May 1997 <http://smt.ucsb.edu/mto/mtohome.html>.

Article in a Magazine

Keillor, Garrison. "Why Did They Ever Ban a Book This Bad?" <u>Salon</u> 13 Oct. 1997. 14 Oct. 1997 <http://www.salon1999.com/feature/>.

Article in an Online Newspaper

"Tornadoes Touch Down in S. Illinois." <u>New York Times on the Web</u> 16 Apr. 1998. 20 May 1998 <http://www.nytimes.com/aponline/a/AP-Illinois-Storms.html>.

Newspaper Editorial

"The Proved and the Unproved." Editorial. <u>New York Times</u> 13 July 1997. 13 July 1997 <http://www.nytimes.com/yr/mo/day/editorial/13sun1.html>.

Review

Koeppel, Fredric. "A Look at John Keats." Rev. of <u>Keats</u>, by Andrew Motion. <u>Nando Times News</u> 16 Apr. 1998. 27 Aug. 1998 <http://www.nando.net/newsroom/ntn/enter/041698/enter30_20804.html>.

Posting to a Discussion List

Merrian, Joanne. "Spinoff: Monsterpiece Theatre." Online posting. 30 Apr. 1994. Shaksper: The Global Electronic Shakespeare Conf. 27 Aug. 1997 <http://www.arts.ubc.ca/english/iemls/shak/MONSTERP_SPINOFF.txt>.
Inman, James. "Re: Technologist." Online posting. 24 Sept. 1997. Alliance for Computers in Writing. 27 Mar. 1998 <acw-1@unicorn.acs.ttu.edu>.

Gopher

Page, Melvin E. "Brief Citation Guide for Internet Sources in History and the Humanities." 20 Feb. 1996. 9 pp. 7 July 1996 <gopher://h-net.msu.edu/00/lists/h-africa/internet-cit>.

Synchronous Communication (MOOs, MUDs)

Inept_Guest. Discussion of disciplinary politics in rhet/comp. 12 Mar. 1998. LinguaMOO. 12 Mar. 1998 <telnet:lingua.utdallas.edu 8888>.

Scholarly Project

<u>Victorian Women Writers Project</u>. Ed. Perry Willett. Apr. 1997. Indiana U. 26 Apr. 1997 <http://www.indiana.edu/~letrs/vwwp/>.

CD-ROM

West, Cornel. "The Dilemma of the Black Intellectual." <u>Critical Quarterly</u> 29 (1987): 39-52. <u>MLA International Bibliography</u>. CD-ROM. Silver Platter. Feb. 1995.

"About <u>Richard III</u>." <u>Cinemania 96</u>. CD-ROM. Redmond: Microsoft, 1996.

Article in Reference Database

"Fresco," <u>Britannica Online</u>. Vers. 97.1.1. Mar. 1997 Encyclopaedia Britannica. 29 Mar. 1997 <http://www.eb.com:180>.

Atwood, Margaret. "Memento Mori-but First. Carpe Diem." Rev. of <u>Toward the End of Time,</u> by John Updike. New York Times Book Review 12 Oct. 1997: 9-10. The New York Times Books on the Web. 1997. The New York Times Company. 13 Oct. 1997 <http://search.nytimes.com/books/97/10/12/reviews/971012.12atwoodt.html>.

Personal E-mail Message

Watkins, Jack. "Collaborative Projects." E-mail to Gabriel Mendoza. 12 April 2000.

Documentation: Parenthetical References, MLA Style

Although you need not acknowledge a source for generally known information such as the dates of the Civil War or the names of the ships that carried Columbus and his followers to the New World, you must identify the exact source and location of each statement, fact, or original idea you borrow from another person or work.

In the text of the research paper, MLA requires only a brief parenthetical source reference keyed to a complete bibliographical entry in the list of works cited at the end of the essay. For most parenthetical references, you will need to cite only the author's last name and the number of the page from which the statement or idea was taken, and, if you mention the author's name in the text, the page number alone is sufficient. This format also allows you to include within the parentheses additional information, such as title or volume number, if it is needed for clarity. Documentation for some of the most common types of sources is discussed in the following sections.

References to Articles and Single-Volume Books

Articles and single-volume books are the two types of works you will be referring to most often in your research paper. When citing them, either mention the author's name in the text and note the appropriate page number in parentheses immediately after the citation or acknowledge both name and page number in the parenthetical reference, leaving a space between the two. If punctuation is needed, insert the mark outside the final parenthesis.

- *Author's Name Cited in Text*

> Marya Mannes has defined euthanasia as "the chosen alternative to the prolongation of a steadily waning mind and spirit by machines that will withhold death or to an existence that mocks life" (61).

- *Author's Name Cited in Parentheses*

> Euthanasia has been defined as "the chosen alternative to the prolongation of a steadily waning mind and spirit by machines that will withhold death or to an existence that mocks life" (Mannes 61).

- *Corresponding Bibliographic Entry*

> Mannes, Marya. <u>Last Rights</u>. New York: Morrow, 1973.

References to Works in an Anthology

When referring to a work in an anthology, either cite in the text the author's name and indicate in parentheses the page number in the anthology where the source is located, or acknowledge both name and page reference parenthetically.

- *Author's Name Cited in Text*

> One of the most widely recognized facts about James Joyce, in Lionel Trilling's view, "is his ambivalence toward Ireland, of which the hatred was as relentless as the love was unfailing" (153).

- *Author's Name Cited in Parentheses*

> This ten-foot dangerous, ugly creature that resembles a dinosaur numbers only somewhere around 5,000-8,000 in the wild but soon will be represented in numerous zoos (Browne C1).

- *Corresponding Bibliography Entry*

> Browne, Malcolm W. "They're Back! Komodos Avoid Extinction." <u>New York Times</u> 1 Mar. 1994: C1, C4.

References to Works of Unknown Authorship

If you borrow information or ideas from an article or book for which you cannot determine the name of the author, cite the title instead, either in the text of the paper or in parentheses, and include the page reference as well.

- *Title Cited in the Text*

> According to an article titled "Going Back to Booze," surveys have shown that most adult alcoholics began drinking heavily as teenagers (42).

- *Title Cited in Parentheses*

> Surveys have shown that most adult alcoholics began drinking heavily as teenagers ("Going Back to Booze" 42).

- *Corresponding Bibliographic Entry*

> "Going Back to Booze." <u>Time</u> 31 Nov. 1999: 41-46.

References to Internet Material

Treat them as you would other material. If the author's name is not available, give the title. Include page and paragraph numbers if they are available; usually they are not.

References in Block Quotations

Quotations longer than four typewritten lines are indented ten spaces or half inch without quotation marks, and their references are put outside end punctuation.

- *Reference Cited after End Punctuation*

      Implicit in the concept of Strange Loops is the
      concept of infinity, since what else is a loop but a way
      of representing an endless process in a finite way? And
      infinity plays a large role in many of Escher's drawings.
      Copies of one single theme often fit into each other,
      forming visual analogues to the canons of Bach.
      (Hofstadter 15)

- *Corresponding Bibliographic Entry*

      Hofstadter, Douglas. <u>Gödel, Escher, Bach: An Eternal
      Golden Braid</u>. New York: Vintage, 1980.

Plagiarism

Careful attention to the rules of documentation will help you avoid *plagiarism:* the unacknowledged use of someone else's words or ideas. It occurs when a writer omits quotation marks when citing the exact language of a source, fails to revise completely a paraphrased source, or gives no documentation for a quotation or paraphrase. The best way to avoid this problem is to be attentive to the following details.

When you copy a quotation directly into your notes, check to be sure that you have put quotation marks around it. If you forget to include them when you copy, you might omit them in the paper as well.

When you paraphrase, keep in mind that it is not sufficient to change just a few words or rearrange sentence structure. You must completely rewrite the passage. One of the best ways to accomplish this is to read the material you want to paraphrase; then cover the page so that you cannot see it and write down the information as you remember it. Compare your version with the original and make any necessary changes in the note. If you cannot successfully rewrite the passage, quote it instead.

The difference between legitimate and unacceptable paraphrases can be seen in the following examples:

- Source

      "What is unmistakably convincing and makes Miller's
      theatre writing hold is its authenticity in respect to the
      minutiae of American life. He is a first-rate reporter; he
      makes the details of his observation palpable."

- Unacceptable paraphrase

      What is truly convincing and makes Arthur Miller's
      theatrical writing effective is its authenticity. He is
      an excellent reporter and makes his observation palpable.

- Legitimate paraphrase

      The strength of Arthur Miller's dramatic art lies in
      its faithfulness to the details of the American scene and
      in its power to bring to life the reality of ordinary
      experience.

Harold Clurman's introduction to *The Portable Arthur Miller*

The differences between these two versions of Clurman's statement are enormous. The first writer has made some token changes, substituting a few synonyms (*truly* for *unmistakably, excellent* for *first-rate*), deleting part of the first sentence, and combining the two parts of the second sentence into a single clause. Otherwise, this is a word-for-word copy of the original, and if the note were copied into the paper in this form, the writer would be guilty of plagiarism. The second writer has changed the vocabulary of the original passage and completely restructured the sentence so that the only similarity between the note and the source is the ideas.

Check to see that each of your research notes has the correct name and page number so that when you use information from that note in your paper, you will be able to credit it to the right source.

Writer's Guidelines: The Research Paper

1. The research paper is a long documented essay based on a thorough examination of a topic and supported by explanations and by both references to and quotations from sources.

2. The research paper is no more difficult than other writing assignments if you select a good topic, use a systematic approach, and do not get behind with your work.

3. A systematic approach involves selecting a topic and making a scratch outline, developing a preliminary bibliography, taking notes keyed to divisions of your topic, creating a detailed outline based on your notes and insights, writing a rough draft with ideas supported by source material, revising the draft as many times as necessary, editing the paper, making a list of the works cited, and writing the final draft.

4. Your library almost certainly mixes traditional and electronic indexes and sources; you should become familiar with them.

5. The MLA forms for works cited are different from those in indexes such as *The Readers' Guide to Periodical Literature.*

6. You can avoid plagiarism by giving credit when you borrow someone else's words or ideas.

Handbook
Writing Effective Sentences

"I have rewritten—often several times—every word I have ever published. My pencils outlast their erasers."

Vladimir Nabokov

© Gary Larson, courtesy Chronicle Features

Subjects and Verbs

T he two most important parts of any sentence are the subject and the verb. The **subject** is who or what causes the action or expresses a state of being. The **verb** indicates what the subject is doing or is being. Many times the subject and verb taken together carry the meaning of the sentence. Consider this example:

The <u>woman</u> <u>left</u> for work.
subject   verb

The subject *woman* and the verb *left* indicate the basic content of the sentence while providing structure.

Subjects

The simple subject of a sentence is usually a single noun or pronoun.

The judge's <u>reputation</u> for order in the courtroom is well known.
simple subject

The complete subject is the simple subject with all its modifiers—that is, with all the words that describe or qualify it.

<u>The judge's reputation for order in the courtroom</u> is well known.
complete subject

To more easily understand and identify simple subjects of sentences, you may want to review the following information about nouns and pronouns. (See Appendix A, p. 474, for more information about all eight parts of speech.)

Nouns

Nouns are naming words. Nouns may name persons, animals, plants, places, things, substances, qualities, or ideas—for example, *Bart, armadillo, Mayberry, tree, rock, cloud, love, ghost, music, virtue.*

Pronouns

A pronoun is a word that is used in place of a noun.

- Pronouns that can be used as subjects of sentences may represent specific persons or things and are called personal pronouns:

I	*we*
you	*you*
he, she, it	*they*

  Example: <u>They</u> recommended my sister for the coaching position.
  subject

- Indefinite pronouns refer to nouns (persons, place, things) in a general way:

each	*everyone*	*nobody*	*somebody*

  Example: <u>Everyone</u> wants a copy of that paragraph.
  subject

- Other pronouns point out particular things:

Singular: *this, that*   Plural: *these, those*

This is my treasure.	*These* are my jewels.
That is your junk.	*Those* are your trinkets.

- Still other pronouns introduce questions:

Which is the best CD player?
What are the main ingredients in a Twinkie?
Who understands this computer command?

Caution: To be the subject of a sentence, a pronoun must stand alone.

This is a treasure. (Subject is *this;* pronoun stands alone.)
This *treasure* is mine. (Subject is *treasure. This* is an adjective—a word that describes a noun; *This* describes *treasure.*)

Compound Subjects

A subject may be compound. That is, it may consist of two or more subjects, usually joined by *and* or *or,* that function together.

The *prosecutor* and the *attorney* for the defense made opening statements.
He and his *friends* listened carefully.
Steven, Juan, and *Alicia* attended the seminar. (Note the placement of commas for three or more subjects.)

Implied Subjects

A subject may be implied or understood. An imperative sentence—a sentence that gives a command—has *you* as the implied subject.

(You) Sit in that chair, please.
(You) Now take the oath.
(You) Please read the notes carefully.

Trouble Spot: Prepositional Phrases

A **prepositional phrase** is made up of a preposition (a word such as *at, in, of, to, with*) and one or more nouns or pronouns with their modifiers: *at the time, by the jury, in the courtroom, to the judge and the media, with controlled anger.* Be careful not to confuse the subject of a sentence with the noun or pronoun (known as the object of the preposition) in a prepositional phrase. The object of a preposition cannot be the subject of a sentence.

The <u>car</u> <u>with the dents</u> is mine.
subject   prepositional
phrase

The subject of the sentence is *car.* The word *dents* is the object of the preposition *with* and cannot be the subject of the sentence.

<u>Most</u> <u>of the pie</u> has been eaten.
subject   prepositional
phrase

The <u>person</u> <u>in the middle</u> <u>of the crowd</u> has disappeared.
   subject   prepositional   prepositional
             phrase   phrase

Trouble Spot: The Words *Here* and *There*

The words *here* and *there* are adverbs (used as filler words) and cannot be subjects.

There is no <u>problem</u>.
           subject

Here is the <u>issue</u>.
          subject

Verbs

Verbs show action or express being in relation to the subject of a sentence.

Types of Verbs

Action verbs indicate movement or accomplishment in idea or deed. Someone can "consider the statement" or "hit the ball." Here are other examples:

She *sees* the arena.
He *bought* the book.
They *adopted* the child.
He *understood* her main theories.

Being verbs indicate existence. Few in number, they include *is, was, were, am,* and *are.*

The movie *is* sad.
The book *was* comprehensive.
They *were* responsible.
I *am* concerned.
We *are* organized.

Verb Phrases

Verbs may occur as single words or as phrases. A **verb phrase** is made up of a main verb and one or more helping verbs such as the following:

is	*was*	*can*	*have*	*do*	*may*	*shall*
are	*were*	*could*	*had*	*does*	*might*	*should*
am		*will*	*has*	*did*	*must*	
		would				

Here are some sentences that contain verb phrases:

The judge *has presided* over many capital cases.
His rulings seldom *are overturned* on appeal.

Trouble Spot: Words Such as *Never, Not,* and *Hardly*

Never, not, hardly, seldom, and so on, are modifiers, not verbs.

The attorney could *not* win the case without key witnesses. (*Not* is an adverb. The verb phrase is *could win.*)

The jury could *hardly* hear the witness. (*Hardly* is an adverb; *could hear* is the verb phrase.)

Compound Verbs

Verbs that are joined by a word such as *and* or *or* are called compound verbs.

> As a district attorney, Sumi *had presented* and *had won* famous cases.

> She *prepared* carefully and *presented* her ideas with clarity.

> We *will go* out for dinner or *skip* it entirely.

Trouble Spot: Verbals

Do not confuse verbs with verbals. **Verbals** are verblike words in certain respects, but they do not function as verbs. They function as other parts of speech. There are three kinds of verbals.

An *infinitive* is made up of the word *to* and a verb. An infinitive provides information, but, unlike the true verb, it is not tied to the subject of the sentence. It acts as a noun or describing unit.

> He wanted *to get* a bachelor's degree.

> *To get* a bachelor's degree was his main objective.

(In the first example, the word *wanted* is the verb for the subject *He*. The word *get* follows *to; to get* is an infinitive.)

A *gerund* is a verblike word ending in *-ing* that acts as a noun.

> *Retrieving* her e-mail was always an exciting experience.

> She thought about *retrieving* her e-mail.

Retrieving in each sentence acts as a noun.

A *participle* is a verblike word that usually has an *-ing* or an *-ed* ending.

> *Walking* to town in the dark, he lost his way.

> *Wanted* by the FBI, she was on the run.

> The *starved* dog barked for food.

In the first example, the word *walking* answers the question *when*. In the second example, the word *wanted* answers the question *which one*. In the third example, *starved* describes the dog. *Walking, wanted,* and *starved* are describing words; they are not the true verbs in the sentences.

Location of Subjects and Verbs

Although the subject usually appears before the verb, it may follow the verb instead:

> Into the court <u>stumbled</u> the <u>defendant</u>.
>   verb   subject

> From tiny acorns <u>grow</u> mighty <u>oaks</u>.
>   verb   subject

> There <u>was</u> little <u>support</u> for him in the audience.
>   verb   subject

> Here <u>are</u> your <u>books</u> and your <u>papers</u>.
>   verb   subject   subject

Verb phrases are often broken up in a question. Do not overlook a part of the verb that is separated from another in a question such as "Where had the defendant gone on that fateful night?" If you have trouble finding the verb phrase, recast the question, making it into a statement form: "The defendant *had gone* where on that fateful night." The result will not necessarily be a smooth or complete statement, but you will be able to see the basic elements more easily.

Can the defense lawyer *control* the direction of the trial?

Change the question to a statement to find the verb phrase:

The defense lawyer *can control* the direction of the trial.

Exercise 1	**FINDING SUBJECTS AND VERBS**

Write the simple subject, without modifiers, in the first blank; write the verb in the second blank. Some sentences have compound subjects, compound verbs, or both; and some sentences have an implied ("you") subject. (See Answer Key for answers.)

1. Early in the morning Neville usually digs clams down on the beach.   _____ _____

2. Never again will I be able to trust my pet python.   _____ _____

3. Berlin and London were bombed heavily during World War II.   _____ _____

4. Perhaps Ahab and you will decide to join us on the cruise to Bermuda.   _____ _____

5. Over by the bench stand Milton and the coach.   _____ _____

6. Several students are applying for that position.   _____ _____

7. Please tell Godot not to be late.   _____ _____

8. William Faulkner, a Nobel Prize winner, wrote mostly about the South.   _____ _____

9. For a long time now I have waited and thought about yelling at him.   _____ _____

10. Whom can we find to take his place as substitute quarterback?   _____ _____

11. There are no longer any customers for sand candles.   _____ _____

12. Where will we find a bagel shop open at this late hour?   _____ _____

13. The players, after losing the game, assembled in the coach's office and elected Kermit their mascot frog captain.   _____ _____

14. By this time next year, we will be living in Mexico.   _____ _____

15. A few of those orders may be delayed until tomorrow.   _____ _____

16. Did you ever wish to remain in the surf all summer?   _____ _____

17. Please buy me that friendship bracelet in the store window. _____ _____

18. His immediate reaction to the unfair proposals was to throw a childlike fit. _____ _____

19. Deep in the Maine woods lies a tired old moose. _____ _____

20. Leave the papers on the desk. _____ _____

Exercise 2	FINDING SUBJECTS AND VERBS

prep first

Write the simple subject, without modifiers, in the first blank; write the verb in the second blank. Some sentences have compound subjects, compound verbs, or both; and some sentences have an implied ("you") subject.

1. The earliest evidence of Chinese writing comes from the Shang dynasty.   *The Shang Dinasty*   *comes*   *evidence*

2. Archaeologists have found and studied hundreds of animal bones and tortoise shells with written symbols on them.   *Archedgo*   *have found*

3. These strange objects are known as oracle bones.   *Objects*   *are known*

4. Priests used them in fortune telling.   *Priests*   *used*

5. People 3,500 years ago developed part of the culture existing in China today.   *People*   *developed*

6. Some of the characters are very much like those in a modern Chinese newspaper.   *the characters*   *are*   *Some*

7. In the Chinese method of writing, each character stands for an idea, not a sound.   *character*   *stands*

8. On the other hand, many of the Egyptian hieroglyphs stood for sounds in their spoken language.   *E. hieroglyphs*   *stood*

9. But there were practically no links between China's spoken language and its written language.   *links*   *were*

10. One might read Chinese and not speak it.   *You might read*   *one all*

11. The Chinese system of writing had one great advantage.   _____ _____

12. People with different dialects in all parts of China could learn the same system of writing and communicate with it.   *People*   *could learn*

13. Thus, the Chinese written language aided the unification of a large and diverse land.   *language*   *aided*

14. The disadvantage of the Chinese system is the enormous number of written characters.   *disadvantage*   *0*

15. A barely literate person needs at least 1,000 characters. _____ _____

16. A true scholar needs about 10,000 characters.

scholar needs

17. For centuries, this requirement severely limited the number of literate, educated Chinese.

requirement limited

18. A noble's children learned to write.

children learned.

19. A peasant's children did not.

children did

20. Consider these ideas as a background to modern educational systems.

You consider

Kinds of Sentences

There are four kinds of basic sentences in English. They are called simple, compound, complex, and compound-complex. The terms may be new to you, but if you can recognize subjects and verbs, with a little instruction and practice you should be able to identify and write any of the four kinds of sentences. The only new idea to master is the concept of the *clause.*

Clauses

A **clause** is a group of words with a subject and a verb that functions as a part or all of a complete sentence. There are two kinds of clauses: independent (main) and dependent (subordinate).

> **Independent Clause:** I have the money.
>
> **Dependent Clause:** When I have the money

Independent Clauses

An *independent (main) clause* is a group of words with a subject and a verb that can stand alone and make sense. An independent clause expresses a complete thought by itself and can be written as a separate sentence.

> She plays the bass guitar.
> The manager is not at fault.

Dependent Clauses

A *dependent clause* is a group of words with a subject and verb that depends on a main clause to give it meaning.

> since Shannon came home (no meaning alone)
>
> <u>Since Shannon came home,</u> <u>her mother has been happy</u>. (has meaning)
>   dependent clause   independent clause
>
> because she was needed (no meaning alone)
>
> <u>She stayed in the game</u> <u>because she was needed</u>. (has meaning)
>   independent clause   dependent clause

Relative Clauses

One type of dependent clause is called a relative clause. A *relative clause* begins with a relative pronoun, a pronoun such as *that, which,* or *who.* Relative pronouns *relate* the clause to another word in the sentence.

> that fell last night (no meaning alone)

> The snow <u>that fell last night</u> is nearly gone. (has meaning)
> dependent clause

In the sentence above, the relative pronoun *that* relates the dependent clause to the subject of the sentence, *snow.*

> who stayed in the game (no meaning alone)

> <u>She was the only one</u> <u>who stayed in the game.</u>
> independent clause   dependent clause

In the sentence above, the relative pronoun *who* relates the dependent clause to the word *one.*

Trouble Spot: Phrases

A **phrase** is a group of words that go together. It differs from a clause in that a phrase does not have a subject and a verb. In the previous section, we discussed prepositional phrases (*in the house, beyond the horizon*) and saw some verbal phrases (infinitive phrase: *to go home;* participial phrase: *disconnected from the printer;* and gerund phrase: *running the computer*).

Types of Sentences

This section covers sentence types according to this principle: On the basis of the number and kinds of clauses it contains, a sentence may be classified as simple, compound, complex, or compound-complex. In the examples in the following table, the dependent clauses are italicized, and the independent clauses are underlined.

Type	Definition	Example
Simple	One independent clause	<u>She did the work well</u>.
Compound	Two or more independent clauses	<u>She did the work well</u>, and <u>she was paid well</u>.
Complex	One independent clause and one or more dependent clauses	*Because she did the work well,* <u>she was paid well</u>.
Compound-complex	Two or more independent clauses and one or more dependent clauses	*Because she did the work well,* <u>she was paid well</u>, and <u>she was satisfied</u>.

Simple Sentences

A **simple sentence** consists of one independent clause and no dependent clauses. It may contain phrases and have more than one subject and/or verb.

> The *lake looks* beautiful in the moonlight. (one subject and one verb)

> The *Army, Navy,* and *Marines sent* troops to the disaster area. (three subjects and one verb)

> *We sang* the old songs and *danced* happily at their wedding. (one subject and two verbs)

My *father, mother,* and *sister came* to the school play, *applauded* the performers, and *attended* the party afterwards. (three subjects and three verbs)

Exercise 3	**WRITING SIMPLE SENTENCES**

Write six simple sentences. The first five have been started for you.

1. The mall _____

_____

2. The parking _____

_____

3. The sale _____

_____

4. After two hours _____

_____

5. Then _____

_____

6. _____

_____

Compound Sentences

A **compound sentence** consists of two or more independent clauses with no dependent clauses. Take, for example, the following two independent clauses:

He opened the drawer. He found his missing disk.

Here are two ways to join the independent clauses to form a compound sentence.

1. The two independent clauses can be connected by a connecting word called a coordinating conjunction. The coordinating conjunctions are *for, and, nor, but, or, yet, so.* (An easy way to remember them is to think of the acronym FANBOYS, which is made up of the first letter of each conjunction.)

He opened the drawer, *and* he found his missing disk.

He opened the drawer, *so* he found his missing disk.

Use a comma before the coordinating conjunction (FANBOYS) between two independent clauses (unless one of the clauses is extremely short).

2. Another way to join independent clauses to form a compound sentence is to put a semicolon between the clauses.

He opened the drawer; he found his missing disk.

Exercise 4   **WRITING COMPOUND SENTENCES**

Write five compound sentences using coordinating conjunctions. The sentences have been started for you. Then write the same five compound sentences without the coordinating conjunctions. Use a semicolon to join the independent clauses.

1. It was the car of her dreams, _____

   _____

2. She used the Internet to find the dealer's cost, _____

   _____

3. She now was ready to bargain, _____

   _____

4. Armed with facts, she went to the dealer, _____

   _____

5. The dealer made an offer, _____

   _____

6. _____

   _____

7. _____

   _____

8. _____

   _____

9. _____

   _____

10. _____

   _____

Complex Sentences

A **complex sentence** consists of one independent clause and one or more dependent clauses. In the following sentences, the dependent clauses are italicized.

> *When lilacs are in bloom,* we love to visit friends in the country.
> (one dependent clause and one independent clause)

Although it rained last night, we decided to take the path *that led through the woods.* (one independent clause and two dependent clauses)

Punctuation tip: Use a comma after a dependent clause that appears before the main clause.

When the bus arrived, we quickly boarded.

A relative clause (see page 373) can be the dependent clause in a complex sentence.

I knew the actress *who played that part in the 1980s.*

Exercise 5	WRITING COMPLEX SENTENCES

Write six complex sentences. The first four have been started for you.

1. Although the job paid well, _____

   _____

2. Before she went to work each day, _____

   _____

3. When she returned home each night, _____

   _____

4. Because her social life was suffering, _____

   _____

5. _____

   _____

6. _____

   _____

Compound-Complex Sentences

A **compound-complex sentence** consists of two or more independent clauses and one or more dependent clauses.

Compound-Complex Sentence:	Albert enlisted in the Army, and Jason, who was his older brother, joined him a day later.
Independent Clauses:	Albert enlisted in the Army Jason joined him a day later
Dependent Clause:	who was his older brother
Compound-Complex Sentence:	Because Mr. Sanchez was a talented teacher, he was voted teacher of the year, and his students prospered.

> **Independent Clauses:** he was voted teacher of the year
> his students prospered
>
> **Dependent Clause:** Because Mr. Sanchez was a talented teacher

---

Exercise 6   **WRITING COMPOUND-COMPLEX SENTENCES**

Write six compound-complex sentences. The first five have been started for you.

1. When he began his research paper, he was confident, but _____

   _____

2. Although his college library offered good traditional sources, he wanted some

   online sources, so _____

   _____

3. After he found sources for background information, he focused on one issue,

   and then _____

   _____

4. When he discovered that an expert in his study lived nearby, he _____

   _____

5. After he wrote his final draft on his word processor, he _____

   _____

6. _____

   _____

   _____

Exercise 7   **IDENTIFYING TYPES OF SENTENCES**

Indicate the kind of sentence by writing the appropriate letter(s) in the blank. (See Answer Key for answers.)

S   *simple*
CP   *compound*
CX   *complex*
CC   *compound-complex*

_____ 1. I left early in the afternoon; I wanted to reach Fresno before dark.

_____ 2. If you wish to see him, you must make an appointment date weeks in
             advance.

_____ 3. Before the opening game of the season, the Boston Celtics had played
             the Los Angeles Lakers two games.

_____ 4. Before you study the plays of that dramatist, you should read some comments by Edith Hamilton.

_____ 5. The shrubs are beginning to grow, but the trees that our neighbor gave to us are dead.

_____ 6. After visiting friends in Albany, we drove on to Pembroke, Massachusetts, and stayed that night in a motel on the east shore of Oldham Pond.

_____ 7. This is the school from which many famous leaders of our country graduated.

_____ 8. Although our campus covers many acres, we do not have sufficient parking areas.

_____ 9. You must be there early in the morning, or you will lose the job to someone else.

_____ 10. I saw the last game that he played in college.

_____ 11. The character delineation in that novel was excellent, but the plot was weak and confusing.

_____ 12. The coach who gave you those suggestions is one of the best ball players with the New York Yankees.

_____ 13. You must return those books to the library at once, or you will be fined.

_____ 14. When I look at the calendar, I realize with a shock that Christmas is only a few weeks away.

_____ 15. The lady entered the store, walked directly to the dress department, handed the waiting clerk a torn dress, and demanded her money back.

_____ 16. Patricia visited her family in Iowa, and I attended school in New York.

_____ 17. It would be unwise for you to demand his resignation before discussing the matter with his superior.

_____ 18. After our glorious stay in Rome, we flew to Egypt and spent the summer studying at the University of Cairo.

_____ 19. They were very late in arriving home; nevertheless, we stayed up and greeted them.

_____ 20. Gerardo would not agree to the proposals.

Exercise 8   **IDENTIFYING TYPES OF SENTENCES**

Indicate the kind of sentence by writing the appropriate letter(s) in the blank.

S   *simple*
CP   *compound*
CX   *complex*
CC   *compound-complex*

_____ 1. Throughout history there have been truth tests for the innocent and the guilty.

_____ 2. Many of these methods relied (unknowingly) on the basic physiological principles that also guided the creation of the polygraph.

_____ 3. For example, one method of lie detection involved giving the suspect a handful of raw rice to chew.

_____ 4. After the suspect chewed for some time, he or she was instructed to spit out the rice.

_____ 5. An innocent person was expected to do this easily, but a guilty person was expected to have grains of rice sticking to the roof of the mouth and tongue.

_____ 6. This technique relied on the increased sympathetic nervous system activity in the presumably fearful and guilty person.

_____ 7. This activity would result in the drying up of saliva.

_____ 8. That, in turn, would cause grains of rice to stick in the mouth.

_____ 9. A similar but more frightening technique involved placing a heated knife blade briefly against the tongue.

_____ 10. An innocent person would not be burned, but the guilty person would immediately feel pain, again because of the relative dryness of the mouth.

_____ 11. A more primitive but functional technique for detecting liars was supposedly used by a Persian king.

_____ 12. He was presumed to have a very special donkey, one that had the ability to tell an innocent person from a guilty one.

_____ 13. When a crime was committed, the suspects would be gathered in a hall next to the room that held the donkey.

_____ 14. According to directions, each suspect entered the room alone, found the donkey in the dark, and pulled its tail.

_____ 15. The donkey did the rest.

_____ 16. If an innocent person pulled the tail, the donkey was said to remain silent.

_____ 17. If a guilty person pulled the tail, the donkey would bray loudly.

_____ 18. In fact, the donkey's tail was dusted with graphite.

_____ 19. The guilty person emerged with clean hands because he or she wanted to avoid detection.

_____ 20. The king knew that the person with clean hands was guilty, and he proceeded with punishment.

Combining Sentences

The simple sentence, the most basic sentence in the English language, can be exceptionally useful and powerful. Some of the greatest statements in literature have been presented in the simple sentence. Its strength is in its singleness of purpose. However, a piece of writing made up of a long series of simple sentences is likely to be monotonous. Moreover, the form may suggest a separateness of ideas that does not serve your purpose well. If your ideas are closely related, some equal in importance and some not, you can combine sentences to show the relationships between your ideas.

Coordination: The Compound Sentence

If you intend to communicate two equally important and closely related ideas, you certainly will want to place them close together, probably in a compound sentence.

Suppose we take two simple sentences that we want to combine:

> I am very tired.

> I worked very hard today.

We have already looked at coordinating conjunctions as a way of joining independent clauses to create compound sentences. Depending on which coordinating conjunction you use, you can show different kinds of relationships. (The following list is arranged according to the FANBOYS acronym discussed in the previous section. Only the first conjunction joins the original two sentences.)

For shows a reason:

> I am very tired, *for* I worked very hard today.

And shows equal ideas:

> I am very tired, *and* I want to rest for a few minutes.

Nor indicates a negative choice or alternative:

> I am not tired, *nor* am I hungry right now.

But shows contrast:

> I am very tired, *but* I have no time to rest now.

Or indicates a choice or an alternative:

> I will take a nap, *or* I will go out jogging.

Yet indicates contrast:

> I am tired, *yet* I am unable to relax.

So points to a result:

> I am tired, *so* I will take a nap.

Punctuation with Coordinating Conjunctions

When you combine two sentences by using a coordinating conjunction, drop the first period, change the capital letter that begins the second sentence to a small letter, and insert a comma before the coordinating conjunction.

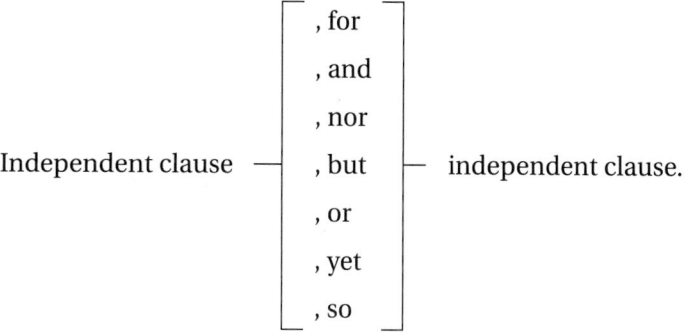

Independent clause — , for / , and / , nor / , but / , or / , yet / , so — independent clause.

Semicolons and Conjunctive Adverbs

In the previous section we saw that a semicolon can join independent clauses to make a compound sentence. Here are two more simple sentences to combine:

> We were late. We missed the first act.

We can make one compound sentence out of them by joining the two clauses with a semicolon:

> We were late; we missed the first act.

We can also use words called conjunctive adverbs after semicolons to make the relationship between the two clauses clearer. Look at how the conjunctive adverb *therefore* adds the idea of "as a result."

> We were late; *therefore,* we missed the first act.

Conjunctive adverbs include the following words and phrases: *also, consequently, furthermore, hence, however, in fact, moreover, nevertheless, now, on the other hand, otherwise, soon, therefore, similarly, then, thus.*

Consider the meaning you want when you use a conjunctive adverb to coordinate ideas.

As a result of: *therefore, consequently, hence, thus, then*

To the contrary or with reservation: *however, nevertheless, otherwise, on the other hand*

In addition to: *moreover, also*

To emphasize or specify: *in fact, for example*

To compare: *similarly*

Punctuation with Semicolons and Conjunctive Adverbs

When you combine two sentences by using a semicolon, replace the first period with a semicolon and change the capital letter that begins the second sentence to a small letter. If you wish to use a conjunctive adverb, insert it after the semicolon and put a comma after it. (However, no comma follows *then, now, thus,* and *soon.*) The first letters of ten common conjunctive adverbs make up the acronym HOT-SHOT CAT.

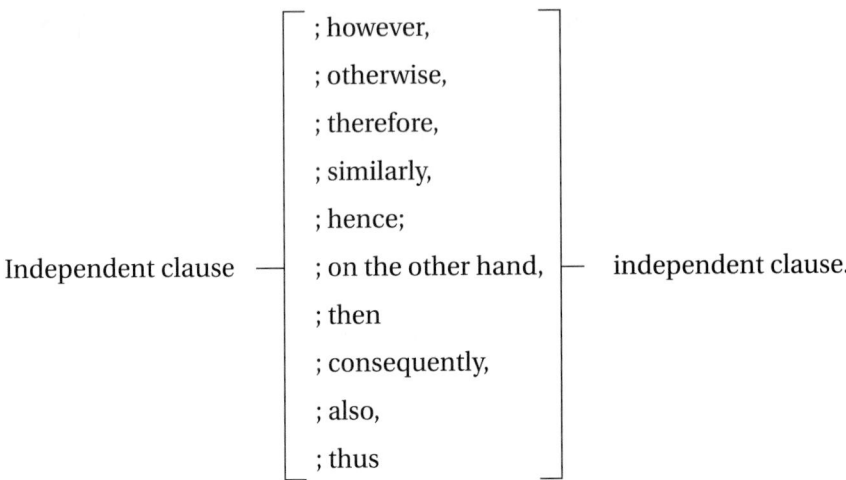

Independent clause
; however,
; otherwise,
; therefore,
; similarly,
; hence;
; on the other hand,
; then
; consequently,
; also,
; thus
independent clause.

Subordination: The Complex Sentence

Whereas a compound sentence contains independent clauses that are equally important and closely related, a complex sentence combines ideas of unequal value. The following two sentences can be combined as either a compound sentence or a complex sentence, depending on whether the writer thinks the ideas are of equal value.

> My neighbors are considerate.
>
> They never play loud music.

Combined as a compound sentence, suggesting that the ideas are of equal value, the new sentence looks like this:

My neighbors are considerate, and they never play loud music.
    independent clause   **independent clause**
      (main idea)   **(main idea)**

Here are the same two ideas combined as a complex sentence, suggesting that the ideas are of unequal value:

Because my neighbors are considerate, they never play loud music.
    dependent clause   **independent clause**
   (less important idea)   **(main idea)**

Although both the compound and complex forms are correct, the complex form conveys the ideas more precisely in this sentence because one idea does seem to be more important—one idea depends on the other.

Thus if you have two sentences with closely related ideas and one is clearly more important than the other, consider combining them in a complex sentence. Compare these two paragraphs:

1. Version 1 contains six simple sentences, implying that the ideas are of equal value:

> (1) I was very upset. (2) The Fourth of July fireworks were especially loud. (3) My dog ran away. (4) The animal control officer made his morning rounds. (5) He found my dog in another part of town. (6) I was relieved.

2. Version 2 consists of two simple sentences and two complex sentences, showing that some ideas are more important than others:

> (1) I was very upset. (2) Because the Fourth of July fireworks were especially loud, my dog ran away. (3) When the animal control officer made his morning rounds, he found my dog in another part of town. (4) I was relieved.

You will probably consider Version 2 superior to Version 1. In Version 1 sentences 2 and 3 are closely related, but 3 is more important. Sentences 4 and 5 are closely related, but 5 is more important. In Version 2 the revision made each pair into a complex sentence.

Although you could combine sentences 1 and 2, the result would be illogical because the wrong idea would be conveyed:

Illogical Combination: I was very upset because the Fourth of July fireworks were especially loud.

The person was very upset because the dog ran away, not because the fireworks were especially loud.

Subordinating Conjunctions

As you learned in the previous section, a complex sentence is composed of one independent clause and one or more dependent clauses. In combining two independent clauses to write a complex sentence, your first step is to decide on a word that will best show the relationship between the clauses. Words that show the relationship of a dependent clause to an independent one are called subordinating conjunctions. The italicized words in the following sentences are subordinating conjunctions. Consider the meaning as well as the placement of each one.

> *Because* the storm hit, the game was canceled.
>
> *After* the storm passed, the dogs began to bark.
>
> *When* she read her poem, they were moved to fits of hysterics.
>
> He did not volunteer to work on the holiday, *although* the pay was good.
>
> No one has visited her *since* she moved into town.
>
> They decided to wait *until* the cows came home.
>
> They refused to work *unless* they were allowed to wear chef's hats.
>
> *Before* the session ended, all the "hep cats" blew some sweet sounds.

Other subordinating conjunctions include the following:

as	*provided that*	*whereas*
as if	*rather than*	*wherever*
even if	*so that*	*whether*
even though	*than*	*while*
if	*whenever*	
in order that	*where*	

Punctuation with Subordinating Conjunctions

If the dependent clause comes *before* the main clause, set it off with a comma.

> Before Mike wrote his final draft, he looked over his outline.

If the dependent clause comes *after* or *within* the main clause, set it off only if the clause is not necessary to the meaning of the main clause or if the dependent clause begins with the word *although, though,* or *even though.*

> We went home *after* the concert had ended.

> He continued painting, *although* he had repainted the cabinet twice.

Punctuation with Relative Pronouns

As you learned earlier, a relative clause begins with a relative pronoun, a pronoun such as *that, which,* or *who.*

> The decision <u>that I made</u> is final.
> **relative clause**

> A student <u>who uses a computer</u> can save time in revising.
> **relative clause**

Set off the dependent (relative) clause with commas when it is not necessary to the sentence. Do not set off the clause if it is necessary for the meaning of the sentence.

> Everyone *who tries* will pass this class. (The dependent clause is necessary because one would not say, "Everyone will pass this class.")

> Rachel, *who tries,* will pass this class. (The dependent clause is not necessary because one can say, "Rachel will pass this class.")

The relative pronoun *which* usually refers to things. The word *which* almost always indicates that a clause is not necessary for the meaning of the sentence. Therefore, a clause beginning with *which* is almost always set off by commas.

> My car, *which* is ten years old, has a flat tire.

The relative pronoun *that* also usually refers to things. However, the word *that* almost always indicates that the clause *is* necessary for the meaning of the sentence. Therefore, a clause beginning with *that* is almost always *not* set off by commas.

> The car *that* has a flat tire is ten years old.

The relative pronouns *who* and *whom,* as well as *whoever* and *whomever,* usually refer to people. Clauses that begin with those relative pronouns are not set off by commas if they are necessary for the meaning of the sentence; if they are not necessary, they are set off.

> A person *who* has a way with words is often quoted. (necessary for the meaning of the sentence)

> My uncle, *whom* I quote often, has a way with words. (not necessary for the meaning of the sentence)

Coordination and Subordination: The Compound-Complex Sentence

At times you may want to show the relationship of three or more ideas within one sentence. If that relationship involves two or more main ideas and one or more supporting ideas, the combination can be stated in a compound-complex sentence (two or more independent clauses and one or more dependent clauses).

<u>Before he learned how to operate a word processor,</u>
dependent clause

<u>he had trouble with his typewritten assignments,</u>
independent clause

but now <u>he produces clean, attractive pages</u>.
independent clause

In our previous discussion of the complex sentence, we presented this group of six sentences:

> I was very upset. The Fourth of July fireworks were especially loud. My dog ran away. The animal control officer made his morning rounds. He found my dog in another part of town. I was relieved.

We then converted the group of six sentences to four:

> I was very upset. Because the Fourth of July fireworks were especially loud, my dog ran away. When the animal control officer made his morning rounds, he found my dog in another part of town. I was relieved.

But what if we wanted to show an even closer relationship of ideas? One solution would be to combine the two complex sentences in this way (the italicized sentence is compound-complex):

> I was very upset. *Because the Fourth of July fireworks were especially loud, my dog ran away; but when the animal control officer made his morning rounds, he found my dog in another part of town.* I was relieved.

Punctuation of Complicated Compound or Compound-Complex Sentences

If a compound or compound-complex sentence has one or more commas in the first clause, you may want to use a semicolon before the coordinating conjunction between the two clauses. Its purpose is to show the reader very clearly the division between the two independent clauses. The preceding example illustrates this use of the semicolon.

Other Ways to Combine Ideas

1. Use an appositive, a noun or a noun phrase that immediately follows a noun or pronoun and renames it.

   > Garth Brooks claims Yukon, Oklahoma, as his home town. He is a famous singer.

   > Garth Brooks, *a famous singer,* claims Yukon, Oklahoma, as his home town.

2. Use a prepositional phrase, a preposition followed by a noun or pronoun object.

   > John Elway led the Denver Broncos to two Super Bowl victories. Both triumphs occurred in the 1990s.

   > John Elway led the Denver Broncos to two Super Bowl victories *in the 1990s.*

3. Drop the subject in the sentence that follows and combine the sentences.

> Emily Dickinson's poetry went mostly unpublished during her lifetime. It was finally discovered and celebrated more than a half century later.

> Emily Dickinson's poetry went mostly unpublished during her lifetime but was finally discovered and celebrated more than a half century later.

4. Use a participial phrase, a group of words that include a participle, which is a verbal that usually ends in *-ing* or *-ed*.

> Michael rowed smoothly. He reached the shore.

> *Rowing smoothly,* Michael reached the shore.

Exercise 9   **COMBINING SENTENCES**

Combine each group of sentences into a single sentence. Use coordination, subordination, or one of the other ways of combining ideas. (See Answer Key for answers.)

1. Cobras are among the most feared of all snakes.
   They are not the deadliest of all snakes.

2. Cobras do not coil before they strike.
   They cannot strike for a long distance.

3. Cobras do not have a hood.
   They flatten their neck by moving their ribs when they are nervous or frightened.

4. Cobras use their poison in two ways.
   One way is by injecting venom with their fangs.
   Another way is by spitting venom at their victims.

5. Human beings will not die from the venom that has been spit.
   It can cause blindness if it is not washed from the eyes.

6. A person can die from a cobra bite.
   Death may come in only a few hours.

7. Snake charmers have long worked with cobras.
   They use only a snake, a basket, and a flute.

8. The snakes cannot hear the music.
   They respond to the rhythmic movements of the charmers.

9. The snake charmers are hardly ever in danger of being bitten.
   They defang the cobras or sew their mouths shut.

10. Most cobras flee from people.
    They attack if they are cornered or if they are guarding their eggs.

Exercise 10	**COMBINING SENTENCES**

Combine each group of sentences into a single sentence. Use coordination, subordination, or one of the other ways of combining ideas.

1. Henry David Thoreau grew tired of living in society.
   He wanted to face his essential self.

2. He built a cabin in the woods.
   He lived there for more than a year.

3. Gilligan had a plan.
   He would float in a shipping crate to Hawaii.

4. It would be a surprise.
   He would send help to his friends on the island.

5. A storm came up.
   Gilligan's craft sank in three feet of water in the lagoon.
   The skipper cried bitter tears over the loss of his little buddy.

6. The professor made a submarine out of coconut shells, Mrs. Howell's corset, Ginger's jewelry, and fish bones.
   Gilligan was rescued.

7. Captain Ahab set sail for the South Seas.
   Captain Ahab had an obsession.

8. He wanted to kill the great white whale.
   The name of the great white whale was Moby Dick.

9. The captain and the whale had their encounter. Moby Dick was easily the victor.

10. Hamlet was sad.
    His father was dead.
    His mother had married his uncle.

11. Hamlet believed that his uncle had killed his father.
    Hamlet plotted to kill his uncle.

12. Romeo and Juliet were young.
    They fell in love.

13. Their families were feuding.
    Romeo and Juliet decided to run away.

14. They tried to trick their families.
    Their plans turned sour.
    They both died.

15. The contestant spun the wheel one more time.
    Vanna White clapped her hands with glee.

16. Pat Sajak made a wry joke about greed.
    Only one letter remained.

17. The wheel stopped.
    The contestant lost his turn.

18. The audience groaned.
    Vanna White slumped, and Pat Sajak comforted her sad heart.

19. Several tabloids have reported that Elvis has not left us.
    He has been sighted in several parts of the country and even on other planets.

20. The tabloids report that the King is just tired and wants privacy.
    They give credit to unnamed reliable sources.

Correcting Fragments, Comma Splices, and Run-Ons

You have learned about subjects and verbs, and you have identified and written different kinds of sentences. With the information you now have, you will be able to spot and correct three problems that sometimes creep into what is otherwise good writing. Those problems are sentence fragments, comma splices, and run-on sentences.

Fragments

A correct sentence signals completeness. The structure and punctuation provide those signals. For example, if I say to you, "She left in a hurry," you do not necessarily expect me to say anything else, but if I say, "In a hurry," you do. If I say, "Tomorrow I will give you a quiz on the reading assignment," and I leave the room, you will merely take note of my words. But if I say, "Tomorrow when I give you a quiz on the reading assignment," and leave the room, you will probably be annoyed, and you may even chase after me and ask me to finish my sentence. Those examples illustrate the difference between completeness and incompleteness.

A **fragment** is a word or group of words without a subject ("Is going to town.") or without a verb "(He going to town.") or without both ("Going to town."). A fragment can also be a group of words with a subject and verb that cannot stand alone ("When he goes to town."). Although the punctuation signals a sentence (a capital letter at the beginning and a period at the end), the structure of a fragment signals incompleteness. If you said it or wrote it to someone, that person would expect you to go on and finish the idea.

Other specific examples of common unacceptable fragments are these:

- *Dependent clause only:* When she came.

- *Phrase(s) only:* Waiting there for some help.

- *No subject in main clause:* Went to the library.

- *No verb in main clause:* She being the only person there.

Acceptable Fragments

Sometimes fragments are used intentionally. When we speak, we often use the following fragments.

- *Interjections:* Great! Hooray! Whoa!

- *Exclamations:* What a day! How terrible! What a bother!

- *Greetings:* Hello. Good morning. Good night. Good evening.

- *Questions:* What for? Why not? Where to?

- *Informal conversation:* Eight o'clock. Really.

In novels, plays, and short stories, fragments are often used in conversation among characters. However, unless you are writing fiction, you need to be able to identify fragments in your college assignments and turn those fragments into complete sentences.

Dependent Clauses as Fragments: Clauses with Subordinating Conjunctions

You have learned that words such as *because, after, although, since, before* (see page 383 for a more complete list) are subordinating conjunctions, words that show the relationship of a dependent clause to an independent one. A dependent clause punctuated like a sentence (capital letter at the beginning; period at the end) is a sentence fragment.

> *While the ship was sinking.*

You can choose one of many ways to fix that kind of fragment.

Incorrect:	They continued to dance. *While the ship was sinking.*
Correct:	They continued to dance *while the ship was sinking.*
Correct:	*While the ship was sinking,* they continued to dance.
Correct:	The shop was sinking. They continued to dance.
Correct:	The ship was sinking; they continued to dance.

In the first two correct sentences above, the dependent clause *while the ship was sinking* has been attached to an independent clause. Note that a comma is used when the dependent clause appears at the beginning of the sentence. In the next two sentences, the subordinating conjunction *while* has been omitted. The two independent clauses can then stand alone as sentences or as parts of a sentence, joined by a semicolon.

Dependent Clauses as Fragments: Clauses with Relative Pronouns

You have also learned that words such as *that, which,* and *who* can function as relative pronouns, words that relate a clause back to a noun or pronoun in the sentence. Relative clauses are dependent. If they are punctuated as sentences (begin with a capital letter; end with a period), they are incorrect. They are really sentence fragments.

> *Which is lying on the floor.*

The best way to fix such a fragment is to attach it as closely as possible to the noun to which it refers.

Incorrect: That new red sweater is mine. *Which is lying on the floor.*

Correct: The new red sweater, *which is lying on the floor,* is mine.

Reminder: Some relative clauses are restrictive (necessary to the meaning of the sentence) and should not be set off with commas. Some are nonrestrictive (not necessary to the meaning of the sentence), as in the example above, and are set off by commas.

Phrases as Fragments

Although a phrase may carry an idea, a phrase is a fragment because it is incomplete in structure. It lacks both a subject and a verb. (See page 369 for verbal phrases, pages 367 and 385 for prepositional phrases, and page 385 for appositive phrases.)

Verbal Phrase

Incorrect: *Having studied hard all evening.* John decided to retire.

Correct: *Having studied hard all evening,* John decided to retire.

The italicized part of the incorrect example is a verbal phrase. As you have learned, a verbal is verblike without being a verb in sentence structure. Verbals include verb parts of speech ending in *-ed* and *-ing.* To correct a verbal phrase fragment, attach it to a complete sentence (independent clause). When the phrase begins the sentence, it is usually set off by a comma.

Prepositional Phrase

Incorrect: *For the past ten hours.* I have been designing my home page.

Correct: *For the past ten hours,* I have been designing my home page.

In this example, the fragment is a prepositional phrase—a group of words beginning with a preposition, such as *in, on, of, at,* and *with,* that connects a noun or pronoun object to the rest of the sentence. To correct a prepositional phrase fragment, attach it to a complete sentence (independent clause). If the prepositional phrase is long and begins the sentence, it is usually set off by a comma.

Appositive Phrase

Incorrect: He lived in the small town of Whitman. *A busy industrial center near Boston.*

Correct: He lived in the small town of Whitman, *a busy industrial center near Boston.*

Incorrect: Many readers admire the work of the nineteenth-century American poet. *Emily Dickinson.*

> **Correct:** Many readers admire the work of the nineteenth-century American poet *Emily Dickinson.*

In these examples, the fragment is an appositive phrase—a group of words following a noun or pronoun and renaming it. To correct an appositive phrase fragment, connect it to a complete sentence (an independent clause). An appositive phrase fragment is set off by a comma or by commas only if it is not essential to the meaning of the sentence.

Fragments as Word Groups Without Subjects or Without Verbs

> **Incorrect:** Kristianna studied many long hours. And received the highest grade in the class. (without subject)
>
> **Correct:** Kristianna studied many long hours and received the highest grade in the class.
>
> **Incorrect:** Few children living in that section of the country. (without verb)
>
> **Correct:** Few children live in that section of the country.

Each sentence must have an independent clause, a group of words that contains a subject and a verb and that can stand alone. As you may recall from the discussion of subjects, a command or direction sentence, such as "Think," has an understood subject of *you.*

Comma Splices and Run-Ons

The comma splice and the run-on are two other kinds of faulty "sentences" that give false signals to the reader. In each instance the punctuation suggests that there is only one sentence, but in fact, there is material for two.

The **comma splice** consists of two independent clauses with only a comma between them:

> *The weather was disappointing, we canceled the picnic.* (A comma by itself cannot join two independent clauses.)

The run-on differs from the comma splice in only one respect: It has no comma between the independent clauses. Therefore, the run-on is two independent clauses with *nothing* between them:

> *The weather was disappointing we canceled the picnic.* (Independent clauses must be properly connected.)

Because an independent clause can stand by itself as a sentence and because two independent clauses must be properly linked, you can use a simple technique to identify the comma splice and the run-on. If you see a sentence that you think may contain one of these two errors, ask yourself this question: "Can I insert a period at some place in the word group and still have a sentence on either side?" If the answer is yes and there is no word such as *and* or *but* following the inserted period, then you have a comma splice or a run-on to correct. In our previous examples of the comma splice and the run-on, we could insert a period after the word *disappointing* in each case, and we would still have an independent clause—therefore, a sentence—on either side.

Four Ways to Correct Comma Splices and Run-Ons

Once you identify a comma splice or a run-on in your writing, you need to correct it. There are four different ways to fix these common sentence problems.

1. **Use a comma and a coordinating conjunction.**

    Incorrect: We canceled the picnic the weather was disappointing. (run-on)

    Correct: We canceled the picnic, *for* the weather was disappointing. (Here we inserted a comma and the coordinating conjunction *for.*)

Knowing the seven coordinating conjunctions will help you in writing sentences and correcting sentence problems. Remember the acronym FANBOYS: *for, and, nor, but, or, yet, so.*

2. **Use a subordinating conjunction.**

    Incorrect: The weather was disappointing, we canceled the picnic.

    Correct: *Because* the weather was disappointing, we canceled the picnic.

By inserting the subordinating conjunction *because,* you can transform the first independent clause into a dependent clause and correct the comma splice. Knowing the most common subordinating conjunctions will help you in writing sentences and correcting sentence problems. Here again is a list of frequently used subordinating conjunctions.

after	*if*	*until*
although	*in order that*	*when*
as	*provided that*	*whenever*
as if	*rather than*	*where*
because	*since*	*whereas*
before	*so that*	*wherever*
even if	*than*	*whether*
even though	*unless*	*while*

3. **Use a semicolon.**

    Incorrect: The weather was disappointing, we canceled the picnic.

    Correct: The weather was disappointing; we canceled the picnic.

    Correct: The weather was disappointing; *therefore,* we canceled the picnic.

This comma splice was corrected by a semicolon. The first correct example shows the semicolon alone. The second correct example shows a semicolon followed by the conjunctive adverb *therefore.* The conjunctive adverb is optional, but, as we have already seen, conjunctive adverbs can make the relationship between independent clauses stronger. Here is a list of conjunctive adverbs you saw on page 382.

however
otherwise
therefore
similarly
hence
on the other hand
then
consequently
also
thus

Do you remember the acronym HOTSHOT CAT, made up of the first letter of each of these common conjunctive adverbs? The acronym will help you remember them. Other conjunctive adverbs include *in fact, for example, moreover, nevertheless, furthermore, now,* and *soon.*

4. Make each clause a separate sentence.

Incorrect: The weather was disappointing, we canceled the picnic.

Correct: The weather was disappointing. We canceled the picnic.

To correct the comma splice, replace the comma with a period and begin the second sentence (the second independent clause) with a capital letter. This method is at once the simplest and most common method of correcting comma splices and run-ons. For a run-on, insert a period between the two independent clauses and begin the second sentence with a capital letter.

Techniques for Spotting Problem Sentences

1. For the fragment, ask yourself: "If someone were to say or write this to me, would I expect the person to add to the statement or rephrase it?"

2. In checking for the comma splice or run-on, ask yourself: "Is there a point in this word group at which I can insert a period and create a sentence on either side?" (The question is not necessary if there is a coordinating conjunction— FANBOYS—at that point.)

3. If you have trouble with comma splices and run-ons, check these constructions as you revise:

   a. A comma preceded by a noun or pronoun followed by a noun or pronoun

   b. A sentence beginning with a subordinating conjunction

4. If you have trouble with fragments, look for these clues:

   a. A word group with a single verb ending in *-ing*

   b. A word group without both a subject and a verb

5. Use the grammar checker on your word processor to alert you to possible problem sentences. Then use instructions from this book to make necessary corrrections.

| **Exercise 11** | **CORRECTING FRAGMENTS, COMMA SPLICES, AND RUN-ONS** |

Write the appropriate identification in each blank. Correct the faulty sentences. (See Answer Key for answers.)

OK   *correct*
CS   *comma splice*
RO   *run-on*
FRAG   *fragment*

_____   1. Youthfulness seems to be a necessity for most television sitcoms that

succeed.

_____   2. Vincent Van Gogh is one of the most famous artists of modern art

during his lifetime he sold only one painting.

_____ 3. Those who say American schools are inferior to European schools and provide only entertainment.

_____ 4. Jazz can express pain and sorrow if played by a skillful musician.

_____ 5. The faculty is not perfect, the administration is weak.

_____ 6. "Commuting is good," Ann said, "it gives you time to think."

_____ 7. The most common flower clusters eaten as vegetables are broccoli and cauliflower.

_____ 8. The instrument of manual operation for shaping metal, wood, or plastics and for holding the work.

_____ 9. Some parents panic when told of the fantastic increase in college costs.

_____ 10. You present real content instead of circling the topic.

_____ 11. Vampire bats sometimes attack persons who are sleeping the bite itself is usually harmless and soon heals.

_____ 12. Words can be studied in several ways, the etymology of words reveals their history.

_____ 13. Birds singing in the sycamore trees.

_____ 14. The silent letter in some words that changes the way the word sounds when it is pronounced.

_____ 15. Uruguay is the smallest republic in South America, it has one of the highest living standards on the continent.

_____ 16. The Danish invasion of England changed the language, another factor was the Norman Conquest.

_____ 17. Football is essentially a spectator sport.

_____ 18. Every young child has a strong need for positive regard that positive regard should be unconditional.

_____ 19. My favorite author is John Steinbeck his best books are about common people.

_____ 20. The problem is a legal one; it is also an ethical one that touches every

member of the community.

| **Exercise 12** | **CORRECTING FRAGMENTS, COMMA SPLICES, AND RUN-ONS** |

Write the appropriate identification in each blank. Correct the faulty sentences.

OK   correct
CS   comma splice
RO   run-on
FRAG   fragment

_____ 1. The male newt glows during the courting season the human male has

no such attraction.

_____ 2. A person's head measures only about an eighth of the body a cartoon

character's head is likely to be a third or a half of the body length.

_____ 3. Although there has been an increase in heart disease among adults.

_____ 4. Their tremendous success in helping adults to read.

_____ 5. The walking catfish has gills it also has lunglike breathing organs.

_____ 6. Friends said his manager was interested in the money, he refused to

believe them.

_____ 7. According to Rollo May, televised entertainment cultivates the spec-

tator role, which leads to feelings of impotence and contributes to

violent behavior.

_____ 8. Keith completed his report, his friends were envious.

_____ 9. Authorities disagree on what makes a car safe; it's more than seat

belts.

_____ 10. The problem difficult to locate.

_____ 11. During an earthquake, if you are outdoors, stay outdoors, if you are

indoors, stay indoors.

_____ 12. I can't wait that long, I'm moving out today.

_____ 13. People's survival seems to depend on their ability to use their wits;

being half-educated won't do.

_____ 14. Joanne needs an automobile she lives a mile from her work, and the
bus service is bad.

_____ 15. Your high sales resistance and your critical mind.

_____ 16. José said, "You're the person I need for my project you want to work,
and you are willing to learn."

_____ 17. People in many societies think that cats bring good fortune, some
people associate cats with bad luck and fear them.

_____ 18. At first, Caligula was a popular emperor then it became apparent that
he was insane.

_____ 19. Janelle said that she considered the movie inferior to others on that
topic.

_____ 20. Although they were not pleased with his work as he tried to learn how
to operate the machine.

| **Exercise 13** | **CORRECTING FRAGMENTS, COMMA SPLICES, AND RUN-ONS** |

Write the appropriate identification in each blank. Correct the faulty sentences.

OK	*correct*
CS	*comma splice*
RO	*run-on*
FRAG	*fragment*

_____ 1. A total institution is a behavior setting, it has certain unique characteristics.

_____ 2. A total institution completely encompassing the individual.

_____ 3. Forming barriers to the types of social intercourse that occur outside
such a setting.

_____ 4. Monasteries, jails, homes for the aged, boarding schools, and military
academies being a few examples of total institutions.

_____ 5. In total institutions the individuals must sleep, play, and work within
the same setting.

_____ 6. These are generally segmented spheres of activity in the lives of most individuals, within a total institution one sphere of activity overlaps others.

_____ 7. Each phase of life taking place in the company of a large group of other people.

_____ 8. Usually, sleeping is done in a barracks, food is served in a cafeteria.

_____ 9. In such activities everyone being treated alike and must perform certain essential tasks.

_____ 10. Activities in an institution tightly scheduled according to a master plan.

_____ 11. With set times to rise, to eat, to exercise, and to sleep.

_____ 12. These institutional characteristics result in a bureaucratic society it requires the hiring of other people for surveillance.

_____ 13. What often results is a split in the groups within an institution into a large, managed group (inmates) and a small supervisory staff.

_____ 14. There tends to be great social distance between the groups, they perceive each other according to stereotypes and have severely restricted communications.

_____ 15. The world of the inmate differing greatly from the outside world.

_____ 16. When one enters a total institution, all previous roles, such as father or husband, are disrupted.

_____ 17. The individual is further depersonalized.

_____ 18. The effects of an institutional setting so all-encompassing that one can meaningfully speak of an "institutional personality."

_____ 19. A persistent manner of behaving compliantly without emotional involvement.

_____ 20. Individual adaptations can be as extreme as psychosis, childlike regression, and depression or as mild as resigned compliance.

Verbs

This section covers the use of standard verbs. To some, the word *standard* implies "correct." A more precise meaning is "that which is conventional among educated people." Therefore, a standard verb is the right choice in most school assignments, most published writing, and most important public speaking situations. We all change our language when we move from these formal occasions to informal ones: We don't talk to our families in the same way we would speak at a large gathering in public; we don't write letters to friends the same way we write a history report. But even with informal language we would seldom change from standard to nonstandard usage.

Regular and Irregular Verbs

Verbs can be divided into two categories, called *regular* and *irregular.* Regular verbs are predictable, but irregular verbs—as the term suggests—follow no definite pattern.

Verbs always show time. Present tense verbs show an action or a state of being that is occurring at the present time: I *like* your hat. He *is* at a hockey game right now. Present tense verbs can also imply a continuation from the past into the future: She *drives* to work every day.

Past tense verbs show an action or a state of being that occurred in the past: We *walked* to town yesterday. Tim *was* president of the club last year.

Regular Verbs

Present Tense

For *he, she,* and *it,* regular verbs in the present tense add an *-s* or an *-es* to the base word. The following chart shows the present tense of the base word *ask,* which is a regular verb.

	Singular	**Plural**
First Person:	I ask	we ask
Second Person:	you ask	you ask
Third Person:	he, she, it asks	they ask

If the verb ends in *-y,* you might have to drop the *-y* and add *-ies* for *he, she,* and *it.*

	Singular	**Plural**
First Person:	I try	we try
Second Person:	you try	you try
Third Person:	he, she, it tries	they try

Past Tense

For regular verbs in the past tense, add *-ed* to the base form:

Base Form (Present)	**Past**
walk	walked
answer	answered

If the base form already ends in *-e,* add just *-d:*

Base Form (Present)	**Past**
smile	smiled
decide	decided

If the base form ends in a consonant followed by *-y,* drop the *-y* and add *-ied.*

Base Form (Present)	Past
fry	fried
amplify	amplified

Regardless of how you form that past tense, regular verbs in the past tense do not change forms. The following chart shows the past tense of the base word *like,* which is a regular verb.

	Singular	Plural
First Person:	I liked	we liked
Second Person:	you liked	you liked
Third Person:	he, she, it liked	they liked

Past Participles

The past participle uses the helping verb *has, have,* or *had* along with the past tense of the verb. For regular verbs, the past participle form of the verb is the same as the past tense.

Base Form	Past	Past Participle
happen	happened	happened
hope	hoped	hoped
cry	cried	cried

Following is a list of some common regular verbs, showing the base form, the past tense, and the past participle. The base form can also be used with such helping verbs as *can, could, do, does, did, may, might, must, shall, should, will,* and *would.*

Regular Verbs

Base Form (Present)	Past	Past Participle
ask	asked	asked
answer	answered	answered
cry	cried	cried
decide	decided	decided
dive	dived (dove)	dived
finish	finished	finished
happen	happened	happened
learn	learned	learned
like	liked	liked
love	loved	loved
need	needed	needed
open	opened	opened
start	started	started
suppose	supposed	supposed
walk	walked	walked
want	wanted	wanted

Irregular Verbs

Irregular verbs do not follow any definite pattern.

Base Form (Present)	Past	Past Participle
shake	shook	shaken
make	made	made
begin	began	begun

Some irregular verbs that sound similar in the present tense don't follow the same pattern.

Base Form (Present)	Past	Past Participle
ring	rang	rung
swing	swung	swung
bring	brought	brought

Present Tense
For *he, she,* and *it,* irregular verbs in the present tense add an *-s* or an *-es* to the base word. The following chart shows the present tense of the base word *break,* which is an irregular verb.

	Singular	Plural
First Person:	I break	we break
Second Person:	you break	you break
Third Person:	he, she, it breaks	they break

If the irregular verb ends in *-y,* you might have to drop the *-y* and add *-ies* for *he, she,* and *it.*

	Singular	Plural
First Person:	I cry	we cry
Second Person:	you cry	you cry
Third Person:	he, she, it cries	they cry

Past Tense
Like past tense regular verbs, past tense irregular verbs do not change their forms. This chart shows the past tense of the irregular verb *do.*

	Singular	Plural
First Person:	I did	we did
Second Person:	you did	you did
Third Person:	he, she, it did	they did

The list on page 401 includes the past tense of many irregular verbs.

Past Participles
Use the past tense form with the helping verbs *has, have,* or *had.*

Here is a list of some common irregular verbs, showing the base form (present), the past tense, and the past participle. Like regular verbs, the base forms can be used with such helping verbs as *can, could, do, does, did, may, might, must, shall, should, will,* and *would.*

Irregular Verbs

Base Form (Present)	Past	Past Participle
arise	arose	arisen
awake	awoke (awaked)	awoken (awaked)
be	was, were	been
become	became	become
begin	began	begun
bend	bent	bent
blow	blew	blown
break	broke	broken
bring	brought	brought
burst	burst	burst
buy	bought	bought
catch	caught	caught
choose	chose	chosen
cling	clung	clung
come	came	come
cost	cost	cost
creep	crept	crept
deal	dealt	dealt
do	did	done
drink	drank	drunk
drive	drove	driven
eat	ate	eaten
feel	felt	felt
fight	fought	fought
fling	flung	flung
fly	flew	flown
forget	forgot	forgotten
freeze	froze	frozen
get	got	got (gotten)
go	went	gone
grow	grew	grown
hang	hung	hung
have	had	had
hit	hit	hit
know	knew	known
lead	led	led
leave	left	left
lose	lost	lost
make	made	made
mean	meant	meant
put	put	put
read	read	read
ride	rode	ridden
ring	rang	rung
see	saw	seen
shine	shone	shone
shoot	shot	shot
sing	sang	sung
sink	sank	sunk
sleep	slept	slept
slink	slunk	slunk

Base Form (Present)	Past	Past Participle
speak	spoke	spoken
spend	spent	spent
spread	spread	spread
steal	stole	stolen
stink	stank (stunk)	stunk
sweep	swept	swept
swim	swam	swum
swing	swung	swung
take	took	taken
teach	taught	taught
tear	tore	torn
think	thought	thought
throw	threw	thrown
thrust	thrust	thrust
wake	woke (waked)	woken (waked)
weep	wept	wept
write	wrote	written

Exercise 14   **SELECTING VERBS**

Cross out the incorrect verb form.

1. Mark (knew/knowed) he could not finish the term paper that semester.

2. They (dragged, drug, drugged) the cart into the back yard.

3. I was sure that I hadn't (ate, eaten) the lobster.

4. When we arrived, the windows were (broke, broked, broken).

5. Vanessa (dive, dived) from the high board and swam over to us.

6. Imelda had (spread, spreaded) the maps out on the table before the meeting.

7. Have they (began, begun) to gather that material this early?

8. Shawna (swimmed, swam, swum) that distance twice last week.

9. The water pipes have (burst, busted, bursted) again.

10. I (ran, runned) over to Colleen's house for help.

"Problem" Verbs

The following pairs of verbs are especially troublesome and confusing: *lie* and *lay,* *sit* and *set,* and *rise* and *raise.* One way to tell them apart is to remember which word in each pair takes a direct object. A direct object answers the question *whom* or *what* in connection with a verb. The words *lay, raise,* and *set* take a direct object.

He *raised* the window. (He *raised* what?)

Lie, rise, and *sit,* however, cannot take a direct object. We cannot say, for example, "He rose the window." In the examples, the italicized words are objects.

Present Tense	Meaning	Past Tense	Past Participle	Example
lie	to rest	lay	lain	I lay down to rest.
lay	to place something	laid	laid	We laid the *books* on the table.
rise	to go up	rose	risen	The smoke rose quickly.
raise	to lift, bring forth	raised	raised	She raised the *question*.
sit	to rest	sat	sat	He sat in the chair.
set	to place something	set	set	They set the *basket* on the floor.

Exercise 15	**SELECTING VERBS**

Cross out the incorrect verb form.

1. The book is (lying, laying) on top of the bureau.

2. Will we (receive, received) your package soon?

3. His recent decision will certainly (change, changed) our policy.

4. When he heard Lenore call, he (rose, raised) and left the room.

5. That dog can (sit, set) in the yard for hours and bark constantly.

6. Marcia (done, did) many chores before she left for school.

7. Why are you (sitting, setting) those plants in the hot sun?

8. My mother (don't, doesn't) understand why Victor takes so long to come home from kindergarten.

9. A stray cat (drowned, drownded) in the river yesterday.

10. The spy (fool, fooled) his captor by disguising himself as a workman.

11. My cousins will (left, leave) Europe soon.

12. We (learn, learned) from his conversation that he did not wish to go again.

13. Kim hasn't been able to (taught, teach) those boys anything.

14. Have you (tryed, tried) to relax for a few minutes this evening?

15. The police officers could not (see, saw) us cross the bridge during the heavy rainstorm.

16. You (lie, lay) down here and rest for a few minutes before class.

17. The cost of those articles has (raised, risen) considerably since the first of the year.

18. Pam (rose, raised) the window and waved to me as I passed.

19. My brother (lay, laid) the money on the table and looked hopefully at Mother.

20. Please (sit, set) the shoes down on the rack and come over here.

Exercise 16   **WRITING SENTENCES WITH TROUBLESOME VERBS**

Use each of these words in a sentence of ten words or more.

1. *lie, lay* (rest), *lain, laid* _____

_____

_____

_____

_____

_____

2. *sit, sat, set* _____

_____

_____

_____

_____

_____

3. *is, was, were* _____

_____

_____

_____

_____

_____

4. *do, does* (or *don't, doesn't*) _____

_____

_____

_____

_____

_____

_____

The Twelve Verb Tenses

Some languages, such as Chinese and Navajo, have no verb tenses to indicate time. English has a fairly complicated system of tenses, but most verbs pattern in what are known as the simple tenses: present, past, and future. Altogether there are twelve tenses in English. The first four charts that follow illustrate those tenses in sentences. The next charts place each verb on a time line. The charts also explain what the different tenses mean and how to form them.

Simple Tenses

Present:	I, we, you, they *drive.* He, she, it *drives.*
Past:	I, we, you, he, she, it, they *drove.*
Future:	I, we, you, he, she, it, they *will drive.*

Perfect Tenses

Present Perfect:	I, we, you, they *have driven.* He, she, it *has driven.*
Past Perfect:	I, we, you, he, she, it, they *had driven.*
Future Perfect:	I, we, you, he, she, it, they *will have driven.*

Progressive Tenses

Present Progressive:	I *am driving.* He, she, it *is driving.* We, you, they *are driving.*
Past Progressive:	I, he, she, it *was driving.* We, you, they *were driving.*
Future Progressive:	I, we, you, he, she, it, they *will be driving.*

Perfect Progressive Tenses

Present Perfect Progressive:	I, we, you, they *have been driving.* He, she, it *has been driving.*
Past Perfect Progressive:	I, we, you, he, she, it, they *had been driving.*
Future Perfect Progressive:	I, we, you, he, she, it, they *will have been driving.*

Simple Tenses

Tense	Time Line	Time	Verb Form

Present
  I <u>drive</u> to work.
 	
  She <u>drives</u> to work.
	past ——— XXX ——— future
	Now
		Present; may imply a continuation from past to future	Present:
			  <u>drive</u>
			  <u>drives</u>

Past I <u>drove</u> to work.	X Now	Past	Past: <u>drove</u>
Future I <u>will drive</u> to work.	X Now	Future	Present preceded by <u>will</u>: <u>will drive</u>

Perfect Tenses

Tense	Time Line	Time	Verb Form
Present Perfect I <u>have driven</u> to work.	past ——— XXX ——— future Now	Completed recently in past; may continue into the present	Past participle preceded by <u>have</u> or <u>has</u>: <u>have driven</u>
Past Perfect I <u>had driven</u> to work before I moved to the city (event).	Event XO Now	Prior to a specific time in the past	Past participle preceded by <u>had</u>: <u>had driven</u>
Future Perfect I <u>will have driven</u> to work thousands of times by December (event).	Event X O Now	At a time prior to a specific time in the future	Past participle preceded by <u>will have</u>: <u>will have driven</u>

Progressive Tenses

Tense	Time Line	Time	Verb Form
Present Progressive I <u>am driving</u> to work.	past —— future **Now**	In progress now	Progressive (-*ing* ending) preceded by <u>is</u>, <u>am</u>, or <u>are</u>: <u>am driving</u>
Past Progressive I <u>was driving</u> to work.	**Now**	In progress in the past	Progressive (-*ing* ending) preceded by <u>was</u> or <u>were</u>: <u>was driving</u>
Future Progressive I <u>will be driving</u> to work.	**Now**	In progress in the future	Progressive (-*ing* ending) preceded by <u>will be</u>: <u>will be driving</u>

Perfect Progressive Tenses

Tense	Time Line	Time	Verb Form
Present Perfect Progressive I <u>have been driving</u> to work.	past —— future **Now**	In progress before now or up to now	Progressive (-*ing* ending) preceded by <u>have been</u> or <u>has been</u>: <u>have been driving</u>
Past Perfect Progressive I <u>had been driving</u> when I began ride-sharing (event).	Event **Now**	In progress before another event in the past	Progressive (-*ing* ending) preceded by <u>had</u>: I <u>had been driving</u>
Future Perfect Progressive By May 1 (event), I <u>will have been driving</u> to work for six years.	Event **Now**	In progress before another event in the future	Progressive (-*ing* ending) preceded by <u>will have been</u>: <u>will have been driving</u>

Exercise 17	SELECTING VERBS

Underline the correct verb form. (See Answer Key for answers.)

1. I wished I (stayed, had stayed) home.

2. I remembered that I (paid, had paid) him twice.

3. After parking their car, they (walk, walked) to the beach.

4. I (have, had) never encountered a genius until I met her.

5. I hoped that we (could have gone, went) to the big game.

6. They know that they (will complete, will have completed) the job before the first snow.

7. We (are considering, consider) the proposal.

8. He told us of the interesting life he (had led, led).

9. We went to the desert to see the cabin they (built, had built).

10. Tomorrow I (drive, will drive) to the supermarket for party items.

Exercise 18	SELECTING VERBS

Underline the correct verb form.

1. The scholars (worked, had worked) many hours before they solved the problem.

2. The shipping clerks wished they (had sent, sent) the package.

3. We (study, are studying) the issue now.

4. We (decide, will decide) on the winner tomorrow.

5. They reminded us that we (made, had made) the same promise before.

6. Before she went to Mexico, Jill (had never been, never was) out of the country.

7. Jake (had been napping, napped) when the alarm sounded.

8. By the time he finished talking, he realized that he (said, had said) too much.

9. At the end of the semester, the course grade (depends, will depend) on your ability to write well.

10. After he retired, I realized how much I (had learned, learned) from working with him.

Subject-Verb Agreement

This section is concerned with number agreement between subjects and verbs. The basic principle of **subject-verb agreement** is that if the subject is singular, the verb should be singular, and if the subject is plural, the verb should be plural. There are ten major guidelines. In the examples under the following guidelines, the simple subjects and verbs are italicized.

1. Do not let words that come between the subject and verb affect agreement.

   - Modifying phrases and clauses frequently come between the subject and verb:

     The various *types* of drama *were* not *discussed.*

     Angela, who is hitting third, *is* the best player.

     The *price* of those shoes *is* too high.

   - Certain prepositions can cause trouble. The following words are prepositions, not conjunctions: *along, with, as well as, besides, in addition to, including, together with.* The words that function as objects of prepositions cannot also be subjects of the sentence.

     The *coach,* along with the players, *protests* the decision.

   - When a negative phrase follows a positive subject, the verb agrees with the positive subject.

     Philip, not the other boys, *was* the culprit.

2. Do not let inversions (verb before subject, not the normal order) affect the agreement of subject and verb.

   - Verbs and other words may come before the subject. Do not let them affect the agreement. To understand subject-verb relationships, recast the sentence in normal word order.

     Are Juan and his *sister* at home? (question form)

     Juan and his *sister are* at home. (normal order)

   - A sentence filler is a word that is grammatically independent of other words in the sentence. The most common fillers are *there* and *here.* Even though a sentence filler precedes the verb, it should not be treated as the subject.

     There *are* many *reasons* for his poor work. (The verb *are* agrees with the subject *reasons.*)

3. A singular verb agrees with a singular indefinite pronoun. (See page 366.)

   - Most indefinite pronouns are singular.

     Each of the women *is* ready at this time.

     Neither of the women *is* ready at this time.

     One of the children *is* not paying attention.

   - Certain indefinite pronouns do not clearly express either a singular or plural number. Agreement, therefore, depends on the meaning of the sentence. These pronouns are *all, any, none,* and *some.*

     All of the melon *was* good.

     All of the melons *were* good.

     None of the pie *is* acceptable.

     None of the pies *are* acceptable.

4. Two or more subjects joined by *and* usually take a plural verb.

> The *captain* and the *sailors were* happy to be ashore.

> The *trees* and *shrubs need* more care.

- If the parts of a compound subject mean one and the same person or thing, the verb is singular; if the parts mean more than one, the verb is plural.

> The *secretary* and *treasurer is* not present. (one)

> The *secretary* and the *treasurer are* not present. (more than one)

- When *each* or *every* precedes singular subjects joined by *and,* the verb is singular.

> Each *boy* and each *girl brings* a donation.

> Each *woman* and *man has asked* the same questions.

5. Alternative subjects—that is, subjects joined by *or, nor, either/or, neither/nor, not only/but also*—should be handled in the following manner:

- If the subjects are both singular, the verb is singular.

> *Rosa* or *Alicia* is responsible.

- If the subjects are plural, the verb is plural.

> Neither the *students* nor the *teachers were* impressed by his comments.

- If one of the subjects is singular and the other subject is plural, the verb agrees with the nearer subject.

> Either the Garcia *boys* or their *father goes* to the hospital each day.

> Either their *father* or the Garcia *boys go* to the hospital each day.

6. Collective nouns—*team, family, group, crew, gang, class, faculty,* and the like—take a singular verb if the verb is considered a unit, but they take a plural verb if the group is considered as a number of individuals.

> The *team is playing* well tonight.

> *The team are getting* dressed.

(In the second sentence the individuals are acting not as a unit but separately. If you don't like the way the sentence sounds, substitute "The members of the team are getting dressed.")

7. Titles of books, essays, short stories, and plays, a word spoken of as a word, and the names of businesses take a singular verb.

> *The Canterbury Tales was written* by Geoffrey Chaucer.

> *Ives is* my favorite name for a pet.

> *Markel Brothers has* a sale this week.

8. Sums of money, distances, and measurements are followed by a singular verb when a unit is meant. They are followed by a plural verb when the individual elements are considered separately.

> *Three dollars was* the price. (unit)

> *Three dollars were* lying there. (individual)

> *Five years is* a long time. (unit)

> The *first five years were* difficult ones. (individual)

9. Be careful of agreement with nouns ending in *-s.* Several nouns ending in *-s* take a singular verb—for example, *aeronautics, civics, economics, ethics, measles, mumps.*

> *Mumps is* an extremely unpleasant disease.
>
> *Economics is* my major field of study.

10. Some nouns have only a plural form and so take only a plural verb—for example, *clothes, fireworks, scissors, trousers.*

> His *trousers are* badly wrinkled.
>
> Marv's *clothes were* stylish and expensive.

Exercise 19	MAKING SUBJECTS AND VERBS AGREE

Cross out the incorrect verb form. (See Answer Key for answers.)

1. Where can you go to find a place where there (is, are) no tin cans to spoil the view?

2. We have no case if neither the police nor the detectives (has, have) produced a suspect.

3. (Has, Have) either of the winners admitted cheating?

4. Every child who camps in the woods (eat, eats) more there than at home.

5. We wanted to be sure all of the dishes (were, was) tasted by everyone.

6. Several, not just one, of his answers (is, are) right.

7. On one occasion, a husband and wife (was, were) elected co-presidents.

8. Macaroni and cheese (is, are) the regular chef's special on Fridays.

9. A photographer knows that each pose and each lighting shift (change, changes) the subject's appearance.

10. Every pen and pencil in the office (has, have) a clip attached.

11. The captain said either the mates or the lieutenant (was, were) able to guide the ship.

12. It looks as if neither the treasury nor the miscellaneous funds (is, are) enough to cover expenses.

13. Old Mt. Triton (attracts, attract) artists every fall.

14. The lawyer always (want, wants) to defend the underdog.

15. The students wait until the faculty (get, gets) in line.

16. *Knots and Splices* (tell, tells) how to make a hammock from cord.

17. Three months (seem, seems) like a long vacation to a businessperson.

18. Aesthetics (is, are) often as much a philosophical consideration as an artistic one.

19. At the end of the conference two hours (is, are) spent on reviewing and summarizing.

20. Cameron asked if mathematics (was, were) different from arithmetic.

Exercise 20   MAKING SUBJECTS AND VERBS AGREE

Cross out the incorrect verb form.

1. Many kinds of poetry (is, are) included.

2. Leticia, one of the best players, (are, is) lost for the season.

3. The cost of those victories (is, are) not soon forgotten.

4. My neighbor, along with fifteen of his rowdy friends, (are, is) noisy almost every night.

5. Cindy Jenkins, not the other Cindy's, (is, are) the one I am talking about.

6. (Is, Are) Teshon and Twalla coming to the party?

7. There (is, are) many questions and few answers.

8. Each of the students (are, is) prepared for the challenge.

9. Neither of the workers (cares, care) who takes the first break.

10. One of the professors (talk, talks) louder than the other.

11. Some of the apple pie (was, were) edible.

12. Some of the apples (was, were) edible.

13. (Do, Does) your car or your shoes need polishing?

14. Neither my shoes nor my car (need, needs) polishing.

15. Make certain that every adult and child (get, gets) the message.

16. The manager and coach (is, are) sitting in the dugout.

17. *Microbe Hunters* (is, are) a famous book about biology.

18. Penneys (celebrate, celebrates) its annual Blue Moon Sale this week.

19. Civics (is, are) my favorite class.

20. The fireworks (explode, explodes) on the stadium infield.

Consistency in Tense

Consider this paragraph:

> We (1) went downtown, and then we (2) watch a movie. Later we (3) met some friends from school, and we all (4) go to the mall. For most of the evening, we (5) play video games in arcades. It (6) was a typical but rather uneventful summer day.

Does the shifting verb tense bother you (to say nothing about the lack of development of ideas)? It should! The writer makes several unnecessary changes. Verbs 1, 3, and 6 are in the past tense, and verbs 2, 4, and 5 are in the present tense. Changing all verbs to past tense makes the paragraph much smoother.

> We went downtown, and then we watched a movie. Later we met some friends from school, and we all went to the mall. For most of the evening, we played video games in arcades. It was a typical but rather uneventful summer day.

In other instances you might want to maintain a consistent present tense. There are no inflexible rules about selecting a tense for certain kinds of writing, but you should be consistent, changing tense only for a good reason.

The present tense is usually used in writing about literature, even if the literature was written long in the past:

> *Moby Dick* is a novel about Captain Ahab's obsession with a great white whale. Ahab *sets* sail with a full crew of sailors who *think* they *are going* on merely another whaling voyage. Most of the crew *are* experienced seamen.

The past tense is likely to serve you best in writing about your personal experiences and about historical events (although the present tense can often be used effectively to establish the feeling of intimacy and immediacy):

> In the summer of 1991, Hurricane Bob *hit* the Atlantic coast region. It *came* ashore near Cape Hatteras and *moved* north. The winds *reached* a speed of more than ninety miles per hour on Cape Cod but then *slackened* by the time Bob *reached* Maine.

Exercise 21   **MAKING VERBS CONSISTENT IN TENSE**

In each sentence, the last verb is the wrong tense. Cross it out and write the correct form above it. (See Answer Key for answers.)

1. Francis Bacon said that reading made a full man.

2. The tutor had gone over the metaphors many times before Dylan take the test.

3. Professor Sydney was always surprised that only a few students in every class knew what an iambic foot was.

4. After having worked in the shoe store for twelve years, Kristin quits to take up computer programming.

5. We heard a crash in the kitchen, but the embarrassed hostess doesn't explain it.

6. Jana has only the bibliography page to complete before the lights went out.

7. No one who has a full-time job got a fellowship next year.

8. Jorgensen proposes in the first act, but he will marry another woman in the second act.

9. The reporter didn't know that *Prudence* was a female name.

10. Whitehead, the philosopher and mathematician, said that imagination was a contagious disease.

11. The minister offered to heal anyone of any illness; then he asks for a love offering.

12. He gives her a beautiful diamond; then she breaks the engagement and kept the diamond.

13. As Pam lectures, she had the habit of twitching her nose.

14. The guide liked our group because jokes were passed back and forth and are really enjoyed.

15. When little Lizzie went to bed crying, Hector comes up to comfort her.

16. Janeen thought we added Alaska because we need more people in the United States.

17. Frank fell asleep before he finishes the last page of the manuscript.

18. The thing we wanted most was to have told him we will always be his friends.

19. Wes thinks he is seeing things when a man handed him the money.

20. We drove past the church where the people were milling around and the minister is shaking everybody's hand.

| Exercise 22 | MAKING VERBS CONSISTENT IN TENSE |

Change the verbs in the following paragraph as necessary to maintain a mostly consistent past tense. (See Answer Key for answers.)

(1) Tarzan spoke to Jane in simple language. (2) His most famous words were "Me Tarzan, you Jane." (3) Before the arrival of Jane, there are only jungle friends for Tarzan. (4) Those animals seldom used the full eight parts of speech. (5) For example, lions seldom utter verbs. (6) Elephants had no patience with prepositions. (7) Chimps condemn conjunctions. (8) Their punctuation was replaced largely by snarls, growls, and breast-beating. (9) Their language is well suited to Tarzan. (10) To him, jungle language was like swinging on a vine. (11) A one-syllable yell is a full oration. (12) Jane never ridiculed his grammar or even his yelling. (13) She holds back criticism of the king of the apes. (14) Despite their difference in language skills, they establish hutkeeping. (15) They were very poor and wore simple garments made of skins. (16) Their main transportation is well-placed hanging vines. (17) Tarzan and Jane had a child. (18) They name him "Boy." (19) Fortunately, they did not have another male child. (20) Such an occurrence could have caused a language gridlock.

| Exercise 23 | MAKING VERBS CONSISTENT IN TENSE |

Change the verbs in the following paragraph as necessary to maintain a mostly consistent past tense.

(1) Once upon a time, a Professor Glen was very popular with his students. (2) He kept long office hours and always speaks nicely to his students on campus. (3) He even bought popcorn for them to munch on during tests. (4) Respecting their sensitivity, he marks with a soothing green ink instead of red. (5) He often told jokes and listened attentively to their complaints about assignments. (6) The leaders of student government elect him teacher of the century. (7) Who would not admire such a person? (8) Then late one semester, a strange and shocking thing happens. (9) Everywhere there were students in despair. (10) Professor Glen no longer speaks

openly to students. (11) During his office hours, he locked his door and posted a pit bull. (12) He marks student papers in flaming scarlet. (13) Instead of popcorn, he gave them hot scorn. (14) He told no more jokes and sneered at their complaints about assignments. (15) He sticks out his tongue at students on campus. (16) He offered good grades for cash. (17) Professor Glen even accepts Visa cards and validated parking. (18) One day the students heard a thumping sound in a classroom closet. (19) Looking inside, they find the true Professor Glen. (20) The other one was an evil twin professor.

Active and Passive Voice

Which of these sentences sounds better?

> Ken Griffey, Jr., slammed a home run.

> A home run was slammed by Ken Griffey, Jr.

Both sentences carry the same message, but the first expresses it more effectively. The subject (*Ken Griffey, Jr.*) is the actor. The verb (*slammed*) is the action. The direct object (*home run*) is the receiver of the action. The second sentence lacks the vitality of the first because the receiver of the action is the subject; the one who performs the action is embedded in the prepositional phrase at the end of the sentence.

The first sentence demonstrates the active voice. It has an active verb (one that leads to the direct object), and the action moves from the beginning to the end of the sentence. The second exhibits the passive voice (with the action reflecting back on the subject). When given a choice, you should usually select the active voice. It promotes energy and directness.

The passive voice, though not usually the preferred form, does have its uses.

- When the doer of the action is unknown or unimportant:

> My car was stolen.

> (The doer, a thief, is unknown.)

- When the receiver of the action is more important than the doer:

> My neighbor was permanently disabled by an irresponsible drunk driver.

> (The neighbor's suffering is the focus, not the drunk driver.)

As you can see, the passive construction places the doer at the end of a prepositional phrase (as in the second example) or does not include the doer in the statement at all (as in the first example). In the first example the receiver of the action (the car) is in the subject position. The verb is preceded by the *to be* helper *was*. Here is another example:

> The book was read by her.   (passive)

> She read the book.   (active)

Because weak sentences often involve the unnecessary and ineffective use of the passive form, the following exercise gives you practice in identifying the passive voice and changing it to active.

| **Exercise 24** | **USING ACTIVE AND PASSIVE VOICE** |

Rewrite these sentences to convert the verbs from passive to active voice. (See Answer Key for answers to 1–5.)

1. A letter has been written by me to you.

2. An honest dollar was never made by his ancestors, and now he is following in their fingerprints.

3. The assignment was approved by the instructor.

4. The instructor was given a much-deserved medal of valor by the president of the student body.

5. Few people noticed that most of the work was done by the quiet students.

6. The ballgame was interrupted by bats catching flies in the outfield.

7. The commotion at the apathy convention was caused by a person who attended.

8. The air was filled with speeches by him.

9. He doesn't have an enemy, but he is hated by all his friends.

10. His lips are never passed by a lie—he talks through his nose.

Strong Verbs

Because the verb is an extremely important part of any sentence, it should be chosen with care. Some of the most widely used verbs are the "being" verbs: *is, was, were, are, am.* We couldn't get along in English without them, but writers often use them when more forceful and effective verbs are available. Consider these examples:

Weak Verb: He *is* the leader of the people.

Strong Verb: He *leads* the people.

Weak Verb: She *was* the first to finish.

Strong Verb: She *finished* first.

| **Exercise 25** | **USING STRONG VERBS** |

Rewrite the following sentences to strengthen the weak verbs. (See Answer Key for answers to 1–5.)

1. He is the writer of that essay.

2. She was the driver of the speeding car.

3. He was the player of the guitar.

4. They were the leaders of the entire region in sales.

5. The medicine was a cure for the cold.

6. The last entertainer was the winner of the award.

7. The yowling cat was the cause of my waking up last night.

8. The mechanic is the fixer of my car.

9. He was in attendance at the computer seminar.

10. She is a shoe salesperson.

Subjunctive Mood

Mood refers to the intention of the verb. Three moods are relevant to our study: indicative, imperative, and subjunctive.

The indicative mood expresses a statement of fact.

> I considered the issue.

> I was tired.

The imperative mood expresses a command (and has a *you* understood subject).

> Go to the store.

The subjunctive mood expresses a statement as contrary to fact, conditional, desirable, possible, necessary, or doubtful. In current English the subjunctive form is distinguishable only in two forms: The verb *to be* uses *be* throughout the present tense and *were* throughout the past tense.

> He requires that we *be* (instead of *are*) on time.

> If she *were* (instead of *was*) the candidate, she would win.

In other verbs, the final *s* is dropped in the third person singular (*he, she, it*) of the present tense to make all forms the same in any one tense.

> I request that he *report* (instead of *reports*) today.

Here are examples of the common forms:

If I *were* (instead of *was*) you, I wouldn't do that. (contrary to fact)

She behaves as if she *were* (instead of *was*) not certain. (doubt)

I wish I *were* (instead of *was* in Texas. (wish)

Exercise 26	**SELECTING SUBJUNCTIVE VERBS**

Underline the subjunctive verbs. (See Answer Key for answers to 1–5.)

1. If I (was, were) going to work, I would give you a ride.

2. I wish I (were, was) on the beach.

3. I demand that you (will return, return) the deposit.

4. They act as if they (are, were) rich.

5. I require that my workers (are, be) on time.

6. You may wish you (are, were) an adult, but you must show your ID.

7. You talk as if winning (was, were) possible.

8. My manager insists that I (be, am) tactful with clients.

9. Suppose, for sake of argument, your statement (was, were) true.

10. Sometimes I wish I (were, was) of the younger generation.

Pronouns

Should you say, "Between you and *I*" or "Between you and *me*"? What about "Let's you and *I* do this" or "Let's you and *me* do this"? Are you confused about when to use *who* and *whom?* Is it "Everyone should wear *their* coat, or *his* coat, or *his or her* coat"? Is there anything wrong with saying, "When *you* walk down the streets of Laredo"?

The examples in the first paragraph represent the most common problems people have with pronouns. This section will help you identify the standard forms and understand why they are correct. The result should be expertise and confidence.

Pronoun Case

Case is the form a pronoun takes as it fills a position in a sentence. Words such as *you* and *it* do not change, but others do, and they change in predictable ways. For example, *I* is a subject word and *me* is an object word. As you refer to yourself, you will select a pronoun that fits a certain part of sentence structure. You say, "*I* will write the paper," not "*Me* will write the paper," because *I* is in the subject position.

But you say, "She will give the apple to *me*," not "She will give the apple to *I*," because *me* is in the object position. These are the pronouns that change:

Subject	**Object**
I	me
he	him
she	her
we	us
they	them
who, whoever	whom, whomever

Subjective Case

	Singular	**Plural**
First Person:	I	we
Second Person:	you	you
Third Person:	he she it	they

who

Subjective-case pronouns can fill two positions in a sentence.

1. Pronouns in the subjective case fill subject positions.

   a. Some will be easy to identify because they are at the beginning of the sentence.

      I dance in the park.

      He dances in the park.

      She dances in the park.

      We dance in the park.

      They dance in the park.

      Who is dancing in the park?

   b. Others will be more difficult to identify because they are not at the beginning of a sentence and may not appear to be part of a clause. The words *than* and *as* are signals for these special arrangements, which can be called incompletely stated clauses.

      He is taller than *I* (am).

      She is younger than *we* (are).

      We work as hard as *they* (do).

The words *am, are,* and *do,* which complete the clauses, have been omitted. We are actually saying, "He is taller than *I am,*" "She is younger than *we are,*" and "We work as hard as *they do.*" The italicized pronouns are subjects of "understood" verbs.

2. Pronouns in the subjective case refer back to the subject.

   a. They follow a form of the verb *to be*, such as *was, were, am, is*, and *are*.

      I believe it is *he.*

      It was *she* who spoke.

      The victims were *they.*

   b. Some nouns and pronouns refer back to an earlier noun without referring back through the verb.

      The leading candidates—Juan, Darnelle, Steve, Kimlieu, and *I*—made speeches.

Objective Case

	Singular	Plural
First Person:	me	us
Second Person:	you	you
Third Person:	him her it	them
	whom	

Objective-case pronouns can also fill two positions in sentences.

1. Pronouns in the objective case fill object positions.

   a. They may be objects after the verb.

     • A direct object answers the question *what* or *whom* in connection with the verb.

      We brought *it* to your house. (*what* did we bring? *it*)

      We saw *her* in the library. (*whom* did we see? *her*)

     • An indirect object answers the question *to whom* in connection with the verb.

      I gave *him* the message. (*to whom* did I give the message? *to him*)

      The doctor told *us* the test results. (*to whom* did the doctor tell the results? *to us*)

   b. Objective-case pronouns are objects after prepositions.

      The problem was clear to *us.*

      I went with Steve and *him.*

2. Objective-case pronouns may also refer back to object words.

      They had the costumes for us—Judy and *me.*

      The judge addressed the defendants—John and *her.*

Techniques for Determining Case

Here are three techniques that will help you decide which pronoun to use when the choice seems difficult.

1. If you have a compound element (such as a subject or an object of a preposition), consider only the pronoun part. The sound alone will probably tell you the answer.

> She gave the answer to Marie and (I, me).

Marie and the pronoun make up a compound object of the preposition *to*. Disregard the noun, *Marie*, and ask yourself, "Would I say, 'She gave the answer *to me* or *to I*'?" The way the words sound would tell you the answer is *to me*. Of course, if you immediately notice that the pronoun is in an object position, you need not bother with sound.

2. If you are choosing between *who* (subject word) and *whom* (object word), look to the right to see if the next verb has a subject. If it does not, the pronoun probably *is* the subject, but if it does have a subject, the pronoun probably is an object.

> The person (*who*, whom) works hardest will win. (*Who* is the correct answer because it is the subject of the verb *works*.)

> The person (who, *whom*) we admire most is José. (*Whom* is the correct answer because the next verb, *admire*, already has a subject, *we*. *Whom* is an object.)

A related technique works the same way. If the next important word after *who* or *whom* in a statement is a noun or pronoun, the correct word will almost always be *whom*. However, if the next important word is not a noun or pronoun, the correct word will be *who*.

To apply this technique, you must disregard qualifier clauses such as "I think," "it seems," and "we hope."

> Tyrone is a natural leader (*who*, whom) has charisma. (*Who* is the correct answer; it is followed by something other than a noun or pronoun.)

> Tyrone is a natural leader (*who*, whom), we think, has charisma. (*Who* is the correct answer; it is followed by the qualifier clause *we think*, which is then followed by something other than a noun or pronoun.)

> Tyrone is a natural leader (who, *whom*) we supported. (*Whom* is the correct answer; it is followed by a pronoun.)

3. *Let's* is made up of the words *let* and *us* and means "you *let us*"; therefore, when you select a pronoun to follow it, consider the two original words and select another object word—*me*.

> Let's you and (I, *me*) take a trip to Westwood. (Think of "You let us, you and me, take a trip to Westwood." *Us* and *me* are object words.)

Exercise 27   **SELECTING PRONOUNS: CASE**

Cross out the incorrect pronoun form. (See Answer Key for answers.)

Compounds

1. José, William, and (she, her) were asked to wait on tables.

2. Did you and (she, her) go to the movies last Saturday evening?

3. They bought those presents for Christine and (he, him).

4. Her mother also sent Alicia and (they, them) additional announcements.

Appositives

5. Let's you and (I, me) do the homework together tomorrow afternoon.

6. Three members of the sophomore class—Kyoko, you, and (she, her)—were chosen to attend the fall conference.

7. They classified two students as incompetent—Lionel and (he, him).

8. (We, Us) married people must be willing to make some compromises to pre-serve our relationships.

9. Will they ask (we, us) women to join their club?

Comparisons

10. My brother is much shorter than (I, me).

11. Kim runs as fast as (she, her).

12. Anne is not as sensible about such things as (they, them).

13. Sam is as reliable as (I, me).

Who, Whom

14. (Who, Whom) do you know at my school?

15. Syd is one person, I believe, (who, whom) we can depend on.

16. (Who, Whom) was to blame for that accident?

17. The young man (who, whom) we met last week is Phil's brother.

18. (Who, Whom) do you believe will win the contest?

Refer Back to Subject

19. It is (I, me) to whom they gave the books.

20. Was it (she, her) you saw at the restaurant?

Exercise 28   SELECTING PRONOUNS: CASE

Cross out the incorrect pronoun form.

1. She did not realize that you and (I, me) would be asked to testify.

2. Give the award to (whoever, whomever) is voted most valuable player.

3. We need one person (who, whom) we can rely on.

4. Would you support (her, she) in the election?

5. Let's you and (I, me) take that trip next year.

6. Everybody but (he, him) was ready for the test.

7. Only two were chosen, Kathy and (he, him).

8. She thinks more clearly than (I, me).

9. Distribute the cards among John, Joe, and (he, him).

10. Gilligan knows the answer better than (we, us).

11. The person (which, who) came will call on you again.

12. You know that much better than (I, me).

13. The police believed (they, them) to be us.

14. The court found (us, we) to be responsible.

15. (Whoever, Whomever) they choose will receive the promotion.

16. I would have taken (she, her) to the meeting.

17. Is it (I, me) you are looking for?

18. Just between you and (I, me), I think we should go.

19. It could have been (he, him) whom you saw.

20. The soldiers (who, whom) they trained were sent to the front.

Pronoun-Antecedent Agreement

Every pronoun refers to an earlier noun, which is called the *antecedent* of the pronoun. The antecedent is the noun that the pronoun replaces. The pronoun brings the reader back to the earlier thought. Here are some examples:

> I tried to buy *tickets* for the concert, but *they* were all sold.

> *Roger* painted a *picture* of a pickup truck. *It* was so good that *he* entered *it* in an art show.

A **pronoun** agrees with its antecedent in person, number, and gender. **Person—** first, second, or third—indicates perspective, or point of view. **Number** indicates singular or plural. **Gender** indicates masculine, feminine, or neuter.

	Subject Words				Object Words	
	Singular	Plural			Singular	Plural
First Person:	I	we		**First Person:**	me	us
Second Person:	you	you		**Second Person:**	you	you
Third Person:	he, she, it	they		**Third Person:**	him, her, it	them
	who				whom	

Agreement in Person

Avoid needless shifting of person, which means shifting of point of view, such as from *I* to *you*. First person, second person, and third person indicate perspectives from which you can write. Select one point of view and maintain it, promoting continuity and consistency. Needless shifting of person, meaning changing perspectives without reasons important for your content and purpose, is distracting and awkward. Each point of view has its appropriate purposes.

First Person

Using the word *I* and its companion forms *we, me,* and *us,* the first-person point of view emphasizes the writer, who is an important part of the subject of the composition. Choose first person for friendly letters, accounts of personal experience, and, occasionally, business correspondence, such as a letter of application for a job, which requires self-analysis.

Observe the presence of the writer and the use of *I* in this example.

> I could tell that the wedding would not go well when the caterers started serving drinks before the ceremony and the bride began arguing with her future mother-in-law. After the sound system crashed, the band canceled and I wished I hadn't come.

Second Person

Using or implying the word *you,* the second-person point of view is fine for informal conversation, advice, and directions. Although it is occasionally found in academic writing, most instructors prefer that you use it only in process analysis, directions in how to do something.

In this example, note that the word *you* is sometimes understood and not stated.

> To juggle three balls, first you place two balls (A and B) in one hand and one ball (C) in the other. Then toss one of the two balls (A), and before you catch it with your other hand, toss the single ball (C) from that hand. Before that ball (C) lands in the other hand, toss the remaining inactive ball (B). Then pick up the balls and repeat the process until balls no longer fall to the ground.

Third Person

Referring to subject material, individuals, things, or ideas, the third-person point of view works best for most formal writing, be it academic or professional. Third-person pronouns include *he, she, it, they, him, her,* and *them.* Most of your college writing—essay exams, reports, compositions that explain and argue, critiques, and research papers—will be from this detached perspective with no references to yourself.

In this example, written in the third person, the name *Bartleby* is replaced by forms of *he.*

> *Bartleby,* one of Herman Melville's most memorable characters, has befuddled critics for more than a century. At a point in *his* life chosen for no obvious reason, *he* decides not to work, not to cooperate with others, and not to leave the premises of *his* employer because *he* "prefers not to." Most readers do not know what to make of *him.*

Correcting Problems of Agreement in Person

Most problems with pronoun agreement in person occur with the use of *you* in a passage that should have been written in the first or third person. If your composition is not one of advice or directions, the word *you* is probably not appropriate and should be replaced with a first- or third-person pronoun.

If you are giving advice or directions, use *you* throughout the passage, but, if you are not, replace each *you* with a first- or third-person pronoun that is consistent with the perspective, purpose, and content of the passage.

Inconsistent:	*I* love to travel, especially when *you* go to foreign countries.
Consistent:	*I* love to travel, especially when *I* go to foreign countries.
Inconsistent:	When *you* are about to merge with moving traffic on the freeway, *one* should not stop *his or her* car.
Consistent:	When *you* are about to merge with moving traffic on the freeway, *you* should not stop *your* car.
Consistent	(using third-person pronouns, including the indefinite pronoun *one*): When *one* is about to merge with moving traffic on the freeway, *one* should not stop *his or her* car.
Consistent	(using third-person plural pronouns to match plural noun): When *drivers* are about to merge with moving traffic on the freeway, *they* should not stop *their* car.

Agreement in Number

Most problems with pronoun-antecedent agreement involve **number.** The principles are simple: If the antecedent (the word the pronoun refers back to) is singular, use a singular pronoun. If the antecedent is plural, use a plural pronoun.

1. A singular antecedent requires a singular pronoun.

   Vincent forgot *his* notebook.

2. A plural antecedent requires a plural pronoun.

   Many *students* cast *their* votes today.

3. A singular indefinite pronoun as an antecedent takes a singular pronoun. Most indefinite pronouns are singular. The following are common indefinite singular pronouns: *anybody, anyone, each, either, everybody, everyone, no one, nobody, one, somebody, someone.*

Each of the girls brought *her* book.

When *one* makes a promise, *one* (or *he or she*) should keep it.

4. A plural indefinite pronoun as an antecedent takes a plural pronoun.

Few knew *their* assignments.

5. Certain indefinite pronouns do not clearly express either a singular or plural number. Agreement, therefore, depends on the meaning of the sentence. These pronouns are *all, any, none,* and *some.*

All of the apple *was* wormy.

All of the apples *were* wormy.

None of the cake *is* acceptable.

None of the cakes *are* acceptable.

6. Two or more antecedents, singular or plural, take a plural pronoun. Such antecedents are usually joined together by *and* or by commas and *and.*

Howard and his *parents* bought *their* presents early.

Students, instructors, and the *administration* pooled *their* ideas at the forum.

7. Alternative antecedents—that is, antecedents joined by *or, nor, whether/or, either/or, neither/nor, not only/but also*—require a pronoun that agrees with the nearer antecedent.

Neither Alex nor his *friends* lost *their* way.

Neither his friends nor *Alex* lost *his* way.

8. In a sentence with an expression such as *one of those _____ who,* the antecedent is usually the plural noun that follows the preposition *of.*

He is one of those *people who* want *their* money now.

9. In a sentence with the expression *the only one of those _____ who,* the antecedent is usually the singular word *one.*

She is the *only one* of the members *who* wants *her* money now.

10. When collective nouns such as *team, jury, committee,* and *band* are used as antecedents, they take a singular pronoun if they are considered as units.

The *jury* is doing *its* best.

When individual behavior is suggested, antecedents take a plural form.

The *jury* are putting on *their* coats.

11. The words *each, every,* and *many a(n)* before a noun make the noun singular.

Each child and *adult* was *his* or *her* own authority.

Each and *every person* doubted *himself* or *herself.*

Many a person is capable of knowing *himself* or *herself.*

Agreement in Gender

The pronoun should agree with its antecedent in **gender,** if the gender of the antecedent is specific. Masculine and feminine pronouns are gender-specific: *he, him, she, her.* Others are neuter: *I, we, me, us, it, they, them, who, whom, that, which.*

The words *who* and *whom* refer to people. *That* can refer to ideas, things, and people, but usually does not refer to individuals. *Which* refers to ideas and things, but never to people.

> My *girlfriend* gave me *her* best advice. (feminine)

> Mighty *Casey* tried *his* best. (masculine)

> The *people* with *whom* I work are loud. (neuter)

Indefinite singular pronouns used as antecedents require, of course, singular pronouns. Handling the gender of these singular pronouns is not as obvious; opinion is divided.

1. Traditionally, writers have used the masculine form of pronouns to refer to the indefinite singular pronouns when the gender is unknown.

> *Everyone* should work until *he* drops.

2. To avoid a perceived sex bias, use *he or she* or *his or her* instead of just *he* or *his*.

> *Everyone* should work until *he or she* drops.

3. Although option 1 is more direct, it is illogical to many listeners and readers, and option 2 used several times in a short passage can be awkward. To avoid those possible problems, writers often use plural forms.

> *All people* should work until *they* drop.

In any case, avoid using a plural pronoun with a singular indefinite pronoun; such usage violates the basic principle of number agreement.

Incorrect:	*Everyone* should do *their* best.
Correct:	*Everyone* should do *his* or *her* best.
Correct:	*People* should do *their* best.

Exercise 29   **MAKING PRONOUNS AGREE**

Cross out the incorrect pronoun form. (See Answer Key for answers.)

1. Before a person can leave this camp, (he or she, they) must get permission from the director.

2. Our high school band gave (their, its) first concert of the season last Friday.

3. Will anyone who has seen that television show please raise (his or her, their) hand?

4. The team won (its, their) first game yesterday.

5. Everyone who was contacted should leave (his or her, their) reports on the president's desk.

6. Gustavo is one of those workers who want (his or her, their) job description changed.

7. Christine was among the passengers (who, which) were lost at sea during the big storm.

8. Chin was afraid of anybody and anything (who, that, which) might interfere with completing the government work.

9. Juan is the only one of that group who keeps (himself or herself, themselves, himself) in good condition.

10. Neither of the women felt that it was (her, their) fault the new machine did not work properly.

11. The sales division has (its, their) offices in Seminole, Oklahoma.

12. The instructor was determined that both of the boys be punished for (his, their) part in hazing the younger boys.

13. Neither Chelsea nor her sisters could finish (her, their) project in time for the exhibition.

14. A student must not be late for class very often if (you, he or she, they) wants a good grade.

15. Either of the women will lend you (her, their) history book to study that assignment.

16. The manager and the owner of the store left (his or her, their) offices open last evening.

17. Either his family or Jung must pay (his, their) semester bills before next week.

18. All students have a right to vote for these candidates, but will (he or she, they) exercise that right in the coming election?

19. A photographer must use the best film in that light if (you, he or she, they) wishes to get good pictures.

20. It is often difficult for someone in that position to justify (himself or herself, themselves).

| **Exercise 30** | **MAKING PRONOUNS AGREE** |

Cross out the incorrect pronoun form.

1. The music was so bad that I wished (I, you) hadn't come.

2. He is the only one of the seven candidates who says that (he, they) will support a tax increase.

3. Concord is a famous historical town; just seeing the Old North Bridge can cause (you, one) to think of a famous battle.

4. Each of the students brought (their, his or her) registration cards to the first class meeting.

5. Neither Mark nor the other players would admit it was (his, their) fault.

6. She is one of those people who are always trying to put (her, their) life in balance.

7. He is the only one of all the staff who will not do (their, his) share of the work.

8. The members of the team are now leaving the stadium under (its, their) own power.

9. Everyone should wait until (they, he or she) is contacted.

10. Going into battle, few seemed to care about (their, his or her) well-being.

11. Everyone should mind (their, his or her) own business.

12. On days like that, (you want, one wants) to be somewhere else.

13. When I was in France, I discovered that (you, one) can't find many fried chicken restaurants.

14. Each of the dogs strained at (its, his or her) leash.

15. She is the only one of the administrators who speaks (her, their) mind.

16. A politician must be responsive to (his or her, their) constituents or lose the next election.

17. Either of the examiners will give you (his or her, their) patient consideration.

18. The secretary and the treasurer must do (their, his or her) best work.

19. The jury voted on (their, its) first case after two hours of deliberation.

20. Every immigrant must deal with the problem of cultural adjustment, as well as (his or her, their) own personal problems.

Pronoun Reference

A pronoun must refer clearly to its antecedent. Because a pronoun is a substitute word, it can express meaning clearly and definitely only if its antecedent is easily identified.

In some sentence constructions, gender and number make the reference clear.

> Kevin and Latisha discussed *his* absences and *her* good attendance. (gender)

If the three older boys in the *club* carry out those plans, *it* will break up. (number)

Avoid ambiguous reference. The following sentences illustrate the kind of confusion that results from structuring sentences with more than one possible antecedent for the pronoun.

Unclear:	Tyler gave Walt *his* money and clothes.
Clear:	Tyler gave his own money and clothes to Walt.
Unclear:	Lynette told her sister that *her* car had a flat tire.
Clear:	Lynette said to her sister, "Your car has a flat tire."

When using a pronoun to refer to a general idea, make sure that the reference is clear. The pronouns used frequently in this way are *this, that, which,* and *it.* The best solution may be to recast the sentence to omit the pronoun in question.

Unclear:	She whistled the same tune over and over, *which* irritated me.
Clear:	She whistled the same tune over and over, a *habit* that irritated me.
Recast:	Her whistling the same tune over and over irritated me.

Exercise 31   **CORRECTING PROBLEMS IN PRONOUN REFERENCE**

Some of the following sentences contain pronouns that are examples of faulty reference; cross out these pronouns and correct them. If the sentence is correct, write OK in the blank. (See Answer Key for answers.)

_____ 1. In small classes, the student is often able to receive individual assistance from his or her professor.

_____ 2. Ibsen's *Hedda Gabler* is a play that still has a powerful dramatic impact.

_____ 3. If the leader is permitted to carry out his so-called policy of security, he will become a dictator.

_____ 4. In large classes, you are often unable to receive individual help.

_____ 5. The professor said to Shan-ting that his short story will soon be published.

_____ 6. To run effectively for office, one needs a great deal of money.

_____ 7. That is Cynthia's house we visited yesterday.

_____ 8. Although Andrew respected the teaching profession, he did not want to be a teacher.

_____ 9. In that college, they have excellent science laboratories.

_____ 10. According to the magazine, one is likely to encounter drunk drivers on the highway after midnight.

_____ 11. Ron gave Joe his message.

_____ 12. Marge told her mother that her ideas were good."

_____ 13. It was one of Larry's poems that we read yesterday.

_____ 14. Julian implied that he would buy the property.

_____ 15. Roy whistled too often and too loud, which constantly irritated me.

_____ 16. Many people do not visit their doctor at least once a year. This may lead to serious illnesses.

_____ 17. My brother enjoys studying law. For that reason, I want to be one.

_____ 18. As a traveler approaches that corner, you should slow down and take great care.

_____ 19. In this pamphlet, it says that campers should bring their own tents and blankets.

_____ 20. Mamood respects his older brother and admires him also.

Exercise 32   CORRECTING PROBLEMS IN PRONOUN REFERENCE

The following sentences contain pronouns that are examples of faulty reference. Correct the sentences.

1. They treated him like a child and that angered him.

2. Noel talked while he was eating, which annoyed his companions.

3. You could disagree with the idea, but it would not be easy.

4. Marcus handed Jim his keys.

5. Jannis told Jannel that her hair was too long.

6. We installed mud flaps, but some of it still got on the fenders.

7. The instructor told the student that his deadline was tomorrow.

8. This is my sister's house, whom you met yesterday.

9. They say the unemployment is causing social problems.

10. Timothy never looked at me when he talked, which made me distrust him.

11. He often interrupted other people, which I found annoying.

12. They regarded him as incompetent, which embarrassed him.

13. You could come to her aid, but would it be appreciated?

14. Franklin told Jeff that his car needed to be repaired.

15. They say that the big bands are coming back.

16. In prison, you have little freedom.

17. This is my uncle's dog, who has a hundred-acre farm.

18. You could build a baseball field, but would it be worth the bother?

19. They say on television that anyone can buy a new car.

20. Hans put his finger into a hole in the dike at the edge of the ocean, but some of it still came in.

Adjectives and Adverbs

Adjectives modify (describe) nouns and pronouns and answer the questions *Which one? What kind?* and *How many?*

> *Which one?* The <u>new</u> <u>car</u> is mine.
>   adj   n

> *What kind?* <u>Mexican</u> <u>food</u> is my favorite.
>   adj   n

> *How many?* A <u>few</u> <u>friends</u> are all one needs.
>   adj   n

Adverbs modify verbs, adjectives, or other adverbs and answer the questions *How? Where? When?* and *To what degree?* Most words ending in *-ly* are adverbs.

> *Where?* The cuckoo <u>flew</u> <u>south</u>.
>   v   adv

> *When?* The cuckoo <u>flew</u> <u>yesterday</u>.
>   v   adv

> *Why?* The cuckoo <u>flew</u> <u>because of the cold weather</u>.
>   v   adv phrase

> *How?* The cuckoo <u>flew</u> <u>swiftly</u>.
>   v   adv

> <u>Without adjectives and adverbs</u>, <u>even</u> John Steinbeck, the <u>famous</u>
>   adv phrase   adv   adj
>
> <u>Nobel Prize–winning</u> author, <u>surely</u> could <u>not</u> have described the
>   adj   adv   adv
>
> <u>crafty</u> octopus <u>very</u> <u>well</u>.
>   adj   adv   adv

We have two concerns regarding the use of adjectives and adverbs (modifiers) in writing. One is a matter of diction, or word choice—in this case, selecting adjectives and adverbs that will strengthen the writing. The other is how to identify and correct problems with modifiers.

Selecting Adjectives and Adverbs

If you want to finish the sentence "She was a(n) _____ speaker," you have many adjectives to select from, including these:

distinguished	dependable	effective	sly
influential	impressive	polished	astute
adequate	boring	abrasive	humorous

If you want to finish the sentence "She danced _____ ," you have another large selection, this time of adverbs such as the following:

bewitchingly	angelically	quaintly	zestfully
gracefully	grotesquely	carnally	smoothly
divinely	picturesquely	serenely	unevenly

Adjectives and adverbs can be used to enhance communication. If you have a thought, you know what it is, but when you deliver that thought to someone else, you may not say or write what you mean. Your thought may be eloquent and your word choice weak. Keep in mind that no two words mean exactly the same thing. Further, some words are very vague and general. If you settle for a common word such as *good* or a slang word such as *neat* to characterize something that you like, you will be limiting your communication. Of course, those who know you best may understand fairly well; after all, certain people who are really close may be able to convey ideas using only grunts and gestures.

But what if you want to write to someone you hardly know to explain how you feel about an important issue? Then the more precise the word, the better the communication. By using modifiers, you may be able to add significant information. Keep in mind, however, that anything can be overdone; therefore, use adjectives and adverbs wisely and economically.

Your first resource in searching for more effective adjectives should be your own vocabulary storehouse. Another resource is a good thesaurus (book of synonyms), either in print form or on a word processor.

Supply the appropriate modifiers in the following exercises, using a dictionary, a thesaurus, or the resources designated by your instructor.

Exercise 33   **SUPPLYING ADJECTIVES**

Provide adjectives to modify these nouns. Use only single words, not adjective phrases.

1. A(n) _____ cat

2. A(n) _____ politician

3. A(n) _____ echo

4. A(n) _____ friend

5. A(n) _____ waiter

6. A(n) _____ conference

7. A(n) ⸺⸺⸺ comedian

8. A(n) ⸺⸺⸺ street

9. A(n) ⸺⸺⸺ school

10. A(n) ⸺⸺⸺ vacation

| **Exercise 34** | **SUPPLYING ADVERBS** |

Provide adverbs to modify these verbs. Use only single words, not adverb phrases.

1. stare ⸺⸺⸺

2. flee ⸺⸺⸺

3. yell ⸺⸺⸺

4. approach ⸺⸺⸺

5. taste ⸺⸺⸺

6. smile ⸺⸺⸺

7. look ⸺⸺⸺

8. leave ⸺⸺⸺

9. cry ⸺⸺⸺

10. eat ⸺⸺⸺

Comparative and Superlative Forms

For making comparisons, most adjectives and adverbs have three different forms: the positive (one), the comparative (comparing two), and the superlative (comparing three or more).

Adjectives

1. Some adjectives follow a regular pattern:

Postive (one)	**Comparative (two)**	**Superlative (three or more)**
nice	nicer	nicest
rich	richer	richest
big	bigger	biggest
tall	taller	tallest
lonely	lonelier	loneliest
terrible	more terrible	most terrible
beautiful	more beautiful	most beautiful

These are usually the rules:

a. Add *-er* to short adjectives (one or two syllables) to rank units of two.

> Julian is *nicer* than Sam.

b. Add *-est* to short adjectives (one or two syllables) to rank units of three or more.

> Of the fifty people I know, Julian is the *kindest.*

c. Add the word *more* to long adjectives (three or more syllables) to rank units of two.

> My hometown is *more beautiful* than yours.

d. Add the word *most* to long adjectives (three or more syllables) to rank units of three or more.

> My hometown is the *most beautiful* in all America.

2. Some adjectives are irregular in the way they change to show comparison:

Positive (one)	Comparative (two)	Superlative (three or more)
good	better	best
bad	worse	worst

Adverbs

1. Some adverbs follow a regular pattern.

Positive (one)	Comparative (two)	Superlative (three or more)
clearly	more clearly	most clearly
quickly	more quickly	most quickly
carefully	more carefully	most carefully
thoughtfully	more thoughtfully	most thoughtfully

a. Add *-er* to some one-syllable adverbs for the comparative form and add *-est* for the superlative form.

> My piglet runs *fast.* (positive)

> My piglet runs *faster* than your piglet. (comparative)

> My piglet runs *fastest* of all known piglets. (superlative)

b. Add the word *more* to form longer comparisons and *most* to form longer superlative forms.

> Judy reacted *happily* to the marriage proposal. (positive)

> Judy reacted *more happily* to the marriage proposal than Nancy. (comparison)

> Of all the women Clem proposed to, Judy reacted *most happily.* (superlative)

c. In some cases, the word *less* may be substituted for *more,* and *least* for *most.*

> Mort's views were presented *less effectively* than Craig's (comparative)

> Of all the opinions that were shared, Mort's views were presented *least effectively.* (superlative)

2. Some adverbs are irregular in the way they change to show comparisons.

Positive (one)	Comparative (two)	Superlative (three or more)
well	better	best
far	farther (distance)	farthest (distance)
	further	furthest
badly	worse	worst

Using Adjectives and Adverbs Correctly

1. Avoid double negatives. Words such as *no, not, none, nothing, never, hardly, barely,* and *scarcely* should not be combined.

   Double Negative: I do *not* have *no* time for recreation. (incorrect)

   Single Negative: I have *no* time for recreation. (correct)

   Double Negative: I've *hardly never* lied. (incorrect)

   Single Negative: I've *hardly* ever lied. (correct)

2. Do not confuse adjectives with adverbs. Among the most commonly confused adjectives and adverbs are *good/well, bad/badly,* and *real/really.* The words *good, bad,* and *real* are always adjectives. *Well* is sometimes an adjective. The words *badly* and *really* are always adverbs. *Well* is usually an adverb.

   To distinguish these words, consider what is being modified. Remember that adjectives modify nouns and pronouns and that adverbs modify verbs, adjectives, and other adverbs.

   Wrong: I feel *badly* today. (We're concerned with the condition of *I.*)

   Right: I feel *bad* today. (The adjective *bad* modifies the pronoun *I.*)

   Wrong: She feels *well* about that choice. (We're concerned with the condition of *she.*)

   Right: She feels *good* about that choice. (The adjective *good* modifies the pronoun *she.*)

   Wrong: Lazarro plays the piano *good.* (The adjective *good* modifies the verb *plays,* but adjectives should not modify verbs.)

   Right: Lazarro plays the piano *well.* (The adverb *well* modifies the verb *plays.*)

   Wrong: He did *real* well. (Here the adjective *real* modifies the adverb *well,* but adjectives should not modify adverbs.)

   Right: He did *really* well. (The adverb *really* modifies the adverb *well.*)

3. Do not use an adverb such as *very, more,* or *most* before adjectives such as *perfect, round, unique, square,* and *straight.*

   Wrong: It is more round.

   Right: It is round.

   Right: It is more nearly round.

4. Do not double forms, such as *more lonelier* or *most loneliest.*

   Wrong: Julie was *more nicer* than Jake.

   Right: Julie was *nicer* than Jake.

5. Do not confuse standard and nonstandard forms of adjectives and adverbs.

- **Accidently.** This is a substandard form of *accidentally.*

- **All ready, already.** *All ready* means "completely prepared." *Already* means "previously."

    We are *all ready* to give the signal to move out. (prepared)

    When he arrived at the station, we had *already* left. (previously)

- **All right, alright.** *All right* (two words) means "correct," "yes," "fine," "certainly." *Alright* is a substandard spelling of "all right.

    Yes, I am *all right* now.

- **All together, altogether.** *All together* means "in a group." *Altogether* means "completely," "wholly," "entirely."

    The boys were *all together* at the end of the field.

    The manuscript is *altogether* too confusing.

Be careful to place such words as *also, almost, even, just, hardly, merely, only,* and *today* in the right position to convey the intended meaning. As these words change position in the sentence, they may also change the meaning of the sentence.

I *only* advised him to act cautiously.
I advised *only* him to act cautiously.
Only I advised him to act cautiously.
I advised him *only* to act cautiously.

| Exercise 35 | SELECTING ADJECTIVES AND ADVERBS |

Cross out the mistake in each sentence and write in the correction above it. (See Answer Key for answers.)

1. Ping-Sim thought his teacher had a most unique method of lecturing.

2. Some jobs are done easier by blind people than by those with sight.

3. It was up to the parents to decide if this kind of movie is real bad for children.

4. The adventure of life is too impossible to discuss.

5. Oscar felt badly about rejection slips but worse about his bank account.

6. Victor was not the stronger of the pair, but he was the best boxer.

7. The whole class thought Kyoka's sunglasses the most perfect they had seen.

8. The suspect became violenter as the police drew nearer.

9. Of all the potential winners, the judges agreed that Miss Idaho was more beautiful.

10. The United States has no central educational authority, but overall it does good.

11. An unambiguous word only can mean one thing.

12. It is real easy to forget that "liquor" used to mean "liquid."

13. Hurtful experiences in childhood don't fade out easy.

14. She said he had all ready ruined his reputation by making her buy her own flowers.

15. A trembling voice may indicate that the speaker does not feel alright.

16. Julian had two ways of starting a speech: One way was with a definition, but the easiest way was with a joke.

17. Sherman choked as if the very words tasted badly to him.

18. Natasha made a real good decision.

19. Erika didn't say the food was terrible; only she said it was bad.

20. On controversial topics, he was all together too easily offended.

| **Exercise 36** | **SELECTING ADJECTIVES AND ADVERBS** |

Cross out the mistake in each sentence and write in the correction above it.

1. I remember one real good experience.

2. It left me feeling alright.

3. Of the two cars I have owned, the '69 Camaro was best.

4. It was also the most beautifulest car I have ever seen.

5. When I drove it, I felt like the most rich person in town.

6. For a year I didn't have no time for anything except polishing my car.

7. I had it painted green so it was real handsome.

8. My name for it was the "Hornet," and when people gave me glances as I drove it, I felt well.

9. I hardly never abused that vehicle.

10. When I finally traded it in, I didn't never look back for fear I would cry.

11. All I can say is that it was most perfect.

12. Later I went back to the dealer, but I was all ready too late.

13. The Hornet had been bought by a young man who thought it was the better of all the cars on the lot.

14. He said he couldn't find no better car anywhere.

15. I could see he felt real good.

16. He and his family were standing altogether.

17. It was no time for me to feel badly.

18. In fact, as I said, I felt alright about the transaction.

19. I didn't shed no tears.

20. That experience is a real happy memory for me.

Dangling and Misplaced Modifiers

Modifiers should clearly relate to the word or words they modify.

1. A modifier that fails to modify a word or group of words already in the sentence is called a **dangling modifier.**

   Dangling: *Walking down the street,* a snake startled him. (Who was walking down the street? The person isn't mentioned in the sentence.)

   Correct: *Walking down the street, Don* was startled by a snake.

   Correct: As *Don* walked down the street, *he* was startled by a snake.

   Dangling: *At the age of six,* my uncle died. (Who was six years old? The person isn't mentioned in the sentence.)

   Correct: *When I was six,* my uncle died.

2. A modifier that is placed so that it modifies the wrong word or words is called a **misplaced modifier.** The term also applies to words that are positioned so as to unnecessarily divide closely related parts of sentences such as infinitives (*to* plus verb) or subjects and verbs.

   Misplaced: The sick man went to a doctor *with a high fever.*

   Correct: The sick man *with a high fever* went to the doctor.

   Misplaced: I saw a great movie *sitting in my pickup.*

   Correct: *Sitting in my pickup,* I saw a great movie.

   Misplaced: Kim found many new graves *walking through the cemetery.*

   Correct: *Walking through the cemetery,* Kim found many new graves.

   Misplaced: I forgot all about my sick dog *kissing my girlfriend.*

   Correct: *Kissing my girlfriend,* I forgot all about my sick dog.

   Misplaced: They tried to *earnestly and sincerely* complete the task. (splitting of the infinitive *to complete*)

   Correct: They tried *earnestly and sincerely* to complete the task.

Misplaced: My neighbor, *while walking to the store,* was mugged. (unnecessarily dividing the subject and verb)

Correct: *While walking to the store,* my neighbor was mugged.

3. Try this procedure in working through Exercises 37 and 38.
    a. Circle the modifier.
    b. Draw an arrow from the modifier to the word or words it modifies.
    c. If the modifier does not relate directly to anything in the sentence, it is dangling, and you must recast the sentence.
    d. If the modifier does not modify the nearest word or words, or if it interrupts related sentence parts, it is misplaced and you need to reposition it.

| **Exercise 37** | **CORRECTING DANGLERS AND MISPLACED MODIFIERS** |

In the blank, write D for dangling modifier, M for misplaced modifier, and OK for correct sentences. Correct the sentences with modifier problems. (See Answer Key for answers.)

_____   1. Interested in my studies, there was no time for romance at school.

_____   2. Falling throughout the night, the snow blocked major highways.

_____   3. The radio announced that a hundred cars were stranded approximately in the snow.

_____   4. The radio announced approximately that a hundred cars were stranded in the snow.

_____   5. My computer never worked properly in spite of following the instructions carefully.

_____   6. After working at the computer all night, the job was still not completed.

_____   7. The students gossiping noisily left the room.

_____   8. Noisily, the gossiping students left the room.

_____   9. By practicing every day, French can be learned in two weeks.

_____ 10. While working in the factory, much money was made.

_____ 11. The doctor told him to stop smoking last week.

_____ 12. While returning from shopping, Debra's promise was remembered and she stopped.

_____ 13. Walking to school, the rain came down heavily.

_____ 14. In our English classes, we only studied grammar on rare occasions.

_____ 15. To be a careful writer infinitive phrases should never dangle.

_____ 16. To protect their hands, gloves were worn by the astronauts.

_____ 17. When only eight years old, my mother took me to Europe.

_____ 18. I only drank a glass of milk.

_____ 19. Jill tried to carefully and constantly avoid making her date jealous.

_____ 20. While recovering in the hospital, my friends brought me flowers.

| Exercise 38 | CORRECTING DANGLERS AND MISPLACED MODIFIERS |

In the blank, write D for dangling modifier, M for misplaced modifier, and OK for correct sentences. Correct the sentences with modifier problems.

_____ 1. When I was only ten years old, my father died.

_____ 2. When ten years old, my father died.

_____ 3. After the game was over, Jean went to the banquet.

_____ 4. Raynelle went after the game was over, to the banquet.

_____ 5. Traveling over the mountain road, the inn was reached.

_____ 6. To climb mountains, one needs strength and equipment.

_____ 7. Driving through the forest, many deer were seen from our car.

_____ 8. After studying it for many weeks, the plan was discontinued.

_____ 9. Searching the computer screen, we found the answer.

_____ 10. After giving it considerable study, the plan of action was discontinued.

_____ 11. Traveling over the mountain road, Ron reached the inn.

_____ 12. The moon cast its spell rising over the mountain, on the lovers.

_____ 13. Rising over the mountain, the moon cast its spell on the lovers.

_____ 14. Ms. Prank wanted to buy a car for her husband with a large trunk.

_____ 15. To miss the construction, a detour was taken.

_____ 16. To miss the construction, Ginny took a detour.

_____ 17. Ginny took, to miss the construction, a detour.

_____ 18. To play basketball well, good eyes and stamina are needed.

_____ 19. After playing all the game, the coach knew that Jean was tired.

_____ 20. It is desirable to usually avoid splitting an infinitive.

Balancing Sentence Parts

We are surrounded by balance. Watch a high-performance jet plane as it streaks across the sky. If you draw an imaginary line from the nose to the tail of the aircraft, you will see corresponding parts on either side. If you were to replace one of the streamlined wings of the jet with the straight and long wing of a glider, the plane would never fly. A similar lack of balance can also cause a sentence to crash.

Consider these statements:

> "*To be* or *not to be*—that is the question." (dash added)

This line from *Hamlet,* by William Shakespeare, is one of the most famous lines in literature. Compare it to the jet in full flight. Its parts are parallel and it "flies" well.

> "*To be* or *not being*—that is the question."

It still vaguely resembles the sleek aircraft, but now a phrase dips like a wing tip. Lurching, the line begins to lose altitude.

> "*To be* or *death is the other alternative*—that is the question."

The writer and the line slam into the ground with a deafening boom, scattering words across the landscape.

The first sentence is forceful and easy to read. The second is more difficult to follow. The third is almost impossible to understand. We understand it only because we know what it should look like from having read the original. The point is that perceptive readers are as critical of sentences as pilots are of planes.

Basic Principles of Parallelism

Parallelism as it relates to sentence structure is usually achieved by joining words with similar words: nouns with nouns, adjectives (words that describe nouns and pronouns) with adjectives, adverbs (words that describe verbs, adjectives, and other adverbs) with adverbs, and so forth.

> *Men, women* and *children* enjoy the show. (nouns)

> The players are *excited, eager,* and *enthusiastic.* (adjectives)

> The author wrote *skillfully* and *quickly.* (adverbs)

You can create parallel structure by joining groups of words with similar groups of words: prepositional phrase with prepositional phrase, clause with clause, sentence with sentence.

> She fell *in love* and *out of love* in a few minutes. (prepositional phrases)

> *Who he was* and *where he came from* did not matter. (clauses)

> *He came in a hurry. He left in a hurry.* (sentences)

Parallelism means balancing one structure with another of the same kind. Faulty parallel structure is awkward and draws unfavorable attention to what is being said.

Nonparallel: Kobe Bryant's reputation is based on his ability in *passing, shooting,* and *he is good at rebounds.*

Parallel: Kobe Bryant's reputation is based on his ability in *passing, shooting,* and *rebounding.*

In the nonparallel sentence, the words *passing* and *shooting* are of the same kind (verblike words used as nouns), but the rest of the sentence is different. You don't have to know terms to realize that there is a problem in smoothness and emphasis. Just read the material aloud. Then compare it with the parallel statement; *he is good at rebounds* is changed to *rebounding* to make a sentence that's easy on the eye and ear.

Signal Words

Some words signal parallel structure. If you use *and,* the items joined by *and* should almost always be parallel. If they aren't, then *and* is probably inappropriate.

> The weather is hot *and* humid. (*and* joins adjectives)
>
> The car *and* the trailer are parked in front of the house. (*and* joins nouns)

The same principle is true for *but,* although it implies a direct contrast. Where contrasts are being drawn, parallel structure is essential to clarify those contrasts.

> He *purchased* a Dodger Dog, *but* I *chose* the Stadium Peanuts. (*but* joins contrasting clauses)
>
> She *earned* an A in math *but failed* her art class. (*but* joins contrasting verbs)

You should regard all the coordinating conjunctions (FANBOYS: *for, and, nor, but, or, yet, so*) as signals for parallel structure.

Combination Signal Words

The words *and* and *but* are the most common individual signal words used with parallel constructions. Sometimes, however, **combination words** signal the need for parallelism or balance. The most common ones are *either/or, neither/nor, not only/but also, both/and,* and *whether/or.* Now consider this faulty sentence and two possible corrections:

> **Nonparallel:** *Either* we will win this game, *or* let's go out fighting.
>
> **Parallel:** *Either we will* win this game, *or we will* go out fighting.

The correction is made by changing *let's* to *we will* to parallel the *we will* in the first part of the sentence. The same construction should follow the *either* and the *or.*

> **Nonparallel:** Flour is used *not only* to bake cakes *but also* in paste.
>
> **Parallel:** Flour is used *not only to bake* cakes *but also to make* paste.

The correction is made by changing *in* (a preposition) to *to make* (an infinitive). Now an infinitive follows both *not only* and *but also.*

Exercise 39   **CORRECTING FAULTY PARALLELISM**

Mark each sentence as P for parallel or NP for nonparallel. Rewrite the sentences with nonparallel structure. (See Answer Key for answers.)

_____   1. They push education aside if it interferes with love or the moment it

is no longer fun.

_____   2. She has to assume responsibility for her own decisions and has her

own duties.

———— 3. Reading the assignment and to take lecture notes are equally important.

———— 4. Benjamin Franklin was a statesman, a writer, and he was also an inventor.

———— 5. Joletta's methods were using puns, listing homonyms, and to tell jokes.

———— 6. The prime minister recommended an increase in taxes and that several fees be increased.

———— 7. Mr. Roberts found teaching in the classroom more inspiring than to manage the school.

———— 8. To give is as important as receiving.

———— 9. The ghouls tried to gain entrance first by persuasion and then to force.

———— 10. The new governor has already shown herself to be not only charming but also a person of political sophistication.

———— 11. Brooke is not only captain of the softball team but also of the fencing team.

———— 12. She was disappointed both in their performance and their attitude.

———— 13. The conscientious objectors came to listen and with questions.

———— 14. Taking the oral examination is usually harder than to write the dissertation.

———— 15. His trouble was that he regarded every doctor as ignorant and a liar.

———— 16. The General Assembly understood neither the speaker's words nor what his purpose was.

———— 17. Tarzan explained both the causes of the deaths and his plan to save the village.

———— 18. General Eisenhower was not only commander of the American forces but also of the Allied armies in Europe.

———— 19. Martin Luther King, Jr., was both a preacher and he was a powerful political influence.

_____ 20. The psychologist recommended plenty of work, friends, and ~~eating~~ good food.

| **Exercise 40** | **CORRECTING FAULTY PARALLELISM** |

Mark each sentence as P for parallel or NP for nonparallel. Rewrite the sentences with nonparallel structure.

_____ 1. Where he had been and his experiences did not matter to the monsignor.

_____ 2. The students, classified employees, and those who teach all bear responsibility.

_____ 3. Rosalyn had two ambitions: to learn and advancing.

_____ 4. Shane wrote the essay swiftly and with skill.

_____ 5. Dean decided that either he must go to work or quit eating.

_____ 6. Jill arrived with happiness. She left sadly.

_____ 7. The weather is hot and it feels muggy.

_____ 8. Neither snow nor sleet will stop me.

_____ 9. To know her is loving her.

_____ 10. This country is known as one of the people, for the people, and run by the people.

_____ 11. Mark McGwire is a famous baseball player and who went from Oakland to St. Louis.

_____ 12. Jazz is a music form based on improvisation, performance, and it uses African rhythms.

_____ 13. Ruthanne decided to either play the saxophone or the clarinet.

_____ 14. Charley gave not only thanks to his parents but also to his fellow students.

_____ 15. Jannelle used both her wits and her courage to survive the ordeal.

_____ 16. To go or not going—that was the question.

_____ 17. Who would go and the mission of the person were major concerns.

_____ 18. The integrity of the whole program depended on what she would say and her reaction.

_____ 19. He intended to go to work, mind his own business, and then he would go home.

_____ 20. He shouted, "Who are you and do you want something?"

Punctuation and Capitalization

Understanding punctuation will help you to write better. If you aren't sure how to punctuate a compound or compound-complex sentence, then you probably will not write one. If you don't know how to show that some of your words come from other sources, you may mislead your reader. If you misuse punctuation, you will force your readers to struggle to get your message. So take the time to review and master the mechanics. Your efforts will be rewarded.

End Punctuation

Periods

1. Place a period after a statement.

    The weather is beautiful today.

2. Place a period after common abbreviations.

Dr.		Mr.	Mrs.	Dec.	a.m.
Exceptions:	FBI	UN	NAACP	FHA	

3. Use an ellipsis—three periods within a sentence and four periods at the end of a sentence—to indicate that words have been omitted from quoted material.

James Thurber, "The Secret Life of Walter Mitty"

    He stopped walking and the buildings . . . rose up out of the misty courtroom. . . .

Question Marks

1. Place a question mark at the end of a direct question.

    Will you go to the country tomorrow?

2. Do *not* use a question mark after an indirect (reported) question.

    She asked me what caused that slide.

Exclamation Points

1. Place an exclamation point after a word or a group of words that expresses strong feeling.

    Oh!   What a night!   Help!   Gadzooks!

2. Do not overwork the exclamation point. Do not use double exclamation points. Use the period or comma for mild exclamatory words, phrases, or sentences.

> Oh, we can leave now.

Commas

Commas to Separate

1. Use a comma to separate main clauses joined by one of the coordinating conjunctions—*for, and, nor, but, or, yet, so.* The comma may be omitted if the clauses are brief and parallel.

> We traveled many miles to see the game, *but* it was canceled.
>
> Mary left and I remained. (brief and parallel clauses)

2. Use a comma after introductory dependent clauses and long introductory phrases (generally, four or more words is considered long).

> *Before the arrival of the shipment,* the boss had written a letter protesting the delay. (two prepositional phrases)
>
> *If you don't hear from me,* assume that I am lost. (introductory dependent clause, an adverbial modifier)
>
> *In winter* we skate on the river. (short prepositional phrase, no comma)

3. Use a comma to separate words, phrases, and clauses in a series.

> *Red, white,* and *blue* were her favorite colors. (words)
>
> He ran *down the street, across the park,* and *into the arms of his father.* (prepositional phrases)
>
> *When John was asleep, when Mary was at work,* and *when Bob was studying,* Mother had time to relax. (dependent clauses)

4. However, when coordinating conjunctions connect all the elements in a series, the commas are omitted.

> He bought apples and pears and grapes.

5. Use a comma to separate coordinate adjectives not joined by *and* that modify the same noun.

> I need a *sturdy, reliable* truck.

6. Do not use a comma to separate adjectives that are not coordinate. Try the following technique to determine whether the adjectives are coordinate: Put *and* between the adjectives. If it fits naturally, the adjectives are coordinate; if it does not, they are not, and you do not need a comma.

> She is a kind, beautiful person.
>
> kind *and* beautiful (natural, hence the comma)
>
> I built a red brick wall.
>
> red *and* brick wall (not natural, no comma)

7. Use a comma to separate sentence elements that might be misread.

> Inside the dog scratched his fleas.
>
> *Inside,* the dog scratched his fleas.

Without benefit of the comma, the reader might initially misunderstand the relationship among the first three words.

Commas to Set Off

1. Use commas to set off (enclose) adjectives in pairs that follow a noun.

   > The scouts, *tired and hungry,* marched back to camp.

2. Use commas to set off nonessential (unnecessary for meaning of the sentence) words, phrases, and clauses.

   > My brother, *a student at Ohio State University,* is visiting me. (If you drop the phrase, the basic meaning of the sentence remains intact.)

   > Marla, *who studied hard,* will pass. (The clause is not essential to the basic meaning of the sentence.)

   > All students *who studied hard* will pass. (Here the clause *is* essential. If you remove it, you would have *All students will pass,* which is not necessarily true.)

   > I shall not stop searching *until I find the treasure.* (A dependent clause at the end of a sentence is usually not set off with a comma. However, a clause beginning with the word *though* or *although* will be set off regardless of where it is located.)

   > I felt unsatisfied, *though we had won the game.*

3. Use commas to set off parenthetical elements such as mild interjections (*oh, well, yes, no,* and others), most conjunctive adverbs (*however, otherwise, therefore, similarly, hence, on the other hand,* and *consequently* but not *then, thus, soon, now,* and *also*), quotation indicators, and special abbreviations (*etc., i.e., e.g.,* and others).

   > *Oh,* what a silly question! (mild interjection)

   > It is necessary, *of course,* to leave now. (sentence modifier)

   > We left early; *however,* we missed the train anyway. (conjunctive adverb)

   > "When I was in school," *he said,* "I read widely." (quotation indicators)

   > Books, papers, pens, *etc.,* were scattered on the floor. (The abbreviation *etc.* should be used sparingly, however.)

4. Use commas to set off nouns used as direct address.

   > Play it again, *Sam.*

   > Please tell us the answer, *Jane,* so we can discuss it.

5. Use commas to separate the numbers in a date.

   > June 4, 1965, is a day I will remember.

6. Do not use commas if the day of the month is not specified, or if the day is given before the month.

   > June 1965 was my favorite time.

   > One day I will never forget is 4 June 1965.

7. Use commas to separate the city from the state. No comma is used between the state and the ZIP code.

> Walnut, CA 91789

8. Use a comma after both the city and the state when they are used together in a sentence.

> Our family visited Anchorage, Alaska, last summer.

9. Use a comma following the salutation of a friendly letter and the complimentary closing in any letter.

> Dear John,
>
> Sincerely,

10. Use a comma in numbers to set off groups of three digits. However, omit the comma in dates, serial numbers, page numbers, years, and street numbers.

> The total assets were $2,000,000.
>
> I look forward to the year 2050.

Exercise 41	USING COMMAS

Insert all necessary commas in the following sentences. (See Answer Key for answers.)

1. Commas are used to separate words phrases and clauses in a series.

2. A strong assertive comma separates coordinate adjectives.

3. After long introductory modifiers a comma is used.

4. A comma is used between independent clauses and a period is usually found at the end of a sentence.

5. After all the meaning of the sentence is often clarified by a comma.

6. Inside the car smelled new and clean.

7. In the beginning of the game there was nothing but noise and chaos.

8. The crazy-looking car was painted pink black green and lavender.

9. Cherise worked at her desk all night but the job was not finished in time.

10. The sharp burning rays of the sun would soon be hidden by the trees.

11. Having finished the banquet the diners moved to the living room.

12. Bach and Handel both born in 1685 were the two greatest baroque composers.

13. Motor racing not horse racing is the more popular sport.

14. "When I was a boy" Arturo said "one dollar a week was enough!"

15. Dwight Jones the salesperson will take your order now.

16. Well that's the way it's going to be!

17. The new car all sleek and shiny was nowhere to be found.

18. He arrived in Tribbey Oklahoma on February 21 1934.

19. The old boxer was only down not out.

20. The Eiffel Tower which is located in Paris is no longer the highest tower in the world.

Exercise 42   **USING COMMAS**

Insert all necessary commas in the following sentences.

1. Dwight Eisenhower a former president spent his winters in Palm Springs.

2. "The fault dear Brutus is not in our stars, but in ourselves. . . ."

3. The ship tall and stately sailed into the harbor.

4. Many writers I believe have died tragic deaths.

5. Percy Shelley a poet drowned off the west coast of Italy.

6. Will Rogers said "I never met a man I didn't like."

7. It is however not up to me to decide your fate.

8. The puppy wet and bedraggled crept under the porch.

9. You will of course have prepared your case ahead of time.

10. My English class coming as it does early in the morning often finds me barely awake.

11. After the game was discussed by the coaches.

12. We must trust each other or we cannot be friends.

13. Outside the house did not appear to be occupied.

14. Lincoln said that this country was "of the people by the people and for the people."

15. If you don't hear from me send the police to this address.

16. Because Linda had opened the package he could hardly expect a surprise.

17. A high rugged brick wall surrounded the manor on all sides.

18. The reporter told them to fear not for she brought them good news.

19. Larry wrapped Frank labeled and Liz addressed each package.

20. The fast steady goat reached the top before we did.

Semicolons

The semicolon indicates a stronger division than the comma. It is used principally to separate independent clauses within a sentence.

1. Use a semicolon to separate independent clauses not joined by a coordinating conjunction.

>   You must buy that car today; tomorrow will be too late.

2. Use a semicolon between two independent clauses joined by a conjunctive adverb such as one of the HOTSHOT CAT words (*however, otherwise, therefore, similarly, hence, on the other hand, then, consequently, accordingly, thus*).

>   It was very late; therefore, I remained at the hotel.

3. Use a semicolon to separate main clauses joined by a coordinating conjunction if one or both of the clauses contain distracting commas.

>   Byron, the famous English poet, was buried in Greece; and Shelley, who was his friend and fellow poet, was buried in Italy.

4. Use a semicolon in a series between items that themselves contain commas.

>   He has lived in Covina, California; Reno, Nevada; Prague, Oklahoma; and Bangor, Maine.

Exercise 43	USING COMMAS AND SEMICOLONS

Each sentence needs one or more semicolons or commas. Insert the appropriate marks. (See Answer Key for answers.)

1. The Bohemians clustered together on Telegraph Hill they shared it with the Italian fishermen.

2. Washington's death was mourned in many countries indeed, many in the United States worshiped his image.

3. It is one thing to dig but it is another thing to live underground.

4. The advertisements show rugged males, all smoking beautiful females, all in bathing suits and luxury cars, all with only two seats.

5. Watson intended to buy only a pair of shoes, a prosaic enough errand, he thought but he actually bought each sibling a gift, one an ivory figurine and the other a delicate fan.

6. Serinda found one page of Ruskin a pleasure but twenty she found a bore.

7. Spring was full of promise of apples, now only pink-white, sweet blossoms pumpkins, still just tiny green marbles and corn, barely showing above the brown earth.

8. Gertrude Stein knew about the people in Paris for she lived there.

9. Professor Anne Parker told us that the life of Joseph was a foreshadowing of the life of Jesus in fact, in comparing their lives, she pointed out thirteen literal and symbolic similarities.

10. One author bases the story on his or her own life, and it need not be an unusual one another analyzes relationships among others, imaginary or real still another concentrates on historical events, commenting as he or she records.

11. F. Scott Fitzgerald was interested in the power of money to buy status in fact he, himself, bought status.

12. Paperwork makes different demands on different people otherwise, Parkinson's law would not work in our office.

13. The critic called Pamela Johnson's novel a shallow romance but she insisted it was a penetrating psychological study.

14. It is impossible to make predictions about a grown dog by studying a mongrel puppy however, a purebred puppy is almost sure to be a duplicate of its parents.

15. Many children are afraid of their grandfathers and I was one of those children.

16. Human beings will try to find their way out of a fire but horses may run into it.

17. He believed he was responsible for me, and he told me I was determined to do things my way, even if it meant failing or humiliating him.

18. The judge had an avid interest in nature and often lived in the open for weeks at a time it cost him his marriage.

19. They were poor people and they lived in the damp chill of an inhospitable island.

20. Thoreau did not want to become a recluse he wanted only to lead a simple life.

Exercise 44   **USING COMMAS AND SEMICOLONS**

Each sentence needs one or more semicolons or commas. Insert the appropriate marks.

1. He was the person I met on the subway I never forget a face.

2. That melon looks fresh but it costs too much.

3. We gave the book to Lorenza however she never opened it.

4. He became king after the abolition of the parliament but his days of power were numbered.

5. Please remain quiet while Carlos reads the announcement you may nap if you like.

6. The best part of the trip was our stay at Yosemite the worst part was the traveling.

7. I found them another house it was similar to the first one they saw.

8. Joline looks somewhat tired I wonder if she is really well.

9. The apple Arek gave me is very sour but it is the thought that counts.

10. Our instructor gave a lecture on constitutional law it was brilliant in expression and content.

11. I did not recommend that novel to Judy she discovered it herself.

12. Will it be our turn next or will we have to wait longer?

13. It was not the whale that destroyed Captain Ahab it was Captain Ahab who destroyed Captain Ahab.

14. I do not feel responsible he had a clear choice in the matter.

15. No one could be wiser than the Zen master we could only study his principles.

16. Luke is the only person who could be so ruthless Joshua comes in a close second.

17. Ramona smiled sweetly as she handed the president the message but he was suspicious.

18. Wendy was only the messenger however he was furious at her instead of at the message.

19. It was a long, cold winter and I was fortunate to work indoors.

20. We sent members notice of the meeting well in advance yet some said they received nothing.

Quotation Marks

Quotation marks are used principally to set off direct quotations. A direct quotation consists of material taken from the written work or the direct speech of others; it is set off by double quotation marks. Single quotation marks are used to set off a quotation within a quotation.

Double Quotation Marks: He said, "I don't remember."

Single Quotation Marks: He said, "I don't remember if she said, 'Wait for me.'"

1. Use double quotation marks to set off direct quotations.

> Erin said, "Give me the book."

> As Edward McNeil writes of the Greek achievement: "To an extent never before realized, mind was supreme over faith."

2. Use double quotation marks to set off titles of shorter pieces of writing such as magazine articles, essays, short stories, short poems, one-act plays, chapters in books, songs, and separate pieces of writing published as part of a larger work.

> The book *Literature: Structure, Sound, and Sense* contains a deeply moving poem entitled "On Wenlock Edge."

> Have you read "The Use of Force," a short story by William Carlos Williams?

> My favorite Elvis song is "Don't Be Cruel."

3. Use double quotation marks to set off slang, technical terms, and special words.

> There are many aristocrats, but Elvis is the only true "King." (special word)

> The "platoon system" changed the game of football. (technical term)

4. Use double quotation marks in writing dialogue (conversation). Write each speech unit as a separate paragraph and set it off with double quotation marks.

> "Will you go with me?" he asked.

> "Yes," she replied. "Are you ready now?"

5. Use single quotation marks to set off a quotation within a quotation.

> Professor Baxter said, "You should remember Shakespeare's words, 'Nothing will come of nothing.'"

6. Do *not* use quotation marks for indirect quotations.

Wrong: He said that "he would bring the supplies."

Right: He said that he would bring the supplies.

7. Do *not* use quotation marks for the title on your own written work. If you refer to that title in another piece of writing, however, you need the quotation marks.

Punctuation with Quotation Marks

1. A period or comma is always placed *inside* the quotation marks.

> Our assignment for Monday was to read Poe's poem "The Raven."

> "I will read you the story," he said. "It's a good one."

2. A semicolon or colon is always placed *outside* the quotation marks.

> He read Robert Frost's poem "Design"; then he gave the examination.

> He quoted Frost's "Stopping by Woods on a Snowy Evening": "But I have promises to keep."

3. A question mark, exclamation point, or dash (see page 457) is placed *outside* the quotation marks when it applies to the entire sentence and *inside* the quotation marks when it applies to the material in quotation marks.

> He asked, "Am I responsible for everything?" (quoted question within a statement)

> Did you hear him say, "I have the answer"? (statement within a question)

> Did she say, "Are you ready?" (question within a question)

> She shouted, "Impossible!" (exclamation)

> Roy screamed, "I'll flunk if I don't read Poe's short story "The Black Cat"! (exclamation that does not belong to the material inside the quotation marks)

> "I hope—that is, I—" he began. (dash)

> "Accept responsibility"—those were his words. (dash that does not belong to the material inside the quotation marks)

4. A single question mark is used in sentence constructions that contain a double question—that is, a quoted question following a question.

> Mr. Martin said, "Did he say, 'Are you going?'"

Italics

Italics (slanting type) is used to call special attention to certain words or groups of words. In handwriting or typing, such words are <u>underlined;</u> however, word processors provide italics.

1. Italicize (underline) foreign words and phrases that are still listed in the dictionary as foreign.

> *nouveau riche*   *Weltschmerz*

2. Italicize (underline) titles of books (except the Bible); long poems; plays; magazines; motion pictures; musical compositions; newspapers; works of art; names of aircraft and ships; and letters, figures, and words.

> I think Hemingway's best novel is *A Farewell to Arms.*

> His source material was taken from *Time, Newsweek,* and the Los Angeles *Times.* (Sometimes the name of the city in titles of newspapers is italicized—for example, the *New York Times.*)

> The *Mona Lisa* is my favorite painting.

3. Italicize (underline) the names of ships, airplanes, spacecraft, and trains.

   Ships: *Queen Mary Lurline Stockholm*

   Spacecraft: *Challenger Voyager 2*

4. Italicize (underline) to distinguish letters, figures, and words when they refer to themselves rather than to the ideas or things they usually represent.

   Do not leave the *o* out of *sophomore.*

   Your *3*'s look like *5*'s.

Dashes

The dash is used when a stronger break than the comma is needed. The dash is typed as two hyphens with no space before or after them (--).

1. Use a dash to indicate a sudden change in sentence construction or an abrupt break in thought.

   Here is the true reason—but maybe you don't care.

2. Use a dash after an introductory list. The words *these, those, all,* and occasionally *such* introduce the summarizing statement.

   English, French, history—these are the subjects I like.

Colons

The colon is a formal mark of punctuation used chiefly to introduce something that is to follow, such as a list, a quotation, or an explanation.

1. Use a colon after a main clause to introduce a formal list, an emphatic or long restatement (appositive), an explanation, an emphatic statement, or a summary.

   The following cars were in the General Motors show: Cadillac, Chevrolet, Buick, Oldsmobile, and Pontiac. (list)

   He worked toward one objective: a degree. (restatement or appositive)

   Let me emphasize one point: I do not accept late papers. (emphatic statement)

2. Use a colon to introduce a formal quotation or a formal question.

   Shakespeare's Polonius said: "Neither a borrower nor a lender be." (formal quotation)

   The question is this: Shall we surrender? (formal question)

3. Use a colon in the following conventional ways: to separate a title and subtitle, a chapter and verse in the Bible, and hours and minutes; after the salutation in a formal business letter; and between the act and the scene of a play.

Title and subtitle:	*Korea: A Country Divided*
Chapter and verse:	Genesis 4:12
Hour and minutes:	8:25 P.M.
Salutation:	Dear Ms. Johnson:
Act and scene:	*Hamlet* III:ii

Parentheses

Parentheses are used to set off material that is of relatively little importance to the main thought of the sentence. Such material—numbers, supplementary material, and sometimes explanatory details—merely amplifies the main thought.

1. Use parentheses to set off material that is not part of the main sentence but is too relevant to omit altogether. This category includes numbers that designate items in a series, amplifying references, explanations, directions, and qualifications.

> Jay offered two reasons for his losing: (1) he was tired, and (2) he was out of condition. (numbers)

> Review the chapters on the Civil War (6, 7, and 8) for the next class meeting. (references)

> Her husband (she had been married about a year) died last week. (explanation)

2. In business writing, use parentheses to enclose a numerical figure that repeats and confirms a spelled-out number.

> I paid twenty dollars ($20) for the book.

3. Use a comma, semicolon, and colon after the parentheses when the sentence punctuation requires their use.

> Although I have not lived here long (I arrived in 1998), this place feels like my only true home.

Use the period, question mark, and exclamation point in appropriate positions depending on whether they go with the material within the parentheses or with the entire sentence.

> The greatest English poet of the seventeenth century was John Milton (1608–1674).

> The greatest English poet of the seventeenth century was John Milton. (Some might not agree; I myself favor Andrew Marvell.)

Brackets

Brackets are used within a quotation to set off editorial additions or corrections made by the person who is quoting.

> Churchill said: "It [the Yalta Agreement] contained many mistakes."

Apostrophes

The apostrophe is used with nouns and indefinite pronouns to show possession; to show the omission of letters and figures in contractions; and to form the plurals of letters, figures, and words referred to as words.

1. A possessive shows that something is owned by someone. Use an apostrophe and -*s* to form the possessive of a noun, singular or plural, that does not end in -*s*.

> man's coat   women's suits

2. Use an apostrophe alone to form the possessive of a plural noun ending in -*s*.

> girls' clothes   the Browns' house

3. Use an apostrophe and *-s* or the apostrophe alone to form the possessive of singular nouns ending in *-s*. Use the apostrophe and *-s* only when you would pronounce the *s*.

> James' hat or (if you would pronounce the *s*) James's hat

4. Use an apostrophe and *-s* to form the possessive of certain indefinite pronouns.

> everybody's idea   one's meat   another's poison

5. Use an apostrophe to indicate that letters or figures have been omitted.

> o'clock (short for *of the clock*)   in the '90s (short for 1990s)

6. Use an apostrophe with pronouns only when you are making a contraction. A contraction is a combination of two words. The apostrophe in a contraction indicates where a letter has been omitted.

> it is = it's
>
> she has = she's
>
> you are = you're

If no letters have been left out, don't use an apostrophe.

> **Wrong:**   The dog bit it's tail.
>
> **Right:**   The dog bit its tail. (not a contraction)
>
> **Wrong:**   Whose the leader now?
>
> **Right:**   Who's the leader now? (a contraction of *who is*)
>
> **Wrong:**   Its a big problem.
>
> **Right:**   It's a big problem. (a contraction of *it is*)

7. Use an apostrophe to indicate the plural of letters, figures, and words used as words.

> Dot your *i*'s.   five *8*'s   *and*'s

Note that the letters, figures, and words are italicized, but the apostrophe and *-s* are not.

Hyphens

The hyphen brings two or more words together into a single compound word. Correct hyphenation, therefore, is essentially a spelling problem rather than one of punctuation. Because the hyphen is not used with any degree of consistency, consult your dictionary for current usage. Study the following as a beginning guide.

1. Use a hyphen to separate the parts of many compound words.

> brother-in-law   go-between

2. Use a hyphen between prefixes and proper names.

> all-American   mid-Atlantic

3. Use a hyphen to join two or more words used as a single adjective modifier before a noun.

> bluish-gray eyes   first-class service

4. Use a hyphen with spelled-out compound numbers up to ninety-nine and with fractions.

twenty-six   two-thirds

Note: Dates, street addresses, numbers requiring more than two words, chapter and page numbers, time followed directly by A.M. or P.M., and figures after a dollar sign or before measurement abbreviations are usually written as figures, not words.

Capitalization

Following are some of the many conventions concerning the use of capital letters in English.

1. Capitalize the first word of a sentence.

2. Capitalize proper nouns and adjectives derived from proper nouns.

   Names of persons:
   Edward Jones

   Adjectives derived from proper nouns:
   a Shakespearean sonnet   a Miltonic sonnet

   Countries, nationalities, races, languages:
   Germany   English   Spanish   Chinese

   States, regions, localities, other geographical divisions:
   California   the Far East   the South

   Oceans, lakes, mountains, deserts, streets, parks:
   Lake Superior   Fifth Avenue   Sahara Desert

   Educational institutions, schools, courses:
   Santa Ana College   Spanish 3   Joe Hill School   Rowland High School

   Organizations and their members:
   Boston Red Sox   Boy Scouts   Audubon Society

   Corporations, governmental agencies or departments, trade names:
   U.S. Steel Corporation   Treasury Department   White Memorial Library
   Coca-Cola

   Calendar references such as holidays, days of the week, months:
   Easter   Tuesday   January

   Historic eras, periods, documents, laws:
   Declaration of Independence   Geneva Convention   First Crusade
   Romantic Age

3. Capitalize words denoting family relationships when they are used before a name or substituted for a name.

He walked with his nephew and Aunt Grace.

but

He walked with his nephew and his aunt.

Grandmother and Mother are away on vacation.

but

My grandmother and my mother are away on vacation.

4. Capitalize abbreviations after names.

> Henry White, Jr.
>
> Juan Gomez, M.D.

5. Capitalize titles of essays, books, plays, movies, poems, magazines, newspapers, musical compositions, songs, and works of art. Do not capitalize short conjunctions and prepositions unless they come at the beginning or the end of the title.

> *Desire Under the Elms*
>
> *Last of the Mohicans*
>
> "Blueberry Hill"
>
> *Terminator*
>
> *Of Mice and Men*

6. Capitalize any title preceding a name or used as a substitute for a name. Do not capitalize a title following a name.

Judge Wong	Alfred Wong, a judge
General Clark	Raymond Clark, a general
Professor Fuentes	Harry Fuentes, the biology professor

Exercise 45   **USING PUNCTUATION AND CAPITALIZATION**

One punctuation mark, a capital letter, or italic type is omitted in each of the following sentences. Insert them as needed. Pairs of quotation marks or dashes are considered one unit. (See Answer Key for answers.)

1. Wyatt Earp said, In two years at Wichita, my deputies and I arrested more than 800 men.

2. It was all in a days work.

3. "We really have no satisfactory synonym for Lebensraum," Cary said.

4. "Its like a miracle of God," Ginny said. "I can rest now."

5. "Just say, Stop now, when you've heard enough," the salesman said.

6. The wind carried its murmur through the trees, and we listened to the crickets chirping louder and louder as the birds chirping softened into silence.

7. In a trite way, its true that the best things are free.

8. Melville's novel Billy Budd was published posthumously.

9. What does Keats mean by "Darkling I listen" in his poem Ode to a Nightingale?

10. Jack Londons books are still widely read in this country and abroad.

11. Will couldn't see the connection between Oxford and Walnut—or could he.

12. Every one of the miners was lost in the cave in.

13. The boy from Germany crossed his *7*s.

14. Joe Louis, Art Aragon, and Rocky Marciano these were my father's favorite fighters.

15. The following citizens in Hiroshima were interviewed a town official, a house-wife, a farmer, a mechanic, and a doctor.

16. Marx and Engels you know who they were understood dialectical materialism much better than the working class did.

17. The romantic Age is not as difficult to teach to this generation as I thought it would be.

18. Those who believed in the Declaration of independence thought that Madison's *Federalist* was too conservative.

19. It's not difficult to think of C. P. Snow as an english scholar, although his field was science.

20. The doctor, Ralph Berger, called aunt Helen to hold his son's head while he stitched it up.

Exercise 46 **USING PUNCTUATION AND CAPITALIZATION**

Twenty punctuation marks are needed in the following paragraphs; the locations are indicated by the numbers. Pairs such as quotation marks and parentheses are considered one unit. Insert the marks as needed.

   ¹   ²   ³   ⁴
Shakespeares age was like ours it was full of change and turmoil" the old gen-
       ⁵   ⁶
tleman said. New ideas were not confined exclusively to one social class one reli-
       ⁷
gion or one political party. Outer space stirred the imaginations of most of the
          ⁸   ⁹   ¹⁰
people not just the astronomers. They went to see Hamlet for fun and they bought
                                                                        ¹¹
all the books available on the strange customs of other cultures. And whos to say
              ¹²   ¹³ ¹⁴   ¹⁵   (14)
that when Hamlets father says I am thy fathers spirit he is any less visible than the
                                        ¹⁶   ¹⁷   ¹⁸
ghosts some people say they see today. There wasnt much Shakespeare didnt know
          ¹⁹   ²⁰
about us. Thats why we still quarrel about the meaning of his plays we are still dis-
                                        (5)
covering the truth about ourselves in them.

Spelling

Spelling Tips

The following tips will help you become a better speller.

1. **Do not omit letters.**
   Many errors occur because certain letters are omitted when the word is pronounced or spelled. Observe the omissions in the following words. Then concentrate on learning the correct spellings.

Incorrect	Correct	Incorrect	Correct
aquaintance	a*c*quaintance	irigation	ir*r*igation
ajourned	a*d*journed	libary	lib*r*ary
agravate	a*g*gravate	paralell	paral*l*el
aproved	a*p*proved	parlament	parl*i*ament
artic	ar*c*tic	paticulaly	pa*r*ticula*r*ly
comodity	co*m*modity	readly	read*i*ly
efficent	effic*i*ent	sophmore	soph*o*more
envirnment	enviro*n*ment	stricly	stric*t*ly
familar	famil*i*ar	unconsious	uncons*c*ious

2. **Do not add letters.**

Incorrect	Correct	Incorrect	Correct
ath*e*lete	athlete	om*m*ission	omission
co*m*ming	coming	pas*t*time	pastime
drown*d*ed	drowned	privile*d*ge	privilege
folk*e*s	folks	simil*i*ar	similar
occa*s*sionally	occasionally	tra*d*gedy	tragedy

3. **Do not substitute incorrect letters for correct letters.**

Incorrect	Correct	Incorrect	Correct
benefi*s*ial	beneficial	offen*c*e	offense
bull*i*tins	bulletins	peculi*e*r	peculiar
*s*ensus	census	re*s*itation	recitation
d*i*scription	description	scre*a*ch	screech
d*e*sease	disease	substan*s*ial	substantial
dissen*t*ion	dissension	surpri*z*e	surprise
it*i*ms	items	techn*a*cal	technical

4. **Do not transpose letters.**

Incorrect	Correct	Incorrect	Correct
alu*nm*i	alumni	p*r*ehaps	perhaps
child*er*n	children	p*e*rfer	prefer
dup*il*cate	duplicate	p*e*rscription	prescription
irreve*la*nt	irrelevant	princip*e*ls	principles
kind*el*	kindle	ye*i*ld	yield

Note: Whenever you notice other words that fall into any one of these categories, add them to the list.

5. **Apply the spelling rules for spelling *ei* and *ie* words correctly.**

    Remember this poem?

    > Use *i* before *e*
    > Except after *c*
    > Or when sounded like *a*
    > As in *neighbor* and *weigh*.

    i before e

achieve	chief	niece	relieve
belief	field	piece	shield
believe	grief	pierce	siege
brief	hygiene	relief	variety

    Except after **c**

ceiling	conceive	deceive	receipt
conceit	deceit	perceive	receive

    Exceptions: either, financier, height, leisure, neither, seize, species, weird

    When sounded like ***a***

deign	freight	neighbor	sleigh
eight	heinous	rein	veil
feign	heir	reign	vein
feint	neigh	skein	weigh

6. **Apply the rules for dropping the final *e* or retaining the final *e* when a suffix is added.**

    Words ending in a silent *e* usually drop the *e* before a suffix beginning with a vowel; for example, *accuse* + -ing = *accusing*. Here are some common suffixes beginning with a vowel: *-able, -al, -age, -ary, -ation, -ence, -ing, -ion, -ous, -ure.*

admire + -*able* = admirable	imagine + -*ary* = imaginary
arrive + -*al* = arrival	locate + -*ion* = location
come + -*ing* = coming	please + -*ure* = pleasure
explore + -*ation* = exploration	plume + -*age* = plumage
fame + -*ous* = famous	precede + -*ence* = precedence

    Exceptions: *dye* + -*ing* = *dyeing* (to distinguish it from *dying*), *acreage, mileage.*

    Words ending in a silent -*e* usually retain the *e* before a suffix beginning with a consonant; for example: *arrange* + -*ment* = *arrangement*. Here are some common suffixes beginning with a consonant: *-craft, -ful, -less, -ly, -mate, -ment, -ness, -ty.*

entire + -*ty* = entirety	manage + -*ment* = management
hate + -*ful* = hateful	safe + -*ly* = safely
hope + -*less* = hopeless	stale + -*mate* = stalemate
like + -*ness* = likeness	state + -*craft* = statecraft

    Exceptions: Some words taking the -*ful* or -*ly* suffixes drop the final *e:*

awe + -*ful* = awful	true + -*ly* = truly
due + -*ly* = duly	whole + -*ly* = wholly

    Some words taking the suffix -*ment* drop the final *e;* for example:

acknowledgment	argument	judgment

Words ending in silent *-e* after *c* or *g* retain the *e* when the suffix begins with the vowel *a* or *o*. The final *-e* is retained to keep the *c* or *g* soft before the suffixes.

advantag*e*ous   notic*e*able
courag*e*ous   peac*e*able

7. **Apply the rules for doubling a final consonant before a suffix beginning with a vowel.**

Words of one syllable:

blot	blotted	get	getting	rob	robbed
brag	bragging	hop	hopped	run	running
cut	cutting	hot	hottest	sit	sitting
drag	dragged	man	mannish	stop	stopped
drop	dropped	plan	planned	swim	swimming

Words accented on the last syllable:

acquit	acquitted	equip	equipped
admit	admittance	occur	occurrence
allot	allotted	omit	omitting
begin	beginning	prefer	preferred
commit	committee	refer	referred
concur	concurring	submit	submitted
confer	conferring	transfer	transferred
defer	deferring		

Words that are not accented on the last syllable and words that do not end in a single consonant preceded by a vowel do not double the final consonant (whether or not the suffix begins with a vowel).

Frequently Misspelled Words

a lot	complete	existence	laboratory
absence	consider	experience	leisure
across	criticism	explanation	length
actually	definitely	extremely	library
all right	dependent	familiar	likely
among	develop	February	lying
analyze	development	finally	marriage
appearance	difference	foreign	mathematics
appreciate	disastrous	government	meant
argument	discipline	grammar	medicine
athlete	discussed	grateful	neither
athletics	disease	guarantee	ninety
awkward	divide	guard	ninth
becoming	dying	guidance	nuclear
beginning	eighth	height	occasionally
belief	eligible	hoping	opinion
benefit	eliminate	humorous	opportunity
buried	embarrassed	immediately	parallel
business	environment	independent	particular
certain	especially	intelligence	persuade
college	etc.	interest	physically
coming	exaggerate	interfere	planned
committee	excellent	involved	pleasant
competition	exercise	knowledge	possible

practical	religious	significant	tried
preferred	repetition	similar	tries
prejudice	rhythm	sincerely	truly
privilege	ridiculous	sophomore	unfortunately
probably	sacrifice	speech	unnecessary
professor	safety	straight	until
prove	scene	studying	unusual
psychology	schedule	succeed	using
pursue	secretary	success	usually
receipt	senior	suggest	Wednesday
receive	sense	surprise	writing
recommend	separate	thoroughly	written
reference	severely	though	
relieve	shining	tragedy	

Confused Spelling and Confusing Words

The following are more words that are commonly misspelled or confused with one another. Some have similar sounds, some are often mispronounced, and some are only misunderstood.

a	An adjective (called an article) used before a word beginning with a consonant or a consonant sound, as in "I ate *a* donut."
an	An adjective (called an article) used before a word beginning with a vowel (*a, e, i, o, u*) or with a silent *h,* as in "I ate an artichoke."
and	A coordinating conjunction, as in "Sara *and* I like Johnny Cash."
accept	A verb meaning "to receive," as in "I *accept* your explanation."
except	A preposition meaning "to exclude," as in "I paid everyone *except* you."
advice	A noun meaning "guidance," as in "Thanks for the *advice.*"
advise	A verb meaning "to give guidance," as in "Will you please *advise* me of my rights?"
all right	An adjective meaning "correct" or "acceptable," as in "It's *all right* to cry."
alright	Not used in formal writing.
all ready	An adjective that can be used interchangeably with *ready,* as in "I am *all ready* to go to town."
already	An adverb meaning "before," which cannot be used in place of *ready,* as in "I have *already* finished."
a lot	An adverb meaning "much," as in "She liked him *a lot,*" or a noun meaning "several," as in "I had *a lot* of suggestions."
alot	Misspelling.
altogether	An adverb meaning "completely," as in "He is *altogether* happy."
all together	An adverb meaning "as one," which can be used interchangeably with *together,* as in "The group left *all together.*"
choose	A present tense verb meaning "to select," as in "Do whatever you *choose.*"

chose	The past tense form of the verb *choose,* as in "They *chose* to take action yesterday."
could of	A misspelled phrase caused by confusing *could've,* meaning *could have,* with *could of.*
could have	Correctly spelled phrase, as in "I could have left."
could've	Correctly spelled contraction of *could have,* as in "He could've succeeded."
affect	Usually a verb meaning "change," as in "Ideas *affect* me."
effect	Usually a noun meaning "result," as in "That *effect* was unexpected."
hear	A verb indicating the receiving of sound, as in "I *hear* thunder."
here	An adverb meaning "present location," as in "I live *here.*"
it's	A contraction of *it is,* as in "*It's* time to dance."
its	Possessive pronoun, as in "Each dog has *its* day."
know	A verb usually meaning "to comprehend" or "to recognize," as in "I *know* the answer."
no	An adjective meaning "negative," as in "I have *no* potatoes."
lead	A present tense verb, as in "I *lead* a stable life now," or a noun referring to a substance, such as "I sharpened the *lead* in my pencil."
led	The past tense form of the verb *lead,* as in "I *led* a wild life in my youth."
loose	An adjective meaning "without restraint," as in "He is a *loose* cannon."
lose	A present tense verb from the pattern *lose, lost, lost,* as in "I thought I would *lose* my senses."
paid	The past tense form of *pay,* as in "He *paid* his dues."
payed	Misspelling.
passed	The past tense form of the verb *pass,* meaning "went by," as in "He *passed* me on the curve."
past	An adjective meaning "former," as in "That's *past* history," or a noun, as in "He lived in the *past.*"
patience	A noun meaning "willingness to wait," as in "Job was a man of much *patience.*"
patients	A noun meaning "people under care," as in "The doctor had fifty *patients.*"
peace	A noun meaning "a quality of calmness" or "absence of strife," as in "The guru was at *peace* with the world."
piece	A noun meaning "part," as in "I gave him a *piece* of my mind."
quiet	An adjective meaning "silent," as in "She was a *quiet* child."
quit	A verb meaning "to cease" or "to withdraw," as in "I *quit* my job."
quite	An adverb meaning "very," as in "The clam is *quite* happy."

receive	A verb meaning "to accept," as in "I will *receive* visitors now."
recieve	Misspelling.
stationary	An adjective meaning "not moving," as in "Try to avoid running into *stationary* objects."
stationery	A noun meaning "paper material to write on," as in "I bought a box of *stationery* for Sue's birthday present."
than	A conjunction, as in "He is taller *than* I am."
then	An adverb, as in "She *then* left town."
their	An adjective (possessive pronoun), as in "They read *their* books."
there	An adverb, as in "He left it *there*," or a filler word, as in "*There* is no time left."
they're	A contraction of *they are*, as in "*They're* happy."
thorough	An adjective, as in "He did a *thorough* job."
through	A preposition, as in "She went *through* the yard."
to	A preposition, as in "I went *to* town."
too	An adverb meaning "exceeding or going beyond what is acceptable," as in "You are *too* late to qualify for the discount," or "also," as in "I have feelings, *too*."
two	An adjective of number, as in "I have *two* jobs."
truely	Misspelling.
truly	An adverb meaning "sincerely" or "completely," as in "He was *truly* happy."
weather	A noun meaning "condition of the atmosphere," as in "The *weather* is pleasant today."
whether	A conjunction, as in "*Whether* he would go was of no consequence."
write	A present tense verb, as in "Watch me as I *write* this letter."
writen	Misspelling.
written	A past participle verb, as in "I have *written* the letter."
you're	A contraction of *you are*, as in "*You're* my friend."
your	A possessive pronoun, as in "I like *your* looks."

Your Spell Checker

Your computer spell checker is an important tool with many benefits and some limitations. With about 100,000 words in a typical database, the spell checker alerts you to problem words in your text that should be verified. If you agree that the spelling of a word should be checked, you can then select from a list of words with similar spellings. A likely substitute word will be highlighted. With a keystroke, you can correct a problem, add your own word to the database, or ignore the alert. With a few more keystrokes, you can type in your own correction, and you can add an unusual spelling or word to the database. You may even be able to program your spell checker to correct automatically your most frequent spelling or typing errors. You will be amazed at how many times your computer will catch misspellings that your eye did not see.

However, the spell checker has limitations. If you intended to type *he* and instead typed *me,* the spell checker will not alert you to a possible problem because the word you typed is spelled correctly. If you use the wrong word, such as *herd* instead of *heard,* the spell checker will not detect a problem. Thus, you should always proofread your writing after you have spell checked it. Do not be lulled into a false sense of spelling security simply because you have a machine on your side. As a writer, you are the final spell checker.

Brief Guide for ESL Students

If you came to this country knowing little English, you probably acquired vocabulary first. Then you began using that vocabulary within the basic patterns of your own language. If your native language had no articles, you probably used no articles; if your language had no verb tenses, you probably used no verb tenses, and so on. Using the grammar of your own language with your new vocabulary may initially have enabled you to make longer and more complex statements in English, but eventually you learned that your native grammar and your adopted grammar were different. You may even have learned that no two grammars are the same, and that English has a bewildering set of rules and an even longer set of exceptions to those rules. The Handbook presents grammar (the way we put words together) and rhetoric (the way we use language effectively) that can be applied to your writing. The following are some definitions, rules, and references that are of special help to writers who are learning English as a second language (ESL).

Using Articles in Relation to Nouns

Articles

Articles are either indefinite (*an, a*) or definite (*the*). Because they point out nouns, they are often called *noun determiners.*

Nouns

Nouns can be either singular (*book*) or plural (*books*) and are either count nouns (things that can be counted, such as "book") or noncount nouns (things that cannot be counted, such as "homework"). If you are not certain whether a noun is a count noun or a noncount noun, try placing the word *much* before the word. You can say, "much homework," so *homework* is a noncount noun.

Rules

- **Use an indefinite article (*a* or *an*) before singular count nouns and not before noncount nouns.** The indefinite article means "one," so you would not use it before plural count nouns.

  Correct: I saw a book. (count noun)

  Correct: I ate an apple. (count noun)

  Incorrect: I fell in a love. (noncount noun)

Correct:	I fell in love. (noncount noun)
Incorrect:	I was in a good health. (noncount noun)
Correct:	I was in good health. (noncount noun)

- **Use the definite article (*the*) before both singular and plural count nouns that have specific reference.**

Correct:	I read the book. (a specific one)
Correct:	I read the books. (specific ones)
Correct:	I like to read a good book. (nonspecific, therefore the indefinite article)
Correct:	A student who works hard will pass. (any student, therefore nonspecific)
Correct:	The student on my left is falling asleep. (a specific student)

- **Use the definite article with noncount nouns only when they are specifically identified.**

Correct:	Honesty (as an idea) is a rare commodity.
Correct:	The honesty of my friend has inspired me. (specifically identified)
Incorrect:	I was in trouble and needed the assistance. (not specifically identified)
Correct:	The assistance offered by the paramedics was appreciated. (specifically identified)

- **Place the definite article before proper nouns (names) of**

  oceans, rivers, and deserts (for example, *the* Pacific Ocean and *the* Red River).

  countries, if the first part of the name indicates a division (*the* United States of America).

  regions (*the* South).

  plural islands (*the* Hawaiian Islands).

  museums and libraries (*the* Los Angeles County Museum).

  colleges and universities when the word *college* or *university* comes before the name (*the* University of Oklahoma).

These are the main rules. For a more detailed account of rules for articles, see a comprehensive ESL book in your library.

Sentence Patterns

The Kinds of Sentences section in this Handbook defines and illustrates the patterns of English sentences. Some languages include patterns not used in standard English. The following principles are well worth remembering:

- **The conventional English sentence is based on one or more clauses, each of which must have a subject (sometimes the implied "you") and a verb.**

Incorrect:	Saw the book. (subject needed even if it is obvious)
Correct:	I saw the book.

- **English does not repeat a subject, even for emphasis.**

Incorrect:	The book that I read it was interesting.
Correct:	The book that I read was interesting.

Verb Endings

- **English indicates time through verbs.** Learn the different forms of verb tenses and the combinations of main verbs and helping verbs.

Incorrect:	He watching the game. (A verb-like word ending in *-ing* cannot be a verb all by itself.)
Correct:	He is watching the game. (Note that a helping verb such as *is, has, has been, will,* or *will be* always occurs before a main verb ending in *-ing.*

- **Take special care in maintaining consistency in tense.**

Incorrect:	I went to the mall. I watch a movie there. (verb tenses inconsistent)
Correct:	I went to the mall. I watched a movie there.

All twelve verb tenses are covered with explanations, examples, and exercises in the Verbs section of the Handbook, pages 398–419.

Idioms

Some of your initial problems with writing English are likely to arise from trying to adjust to a different and difficult grammar. If the English language used an entirely systematic grammar, your learning would be easier, but English has patterns that are both complex and irregular. Among them are idioms, word groups that often defy grammatical rules and mean something other than what they appear to mean on the surface.

The expression "He kicked the bucket" does not mean that someone struck a cylindrical container with his foot; instead, it means that someone died. That example is one kind of idiom. Because the expression suggests a certain irreverence, it would not be the choice of most people who want to make a statement about death; but if it is used, it must be used with its own precise wording, not "He struck the long cylindrical container with his foot," or "He did some bucket-kicking." Like other languages, the English language has thousands of these idioms. Expressions such as "the more the merrier" and "on the outs" are ungrammatical. They are also very informal expressions and therefore seldom used in college writing, although they are an indispensable part of a flexible, effective, all-purpose vocabulary. Because of their twisted meanings and illogic, idioms are likely to be among the last parts of language that a new speaker learns well. A speaker must know the culture thoroughly to understand when, where, and how to use slang and other idiomatic expressions.

If you listen carefully and read extensively, you will learn English idioms. Your library will have dictionaries that explain them.

More Suggestions for ESL Writers

1. Read your material aloud and try to detect inconsistencies and awkward phrasing.

2. Have others read your material aloud for the same purposes.

3. If you have severe problems with grammatical awkwardness, try composing shorter, more direct sentences until you become more proficient in phrasing.

4. On your Self-Evaluation Chart, list the problems you have (such as articles, verb endings, clause patterns), review relevant parts of the Handbook, and concentrate on your own problem areas as you draft, revise, and edit.

Exercise 47	CORRECTING ESL PROBLEMS

Make corrections in the use of articles, verbs, and phrasing. (See Answer Key for answers.)

George Washington at Trenton

One of most famous battles during the War of Independence occur at Trenton, New Jersey, on Christmas Eve of the 1776. The colonists outmatched in supplies and finances and were outnumbered in troop strength. Most observers in other countries think rebellion would be put down soon. British overconfident and believe there would be no more battles until spring. But George Washington decide to fight one more time. That Christmas, while large army of Britishers having party and thinking about the holiday season, Americans set out for surprise raid. They loaded onto boats used for carrying ore and rowed across Delaware River. George Washington stood tall in lead boat. According to legend, drummer boy floated across river on his drum, pulled by rope tied to boat. Because British did not feel threatened by the ragtag colonist forces, they unprepared to do battle. The colonists stormed living quarters and the general assembly hall and achieved victory. It was good for the colonists' morale, something they needed, for they would endure long, hard winter before fighting again.

Appendixes

"For excellence, the presence of others is always required."

Hannah Arendt

THE QUIGMANS   by Buddy Hickerson

"We're not exactly on the cutting edge of surgical techniques here. We're mostly into licking the wounds clean."

B. Hickerson, copyright 1997. Los Angeles Times Syndicate. Reprinted by permission.

Appendix A   Parts of Speech

To classify a word as a part of speech, we observe two simple principles:

- The word must be in the context of communication, usually in a sentence.

- We must be able to identify the word with others that have similar characteristics—the eight parts of speech: nouns, pronouns, adjectives, verbs, adverbs, prepositions, conjunctions, or interjections.

The first principle is important because some words can be any of several parts of speech. The word *round,* for example, can function as five:

1. I watched the potter *round* the block of clay. (verb)

2. I saw her go *round* the corner. (preposition)

3. She has a *round* head. (adjective)

4. The astronauts watched the world go *round.* (adverb)

5. The champ knocked him out in one *round.* (noun)

Nouns

- **Nouns are naming words.** Nouns may name persons, animals, plants, places, things, substances, qualities, or ideas—for example, *Bart, armadillo, Mayberry, tree, rock, cloud, love, ghost, music, virtue.*

- **Nouns are often pointed out by noun indicators.** These noun indicators—*the, a, an*—signal that a noun is ahead, although there may be words between the indicator and the noun itself.

the slime	*a* werewolf	*an* aardvark
the green slime	*a* hungry werewolf	*an* angry aardvark

Pronouns

A **pronoun** is a word that is used in place of a noun.

- Some pronouns may represent specific persons or things:

I	she	they	you
me	her	them	yourself
myself	herself	themselves	yourselves
it	he	we	who
itself	him	us	whom
that	himself	ourselves	

- Indefinite pronouns refer to nouns (persons, places, things) in a general way:

each	everyone	nobody	somebody

- Other pronouns point out particular things:

Singular	**Plural**
this, that	*these, those*
This is my treasure.	*These* are my jewels.
That is your junk.	*Those* are your trinkets.

- Still other pronouns introduce questions.

  Which is the best CD player?

  What are the main ingredients of a Twinkie?

Verbs

Verbs show action or express being in relation to the subject of a sentence. They customarily occur in set positions in sentences.

- **Action verbs** are usually easy to identify.

    The aardvark *ate* the crisp, tasty ants. (action verb)

    The aardvark *washed* them down with a snoutful of water. (action verb)

- The **being verbs** are few in number and are also easy to identify. The most common *being* verbs are *is, was, were, are,* and *am.*

    Gilligan *is* on an island in the South Pacific. (being verb)

    I *am* his enthusiastic fan. (being verb)

- The form of a verb expresses its tense, that is, the time of the action or being. The time may be in the present or past.

    Roseanne *sings* "The Star-Spangled Banner." (present)

    Roseanne *sang* "The Star-Spangled Banner." (past)

- One or more **helping verbs** may be used with the main verb to form other tenses. The combination is called a *verb phrase.*

    She *had sung* the song many times in the shower. (Helping verb and main verb indicate a time in the past.)

    She *will be singing* the song no more in San Diego. (Helping verbs and main verb indicate a time in the future.)

- Some helping verbs can be used alone as main verbs: *has, have, had, is, was, were, are, am.* Certain other helping verbs function only as helpers: *will, shall, should, could.*

The most common position for the verb is directly after the subject or after the subject and its modifiers.

    At high noon only two men (subject) *were* on Main Street.

    The man with the faster draw (subject and modifiers) *walked* away alone.

Adjectives

Adjectives modify nouns and pronouns. Most adjectives answer the questions *What kind? Which one?* and *How many?*

- Adjectives answering the **What kind?** question are descriptive. They tell the quality, kind, or condition of the nouns or pronouns they modify.

    red convertible   *dirty* fork
    noisy muffler   *wild* roses
    The rain is *gentle.*   Bob was *tired.*

- Adjectives answering the **Which one?** question narrow or restrict the meaning of a noun. Some of these are pronouns that become adjectives by function.

    my money   *our* ideas   the *other* house
    this reason   *these* apples

- Adjectives answering the **How many?** question are, of course, numbering words.

> *some* people   *each* pet   *few* goals
> *three* dollars   *one* glove

- The words *a, an,* and *the* are adjectives called *articles.* As "noun indicators," they point out persons, places, and things.

Adverbs

Adverbs modify verbs, adjectives, and other adverbs. Adverbs answer the questions *How? Where? When?* and *To what degree?*

Modifying Verbs: They <u>did</u> their work <u>quickly.</u>
                           v   adv

Modifying Adjectives: They were <u>somewhat</u> <u>happy.</u>
                           adv   adj

- Adverbs that answer the **How?** question are concerned with manner or way.

  She ate the snails *hungrily.*

  He snored *noisily.*

- Adverbs that answer the **Where?** question show location.

  They drove *downtown.*

  He stayed *behind.*

  She climbed *upstairs.*

- Adverbs that answer the **When?** question indicate time.

  The ship sailed *yesterday.*

  I expect an answer *soon.*

- Adverbs that answer the **To what degree?** question express extent.

  She is *entirely* correct.

  He was *somewhat* annoyed.

Most words ending in *-ly* are adverbs.

    He completed the task <u>skillfully.</u>
                                  adv

    She answered him <u>courteously.</u>
                               adv

However, there are a few exceptions.

    The house provided a <u>lovely</u> view of the valley.
                                  adj

    Your goblin mask is <u>ugly.</u>
                             adj

Prepositions

A **preposition** is a word or words that function as a connective. The preposition connects its object(s) to some other word(s) in the sentence. A preposition and its object(s)—usually a noun or pronoun—with modifiers make up a **prepositional phrase.**

Bart worked <u>against</u> great <u>odds.</u>

prep   object

prepositional phrase

Everyone <u>in</u> his <u>household</u> cheered his effort.

prep   object

prepositional phrase

Some of the most common prepositions are the following:

about	before	but	into	past
above	behind	by	like	to
across	below	despite	near	toward
after	beneath	down	of	under
against	beside	for	off	until
among	between	from	on	upon
around	beyond	in	over	with

Some prepositions are composed of more than one word and are made up from other parts of speech:

according to	as far as	because of	in spite of
ahead of	as well as	in back of	instead of
along with	aside from	in front of	together with

A storm is forming <u>on</u> the <u>horizon</u>.

prep   object

prepositional phrase modifying <u>is forming</u>, a verb phrase

adverb

Caution: Do not confuse adverbs with prepositions.

I went *across* slowly. (without an object—adverb)

I went *across* the field. (with an object—preposition)

We walked *behind* silently. (without an object—adverb)

We walked *behind* the mall. (with an object—preposition)

Conjunctions

A **conjunction** connects and shows a relationship between words, phrases, or clauses. A phrase is two or more words acting as a part of speech. A clause is a group of words with a subject and a verb. An independent clause can stand by itself: *She plays bass guitar.* A dependent clause cannot stand by itself: *when she plays bass guitar.*

There are two kinds of conjunctions: coordinating and subordinating.

Coordinating conjunctions connect words, phrases, and clauses of equal rank: noun with noun, adjective with adjective, verb with verb, phrase with phrase, main clause with main clause, and subordinate clause with subordinate clause. The seven common coordinating conjunctions are *for, and, nor, but, or, yet,* and *so.* (They form the acronyn FANBOYS.)

Two Nouns: Bring a <u>pencil</u> <u>and</u> some <u>paper.</u>

noun   conj   noun

Two Phrases: Did she go <u>to the store</u> <u>or</u> <u>to the game?</u>

prep phase   conj   prep phrase

Paired conjunctions such as *either/or, neither/nor,* or *both/and* are usually classed as coordinating conjunctions.

<u>Neither</u> the coach <u>nor</u> the manager was at fault.
conj   conj

Subordinating conjunctions connect dependent clauses with main clauses. The most common subordinating conjunctions include the following:

after	because	provided	whenever
although	before	since	where
as	but that	so that	whereas
as if	if	till	wherever
as long as	in order that	until	
as soon as	notwithstanding	when	

Sometimes the dependent clause comes *before* the main clause where it is set off by a comma.

<u>Although</u> <u>she</u> <u>was</u> in pain, she stayed in the game.
conj   sub   v
dependent clause

Sometimes the dependent clause comes **after** the main clause, where it usually is *not* set off by a comma.

She stayed in the game <u>because</u> <u>she</u> <u>was needed</u>.
conj   sub   v
dependent clause

Caution: Certain words can function as either conjunctions or prepositions. It is necessary to look ahead to see if the word introduces a clause with a subject and verb—conjunction function—or takes an object—preposition function. Some of the words with two functions are these: *after, for, since, until.*

After the concert was over, we went home. (clause follows—conjunction)

After the concert, we went home. (object follows—preposition)

Interjections

An **interjection** conveys strong emotion or surprise. When an interjection appears alone, it is usually punctuated with an exclamation mark.

Awesome!   Curses!   Cowabunga!   Yaba dabba doo!

When it appears as part of a sentence, an interjection is usually followed by a comma.

Oh, I did not consider that problem.

The interjection may sound exciting, but it is seldom appropriate for college writing.

| **Exercise 1** | **IDENTIFYING PARTS OF SPEECH** |

Identify the part of speech of each italicized word or group of words by placing the appropriate abbreviations in the blanks. (See Answer Key for answers.)

n	noun	*pro*	pronoun
v	verb	*adj*	adjective
adv	adverb	*prep*	preposition
conj	conjunction		

1. I could *never* do *that* hard work at my age. _____ _____

2. We *must leave* for the seashore at once *before* the shower. _____ _____

3. *Until* Steve signs the checks, *we* must remain here. _____ _____

4. *These* men are anxiously awaiting your *instructions*. _____ _____

5. What is the *price* of those new *foreign* cars? _____ _____

6. Your *sister* is later than *you* this time. _____ _____

7. The coach is always *nervous before* the game begins. _____ _____

8. The *Norwegian* people protested the visit *of* the alleged terrorist. _____ _____

9. *I* shall have been absent a week *tomorrow*. _____ _____

10. That *reckless* driver hurt only *himself* in the accident. _____ _____

11. Her attitude *toward* the suspension of the students was *somewhat* cool. _____ _____

12. We *found* the answer to those difficulties *since* he was last present. _____ _____

13. Joan is much *wiser* now, *and* she will never forget the lesson. _____ _____

14. We saw the ship *that* was in the *collision*. _____ _____

15. *Behind* the store is a *winding* road that leads to the farms. _____ _____

16. *If* you wish, I *will take* down his message for you. _____ _____

17. A *group* of students *asked* to see those new paintings earlier. _____ _____

18. When Kristin had finished talking, she came *over* to *my* side of the room. _____ _____

19. *Certainly*, you may see *his* answers. _____ _____

20. I will *not* agree to *your* criticism. _____ _____

| **Exercise 2** | **IDENTIFYING PARTS OF SPEECH** |

Identify the part of speech of each italicized word or group of words by placing the appropriate abbreviations in the blanks.

n	*noun*	*pro*	*pronoun*
v	*verb*	*adj*	*adjective*
adv	*adverb*	*prep*	*preposition*
conj	*conjunction*		

1. *According to* legend, silk *was discovered* by Empress Hsi Ling-shi. _____ _____

2. Empress Hsi Ling-shi *lived around* 2500 B.C. _____ _____

3. *One* day while walking, *she* saw a mulberry tree covered with caterpillars. _____ _____

4. The *caterpillars* were eating the *mulberry* leaves. _____ _____

5. A few days *later* she saw the branches filled *with* the caterpillars' cocoons. _____ _____

6. She plucked a cocoon *from* a branch and *took* it home. _____ _____

7. *There* she placed *it* in a pot of water. _____ _____

8. She *watched as* it loosened into a web. _____ _____

9. She picked the *web apart*. _____ _____

10. She discovered that *it* was a *long* thread of silk. _____ _____

11. The process of making silk *became* China's *special* secret. _____ _____

12. The *secret lasted* for the next 3,000 years. _____ _____

13. Foreign gold poured *into* China from the *silk* trade. _____ _____

14. To pass on the secret of silk-making *to* the *outside* world was forbidden. _____ _____

15. Betraying the secret was punishable *by death*. _____ _____

16. *Anyone* who has ever seen or worn a garment of pure silk knows why the Chinese had to guard *their* invention so jealously. _____ _____

17. Silk is *petal* soft and lighter than the *sheerest* cotton. _____ _____

18. It is *stronger* than *some* kinds of steel thread of equal thickness. _____ _____

19. Silk *drapes* and flows *gracefully*. _____ _____

20. It can be dyed to *richer* hues than any other natural *fabric*. _____ _____

Exercise 3   SUPPLYING AND IDENTIFYING WORDS IN CONTEXT

Bubba and Lisa LaRue made a handsome couple at their wedding. Everyone had said so. But now, after seven years of marriage, they are not always happy with each other. After one heated argument, Lisa left, and Bubba sat down with his guitar to write a song describing their situation.

Fill in the blanks with words that you think would fit the context of the song. Then identify the part of speech of each of your choices by placing the appropriate abbreviation in the blanks at the left. The lines from the songs have been converted to sentences and may seem a bit less lyrical than Bubba's inspired original creation, "You Hurt My Feelings."

_____ You always burn my (1) _____ TV dinners.

_____ You (2) _____ my brand-new station-wagon car.

_____ You said (3) _____ didn't like to do housekeeping.

_____ By accident you broke my best (4) _____ .

_____ _____ You went (5) _____ and spent my hard-earned (6) _____ .

_____ _____ Then you (7) _____ a dozen bouncing (8) _____ .

_____ _____ And then (9) _____ had to go and hurt my (10) _____

_____ when you ran (11) _____ with my best friend named Tex.

Chorus:

_____ _____ You (12) _____ my feelings, and I'm feeling (13) _____ .

_____ _____ You hurt my (14) _____ (15) _____ I'm feeling sad. You

hurt my feelings, ran away with my friend.

_____ _____ (16) _____ hurt my feelings, and (17) _____ is the end.

_____ You went out drinking on my (18) _____ .

_____ _____ Then you (19) _____ my mother is a (20) _____ .

_____ You made (21) _____ of my special mustache.

_____ You (22) _____ it gives you a funny itch.

_____ You broke all my Dolly Parton (23) _____ .

_____ Then you went (24) _____ dancing with your ex.

_____ And then you had to go and (25) _____ my feelings

_____ when you ran away with my best (26) _____ named Tex.

Chorus:

You hurt my feelings, and I'm feeling sad.

———— ———— You hurt my (27) ———— , and I'm feeling (28) ———— .

———— You (29) ———— my feelings, and I'm feeling sad

———— because Tex was the best (30) ———— I ever had.

Scale for correctly labeled parts of speech (have your instructor check your answers):

0–10 = need help with grammar

11–20 = starting to catch on to parts of speech

21–25 = becoming highly capable with parts of speech

26–30 = excellent knowledge of parts of speech

Scale for correct answers (exact matches or close enough, as determined by your instructor) of word selections.

0–10 = need help with basic song writing

11–20 = ready for simple ditties

21–25 = becoming highly capable in dealing with sentimentality

26–30 = ready for advanced country song writing

Appendix B   Taking Tests

Good test-taking begins with good study techniques. These techniques involve, among other things, how to read, think, and write effectively. Those skills have been covered in this book. Here we will discuss only a few principles that apply directly and immediately to the test situation.

At the beginning of the semester, you should discover how you will be tested in each course. Match your note-taking and underlining of texts to the kind or kinds of tests you will take. Objective tests will usually require somewhat more attention to details than will subjective or essay tests.

For both types of tests—and you will probably have a combination—you should carefully apportion your time, deciding how much to spend on each section or essay and allowing a few minutes for a quick review of answers. For both, you should also read the directions carefully, marking key words (if you are permitted to do so) as a reminder to you for concentration.

Objective Tests

Here are some tips on taking objective tests.

- Find out whether you will be graded on the basis of the number of correct answers or on the basis of right-minus-wrong. This is the difference: If you are graded on the basis of the number of correct answers, there is no penalty for guessing; therefore, if you want the highest possible score, you should leave no blanks. But if you are graded on the basis of right-minus-wrong (meaning one or a fraction of one is subtracted from your correct answers for every miss), then answer only if the odds of being right are in your favor. For example, if you know an answer is one of two possibilities, you have a 50 percent chance of getting it right; consequently, guess if the penalty is less than one because you could gain one by getting it right and lose less than one by getting it wrong. Ask your teacher to explain if there is a right-minus-wrong factor.

- If you are going to guess and you want to get some answers correct, you should pick one column and fill in the bubbles. By doing that, you will almost certainly get some correct.

- Studies show that in a typical four-part multiple choice tests section, more answers are B and C than A and D.

- Statements with absolutes such as *always* and *never* are likely to be false, whereas statements with qualifications such as *usually* and *probably* are likely to be true.

- If you don't know an answer, instead of fixating on it and getting frustrated, mark it with what seems right, put a dot alongside your answer, and go back later for a second look if time permits.

- When (and if) you go back to check your work, do not make changes unless you discover that you obviously marked one incorrectly. Studies have shown that first hunches are usually more accurate.

Subjective or Essay Tests

Here are some tips on taking subjective tests.

- Consider the text, the approach taken by the instructor in lectures, and the overall approach in the course outline and try to anticipate essay questions. Then, in your preparation, jot down and memorize simple outlines that will jog your memory during the test if you have anticipated correctly.

- Remember to keep track of time. A time-consuming A+ essay that does not allow you to finish the second half of the exam will result in a failing grade.

- Study the essay questions carefully. Underline key words. Each essay question will have two parts: the subject part and the treatment part. It may also have a limiting part. If you are required, for example, to compare and contrast President Jimmy Carter and President George Bush on their environmental programs, you should be able to analyze the topic immediately in this fashion:

The *subject* is President Carter and President Bush.

The *limitation* is their environmental programs.

The *treatment* is comparison and contrast.

Hence, you might mark the question in this fashion:

treatment   limitation

(Compare and contrast) the (environmental programs) of

subject

(President Carter and President Bush)

The treatment part (here "compare and contrast") may very well be one of the forms of discourse such as definition, classification, or analysis, or it may be something like "evaluate" or "discuss," in which a certain form or forms would be used. Regardless of what the treatment word is, the first step is to determine the natural points of division and to prepare a simple outline or outline alternative for organization.

- In writing the essay, be sure to include specific information as support for your generalizations.

Appendix C   Writing a Job Application Letter and a Résumé

Two forms of practical writing that you may need even before you finish your college work are the job application letter and the résumé. They will often go together as requirements by an employer. In some instances, the employer will suggest the form and content of the letter and résumé; in others, you will receive no directions and should adjust your letter and résumé to match the requirements and expectations as you perceive them. The models on pages 485 and 486 are typical of what job applicants commonly submit.

Job Application Letter

The following basic guidelines will serve you well:

- Use standard letter-size paper and type.

- Do not apologize, and do not brag.

- Do not go into tedious detail, but do relate your education, work experience, and career goals to the available job.

- Begin your letter with a statement indicating why you are writing the letter and how you heard about the job opening.

- End the letter by stating how you can be contacted for an interview.

Résumé

Employers are especially concerned about your most recent work experiences and education, so include them first, as indicated in the example on page 486. The heading "College Activities" can be replaced with "Interests and Activities." Your main concern is presenting relevant information in a highly readable form. Always end with a list of references.

203 Village Center Avenue
Glendora, CA 91740
July 11, 1999

Mr. Roy Ritter
Computers Unlimited
1849 N. Granada Avenue
Walnut, CA 91789

Dear Mr. Ritter:

I am responding to your advertisement in the Los Angeles *Times* for the position of salesperson for used computers. Please consider me as a candidate.

In one more semester I will have completed my Associate in Arts degree at Mt. San Antonio College with a major in business management and a minor in computer technology.

My experience relates directly to the job you offer. As a result of my part-time work for two years as lab technician at my college, I have come to know the operations of several different computers. I have also learned to explain the operations to people who have very little knowledge of computers. In my business classes, I have studied the practical approaches to advertising and sales while also learning theory. Each semester for the past two years, I have worked in the college bookstore, where I helped customers who were buying various products, including computers.

This job would coincide perfectly with my work at school, my work experience, and even my goal of being a salesperson with a large company.

Enclosed is my résumé with several references to people who know me well. Please contact them if you want information or if you would like a written evaluation.

I am available for an interview at your request.

Sincerely yours,

Benjamin Johanson
Benjamin Johanson

Benjamin Johanson
203 Village Center Avenue
Glendora, CA 91740
(626) 987-5555

WORK EXPERIENCE
Lab Assistant in the Mt. San Antonio College Computer Lab   1997–99
Sales Clerk in the Mt. San Antonio College Bookstore   1997–99

EDUCATION
Full-time student at Mt. San Antonio College   1997–99
High school diploma from Glendora High School   1997

COLLEGE ACTIVITIES
Hackers' Club (1996–98)
Chess Club (1996–98)
Forensics Club (1997–99)—twice a regional debate champion

REFERENCES

Stewart Hamlen
Chairperson, Business Department
Mt. San Antonio College
Walnut, CA 91789
(909) 594-5611, ext. 4707

Howard McGraw
Coach, Forensics Team
Mt. San Antonio College
Walnut, CA 91789
(909) 594-5611, ext. 4575

Bart Grassmont
Human Resources Director, Bookstore
Mt. San Antonio College
Walnut, CA 91789
(909) 594-5611, ext. 4706

Answer Key

Chapter 2
Exercise 1

1. <u>Students who cheat in school</u> <u>may be trying to relieve certain emotional</u>

              S   T

<u>pressures.</u> (E)

2. <u>Shakespeare</u> <u>was an Elizabethan writer.</u> (I)

     S   T

3. <u>The quarterback in football and the general of an army</u> <u>are alike in significant</u>

                   S   T

<u>ways.</u> (E)

4. <u>Animals</u> <u>use color chiefly for protection.</u> (E)

   S   T

5. <u>Portland</u> <u>is a city in Oregon.</u> (I)

   S   T

6. <u>Life in the ocean</u> <u>has distinct realms.</u> (E)

       S   T

7. <u>Rome</u> <u>has had a glorious and tragic history.</u> (I)

   S   T

8. <u>Boston</u> <u>is the capital of Massachusetts.</u> (I)

   S   T

9. <u>The word *macho*</u> <u>has a special meaning to the Hispanic community.</u> (E)

       S   T

10. <u>The history of plastics</u> <u>is exciting.</u> (I)

        S   T

Chapter 3
Exercise 3

Pain Unforgettable

James Hutchison

One evening in 1968 while I was working the swing shift at the General

Tire Recapping Plant, I ~~came up with~~ ^{experienced} the greatest pain of my life because of a

terible accident. Raw rubber was heated up in a large tank, ^{prior} ~~Pryor~~ to its being

fed into an extruder. |I was recapping large off-road tires.| ^{While} The lowering plat-

form was in the up position, the chain snapped, ^{sending} ~~It sent~~ the heavy platform crashing down into the tank. This caused a huge wave of steaming water to

surge out of the tank. Unfortunately, I was in its path the wave hit my back just
~T~
above my waist. The sudden pain ~~shook me up.~~ I could not move. My clothes
took my breath away
were steaming ~~I freaked out.~~ Co-workers ran to my aid and striped the hot
and I could only stand there and scream   ~p~

clothing from my body, taking skin as they did. I lay face down on the plant

floor, naked and shaking for ~~a long time.~~ The paramedics ~~came to pick me up.~~
what seemed like eternity   arrived to transport me to the hospital

The painful experience is still ~~scary when I think about it.~~
~i~   with me as a nightmare memory

Handbook

Exercise 1

1. Neville, digs
2. I, will be
3. Berlin/London, were bombed
4. Ahab/you, will decide
5. Milton/coach, stand
6. students, are applying
7. (you), tell
8. William Faulkner, wrote
9. I, have waited/thought
10. we, can find
11. customers, are
12. we, will find
13. players, assembled/elected
14. we, will be living
15. few, may be delayed
16. you, did wish
17. (you), buy
18. reaction, was
19. moose, lies
20. (you), leave

Exercise 7

1. CP	5. CC	9. CP	13. CP	17. S
2. CX	6. S	10. CX	14. CX	18. S
3. S	7. CX	11. CP	15. S	19. CP
4. CX	8. CX	12. CX	16. CP	20. S

Exercise 9

(Answers may vary.)

1. Although cobras are among the most feared of all snakes, they are not the deadliest of all snakes.

2. Cobras do not coil before they strike; therefore, they cannot strike for a long distance.

3. Cobras do not have a hood, but they flatten their neck by moving their ribs when they are nervous or frightened.

4. Cobras use their poison by injecting venom with their fangs and by spitting venom at their victims.

5. Although human beings will not die from the venom that has been spit, it can cause blindness if it is not washed from their eyes.

6. A person can die from a cobra bite, and death may come in only a few hours.

7. Snake charmers have long worked with cobras; they use only a snake, a basket, and a flute.

8. The snakes cannot hear the music, but they respond to the rhythmic movements of the charmers.

9. The snake charmers are hardly ever in danger of being bitten because they defang the cobras or sew their mouths shut.

10. Most cobras flee from people, but they attack if they are cornered or if they are guarding their eggs.

Exercise 11

1. OK
2. RO;   art. During
3. FRAG;   entertainment are wrong.
4. OK
5. CS;   perfect, and
6. CS;   said. "It
7. OK
8. FRAG;   work is a lathe.
9. OK
10. OK
11. RO;   sleeping, but
12. CS;   ways;
13. FRAG; sing
14. FRAG; words changes
15. CS;   America, but
16. CS;   language;
17. OK
18. RO;   for positive regard, and
19. RO;   Steinbeck. His
20. OK

Exercise 17

1. had stayed
2. had paid
3. walked
4. had
5. could have gone
6. will have completed
7. are considering
8. had led
9. had built
10. will drive

Exercise 19

1. are
2. have
3. Has
4. eats
5. were
6. are
7. were
8. is
9. changes
10. has
11. was
12. are
13. attracts
14. wants
15. get
16. tells
17. seems
18. is
19. are
20. was

Exercise 21

1. makes	5. didn't	9. is	13. has	17. finished
2. took	6. go	10. is	14. were	18. would
3. is	7. will get	11. asked	15. came	19. hands
4. quit	8. marries	12. keeps	16. needed	20. was

Exercise 22

	From	To			From	To
1.	OK			11.	is	was
2.	OK			12.	OK	
3.	are	were		13.	holds	held
4.	OK			14.	establish	established
5.	utter	uttered		15.	OK	
6.	OK			16.	is	was
7.	condemn	condemned		17.	OK	
8.	OK			18.	name	named
9.	is	was		19.	OK	
10.	OK			20.	OK	

Exercise 24

1. I have written a letter to you.

2. His ancestors never made an honest dollar, and now he is following in their fingerprints.

3. The instructor approved the assignment.

4. The president of the student body gave the instructor a much-deserved medal of valor.

5. Few people noticed that the quiet students did most of the work.

Exercise 25

1. He wrote that essay.

2. She drove the speeding car,

3. He played the guitar

4. They led the entire region in sales.

5. The medicine cured the cold.

Exercise 26

1. were
2. were
3. return
4. were
5. be

Exercise 27

1. she	5. me	9. us	13. I	17. whom
2. she	6. she	10. I	14. Whom	18. Who
3. him	7. him	11. she	15. whom	19. I
4. them	8. We	12. they	16. Who	20. she

Exercise 29

1. he or she	5. his or her	9. himself	13. their	17. his
2. its	6. their	10. her	14. he or she	18. they
3. his or her	7. who	11. its	15. her	19. he or she
4. its	8. that	12. their	16. their	20. himself or herself

Exercise 31

	From	**To**
1.	OK	
2.	OK	
3.	OK	
4.	you are	one is
5.	that his	, "Your short story will . . ."
6.	OK	
7.	That . . . yesterday.	That house belongs to Cynthia, whom we visited yesterday.
8.	OK	
9.	In . . . have	That college has
10.	OK	
11.	his message.	the message he had taken him.
12.	told . . . good."	said to her mother, "Your ideas are good."
13.	OK	
14.	OK	
15.	which	a practice that
16.	This may	This omission may

17. one.	a lawyer.
18. you	he or she
19. In . . . it	This pamphlet
20. OK	

Exercise 35

	From	**To**
1.	most unique	unique
2.	easier	more easily
3.	real	really
4.	too impossible	impossible
5.	badly	bad
6.	best	better
7.	most perfect	most nearly perfect
8.	violenter	more violent
9.	more beautiful	the most beautiful
10.	good	well
11.	only can mean one	can mean only one
12.	real	really
13.	easy	easily
14.	all ready	already
15.	alright	all right
16.	easiest	easier
17.	badly	bad
18.	real	really
19.	only she	she only
20.	all together	altogether

Exercise 37

1. D; Interested in my studies, I had
2. OK
3. M; that approximately a hundred
4. M; that approximately a hundred
5. D; in spite of my
6. D; night, I still had not completed the job.
7. M; Gossiping noisily, the students
8. M; Gossiping noisily, the students

9. D;   By practicing every day, one can learn French in two weeks.

10. D;   While working in the factory, we made much money.

11. M;   Last week, the doctor told him to stop smoking.

12. D;   Debra remembered her promise

13. D;   As we walked to school,

14. M;   we studied grammar only

15. D;   To be a careful writer, one should never write dangling infinitive phrases.

16. M;   To protect their hands, astronauts wore gloves.

17. D;   When I was only

18. M;   I drank only

19. M;   Jill tried carefully and constantly to avoid

20. D;   While I was recovering

Exercise 39

1. NP;   or if it is no longer fun

2. NP;   and for her own behavior.

3. NP;   taking lecture notes

4. NP;   and an inventor.

5. NP;   and telling jokes.

6. NP;   and an increase in several fees.

7. NP;   than managing

8. NP;   Giving is

9. NP;   then by force.

10. NP;   but also politically sophisticated.

11. NP;   captain not only of

12. NP;   in both their

13. NP;   and to ask questions.

14. NP;   than writing

15. NP;   and untruthful.

16. NP;   nor his purpose.

17. P

18. NP;   commander not only of

19. NP;   and a powerful

20. NP;   and good food.

Exercise 41

1. words, phrases,

2. strong,

3. modifiers,

4. clauses,

5. all,

6. Inside,

7. game,

8. pink, black, green,

9. night,

10. sharp,

11. banquet,

12. Handel, both born in 1685,

13. Motor racing, not horse racing,

14. boy," Arturo said,

15. Jones, the salesperson,

16. Well,

17. car, all sleek and shiny,

18. Tribbey, Oklahoma, on February 21, 1934.

19. down,

20. Tower, which is located in Paris,

Exercise 43

1. Hill;

2. countries;

3. dig,

4. smoking; beautiful females, all in bathing suits;

5. thought;

6. pleasure,

7. blossoms; pumpkins, still just tiny green marbles;

8. Paris,

9. Jesus;

10. one; another analyzes relationships among others, imaginary or real;

11. status; in fact,

12. people;

13. romance,

14. mongrel puppy;

15. grandfathers,

16. fire,

17. me;

18. time;

19. people,

20. recluse;

Exercise 45

1. "In . . . men."

2. day's

3. Lebensraum

4. It's

5. 'Stop now,'

6. birds'

7. it's

8. Billy Budd

9. "Ode . . . Nightingale"?

10. London's

11. he?

12. cave-in

13. *7*'s

14. Marciano—

15. interviewed:

16. Engels— . . . were—

17. Romantic

18. Independence

19. English

20. Aunt

Exercise 47

George Washington at Trenton

One of *the* most famous battles during the War of Independence ~~occur~~ *occurred* at Trenton, New Jersey, on Christmas Eve of t~~h~~e 1776. The colonists *were* outmatched in supplies and finances and ~~were~~ outnumbered in troop strength. Most observers in other countries ~~think~~ *thought the* rebellion would be put down soon. *The* British ~~is~~ *were* overconfident and ~~believe~~ *believed* there would be no more battles until spring. But George Washington ~~decide~~ *decided* to fight one more time. That Christmas, while *a* large army of Britishers *were* having *a* party and thinking about the holiday season, *the* Americans set out for *a* surprise raid. They loaded onto boats used for carrying ore and rowed across *the* Delaware River. George Washington stood tall in *the* lead boat. According to legend, *the* drummer boy floated across *the* river on his drum, pulled by *a* rope tied to *a* boat. Because *the* British did not feel threatened by the rag-tag colonist forces, they *were* unprepared to do battle. The colonists stormed *the* living quarters and the general assembly hall and achieved victory. It was good for the colonists' morale, something they needed, for they would endure *a* long, hard winter before fighting again.

Appendix A
Exercise 1

1. adv, adj
2. v, prep
3. conj, pro
4. adj, n
5. n, adj
6. n, pro
7. adj, conj
8. adj, prep
9. pro, adv
10. adj, pro
11. prep, adv
12. v, conj
13. adj, conj
14. pro, n
15. prep, adj
16. conj, v
17. n, v
18. adv, adj
19. adv, adj
20. adv, adj

Text Credits

"Frankie and Johnnie," from *American Favorite Ballads: Tunes and Songs Sung by Peter Seeger*. Edited by Irwin Silver and Ethel Raim. Copyright © 1961 (Renewed) Oak Publications, a division of Music Sales Corporation International. Copyright Secured. All Rights Reserved. Reprinted by permission.

Jeffrey M. Bernbach, "Sex Discrimination," from *Job Discrimination: How to Fight, How to Win*. 1996, Crown Trade Paperbacks, pp. 43-48 (top). Reprinted with permission of Perkins, Rubie Associates and the author.

Ellen Bravo and Ellen Cassedy, "Is It Sexual Harassment?" *Redbook*, July 1992. A new 1999 edition has been published by 9 to 5 Work Women Education Fund. Reprinted by permission of the authors.

Suzanne Britt, "Neat People vs. Sloppy People," *Show and Tell*. Reprinted by permission of the author

Lynn Bulhman, "Road Warriors," Waco [TX] *Tribune-Herald*, May 25, 1997, author Lynn Bulhman staff writer. Reprinted with permission of the *Waco Tribune-Herald*.

José Antonio Burciaga, "Tortillas." Copyright José Antonio Burciaga. Reprinted by permission of Cecilia P. Burciaga.

Willi Coleman, "Closets and Keepsakes," from *Double Stitch: Black Women Write about Mothers and Daughters*, edited by Patricia Bell-Scott et al. Harper Perennial 1993. Reprinted with the permission of the author.

Barbara Ehrenriech, "In Defense of Talk Shows," *Time*, December 4, 1995. © 1995 Time, Inc. Reprinted by permission.

C. Edward Good and William Fitzpatrick, "A Successful Interview." Prima Publishing, 1993. Reprinted with permision of the authors.

Preston Gralla, "Fast, Sleek and Shiny: Using the Internet to Help Buy New Cars," from *The Complete Idiot's Guide to Online Shopping*. Reprinted with permission from Macmillan Computer Publishing.

William Heat-Moon, "In the Land of 'Coke-Cola'," from *Blue Highways: A Journey into America* by William Least Heat-Moon. Copyright © 1982, 1999 by William Least Heat-Moon. By permission of Little, Brown and Company (Inc.).

Fred M. Hechinger, "The First Step in Improving Sex Education: Remove the Hellfire," *The New York Times*, May 24, 1989, Section 2, p. 9, Column 1. Copyright © 1989 by The New York Times Co. Reprinted by permission.

Mary Ann Hogan, "Why We Carp and Harp." *Los Angeles Times*. March 10, 1992. Copyright 1992 by Mary Ann Hogan. Reprinted with permission of the author.

Donna Brown Hogarty, "How to Deal with a Difficult Boss." Reprinted with permission from July 1993 *Reader's Digest*.

Charles Krauthammer, "Of Headless Mice . . . and Men," from *Time*, January 19, 1998. Reprinted by permission.

Charles Krauthammer, "The New Prohibitionism," from *Time*, October 6, 1997. © 1997 Time, Inc. Reprinted by permission.

David Levine, "I'm Outta Here" from *Seventeen*. David Levine is a freelance writer and author living in Saratoga Springs. He has written for the *New York Times, New York Daily News, Sports Illustrated* and dozens of others. Author of "Life on the Rim" (Macmillan, 1990).

Kesaya E. Noda, "Growing Up Asian in America." Reprinted by permission of the author, Kesaya E. Noda, from *Making Waves*, by Asian Women United of California, © 1989 by Asian Women United.

Russell B. Nye, "Eight Ways of Looking at an Amusement Park" (last paragraph [#33] from a long essay)—as appeared in *The Journal of Popular Culture*, 1981. Reprinted with permission of Popular Press.

Anna Quindlen, "Raised on Rock-and-Roll," *The New York Times*, February 25, 1987. Copyright © 1987 by The New York Times Co. Reprinted by permission.

Irwin Shaw, "The Girls in Their Summer Dresses," from *Five Decades* by Irwin Shaw. Copyright 1978 Irwin Shaw. Reprinted with permission. © Irwin Shaw

Jill Smolowe, "Intermarried . . . With Children," *Time*, Fall 1993 (special issue), pp. 64-65. © 1993 Time, Inc. Reprinted with permission.

Lee Little Soldier, "Cooperative Learning and the Native American Student," from Lee Little Soldier, *Phi Delta Kappan*, October 1989. Copyright © 1989. Reprinted by permission of the author.

Gary Soto, "The Pie" from *A Summer Life*, © 1990 University Press of New England by permission of the University Press of New England.

Robert J. Trotter, "How Do I Love Thee?" from *The Three Faces of Love*, September 1986, p. 47. Reprinted with permission from *Psychology Today* magazine. Copyright © 1986, Sussex Publishers, Inc.

Luis Torres, "Los Chinos Discover El Barrio," May 11, 1989. Reprinted by permission of Luis Torres, a Los Angeles–based journalist.

U. S. News and World Report, "A Hole in the Head?" November 3, 1997. Copyright *U.S. News and World Report*. Reprinted with permission.

Eudora Welty, excerpt from "A Worn Path" in *A Curtain of Green and Other Stories* copyright 1941 and renewed 1969 by Eudora Welty. Reprinted by permission of Harcourt, Inc.

Larry Woiwode, "Ode to an Orange." Reprinted by permission of Donadio & Olson, Inc. Copyright 1986 by Larry Woiwode.

Elizabeth Wong, "The Struggle to Be an All American Girl." Reprinted by permission of the author.

Two dictionary definitions—*indigenous* and *native*. Webster's Ninth New Collegiate Dictionary. Extract reprinted by permission. From *Webster's Ninth New Collegiate Dictionary* © 1991 by Merriam–Webster, Inc., publisher of the Merriam Webster (®) dictionaries.

Author and Title Index

497

Subject Index